SIR WILLIAM LAIRD CLOWES was born in 1865 and made his reputation as naval correspondent of *The Times* between 1890 and 1895. He was a member of the Navy League and involved in the agitation for greater naval resources, and his anonymous articles which appeared in the *Daily Graphic* in 1893 undoubtedly influenced the naval Estimates.

He wrote and compiled this seven-volume history of the Royal Navy between 1897 and 1903, involving a number of distinguished contemporary writers to assist him. From America he employed Captain Mahan, author of *The Influence of Sea Power upon History*, and Theodore Roosevelt who covered the history of the war with the United States. Sir Clements Markham, President of the Royal Geographical Society, dealt with the history of voyages and discoveries, and H W Wilson, author of *Battleships in Action*, described many of the minor naval operations.

Walter Webb, R.A.

The Battle of Navarin.

From the painting by R. A. Thomas, by permission of the Rev. R. W. J. Smart.

The Royal Navy

A History

From the Earliest Times to the Present

By

Wm. Laird Clowes

Fellow of King's College, London; Gold Medallist U.S. Naval Institute;
Hon. Member of the Royal United Service Institution

Assisted by

Sir Clements Markham, K.C.B., P.R.G.S.
Captain A. T. Mahan, U.S.N.
Mr. H. W. Wilson
Col. Theodore Roosevelt, President of the United States
etc.

In Seven Volumes

VOL. VI.

CHATHAM PUBLISHING

LONDON

PUBLISHER'S NOTE

In the original edition the four photogravure plates and
four full-page illustrations faced the text pages as
listed on page xiii. In this edition these illustrations are
collected at the back of the book after page 550, in the
order in which they appeared in the first edition.

Published in 1997 by
Chatham Publishing,
1 & 2 Faulkner's Alley, Cowcross Street,
London EC1M 6DD

Chatham Publishing is an imprint of
Gerald Duckworth and Co Ltd

First published in 1901 by
Sampson Low, Marston and Company

ISBN 1 86176 015 9

A catalogue record for this book is available from the British Library

Printed and bound in Great Britain by Biddles Ltd, Guildford, Surrey

INTRODUCTION TO VOLUME VI.

WHEN, in June, 1899, I wrote the Introduction to Volume IV. of this History, I announced that, at my urgent instance, the Publishers had generously agreed to allow me to extend the work from five volumes to six. Since then much has happened. It was permissible to hope that the remaining eighteen months of the nineteenth century, and, in fact, the concluding years of her late Majesty's most glorious reign, would be spent in peace; yet scarcely was Volume IV. in the hands of the public ere there broke out in South Africa one of the most troublesome and tedious wars in which the British Empire has ever been engaged; and, not long afterwards, it became necessary to embark upon extensive operations in China. On both scenes of action the Navy has borne an onerous and honourable part, and has done magnificent work which cannot fitly be described save at some length.

Since, therefore, I am anxious to complete the History up to the end of the nineteenth century, and, at the same time, to do such justice as I can to the services of the Navy as well at the close as at the beginning and middle of that eventful hundred years, I have again induced my Publishers, Messrs. Sampson Low, Marston & Co., Ltd., to agree to an extension of the plan of the book. It will now consist of seven volumes, and will bring the story up to the end of the year 1900, a date which, for practical purposes, is synchronous with that of the end of the Victorian era. This arrangement has permitted me to deal at somewhat greater length than at first I deemed possible with all the previous operations in China, with the naval side of the war with Russia, and with many minor affairs which well deserve to be chronicled with some fulness.

The present volume is concerned with the war with the United States in 1812–15, and with the development and work of the Royal

Navy from that time onwards until the conclusion of the war with Russia. For it are responsible Colonel Roosevelt, now President of the United States, Sir Clements Markham, and myself.

Colonel Roosevelt, when he kindly promised to write for me the interesting and suggestive chapter which is to-day before the reader, was not even Vice-President. He was only President of the Board of Police Commissioners of New York. Even when he completed the chapter, and corrected the proof-sheets of it, he was only Assistant-Secretary of the United States' Navy. I feel it my duty to mention these facts in order that I may make clear to his countrymen, should they be curious in the matter, that although the name of the President of the United States is affixed to the chapter, the opinions expressed in it are those, rather, of a naval administrator who, be it remembered, when little more than a boy, wrote what was then the best American account of the war which he now describes again, more briefly, it is true, yet by the light of fuller knowledge. Since the days of his service in the Navy Department, Theodore Roosevelt, already sportsman, big-game hunter, zoologist, and politician, has gained equal distinction as a soldier and as a statesman. The sorrowful circumstances which in the last few days have led him so suddenly to the Presidency must, I fear, confine his wonderful energies to one channel only for some time to come. I am very fortunate in having secured, at a comparatively quiet period of his most active career, the assistance of so brilliant, able, and busy a man.

In his book, 'The Naval War of 1812,' published when he was but four-and-twenty, Theodore Roosevelt dealt with the struggle from the exclusively American point of view. He has now attacked the subject from the more purely critical side; and I do not hesitate to say that he has produced a piece of work which, while fair-minded and generous to a degree, is as remarkable for its analytical insight as for its impartial plain speaking. He indicates very clearly why the United States beat Great Britain so frequently in the earlier actions of the war, and why, in spite of American successes, the Great Republic, with a navy as it was then constituted and managed, could never hope for decisive victory. The lessons which he deduces from the history of the war should be as valuable to Britons as to his own people: and, believing as I do in the high mission of the races concerned, I trust that both may equally profit by my friend's clear-sighted conclusions.

Many of the interesting American portraits which illustrate President Roosevelt's chapter are reproduced from originals which have been most kindly lent me by Mr. Henry Carey Baird, of Philadelphia, to whose voluntary co-operation I owe much.

Sir Clements Markham contributes the two chapters which describe the naval voyages and discoveries of 1803–15, and 1816–56. In the second of these chapters, the President of the Royal Geographical Society tells, I may remind the reader, of services *quorum pars fuit*; for although, perhaps, the fact is not generally remembered, Sir Clements was for eight years in the Navy, and was himself with one of the most interesting Arctic expeditions of that period.

For the remaining part of the volume I am alone responsible. The active services of the Navy between the years 1816 and 1856 were, speaking generally, of a character somewhat different from that which chiefly marks the work of the fleet up to the close of the Napoleonic wars; but I do not know that they are less interesting, or less usefully suggestive. In the forty years, British admirals fought no great pitched battles with formidable foes; and although the period is that of Algier, Navarin, St. Jean d'Acre, and Sebastopol, it is more especially the period of small wars with uncivilised peoples, of steady, but nearly noiseless, extension of the Empire, and of onerous policing of the ocean. It witnessed the practical extinction of piracy, and of the over-sea slave trade; and, in connection with those subjects, there will be found in the following pages the record of many almost forgotten deeds of heroism. It witnessed also many scarcely-remembered exploits which were undertaken in defence of British interests in all parts of the world, and for the protection and advancement of British trade. The reader will perceive, perhaps with some surprise, that although the period was, upon the whole, one which it is customary to call a time of peace, scarcely a year of it passed without seeing the Navy actively and gallantly engaged in some corner of the world.

For assistance rendered to me in connection with Chapters XLIII. and XLIV., and with the Appendices, I have gratefully to acknowledge my indebtedness to, among others, Admiral of the Fleet the Rt. Hon. Lord John Hay, Sir J. E. Commerell, and Sir A. McL. Lyons; Admirals Sir E. G. Fanshawe, Sir E. Ommanney, Sir H. Chads, the Rt. Hon. Sir J. C. D. Hay, Bart., Sir G. O. Willes, and Henry Boys; Paymasters-in-Chief J. W. M. Ashby, and

R. R. A. Richards ; Fleet-Paymaster Frederick Cleeve ; and Chaplain the Rev. A. G. Kealy, R.N. ; some of whom are now, alas, no more. I have also to express my gratitude to the Navy Department, Washington; the Marine-Section of the K. und K. Reichs-Kriegs-Ministerium (through the courtesy of my old friend Captain Leopold Ritter von Jedina, of the Aust.-Hung. Navy) ; the Imperial Russian Admiralty ; and the Ministry of Marine in Paris.

Once more I have to apologise for the delayed appearance of a volume, and to beg both my most patient and kindly Publishers and the public to excuse it on the ground of my continued ill-health. I have personally undertaken the indexing of the previous five volumes. To my regret, I have been obliged to entrust the laborious task of indexing the present volume to another hand ; but I have been fortunate in securing for the work the services of Miss E. M. Samson, to whom my thanks are due for the manner in which she has carried out what I know to be a most difficult undertaking.

AVAL DU CREUX, SARK.
    Sept. 15, 1901.

ADDENDUM.

The following paragraph, which should have preceded the paragraph, on p. 277, beginning " The year 1837," was accidentally omitted when the copy was sent to the printers :—

In spite of the operations of Chads, the Malays continued to give trouble to the Indian Government, whose province it then was to superintend relations with the tribes of the Archipelago; and, early in 1837, Captain Robert Contart M'Crea, of the *Zebra*, 16, was ordered, in consequence of representations from Calcutta, to capture a contumacious Malay chief, the ex-rajah of Quedah, who had taken refuge at Bruas, on the coast of Perak, and to convey him as prisoner to Penang. M'Crea executed the service in the month of April, but not without difficulty. His boats, which he led in person, had to approach the chief's hiding-place along a narrow and tortuous stream, both sides of which were fringed with dense jungle, and then to sustain a sharp action for an hour and a half with a brig, and with a strong and well-manned stockade. The affair cost heavy loss to the attackers, and still heavier to the defenders, but was so ably carried out that the East India Company subsequently presented M'Crea with a piece of plate in token of its satisfaction.

CONTENTS.

VOLUME VI.

————◆◆◆————

CHAPTER XLI.

CHAPTER XLII.

CHAPTER XLIII.

CHAPTER XLIV.

PUBLISHER'S NOTE

The photogravure plates and four full-page illustrations listed below
appear in this edition at the back of the book, after page 550.

LIST OF ILLUSTRATIONS.

VOLUME VI.

———◆———

PHOTOGRAVURE PLATES.

FULL-PAGE ILLUSTRATIONS.

ILLUSTRATIONS IN THE TEXT.

NAVAL HISTORY.

CHAPTER XLI.

THE WAR WITH THE UNITED STATES, 1812–15.

THEODORE ROOSEVELT,
Vice-President of the United States of America.

OUTBREAK OF THE WAR: Causes of hostility—American unpreparedness—Jefferson's peace policy—Irritation engendered by facilities for naturalisation—The Milan and Berlin decrees, and the Orders in Council—Hardships brought about by the edicts—Cleveland's experiences—Basil Hall's testimony—British seamen in the American marine—American seamen pressed by the British—Berkeley's order—Affair of the *Leopard* and the *Chesapeake*—Jefferson's " commercial war "—Napoleon's duplicity—British blockade of the American coasts—Affair of the *President* and the *Little Belt*—Declaration of war—Indifference of the American people—British over-confidence—Efficiency of the United States navy—Ships of the United States—Tonnage and armament—Superiority of the American frigate—The American *personnel*—British seamen in the American navy—Poorness of British gunnery. THE EARLY AMERICAN VICTORIES: The *President* and the *Belvidera*—The *Essex* and the *Alert*—The *Constitution* and the *Guerrière*—The *Wasp* and the *Frolic*—The *United States* and the *Macedonian*—The *Constitution* and the *Java*—The *Hornet* and the *Peacock*—American privateers—Effects of commerce-destroying—British discouragement—Admiralty precautions—Jurien de La Gravière on the war. THE TURN OF THE TIDE: The American coast blockaded—Effect of the blockade—Raids on the coast—Retaliation by the privateers—Failure of expectations on both sides—Fleets the true commerce-destroyers—The *Shannon* and the *Chesapeake*—The power of good organisation—The *Pelican* and the *Argus*—The *Enterprise* and the *Boxer*—Failure of the attack on Norfolk—Outrages at Hampton—Inadequacy of the American gunboats—The *Junon* in Delaware Bay—Attack on the *Asp*—Capture of the *Surveyor*—Affair in the Stone River—Capture of the *Lottery*—Polkinghorne and the privateers—Cochrane succeeds Warren—Cruise of the *Essex*—The *Phœbe* and *Cherub*, and the *Essex* and *Essex Junior*. THE WARFARE ON THE LAKES: The forces opposed—Lake Ontario—Defence of Sackett's Harbour—Capture of the *Julia* and *Growler*—Chauncey and Yeo—The affair at Big Sandy Creek—A contest of shipbuilding—Lake Erie—Cutting out of the *Caledonia*—Barclay and Perry—Battle of Lake Erie—American repulse at Macinaw—Capture of the *Tigress* and *Scorpion*—Cutting out affair at Port Erie—Lake Champlain—Capture of the *Growler*—Macdonough and Downie—Battle of Plattsburg Harbour. THE BLOCKADE AND THE CRUISERS: Destruction of Barney's gunboats—Capture of Washington—Gordon at Alexandria—Repulse at Baltimore—Lockyer in Lake Borgne—Repulse at Fort Bowyer—The case of the *Erebus*—Increase of American privateering—The *Chasseur*, of Baltimore—British indignation—Capture of the *St. Lawrence*—The *General Armstrong*—The *Prince de Neufchâtel*—Capture of the *Frolic*—The *Peacock* and the *Epervier*—The *Wasp* and the *Reindeer*—The *Wasp* and the *Avon*—Loss of the *Wasp*—The *Endymion* and the *President*—Capture of the *Levant* and *Cyane*—Escape of the *Constitution*—The *Hornet* and the *Penguin*—Escape of the *Hornet*—The *Peacock* and the *Nautilus*—End of the war—Novel weapons in the American navy—A drawn quarrel.

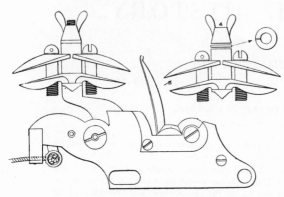

DOUGLAS'S DOUBLE (REVERSIBLE) FLINT LOCK,
FOR GUNS OR MORTARS, CA. 1818.
(*From Ch. Dupin.*)

IT is often difficult to realise that, in a clash between two peoples, not only may each side deem itself right, but each side may really be right from its own standpoint. A healthy and vigorous nation must obey the law of self-preservation. When it is engaged in a life and death grapple with a powerful foe, it cannot too closely scan the damage it is incidentally forced to do neutral nations. On the other hand, it is just as little to be expected that one of these neutral nations, when wronged, will refrain from retaliation merely because the injuries are inflicted by the aggressor as a regrettable, but necessary, incident of a conflict with some one else.

This holds true of the bickering war between Britain and America which closed the gigantic Napoleonic struggles. During nearly a quarter of a century of tremendous warfare, Britain and France stood as opposing champions in a struggle which dwarfed all previous contests and convulsed the entire civilised world. As has been seen, every other nation of Europe was at one time or another drawn into this struggle, and almost every other nation sided now with one, and now with the other, of the great central pair of combatants. Russia and Spain, Austria and Prussia, Holland and Turkey, appeared, now as the subservient allies, now as the bitter enemies, of Republican and Imperial France. The Island Monarchy alone never wavered, and never faltered. In the countless shifting coalitions framed against France, there was always one unshifting figure, that of Britain. Kaiser and King, Tsar and

Cortes, might make war, or sue for peace; but, save for one brief truce, the people of Britain never for a moment relaxed that deadly strain of hostility which at last wore out even Napoleon's giant strength.

It was a life and death struggle; and to win, Britain had to spend her gold, her ships, and her men like water. Where she was thus lavish of her own wealth and her own blood, it was not to be expected that she would pay over-scrupulous heed to the exact rights of others, above all if these rights were exercised seriously to her own disadvantage. While the fight stamped to and fro, the combatants were far too busy with one another to care whether or not they trampled on outsiders. In the grim, relentless, long-drawn warfare, neither side had any intention of throwing away a chance by quixotic over-regard for the rights of others; and both sides were at times seriously to blame for disregarding these rights on occasions when to regard them would not have been quixotic at all, but an evidence of sound common-sense.

The scarlet-clad armies of Britain played a great part in the closing years of the struggle, and developed as their leader the chief of all the generals who fought under or against Napoleon. Nevertheless it was the Navy of Britain, it was the British sea power, which threw the deciding weight into the contest. The British Navy destroyed the fleets of France and the fleets of the Spanish, Dutch, and Danish allies of France, and blockaded the French ports, and the ports of all powers that were not hostile to the French. In order to man the huge fleets with which she kept command of the seas, England was forced to try every expedient to gather sailors; and in order to make her blockade effective she had to lay a heavy hand on the ships of those neutral powers that found their profit in breaking the blockade.

The United States of America was the only neutral power which at once both tended to drain the British Navy of a certain number of its seamen, and at the same time offered in her own seamen a chance for that same Navy to make good the loss. Moreover, it was the one neutral nation which throve apace during the years of European warfare by trading with the hostile powers. So long as they were not too much harassed, the American merchants and seamen were greatly benefited by the war in Europe. The destruction of the French merchantmen by the British warships, and the constant harrying of the British merchantmen by the French privateers, tended to drive trade into neutral bottoms; and America was the only neutral nation prepared to profit greatly by this tendency. She made the loss of England her gain. Her merchants shipped cargoes to French ports; and her merchant captains, as their trade grew apace, and as they became short-handed, welcomed eagerly all British seamen, deserters or otherwise, who might take service under the American flag in the hope of avoiding the press-gang and the extreme severity of British naval discipline.

The Americans were merely exercising their rights; but naturally their attitude exasperated not only Britain, but also France. Each of the two main combatants was inclined to view with suspicion the neutral who made a cold-blooded profit out of the sufferings of both. Each took harsh, and often entirely unjustifiable, measures to protect himself. Each in his action was guided very naturally by his own interests as he saw them. It was Britain with which America ultimately came to blows, because Britain possessed far greater power of inflicting injury; but, according to his capacity, Napoleon showed a much more callous disregard for American rights.

The British claimed the right to forbid vessels to sail to or from ports which they announced as blockaded, and to search neutral ships for contraband goods. They also acted upon the doctrine that "once a subject, always a subject," and that their warships could at any time take British sailors, wherever found, on the high seas. The intense vexation and heavy loss caused by the right of search need not be dwelt upon. The impressment of American seamen was an even more serious business. Thousands of British sailor-men were to be found on American vessels. Britain re-claimed these at every opportunity; but she did not rest content with this. Each British war vessel regarded itself as the judge as to whether the members of the crew of a searched vessel were British or Americans. If the captain of such a war vessel were short-handed, he was certain to resolve all doubts in his own favour; and, consequently, thousands of impressed Americans served, sorely against the grain, in British warships.

The whole situation was one that could not but provoke intense irritation. There was much fraud in the naturalisation of British seamen as Americans; and, on the other hand, there was much brutal disregard of the rights of American sailors by British war-ships. The American merchant cared nothing for the contestants, save that he wanted to sell his goods where he could get the best price; while the British officer was determined that the American should not render help to France. From their respective standpoints, each nation had much to say in its own favour. Consistently with retaining her self-respect, America could not submit quietly to the injuries she received. On the other hand, Britain could not afford, because of any consideration of abstract right, to allow any neutral nation to furnish Napoleon with another weapon. War was almost inevitable.

At the time each people as a whole of course firmly believed that its own cause was entirely righteous, and that its opponents were without any moral justification for their acts; though the best-informed Englishmen, those who managed the councils of their country, evidently felt at bottom an uneasy sense that their course was not entirely justifiable, as was shown by the too tardy repeal of the Orders in Council. The difference in feeling caused by the difference of point of view was illustrated by the attitudes of the British and Americans towards one another in 1812 and 1862 respectively. In 1812 the bolder American merchants embarked eagerly in the career of running cargoes into the ports of blockaded France, precisely as half a century later the British of the stamp of Hobart Pasha swarmed forward to command the blockade-runners which plied between the British ports and the ports of the Southern Confederacy. At the earlier date the Americans resisted and the British upheld the right of search; fifty years later it was the American, Wilkes, who exercised the right, while the British made ready for instant war unless the deed should be disavowed.

It was entirely natural that Great Britain should strive in every way possible to minimise the aid which America, by the exercise of her rights as a neutral, gave to France. It was equally natural that the more reckless and overbearing spirits among the British naval officers, while carrying out this policy, should do deeds that were entirely indefensible, and which could not but inflame the Americans to madness. No American ship was safe from confiscation, no American seaman was safe from impressment, either on the high seas, or on the American coast; and insult and outrage followed one another in monotonous succession.

The nation which submitted without war to such insults erred on the side of tame submission, not of undue truculence. But it must be remembered that France was all the time, according to her capacity, behaving quite as badly as Great Britain. Her sea strength had been shattered by Britain, so she could not do America anything like as much harm ; but no British Minister vied with Napoleon in vicious and treacherous disregard of the rights of both friend and foe. Nevertheless, France offered the chance of making money, and Britain did not. Britain could do her own carrying trade, while the carrying trade of France was largely in American bottoms. Many Americans were delighted to balance against the insults and injuries they received from the mighty combatants, the profits which flowed into their coffers only because the combat did not cease.

There was but one possible way by which to gain and keep the respect of either France or Britain : that was by the possession of power, and the readiness to use it if necessary ; and power in this case meant a formidable fighting navy. Had America possessed a fleet of twenty ships of the line, her sailors could have plied their trade unmolested ; and the three years of war, with its loss in blood and money, would have been avoided. From the merely monetary standpoint such a navy would have been the cheapest kind of insurance ; and morally its advantages would have been incalculable, for every American worth the name would have lifted his head higher because of its existence. But unfortunately the nation lacked the wisdom to see this, and it chose and re-chose for the Presidency Thomas Jefferson, who avowed that his "passion was peace," and whose timidity surpassed even his philanthropy. Both Britain and America have produced men of the "peace at any price" pattern ; and in America, in one great crisis at least, these men cost the nation more, in blood and wealth, than the political leaders most recklessly indifferent to war have ever cost it. There never was a better example of the ultimate evil caused by a timid effort to secure peace, through the sacrifice of honour and the refusal to make preparations for war, than that afforded by the American people under the Presidencies of Jefferson and Madison. The "infinite capacity of mankind to withstand the introduction of knowledge" is also shown by the fact that this lesson has not only been largely wasted, but has even been misread and misinterpreted. National vanity, and the party spirit which resolutely refuses to see crimes committed against the nation by party heroes, are partly responsible for this. The cultivation of a political philosophy which persistently refuses to accept facts as they are, and which in America is no dearer to the unlettered demagogue than to the educated, refined theorist whose knowledge of political affairs is evolved in the seclusion of his own parlour, has also operated to prevent Americans from learning the bitter lessons which should be taught from the war of 1812. The wealthy man who cares only for mercantile prosperity, and the cultivated man who forgets that nothing can atone for the loss of the virile fighting virtues, both also forget that, though war is an evil, an inglorious or unjustifiable peace is a worse evil. As for England, she knows little or nothing about the war, and so of course has been equally blind to its lessons. In one way, however, England does not so much need to be taught these lessons, for there are few of her politicians or publicists of any note who fail to see the necessity of her possessing a navy more formidable than any other navy on the face of the globe.

These men had numerous prototypes in the first decade of the present century. The Federalists, who were crystallised into a party under Washington, did have some appreciation of the fact that peace is worth nothing unless it comes with sword girt on thigh. Accordingly, in 1798 and 1799, under the spur of the quasi-war with France and the depredations of the Moorish pirates, the Federalists set out to build a navy. They only made a beginning. The people behind them were too ignorant and too short-sighted to permit the building of the great ships of the line which could alone decide a war; but they did build half-a-dozen frigates, which were the best of their kind in existence. In 1801, however, the Jeffersonian democrats came into power, and all work on the navy stopped forthwith. Jefferson hated and dreaded war; and he showed the true spirit of the non-military visionary in striving to find some patent substitute for war, or, if war could not be avoided, then some patent substitute for the armies and fleets by which war must be fought. Fatuously unable to learn the lesson taught by the revolutionary contest, he hoped to find in levies of untrained militia a substitute for a regular army. As for the navy, he at one time actually hoped to supply its place by a preposterous system of what may be called horse-gunboats, that is, gunboats which could be drawn ashore and carried on wheeled vehicles to any point menaced by a hostile fleet. Men who get discouraged by the attitude of latter-day politicians may draw some hope and comfort from the reflection that the nation actually lived through the experiment of trying Jefferson's ideas. Nevertheless, the trial of this same experiment caused bitter loss and mortification.

At the present day no student of international law would justify
the attitude of Great Britain in the quarrel; but the international
standard was different among nations at the beginning of the
nineteenth century; and, moreover, Great Britain was fighting
for her life, and nice customs curtesy to great crises as well as
to great kings.

The United States was still primarily a country of dwellers on
the sea-coast. The bulk of the population lay along the Atlantic
sea-board. There were but three states west of the Alleghanies—
Kentucky, Tennessee, and Ohio; and all three were still frontier
commonwealths. From Salem to Savannah the men of every seaport city—and as yet there were no cities of note which were not
seaports—looked upon foreign trade as the surest means to wealth
and social distinction. American shipwrights were already famous:
readers of that delightful book, 'Tom Cringle's Log,' will recall
at once the way in which Scott speaks of the swift American
schooners; and their full-rigged ships also were among the best
of their kind on the ocean. Under the stimulus given by the
European war to their trade the merchants embarked more and
more eagerly in foreign ventures, and ships were turned out of the
yards in ever-increasing numbers. From Maine to Maryland there
was a hardy population of sailor-folk, who manned, not only the
merchantmen, but also the fishing-fleet and the whalers that went
to the North Atlantic and the South Seas. Under the abnormal
growth of the American merchant marine, however, the growth
of the sailor population was outstripped, and it became impossible
to man American ships purely with American seamen. Seamen are
roving creatures at all times, and in every country they shift readily
from one flag to another. Seafarers from various European states,
notably from Portugal and the Scandinavian countries, found their
way in numbers aboard the American ships; but it was the sailors
of the British Islands who formed the chief resource in making up
any deficiency in the numbers of the native Americans. The needs
of Britain's gigantic Navy were very great, and every method was
resorted to in order to keep level its quota of men. Life on a
British warship was hard, and the British seamen lived in terror
of the press-gang. Readers of Marryat's novels will remember
the large part this institution played in the sea life of that period.
Wages on board the American ships were high, and the service not
particularly severe. In consequence, British seamen entered the

American merchant marine literally by thousands. The easy naturalisation laws of the country were even more easily circumvented. There was very little difficulty indeed in any British seaman getting naturalisation papers as an American. The captains of British war vessels were continually meeting in the American ports scores of British seamen who passed them by with insolent defiance, confident in their possession of American naturalisation papers.

Seeing that this occurred at the very time when American trading ships were crippling their British rivals by their competition, and were furnishing supplies to Britain's dreaded and hated rival, the anger alike of British Government officials, of British merchants, and of British naval officers, can be readily understood. It was sufficiently irritating to see an American ship carry to a French port goods which the British wished to keep out of that port, and which, in happier circumstances, might have been in a British bottom; but it was still more exasperating to know that this very ship might number among her crew a considerable proportion of British seamen, at a time when the British fleets needed every man they could crimp or press. Moreover, such a system of neutral trade and of easy naturalisation put a premium upon perjury, and the British grew to look with suspicion upon every statement of an American merchant master, and every paper produced by an American merchant seaman.

The French had little in the way of a grievance against the Americans. Very few French seamen served under the American flag, certainly not enough to be of any consequence to the French navy. The French trade that was driven into American bottoms would otherwise have been extinguished. On the other hand, American merchantmen performed a real service to France when they entered the French ports. There was one point, however, on which the American attitude was precisely as exasperating to France as to Britain, and for the same reason. As regards their dealings with the insurgent negroes of Haiti and with the effort to blockade the Haitian ports, the French stood toward the Americans just as Britain stood toward them in regard to France. In each case the American merchants showed, as might have been expected, the same desire to send their cargoes to the people who wished to pay for them, without regard to the rights or wrongs of any struggle in which these people might be engaged. The Americans sent small fleets of merchantmen to carry goods to the negroes in Haiti, who were engaged in a life and death fight with the French, just as they sent far larger fleets of merchantmen to carry goods to the French, in their deadly grapple with the British; and the French felt as aggrieved in the one case as the British did in the other.

But the case of Haiti was exceptional. Speaking generally, no harm, and, on the contrary, much good, resulted to France from the American neutral trade. Nevertheless, Napoleon adopted toward the Americans a course quite as brutal as the British attitude, and more treacherous. In this he was mainly actuated by a desire to force the Americans into war with Great Britain; but he was swayed by various and complicated motives from time to time—motives which it would be impossible to discuss at proper length here. The intentions of the French people toward the American Republic, as shown by the actions of the French Emperor, were as bad as could be.

The policy of the two nations towards America was promulgated in a series of edicts—those of Napoleon taking the form of Decrees dated at Milan, Berlin, and elsewhere; and those of the advisers of King George appearing as Orders in Council. At different times widely different interpretations were put upon every decree and order, according to the strenuousness of the American protest, and the degree of exasperation of Britain or France. Napoleon in particular, whenever it suited him, interpreted his own decrees in a sense directly opposite to their palpable purport; or, if there was a momentary gain in view, simply denied that he had ever issued them. In Britain the followers of Fox were supposed to be more friendly to America than the followers of Pitt. In theory they were; but in practice the attitudes of the two parties were not materially different. The essential features of the Orders in Council were, that they prohibited American ships from trading with France, unless they first cleared from some British port; and they declared the coast of most of continental Europe to be blockaded, and provided for the seizure of American vessels bound thither. They also imposed similar restrictions upon the very lucrative trade of America with the West Indian Islands. Napoleon's decrees, on the other hand, provided that any American vessel which touched at a British port, or submitted to search by a British cruiser, should be treated as hostile, and be confiscated accordingly. Each nation asserted its right to claim its own seamen, as a matter of course.

These two series of edicts, if fully carried out, meant the absolute annihilation of the American merchant marine so far as foreign commerce was concerned, for almost every country in the world was engaged on one side or the other in the Napoleonic struggles. In point of intent, the action of the French was a little the worse; and some of Napoleon's seizures of American vessels in European ports were marked by a bad faith which made them peculiarly repulsive. The attitude of each nation amply warranted America in declaring war on both. This was the course which was actually proposed in Congress, and which should have been followed. But it was perhaps too much to expect that the struggling transatlantic republic, which, in point of regular navy and army, hardly ranked as a fifth-class power, should at the same time throw down the glove to the two greatest empires of the world. Moreover, the Americans very naturally cared much less what the French and British meant to do, than what they actually did; and when it came to doing, the British were vastly better fitted than the French to carry out their threats.

French privateers and cruisers occasionally mishandled an American vessel, and both ships and cargoes were confiscated when in French ports, sometimes even on a large scale; but it was not for the self-interest of the French to molest overmuch the only neutrals who could bring them the goods of which they stood in need; and there was practically no trouble about the French impressing seamen from American ships, because there were very few Frenchmen in these ships, and those few could not hope to disguise their nationality. The American seaman was inclined to look down upon the French, but he had not much cause either to fear or hate them.

With the British, all this was different. In the first place, the Englishman cordially disliked the American, because the American was feeding his foes, and was robbing him both of his men and of his trade. The fraudulent naturalisation of British seamen was carried on openly in most American ports; and the American flag was used to protect, not merely American skippers engaged in carrying goods, which the British said should not be carried, to France, but also not a few Frenchmen and Spaniards, and a larger number of recreant Britons, who wished to share the profits of the business. The British ships of war were chronically undermanned, and every commander had good reason to believe that almost all

American merchant vessels contained some British seamen to whose service he felt he was lawfully entitled. It was an article of faith with him, as with his country, that he had a right to take these seamen wherever he found them on the ocean. As a rule he disliked, and half despised, the Americans;[1] he was puzzled and angered by the chicanery of fraudulent naturalisation papers and the like wherewith they sought to baffle him; and in revenge he took refuge in brutality. He was himself the judge as to whether or not he was satisfied in regard to the nationality of any given seaman; and he always gave himself the benefit of the doubt— even when there was no doubt. Not only did he impress British seamen who had been fraudulently naturalised as Americans, but quite as often he impressed British seamen who had been properly naturalised and were American citizens, and, even more often, American citizens who were such by birth, and not merely by adoption. The two peoples could not always with entire certainty be told apart; and when the British captain was short-handed he did not endeavour to tell them apart. Many thousands of British seamen served in the American merchant marine; but there were several thousand American seamen who had been impressed into British ships of war. One of the commonest incidents of the time was for an American merchantman to be left helpless on the high seas, unable to reach her port of destination, because the majority of the crew had been taken off by some British man-of-war.

In one of Cooper's sea novels, 'Miles Wallingford,' the action of the story centres upon the experience of an American merchant captain with a British frigate and a French privateer; and, like many another good novel, it is as essentially true to life as any professed history. When not long from New York, the ship was overhauled by a British frigate and sent into a British port as a prize, on the ground that she was sailing for a German port under French influence, and that there was some doubt as to the cargo

---

[1] Although a feeling of dislike for one another may have animated officers and men on both sides, such feeling was by no means universal; and there are many examples of warm private friendships having subsisted before the war between British and American naval officers, and having been continued after it, even in spite of hostile meetings having occurred during the conflict. A notable example of this kind of friendship is to be found in the long and affectionate intimacy which subsisted between Captain Isaac Hull, U.S.N., and Captain James Richard Dacres (2), R.N., an intimacy heightened rather than decreased by the conduct of both on the occasion of the capture of the *Guerrière* by the *Constitution.*—W. L. C.

papers; while most of the crew, Americans and foreigners alike, were taken aboard the frigate. By surprise, the remaining Americans re-captured the ship from the British prize crew, only to have their ship overhauled anew by a French privateer, and again declared to be a prize, upon the ground of having been previously captured by the British. The Americans once more succeeded in regaining posses-sion of the vessel; but, having only four hands with which to work her, she was cast away; so that the voyage ended with the ruin of the owner of the ship, and the impressment of her entire crew.

This particular incident only occurred in a novel; but it was of a kind which occurred hundreds of times in actual life. It was but rarely that an American merchant captain of that day did any writing; yet one out of the very many Salem shipmasters has left a record of his ocean trips at the end of the last and the beginning of the present centuries.[1] He usually owned the ship he navigated, and her cargo also; and he sailed at different times to the chief ports of Europe and Asia, and also to many a coast where the ports were open roadsteads and the inhabitants bloodthirsty savages. He was able to hold his own against mutineers, savages, and pirates; but he was twice brought to ruin by civilised France and Great Britain.

In 1807, when trading to the West Indies, after having already been repeatedly searched by British cruisers, he was taken by Rear-Admiral the Hon. A. F. I. Cochrane, and his ship was con-demned by a rascally little court at Tortola, whither he was sent because a more respectable court would doubtless have released him. The confiscation of his goods stripped him to the bone, so that he had to begin life over again; and, in writing of the event in after years, he remarked: " Compelled to navigate for the support of my family, and deprived in consequence of superintending the education of my children, worn with anxiety and sick at heart with hope deferred, it will be seen that I was for many years an exile from all that rendered life dear and desirable; and this as a consequence of the robbery of my hard-earned fortune by Admiral Cochrane."

Two years later he again got a ship, which he took to Naples, whither he was enticed, with a number of other American merchant-men, by one of the treacherous proclamations of Napoleon. Having got the ships into his power, Napoleon, acting through Murat,

---

[1] 'Voyages of an American Navigator.' By Richard J. Cleveland, pp. 124, 143.

had them all seized and confiscated, without even the formality of a trial. In comparing the two disasters the sufferer commented upon the difference between them as being of not much more consequence than the distinction between " the act of the highwayman who demands your money at the muzzle of a pistol, and that of the swindler who robs you under the form of law." The marvel is, not that such outrages were resented, but that they were ever endured.

No better description of the attitude of the two parties, British and American, toward one another was ever given than is contained in the writings of a most gallant British officer, Captain Basil Hall, R.N. In 1831 he published two little volumes of 'Voyages and Travels,' which contained a chapter called "Blockading a Neutral Port." In this he described what he saw when a Midshipman on board the 50-gun ship *Leander*, while she was lying off New York harbour, to carry out the instructions of the British Government as to supervising the American trade with France. I quote at some length, condensing a little, from his description because it is the best ever given by a responsible authority of what really occurred under the Orders in Council ; and it is written with entire good temper and truthfulness :—

" The blockading service at any time is a tedious one ; but upon this occasion we contrived to enliven it in a manner which, whether legitimate or not, was certainly highly exciting, and sometimes rather profitable, to us.

" With the outward bound vessels we had little to do, but with those which came from foreign parts, especially from France, then our bitter enemy, we took the liberty—the American said the improper liberty. The ships we meddled with, so much to the displeasure of the Americans, were those which, to outward appearance, belonged to citizens of the United States, but on board which we had reason, good or bad, to suspect there was cargo owned by the enemy. Nothing appears to be so easy as to forge a ship's papers or to swear false oaths ; and, accordingly, a great deal of French property was imported into America in vessels certainly belonging to the United States, but covered, as it was called, by documents implying an American or neutral right in it. In the very same way, I suppose, much Spanish property was for a long course of years imported into South America in English bottoms when Spain was at war with her colonies. England in that case acted the part of a neutral, and learned in like manner for the lucre of gain to trifle with all the obligations of an oath. The adroit neutral, by watching his time, can always minister to the several necessities of the combatants, sometimes to one and sometimes to the other, according as the payment is good or bad, and in such a manner as to be sure of his own profit, reckless at whose cost. At the same time he must naturally lay his account with provoking the displeasure of the powers at war, who in their turn will, of course, do all they possibly can to prevent the neutral from lending assistance to their opponents respectively.

" Conflicting nations accordingly have always claimed, and, when they can, will never cease to enforce, this right of searching neutral ships in order to discover whether or not there be enemies' property on board.

"Every morning at daybreak during our stay off New York we set about arresting the progress of all vessels we saw, firing off guns to the right and left, to make every ship that was running in heave to, or wait until we had leisure to send a boat on board 'to see,' in our lingo, 'what she was made of.' I have frequently known a dozen, and sometimes a couple of dozen, ships lying a league or two off the port, losing their fair wind, their tide, and, worse than all, their market, for many hours, sometimes the whole day, before our search was completed. I am not now inquiring whether all this was right, or whether it was even necessary, but simply describing the fact.

"When any circumstances in the ship's papers looked suspicious, the boarding officer brought the master and his documents to the *Leander*, where they were further examined by the Captain; and, if anything more important was then elicited by the examination of the parties or their papers to justify the idea that the cargo was French and not American, as was pretended, the ship was forthwith detained. She was then manned with an English crew from the ships of war and ordered off to Halifax, to be there tried in the Admiralty Court.

"One can easily conceive how this sort of proceeding, in every possible case, must be vexatious to the neutral. If the cargo be all the while, *bonâ fide*, the property of the neutral whose flag it is sailing under, the vexation caused by this interruption to the voyage is excessive. In the event of restoration or acquittal, the owner's loss, it is said, is seldom, if ever, adequately compensated for by the awarded damages.

"We detained, at that period, a good many American vessels on the ground of having French or Spanish property on board. Three or four, I remember, were restored to their owners by the decision of the Admiralty Court; and two of them were forcibly recaptured by the Americans on their way to Halifax. On board one of these ships the master and the few hands left in her to give evidence at the trial rose in the night, overpowered the prize master and his crew, nailed down the hatches, and having put the helm up, with the wind on land, gained the coast before the scale of authority could be turned.

"There was another circumstance, connected with our proceedings at that time, of still more serious annoyance to the Americans, and one requiring in its discussion still greater delicacy of handling. I need hardly mention that I allude to the impressment of those seamen who were found serving on board American merchant ships, but who were known to be English subjects. It seems quite clear that, while we can hold it, we will never give up the right of search, or the right of impressment. We may, and ought certainly to, exercise so disagreeable a power with such temper and discretion as not to provoke the enmity of any friendly nation. But at the time I speak of, and on board our good old ship the *Leander*, whose name I was grieved, but not surprised, to find was still held in detestation three or four and twenty years afterwards at New York, I am sorry to own we had not much of this discretion in our proceedings; or, rather, we had not enough consideration for the feelings of the people we were dealing with. We have since learned to respect them more—or, as they prefer to express it, they have since taught us to respect them: be it either way, it matters not much; and if it please the Americans more to say they have instructed us in this point of good manners, than to allow that we have come to a knowledge of better habits, well and good.

"To place the full annoyance of these matters in a light to be viewed fairly by English people: let us suppose that the Americans and French were to go to war, and that England for once remained neutral, and that an American squadron stationed itself off Liverpool. If the American ships were to detain off the port, within a league or so of the lighthouse, every British ship coming from France or from a French colony; and if, besides looking over the papers of these ships to see whether all was regular, they were to open every private letter in the hope of detecting some trace of French ownership in the cargo, what should we say? If, out of twenty ships, one or two were to be completely diverted from their course from time to time, and sent off under a prize master to New York for adjudication, I wonder how the Liverpool folks would like it?

Conceive, for instance, that the American squadron employed to blockade the French ships in Liverpool were short-handed, but, from being in daily expectation of bringing their enemy to action, it had become an object of great consequence with them to get their ships manned. And suppose, likewise, that it was perfectly notorious to all parties that on board every English ship, arriving or sailing from the port in question, there were several American citizens calling themselves Englishmen, and having in their possession 'protections' or certificates to that effect sworn to in regular form, but all known to be false. If the American man-of-war, off the English port, were then to fire at and stop every ship, and, besides overhauling her papers and cargo, were to take out any seamen, to work their own guns withal, whom they had reason, or supposed, or said they had reason, to consider American citizens, or whose country they guessed from dialect or appearance, I wish to know with what degree of patience this would be submitted to on the Exchange at Liverpool, or anywhere else in England.

"In putting a parallel case to ours off New York, and supposing Liverpool to be blockaded by the Americans, on the ground of having to watch some French ships, I omitted to throw in one item which is necessary to complete the parallel. In 1804, when we were blockading the French frigates in New York, a casual shot from the *Leander* hit an unfortunate ship's mainboom; and the broken spar, striking the mate, John Peirce by name, killed him instantly. The sloop sailed on to New York, where the mangled body, raised on a platform, was paraded through the streets in order to augment the vehement indignation, already at a high pitch, against the English. Now, let us be candid to our rivals, and ask whether the Americans would have been worthy of our friendship, or even of our hostility, had they tamely submitted to indignities which, if passed upon ourselves, would have roused not only Liverpool, but the whole country into a towering passion of nationality?"

The British Minister, Erskine, laid the situation fairly before his Government, writing to them that American ill-will was naturally excited by the "insulting behaviour" of British captains "in the very harbours and waters of the United States," while the whole coast was blockaded as if in time of war, and every American ship vigorously searched in sight of the shore.[1]

According to the best estimate, some twenty-five hundred British seamen were drawn annually into the American merchant marine; and, on the other hand, about a thousand seamen, supposed to be British, but in large part American, were impressed from American merchantmen by British warships every year; while hundreds of these merchantmen were seized by British cruisers, not merely on the high seas, but within gunshot of the American coast. The Americans clamoured in anger, but took no effectual steps in retaliation. The seafaring people were willing to risk a war; but the merchants were not, for, after all, the neutral trade was very remunerative, and, inasmuch as they pocketed the profits, they were willing to pocket the accompanying insults and injuries. Even the outrages on the coast met with no more response than the tedious protests of diplomacy, and an occasional outburst of indignation in some

[1] Adams, iv. 143.

town which refused for the moment to furnish provisions to a
peculiarly offensive British frigate.   It could hardly be deemed very
spirited retaliation, this refusal to give green vegetables to the men
who slew or imprisoned American citizens.   But finally something
occurred which really did rouse the whole nation, for the British
suddenly extended their theory of the right of search so as to
include, not merely the merchant vessels, but the warships of the
United States.

ADMIRAL THE HON. SIR GEORGE CRANFIELD BERKELEY, G.C.B.
(From Ridley's lithograph after the portrait by Miss Paye.)

The British ships on the American coast were under the command of Vice-Admiral the Hon. George Cranfield Berkeley, who
was stationed at Halifax.   Desertions were rife from among these
ships, and, indeed, were not infrequent from the American ships
themselves.   Naturally, whenever a British ship was lying off an
American port, the American seamen aboard her were eager for a
chance to get ashore and desert; and some of the British seamen
were delighted to follow suit.   In 1807 the Admiral issued an order
reciting the fact that a certain number of deserters had escaped

from various British vessels, which he enumerated, and directed the captains of the ships under him to reclaim these deserters wherever found; specifically ordering them to search even an American man-of-war which might be suspected of having them aboard. At that time a British squadron, including both two-deckers and frigates, lay off Norfolk. When they received the news, the American frigate *Chesapeake* was about to put to sea. She had aboard her one of the deserters alluded to, and the 50-gun ship *Leopard*, Captain Salusbury Pryce Humphreys, was despatched to overhaul her and re-claim him.

The *Chesapeake* rated thirty-eight guns, and on this voyage carried forty. She was inferior in strength to the *Leopard*, about in the proportion that a 38-gun frigate was inferior to a 44; that is, the inferiority was not such as to warrant her striking without resistance. The *Chesapeake* was under the command of Captain James Barron when she put out; and, of course, neither he nor anyone else aboard her dreamed that there was the slightest fear of attack from the British ships which were lying at anchor or cruising in the harbour. The *Chesapeake's* decks were lumbered up, and none of her guns were ready for action, for they were without gunlocks, and could only be fired by means of slow matches, or of firing-irons previously heated in the fire. When the *Leopard* approached, Barron still felt no suspicion of the errand on which she came, and he was dumbfounded when he was informed of the purpose to search his ship. It was, of course, a proposition to which no naval officer who did not wish to be hanged for cowardice or treason could submit; and Barron refused. After a few minutes' hesitation, he began to prepare for defence; but, long before the preparations were completed, the *Leopard* opened fire. After submitting to three broadsides, which killed or wounded twenty-one men, the *Chesapeake* struck. She had been able to fire in return but a single gun, which Lieutenant William Henry Allen discharged by means of a hot coal which he brought in his hands from the galley. The British then boarded her, and took out four deserters from British ships, three of these deserters being Americans, and only one a British subject; and the *Chesapeake* returned to port in an agony of shame and rage. Captain Barron was court-martialled, but was acquitted of all charges save neglect to utilise fully the short period given him by the *Leopard* in which to make ready for the fight. Decatur, however, always considered him more blameworthy than was shown by the judgment; and in after life the quarrel between the two men gave rise to a duel in which Decatur was slain.

The event was a terrible tragedy; but one touch of comedy was supplied by Admiral Berkeley's letter approving the deed. In this he warned Captain Humphreys, of the *Leopard*, not to pay heed to American criticism of a feat which was as lawless as any deed of piracy ever committed on the high seas, because he "must make

REAR-ADMIRAL SIR SALUSBURY PRYCE DAVENPORT (PREVIOUSLY HUMPHREYS), KT., C.B., K.C.H.

(After Page's lithograph, in the 'Naval Chronicle,' 1812, of Humphreys as a Post-Captain.)

allowances for the heated state of the populace in a country where law, and every tie both civil and religious, is treated so lightly." [1]

Such an outrage convulsed the whole country for the moment, and spurred to action even Jefferson, the most timid and least warlike of presidents; but Jefferson, even when angry, was utterly unable to uphold the honour or dignity of the nation in any dispute with a foreign power. Though he led the people wrong, it must be remembered that they were more than willing to

[1] Marshall; 'Naval Biography,' ii. 895.

follow his lead; for the Americans of that day lacked national feeling, and were possessed of a party spirit rendered more than usually ignoble because of the fact that the rival factions fought under the badges of France and England, and considered all American questions solely from the standpoint of the foreign nation whose interests they happened to champion. The President, the Congress, and the people as a whole all showed an unworthy dread of the appeal to arms.

Instead of declaring war, Jefferson put in practice one of his favourite schemes, that of commercial war, as he called it. In other words, he declared an embargo on all American shipping, refusing to allow any of it to leave American ports, and hoping thus so to injure the interests of England and France as to force them to refrain from injuring America: a futile hope, rightly destined to meet with the failure which should attend the efforts of men and of nations that lack that most elementary and needful of all virtues, the orderly courage of the soldier. The temper of Jefferson's mind, and the extraordinary military foolishness of the American people as a whole, may be gathered from the fact that, in preparing for war, all he could suggest was that the ships of war should be laid up so as not to tempt the enemy to capture them; and that the United States should rely upon the worthless militia on shore, and the flotillas of equally worthless gunboats along the coast.[1] The British Government, through Canning, disavowed Berkeley's act and recalled him, but accompanied the disavowal with requests and demands in connection with the Orders in Council which were in themselves almost as great insults. Jefferson could not make his embargo work. It did some damage to Great Britain and France, but by no means enough to force either to yield, while it wrought such ruin in America as very nearly to bring about a civil war. It was a mean and ignoble effort to avoid war; and it spoke ill for its promoters that they should prefer it to the manlier course which would have appealed to all really brave and generous natures. At the very end of his administration Jefferson was forced to submit to the repeal of his pet measure, and the substitution of a non-intercourse act, which merely forbad vessels to sail direct to France or England : a measure which, if it accomplished no more good, at least did very much less harm.

The British Government resolutely declined to withdraw the

[1] Adams, iv. 159.

Orders in Council, or to abandon the impressment of seamen from American ships; but, inasmuch as the measures taken by the American government bore equally heavily against France and Britain, they ceased to blockade the American ports, or to exercise the right of search on the American coasts; for they insisted that America must not favour France at the expense of Britain, and hope to escape retaliation. An interminable diplomatic wrangle followed, the British and the French alike accusing the Americans of favouring their opponents; and the Americans endeavouring to persuade each set of combatants that its conduct was worse than that of the other, and should be abandoned. Finally, in 1810, Napoleon made in the last and worst of his decrees certain changes which the Americans thought were equivalent to a repeal. Napoleon and his administrators were steeped in such seething duplicity, mendacity, and corruption, that negotiations with the French at that period afforded a peculiarly difficult problem. He allowed one set of public officials to issue mandates showing that the repeal of the decrees was real, and he permitted action to be taken in accordance with these mandates; while another set of officers, or even the same set on some other occasion, might ignore the alleged repeal and enforce the original decrees. Just prior to going through the form of a pretended repeal, he had enforced a sweeping confiscation of American ships by an act of gross treachery, and he evaded making restitution for this; while, later, one of his squadrons burned American merchant vessels at sea. However, on the assumption that the repeal of the obnoxious decrees had been declared, the American government discontinued the operation of the non-intercourse law as against France. Thereupon the British Government, insisting that the decrees had really not been repealed, renewed the blockade of the American coast, and there began once more the familiar series of outrages; American ships being confiscated, and American sailors impressed, off the mouth of American harbours, and within gunshot of the American shore. Even the greed of gain, and the timidity of the doctrinaire politicians who believed in a conquest to be achieved purely by peace, could not withstand this, and the war spirit rose steadily among the American people; although without that accompaniment of forethought, and of resolute, intelligent preparation, the lack of which tends to make war spirit merely bluster.

At the time the conduct of the French was in intention rather worse than that of the English, and the damage which the French inflicted on the property within their clutches was almost as great; but they had made a pretence of repealing the obnoxious decrees, whereas Great Britain positively declined to repeal the Orders in Council, or to abandon the right of impressment. Moreover, what was far more important, the French were remote and could not do the damage they wished, whereas the British warships were in sight of the American coast, and their actions were the every-day theme of indignant comment. In such circumstances it was inevitable that the people, smarting under their wrongs, should feel inclined to revenge them against the nearer and more obvious aggressor; though this did not excuse the American government for the failure to take a stand as decided against France as against Great Britain.

In 1811 there occurred another collision between armed ships of the two nations. The great frigate, *President*, under the command of Captain John Rodgers, encountered the British sloop of war *Little Belt*, under the command of Commander Arthur Batt Bingham, not very far from the scene of the *Chesapeake's* humiliation. The encounter took place at night, under a misunderstanding which each alleged to be the fault of the other. Shots were exchanged, and a regular fight, lasting about a quarter of an hour, took place, when the *Little Belt*, which was not of a quarter the force of her antagonist,[1] was of course silenced, having thirty-two of her men either killed or wounded. Not a man was touched on board the *President*.[2] Each accused the other of having fired the first shot and brought on the action. But, taking into account the great disparity in force between the combatants, and the further fact that Rodgers carried a letter of instructions from the Secretary of the Navy, which, in effect, directed him to err on the side of aggressiveness rather than to run any risk of a repetition of the *Chesapeake* affair, it is difficult not to come to the conclusion that the *President* was the offender. The incident deeply exasperated the British captains along the coast, while it put the Americans in high feather. They accepted it as an offset to the *Chesapeake* affair, and no longer dwelt much upon the need of redress for the latter.

All of this really rendered war inevitable; but as the American government grew more, the British Government grew less, ready to

---

[1] The *Little Belt* carried eighteen 32-pr. carronades and two 9-prs., with a complement of 121 men and boys; the *President*, a " 44-gun" frigate, seems to have mounted thirty-two 24-prs. and twenty-four 42-pr. carronades.—W. L. C.

[2] Rodgers's letter, May 23rd, 1811; Secretary Hamilton to Rodgers, June 9th, 1810; Bingham's letter, May 23rd, 1811.

appeal to the sword. Finally, in June 1812, Madison sent in his declaration of war, the two chief grievances alleged being the right of search and the impressment of seamen. Almost at the same time, and therefore too late to do any good, the British Government repealed the Orders in Council : a step which, if taken a year before, would not only have prevented war, but very possibly would have made America declare war on France.

Deeply to the national discredit, the American government and people had made no adequate preparation for the conflict into which they plunged. The statesmen who had been in control of the administration for the last dozen years, Jefferson and his followers, were utterly incompetent to guard the national honour when menaced by a foreign Power. They were painfully unable to plan or carry out proper measures for national defence. The younger democratic-republican leaders, men like Clay and Calhoun, were unlike their elders in being willing to fight, but they had not the slightest conception what war meant, or how to meet the formidable foe to whom they had thrown down the glove. Instead of keeping quiet and making preparations, they made no preparations, and indulged in vainglorious boastings. Clay asserting that the militia of Kentucky alone would conquer Canada ; and Calhoun, that the conquest would be made almost without an effort. The memory of these boasts must have cost bitter mortification to the authors a couple of years later. The people as a whole deserved just the administrative weakness with which they were cursed by their chosen rulers. Had Jefferson and the other leaders of popular opinion been wiser and firmer men, they could have led the people to make better preparations ; but the people themselves did not desire wiser or better leadership. The only party which had ever acted with dignity in foreign affairs, or taken proper measures for the national defence and national honour, was the party of the Federalists ; and the Federalists had sunk into a seditious faction, especially in New England, where discontent with the war reached a treasonable pitch before it ended.

Though at the last the British Government had seemed reluctant to go into the war, anticipating no good from it, no question as to the result crossed the mind of any British statesman, soldier or sailor. The *Morning Post*, the organ of the Government, expressed the general feeling when it said in an inspired article that " a war of a very few months, without creating to " (England) " the expense of a single additional ship, would be sufficient to convince" (America) "of her folly by a necessary chastisement of her insolence and audacity." [1] Indeed, there was one factor which both sides agreed at the outset could be neglected, and that was the American navy. The British could hardly be said to have considered it at all; and American statesmen so completely shared the British belief in British invulnerability at sea, that there was a general purpose to lay up the American ships in port; and this course was only prevented by the striking victories with which the navy opened its career.

The American navy itself did not in the least share the feelings of its friends and foes. The officers knew that their ships were, on the whole, better built and better armed than any foreign ships of their classes; and they had entire confidence in their own training and courage, and in the training and courage of the men under them. The navy had been in existence only fourteen years. It was probably fortunate that the service of none of the officers extended back to the revolutionary struggle, when the American warships were really, for the most part, merely ill-disciplined privateers. The first experience of the navy, in the struggle with France, had been honourable. A French frigate and corvette were captured in single fight, while the West Indian seas were almost cleared of French privateers, and no American vessel was lost. Then came the war with the Barbary States, which lasted four years, and was a still better training school; for though it was mostly a wearisome blockade, yet there were bombardments, single ship encounters—in which the vessels of the Moorish pirates were captured—and desperate cutting-out expeditions, in which the Yankee cutlass proved an over-match for the Moorish scimitar. It was in that war that the commanders who later won distinction against the lords of the sea, gained their first experience of hard and dangerous fighting, and of commanding men in action. They improved the experience thus gained by careful training in time of peace.

In 1812 the American navy regarded itself with intelligent and resolute self-confidence. The people at large not merely failed to possess this confidence, but also showed criminal negligence in refusing to build up a navy. The very Congress which declared for war actually voted down a bill to increase the navy by twelve battleships and twenty frigates. The Federalists supported the proposition, but the great bulk of the dominant party, though

[1] *Morning Post*, November 12th, 1807.

clamorous for war, yet declined to take the steps which alone could
have justified their clamour; and in so doing they represented only
too well the people behind them.   Their conduct was humiliating
to the national honour: it was a crime, and it left a stain on the
national character and reputation.   Contempt is the emotion of all
others which a nation should be least willing to arouse; and contempt was aroused by the attitude of those Americans who, in 1812
and before, refused to provide an adequate navy, and declined to put
the country into shape which she ld render it fit for self-defence.
There are plenty of philanthropists and politicians in the America
of to-day who show the same timid, short-sighted folly, and supine
indifference to national honour; nor is the breed wholly lacking in
England.

In 1812 the navy of the United States, exclusive of two or three
condemned hulks and a score or so of worthless gunboats, consisted
of the following vessels :—

RATE. (GUNS.)	NAME.	CLASS.	DATE OF BUILDING.	TONNAGE.
44	United States	Frigate	1797	1576
44	Constitution	„	1797	1576
44	President	„	1800	1576
38	Constellation	„	1797	1265
38	Congress	„	1799	1268
38	Chesapeake	„	1799	1244
32	Essex	„	1799	860
28	Adams	Corvette	1799	560
18	Hornet	Ship-sloop	1805	480
18	Wasp	„	1806	450
16	Argus	Brig-sloop	1803	298
16	Syren	„	1803	250
14	Nautilus	„	1803	185
14	Vixen	„	1803	185
12	Enterprise	Brig	1799	165
12	Viper	„	1810	148

Tonnage was at that time reckoned arbitrarily in several different
ways.   One of the tricks of naval writers of the period, on both
sides, was to compute the tonnage differently for friendly and foreign
ships, thus making out the most gratifying disparity in size, for the
benefit of the national vanity.[1]

[1] The British method of computing tonnage being different from the American,
and even the methods of measurement being different, it is not possible to make an
absolutely accurate comparison of the tonnage of the combatants.   According to the
British methods, the American frigates would measure from 100 to 150 tons less than
the figures given above.   I have discussed the matter fully in the appendix to my
'Naval War of 1812.'   James, the British historian, is one of the writers who, especially

The four smallest brigs were worthless craft originally altered from schooners. The other twelve vessels were among the best of their respective classes afloat. At that time there were two kinds of guns in use in all navies : the long gun and the carronade.[1] The carronade was short and light, but of large calibre. At long ranges it was useless ; at short ranges, owing to the greater weight of the shot, it was much more useful than a long gun of less calibre. American sloops and brigs were armed only with carronades, save for two long bow-chasers ; frigates were armed with long guns on the main-deck, and with carronades and two long bow-chasers on the quarter-deck and forecastle, or what the Americans called the spar-deck. The only exception to this rule was the *Essex*, which was armed with forty 32-pr. carronades and six long 12's. In comparing the relative force of any pair of combatants, the most important item is the relative weight of metal in broadside ; but, in considering this, allowance must always be made for the difference between carronades and long guns, the latter being, relatively to their calibre, much more powerful and efficient weapons. The annalist of each side usually omits all considerations of this kind when they tell against their own people.

The only other class of ocean vessels used by the Americans during the war may as well be alluded to here. It consisted of a class of fine ship-sloops, of 509 tons, each carrying twenty-two guns, which put to sea in 1814.

Almost all the American ships carried more guns than they rated. The 44-gun frigate usually carried fifty-four, consisting of thirty long 24's on the main-deck, and on the spar-deck two long bow-chasers, and either twenty or twenty-two carronades—32-pounders in the *Constitution*, and 42-pounders in the *President* and the *United States*. The *Constellation*, *Congress*, and *Chesapeake* carried forty-eight guns, twenty-eight long 18's on the main-deck, and on the spar-deck two long 18's, and eighteen 32-pr. carronades. The ship-sloops carried 32-pr. carronades, and long 12's for bow-chasers. The brig-sloops carried 24 or 18-pr. carronades, according to their size.

---

in dealing with the lake flotillas, adopts different standards for the two sides ; and his latest editor has attempted to justify him, by ignoring the fact that the question is, not as to the accuracy of James's figures by any one standard, but as to his using two different standards as if they were the same.

[1] For fuller information as to the carronade, *see* Vol. III., pp. 330–333.—W. L. C.

The British vessels with which the American ships most frequently came in contact were the 38-gun frigates and the 18-gun brig-sloops. The 38-gun frigates were almost exactly similar in size and armament to the American ships of the same rate. The brig-sloops were somewhat less in size than the *Hornet* ; they were supposed to carry eighteen guns, two bow-chasers and sixteen 32-pound carronades.

The system of rating, like the system of measuring tonnage, was thus purely artificial. The worst case of underrating in the American navy was that of the *Essex*, which rated thirty-two and carried forty-six guns, so that her real, was 44 per cent. in excess of her nominal force. Among the British ships with which the Americans came in contact, the worst case of underrating was the *Cyane*, which was rated at twenty-two and carried thirty-three guns, making a difference of 50 per cent. The *Wasp* carried eighteen guns, the *Hornet* twenty. The English brig-sloops almost always carried one light carronade beyond their rating, and sometimes, in addition, a light stern-chaser, or two bow-chasers, thrust into the bridle ports.

The conflicts which at the time and afterwards attracted most attention were the first three frigate fights, all of which took place between the American 44's and the British 38's. In each case the American ship was markedly superior in force. The countrymen of each combatant tried, on the one side, to enhance the glory of the victory by minimising this difference in force, and, on the other, to explain away the defeat by exaggerating it. The Americans asserted, not merely in their histories, but even by resolutions in Congress, that the ships were practically equal in force, which a glance at the figures given above will show to be an absurd untruth. The British, on the other hand, sought consolation in declaring that the American frigates were " disguised line-of-battle ships." This has been solemnly repeated at intervals to the present day. It is of course pure nonsense. The American 44's were the finest frigates afloat ; but there had already been 24-pounder frigates, not only in the British, but also in the French and Danish navies. One of the British frigates with which the Americans came in contact was the 40-gun frigate *Endymion*. The *Endymion*, like the *Constitution*, carried long 24's on her main-deck, and 32-pound carronades on her spar-deck. In 1815 she had fifty-one guns, including a shifting 24-pound carronade, making a broadside of 698 pounds. The *Constitution* that year carried fifty-two guns, and threw a broadside of 704 pounds. The difference in weight of metal was therefore just six pounds, or one per cent., which is certainly not enough to mark the difference between a 40-gun frigate and a "disguised line-of-battle ship." As a matter of fact, the difference between the force and the rating was greater in the case of the *Endymion* than in that of the *Constitution*.

The United States was not the first nation that invented the heavy frigate, but was the first to use it effectively. The French 24-pounder carried a ball about five pounds heavier than that of the American 24, and the 36-pound carronade which the French put on their spar-decks carried a heavier ball than the American or British 42-pounder; for the French pound was about 15 per cent. heavier than the English. Nevertheless the French, as well as the Dutch and Danish, heavy 24-pounder frigates had failed to distinguish themselves, and had been captured by the British just as easily as the 18-pounder frigates. In consequence, the belief was general that the 18-pounder frigates were really better as fighting machines than those with 24-pounders. The American successes upset this theory, because the Americans built heavy frigates which were even better than those built by the French and Dutch, and put into them officers and seamen who were able to handle and fight them as no frigates at that time were handled or fought by any other nation.

The size and seaworthy qualities, and the excellent armament of the American vessels did the utmost credit, both to those who had planned them, and to those who had built them. There was one point in which there was a falling off as compared with the British. The American foundries were not very good, and in consequence the guns were more liable to accidents; and almost all the shot were of light weight, the shortage varying from two or three to as much as ten per cent. As a result, the real weight of the American broadside was always somewhat less than the nominal.

The *personnel* of the American navy consisted of 500 officers, but twelve of whom were captains, and 5230 seamen and boys, of whom 2346 were destined for the cruising war vessels, the remainder being for service at the forts and navy yards, in the gun-boats, and on the lakes. The officers were almost exclusively native Americans. In the crews native Americans also overwhelmingly predominated; there were, however, a certain number of foreigners aboard almost every vessel, the proportion of English being probably larger than that of any other nationality, in spite of the fact that Great Britain was the country with which the Americans were at war. This proportion of foreigners, and especially of Englishmen, varied in the different ships. The captains, under instructions from the Secretary of the Navy, got rid of as many English as possible at the outbreak of the war, fearing lest they might be reluctant to fight against their countrymen. A good many remained, possibly as many as ten or even fifteen per cent. of the total in some of the ships, but certainly a smaller percentage on the average.

The British Navy was so large as to put all comparison between it and that of the United States out of the question. But the British Navy could not be diverted from the use to which it had so long been put. It was a knife at the throat of Napoleon, and it could not be taken away. However, this applied only to the great fleets, and there was no need of great fleets for use against America. A few two-deckers, and a score or two of frigates would, it was believed, suffice to keep in check the entire American navy, and to blockade all the important American ports.

The British Navy stood at the height of its splendour and triumph, and higher than any other navy either before or since. During twenty years of almost uninterrupted warfare it had cowed or destroyed the navies of all other European powers. In fleet action after fleet action it had crushed to atoms the sea might of France, of Spain, of Holland, and of Denmark; in hundreds of single ship fights, in which the forces engaged on each side were fairly equal, the monotonous record of Britain's triumphs had been broken by less than half-a-dozen defeats. The British officers felt absolute confidence in their prowess, and they despised their new foes. As a whole they had begun to pay less attention to gunnery since Nelson's death; and this lack of care and their overwhelming pride and self-confidence—good qualities, but bad if carried to excess—made them less fit than formerly to contend on equal terms for the mastery of the ocean with enemies more skilful than any they had yet encountered. Their European antagonists had been completely cowed, and always entered into a fight half beaten in advance; but in the Americans they had to meet men of a different mettle.

In June, 1812, there were half-a-dozen British frigates, and one old two-decker, the *Africa*, 64,[1] immediately off the American coast. Had the American ships been ready they could doubtless have overcome these, even when collected into a squadron, as they were as soon as the news of the outbreak of the war became known. Such a victory over a squadron would have been an incalculable benefit to the Americans; but the administration had no thought of such action. It wished to lay up the American frigates in port, and was only prevented from doing so by the urgent remonstrances of two of the naval captains. The Secretary of the Navy wrote letters to Captain Isaac Hull urging him to act, even against a single foe, with timid caution; but Hull, fortunately, was willing to bear the responsibility which his superior shirked.[2] However, even a bold administration could have done little at the moment. The ships were not ready, and all that could be done was to send Captain John Rodgers on a cruise with his own frigate, the *President*, 44, the *United States*, 44, Captain Stephen Decatur, the *Congress*, 38, Captain John Smith, the *Hornet*, 18, Captain James Lawrence, and the *Argus*, 16, Captain Arthur Sinclair. Rodgers put to sea on June 21st, hoping to strike the West Indies' homeward-bound fleet.[3] Two days out of the port he encountered the British frigate *Belvidera*, 36, Captain Richard Byron (2).[4] Byron had been informed of the likelihood of war by a New York pilot boat; and as soon as he made out the strange ships he stood away before the wind. The Americans made all sail in chase, the *President*, a very fast ship off the wind, leading, and the *Congress* coming next.

At noon the *President* was within less than three miles of the *Belvidera*, steering N.E. by E. As the *President* kept gaining, Byron cleared for action, and shifted to the stern ports two long 18's on the main-deck and two 32-pound carronades on the quarter-deck. At 4.30[5] Commodore Rodgers himself fired the *President's* starboard forecastle bow-chaser; the corresponding main-deck gun was next discharged; and then Rodgers fired his gun again. All three shots struck the stern of the *Belvidera*, killing and wounding nine men; but when the *President's* main-deck gun was discharged

[1] The *Africa*, built in 1781, was, in 1812, flagship of Vice-Admiral Herbert Sawyer (2), who, since 1810, had been Commander-in-Chief on the Halifax station.— W. L. C.

[2] Ingersoll's 'Second War between the United States and Great Britain,' i. 377, 381.

[3] Captain John Rodgers to the Secretary of the Navy, Sept. 1st, 1812.

[4] Brenton, v. 46.

[5] Cooper, ii. 151.

for the second time it burst, blowing up the forecastle deck and killing and wounding sixteen men, among them the Commodore himself, whose leg was broken. Nothing causes more panic than such an explosion, for every gun is at once distrusted; and in the midst of the confusion Byron opened his stern-chaser, and killed or wounded six men more. Had the *President* pushed steadily on, using only her bow-chasers until she closed, she would probably have run abreast of the *Belvidera*, which could not then have successfully withstood her; but, instead of doing this, she bore up and fired her port broadside, doing little damage; and this manœuvre she repeated again and again; while the *Belvidera* kept up a brisk and galling fire with her stern-chasers, and her active seamen repaired the damage done by the *President's* guns as fast as it occurred.[1] Byron cut away his anchors, the barge, yawl, gig, and jolly-boat, and started fourteen tons of water, gradually shifting his course, and beginning to draw ahead, and the *President*, which had lost much ground by yawing to deliver her broadsides, could not regain it.[2] The upshot of it was that Captain Byron escaped and got safely into Halifax on June 27th, having shown himself to be a skilful seaman and resolute commander.[3] Subsequently, when engaged in the blockade of the Chesapeake, he proved himself to be as humane and generous to non-combatants as he was formidable to armed foes.

Rodgers's squadron continued its cruise, but returned home two months later without accomplishing anything save the capture of a few merchantmen. When Byron brought the news of the war to Halifax, a squadron of ships [4] was immediately despatched to cruise against the United States, under the command of Captain Philip Bowes Vere Broke, of the *Shannon*. Meanwhile the *Essex*, 32, had to put to sea under Captain David Porter, after he had in vain implored the Navy Department to allow him to change her main-deck carronades for long guns. She cut out a transport with a couple of hundred soldiers from a convoy of troopships bound to Quebec, under the protection of the British frigate *Minerva*, 32,

---

[1] James, vi. 119.

[2] Sir Howard Douglas, 'Naval Gunnery,' 419 (3rd edition).

[3] In this affair, Lieutenants John Sykes (2), William Henry Bruce (2), who was wounded, and the Hon. George Pryse Campbell, and the Master, Mr. James Kerr, of the *Belvidera*, specially distinguished themselves. (Byron's Disp.)—W. L. C.

[4] *Africa*, 64, *Shannon*, 38, *Belvidera*, 36, and *Æolus*, 32, subsequently reinforced by the *Guerrière*, 38. The squadron left Halifax on July 5th.—W. L. C.

Captain Richard Hawkins; and she captured the British ship-sloop *Alert*, 16,[1] Commander Thomas Lamb Polden Laugharne, after an exchange of broadsides, made prize of eight merchantmen, and then returned to New York.[2]

On July 12th another ship, destined to become one of the most famous in the American navy, put out of the Chesapeake. This was the 44-gun frigate *Constitution*, affectionately known as "Old Ironsides." She was commanded by Captain Isaac Hull, than whom there was no better single ship commander in the service. Her crew was almost entirely new, drafts of men coming on board up to the last moment; but they were of excellent stuff, being almost all native Americans, cool, handy, intelligent, and eager to learn their duties. Under the care of the experienced officers and under-officers they were got into shape as men-of-war's men without the slightest trouble. Just before starting, Hull wrote to the Secretary of the Navy: "The crew are as yet unacquainted with a ship of war, as many have but lately joined, and have never been on an armed ship before. . . . We are doing all we can to make them acquainted with their duties, and in a few days we shall have nothing to fear from any single-decked ship." [3]

There was need of hurry. On the afternoon of July 16th, when some leagues off Barnegat, Hull sighted Captain Broke's squadron, which had just previously captured the American brig *Nautilus*, 14. This squadron then consisted of the *Shannon*, 38, Captain Broke, the *Belvidera*, 36, Captain Richard Byron, the *Guerrière*, 38, Captain James Richard Dacres (2), the *Africa*, 64, Captain John Bastard, and the *Æolus*, 32, Captain Lord James Nugent Boyle Bernards Townshend. The *Guerrière* became separated from the rest of the squadron, and the *Constitution* beat to action and stood toward her, the wind being very light. The *Guerrière* also stood toward the *Constitution*, but, early on the 17th, when only half a mile away, she discovered the rest of the British squadron on her lee beam. She signalled to these vessels, and they did not answer—a circum-

---

[1] The *Alert* was one of twelve colliers which had been purchased into the Navy in 1804, and fitted with 18-pr. carronades. In 1812 two only of these craft, the *Alert* and the *Avenger*, remained on the list. In the brief action the *Alert* had three men wounded. Laugharne, his Master, and his Purser were most honourably acquitted for the loss of the ship; but the first lieutenant, Andrew Duncan, was dismissed the service for misbehaviour.—W. L. C.

[2] Navy Department MSS., 'Captains' Letters,' 1812, vol. ii., No. 128, etc.

[3] Navy Department MSS., 'Captains' Letters,' 1812, ii. No. 85.

stance which afterwards caused a sharp controversy among the
Captains; whereupon, concluding that they were Commodore
Rodgers's squadron, she tacked and stood away from the *Constitution* some time before discovering her mistake.   It was now nearly
daylight.

As morning broke all the British ships were in chase of the
Constitution, heading eastward.   At 5.30 it fell entirely calm, and
Hull rigged four long 24's aft to serve as stern-chasers.   At 6 A.M.
the *Shannon*, the nearest frigate, tried a few shots, which fell short.
Then most of the boats of the squadron were got out to tow her,
and she began to gain on the American.   Hull tried kedging.   All the
spare rope was bent on to the cables and payed out into the cutters,
and a kedge was run out half a mile ahead and let go; whereupon the
crew clapped on and walked away with the ship, overrunning and
tripping the kedge as she came up with the end of the line.[1]   Meanwhile fresh lines and another kedge were carried ahead, and the
frigate glided away from her pursuers.   From time to time there
were little puffs of air, and every possible advantage was taken of
each.   At one time the *Guerrière* opened fire, but her shot fell
short.   Later in the day the *Belvidera*, observing the benefit which
the *Constitution* had derived from warping, did the same, and,
having men from the other frigates to help him, she got near enough
to exchange bow and stern-chasers;[2] but fear of the American guns
rendered it impossible for either the *Belvidera* or the *Shannon* to
tow very near.

The *Constitution's* crew showed most excellent spirit, the officers
and men relieving one another regularly, and snatching their sleep on
the decks.   All through the afternoon and until late in the evening
the towing and kedging went on, the British ships being barely
out of gunshot.   Then a light breeze sprang up, and, the sails of
the *Constitution* being handled with consummate skill, she gradually
drew away, and throughout the following day continued to gain.
In the evening there came on a heavy rain squall, of which Hull
took such skilful advantage that he greatly increased his lead.   At
8.15 on the morning of the 20th, the British ships gave up the
pursuit.   During the three days' chase Hull had shown skill and
seamanship as great as would be demanded by a successful battle,
and his men had proved their hardihood, discipline, and readiness

[1] Cooper is the best authority for this chase.
[2] Marshall's ' Naval Biography,' ii. 626.

for work. If they could do as well with the guns as with the sails, Hull's confidence in his ability to meet any single-decker was more than justifiable; and Hull was eager to try the experiment. He did not have long to wait.

The *Constitution* put into Boston, and on August 6th made sail to the eastward. Hull acted without orders from the Department, for the administration was as yet uncertain as to whether it could afford to risk its frigates in action. But Hull himself wished for nothing so much as a chance to take the risk, and he knew that, not being one of the senior officers, he would speedily be superseded in the command of the *Constitution*. Accordingly, he sailed, right in the track of the British cruisers, to the coast of Nova Scotia, where the British fleet had its headquarters. In the afternoon of the 19th, in latitude 40° 30′ N. and 55° W., he made out a frigate bearing E.S.E. and to leeward.[1] She proved to be his old acquaintance, the *Guerrière*, under Captain James Richard Dacres (2).[2] It was a cloudy day, and the wind blew fresh from the N.W. The *Guerrière* backed her maintopsail, and waited for the *Constitution*, which shortened her sail to fighting rig, and ran down with the wind nearly aft. The *Guerrière* was on the starboard tack, and at 5 o'clock she opened with her weather guns, the shot falling short. She then wore round and fired her port broadside, the shot this time passing over the *Constitution*.[3] As she again wore to fire her starboard battery, the *Constitution* yawed a little and fired two or three of her port bow-guns. Three or four times the *Guerrière* repeated this manœuvre, wearing and firing alternate broadsides with little or no effect; while the *Constitution* yawed to avoid being raked, and occasionally fired one of her bow-guns. The distance was very great, however, and little or no damage was caused. At 6 o'clock the *Guerrière* bore up and ran off with the wind almost astern on her port quarter under her topsails and jib. The *Constitution* set her main-topgallantsail and foresail, and at 6.5 P.M. closed within half pistol-shot distance on her adversary's port beam.[4] Then for the first time the action began in earnest, each ship firing as the guns bore. By 6.20[5] the two were fairly abreast, and the *Con-*

---

[1] Letter of Captain Isaac Hull, Aug. 28th and 30th, 1812.
[2] Letter of Captain Dacres, Sept. 7th, 1812.
[3] Navy Department MSS., 'Logbook of *Constitution*,' vol. ii.
[4] 'Autobiography of Commodore Morris,' p. 164.
[5] 6.5 P.M. by the *Guerrière's* time.—W. L. C.

stitution shot away the *Guerrière's* mizenmast, which fell over the starboard quarter, knocking a big hole in the counter, and brought the ship round against her helm.   The British ship was being cut

AMERICAN COMMEMORATION MEDAL OF THE CAPTURE OF THE "GUERRIÈRE" IN 1812.

to pieces, while the American had hardly suffered at all.   The *Constitution*, finding that she was ranging ahead, put her helm aport and luffed short round her enemy's bows, raking her with the starboard guns; then she wore, and again raked with her port

battery. The Englishman's bowsprit got foul of the American's
mizen-rigging, and the vessels then lay with the *Guerrière's* starboard bow against the *Constitution's* port quarter.[1] The Englishmen's bow-guns played havoc with Captain Hull's cabin, setting
fire to it; and on both sides the boarders were called away. The
British ran forward, but Captain Dacres relinquished the idea of
attacking when he saw the crowds of men on the American's
decks;[2] while the *Constitution's* people, though they gathered aft
to board, were prevented by the heavy sea which was running.
Both sides suffered heavily from the closeness of the musketry fire;
indeed, it was at this time that almost the entire loss of the *Constitution* occurred. In the *Constitution*, as Lieutenant William S.
Bush of the marines sprang upon the taffrail to leap on the *Guerrière's*
deck, a British marine shot him dead; Charles Morris, the first lieutenant, and John C. Alwyn, the master, had also both leaped on the
taffrail, and both were at the same moment wounded by the musketry
fire. In the *Guerrière* almost all the men on the forecastle were
picked off. Captain Dacres himself was shot and wounded by one
of the American mizentop men while he was standing on the starboard forecastle hammocks cheering on his crew; the first and
second lieutenants, Bartholomew Kent and Henry Ready, and the
master, Robert Scott, were also shot down. The ships gradually
worked round until they got clear. Immediately afterwards the
Guerrière's foremast and mainmast went by the board, leaving her
a defenceless hulk, rolling her main-deck guns into the water. At
6.30 the *Constitution* ran off for a little distance, and lay to until she
had repaired the damages to her rigging. Captain Hull then stood
under his adversary's lee, and the latter struck at 7 P.M., just two
hours after she had fired the first shot; the actual fighting, however,
occupied but little over twenty-five minutes.

The *Constitution* was a very much heavier ship than the
Guerrière. She carried thirty-two long 24's and twenty-two
32-pr. carronades, while the *Guerrière* carried thirty long 18's, two
long 12's, and eighteen 32-pr. carronades; the *Constitution's* crew
numbered 456 all told, while the *Guerrière's* numbered but 282,
and 10 of these were Americans, who refused to fight against
their countrymen, and whom Captain Dacres, very greatly to his
credit, permitted to go below. Fourteen of the *Constitution's* men

[3] Cooper in *Putnam's Magazine*, i. 475.
[2] Dacres's address to the court-martial at Halifax.

and 79 of the *Guerrière's* were killed or wounded.[1]   The damage done to the *Constitution* was trifling, while the *Guerrière* was so knocked to pieces that she had to be abandoned and burned by the victors, who then set sail for Boston, which they reached on August 30th.   "Captain Hull and his officers," wrote Captain Dacres, "have treated us like brave and generous enemies; the greatest care has been taken that we should not lose the smallest trifle."

Rarely has any single-ship action caused such joy to the victors, such woe to the vanquished.   The disparity of force between the combatants was very nearly in the proportion of three to two. Against such odds, when there was an approximate equality in courage and skill, neither Dacres [2] nor any other captain in the British Navy could hope to succeed.   But hitherto the British had refused to admit that there was or could be any equality of courage and skill between them and their foes.   Moreover, the disparity in loss was altogether disproportionate to the disparity in force.   No one could question the gallantry with which the British ship was fought; but in gunnery she showed at a great disadvantage compared to the American, and she was not handled with as much judgment.   Like all the other British captains on the American coast, Dacres had been intensely eager to meet one of the large American frigates, and no doubt of his success had crossed his mind. British captains, in single-ship contests, had not been accustomed to weigh too nicely the odds against them; and in the twenty years during which they had overcome the navies of every maritime power in Europe they had repeatedly conquered in single fight where the difference in force against them had been far heavier than in this instance.   This was the case when, in 1799, the British 38-gun 18-pr. frigate *Sibyl* captured the French 44-gun 24-pr. frigate *Forte;* when, in 1805, the *Phœnix*, 36, captured the *Didon*, 40; when, in 1808, the *San Fiorenzo*, 36, captured the *Piedmontaise*, 40; and in many other instances.   The exultation of the Americans was as natural as was the depression of the British; though both feelings were exaggerated.

[1] The *Guerrière* lost 15 killed, including Lieutenant Henry Ready, and 63 (6 mortally) wounded, including Captain Dacres, Lieutenant Bartholomew Kent, Master Robert Scott, Master's Mates Samuel Grant and William John Snow, and Midshipman James Enslie.—W. L. C.

[2] Captain Dacres was tried at Halifax on October 2nd, and, with his officers and crew, unanimously and honourably acquitted.—W. L. C.

Captain Hull owed his victory as much to superiority of force as to superiority of skill; but in the next sea fight that occurred the decisive difference was in skill. On October 18th the American 18-gun ship-sloop *Wasp*, Captain Jacob Jones, mounting sixteen 32-pr. carronades and two long 12's, with 137 men all told, sailed from the Delaware. She went south-eastward to get into the track of the West India vessels; and on the 16th ran into a heavy gale in which she lost her jib-boom, and two men who were on it. On the 17th the weather had moderated somewhat, and late in the evening she descried several sails in latitude 37° N. and longitude 65° W.[1] These were a convoy of merchantmen guarded by the British 18-gun brig-sloop *Frolic*, carrying sixteen 32-pr. carronades, two long 6's and two 12-pr. carronades, with a crew of 110 men. She was under the command of Commander Thomas Whinyates, and had also suffered in the gale of the 16th, in which her mainyard had been carried away.[2] The morning of the 18th was almost cloudless, and the *Wasp* bore down on the convoy under short fighting canvas; while the *Frolic* hauled to the wind under her boom-mainsail and close-reefed foretopsail, the merchantmen making all sail to leeward. At 11.30 A.M. the action began, the two ships running parallel on the starboard tack within sixty yards of one another, the *Wasp* firing her port and the *Frolic* her starboard guns. By degrees the ships fell off until they were almost before the wind. There was a heavy sea running, which caused the vessels to pitch and roll; and the two crews cheered loudly as the ships wallowed through the water. Clouds of spray dashed over both crews, and at times the muzzles of the guns were rolled under;[3] but in spite of the rough weather the batteries were well served. The *Frolic* fired far more rapidly than the *Wasp*, delivering three broadsides to her opponent's two, and shooting while on the crests of the seas. The shot, in consequence, tended to go high. In the *Wasp* the captains of the guns aimed with skill and precision, as the engaged side of their ship was getting down. They therefore fired into their opponent's hull; so that, though they fired fewer shots, a much larger proportion hit. Four minutes after the action began, the *Wasp's* maintopmast was shot away and fell with its yard

---

[1] Letter of Captain Jones, Nov. 24th, 1812. The American letters can generally be found in 'Niles's Register.'

[2] Captain Whinyates' letter, Oct. 18th, 1812.

[3] 'Niles's Register,' iii. 324.

across the port foretopsail braces, rendering the head-yards unmanageable. Ten minutes later the gaff and mizen-topgallantmast
came down; and twenty minutes after the action had begun, every
brace and most of the rigging was shot away, so that it was almost

AMERICAN COMMEMORATION MEDAL, BY SPENCER, OF THE CAPTURE OF THE
"FROLIC," IN 1812.

impossible to brace any of the yards. But while the *Wasp* suffered
thus aloft, the *Frolic* was suffering far more heavily below. Her gaff
and her head braces were shot away, and her lower masts wounded;
but her hull was cut to pieces. The slaughter was very great

among her crew; nevertheless, the survivors fought on with splendid
courage.   Gradually the *Wasp* forged ahead, while the two vessels
drew closer together, so that at last the Americans struck the
Frolic's side with their rammers in loading.   The *Frolic* then fell
aboard her antagonist, her jibboom coming in between the main and
mizen-rigging of the *Wasp*, and passing over the heads of Captain
Jones and Lieutenant James Biddle as they stood near the capstan.
The brig was raked from stem to stern; and in another moment
the Americans began to swarm along the *Frolic's* bowsprit, though
the roughness of the sea rendered the boarding very difficult.   A
New Jersey sailor, Jack Lang, was the first man on the bowsprit.
Lieutenant Biddle then leaped on the hammock cloth to board; but
one of the midshipmen who was following him seized his coat-tails
and tumbled him back on deck.   At the next swell he succeeded in
getting on the bowsprit behind Jack Lang and another seaman, and
he passed them both on the forecastle; but there was no one
to oppose him.   Not twenty of the British were left unhurt, and
most of those were below.   The man at the wheel was still at
his post, doggedly attending to his duty, and two or three more
were on deck, including Captain Whinyates and Lieutenant Frederick
Boughton Wintle, both so severely wounded that they could not
stand without support.   It was impossible to resist longer, and
Lieutenant Biddle lowered the flag at 12.15, after three-quarters of
an hour's fighting.

A minute or two afterwards the *Frolic's* masts went by the
board.   Every one of her officers was wounded, two of them mortally.[1]   The *Wasp* lost but ten men, chiefly aloft.   Nevertheless,
the desperate defence of the *Frolic* in the end accomplished the
undoing of her foe, for in a few hours a British 74, the *Poictiers*,
Captain John Poo Beresford, hove in sight, and captured both victor
and vanquished, the *Wasp* being too much cut up aloft to make her
escape.

The two ships were of practically equal force: in broadside the
British used ten guns to the American's nine, and threw a few
pounds more weight of metal, while they had twenty-five fewer
men.   The disparity in loss was enormous.   The *Frolic* was

[1] The *Frolic* went into action with 110 men and boys all told on board. Of these,
15 were killed and 47 wounded, besides some who were slightly hurt. Among the
wounded were Commander Whinyates, Lieutenants Charles M'Kay (mortally), and
Frederick Boughton Wintle, and Master John Stephens (mortally).—W. L. C.

desperately defended; no men in any navy ever showed more courage than Captain Whinyates and his crew. The battle was decided by gunnery, the coolness and skill of the Americans, and the great superiority in the judgment and accuracy with which they fired, giving them the victory. Their skill was rendered all the more evident by the extreme roughness of the sea, which might have been expected to prevent, and, in the case of the *Frolic*, actually did prevent, very great accuracy of aim. In forty-five minutes the American ship cut her antagonist to pieces, conquering a foe who refused to admit defeat until literally unable to return a blow.

On October 8th Commander Rodgers left Boston, on his second cruise, with the *President, United States, Congress,* and *Argus.* Three days out they separated. The *President* and *Congress* cruised together, nearly crossing the Atlantic, but did nothing more than capture a dozen merchantmen, though they twice chased British frigates—once the *Nymphe*, 38,[1] once the *Galatea*, 36.[2] They returned to Boston on December 31st. The *Argus* got in about the same time, having herself been chased for three days by a British frigate.[3] She had to start her water and cut away her boats and anchors to escape; but she kept her guns, and during the chase actually succeeded in taking and manning a prize, though the delay allowed the pursuer to get near enough to open fire as the vessels separated.

The fourth ship of Rodgers's squadron met with greater luck. This was the frigate *United States*, 44, Captain Stephen Decatur. She was a sister ship to the *Constitution*, but mounted 42-pr. carronades instead of 32's, and had a crew of 478 officers and men all told. On October 25th, in latitude 29° N. and longitude 29° 30′ W., she descried a sail on her weather-beam, twelve miles distant.[4] This was the British 38-gun frigate *Macedonian*, Captain John Surmam Carden. Unlike the *Guerrière*, which had been captured from the French, she was a new oak-built ship, rather larger than any of the American 18-pr. frigates. She carried a crew of 301 men all told. Her armament was like the *Guerrière's*, except that she had two

---

[1] Captain Farmery Predam Epworth. The *Nymphe* was sighted and chased on October 10th.—W. L. C.

[2] Captain Woodley Losack. The *Galatea* was sighted on October 31st.—W. L. C.

[3] Letter of Captain Arthur Sinclair, Jan. 4th, 1813.

[4] Letter of Captain Decatur, Oct. 30th, 1812.

long 18's fewer on the main-deck, and two long 9's extra on the spar-deck. Like the *Guerrière*, she had an 18-pr. carronade extra, so that she presented twenty-five guns in broadside, throwing 547 pounds of shot; while the *United States* had twenty-seven guns in broadside, throwing nominally 846 pounds of shot, although owing to the short weight of metal the actual broadside was probably under 800.

CAPTAIN STEPHEN DECATUR, JUN., U.S.N.

(From A. B. Durand's engraving of the portrait by T. Sully.)

The *Macedonian* was reputed to be a crack ship. Captain Carden had exercised every care to gather a crew of picked, first-rate men. He had also taken every opportunity to get rid of all the shiftless and slovenly seamen. Both he himself and his first lieutenant, David Hope, were merciless disciplinarians, and kept the crew in order by the unsparing use of the lash, in which they seemed positively to delight. They were feared even more than they were hated, and the discipline of the ship was seemingly perfect ; but they made the men under them detest the service.[1]

Lieutenant Hope said afterwards that the state of discipline on board was excellent ; and that in no British ship was more attention paid to gunnery.[2] The results of the action showed, however, that the discipline was that of a martinet, and that in intelligence and judgment the gunners of the *Macedonian* could not compare with those in the *United States*, where the sailors were admirably drilled, and yet were treated so humanely that the captured crew speedily wished to enlist among them.

Captain Carden knew nothing of the defeat of the *Guerrière*, and was most anxious to engage the *United States*. Once, while at Norfolk before the war, he and Decatur had met and joked one another as to which ship would win if they met in battle. The *Macedonian's* people were entirely confident of victory, although among the crew there was a generally expressed wish that the antagonist were a French, instead of an American, frigate, because they knew that they could whip the French, and they had learned from the Americans on board that the Yankee frigates carried heavy metal.

Of these American seamen there was a considerable number among the crew of the *Macedonian*. A British seaman, who served long on the *Macedonian*, in writing out his reminiscences in after-life, gave a vivid picture of how they happened to be on board. In one place he described the work of the press-gang at a certain port, adding " among (the impressed men) were a few Americans ; they were taken without respect to their protections, which were often taken from them and destroyed ; some were released through the influence of the American Consul ; others, less fortunate, were carried to sea, to their no small chagrin." When the ship was at Norfolk, as already mentioned, the sailors were denied all liberty to get on shore for fear lest they should desert. " Many of our crew were Americans ; some of these were pressed men ; others were much dissatisfied with the severity, not to say cruelty, of our discipline ; so that a multitude

---

[1] 'Thirty Years from Home, or a Voice from the Main-deck, being the Experience of Samuel Leech,' fifteenth edition, 1847, pp. 89, 99, etc.   Leech was an Englishman who was a sailor in the *Macedonian ;* he afterwards entered the United States service, with others of the *Macedonian's* crew. He belonged to the British Nonconformist type, which has so many points in common with the average American citizen.   His rambling reminiscences are by no means without value.

[2] Marshall's ' Navy Biography,' ii. 1018.

of the crew were ready to give leg-bail, as they termed it, could they have planted their feet on American soil." [1] Before going into action some of these Americans requested permission not to fight against their countrymen; but Captain Carden, unlike Captain Dacres, refused to grant this permission, and ordered them to the guns under penalty of death. One or two of them were killed in the action. The crew of the *United States* was mainly composed of native Americans, but among the foreigners on board there were a number of Englishmen, as well as many Americans, who had served in the British fleet.[2] All did their duty equally well.

As soon as it was evident what the *United States* was, the *Macedonian* beat to quarters, the bulkheads were knocked away, the guns were cast loose, and in a few minutes all was ready. In the excitement of the battle the men forgot their wrongs, real and fancied, and went into action in good spirits; and throughout the fight they continued to cheer heartily. The junior midshipmen were stationed below on the berth-deck with orders to shoot any man who ran from his quarters; and the captain exhorted the men to show fidelity and courage, quoting Nelson's famous words, "England expects every man to do his duty." [3]

The *Macedonian* then bore down toward the *United States*, which stood toward her with the wind a little forward of the port-beam. Captain Carden, from over-anxiety to keep the weather-gage,[4] hauled by the wind, and passed far to windward of the

---

[1] Leech, pp. 80, 102.

[2] "That Britons were opposed to Britons in the *Macedonian* action is no less true than lamentable. Most of her gallant defenders recognised old shipmates in the British Navy among those who had fought under the American flag. We have already stated that a quartermaster discovered his first cousin in the person of a traitor Two other seamen met with brothers from whom they had been long separated; and Mr. James, in his ' Naval History,' informs us that an officer's servant, a young lad from London, named William Hearne, found his own brother among the *United States'* crew. . .
It is also worthy of remark that many of the guns on board the *United States* were named after British ships, and some of our most celebrated naval commanders. Captain Carden, observing ' Victory' painted on the ship's side over one port, and ' Nelson ' over another, asked Commodore Decatur the reason of so strange an anomaly. He answered: ' The men belonging to those guns served many years with Lord Nelson, and in the *Victory*. The crew of the gun named ' Nelson ' were once bargemen to that great chief. . . .' "—Marshall : ' Nav. Biog.' ii. 1019. But it does not necessarily follow that men who had served with Nelson were British subjects; and it is admitted on both sides that before 1812 very many Americans had served with honour in the British Navy.—W. L. C.

[3] Leech, 127, etc.

[4] Sentence of court-martial held on board the *San Domingo*, 74, at Bermuda, May 27th, 1813.

American. Decatur eased off and fired a broadside, which fell short; he then held his luff, and, the next time he fired, his long main-deck guns, the only ones used, told heavily. The Englishman responded with his long 18's, but soon found that at long bowls the American had the advantage, not only in weight of metal, but also in rapidity of fire, for the broadsides of the *United States* were delivered almost twice as fast as those of the *Macedonian*.[1] Captain Carden soon altered his mind and tried to close; but he had lost his chance by keeping his wind in the first place, and, when he bore up and down with the wind on his port-quarter, he exposed himself to heavy punishment. The *United States* at 10.15 A.M. led her maintopsail aback and used her whole port broadside. The British ship replied with her starboard guns, hauling up to do so, while the American alternately eased off and came to, keeping up a terrific fire. The guns of the *Macedonian* caused some damage to the American's rigging, but hardly touched her hull, while Carden's ship suffered heavily both below and aloft, and her decks began to look like slaughter-pens. The British sailors fought like tigers — some stripped to the shirt, others to the naked skin. Those who were killed outright were immediately thrown overboard. One man, who was literally cut almost in two by a shot, was caught as he fell by two or three of his shipmates, and, before the last flicker of life had left him, was tossed into the sea. Lieutenant Hope showed that, though a cruel task-master, he at least possessed undaunted courage. He was wounded, but as soon as the wound was dressed returned to the deck, shouting to the men to fight on; and he alone advised against striking the flag, preferring to see the ship sink beneath him.[2] The *Macedonian* gradually dropped to leeward, while the American forereached until the firing ceased. Finding herself ahead and to windward, the *United States* tacked and ranged up under the *Macedonian's* lee, at 11.15, when the latter struck her colours, an hour after the action began.

The *United States* had suffered very little. Some of her spars were wounded, and the rigging was a good deal cut up; but her hull had not been touched more than two or three times. As the ships were never close enough to be within fair range of grape and musketry, only a dozen of her men were killed and wounded. The *Macedonian*, on the other hand, had received over a hundred shots

---

[1] James, vi. 169.   [2] Leech, 131.

in her hull; her mizenmast and her fore and maintopmasts were shot away, and on the engaged side all her carronades but two, and two of her main-deck guns, were dismounted, while one hundred and four [1] of the crew were either killed or wounded.[2]

When the Americans came on board to take possession, the British crew, maddened by the sight of their dead comrades, heated with the fury of the battle, and excited by rum they had obtained from the spirit-room, evinced a tendency to fight their captors. But the latter showed so much good humour, and set to work with such briskness to take care of the wounded and put the ship to rights, that the two crews soon became the best of friends, and ate, drank, sang, laughed, and yarned together with hearty goodwill. A rather unexpected result was that the majority of the captive crew soon showed a disposition to enlist in the American navy, especially when they found out how much more kindly the seamen were treated in the American ships. The Americans, however, not only refused to enlist them, but also kept close guard over them to prevent their escape, as it was wished to send them to England in a cartel to exchange for American prisoners.[3] However, in one way or another most of them managed to get away, a few only venturing to enlist in the American navy, as death would naturally be their portion if they were recaptured and recognised by the British.

Decatur discontinued his cruise to take back his prize to the United States. He reached New London in safety, and the *Macedonian* became part of the American navy.

In this fight the *Macedonian's* only superiority over the *United States* was speed. In force she was very much inferior, about in the proportion of three to two, so that only marked superiority in seamanship and gunnery could have given her the victory. As a matter of fact, however, the superiority was the other way. Decatur handled his ship faultlessly, and William Henry Allen, first lieutenant of the *United States*, had trained the men to the highest

[1] The killed numbered 38, including Boatswain James Holmes, Master's Mate Thomas James Nankivel, and Mr. Dennis Colwell, schoolmaster. Among the 68 wounded were Lieutenants David Hope and John Bulford, Master's Mate Henry Roebuck, Midshipman George Greenway, and Mr. Francis Baker, first-class volunteer. Captain Carden and his officers and men, upon trial for the loss of the ship, were most honourably acquitted, the court specially commending Carden's gallantry, and the good conduct and discipline of all concerned.—W. L. C.

[2] Captain Carden's Letter, Oct. 28th, 1812.

[3] Leech. He is the authority for most of the incidents of the action, as seen from the *Macedonian*.

point of efficiency in the use of the guns.   The gun practice of the
Macedonian's crew was apparently poor, but this was probably as
much the fault of the Captain as of the gunners, for he first kept
off too far, so as to give all possible advantage to the 24-pounders of
the Americans, and then made his attack in such a manner as to
allow his skilful adversaries to use their guns to the best advantage.
The *Macedonian* was bravely fought, and was not surrendered until
there was no hope of success left.   Still, the defence was not so
desperate as that of the *Essex*, nor indeed did the ship lose so
heavily as the *Java* or *Chesapeake*.   Captain Carden had bravely
encountered heavy odds, for during the preceding twenty years the
traditions of the British Navy had taught him that it was possible
to win against such odds.   This had been proved scores of times in
single fight at the expense of the French, the Spaniards, the Dutch,
the Danes, and the Turks.   But only a real superiority in skill could
have warranted the effort.   An eminent British officer, Sir Howard
Douglas, sums up the action very justly, though he ascribes wholly
to inferior gunnery what should be in part ascribed to lack of
judgment on the side of the commanding officer.   He says :—

"As a display of courage the character of the service was nobly upheld; but we
would be deceiving ourselves were we to admit that the comparative expertness of the
crews in gunnery was equally satisfactory.   Now, taking the difference of effect as
given by Captain Carden, we must draw this conclusion—that the comparative loss in
killed and wounded (104 to 12), together with the dreadful account he gives of the
condition of his own ship, while he admits that the enemy's vessel was in comparatively
good order, must have arisen from inferiority in gunnery, as well as in force."

Elsewhere the same writer comments upon the dangers to which
encounters with skilful opponents exposed captains who had been
led by repeated triumphs over men of inferior discipline and ability
to feel that defeat was out of question, and to " contemn all
manœuvring as a sign of timidity."   It was the old lesson of the
ill effects of over-confidence, complicated by the effects of following under wrong conditions the course which a great man had
followed under right ones.   Timid manœuvring was an error,
especially in the presence of an unskilful or inferior foe ; and it was
to such manœuvring that Nelson alluded when—or if—he said,
" Never mind manœuvring—go at them."   Nelson knew very well
when to manœuvre and when not to, and his own genius and the
skill of his captains and seamen enabled him to defy heavy odds.
But it was a very different thing for would-be imitators of Nelson's

tactics who lacked his genius, and who had to encounter superiority in skill as well as superiority in physical force.

On October 26th [1] the *Constitution*, Captain William Bainbridge and the *Hornet*, Captain James Lawrence, sailed ; and, after cruising to and fro, arrived off San Salvador on December 13th. There they found a British ship of twenty guns, the *Bonne Citoyenne*, Captain Pitt Burnaby Greene, almost exactly of the *Hornet's* force, and Lawrence challenged her captain to single fight, the *Constitution* giving the usual pledges not to interfere. The challenge was refused, for a variety of reasons ; among others, because the *Bonne Citoyenne* was carrying home half a million pounds in specie. Leaving the *Hornet* to blockade her, Bainbridge ran off to the southward.

At 9 A.M. on December 29th, while the *Constitution* was running along the coast of Brazil about thirty miles off shore, in latitude 13° 6′ S. and longitude 32° W.,[2] she made out the British frigate *Java*, Captain Henry Lambert, inshore and to westward.[3] The *Java* at once bore down in chase, while the *Constitution* stood toward her on the starboard tack.[4] The *Java* was of the same strength as the *Guerrière*, except that she had a crew of about four hundred men,[5] and carried two long guns less, and two carronades more.[6] The *Constitution* had sent ashore two of her carronades, and had four hundred and seventy-five men in her crew.

The *Java* was much the swifter ship, for the weak point in all

---

[1] James says that the *Constitution* and *Hornet* left Boston on October 30th.— W. L. C.

[2] James (vi. 126) gives the time of sighting as 2 P.M. (an obvious error), and the position as lat. 13° 6′ S., long. 30° W.—W. L. C.

[3] Letter of Captain Bainbridge, Jan. 3rd, 1813.

[4] Letter of Lieutenant Henry Ducie Chads, Dec. 31st, 1812.

[5] James explains that on August 17th, 1812, the *Java*, 38 (ex-*Renommée*), had been commissioned at Portsmouth to carry to Bombay the newly-appointed governor, Lieut.-General Hislop and a supply of stores ; and says that her ship's company included about 60 raw Irish landsmen, and 50 disaffected seamen from the *Coquette*, 18, besides a considerable number of Marine Society boys—in all, 397 persons of every description, mainly inexperienced. She had sailed from Spithead on November 12th, in charge of two Indiamen, and, on December 12th, had captured the American merchantman *William*, into which she had put a prize crew of 20, all told. The Indiamen had afterwards parted company, and the *Java* had put into San Salvador for water.—W. L. C.

[6] *See* Roosevelt's 'Naval War of 1812,' p. 126, for full discussion of the figures given above. The official accounts contradict one another flatly. The reason for the great number of men aboard the *Java* was because she was carrying part of the crews for three other British ships.

the American 44's was their lack of speed. In point of physical force the combatants stood more nearly on an equality than in either of the other frigate duels, the odds being about five to four, or rather less—odds which were a heavy handicap to the *Java*, but which were not such as to render the contest by any means hopeless if the weaker party were even slightly superior in skill and fighting efficiency.

CAPTAIN WILLIAM BAINBRIDGE, U.S.N.

(*From G. Parker's engraving, after the portrait by J. W. Jarvis.*)

The *Constitution* stood away from the land towards the S.E., while the *Java* made sail on a parallel course to windward, and gained rapidly. At half-past one the *Constitution* shortened her canvas to fighting rig, and ran easily off on the port tack. The *Java* also shortened sail, and came down off the wind toward her adversary's weather quarter. The colours of the two ships floated from every mast in proud defiance, the decks were cleared to fighting trim, and the men stood ready at quarters. At 2 P.M. they opened fire at long range, the British with the lee and the Americans with the weather guns. The firing was very spirited, and at the beginning the ships suffered about equally, for the first broadside of the *Java* was well aimed, killing and wounding several of the *Constitution's* crew. The Englishman kept edging down until he got well within range of grape and musketry. Being swifter, he soon forereached, intending to wear across his antagonist's bow and rake him; but Bainbridge anticipated the movement, and himself wore in the smoke. The two antagonists again ran off side by side, with the wind on their starboard beams, the Englishman still a-weather, and steering freer than the *Constitution*, which had luffed to close.[1] The action went on at pistol-shot distance; but in a few minutes the *Java* again forged ahead out of the weight of her adversary's fire, and then kept off as before; and, as before, the *Constitution* avoided this by wearing, both ships once more coming round with their heads to the east, the American still to leeward. The *Java* kept the advantage of the wind, and still forereached a little; and she sought to rake the *Constitution* as the latter from time to time luffed in the endeavour to close; but after the first broadside or two her gunnery had fallen off. Most of the loss which she inflicted was inflicted early in the action.

Bainbridge, finding that his foe outsailed him, and that he was therefore constantly in danger of being raked, set the *Constitution's* foresail and mainsail, and came up close on the *Java's* lee beam. The weight of his fire then told heavily, and among other losses the *Java's* jib-boom and the end of her bowsprit were carried away. The *Constitution* in her turn forged ahead, and again wore on the smoke. The *Java* hove in stays, but the loss of her headsail made her fall off very slowly; and the American frigate, passing across her stern two cable-lengths away, raked her heavily. As the *Java* fell off she replied with her port guns, and the two vessels bore up, and ran off with the wind nearly aft, the *Java* still to windward. She was suffering heavily, and the *Constitution* very little. The ships were well within musketry range, and the British lost many men by the fire from the American topmen, and still more from the round and grape; but the crew showed no signs of flinching, and fought on like tigers. Captain Lambert saw that he was beaten at the guns, and that he was being cut to pieces both below and aloft;

---

[2] Navy Departmental MSS., Log of *Constitution*.

and he resolved to try boarding. The helm was put a-weather, and the *Java* came down for the *Constitution's* main-chains. The boarders and Marines gathered in the gangways and on the fore-castle, the boatswain having been ordered to cheer them with his pipe that they might make a clean spring.[1] But boarding was a hazardous experiment to try against an enemy not already well beaten at the guns. As the *Java* came down, the Americans raked her with terrible effect, taking out her foremast and maintopmast. The stump of the *Java's* bowsprit caught in the *Constitution's* mizen-rigging, and she was raked again, while the American marines and topmen, by their steady fire, prevented any effort to board.

Finally the ships got clear; and once again they ran off abreast. Again the *Constitution* forereached, and, wearing, luffed up under the *Java's* quarter, raked her with the starboard guns, and wore again, recommencing the action with her port battery. Once more the vessels were abreast, and the action went on as furiously as ever, the *Java* refusing to acknowledge defeat. The wreck of her top-hamper lay over her starboard side, taking fire every few minutes; and at that time her able and gallant commander was mortally wounded by a ball fired by one of the American maintop men.[2] Lieutenant Henry Ducie Chads then took the command, though painfully wounded. The British sailors continued to fight with un-daunted resolution, cheering lustily; but nothing could stand against the cool precision of the Yankee fire. The decks of the *Java* looked like a slaughter-house; one by one her masts fell; her guns were silenced; and she lay a sheer hulk on the water, when, at 4.5 P.M., the *Constitution*, thinking that her adversary had struck, ceased firing and passed out of action to windward. There she spent an hour in repairing damages and securing her masts; then, in practically as good condition as ever, she stood towards her foe, who struck his flag.

The American ship had suffered but little either in hull or aloft, and, after an hour of repairs, was again in good fighting trim. Thirty-four of her crew were killed or wounded,[3] for the *Java* had been more skilfully handled and more stubbornly fought than either the *Guerrière* or the *Macedonian*. The British ship was a riddled and

---

[1] Minutes of court - martial held on board H.M.S. *Gladiator*, Portsmouth, April 23rd, 1813.

[2] Report of the Surgeon of the *Java*.

[3] Report of the Surgeon of the *Constitution*.

dismasted hulk. "The *Java* sustained unequalled injuries beyond the *Constitution*," ran the statement of one of her officers.[1] One hundred and twenty-four of those on board her were killed or wounded.[2]   Captain Bainbridge reported that the *Java* was "ex-ceedingly well handled and bravely fought," and paid a deserved tribute to the worth and bravery of Captain Lambert;[3] while Lieutenant Chads in his report stated that "our gallant enemy has treated us most generously," and Lieutenant-General Hislop presented Bainbridge with a handsome sword. Owing to the dis-tance from home, the *Java* was destroyed, and the *Constitution* presently returned to the United States.

The fight was remarkable because of the rather complicated nature of the manœuvres, and the skill with which they were performed.   As regards the tactical ability with which the ships were handled, there was nothing to choose ; and certainly no men could have fought more gallantly than the *Java's* crew; but there was a very great difference in the comparative efficiency of the two crews as fighting machines, especially in gunnery.   The differ-ence in the damage done was utterly out of proportion to the difference in force.   Probably the material of the *Constitution's* crew was slightly better than that of the *Java*, for the seafaring folk from among whom it was recruited were peculiarly handy and resourceful, and they enlisted freely in the American ships, regarding the quarrel as peculiarly their own; while the British frigates were manned by pressed men from many different sources, who were full of fight, but who had little cause to love their task-masters.   The main reason for the difference in fighting efficiency, however, was that one crew

[1] 'Naval Chronicle,' xxix. 432.

[2] The *Java* went into action with a crew of 377 all told, including supernumeraries, 20 others having been sent on board the *William*.   Of these, 22 were killed, and 102 wounded.   Among the killed were Master's Mates Charles Jones, Thomas Hammond, and William Gascoigne, Midshipmen William Salmond and Edward Keele, and Clerk (supernumerary) Thomas Joseph Matthias.   Among the wounded were Captain Henry Lambert (who died on January 4th, 1813), Lieutenant Henry Ducie Chads, Master Batty Robinson, Second Lieutenant David Davies, R.M., Boatswain James Humble, and four Midshipmen, besides, among the supernumeraries, Commander John Marshall, Lieutenant James Saunders, Master's Mate William Brown, and General Hislop's aide-de-camp.   Midshipman Keele, who was only thirteen years of age, was not killed outright, but died in a few hours.   Mr. Humble lost a hand, and had a wound near the elbow, but, after having a tourniquet put on, returned to his duty.—W. L. C.

[3] Captain Henry Lambert had received his post commission on April 10th, 1805. —W. L. C.

had been carefully trained, and the other had not.   The *Java's*
crew had been on board her six weeks, and, when the *Constitution*
fought her first battle, the crew had been on board her only five
weeks ; but the *Constitution's* crew from the very beginning were
incessantly practised in firing, both with blank cartridges and also
at a target; whereas the *Java*, during the entire six weeks, had fired
but six broadsides, all of blank cartridges, and her crew had been
exercised only occasionally even in pointing the guns.   Thus the
Americans were trained to shoot with a precision entirely foreign to
their opponents.   Moreover, they were better trained to play different
parts, so that, for instance, the sudden loss of a gun captain did not
demoralise the rest of the crew, who were able immediately to supply
his place from among themselves.   The petty officers, also, among
the Americans were better paid than in the British ships, and were
of a better class ; and the American officers showed greater zeal and
intelligence in getting their men into order, and in drilling them in
the essentials, never losing sight of the fact that efficiency in fighting
was the first consideration, to which all considerations of show
came second.

The *Hornet* continued to blockade the *Bonne Citoyenne* until
January 24th, 1813, the latter still refusing to fight and jeopardise
the treasure she had on board.   Then the *Montagu*, 74,[1] arrived,
and the *Hornet*, under cover of the darkness, stood out to sea.   She
made a few prizes, one of much value.   On February 24th, 1813, near
the mouth of the Demerara River, Captain Lawrence, being near
shore, discovered a man-of-war brig lying at anchor; and while
beating round Caroband bank in order to get at her, he discovered
another man-of-war brig edging down on his weather quarter.[2]
Both were British.   The one at anchor was the *Espiègle*, of sixteen
32-pr. carronades, and two 6 prs., Commander John Taylor (1) ; the
other was the *Peacock*, Commander William Peake, which for some
unknown reason had exchanged her 32-pr. carronades for 24's.[3]
She had left the *Espiègle's* anchorage that morning at ten o'clock.
The *Hornet* at once turned to attack the newcomer, being anxious
to get rid of her before her companion inside the bar could come to
her assistance.

[1] Captain Manley Hall Dixon, bearing the flag of Rear-Admiral Manley Dixon
commanding on the Brazilian station.—W. L. C.

[2] Letter of Captain Lawrence, March 20th, 1813.

[3] James, vi. 194 (Ed. 1837).

At 4.20 P.M. the *Peacock* hoisted her colours, and the *Hornet* beat to quarters and cleared for action. Lawrence kept close hauled to get the weather-gage. When he was sure that he could weather the enemy, he tacked at 5.10 and stood toward her, hoisting his colours. The ship and the brig were now both on the wind—the *Hornet* on the starboard, and the *Peacock* on the port, tack. At 5.25 they exchanged broadsides as they passed one another, but a few yards distant, in opposite directions, the Americans firing their lee, and the British their weather guns, as they bore. The contrast in the gunnery of the two crews was almost absurd. As the British were using the weather battery, the guns, unless somewhat depressed, were sure to throw the shot high, and for this the crews made no allowance. Not a shot penetrated the *Hornet's* hull, the entire broadside passing through the rigging. One of her men in the mizen-top was killed by a round shot, and two in the main-top were wounded; [1] a few ropes were cut, the foremast was wounded, and some holes were made in the sails; but her fighting efficiency was not impaired in the slightest degree. On the other hand, the *Hornet's* guns, being fired from the lee side of the ship, naturally shot low, and her men aimed as if at drill, almost every shot striking the *Peacock's* hull, while, inasmuch as the *Peacock* was heeled over, many of them struck below the water-line, making holes through which the water gushed in torrents as soon as the brig was again on an even keel.

When the two vessels were clear, Captain Peake put his helm hard up and wore, firing his starboard guns; but Lawrence had watched him closely, and himself bore up, and at 5.35 ran the Englishman close aboard on the starboard quarter. Another broadside, added to the musketry fire, did the business. Captain Peake fell; and at 5.39, [2] just fourteen minutes after the first shot, the *Peacock* surrendered. Immediately afterwards her main-mast went by the board, and she began to settle, hoisting her ensign union down as a signal of distress. Both vessels cast anchor; and Lieutenant Shubrick, being sent on board the prize, reported her sinking. Lieutenant Connor was then sent in another boat to try to save the brig; but though the captors threw the guns overboard, plugged the shot holes, and worked the pumps, the water gained so rapidly

---

[1] Navy Departmental MSS., Logbook of *Hornet*, *Wasp*, and *Argus*, 1809–1813.
[2] British accounts, and James, make the action to have lasted from 5.25 to 5.50 P.M.—W. L. C.

that the attempt was abandoned, and the *Hornet's* officers used what remained of the fading tropical twilight in removing the wounded and prisoners. Just as dark fell the brig suddenly sank, in water which was so shallow that her foretop remained above the surface. There was, of course, much confusion. Three of the *Hornet's* men and nine prisoners went down with the *Peacock*. Four other prisoners lowered the stern-boat and escaped unobserved to the land, while four more saved themselves by running up the rigging into the foretop. Lieutenant Connor and the rest of the *Hornet's* men who were on board, and the remainder of the *Peacock's* crew, who had not been shifted, escaped by jumping into the launch which was lying on the booms, and paddling her towards the ship with pieces of boards.

Seven of the *Hornet's* men and six of the *Peacock's* were on the sick list, leaving fit for action one hundred and thirty-five of the former,[1] and one hundred and twenty-two of the latter.[2] The *Hornet* carried twenty, and the *Peacock* nineteen[3] guns, each presenting ten in broadside; but, as already mentioned, the *Peacock's* carronades were 24's, and the *Hornet's* 32's. There was a very real disparity in force, but in this particular instance the disparity in force in no way affected the result. The *Peacock's* guns simply did not hit, so that their calibre was a matter of no possible consequence. The *Hornet* was hardly scratched, and lost but three men, all aloft; while the *Peacock* was sunk in fourteen minutes, nearly one-third of her crew being killed or wounded.[4] She was bravely fought, but her gunnery was phenomenally bad. It appears that she had long been known as "the yacht" on account of the tasteful arrangement of her deck. The breechings of the carronades were lined with white canvas, and nothing could exceed in brilliancy the polish upon the traversing bars and elevating screws.[5] Of course, a slovenly ship does not often make a good fight, for slovenliness is an indication of laziness, carelessness, and inefficiency; but man—and above all the fighting man—shall not live by neatness alone, nor yet merely by

[1] Letter of Lieutenant Connor, April 26th, 1813.

[2] Letter of Lieutenant Frederick Augustus Wright, April 19th, 1813.

[3] According to James, the *Peacock* mounted only sixteen 24-pr. carronades, and two long 6-prs., and had nine, not ten, guns in broadside.—W. L. C.

[4] Of her crew of 122 men and boys, the *Peacock* had five killed, including Commander Peake, a Commander of January 21st, 1806, and 33 wounded, three mortally.—W. L. C.

[5] James, vi. 194 (Ed. 1837).

precision in the performance of duties not connected with the actual
shock of arms.   Commander Peake had committed the not un-
common mistake of confounding the incidents and the essentials of
discipline.

Throughout the fight the *Espiègle* was but four miles distant,[1]
and was plainly visible from the *Hornet*; but for some reason, which
never was fully explained, her Commander did not observe anything,
and knew nothing of the action until the next day.   Lawrence, of
course, took it for granted that he must know, and would shortly
come out; and, by nine o'clock in the evening, new sails had been
bent on, and the decks cleared, so that the *Hornet* was again ready
for action.   She was then, however, overcrowded with people and
short of water, and, as the *Espiègle* showed no signs of coming out,[2]
the *Hornet* stood for home, which she reached in March.   On their
arrival at New York the officers of the *Peacock* published a card
expressing their appreciation of the way in which they and their
men had been treated.   The note ran in part, " We ceased to consider ourselves prisoners, and everything that friendship could dictate
was adopted by you and the officers of the *Hornet* to remedy
the inconvenience we would otherwise have experienced from the
unavoidable loss of the whole of our property and clothes owing
to the sudden sinking of the *Peacock*." [3]

So far the American navy had achieved success beyond what
any one could have either hoped for or dreaded, and the British
government had paid dearly for its contemptuous disregard of the
power of the United States at sea.   It was utterly unprepared for
the skill and energy shown by the Americans.   More ships of the

---

[1] Upon this point there is, however, a conflict of evidence.   Lieutenant Frederick
Augustus Wright, of the *Peacock*, testified that the *Espiègle* " was not visible from the
look-outs stationed at the *Peacock's* mastheads for some time previous to the commencement of the action."   James, too, says (vi. 194, ed. 1837): " The wreck of the *Peacock* was
visible for a long time after the action, and bore from Point Spirit, which is about six
miles to the eastward of the entrance to Demerara river, N.E. by E.; making the
distance between the *Espiègle* and *Peacock*, during the action, nearly 24 miles."—
W. L. C.

[2] Commander John Taylor (1), of the *Espiègle*, was tried at Portsmouth, in 1814,
on various charges, and was, in consequence, dismissed the service; but though the
charges included a count of having failed in his duty when he was in pursuit of the
Hornet, it was held that that particular charge was not proved.   Commander Taylor
was reinstated, as " the junior Commander," in 1817.   (Marshall, iv., pt. iii. 537, and
the Navy Lists.)—W. L. C.

[3] This and the other letters are given in full in ' Niles's Register ' for this and the
following months.

line and frigates were gradually assembled on the American coast;
but, during the first eight months or thereabouts, no effective
blockade was established, and the American cruisers slipped in
and out as they wished. The British picked up a couple more
American brigs, the *Viper* and the *Vixen*,[1] and captured many
American merchantmen, but this was all.

The offensive powers of the Americans were displayed not merely
in the use of their regular war-vessels, but in the careers of the
privateers. The mere declaration of war with Great Britain meant
the destruction for the moment of the major part of the foreign
trade of America; and the more daring spirits who had formerly
gone into this trade at once turned to the business of privateering.
The American privateers swarmed out into the Atlantic, and
especially round the West India Islands, the trade with which was
at that period very profitable to England. At times, in the past,
the French privateers had inflicted very great damage upon British
trade, but the British men-of-war had so completely gained
the upper hand of their adversaries that very few French ships,
public or private, were left at sea. The activity and success of
the American privateers, therefore, took the British government
and the British mercantile interest completely by surprise. Hundreds of merchantmen were captured in the Atlantic, and in the
West Indies the privateers cut vessels out of harbours protected
by batteries, and landed to plunder the plantations. The island of
Jamaica was for some time practically blockaded by them. At first
the British warships could do little with them; and the merchants
cried out bitterly because of the failure to protect them.

As rapidly as possible the British naval authorities gathered the
swiftest frigates and sloops to employ against these cruisers; and
there resulted a process of natural selection so severe that the type of
privateer soon became altered. At the outset almost any craft was
used; but before the first year of the war had closed all the small and
slow vessels were captured or shut up in port, and a peculiar species
of craft was developed. She was of large size, with a numerous
crew, so as to man the prizes, and was armed with one heavy gun,
or "long tom," and several lighter pieces for use at close quarters.

---

[1] The *Viper*, 16, Lieut. J. D. Henby, was captured on January 17th, 1813, by the
Narcissus, 32, Capt. John Richard Lumley. The *Vixen*, 12, Lieut. Geo. U. Read, had
been taken on the previous November 22nd, by the *Southampton*, 32, Capt. Sir James
Lucas Yeo.—W. L. C.

She was sometimes a schooner, and sometimes a brig or a ship, but always built on fine lines, and with extreme lightness, so as to possess astonishing speed.   There were no more beautiful craft in existence than these graceful, venomous, swift-sailing privateers; and as commerce destroyers they had not then their equals in the entire world.[1]

The first nine months of the war ended with the balance entirely in favour of the Americans.   Even at the outbreak of hostilities the British had, scattered along the American coast and among the West India Islands, three or four times as many ships as there were in the American navy, and to those there had been added many others, including heavy two-deckers; but they had not settled down to any definite plan for seriously interfering with the cruises of the regular warships, or for sweeping the privateers from the seas.   The American trade had suffered severely; but so had the British.   Infinitely more important, however, than such material suffering, short of actual crippling, were the shame and smart felt by the British public at the American naval victories.   Commerce destroying was annoying and vexatious, and it might prove sufficiently serious to incline an already disheartened combatant to peace; but no amount of destruction of commerce could cripple a thoroughly resolute antagonist, nor, giving heart to the nation which inflicted the loss, make it thrill with that warlike pride and determination to conquer which do so much toward winning victory. The two prime objects to be attained in successful warfare are to cripple the antagonist and to give heart and confidence to one's own side.   The first object could not be attained by the little American navy, for it was powerless to inflict appreciable damage to the colossal sea might of England; but the second object it could and did achieve.   On land the American attempts to invade Canada resulted in humiliating disasters, and the effects of the victorious sea fights were very great in offsetting the mortification and depression which those disasters caused.

In England the sea fights caused as much excitement as in America, though of a wholly different kind.   Neither the British government nor the British people, and least of all the British

---

[1] Adams, vols. vii. and viii., has treated better than any other historian the careers and importance of the privateers.   If he could have seen Mahan's book before writing his own, he would doubtless have laid more stress on the unsatisfactory results of trying to substitute commerce destroyers for fighting ships.

Navy, had dreamed it possible that on sea they would suffer any serious annoyance from America. The prowess of the American frigates and sloops, the hawk-like predatory speed of the American privateers, and the energy displayed by men-of-warsmen and privateersmen alike, were so many disagreeable surprises. The material loss to the merchants was heavy, whereas the material loss to the navy was trifling, so far as affecting Great Britain's naval strength was concerned. Nevertheless, it was this last loss which infinitely outweighed the other, as was inevitable and proper with a proud, self-confident, and warlike nation. In seven months Great Britain had suffered from the infant navy of the United States, in five single-ship contests, severer moral loss than she had suffered in all the single-ship contests of the preceding twenty years' warfare with the nations of Europe.

Such a result was almost paralysing, and naturally produced inordinate boastfulness and self-exaltation on the one side, and bitter shame and anger on the other. The victors, the greater to exalt their glory, sought to minimise the difference of force in their favour, and insisted that the contending ships were practically on an equality ; which was not only absurdly untrue, but a discredit to their own intelligence, for, of course, it was highly to the credit of America to have built ships more efficient than any then afloat. The vanquished, to extenuate their defeats, attributed them entirely to the difference in force, and enormously exaggerated this, crying out that the American 44's were " disguised 74's," and that building them was a characteristic piece of " Yankee cunning " to lure brave British captains into unequal combat. The attention paid in Parliament and in the London press to these victories was a sufficient tribute to their importance. The *Times*, smarting under the need to lay stress upon a difference in force which British seamen had been accustomed to disregard, wrote,

" Good God! that a few short months should have so altered the tone of British sentiment! Is it true, or is it not, that our Navy was accustomed to hold the American in utter contempt ? Is it true, or is it not, that the *Guerrière* sailed up and down the American coast with her name painted in large characters on her sails, in boyish defiance of Commodore Rodgers ? "

Eighty-five British ships were on the American station at the beginning of hostilities.

" We have since sent out more line-of-battleships and heavier frigates. Surely we must now mean to smother the American Navy. A very short time before the capture of the *Guerrière,* an American frigate was an object of ridicule to our honest tars. Now the prejudice is actually setting the other way, and great pains seem to be taken by the friends of ministers to prepare the public for the surrender of a British 74 to an opponent lately so much contemned."

The *Pilot,* the chief maritime authority, gave full expression to the feelings with which the British public generally regarded these events :—

"The public will learn, with sentiments which we shall not presume to anticipate, that a third British frigate has struck to an American. This is an occurrence which calls for serious reflection—this, and the fact stated in one paper of yesterday, that *Lloyd's List* contains notice of upwards of five hundred British vessels captured in seven months by the Americans, five hundred merchantmen, and three frigates! Can these statements be true, and can the English people hear them unmoved? Any one who had predicted such a result of an American war this time last year would have been treated as a madman or a traitor. He would have been told, if his opponents had condescended to argue with him, that long ere seven months had elapsed the American flag would be swept from the seas, the contemptible navy of the United States annihilated, and their maritime arsenals rendered a heap of ruins. Yet down to this moment not a single American frigate has struck her flag. They insult and laugh at our want of enterprise and vigour. They leave their ports when they please, and return to them when it suits their convenience; they traverse the Atlantic; they beset the West India Islands; they advance to the very chops of the Channel; they parade along the coasts of South America; nothing chases, nothing intercepts, nothing engages them but to yield them triumph."

Canning, in open Parliament, expressed the bitter anger felt by the whole governing class. He stated that the loss of the frigates had affected the country as it could be affected only by the most violent convulsions of nature, and he returned to the subject again and again, saying, " It never entered into my mind that the mighty naval power of England would be allowed to sit idle while our commerce was swept from the surface of the Atlantic." And again, " It cannot be too deeply felt that the sacred spell of the invincibility of the British Navy was broken by these unfortunate captures."

Most significant of all was the fact that the Admiralty issued an order forbidding the 18-pounder frigates thereafter to do battle with the American 24-pounder frigates. This was not a confession of inferiority, as has been said by some American writers; but it was distinctly a renunciation of any claim of superiority. The American 44 was no more superior to the British 38-gun frigate than the French 74 was to the English 74, for the main-deck battery of the French two-decker carried a gun which threw a shot weighing forty-three English pounds, whereas the main-deck guns of the

British ships of the line were only 32's.   The difference, therefore, was greater in favour of the French ships of the line, as compared with their British opponents, than the difference between the victor and the vanquished in the famous single-ship duels of 1812.   The victories of Nelson and Jervis had been gained against odds much greater than those encountered by the frigates which succumbed to the *Constitution* and the *United States.*   Time and again, moreover, the British had won against odds as great, or greater, in single combat.   The French 18-pounder gun threw a shot weighing twenty-one pounds English; whereas, owing to the short weight of the American shot, the American 24-pounder usually threw but a little over twenty-two; so that, as compared with the old opponents whom the British frigate captains had so often vanquished, their new American foes threw but one and one-half pound more metal from each gun of the main battery.

The difference in the size and stoutness of the ships, in the numbers of the crews, and in the calibre of the guns accounted for much in the result, but it by no means accounted for all; and in the two sloop actions it was of little or no moment.   The other element, which entered quite as decisively into the contest, was the superior efficiency of the Americans, especially in gunnery.   The British had grown over-confident and careless.   They had learned to lean over-much upon what Canning called "the sacred spell of the invincibility of the British Navy," and they needed to learn the lesson that this sacred spell can always be readily broken by any opponent who, with equal courage, shows superiority in skill, and especially in cool forethought and preparation.   Superiority in courage and skill combined can wrest victory from great odds, and no amount of skill will atone for the lack of daring, of unflinching resolution, and of dogged capacity to stand punishment; but where courage is equal, skill will always win; and where courage and skill are both equal, then the side which has the best ships and guns will overwhelm the other, no matter what may be the flags under which the combatants fight.

The best commentary on the five victories thus far described is that given by the French Admiral, Jurien de La Gravière; and it is significant of the profound impression they created that, in a work devoted to the gigantic naval battles of the fleets that fought under and against Nelson, a French admiral, to whom the contest between the British and the Americans had no other interest than the lesson it taught, should have devoted so much space to these duels, singling them out above all the other single-ship contests of the twenty-five years' war.

"When the American Congress declared war on England in 1812," he says,[1] "it seemed as if this unequal conflict would crush her navy in the act of being born; instead, it but fertilised the germ. It is only since that epoch that the United States has taken rank among maritime powers. Some combats of frigates, corvettes, and brigs, insignificant without doubt as regards the material results, sufficed to break the charm which protected the standard of St. George, and taught Europe what she could have already learned from some of our combats, if the louder noise of our defeats had not drowned the glory, that the only invincibles on the sea are good seamen and good artillerists.

"The English covered the ocean with their cruisers when this unknown navy, composed of six frigates and a few small craft hitherto hardly numbered, dared to establish its cruisers at the mouth of the Channel, in the very centre of the British power. But already the *Constitution* had captured the *Guerrière* and *Java*, the *United States* had made a prize of the *Macedonian*, the *Wasp* of the *Frolic*, and the *Hornet* of the *Peacock*. The honour of the new flag was established. England, humiliated, tried to attribute her multiplied reverses to the unusual size of the vessels which Congress had had constructed in 1799, and which did the fighting in 1812. She wished to refuse them the name of frigates, and called them, not without some appearance of reason, disguised line-of-battle ships. Since then all maritime powers have copied these gigantic models, as the result of the war of 1812 obliged England herself to change her naval material; but if they had employed, instead of frigates, cut-down 74's, it would still be difficult to explain the prodigious success of the Americans. . . .

"In an engagement which terminated in less than half an hour, the English frigate *Guerrière*, completely dismasted, had fifteen men killed, sixty-three wounded, and more than thirty shot below the water-line. She sank twelve hours after the combat. The *Constitution*, on the contrary, had but seven men killed and seven wounded, and did not lose a mast. As soon as she had replaced a few cut ropes and changed a few sails, she was in condition, even by the testimony of the British historian, to take another *Guerrière*. The *United States* took an hour and a half to recapture the *Macedonian*, and the same difference made itself felt in the damage suffered by the two ships. The *Macedonian* had her masts shattered, two of her main-deck and all her spar-deck guns disabled, more than a hundred shots had penetrated the hull, and over a third of the crew had suffered by the hostile fire. The American frigate, on the contrary, had to regret but five men killed and seven wounded; her guns had been fired each sixty-six times to the *Macedonian's* thirty-six. The combat of the *Constitution* and the *Java* lasted two hours, and was the most bloody of these three engagements. The *Java* only struck when she had been razed like a sheer hulk; she had twenty-two men killed and one hundred and two wounded.

*　　　*　　　*　　　*　　　*

"This war should be studied with unceasing diligence; the pride of the two peoples to whom naval affairs are so generally familiar has cleared all the details and laid bare all the episodes; and through the sneers which the victors should have spared, merely out of care for their own glory, at every step can be seen the great truth, that there is only success for those who know how to prepare it.

*　　　*　　　*　　　*　　　*

"It belongs to us to judge impartially these marine events, too much exalted

<hr>

[1] 'Guerres Maritimes,' ii. 284 (edition of 1881).

perhaps by a national vanity one is tempted to excuse. The Americans showed in the war of 1812 a great deal of skill and resolution; but if, as they have asserted, the chances had always been perfectly equal between them and their adversaries, if they had only owed their triumphs to the intrepidity of Hull, Decatur, and Bainbridge, there would be for us but little interest in recalling the struggle. We need not seek lessons in courage outside of our own history. On the contrary, what is to be well considered is that the ships of the United States constantly fought with the chances in their favour, and it is on this that the American Government should found its true title to glory. . . . The Americans in 1812 had secured to themselves the advantage of a better organisation (than the English)."

After speaking of the heavier metal and greater number of men of the American ships, he continues :—

" And yet only an enormous superiority in the precision and rapidity of their fire can explain the difference in the losses sustained by the combatants.

" The American fire showed itself to be as accurate as it was rapid. On occasions when the roughness of the sea would seem to render all aim excessively uncertain, the effects of their artillery were not less murderous than under more advantageous conditions.

" Nor was the skill of their gunners the only cause to which the Americans owed their success. Their ships were faster ; the crews, composed of chosen men, manœuvred with uniformity and precision ; their captains had that practical knowledge which is only to be acquired by long experience of the sea ; and it is not to be wondered at that the *Constitution*, when chased during three days by a squadron of five English frigates, succeeded in escaping, by surpassing them in manœuvring and by availing herself of every ingenious resource and skilful expedient that maritime science could suggest . . . . To a marine exalted by success, but rendered negligent by the very habit of victory, the Congress only opposed the best of vessels and most formidable of armaments."

Throughout the year 1812, and the beginning of the year 1813, Britain had made no effective use whatever of her tremendous power at sea, so far as the United States was concerned. She had suffered from overweening self-confidence in her own prowess, and from overweening contempt for her foe. During the first year of war the utter futility of the American land attacks on Canada could fairly be matched by the utter inefficiency of the efforts of the British both to destroy the little American navy, and to employ their own huge Navy so as to make it a determining factor in the struggle. But by the spring of 1813 this was changed. The British were a practical people, and they faced facts—thereby showing capacity to turn these facts to their own advantage. The dream of British naval invincibility, the dream that the British warships could win against any reasonable odds, was a pleasant dream, and the awakening was extremely disagreeable. Nevertheless, a dream it was, and the British recognised it as such, and acted accordingly, with the natural result that thereafter the Americans

suffered more than the British at sea.   The 18-pounder frigates
were forbidden to engage single-handed the 24-pounder frigates of
the Americans,[1] and where possible they were directed to cruise in
couples, or in small squadrons, so as to be able with certainty to
overpower any single antagonist, great or small.   No sufficient steps
were taken to bring the average standard of fighting efficiency,
especially in gunnery, up to the American level, and in consequence
there were some defeats yet in store; but the best captains in the
British Navy were already as good as any to be found in America,
or anywhere else, and it was now the turn of the Americans to
suffer from over-confidence, while the British, wherever possible,
made dexterous use of their superior forces.   After this period no
British frigate was captured, while three American frigates surrendered, one to an opponent of superior fighting efficiency, and the
other two to superior force, skilfully used.   The American sloops
did better, but even their career was chequered by defeat.

The important factor on the British side was the use of the
Navy to blockade the American coast.   When war was declared,
the Napoleonic struggle was at its height, and the chances seemed
on the whole to favour Napoleon.   But, by the spring of 1813, the
Grand Army had gone to its death in the snowclad wastes of Russia,
and Wellington had completely bested the French marshals in
Spain, so that it was merely a question of time as to when he
would invade France.   In Germany the French were steadily losing
ground; and all the nations of Europe were combining for the
overthrow of that splendid, evil, and terrible genius before whom
they had so long cowered.   Britain could, therefore, afford to turn
her attention to America in earnest.   As yet she could not spare
adequate land forces, but she could and did spare a sufficiency of
battleships, frigates, and sloops to make a real blockade of the
American coast.   After May 1813 the blockade was complete from
New York southward.   In the autumn it was extended further east;
but it was not until the following year that it was applied with the
same iron severity to the New England coast, for the British
government hoped always that the seditious spirit in New England
would manifest itself in open revolt.

After the blockade had been once established, commerce ceased;
and the only vessels that could slip out were the fast-sailing privateers

---

[1] The order recites that they are "forbidden to engage" and are to "retreat" from
such a foe.—'The Croker Papers,' i. 44.

and regular cruisers, whose captains combined daring, caution, and skill in such equal proportions as to enable them to thread their way through the innumerable dangers that barred the path. The privateers frequently failed, and even the regular cruisers were by no means always successful; while the risks were too great for merchantmen habitually to encounter them. Georgia touched Florida, and so could do a little trade through the Spanish dominions; and the northern New England coast lay open for some time to come; but elsewhere the ships rotted at the ports, though the shipwrights found employment in building the swift privateers, and the sailor-folk in manning them.

The white-sailed British frigates hovered in front of every seaport of note, standing on and off with ceaseless, unwearying vigilance by day and night, in fair weather and foul, through the summer and through the winter. In the great estuaries fleets rode at anchor, or sailed hither and thither menacing destruction. No town, large or small, could deem itself safe; and every great river was a possible highroad for the entrance of the enemy. There was not a strip of the American coast over which the Americans could call themselves masters, seaward of the point where the water grew deep enough to float a light craft of war.

The one lesson which should be most clearly taught by this war is the folly of a nation's relying for safety upon anything but its own readiness to repel attack; and, in the case of a power with an extended seaboard, this readiness implies the possession of a great fighting navy. The utter failure of Jefferson's embargo and his other measures of what he termed "peaceable coercion," teach their part of the lesson so plainly that it would seem impossible to misread it; but the glory won by their little navy has tended to blind Americans to the fact that this navy was too small to do anything except win glory. It lacked the power to harm anything but Britain's pride, and it was too weak to parry a single blow delivered by the British along the coast, when once they realised that their task was serious, and set about it in earnest. Twenty ships-of-the-line, as good of their kind as were the frigates and sloops, would have rendered the blockade impossible, even if they had not prevented the war; and, judged merely from the monetary standpoint, they would have repaid to the nation their cost a thousand times over by the commerce they would have saved, and the business losses they would have averted. As it was, the Americans were utterly powerless to offer any effective resistance to the British blockade; for it is too late to try to build a fleet, or take any other effective steps, when once the war has begun. The nerveless administration at Washington did not even take steps to defend the capital city.

It is the fashion to speak of the people as misrepresented by the politicians; but in this case certainly the people deserved just the government they had. Indeed, it is curious and instructive as well as melancholy to see how powerless the Americans as a whole were to make good the shortcomings of which they had been guilty prior to the declaration of war. It is especially instructive for those Americans, and indeed those Englishmen, who are fond of saying that either country needs no protection merely because it cannot be directly invaded by land, and who try to teach us that the immense reserve strength which each nation undoubtedly possesses can be immediately drawn on to make good any deficiencies in preparation at the outbreak of a war. This is much like telling a prize-fighter that he need not train because he has such an excellent constitution that he may draw on it to make good defects in his preparation for the ring. The truth seems to be that, in naval matters especially, nothing can supply the lack of adequate preparation and training before the outbreak of war. The lead which is lost at the beginning cannot be regained save by superhuman effort, and after enormous waste of strength. It is too late to mature plans for defence when the enemy is close at hand, for he continually breaks up and renders abortive the various little movements which, if given time, would become formidable. There is more chance of remedying defective preparation on land than on sea, merely because the fighting machinery for use on the sea is so delicate and complicated that ample opportunity must be given, not merely to produce it, but to learn to use it aright. This was true in the days of the American and French Revolutions; it is infinitely truer now, when the fleets of Rodney and Nelson have been left as far behind modern navies as they stood ahead of the galleys of Alcibiades and Hanno.

The failure of the Americans to devise any adequate measure for breaking the British blockade is partially due to this fundamental difficulty in making preparations when the time for preparation has passed. There was also a curious supineness among the people as a whole, which was, if anything, even more noticeable among those States which were clamorous for war than among those which, to

their deep discredit, clamored for peace. Virginia and the Southern
States did not falter in their determination to continue the war,
and the New England States betrayed an utter lack of patriotism
in their councils, and greatly hampered the national government in
its feeble efforts to uphold the national honour. Nevertheless,
astounding to relate, the New England States actually did more
than the South Atlantic States in the war itself, and this, not
because they did so much, but because the South Atlantic States
did so little. Massachusetts and Virginia were the typical States
of their two sections, and Massachusetts gave more men and
more money to carry on the war than did Virginia, apart from
furnishing a very large proportion of the sailors who manned the
war ships and privateers, while Virginia furnished hardly any. Not
even the continual presence of the British at their very doors could
rouse the Virginians to respectable resistance ; and the Marylanders
were not much better. It was in the Chesapeake that the main part
of the blockading fleet lay ; it was along the shores of that great bay
that the ravages of the British were most severely felt ; yet the
Virginians and Marylanders, during the two years when the enemy
lay on their coasts, insulting them at will, never organised any
attack whatsoever upon them, and took inadequate and imperfect
measures even for defence. The truth seems to be that the nation
was yet in the gristle, and that its awkward strength was useless, as
it could not be concentrated or applied to any one object. There
was no public training, and indeed no public feeling, which could
put at the disposal of the national government large bodies of disciplined men sufficient for effective use to a given end ; and the men
in control of the national government had been bred in a political
school which on its administrative side was so silly that they could
not have used this power even had it been given them. New York
and Philadelphia were never directly menaced during the war ; but
once or twice they thought they were, and the way in which they
proposed to meet the danger was by setting the citizens to labour on
earthworks in the neighbourhood, each profession, trade, or association going out in a body on some one day—the lawyers on one day,
the butchers on another, the United Irishmen on another, and so on
and so on. This conception of the way to perform military duty
does not require comment ; it would be grossly unfair to compare it
with the attitude even of unwarlike mediæval burghers, for after all
the mediæval burghers had some idea of arms, and the shop-keepers,

day-labourers, and professional men of New York and Philadelphia had not.

Where such was the conception of how to carry on the war, there is small cause for wonder that the war was allowed to carry on itself pretty much as it pleased. Had the people displayed the energy, the resolution, and the efficiency which their descendants on both sides showed half a century later in the Civil War, no amount of courage or of military sagacity on the part of the British could have prolonged the contest for any length of time. But there was no such showing. No concerted or resolute effort was made by the people as a whole. Individual shipbuilders and contractors showed great energy and capacity. Individual ship-captains at sea, individual generals on land, did remarkably well, showing military aptitude of a high order : and every such commander, by sea or by land, was able to make the seamen or the troops under him formidable and well-disciplined fighters in an astonishingly short space of time ; for the Americans, whether afloat or on shore, were cool, hardy, resolute, and fertile in resources and expedients. But no commander ever had more than a small squadron or a diminutive army with which to work, for the great mass of the Americans did nothing to bring the war to a close. The task, about which the people as a whole refused seriously to concern themselves, and which the government lacked decision and character to perform, was left to the shipwrights, to the seafaring folk, to the admirably trained officers of the little regular navy, and, on shore, to such commanders and troops as the campaigns themselves gradually developed : and all acted more or less independently of one another, or with only such concert as their own intelligence demanded.

The pressure brought to bear on America by the British blockade was exceedingly effective, but it was silent, and so historians have tended to forget it. They have chronicled with pride or regret, according to their nationality, the capture of an occasional British by an American sloop, but they have paid little heed to the ceaseless strain on the American resources caused by the blockade. Its mere existence inflicted a direct material loss to the American people a hundredfold greater than the entire American navy was able to inflict on Great Britain from the beginning to the end of its gallant career in this war. The very fact that the workings of the blockade were ceaseless and almost universal makes it difficult to realise their importance. It told heavily against the coasting trade, though less heavily than against foreign commerce ; and it revived an almost archaic industry, that of the waggoners, who travelled slowly, parallel with the coast-line, to carry with an infinitely greater labour and expense the goods that had formerly gone in the sloops and schooners. The return to this primitive method of interchange implied much of the suffering of primitive times, for it meant that one part of the country might lack the necessaries of which another part possessed an over-abundance. As soon as the blockade was established it created the widest inequalities in the prices of commodities in different parts of the country.[1] Flour cost nearly three times as much in Boston as in Richmond, and rice four times as much in Philadelphia as in Charleston, while imported articles like sugar rose five-fold in price. Exports practically ceased by the close of 1813. In that year they amounted to but two hundred thousand dollars in New York as against over twelve million in the year preceding the outbreak of the war, while, during the same period, Virginia's original exports of five million dollars fell off to twenty thousand. The import duties diminished with even greater rapidity, until finally they could only be raised in New England. The ruin was widespread. As yet the people of the United States were not manufacturers, but small farmers, traders, and seafarers. The trader of the towns saw all his trade destroyed, and could give no employment to the sailors who had formerly worked for him ; while the farmer grew crops which could not be moved to any remunerative market, so that no ready money came in to him ; and yet for whatever he needed, save what he himself produced, he had to pay five times as much as formerly.

The coast dwellers in Virginia and Maryland were forced to experience, not merely the weight of the blockade, but also actual physical contact with the enemy. Another British squadron lay in the Delaware, and forays were made here and there along the coast. New York was blockaded, but very little was done save to put a stop to commerce. There was another squadron at Nantucket, with Sir Thomas Masterman Hardy, Nelson's flag captain, as commodore. Hardy's ships closed southern New England to the world, but they did very little in the way of attacking or harassing the coast itself, for Hardy, one of the most gallant captains who ever lived, a man who had won his spurs in the greatest sea fights of all time, and who prided himself on his ability to meet armed

[1] Adams, vii. 263.

foes in battle, felt impatient at mere marauding, and countenanced it with reluctance.

The directly opposite policy was pursued in Chesapeake Bay. There Admiral Sir John Borlase Warren was in command, but the chief work was done by Rear-Admiral Sir George Cockburn. Cockburn organised a few of the lightest ships of Warren's fleet, and some captured schooners, into a flotilla with which he could penetrate at will the creeks and rivers. He was a capable, brave, energetic man, hating his foes and enjoying his work; and he carried out with scrupulous fidelity the order to harass the American coast. Not merely did he attack any militia that might from time to time assemble, but he also destroyed towns and hamlets, and worked widespread havoc throughout the country that lay within striking distance of tide-water. Houses were burned, farms plundered, stores pillaged, and small towns destroyed, while the larger places, and even Baltimore, were thrown into a panic which caused the inhabitants to neglect their business, but did not cause them to take such efficient measures for self-defence as the exercise of reasonable forethought would have demanded. Usually Cockburn and his followers refrained from maltreating the people personally, and most of the destruction they caused was at places where the militia made some resistance; but, when plundering once began, it was quite impossible for the officers to restrain some of the very men who most needed restraint.

The people were of course greatly exasperated at the marauding, and the American newspapers far and near, and most American writers then and afterwards, were loud in their denunciation of the Rear-Admiral and his methods. Exactly how far these were or were not defensible, it is difficult to say. It is of course a mere matter of convention to discriminate between the destruction of private property on sea and on land. Armed vessels, British and American, destroyed or captured any private property of the enemy which they could find afloat; and if there were sufficient cause, or if there were an object of sufficient importance to be attained, the combatants were certainly warranted in destroying such property ashore. Cockburn's course was in many respects the same as that of Sheridan's at one crisis in the Civil War; and there was certainly little in it to warrant the warmth of the execrations heaped upon him by his foes—which were indeed somewhat in the nature of a tribute to his efficiency. At the same time it may be admitted that

his work was not of the kind in which the best type of fighting
man would find any pleasure, or which he would carry on longer
than was absolutely necessary; and for some of the revolting
details there was small excuse.   There is room for question
as to whether the comparatively trifling loss inflicted on the
Americans did much beyond irritating them.   It certainly failed
to cow them, though equally certainly it failed to rouse them to
effective resistance.

In short, it may be doubted whether the course followed by
Cockburn reflected any particular credit upon, or caused much, if
any, benefit to, the British side.   There can be no doubt, however,
of the discredit attaching to the Americans for their conduct.   A
people which lets its shores be insulted with impunity incurs, if
not greater blame, at least greater contempt, than the people which
does the plundering.   If here and there Cockburn burned a hamlet
or two which he ought to have spared, his offence was really small
when compared with the disgrace brought on the American name
by the supineness shown by the people of the threatened neighbour-
hoods.   They did nothing effectively of any kind for their own
defence.   Indeed, for the most part they did nothing at all, except
gather bodies of militia whenever there was an alarm, and so keep
the inhabitants constantly worried and harassed by always calling
them to arms, and yet merely providing almost worthless defenders.
And the nation as a whole was as much to blame as the States
directly menaced.

The retaliation of the Americans took the form of privateering.
By the time the blockade began to be effective, the American
privateers had developed into a well-recognised type.   Small vessels
had been abandoned.   Brigs and ships were common, and so were
schooners of large size.   Everything was sacrificed to speed; and
the chief feature of the armament was the single long-range gun,
fitted to bring-to a fleeing merchantman at a considerable distance.
The privateers thus had neither the armament nor the build, not
to speak of the discipline, which would have enabled them to withstand regular men-of-war of the same size in close action, although
the crews were large, the better to man the prizes.   In other words,
the privateer was a commerce destroyer pure and simple, built to
run and not to fight; although, even as a commerce destroyer,
she was less effective than a government vessel would be, because
she was built to make money in a particularly risky species of

gambling; and so, instead of destroying prizes, she sought to send them in, with the result that nearly half were recaptured when once the British began to make their blockade effective. A good many privateers went out from the ports of the Southern States, and Baltimore was a famous centre for them; but the great majority sailed from the New England and Middle States.

The ravages of these privateers were very serious.[1] The British trade suffered heavily from them, much more than from the closing of the American ports—the argument upon which Jefferson had placed so much reliance in his vain effort to bring Britain to terms. In fact, the closing of the American ports by the war made comparatively little difference to England, because it was almost immediately accompanied by the opening of the trade with continental Europe. The crushing disasters that befell Napoleon's great army in Russia meant the immediate relaxation of his system in the Baltic; and after he was driven out of Germany, toward the close of 1813, all the German ports were again thrown open to the British merchants, so that their trade grew by leaps and bounds, and the loss of the American market was far more than made good by the gain of markets elsewhere. After the overthrow of France, in the spring of 1814, England was left without an enemy, excepting the United States, and her commerce went where it pleased, unharmed except by the American privateers.

When she was thus left free to use her vast strength solely against America, it seemed inevitable that the latter should be overthrown. But, in the war of 1812, what seemed probable rarely came to pass; and the failures on both sides caused the utmost astonishment at the time, and are difficult to fully explain now. At the outbreak of the war the general opinion in America was that Canada would speedily be conquered; and the general opinion in Europe was that the United States' navy would be brushed from the sea, and that the American privateers would be got under just as those of France had been got under. Neither expectation was fulfilled. During the first two years the Americans made no headway in the effort to conquer feebly-held Canada. When, in 1814, Britain turned her undivided attention to an enemy which with one hand she had held at bay for two years, the inevitable out-

---

[1] Adams, in his 'History,' gives the best account both of the blockade and the privateers. The details of some of the voyages of the latter are preserved in Coggeshall's 'History of American Privateers.'

come seemed to be her triumph; yet she in her turn failed in her aggressive movements against the United States just as America had failed in her aggressive movements against Canada, and her giant Navy proved unequal to the task of scourging from the seas the American men-of-war and privateers. Contrary to her experience in all former wars with European powers, she found that the American privateers were able to operate far from their base, and to do great damage without any great fighting navy to back them up; and as the war progressed they grew ever bolder in their ravages round the coasts of the British Isles themselves.

There are two lessons, which at first sight seem contradictory, to be learned from the history of the privateers in this war. In the first place, their history does teach that very much can be accomplished by commerce destroying, if more directly efficient methods cannot be used. The American privateers rendered invaluable service to their country by their daring, and the severity of their ravages. In those days sailing vessels were not hampered as vessels would be hampered under like conditions in the days of steam; they did not need coaling stations, and there was much less danger of their getting out of repair. The American privateer was a faster ship than any previously seen on the waters, and she was more daringly and skilfully handled than any ships of her kind had ever been handled by Europeans. She could usually overtake any merchantmen, and usually escape any man-of-war. Of course, in the end she was almost certain to encounter some man-of-war from whom she could not escape; but this might not be until after several profitable voyages; and though, on the average, privateering was a business in which the losses equalled the gains, yet the chances of success were as great as the risks, and it was a kind of gambling which appealed peculiarly to adventurous spirits. The commerce destroying put a severe strain on the British mercantile and seafaring communities.

Nevertheless, admitting and emphasising all this does not mean the admission that privateering was the way in which America could best have used her strength. The privateers did great and real damage to England, and though at first they caused more irritation than alarm, they inflicted such punishment upon the merchants and the seamen as materially to increase the disposition of the British for peace. But what they accomplished cannot be compared with what was accomplished by the British Navy. The

American privateers harassed the commerce of England, but the British blockading fleet destroyed the commerce of America. The ravages of the one inclined the British people to peace; but the steady pressure of the other caused such a bitter revolt against the war in parts of America as nearly to produce a civil conflict. The very success of the privateers was a damage to the American navy, for all the seamen wished to enlist on board them instead of on board the regular ships of war. Regular ships were better commerce destroyers, and, above all, battleships would have accomplished far more, had the energies of the nation been turned towards their production instead of to the production of private armed ships. In the coast towns the number of seamen who served on board the privateers could have manned scores of fast government vessels built on the same lines; and, as these vessels would not have tried to save their prizes, they would have inflicted more damage on the enemy. Undoubtedly this would have been an advantage so far as it went; and perhaps, after the outbreak of the war, it was too late to try to build a great fighting fleet. But in reality what was needed was an infinitely more radical change. The substitution of the government commerce destroyer for the privateer would have done some good, but it could not have accomplished anything decisive. What was needed was the substitution for all these commerce destroyers of a great fighting fleet. Such a fleet by its mere existence would doubtless have prevented the war. It would certainly, if handled as well as the frigates, sloops, and privateers were handled, have prevented a blockade, even if war had been declared; and American commerce, instead of being destroyed outright, would merely have suffered heavily, just as the British commerce suffered. The men employed in the privateers would have manned enough ships of the line to have brought all this about. A fighting fleet would have prevented the losses and humiliations which the commerce destroyers were utterly powerless to avert. Moreover, it would have done more real and lasting damage than the commerce destroyers could possibly do. Commerce destroying was a makeshift. It was a very useful makeshift, and much good came from the way in which it was utilised; but it must not be forgotten that it was only a makeshift, and that the commerce destroyers were in no sense satisfactory substitutes for great fighting ships of the line, fitted to wrest victory from the enemy by destroying his powers, both of offence and defence, and able to keep the war away from the home coasts.

The reverses which the British Navy had encountered in all the earlier sea fights were mortifying to a degree. It was now the turn of the Americans to suffer similar mortifications. Perhaps the chief cause of the British disasters had been an ignorant self-confidence combined with an equally ignorant contempt of the enemy, which rendered the British indifferent to odds, and indifferent also to that thorough training which could alone make their ships into efficient fighting machines. The same undue self-confidence and undue disregard for the prowess of the enemy were now to cause the

CAPTAIN JAMES LAWRENCE, U.S.N.

(*From an engraving by Edwin.*)

Americans the loss of one of their frigates and the death of one of their most gallant captains.

In May, 1812, Captain James Lawrence, the commander of the *Hornet*, was promoted to the command of the *Chesapeake*, 38, which was being fitted out at Boston. Her crew had just been discharged, and, as she was regarded as an unlucky ship, and as there had been much dissatisfaction over their failure to get prize money, many of the crew refused to re-enlist, preferring to ship in some of the numerous privateers. A few of the *Constitution's* old crew came on board, and those, and the men who had been in the *Chesapeake* during her former voyage, were excellent material. The rest were raw hands, including an unusually large number of

foreigners. About forty of these were British. There were also
a number of Portuguese, one of whom, a boatswain's mate, almost
brought about a mutiny among the crew, which was only pacified
by giving the men prize cheques. The last draft of the new
hands was not only entirely untrained, but also came on board so
late that when the ship was captured their hammocks and bags
were still lying in the boats stowed over the booms. A man like
Lawrence would speedily have got such a crew into shape. A cruise
of a very few weeks would doubtless have enabled him to put the
ship in as good trim as the *Hornet* was when under his command.
But she was in no condition to meet an exceptionally good frigate
before she was eight hours out of port. Even his officers, with
one exception, were new to the ship, and the third and fourth
lieutenants were not regularly commissioned as such, but were only
midshipmen, acting for the first time in higher positions. Lawrence
himself was of course new to both the officers and the crew.

In such circumstances it was clearly his duty to try to avoid an
encounter with the enemy until his ship should be in good condition
to fight. Unfortunately for him, however, his experiences in the
war had given him the same unreasonable feeling of superiority over
his foes as the latter had themselves felt a year earlier. He had
spent three weeks in blockading a sloop-of-war, the *Bonne Citoyenne*,
which was of equal force with his own, and which yet resolutely
declined to fight. He had captured another sloop-of-war which
was, it is true, inferior in force, but which was also infinitely
inferior in point of fighting efficiency ; and this capture had been
made in spite of the presence of another sloop-of-war, which, nevertheless, did not venture out to attack him. He had, as he deemed,
good ground to believe that his foes were so much inferior in
prowess as to make success almost certain. Indeed, had the frigate
which he was about to attack been no more formidable, as regards
the skill of her captain and the training of her crew, than the ships
which the Americans had hitherto encountered, Lawrence's conduct
might very possibly have been justified by the result.

But the British frigate *Shannon*, 38, which was then cruising
off Boston harbour, was under Captain Philip Bowes Vere Broke,
who had commanded her for seven years, and who was one of the
ablest captains in the British service. A British naval historian
has explained why it was that the *Shannon* proved herself so much
more formidable than her sister frigates.

"There was another point in which the generality of the British crews, as compared with any one American crew, were miserably deficient: that is, skill in the art of gunnery. While the American seamen were constantly firing at marks, the British seamen, except in particular cases, scarcely did so once in a year; and some ships could be named on board which not a shot had been fired in this way for upward of three years. Nor was the fault wholly the captain's. The instructions under which he was bound to act forbade him to use, during the first six months after the ship had received her armament, more shots per month than amounted to a third in number of the upper-deck guns; and after these six months only half the quantity. Many captains never put a shot in the guns till an enemy appeared; they employed the leisure time of the men in handling the sails and in decorating the ship."

REAR-ADMIRAL SIR PHILIP BOWES VERE BROKE, BART., K.C.B.

(*From Blood's lithograph after a portrait painted about 1814, when Broke was a Post-Captain.*)

Captain Broke was not one of this kind.

"From the day on which he had joined her, the 14th of September, 1806, the *Shannon* began to feel the effect of her captain's proficiency as a gunner, and zeal for the service. The laying of the ship's ordnance so that it may be correctly fired in a horizontal direction is justly deemed a most important operation, as upon it depends in a great measure the true aim and destructive effect of every future shot she may fire. On board the *Shannon*, at her first outfit, this was attended to by Captain Broke in person. . . . . By draughts from other ships, and the usual means to which a British man-of-war is obliged to resort, the *Shannon* got together a crew; and in the course of a year or two, by the paternal care and excellent regulations of Captain Broke, an undersized, not very well disposed, and, in point of age, rather motley ship's company became as pleasant to command as they would have been dangerous to meet." [1]

The *Shannon's* guns were all carefully sighted ; and, moreover, " every day, for about an hour and a half in the forenoon, when not prevented by chase or the state of the weather, the men were exercised at training the guns, and for the same time in the after-noon in the use of the broad-sword, pike, musket, etc. Twice a week the crew fired at targets, both with great guns and with musketry ; and Captain Broke, as an additional stimulus beyond the emulation excited, gave a pound of tobacco to every man that put a shot through the bull's-eye." He would frequently have a cask thrown overboard, and suddenly order some one gun to be manned to sink the cask.

Captain Broke had sent a challenge to Captain Lawrence, ex-pressing a willingness to meet the latter in a duel in any latitude and longitude he might appoint ; for Broke did not expect to be given the great advantage of meeting his antagonist just as the latter was leaving port, and before her crew were in fighting trim ; and he possessed a justifiable confidence in the ability of the ship which he commanded to hold her own in any circumstances. It may be mentioned that this letter of challenge was worthy of the gallant writer, being a model of courtesy, manliness, and candour. Un-fortunately for Lawrence, he never received it ; and he stood out to engage the *Shannon* at mid-day of June 1st, 1813.[2] Afterwards it was alleged that he engaged against his judgment ; but this was undoubtedly not the case. The British frigate was in sight in the offing, and he sailed out to attack her in the confident hope of victory.

The two ships were very evenly matched, but what superiority there was was on the American side. The *Chesapeake* carried fifty guns—twenty-eight long 18's on the gun-deck, and, on the spar-deck two long 12's, one long 18, one 12-pr. carronade, and eighteen 32-pr. carronades. There were on board her 379 men all told. The *Shannon* carried fifty-two guns—twenty-eight long 18's on the gun-deck, and, on the spar-deck, four long 9's, one long 6, three 12-pr. carronades, and sixteen 32-pr. carronades, with a crew of 330 men. In guns the two ships were practically equal, but

---

[1] James, vi. 196 (Ed. 1837).

[2] Navy Department MSS., 'Captains' Letters,' vol. xxix. No. 1 ; Lawrence's letter, June 1st, 1813.

in crew the Americans were superior by fifty men, which, in an engagement at close quarters, ought to have given them the upper hand, if the two crews had been likewise equal in fighting capacity.[1]

At noon the *Chesapeake* weighed anchor, stood out of Boston harbour, and an hour later rounded the lighthouse. The *Shannon* stood off under easy sail. She reefed her topsails, and alternately hauled up and again bore away. With her foresail brailed up, and her maintop-sail braced flat and shivering, she surged slowly through the quiet seas, while the *Chesapeake* came down with towering canvas, and the white water breaking under her bow. When Boston lighthouse bore west, distant six leagues, the *Shannon* again hauled up, with her head to the south-east, and lay-to under fighting canvas, stripped to her topsails, topgallant-sails, jib, and spanker. The breeze freshened, and as the *Chesapeake* neared her foe, she took in her studding-sails, topgallant-sails, and royals, got her royal yards on deck, and came down very fast under topsails and jib. At 5.30 P.M., to keep under command and be able to wear if necessary, the *Shannon* put her helm alternately a-lee and a-weather, first keeping a close luff, and then again letting the sails shiver. The *Chesapeake* had hauled up her foresail; and, with three ensigns flying, she steered straight for the *Shannon's* starboard quarter. For a moment Broke feared lest his adversary might pass under the *Shannon's* stern, rake her, and engage her on the quarter; but the American captain sought only a yardarm and yardarm action, to be decided by sheer ability to give and take punishment. He luffed up fifty yards from the *Shannon's* starboard quarter, and squared his mainyard. On board the *Shannon* the captain of the 14th gun, William Mindham, had been ordered not to fire until it bore into the second main-deck port forward. At 5.50 it was fired, and then the other guns in quick succession from abaft forward, the *Chesapeake* replying with her whole broadside. At 5.53, Lawrence, finding that he was forging ahead, hauled up a little. The *Chesapeake's* guns did murderous damage, but the ship herself suffered even more. The men in the *Shannon's* tops could hardly see the deck of the American frigate through the cloud of shivered and splintered wreck that was flying across it. Man after man was killed at the wheel; the fourth lieutenant, the master, and the boatswain fell;

---

[1] Letters of Lieutenant George Budd and Captain Broke, and Brighton's 'Memoir of Admiral Broke.'

and, six minutes after the first gun had been fired, the jib-sheet and foretop-sail tie were shot away, and the spanker brails loosened so that the sails blew out, and the ship came up into the wind somewhat. Her quarter was then exposed to her antagonist's broadside, which beat in her stern ports and swept the men from the after-guns. One of the arms-chests on the quarter-deck was blown up by a hand-grenade thrown from the *Shannon*, the smoke shrouding everything from sight for a moment.[1] Broke saw that the *Chesapeake* had stern-way on and was paying slowly off; so he put his helm a-starboard and shivered his mizen-topsail, to keep off the wind and delay the boarding. But at that moment the *Shannon's* jib-stay was shot away (for some of the *Chesapeake's* guns still bore), and, her headsails becoming becalmed, she went off very slowly. In consequence, at six o'clock, the two frigates fell on board one another, the *Chesapeake's* quarter pressing upon the *Shannon's* side just forward of the starboard main-chains; and they were kept in this position by the fluke of the *Shannon's* anchor catching in the *Chesapeake's* quarter port.

The *Shannon's* crew had suffered severely, and her decks were running thick with blood; but the trained and seasoned seamen stood to their work with grim indifference. Broke ran forward as the frigates ground against one another. He saw that the Americans were flinching from their quarter-deck guns, and at once ordered the ships to be lashed together, the great guns to cease firing, and the boarders to be called. The boatswain, Mr. Stevens, who had fought in Rodney's action, was foremost in fastening the frigates together, though, as he finished his work, an American seaman hacked his right arm off with a blow from a cutlass.

All was confusion and dismay on board the *Chesapeake*. Lieutenant Augustus Charles Ludlow had been mortally wounded and carried below. Lawrence himself, while standing on the quarter-deck, fatally conspicuous by his full-dress uniform and commanding stature, was shot as the vessels closed by Lieutenant John Law of the Royal Marines. He fell dying, and was carried below, exclaiming, "Don't give up the ship"—a phrase that has since become proverbial among his countrymen. The acting third lieutenant, a midshipman, who was a devoted admirer of Lawrence, helped to carry him below, instead of remaining at his post as he

---

[1] Navy Department MSS., "Captains' Letters," vol. xxix. No. 10; Bainbridge's letter, June 2nd, 1833.

should have done.[1] When he returned it was too late. Indeed, one or two of the younger officers were stunned and demoralised by the succession of disasters.

While the confusion was at its height, Captain Broke stepped from the *Shannon's* gangway rail on to the muzzle of the *Chesapeake's* aftermost carronade, and thence over the bulwark on to her quarter-deck, followed by about twenty men. As the British came on board, the men on the *Chesapeake's* spar-deck, who had suffered more heavily than any others, whose officers had all been killed or wounded, and who had not the discipline to take unmoved such heavy punishment, deserted their quarters. The Portuguese boat-swain's mate removed the gratings of the berth-deck and ran below, followed by many of the crew. On the quarter-deck, almost the only man who made any resistance was the chaplain, Mr. Samuel Livermore, who advanced, firing his pistol at Broke; and Broke in return cut him down with a single stroke. On the upper-deck the only men who behaved well were the marines; but of their original number of forty-four men, fourteen, including Lieutenant James Broom and Corporal Dixon, were dead, and twenty, including Sergeants Twin and Harris, wounded; so that there were left but one corporal and nine men, several of whom had been knocked down and bruised, though they were later reported unwounded. There was thus hardly any resistance, Captain Broke stopping his men for a moment until they were joined by the rest of the boarders under Lieutenants George Thomas L. Watt and Charles Leslie Falkiner. The *Chesapeake's* mizen-top men began firing at the boarders, mortally wounding Midshipman John Samwell, and killing Lieutenant Watt; but one of the *Shannon's* long 9's was pointed at the top and cleared it out, being assisted by the British main-top men under Midshipman Cosnahan. At the same time the men in the *Chesapeake's* main-top were driven out of it by the fire of the *Shannon's* fore-top men under Midshipman William Smith (5).

The Americans on the main-deck now for the first time learned that the British had boarded, as the upper-deck men came crowding down; and Lieutenant George Budd sprang up, calling on his people to follow him. A dozen veterans tumbled up after him, and, as they

---

[1] See minutes of court-martial on the loss of the *Chesapeake*, given in Ingersoll, i. 396.

reached the spar-deck, Budd led them against the British who were coming along the gangways. For a moment, under the surprise of the attack, the assailants paused, the British purser, Mr. George Aldham, and Captain's Clerk, Mr. John Dunn, being killed; but they rallied at once, and the handful of Americans were cut down or dispersed, Lieutenant Budd being wounded and knocked down the main hatchway. "The enemy," wrote Captain Broke, "fought desperately, but in disorder." Lieutenant Ludlow, already mortally wounded, heard the shouts and the stamping overhead, and he struggled up on deck, sword in hand. Two or three men followed him; but the rush of the boarders swept them away like chaff, and the dying Ludlow was hewn down as he fought. On the forecastle a few seamen and marines turned at bay. Captain Broke was still leading his men with the same brilliant personal courage which he had all along shown. Attacking the first American, who was armed with a pike, he parried a blow from it and cut down the man; attacking another, he was himself cut down, and only saved by the seaman Mindham, already mentioned, who slew his assailant. One of the American marines brained an Englishman with his clubbed musket; and so stubborn was the resistance of the little group, that, for a moment, the assailants recoiled; but immediately afterwards they closed in and slew their foes to a man. The British fired a volley or two down the hatchway, in response to a couple of shots fired up, whereupon all resistance came to an end; and at 6.5, just fifteen minutes after the first gun had been fired, and not five minutes after Captain Broke had boarded, the colours of the *Chesapeake* were struck. Of her crew sixty-one were killed or mortally wounded, including her captain, her first and fourth lieutenants, the lieutenant of marines, the master, boatswain, and three midshipmen; and eighty-five were severely or slightly wounded, including both her other lieutenants, five midshipmen, and the chaplain: a total of one hundred and forty-eight. Of the *Shannon's* men, thirty-three were killed outright or died of their wounds, including her first Lieutenant, George Thomas L. Watt; Purser, George Aldham; Captain's Clerk, John Dunn; and Midshipman John Samwell; and fifty were wounded, including the Captain himself and the Boatswain, Mr. William Stevens: total, eighty-three. The *Chesapeake* was taken into Halifax, where Captain Lawrence and Lieutenant Ludlow were both buried with military honours. Captain Broke was made a baronet, very deservedly, and Lieutenants Wallis[1] and Falkiner[2] were both made commanders.

The battle had been as bloody as it was brief. When the *Chesapeake* surrendered, her crew had suffered a much heavier relative loss than the crews of the *Guerrière*, the *Macedonian,* or

PROVO WILLIAM PARRY WALLIS, ÆT. 22.

(By permission, from an engraving, published in the " Strand Magazine," after a portrait painted in 1813.)

SIGNATURE OF SIR PROVO WILLIAM PARRY WALLIS, G.C.B., ADMIRAL OF THE FLEET.

(From a letter written to the Author on June 2nd, 1890, *when Sir Provo was in his* 100th *year.)*

even the *Java.* The *Shannon* had not only suffered a heavier loss than befell the victorious ship in any other single ship duel of

[1] Provo William Parry Wallis : born, 1791; Lieutenant, 1808 ; Commander, 1813 ; Captain, 1819 ; Rear-Admiral, 1851 ; Vice-Admiral, 1857 ; Admiral, 1863 ; Admiral of the Fleet, 1877 ; died senior of that rank, and G.C.B., February 13th, 1892, being in his hundred and first year. (Life by Bright.)—W. L. C.

[2] Charles Leslie Falkiner : born, 1791 ; Lieutenant, 1810 ; Commander, 1813 ; retired with the rank of Captain, 1848 ; succeeded his brother as a Baronet ; died, 1858. —W. L. C.

the war, but had also suffered a loss as severe as that which had been held to justify the surrender of more than one vessel—the *Argus* and the *Epervier*, for instance, and even the *Guerrière*. The action was fought at such close quarters and under such conditions that there was no room for manœuvring, and, so far as the first broadside was concerned, no room for display of any very great difference in gunnery, provided each side was moderately efficient. Beyond question, Broke's men were far more skilful in the handling of the guns; but this was only one of the factors which went to make up the victory. It was a terrific, punishing fight, entered into on conditions that ensured the taking as well as the giving of very hard blows. Such a fight is not merely a test of pluck : it is a test, above all others, of training and discipline, and of cool-headed readiness to repair injuries and take advantage of shifting opportunities. The heavy loss on board the *Shannon* did not confuse or terrify the thoroughly trained men, disciplined to place implicit reliance in their leaders. A somewhat greater loss on board the *Chesapeake* disheartened the raw hands among the crew, and created such confusion that there was no immediate readiness to remedy any temporary disaster; while even the officers, being new to one another and to the ship, and some of them being very young, were not able to do their best. American writers have been fond of saying that the defeat of the *Chesapeake* was due to accident, especially to the loss of the jib-sheet and foretop-sail tie, which brought her up into the wind, and exposed her to a raking fire. This statement is simply not true. Such accidents are bound to occur in battle; and a skilled captain and crew will remedy them when they occur in their own ship, and will take advantage of them when they occur to the enemy. The victory was not in the slightest degree to be attributed to accident,[1] though it may have been slightly hastened by it. Trained skill and good discipline won, as they had so often won before. There was no lack of courage on the defeated side; the heavy death-roll shows that. Nearly every American officer was killed or wounded, and so were three-fourths of the marines, and half the veterans of the crew.

Nor did the boarding win the victory. When the ships came together the *Chesapeake* was already beaten at the guns. She had been struck, all told, by three hundred and sixty-two shot of every

---

[1] Cooper is of little use for this action; and the "accident" theory is a favourite with most American writers.

description, and the *Shannon*, by about one hundred and fifty-eight. Had the ships not come together, the fight would have been longer, and the loss greater and more nearly equal; but the result would have been the same. The *Chesapeake's* crew had been together and on board her only as many hours as the *Shannon's* had been years, and the result was what might have been foreseen, when the Captain of the *Shannon* had spent his time to such good advantage in training his crew. It is worth noticing that the only thoroughly disciplined set of men on board the *Chesapeake*, the marines, behaved with superb courage and fought to the last, very few of them escaping entirely unscathed. Complaint was made at the time against the Portuguese and other foreigners among the crew, and notably against the Portuguese boatswain's mate. It appears that at the time of the boarding they did not do very well, the boatswain's mate in particular showing cowardice; but it is idle to ascribe the defeat in any way to their action. The *Chesapeake* was beaten before the boarding took place; and her men had suffered too severe a loss, and were too demoralised, to oppose successful resistance to gallant Captain Broke and his veterans.

Admiral de La Gravière comments on this fight as follows, and his criticism is entirely just :—

"It is impossible to avoid seeing in the capture of the *Chesapeake* a new proof of the enormous power of a good organisation, when it has received the consecration of a few years' actual service on the sea. On this occasion, in effect, two captains equally renowned, the honour of two navies, were opposed to each other in two ships of the same tonnage and number of guns. Never had the chances seemed better balanced; but Sir Philip Broke had commanded the *Shannon* for nearly seven years, while Captain Lawrence had only commanded the *Chesapeake* for a few days. The first of these frigates had cruised for eighteen months on the coast of America; the second was leaving port. One had a crew long accustomed to habits of strict obedience; the other was manned by men who had just been engaged in mutiny. The Americans were wrong to accuse fortune on this occasion. Fortune was not fickle—she was merely logical. The *Shannon* captured the *Chesapeake* on the 1st of June, 1813; but on the 14th of September, 1806, the day when he took command of his frigate, Captain Broke had begun to prepare the glorious termination of this bloody affair."

No single ship action of the war attracted greater attention than this, and none reflected greater credit on the victor. After five ships in succession had been captured in single fight by the enemy, without one victory to relieve the defeats, Captain Broke, in sight of the enemy's coast, off the harbour of one of his chief seaports, had

---

[1] 'Guerres Maritimes,' ii. 272.

captured single-handed a frigate nominally of equal, and in reality of slightly superior, force.   He himself was very badly wounded, and was never again able to go into active service.[1]   His victory was celebrated with almost extravagant joy throughout Britain.   The exultation of the British was as great as had been their previous depression.   No other British Captain has ever won such honour by a single ship action.   No other fight between frigates has ever been so enthusiastically commemorated by the victor's countrymen. Captain Broke was made a baronet.   Nelson, for the battle of the Nile, was only raised to the lowest rank of the peerage ; and fifty years later, as we learn from ' Tom Brown at Rugby,' the glory of the *Shannon* and her commander was a favourite theme for song among British schoolboys.

In America the news of the result caused widespread grief and dismay.   A year had made the Americans feel the same unjustifiable self-confidence that the British had felt at the outbreak of the war, and the *Shannon's* victory shattered the one as the frigate and sloop actions of 1812 had shattered the other.   In each case the exultation of the victors was an unconscious expression of the high esteem in which they had held the prowess of the vanquished.   The excitement caused by the capture of the *Guerrière* was proof of the commanding position of the British Navy ; the joy over the capture of the *Chesapeake* showed the point to which the prowess of the Americans had raised the general estimate of American ships-of-war.

The lesson of the *Chesapeake* was not to stand alone.   The American brig sloop *Argus*, 16, commanded by Lieutenant William Henry Allen, had crossed the ocean in June, carrying the American minister to France.   On July 14th, 1813, she put out again from Lorient, and cruised in the chops of the English Channel, and then along the coast of Cornwall and into St. George's Channel.   She captured and burnt ship after ship, creating the greatest consternation among the merchants.   The labour was very severe, the men getting hardly any rest.   On the night of August 13th a brig laden with wine from Oporto was taken, and many of the crew got drunk. At five o'clock on the following morning, a large brig-of-war, which proved to be the British brig sloop *Pelican* under Commander John

---

[1] Philip Bowes Vere Broke : born, 1776 ; Lieutenant, 1795 ; Commander, 1799 ; Captain, 1801 ; Baronet, November 2nd, 1813 ; K.C.B., January 2nd, 1815 ; Rear-Admiral, 1830 ; died, 1841.—W. L. C.

Fordyce Maples,[1] was descried standing down under a cloud of canvas. St. David's Head bore east five leagues.

The *Argus* was a very swift brig, with loftier masts and longer spars than the *Pelican*, though the latter was considerably heavier; and she was armed only with 24-pr. carronades as against the 32's of the *Pelican*. The odds against her were about the same as they had been against the *Peacock* or the *Java ;* but Allen, who had been Decatur's first lieutenant when the *Macedonian* was captured, was as confident of victory as Lawrence had been, and he had no intention of taking advantage of his superiority of speed to avoid combat. The *Argus* shortened sail and waited until the *Pelican* was nearly aft, and but a pistol-shot off. Then, at 6 A.M., she wore and fired her port guns, the *Pelican* responding with her starboard battery.[2] Immediately after the beginning of the action a round shot carried off Allen's leg, inflicting a mortal wound ; but he stayed on deck until he fainted from loss of blood. Soon afterwards the first lieutenant, William Henry Watson, was wounded by a grape-shot and carried below ; and the second lieutenant, Mr. U. H. Allen, was left to fight the brig. The firing was very heavy, especially from the *Pelican ;* but most of it went high, on both sides. At 6.14 Commander Maples bore up to pass astern of his antagonist ; but Lieutenant Allen luffed into the wind and threw the maintop-sail aback so as to come square across his antagonist's bows. From this position he raked the *Pelican* with his broadside ; but the guns were badly aimed, and did little damage. The ships again ran off side by side, the fire continuing as furiously as ever ; but the *Argus* began to suffer so much in her rigging that she became unmanageable, and fell off before the wind. The *Pelican* then passed under her stern, raked her heavily, ranged up on her starboard quarter, and raked her again and again ; for it was no longer possible to handle her. The *Argus* suffered heavily aloft : her crew escaped without severe slaughter, but began to show symptoms of demoralisation, not behaving as well as the gallantry and seamanship of her officers would seemingly have warranted. In a few moments the *Pelican* passed her foe's broadside, and took a position on her starboard bow. At 6.45, three-quarters of an hour after the action had begun, the brigs fell

---

[1] The *Pelican* had anchored at Cork on August 12th, after a cruise, and had at once been ordered to sea again in quest of the *Argus*. She had, therefore, taken necessary stores on board, and sailed within fourteen hours.—W. L. C.

[2] Minutes of court of inquiry into loss of *Argus*, March 1815.

together, and the *Argus* struck just as the British were about to board.[1]

The *Pelican* carried twenty-one guns, including sixteen 32-pound carronades, four long 6's, and one 12-pound carronade. The *Argus* carried twenty guns—eighteen 24-pound carronades and two long 12's.[2] The crew of the *Pelican* consisted of 113 men, the crew of the *Argus* of 104. Seven men were killed and wounded in the *Pelican*, among the killed being Master's Mate William Young, and twenty-four in the *Argus*. Both ships were tolerably well cut up. The difference in force was less than as five to four; whereas the difference in loss was greater than three to one. In other words, the *Pelican* displayed superiority in efficiency as well as superiority in weight. The *Argus* made a distinctly poor fight. She did not inflict much damage, and though the officers behaved well, most of them being killed or wounded, the crew had lost less than a fourth of their number when they surrendered. The *Pelican* herself did not show to much advantage, her gunnery being poor. In short, the action was directly the reverse of that between the *Chesapeake* and the *Shannon*. Broke won because he did even better than his gallant and skilful antagonist; but the *Pelican* won, although she did poorly, because her antagonist did very badly indeed. The shortcomings of the *Argus* have never been adequately explained, for her commander was a man of proved courage and ability. It was afterwards stated that her powder was poor, and that her crew were over-tired, and some of them intoxicated.[3] It seems evident that Lieutenant Allen had become over-confident, and had let his men fall off in their gunnery, and yet had engaged a heavier antagonist when his people were worn out with fatigue.[4]

---

[1] Letter of Maples, Aug. 14th, 1813.

[2] James gives the armament of the two brigs thus :—

Pelican.		*Argus.*	
16	32-pr. carrs.	18	24-pr. carrs.
2	long 6-prs.	2	long British 12-prs.[2]
1	12-pr. boat carr.[1]		
2	brass 6-prs.[1]		

Broadside weight of metal, 262 lbs.   Broadside weight of metal, 228 lbs.

[1] Not reckoned as part of the broadside. The 6-prs. were in the stern ports, where they inconvenienced the man at the helm.

[2] The 12-prs. were in her bridle ports, and not in her broadside.   —W. L. C.

[3] Cooper; and minutes of court of inquiry.

[4] Lieutenant W. H. Allen, of the *Argus*, after having his thigh amputated, died at Plymouth on August 18th, and was buried there on the 21st. Commander Maples was posted on August 23rd, as a reward for his success. He died, after retirement with the rank of Rear-Admiral, in 1847.—W. L. C.

The next engagement was in favour of the Americans. The only one of the small American gun-brigs left was the *Enterprise*, Lieutenant William Burrows. Two bow-chasers had been crowded into her bridle-ports, and she was overmanned, mounting fourteen 18-pr. carronades and two long 9's, with a crew of 120 men. She was a very lucky little vessel, both before and after the engagement now to be told, and, though a dull sailer, of weak force, she managed to escape capture, and in her turn captured a number of British privateers. One of these privateers, mounting fourteen long 9's with a crew of seventy-nine men, showed fight, and only struck after receiving a broadside which killed and wounded four of her crew. Later, being chased by a frigate, the *Enterprise* had to throw overboard all her guns but two in order to escape.

In the summer of 1813 she was kept cruising off the eastern coast to harass the Nova Scotian and New Brunswick privateers. On September 5th, while standing along shore near Penguin Point, a few miles to the eastward of Portland, Maine, she descried at anchor inside the British gun-brig *Boxer*, Commander Samuel Blyth, of about her own size, but with two carronades less,[1] and only sixty-six men in crew. The *Boxer* at once hoisted ensigns, fore and aft, and bore up for the *Enterprise*, which was then standing in on the starboard tack ; but, when the two brigs were still four miles apart, it fell calm.[2] At mid-day a breeze sprang up from the south-west, giving the *Enterprise* the weather-gage ; and she manœuvred for some time before closing, in order to try the comparative rates of sailing of the vessels. At 3 P.M. Lieutenant Burrows hoisted three ensigns, shortened sail, and edged away towards the *Boxer*. Commander Blyth had nailed his colours to the mast, telling his men that they should never be struck while he had life in his body ;[3] and his little brig was steered gallantly into action. Both crews were in good spirits, and they cheered loudly as the brigs neared one another. At a quarter-past three, when the two brigs were on the starboard tack not a half pistol-shot apart, they opened fire, the Americans using the port, and the British, the starboard guns. Both broadsides were very destructive, and the two commanders fell at the very beginning of the action. Commander Blyth was killed by an 18-pound shot, which passed through his body while he was standing on the quarter-deck.

---

[1] The *Boxer*, moreover, had two long 6's, instead of long 9-prs.—W. L. C.
[2] Letter of Lieutenant Edward R. McCall, U.S.N., Sept. 5th, 1813.
[3] 'Naval Chronicle,' xxxii. 462.

The second in command, Lieutenant David M'Creery, continued
to fight the brig. At almost the same time Lieutenant Burrows
fell. He had laid hold of a gun-tackle fall to help the crew of a
carronade to run out the gun. In doing so he raised one leg
against the bulwark, and a canister-shot struck his thigh, glancing
into his body and inflicting a fearful wound.[1] In spite of the pain,
he refused to be carried below, and lay on the deck calling out to
the men, and cheering them to the fight. Lieutenant Edward R.

COMMANDER SAMUEL BLYTH, R.N.

(From Blood's portrait in the "Naval Chronicle," 1814.)

M'Call took command in his place. After a quarter of an hour's
yardarm and yardarm work, the *Enterprise* ranged ahead, rounded
to on the starboard tack, and raked the *Boxer*. She shot away the
Boxer's main topmast and topsail-yard; but the British crew kept
up the fight bravely, with the exception of four men, who deserted
their quarters and were afterwards court-martialled for cowardice.
However, there was now no chance of success. The *Enterprise* set
her foresail, so as to keep on the starboard bow of the *Boxer*, and

[1] Cooper, ii. 259.

raked her until she surrendered, half an hour after the fight began, she being then entirely unmanageable and defenceless. Lieutenant Burrows would not go below until he had received the sword of his adversary, when he exclaimed, " I am satisfied ; I die contented."

Both brigs had suffered severely, especially the *Boxer*, which had been hulled repeatedly. The *Enterprise's* injuries were chiefly aloft. The difference in loss of men was less than the difference in damage to the brigs. Twelve of the Americans and twenty-one of the British were killed or wounded. The British court-martial attributed the defeat of the *Boxer* " to a superiority in the enemy's force, principally in the number of men, as well as to a greater degree of skill in the direction of her fire, and to the destructive effects of the first broadsides." [1] The main factor was the superiority in force, the difference in loss being very nearly proportional to it. Both sides fought with equal bravery ; and the difference in skill, though appreciable, was not marked. At a naval dinner given at New York shortly afterwards one of the toasts offered was, " The crew of the *Boxer* ; enemies by law, but by gallantry brothers." The two commanders were both buried at Portland with all the honours of war. [2]

The fight had taken place so close to the shore that it could be both seen and heard. Among those who listened to the guns was Longfellow, who long afterwards commemorated the battle in verse. Commander Blyth was a man of high personal courage, noted for his gentleness and courtesy. He had been one of Captain Lawrence's pall-bearers, and, shortly before his death, had been publicly thanked by the militia commander of one of the Maine districts for the kindness and humanity which he had shown to the inhabitants.

The blockade of the American coast as a whole was far more important than any of the single ship actions ; but the incidents to relieve the monotony were so few that there is little to chronicle beyond the fact of the blockade itself, and the further fact that it told upon every article which any American bought or sold, and that it put every man to such trouble and inconvenience, if not to such positive want, as to cause formidable discontent. It was the mere presence of the ships that accomplished this—their ceaseless standing

[1] Minutes of court-martial on board H.M.S. *Surprise,* Jan. 8th, 1814.

[2] Commander Samuel Blyth, born in 1783, had held his rank since September 5th, 1811. If my memory of the spot serves me aright, a single tree overshadows the graves of both commanders.—W. L. C.

to and fro off the coast and at the mouths of the harbours. American merchant vessels had been almost driven from the ocean, although many ran in and out of the New England ports, until, within the closing months of the war, the blockade was applied to New England also in all its rigour. On the high seas the British took many American ships ; but they were mostly privateers, or the prizes of privateers, for there were not many merchantmen to capture. No vigilance by the blockading squadrons could prevent many cruisers, public and private, built especially to run and to fight, from slipping out of port; and, of the prizes, enough got in to pay well in a certain proportion of cases ; but mere cargo ships had to undergo such risks that they could only be compensated for by trebling and quadrupling the prices of the cargoes. The weary sameness of the blockade was broken by occasional descents to harry the coast, or by cutting-out expeditions against gunboats and privateers. Of course, these were mere incidents, valuable chiefly as relieving the monotony of the life, though, in the case of the descents, they had a certain effect in harassing and worrying the Americans. Even the damage done by these expeditions, however, probably caused as much anger as willingness to come to terms. It was the constant pressure of the blockade itself that counted, together with the opportunities which it offered for descents in force, rather than the mere harrying expeditions.

It was early in April, 1813, when Rear-Admiral George Cockburn first began to harry the shores of the Chesapeake in earnest. His little flotilla was manned by but four or five hundred men ; yet he stationed himself at the mouth of the Susquehanna and supplied the whole British fleet with provisions from American towns and farms; and no effort worth speaking of was made to molest him. All Maryland was fiercely excited and angered ; but Maryland had to learn the lesson that, after war has begun, it is impossible to do much by improvised means of defence against a trained enemy who can choose his own point of attack. The militia here and there gathered for resistance ; but Cockburn's veterans, sailors and soldiers, dispersed them with the utmost ease. He destroyed a large cannon foundry, he burned all the towns where there was any resistance, and, early in May, he brought back his flotilla to Sir John Borlase Warren, having had but one man wounded during the month which he had spent working his will among the Marylanders. The American newspapers denounced him bitterly as a buccaneer ; but they should have denounced even more severely themselves and their political leaders. It was a bitter disgrace to the American people that they should be powerless to resent or repel such insults to their shores; and it was a severe commentary on their folly in having refused in the past, and even at the time refusing, to organise the thoroughly trained forces by sea and land which alone could prevent or avenge such a catastrophe.

This expedition showed that the villages and country districts were completely at the mercy of the British. There were three towns of importance, Baltimore, Washington, and Norfolk, which were also within striking distance of the fleet; and, in June, Warren made up his mind to attack one of these. He chose Norfolk, because there was the Portsmouth Navy Yard, and there lay the *Constellation* frigate. The expedition, however, miscarried, although the Admiral had at his disposal three thousand troops and thirteen war vessels. The land forces became entangled among some deep creeks, and re-embarked without making any serious effort to carry out their part of the programme. The attack by the Navy was made in a division of fifteen boats with seven hundred men, under the command of Captain Samuel John Pechell of the *San Domingo*, 74. Captain John Martin Hanchett, of the *Diadem* frigate, led the way in his launch. The point chosen for attack was Craney Island, where a battery of six 18-prs. had been erected and put in charge of a hundred sailors and fifty marines from the *Constellation*, under Lieutenants Neale, Shubrick, Saunders, and Breckinbridge of that ship.[1] The water was shallow, and the attack was not pushed with the resolution ordinarily displayed by the British Navy in an enterprise of the kind. The *Constellation's* men reserved their fire until the British were close in, when they opened with destructive effect. While still more than seventy yards from the guns, the *Diadem's* launch grounded. Three of the boats were sunk by shot, but remained above water, as it was so shallow; and, in the heat of the fight, some of the *Constellation's* crew, headed by Midshipman Tatnall, waded out and took possession.[2] Some of the crews surrendered and went ashore with their captors; the others escaped to the remaining boats, which immediately afterwards made off in disorder, having lost ninety-one men.[3] The assailants

---

[1] Letter of Captain John Cassin, June 23rd, 1813.
[2] 'Life of Commodore Josiah Tatnall,' by Charles C. Jones, p. 17.
[3] James, vi. 233 [Ed. 1837.]

afterwards strove to justify themselves by asserting that the bottom was covered with slime and mud too deep to admit of their getting on shore; but this was certainly not the case, as it did not prevent Tatnall and his companions from wading out to them, and from returning in safety with the prisoners. The Americans suffered no loss.

This took place on June 22nd, 1813. Smarting under the repulse, Warren, on the 25th, sent Cockburn, accompanied by a land force under Major-General Sir Sydney Beckwith, to attack Hampton village. The militia on that occasion gave Beckwith a rather stout fight, killing and wounding some fifty men before they were dispersed. The town was then taken and destroyed with circumstances of horrible outrage. Lieutenant-Colonel C. J. Napier, of the 102nd Regiment, commanded Beckwith's advance, and prevented his men from joining in the deeds of the " miscreants," as he called them. He wrote, with intense indignation, that the troops perpetrated with impunity " every horror—rape, murder, pillage—and not a man was punished;" and he blamed Sir Sydney for not hanging several of the villains.[1] Nothing was done, however; and the affair caused bitter anger in America, leading to reprisals and counter-reprisals on the Canadian frontier. Although none of the offenders were punished, both Sir John Warren and General Beckwith took steps to prevent any repetition of the outrages, dismissing from the service a regiment of French deserters in British pay, who were alleged to be the chief offenders.[2] During the remainder of the year Warren cruised off Chesapeake Bay and at the mouth of the lower Potomac, keeping Virginia and Maryland in a state of incessant alarm; which makes it all the more wonderful that those States were not roused to take measures for efficient defence. Cockburn sailed south to harry the coast of the Carolinas and Georgia. Colonel Napier went with him to North Carolina to take part in the descents, and left on record

[1] ' Life of General Sir Charles James Napier,' i. 221, 225.

[2] James (vi. 234, ed. 1837), while admitting that outrages were committed, makes a feeble attempt to minimise them by quoting from the Georgetown *Federal Republican*, of July 7th, 1813, the following : " The statement of the women of Hampton being violated by the British turns out to be false. A correspondence upon that subject, and the pillage said to have been committed there, has taken place between General Taylor and Admiral Warren. Some plunder appears to have been committed, but it was confined to the French troops employed." If the outrages were perpetrated by troops in British pay, Britain was, unhappily, responsible for what occurred ; and Napier's testimony puts the question of outrage beyond challenge.—W. L. C.

his distaste for what he called " a necessary part of our job, viz.,
plundering and ruining the peasantry . . . (for) no outrages have
been authorised on persons, though much on property, unavoidably."

Meanwhile the American gunboats had on one or two occasions
made efforts to harass the British blockading squadrons, with
ludicrously futile results.   The gunboats were sloop or schooner-
rigged, and armed with one or two long heavy guns, and occasionally with light carronades to repel boarders.   The larger gunboats
were useful in convoying parties of small coasting vessels from one
port to another; and they interfered with the British boats and
tenders, and also kept privateers off the coast.   The smaller gunboats,
which were chiefly employed in attacks on the frigates, had been
built in accordance with Jefferson's theory of coast protection, and
they proved utterly worthless.   They trusted mainly to their sweeps
for motive power, and each was usually armed with a long 12 or
18-pounder.   They could be used only in an almost absolute calm,
for in any wind it was not only impossible to fire, but also difficult
to keep the boats right side up.   Both officers and men hated the
gunboat service, and were so convinced of the uselessness of the
vessels that they made but half-hearted attempts to do anything
with them.   The gunboats were much smaller and in every way
inferior to the big Danish gunboats, which, during the same period,
did at times efficient work on the coast of Denmark.   That the
fault lay in the boats themselves, and not in the crews who manned
them, was proved by the great gallantry with which the latter
afterwards behaved at Bladensburg.

On June 20th fifteen gunboats attacked the *Junon*, 38, Captain
James Sanders, while she lay becalmed in Hampton road.   The
gunboats anchored while still at a very long range, and promptly
drifted round, so that they could not shoot.   They then got under
way, and gradually drew nearer the *Junon*.   A long-range cannonade
followed, in which the *Junon* was very slightly injured, and the
gunboats suffered not at all; but as soon as a slight breeze sprung
up, the *Barrosa*, 36, Captain William Henry Shirreff, approached,
and promptly drove off the flotilla; for as soon as they felt the
effects of the breeze the gunboats became useless, and could only
retire.   The only loss they suffered was one man killed and two
wounded, from the *Barrosa's* fire.

On that occasion the *Junon* did little better than the gunboats;
but she had her revenge a month later.   On July 29th she was

in Delaware Bay with the ship-sloop *Martin*, 18, Commander Humphrey Fleming Senhouse, when the latter grounded on the outside of Crow's Shoal. The frigate anchored within supporting distance ; and shortly afterwards the two ships were attacked by a flotilla of ten American gunboats. Besides the usual disadvantages of gunboats, these particular ones suffered under an additional handicap, for their powder was so bad that all of the officers had joined in a solemn protest to the Navy Department, and had stated that it was unfit for service.[1] The flotilla kept at a distance which permitted an hour's cannonading with no damage to anybody, their own shot failing to reach even the brig, while those of the frigate occasionally passed over them. During the firing, gunboat No. 121, Sailing-Master Shead, drifted a mile and a half away from her consorts. This gave the British an opportunity, of which they took prompt advantage. They made a dash for No. 121 in seven boats, containing one hundred and forty men, under the command of Lieutenant Philip Westphal. Mr. Shead anchored, and made an obstinate defence ; but at the second discharge of his long-gun the carriage was almost torn to pieces, and he was reduced to the use of small-arms.[2] The British boats advanced steadily, firing their boat carronades and musketry, and carried the gunboat by boarding, though not without a loss of three killed or mortally wounded, and four wounded, while seven of the twenty-five members of the gunboat's crew suffered likewise.

At about the same time the boats of the British brig-sloops *Contest* and *Mohawk*, under the command of Lieutenant Rodger Carley Curry, made an attack on the little gunboat *Asp*, 3, commanded by Midshipman Sigourney, when she was moored in Yeocomico Creek, out of the Chesapeake, on July 11th. After a murderous conflict, in which eleven Americans, including Mr. Sigourney, and eight British, including Lieutenant Curry, were killed or wounded, the British carried the *Asp* and set her on fire. However, the surviving Americans, nine in number, escaped to the shore, rallied under Midshipman McClintock, and, as soon as the British retired, boarded the *Asp*, put out the flames, and got her into fighting order.[3] They were not again molested.

---

[1] Navy Department MSS., 'Masters Commandants' Letters,' 1813, No. 3 ; enclosed in letter of Master-Commandant Samuel Angus.

[2] Letter of Mr. Shead, Aug. 5th, 1813.

[3] Letter of Midshipman McClintock, July 15th, 1813 ; also James, vi. 236 (Ed. 1837).

Shortly before this, on June 12th, the boats of the British frigate *Narcissus*, 32, Captain John Richard Lumley, containing fifty men under the command of Lieutenant John Cririe, captured the little cutter *Surveyor*, 6, under Mr. William S. Travis, with a crew of fifteen men, as she lay in York River, out of the Chesapeake.[1] The struggle was brief but bloody, five Americans and nine British being killed or wounded. Lieutenant Cririe led his men with distinguished gallantry, and proved himself a generous victor, for he returned Mr. Travis's sword with a letter running : " Your gallant and desperate attempt to defend your vessel against more than double your number on the night of the 12th instant excited such admiration on the part of your opponents as I have seldom witnessed . . . and I am at a loss which to admire most—the previous arrangements on board the *Surveyor*, or the determined manner in which her deck was disputed inch by inch."

In January, 1814, the little United States coasting schooner *Alligator*, of four guns and forty men, Sailing-Master R. Bassett, was attacked by the boats of a British frigate and brig, after night-fall, while lying at anchor in the mouth of the Stone River, South Carolina. Two of her men were killed and two wounded; but the boats were beaten off with severe loss, one of them being captured.[2]

Besides these engagements with the United States' armed vessels, boat-parties from the British two-deckers and frigates destroyed many privateers and merchantmen all along the coast from New England to Georgia, as well as on the high seas. Some of the privateers showed fight; and of them some behaved with courage that would have done credit to any ship in the regular navy, while others betrayed panic or inefficiency which would have disgraced the worst ship in the worst regular navy afloat. In short, they were the militia of the sea, and they could not be depended upon for steady fighting, though at times their feats were brilliant to a degree; for, unlike the militia of the land, they were trained to the profession of arms, and they followed by choice a pursuit of peril and hazard.

A good example of the wide variety in behaviour of the privateers under similar circumstances was afforded by two incidents which occurred in Chesapeake Bay early in 1813. On February 8th nine boats, with two hundred men under the command of Lieutenant

[1] Letter of W. S. Travis, June 16th, 1813.
[2] Letters of Bassett, Jan. 31st, 1814, and Commander J. H. Dent, Feb. 21st, 1814.

Kelly Nazer, from the four British frigates, *Belvidera*, *Maidstone*, *Junon*, and *Statira*, were sent against the schooner *Lottery*, John Southcomb, master, a letter of marque of six 12-pounder carronades, and twenty-five men, bound from Baltimore to Bordeaux. A calm came on, enabling the boats to overtake the schooner; and they spread out, then closing in with a rush. The schooner[1] was speedily carried, but only after an obstinate struggle, in which Southcomb and nineteen of his crew, together with six of the assailants, were killed or wounded. Southcomb, mortally wounded, was taken on board the *Belvidera*, where Captain Richard Byron (2) treated him with the kind and considerate courtesy which always marked that brave officer's dealings with his foes; and, when Southcomb died, his body was sent ashore with every mark of respect due to a brave officer. Captain Stewart, of the *Constellation*, wrote Captain Byron a letter thanking him for his generous conduct.[2]

On March 16th, 1813, a smaller British division of five boats and one hundred and five men, commanded by Lieutenant James Polkinghorne, attacked the privateer schooner *Dolphin*, and the letters of marque *Racer*, *Arab*, and *Lynx*, mounting all told thirty guns, with an aggregate of one hundred and sixty men. Polkinghorne's force was greatly inferior: nevertheless it dashed in with the utmost gallantry, and the privateersmen speedily became panic-stricken. The *Arab* and *Lynx* surrendered at once. The *Racer* was carried, after a sharp struggle in which Polkinghorne was wounded; and her guns were turned on the *Dolphin*. Most of the latter's crew jumped overboard. A few rallied round their captain, but they were at once scattered as the British seamen came on board.[3] It was an unusually brilliant and daring cutting-out expedition.[4]

The American gunboats occasionally captured British privateers, and on more than one occasion cut them out, when they were becalmed or at anchor, with boat-parties; but they did nothing

[1] The *Lottery* was added to the Royal Navy as the *Canso*, 16.—W. L. C.

[2] The whole correspondence is given in full in ' Niles's Register,' February and March numbers.

[3] See Niles for this; also James's ' Naval Occurrences.'

[4] In this affair, besides Lieutenant Polkinghorne, Lieutenant William Alexander Brand, Lieutenant William Richard Flint, R.M., Midshipman John Sleigh, and 7 men were wounded. In spite of its gallant nature, no medal was ever granted for it. The Americans lost 16 killed and wounded. The *Racer* became the *Shelburne*, 14, and the *Lynx*, the *Musquedobet*, 14, in the Royal Navy. Polkinghorne was not made a Commander until June 27th, 1814. He was posted on August 25th, 1828, and died on January 9th, 1839.—W. L. C.

of any especial note in that way. They also at times cut off
tenders to the British war vessels, or interfered with the British
cutting-out expeditions.

In the spring of 1814 the command of the British fleet on
the coast of North America was given to Vice-Admiral Sir Alexander
Forester Inglis Cochrane.[1]   The main British force continued to
lie in the Chesapeake.

During 1813 and 1814 the blockade of the American coast was

ADMIRAL THE HON. SIR ALEXANDER FORESTER INGLIS COCHRANE, G.C.B.
(*From the portrait in Brenton's History.*)

so severe that only occasionally could American frigates get to
sea; and those that did get to sea failed to accomplish anything.
Once or twice one of the American 44's chased a British 18-pounder
frigate and failed to come up with her; and once or twice they were
themselves chased by a couple of 18-pounder frigates and escaped.

[1] Admiral Sir John Borlase Warren, whom Cochrane superseded, was only sixty-
one years of age, but was very infirm. Cochrane was but fifty-six.—W. L. C.

They captured a few merchantmen and picked up one or two small British cruisers, while two or three small American cruisers, brigs, or schooners were lost in the same way ; but nothing of importance happened to any American frigates, with one exception.

That exception was the *Essex*, 32, Captain David Porter, which spent most of the year 1813 in the Pacific. The *Essex* had left the United States on October 28th, 1812. As she expected to make a very long cruise, she carried an unusual quantity of provisions, and sixty more men than ordinarily, so as to man any ships which she might capture. She cruised in the South Atlantic for two or three months, capturing some valuable prizes. Porter then decided on the very bold course of doubling Cape Horn, and striking at the British whalers in the Pacific.

This was practically going into the enemy's waters, for there were no stations where the *Essex* could refit in safety, while South America and South-Eastern Asia were full of ports friendly to the British. No American frigate had ever before gone into the Pacific ; and, during all the long European warfare, no one of Great Britain's enemies had ventured to attack her in the remote South Seas.

At the end of the winter the *Essex* doubled the Horn, and sailed into the harbour of Valparaiso. On March 20th she captured a Peruvian corsair, the *Nereyda*, which had been harassing American whalers. Porter threw her guns and small-arms overboard, and sent her into port. The Spanish colonies were at that time in open revolt against Spain, both sides bidding for the favour of Britain ; and there was lawlessness throughout the South Seas. The American whalers had been in great danger of capture, but Porter's appearance saved them. He cruised hither and thither to the different islands and archipelagoes most frequented by whaling vessels ; and, as by-play, he took part in the wars of the savages. He saved all the American whalers, and did not cost the government a dollar, supplying everything from his prizes—sails, guns, anchors, provisions, medicine, and even money to pay the officers and the men. He completely broke up the British whaling trade in the Pacific, capturing or destroying four thousand tons of shipping, and making prisoners of four hundred men. One or two of the prizes he turned into tenders ; and these and the boat-parties had one or two smart skirmishes in capturing such of the whalers as were armed letters of marque.[1]

---

[1] In Porter's own book this cruise is described at length.

Early in January, 1814, he returned to the South American coast, and again made the harbour of Valparaiso. One of the captured whalers, rechristened the *Essex Junior*,[1] was in company as a tender. On February 8th the British frigate *Phœbe*, 36, Captain James Hillyar, accompanied by the ship-sloop *Cherub*, 18, Commander Thomas Tudor Tucker, made their appearance in the harbour. They had been sent to the Pacific especially to capture

CAPTAIN DAVID PORTER, U.S.N.
(After a crayon portrait by J. Wood.)

Porter, to break up the American whaling trade, and to destroy the American fur-stations at the mouth of the Columbia. When they came into the harbour Porter was afraid that they might try to carry the *Essex* out of hand without regard to the neutrality laws. The *Essex* was put in fighting trim. The *Phœbe* came so near her —whether by accident, as Hillyar asserted, or by design, as Porter insisted, cannot be said—that a collision seemed imminent; but

[1] Previously the *Atlantic*.—W. L. C.

neither captain was willing to begin the fray, and the peace of the port was not broken.

The British ships began a blockade of the port which lasted over a month. Porter was anxious to meet the *Phœbe* alone, and Hillyar was equally determined to use the advantage which his two ships gave him. He was quite right in refusing single combat except on his own terms. The *Phœbe* was armed like the *Essex* with forty-six guns; but on her main-deck she carried long 18's, so that at a distance she could cut the *Essex* to pieces without suffering any material loss or damage. Her crew consisted of over three hundred men, while that of the *Essex* numbered but· two hundred and fifty-five. But, on the occasions when he sought a single combat, Porter took the crew of the *Essex Junior* on board, which gave him sixty men additional. In such circumstances the widely different armaments of the two frigates made it difficult to foretell the result of a combat between them. In ordinary circumstances, and taking into account the ordinary chances and vicissitudes of naval warfare, the *Phœbe's* armament was beyond all comparison the better; but the *Essex* was the swifter ship, and at close quarters her carronades threw, of course, a greater weight in broadside than the long-guns to which they were opposed, while, when she had the crew of the *Essex Junior* on board, the complements of the two ships were about equal, while the crew of the *Essex* had been especially trained with a view to boarding. If his speed had enabled him to close, Porter would have had more than an even chance of winning; whereas he had no chance at all in action at a distance. Hillyar was not in the South Pacific as a naval knight-errant. His business there was to capture the *Essex*. It would have been folly to risk the result on a doubtful single ship duel, instead of utilising his superiority in force, and trying to get his antagonist at a disadvantage. The *Cherub* was a small frigate-built sloop, mounting twenty-six guns, with a crew of about 160 men. All her guns were carronades, excepting two long bow-chasers.

Toward the end of March Porter decided to run out of harbour on the first opportunity, so as to draw away his two antagonists in chase, and let the *Essex Junior* escape; for Porter had satisfied himself that his ship was faster than either of the British ships. After he had come to this conclusion, the two vessels were kept always ready, the *Essex* having only her proper complement of 255 men on board.

On March 28th it came on to blow from the south, and the *Essex* parted her cables. She then got under way and made sail, Porter having determined to put his plan in operation. The British vessels were close in with the weathermost point of the bay, and Porter hauled up to pass to windward of them. Just as he was rounding the outermost point, and when safety was almost within his grasp, a heavy squall struck the *Essex*, and her main topmast went by the board. Porter then committed a grave error. David Glasgow Farragut,[1] then a midshipman, and afterwards the greatest admiral of the American navy, was on board the *Essex ;* and in after-life he always expressed the opinion that she should have run before the wind, which had shifted, and have tried to escape into the open sea ; for Farragut believed that, even with her topmast out, she would have been faster before the wind than the *Phœbe*, and certainly much faster than the *Cherub*. This at least would have given her a chance to escape : otherwise she had no chance at all.[2]

However, the *Essex* tried to get back to the harbour, and failing, because of her crippled condition, she anchored, at 3.40 P.M., in a small bay three miles from Valparaiso, and half a mile from a detached Chilian battery. She was within pistol-shot of the shore, and was as much entitled to the benefit of neutral rights as when in Valparaiso harbour ; but neutral rights have shifting values, and Hillyar had no idea of letting his foe escape when disabled and within his grasp.

The *Phœbe* and *Cherub* bore down upon the *Essex*, covered with ensigns, union jacks, and motto flags ; and the *Essex* made ready to receive them, her flags flying from every mast.[3] The fight was begun before the springs could be got on her cables. Hillyar made his attack with extreme caution, taking his frigate under the stern of the *Essex*, while the *Cherub* took her position on the American's starboard bow. The action began soon after four in the afternoon. The *Essex's* bow-chasers speedily drove off the *Cherub*, which ran

---

[1] David Glasgow Farragut, born in Tennessee, of part Spanish ancestry, July 5th, 1801 ; gained undying fame as a naval commander in the American Civil War, 1861–65, notably at New Orleans and in Mobile Bay ; was the first officer to be given the rank of Admiral in the United States Navy ; visited Europe, 1867–68 ; died in New York, August 14th, 1870. *Life* by L. Farragut, by Headley, and by Mahan.— W. L. C.

[2] 'Life of Farragut,' by his son, Loyall Farragut, pp. 37–46.

[3] Letters of Captain Hillyar, March 30th, 1814, and Captain Porter, July 3rd, 1814.

down and stationed herself near the *Phœbe*. The latter opened
with her broadside of long 18's from a position in which not one of
Porter's guns could reach her.   Three times springs were got on the
cables of the *Essex*, in order to bring her round until her broadside bore ; but in each instance they were shot away.   Three long
12's were then got out of the stern-ports ; and with these a brisk fire
was kept up, aimed especially at the rigging of the British ships.
A good many of the *Essex's* crew were killed during the first five
minutes, before she could bring any guns to bear ; but afterwards she
did not suffer much.   Meanwhile her own long 12's were so well
handled that, after a quarter of an hour's firing, the *Phœbe* and
Cherub were actually driven off.   They wore, and again began with
their long-guns, but found themselves at too great range to accomplish anything ; and about half an hour after the first shot had been
fired, the British ships hauled out of the fight for the time being.
" Our first fire . . . produced no visible effect ; our second . . .
was not apparently more successful ; and, having lost the use of
our main-sail, jib, and main-stay, appearances were a little in-
auspicious," wrote Captain Hillyar in his official report.

    The damages were soon repaired, and the two ships stood back
for the *Essex*.   The *Phœbe* anchored off her port quarter, at about
5.35 P.M., while the *Cherub* kept under way, using her long bow-
chasers.   They were out of reach of Porter's carronades, his long-
guns would not bear, and the enemy was gradually knocking the
Essex to pieces without suffering any damage in return.   This could
not be borne, and at 5.50 Porter severed his cable and tried to close
with his antagonists.   His rigging and sails were cut almost to
pieces.   Still, the *Essex* drove down on her assailants, and for the
first time got near enough to use her carronades.   After exchanging
a couple of broadsides, the *Cherub* hauled out of the fight, and the
Phœbe also edged off.   The latter now possessed the superiority of
sailing, for her foe was almost helpless, and so Hillyar was able to
choose his own distance.   Again he opened with his long 18's, out
of range of the *Essex's* carronades.   All that Porter could do was
to reply with his long 12's.   There was no hope of success left, but
the *Essex* was not yet ready to surrender.

    From that point on it was a slaughter rather than a battle.
The carnage in the American frigate made her decks look like
shambles.   Throughout the entire war no ship on either side was so
desperately defended as the *Essex*, taking into account the frightful

odds against which she fought; indeed, the *Frolic*, the *Reindeer*, and the *Lawrence* were the only ships which in this respect deserved any comparison with her. Captain Hillyar in his official report says, "The defence of the *Essex*, taking into consideration our superiority of force, and the very discouraging circumstances of her having lost her main topmast, and being twice on fire, did honour to her brave defenders, and fully evinced the courage of Captain Porter and those under his command." A middle-aged man, cool and wary, he very properly declined to expose his men to needless danger; but his first Lieutenant, William Ingram, a hot-headed, impulsive young fellow, begged him to close and run Porter aboard, for it was "deliberate murder" to lie off at long range and use a defenceless foe as a target. Poor gallant Ingram was himself slain in the fight, a splinter striking him in the head as he stood by the rail.

Midshipman Farragut was naturally enough very much impressed by his baptism of fire, and he has preserved for us most of what we know of what occurred on board the *Essex* during the time of slaughter that preceded her surrender.

One gun was manned three times, fifteen men being slain at it. Its captain alone escaped without a wound. As Farragut stood by another gun, he saw four of its crew killed by a single ball. There were but one or two instances of flinching. The wounded, many of whom were killed by flying splinters while under the hands of the doctors, cheered on their comrades, and themselves worked the guns until the mortal weakness came upon them. At one of the guns was a young Scotsman named Bissly, who had one leg shot off close to the groin. Using his handkerchief as a tourniquet, he said, turning to his American shipmates, "I left my own country and adopted the United States to fight for her. I hope I have this day proved myself worthy of the country of my adoption. I am no longer of any use to you or to her, so good-bye!" With these words he leaned on the sill of the port and threw himself overboard. Among the very few men who flinched was one named William Roach. Porter sent one of his midshipmen to shoot him, but he was not to be found. He was discovered by a man named William Call, whose leg had been shot off and was hanging by the skin, and who dragged the shattered stump all round the bag-house, pistol in hand, trying to get a shot at the fellow. A singular feature of Roach's cowardice was that on previous occasions he had

shown much courage. He could fight well when there was a hope
of victory, but he flinched in the awful hour of disaster. Lieutenant
J. G. Cowell had his leg shot off above the knee, and his life might
have been saved had it been amputated at once ; but the surgeons
had already rows of wounded men waiting for them, and when it
was proposed to him that he should be attended to out of order, he
replied, " No, doctor, none of that—fair play's a jewel ! One man's
life is as dear as another's. I would not cheat any poor fellow out of
his turn."

Finding it hopeless to try to close, Porter stood for the land,
intending to run the *Essex* ashore and burn her. But when she had
drifted close to the bluffs, the wind suddenly shifted, took her flat
aback, and paid her head off shore, exposing her to a raking fire. At
that moment Lieutenant John Downes, commanding the *Essex
Junior*, pulled out in a boat, in spite of the cannonade, to see if
he could do anything. Three of the men with him, including
an old boatswain's mate named Kingsbury, had come out expressly
" to share the fate of the old ship " ; so they remained on board,
and in their places Lieutenant Downes took some of the wounded
ashore under a heavy fire. The shift of the wind gave Porter
a faint hope of closing ; and once more the crippled and riddled
Essex was headed for her foes. But Hillyar put his helm up
to avoid close quarters. The battle was his already, and he was
too good an officer to leave anything to chance. Seeing that he
could not close, Porter had a hawser bent on the sheet-anchor,
which he let go. This brought the ship's head round, keeping
her stationary ; and, from such of her guns as were not dismounted and had men enough left to man them, a broadside was
fired at the *Phœbe*. The wind was now very light, and the *Phœbe*,
whose masts were seriously wounded, and which had suffered
much aloft, beside receiving a number of shot between wind and
water, thus being a good deal crippled, began to drift slowly to
leeward. Porter hoped that she would drift out of gunshot ; but
even this chance was lost by the parting of the hawser, which left
the *Essex* at the mercy of the British vessels. Their fire was
deliberate and destructive, and could only be occasionally replied
to by a shot from one of the American's long 12's. The ship
caught fire, and the men came tumbling up from below with their
clothes burning. To save the lives of some of them they were ordered
to jump overboard ; and others, thinking it a general order, followed

suit, leaping into the sea and trying to swim to the land. Some failed, and were drowned. Others succeeded : among them being one man who had sixteen or eighteen pieces of iron in his leg, scales from the muzzle of a gun. The old boatswain's mate, Kingsbury, was one of those who escaped by swimming to shore, though he was so burned that he was out of his mind for several days.

The frigate had been cut to pieces above the water-line, although, from the smoothness of the sea, she was not harmed enough below it to reduce her to a sinking condition. The carpenter reported that he alone of his crew was fit for duty : the others were dead or disabled. One of the lieutenants had been knocked overboard by a splinter and drowned. He had as a servant a little negro boy, who, coming on deck and hearing of the disaster, deliberately leaped into the sea and shared his master's fate. Another of the lieutenants was also knocked overboard, but was not much hurt, and swam back to the ship. The only commissioned officer left on duty was Lieutenant Decatur McKnight. Of the two hundred and fifty-five men on board, fifty-eight had been killed, sixty-six wounded, and thirty-one drowned, while twenty-four had succeeded in reaching shore. Only seventy-six men were left unwounded, and many of them had been bruised or otherwise injured. Porter himself had been knocked down by the windage of a passing shot. Farragut had been acting as powder-boy, messenger, and everything else. While he was on the ward-room ladder, going below for gun-primers, the captain of the gun directly opposite the hatchway was struck full in the face by an 18-pounder shot, and tumbled back on him. They fell down the hatch together, Farragut being stunned for some minutes. Later, while standing by a man at the wheel, an old quarter-master named Francis Bland, a shot, coming over the fore yard-arm, took off the quarter-master's right leg, carrying away at the same time one of Farragut's coat-tails.

Nothing remained to be done ; and at twenty minutes past six the *Essex* surrendered. The *Phœbe* had lost four killed, and seven wounded ; the *Cherub*, one killed, and three, including Commander Tucker, wounded ; or fifteen all told.

Captain Porter in his letter spoke very bitterly of Hillyar's violation of the neutrality, and sneered at his excessive caution before and during the fight. Most American writers, including even Farragut, have repeated the denunciations and the sneers. Captain Hillyar did, of course, break the neutrality laws in circumstances

which made their violation peculiarly irritating ; for he paid respect
to them so long as Porter was in good fighting trim, and broke them
the minute the enemy was crippled and could be attacked with safety.
But as yet respect for international law does not stand on a level
with respect for the law of one's own land ; and the chief thing to
be considered is whether the irritation caused by the violation of
neutrality will compensate for the advantage gained.   In this case
the capture of the *Essex* certainly compensated for any injury done
to the feelings of Chili ; and the circumstances in which the
violation of neutrality took place, though not creditable, were no
more discreditable than those which attended the capture of the
Confederate steamer *Florida* by a Northern cruiser in the American
Civil War.

Before the action Hillyar seems to have been rather over-cautious,
showing, perhaps, too much hesitation about engaging the *Essex*
without the assistance of the *Cherub*.   The *Essex* was the faster
ship ; and this over-caution would have resulted in her escape had it
not been for the accident which caused the loss of her top-mast.
But, in the action itself, Hillyar's conduct was eminently proper.   It
would have been foolish, by coming to close quarters, to forego the
advantage which his entire masts and better artillery gave him.
He treated his prisoners with the utmost humanity and kindness.
Says Sir Howard Douglas, " The action displayed all that can reflect
honour on the science and admirable conduct of Captain Hillyar and
his crew, which, without the assistance of the *Cherub*, would have
insured the same termination.   Captain Porter's sneers at the
respectful distance the *Phœbe* kept are in fact acknowledgments
of the ability with which Captain Hillyar availed himself of the
superiority of his arms."

Following the defeat of the *Essex* came the destruction of the
American fur-posts on the Columbia, and of what was left of the
American whaling trade in the South Seas.   The *Essex* had made a
romantically daring cruise, and had ended her career by an exhibition
of fighting which, for dauntless courage, could not be surpassed.   She
had inflicted much damage on her foes, and had given great
temporary relief to American interests ; but the fact remained that
her cruise ended in disaster, and in the sweeping of the American
flag from the Pacific.   It is a very old truth, though one which
many legislators seem slow to learn, that no courage and skill on
the part of sea-officers can atone for insufficiency in the number,

and inefficiency in the quality, of ships. To do permanent damage to British interests in the Pacific, or anywhere else, the Americans would have needed, even aside from a fleet of battle-ships, a goodly number of frigates as formidable as those with which they won their early victories.

Besides the ocean ones, both the United States and Great Britain possessed inland seaboards ; for the boundary line between the United States and Canada traversed the extreme northern end of Lake Champlain, and went along the middle of Lakes Ontario, Erie, Huron, and Superior. These inland waters were the scenes of important naval engagements—important, that is, in their effects, though they were waged between diminutive flotillas. East of Lake Champlain practically to the ocean, and westward of it nearly to Lake Erie, stretched a wooded wilderness, impassable for armies. In consequence, the effort to invade either territory had to be made in the neighbourhood of one of the lakes ; and the control of the latter was important to the success of any offensive operations whatsoever, and was indispensable to their success if they were to be conducted on a large scale.

The naval warfare on the lakes, therefore, differed in several points from the naval warfare on the ocean. On the lakes, the success of a sea fight might, and did, determine the success or the failure of military operations the outcome of which would have great weight upon the result of the war ; whereas, on the ocean, no success which the American warships could win could possibly have any other than a moral effect. In the next place, on the lakes special flotillas had to be constructed, so that there the enormous British preponderances in sea-might did not prevail. Finally, the crews themselves were made up of more or less heterogeneous elements ; and there was little difference between them in point of skill.

The country around Lake Champlain was reasonably well settled on both the Canadian and American sides, though very remote from the centres of population. Both sides of Lake Erie were still chiefly wooded wilderness. On Lake Ontario the Canadian side had been longer settled, and was more thickly populated than the American. Moreover, it was easier of access, for the great river St. Lawrence connected it with the sea. The American outposts, however, could keep up their connection with the coast districts only through the Mohawk Valley, which in its upper part merged into a forest that stretched to the lakes unbroken, save by occasional clearings and squalid log hamlets, while the roads were very bad. On Lake Champlain both sides were entirely unprepared. On Lake Ontario and Lake Erie the British were very much ahead. They had on Lake Ontario a squadron of six ships, brigs, and schooners, mounting from eight to twenty-two guns each; while the United States had only one brig, the *Oneida*, of sixteen guns. On Lake Erie the British had another squadron of six ships—brigs and schooners of from two to seventeen guns each.

It is quite impossible, and also quite needless, to fully detail the make, rig, armament, and complement of all the vessels employed, for some of the regularly built warships, and many of the sloops and schooners purchased and used as such, changed from time to time, not only in their rig, their armament, and their complement, but even in their names. Drafts of men from the regular navies of both nations were soon sent up to the lakes; but there were not enough regular men-of-wars' men to man the ships on either side, and the deficiency was supplied by the use of Canadian and American lake sailors, of militia, and of regular troops. One result of this mixed character of the force was that the superiority in training, and especially in gunnery, shown by the American on the ocean was not shown by the American on the lakes. There was little in the lake actions to show any difference in skill, as regards either the management of the sails or the handling of the guns; and in daring, resolution, and courage there was also a practical equality. It was largely a test of the comparative merit and energy of the shipwrights. As the operations on the three lakes were entirely independent of one another, they can be considered separately.

Lake Ontario was the body of water on which the largest squadrons were gathered by both sides, and the land in its neighbourhood was the centre of operations in the Canadian campaigns; and, accordingly, this lake should have been the scene of the most important and decisive actions. Such was not the case, however, largely owing to the extremely cautious nature of the two men who respectively commanded the British and the American squadrons when they were finally put into fighting trim.

In 1812, when the war broke out, the Canadian squadron of six ships, mounting about eighty guns, was under the command of a provincial officer named Earle, who was not in the British regular service. The American brig *Oneida*, 16, Lieutenant Melancthon Thomas Woolsey, was stationed at Sackett's Harbour, the American headquarters on the lake, which was protected by a little battery mounting one long 32-pounder. On July 15th Earle's squadron made a feeble attack on the harbour. Woolsey landed some of the *Oneida's* carronades, and beat off the attack without much difficulty, the long 32 being the gun most used. On the retreat of the Canadian

CAPTAIN ISAAC CHAUNCEY, U.S.N.

(From D. Edwin's engraving, after the portrait by J. Wood.)

flotilla, Woolsey prepared to take the offensive. By capture and purchase he procured six schooners, in which he mounted twenty-four long guns.

In September, 1812, Captain Isaac Chauncey arrived to supplant him in the supreme command. A party of ship-carpenters, officers, and seamen, with guns, stores, etc., followed him to the harbour; and preparations were at once made to build some efficient ships. Meanwhile Chauncey took the lake with the little squadron already prepared by Lieutenant Woolsey. The Canadian flotilla was of double his force, but, as already said, it really formed only a species of water militia, and was not capable of making head against regular seamen of the United States navy, just as at the same time the American militia proved unable to make head against the British regulars on land. Chauncey not only chased the Canadian squadron off the lake, but also attacked it when it took refuge under the batteries of Kingston, which was the naval headquarters on the Canadian side. No serious results followed on this attack, any more than on the previous attack on Sackett's Harbour; but it was note-worthy that it should have been made at all, when the attacking force was so greatly inferior.

During the winter both sides made preparations for the warfare in the spring. The lake service was very unpopular with the Americans, so that it proved difficult to get men to volunteer for it at all. The only way they were persuaded to come was by inducing them to serve under officers whom they liked, and who went with them. In the British service this particular difficulty was not en-countered, as men could be sent wherever the Admiralty ordered ; but the demands of the great ocean fleets were so stringent that it was hard to spare men for the service on these remote inland waters. However, by May, 1813, five hundred British seamen had been sent up under Captain Sir James Lucas Yeo. Two ships were being built at Sackett's Harbour by the Americans, and two others, of twenty-four guns each, by the British at York and Kingston, at opposite ends of the lake. Thanks to the energy of Mr. Henry Eckford, the head builder, the work on the American side was pushed with greater rapidity, and larger and somewhat better ships were built. In addition to the new ships, Sir James kept the five best of the original Canadian squadron, and Chauncey kept the *Oneida,* and purchased a dozen schooners. When the two squadrons were completely ready, Chauncey had a great superiority in long-guns and Sir James in carronades. In smooth weather, therefore, when Chauncey could choose his distance, he possessed much advantage; but whereas all the British ships were regularly built for men-of-war, and sailed well in rough weather, Chauncey's schooners were without bulwarks, and were rendered so top heavy by their guns that, in a sea-way, the latter could not be used at all.

In the spring of 1813 the Americans, thanks to the energy with which their shipwrights had worked, were able to take the lake first.

On April 27th Chauncey's squadron joined in the attack on York, whither he convoyed some 1700 troops under the immediate command of General Pike. The attack was successful: the 24-gun ship, which had been almost completed, was burned, many military and naval stores were destroyed, and the 10-gun brig *Gloucester* was captured and taken back to Sackett's Harbour.[1]

On the 27th of May Chauncey's squadron again took part, with Colonel Scott of the land forces (which were conveyed in troop-ships and in the craft which had been captured at York), in a successful attack on Fort George.[2] The result of this attack was that the British troops evacuated the entire Niagara frontier, thereby enabling Captain Oliver Hazard Perry to get into Lake Erie with five small vessels which became the nucleus of the American force on that water. Up to that time they had not been able to get past the British batteries into the lake.

These attacks on York and Fort George had been well executed; but no great fighting capacity was needed, the assailants being in very much greater force than the assailed. Hitherto the British flotilla had not been strong enough to interfere with the Americans, though the largest American ship was still in the dock at Sackett's Harbour; but, at about the time when Chauncey's squadron was at Fort George, the British ship which had been built at Kingston was launched, and this made the British squadron superior in strength for the moment. Sir James Lucas Yeo, together with Sir George Prevost, the Commander-in-Chief of the land forces in Canada, decided to strike a blow at Sackett's Harbour, and destroy the big American ship there, so ensuring their superiority in force on the lake for the remainder of the season. On May 27th they embarked, and on the following day captured some boats which were transporting troops to Sackett's Harbour. On the 29th Sir George and Sir James made their attack on the harbour, which was defended by General Jacob Brown. The defences of the port consisted merely of the one-gun battery and a block-house. The attack resulted in a rather bloody repulse, though at one time it seemed on the point of succeeding.[3] The attacking force was relatively very much

---

[1] Letter of Chauncey, April 28th, 1813; Lossing's 'Field-Book of the War of 1812,' p. 581.

[2] Chauncey's letter, May 29th, 1813; James's 'Military Occurrences,' i. 151.

[3] The British, however, succeeded in burning the *Gloucester*, 10, which had been captured at York.—W. L. C.

weaker than were the Americans at Fort George and York, but it was certainly strong enough to have succeeded if properly handled; and the failure caused much recrimination between the followers of Sir James and Sir George.[1]

During June Yeo kept the lake undisputed, and actively co-operated with the British army in the operations which resulted in the humiliating repulse of the American General Wilkinson's expedition into Canada. In July Chauncey once more took the lake, his new ship being ready. Throughout August and September the two squadrons were facing one another on the lake, each commander manœuvring with a caution that amounted to timidity. In smooth water and with all the ships in action, Chauncey undoubtedly possessed the superiority in force; but on the 8th of August he received a severe lesson as to the unseaworthiness of his schooners, for the two largest went to the bottom in a heavy gust of wind, their guns breaking loose when they heeled over. Moreover, as the ships were of widely different types, it was only possible to get them all into action by causing one half of the squadron to tow the other half.

On August 10th there occurred the one encounter in which either side can be said to have shown anything approaching to brilliancy; and all the credit must be given to the British. Yeo, after two days of cautious manœuvring, finally made a night attack on Chauncey's squadron. Chauncey, partly owing to his own blunder and partly to the blunder of two of his schooners, the *Julia* and *Growler*, allowed the latter to be cut off, and they were both of them captured by Yeo, who deserved great praise.[2]

For the next six weeks the skirmishes on the lakes continued, each commander in his official letters stoutly maintaining that he was chasing the other. As a matter of fact, Yeo was determined only to fight in heavy, and Chauncey only in light weather. On September 11th a long-range skirmish occurred at the mouth of the Genesee River. The heavy guns of the American schooners gave their side the advantage in this affair, but nothing decisive resulted.[3]

On September 28th the squadrons again came into contact near

---

[1] Letter of Adjutant-General Baynes, May 30th, 1813; James's 'Military Occurrences,' i. 173.

[2] Letters of Yeo, Aug. 10th, 1813, and Chauncey, Aug. 13th, 1813.

[3] Letters of Yeo, Sept. 12th, 1813, and Chauncey, Sept. 13th, 1813.

York Bay.   On that occasion the Americans were to windward; and
Chauncey at last made up his mind to try a real fight.   But Yeo
succumbed with very little resistance.   The American vessels
suffered hardly at all.   Chauncey led his squadron in the *Pike*,
much the heaviest vessel in either squadron.   Yeo's ship, the
Wolfe, speedily had her main and mizen top-masts shot away;
whereupon Yeo crowded all sail forward, and hastily got out of
the combat, leaving his retreat to be covered by the *Royal George*,
Captain William Howe Mulcaster.   Mulcaster luffed across the
Wolfe's stern, and stood the brunt of the action until his commodore was in safety, when he himself followed suit, having
lost his fore topmast.   For an hour the American ships followed,
and then relinquished the pursuit when the British were running
into the entirely undefended port of Burlington Bay, whence escape
would have been impossible.[1]   The only loss inflicted by the British
guns had been to the American schooner *Tompkins*, under Lieutenant Bolton Fitch, who shared with Captain Mulcaster what
there was of glory in the day.   The fight, or skirmish, such as it
was, was decisive in so far as concerned any further attempts by
Yeo to keep the lake that season, for thereafter his squadron
remained in Kingston, part of the time blockaded by Chauncey.
But Chauncey deserved no credit for the action.   He possessed an
undoubted superiority in force, and his opponents made very little
resistance, so that the victory was cheap; and his conduct in
abandoning the pursuit and thereby losing the fruits of the victory
was inexplicable.   He did not order his swifter vessels to cast off
the slower ones which they were towing, so he could not overtake
the fleeing enemy; and he did not follow them into the open roadstead where they sought refuge.   He afterwards alleged that he
feared to make the attack in Burlington Bay lest the wind should
blow up to a gale and drive both squadrons ashore; and that he
hoped to be able to make another attack at a more suitable time.
Such excuses simply serve to mark the difference between the commander who allows caution to degenerate into irresolution, and the
bold leader of men.   Chauncey had missed the great opportunity of
his life.

In 1814 the contest degenerated into one of shipbuilding merely.

---

[1] Letter of Chauncey, Sept. 28th, 1813; Brenton, ii. 503.   Unfortunately, the
British Admiralty had at that time adopted the rule of not publishing official accounts
of defeats, so there is no printed letter of Yeo's.

The shipwrights under Yeo and Chauncey began to build huge frigates and to lay down battleships, while the schooners were no longer included in the cruising squadrons.[1] Chauncey had re-captured the *Julia* and the *Growler* in a successful attack upon some British transports. The *Growler*, however, was again captured on May 3rd, 1814, when Yeo, who took the lake first, began a successful attack on Oswego,[2] the British troops being under the command of Lieutenant-Colonel Fischer.[3] Yeo then blockaded Sackett's Harbour. On May 30th he sent an expedition of six boats with seven guns and one hundred and eighty men, under Commanders Stephen Popham and Francis Brockell Spilsbury, to attack an American convoy under Captain Woolsey which was bringing up guns and cables for the new American frigates. Woolsey ran into Big Sandy Creek, eight miles from the harbour, where he was joined by some militia and a company of light artillery, under Major Appling. The British force was absurdly inadequate for the duty to which it was assigned; Americans had every advantage of position, and outnumbered the attacking party. Woolsey and Appling arranged an ambush, and, with the loss of only one man slightly wounded, killed[4] or captured the entire body of assailants.[5]

On July 6th Yeo raised the blockade, and, for six weeks, nothing was done except that Lieutenant Francis Gregory, U.S.N., twice led daring and successful cutting-out expeditions, in one of which he captured a British gunboat, and in the other destroyed a 14-gun schooner which was nearly ready for launching. In August, Com-

---

[1] On April 15th, there were launched, by the British, at Kingston, the *Prince Regent*, 58, and the *Princess Charlotte*, 42. On May 1st the Americans, at Sackett's Harbour, launched the *Superior*, 62, and on June 11th, the *Mohawk*, 48.—W. L. C.

[2] In the capture of Oswego, the British lost 18 killed and 64 wounded, among the former being Captain William Holtoway, R.M., and among the latter Captain William Howe Mulcaster, Commander Stephen Popham, and Lieutenant Charles William Griffith Griffin. The American loss was 6 killed, 38 wounded, and 25 missing. Three schooners and seven guns were carried away by the victors, and a schooner and six guns were destroyed.—W. L. C.

[3] Yeo's letter, May 17th, 1814.

[4] The attacking party consisted of 180 seamen and Royal Marines. It lost 18 killed and 50 badly wounded, among the latter being Lieutenants Thomas S. Cox and Patrick M'Veagh, R.M. Popham's official letter ended: "The exertions of the American officers of the rifle corps commanded by Major Appling, in saving the lives of many of the officers and men whom their own men and the Indians were devoting to death, were conspicuous, and claim our warmest gratitude."—W. L. C.

[5] Letters of Woolsey and Appling, June 1st and May 30th, 1814.

modore Chauncey's vessels having been built, Captain Yeo in
his turn promptly retreated to port, where he was blockaded. The
difference in force against Yeo was about 15 per cent., and he
declined to fight with these odds against him. A little later, in
October, his two-decker, the *Prince Regent*, 58, being completed, Yeo
in his turn took the lake; and the equally cautious Chauncey
promptly retired to Sackett's Harbour.

Chauncey varied the game by quarrelling with General Brown,
alleging that the latter was making a "sinister attempt" to
subordinate the navy to the army.[1] He insisted—wherein he was
quite right—that his proper objective was the enemy's fleet, and
that he could best serve the army by destroying the British vessels.
This was true enough; but the timid and dilatory tactics employed
by both Chauncey and Yeo were such as to render it certain that
neither would ever inflict a serious blow on the other, for neither
would fight unless the odds were largely in his favour; and when
such was the case, he could not persuade his opponent to meet him;
so that the best either could do was to assist the army in the way
against which Chauncey protested. Both Chauncey and Yeo were
good organisers: each in turn assisted the land forces on his side
more or less by getting control of the lake; but, towards the end,
the contest became almost farcical, for it was one of ship-building
merely, and the minute either party completed a new ship the
other promptly retired into harbour until able in turn to complete a larger one.

On Lake Erie the course of events was very different, for the
commanders on that sheet of water displayed none of the extreme
and timid caution which characterised the two commodores on
Lake Ontario.

At the outbreak of the war the British squadron on Lake
Ontario consisted of the *Queen Charlotte*, 16, *Lady Prevost*, 12,
Hunter, 10, *Caledonia*, 2, *Little Belt*, 2, and *Chippeway*, 2. These
were all manned by Canadians, and, like the vessels on Lake
Ontario, were not part of the British regular Navy, but formed a
species of water militia. The American navy was not represented
on Lake Erie at all; but Hull's army at Detroit had fitted out a
small brig, the *Adams*, armed with six 6-pounders, which fell into
the hands of the British when Hull and his army were captured

---

[1] Niles, vii. 12, vi.

by the gallant British General Brock. The *Detroit*, ex *Adams*, was then put in charge of Lieutenant Rolette, R.N., assisted by a boatswain, and was provided with a crew of fifty-six men. She was in company with the *Caledonia*, a small brig mounting two guns, with a crew of twelve Canadians under Mr. Irving. In all the fighting on the upper lakes the bulk of the British crews was composed of Canadians and of British soldiers; whereas on Lake Ontario the ships were manned by British sailors from the fleet.

The *Detroit* and the *Caledonia*, carrying a very valuable cargo of furs and about forty American prisoners, moved down the lake, and on October 7th, 1812, anchored under the guns of the British Fort Erie.

AMERICAN MEDAL COMMEMORATIVE OF THE BATTLE OF LAKE ERIE, 1813.

Commander Jesse D. Elliott, U.S.N., had already been sent to Lake Erie to construct a naval force. On the very day on which the two brigs came to anchor under the British fort the first detachment of the American seamen, fifty-one in number, arrived at Black Rock, on the American side, where Elliott was stationed. They had no arms; but sabres, pistols, and muskets were supplied by the commander of the land forces, who also detailed seventy soldiers under Captain Towsen to act with Elliott, the total force being 124.[1] On the 9th, Elliott, acting with great promptness and decision, left in two large boats, one under his own command, the other under Towsen, intending to cut out the British vessels. After two hours' rowing the boats reached the brigs. Elliott

[1] Letter of Elliott, Oct. 5th, 1812; Lossing, p. 385.

took his own boat alongside the *Detroit* and boarded her before the surprised crew knew their danger, though there was a scuffle in which one American was killed and one wounded. The noise roused the Canadians in the *Caledonia*, and they made more resistance to the other boat. However, it was too late, and the *Caledonia* was carried with a rush, all twelve of the Canadians being cut down or made prisoners. Five of the Americans were killed or wounded. The *Caledonia* was brought back in safety to the American side, but the *Detroit* had to be destroyed.

This ended the naval operations of 1812 on Lake Erie, except that the American Commander Angus, with eighty sailors, took part in one of the abortive attacks made by the American General Smith on some of the British batteries. Late in the winter Commodore Oliver Hazard Perry arrived and took command.

Commander Robert Heriot Barclay (actg.), R.N., was appointed commander of the British forces on Lake Erie, in May, 1813. He began to build a 20-gun ship at Amherstburgh. Some seventy sailors from the British Navy were sent to him, and there were about twice that number of Canadian sailors already in the flotilla. The remainder, at least half, of his men were soldiers sent from the British army on shore.

Perry began the construction of two 20-gun brigs at Presqu'-isle, now Erie. Over one-half of the men who manned his squadron were seamen from the regular navy on the Atlantic coast; about a third were soldiers and marines; and about a tenth were volunteers from among the frontiersmen around the lake.

The crews and vessels on both sides were of the order of make-shifts, although the splendid courage and efficiency with which the men fought was a sufficient proof that there was no difficulty in bringing such material up to the highest standard; for the British and American seamen from the ocean, the American and Canadian frontiersmen and lake sailors, and the soldiers from both armies, who formed the crews, offered fine fighting stuff.

The lake vessels were very much shallower than those used for the deep seas. Their tonnage was estimated arbitrarily, on the supposition that, like the ordinary ocean vessels, they were deep in a given proportion to their length and breadth. If allowance were made for the shallowness of the lake vessels, their tonnage would be of course very much less. Thus, making such allowance, the British 20-gun ship built by Barclay, which he christened the *Detroit*, was of only 305 tons, while, if estimated in the usual manner, it was of 490. The two brigs *Lawrence* and *Niagara*, which Perry was building, were similarly of either 300 or 480 tons. However, the tonnage was really a matter of small moment in war vessels, except to indicate the size above the water-line, for they carried no cargoes; so that the tonnage of the lake vessels may as well be reckoned as though it were a case of ordinary ocean vessels. Reckoning thus, Barclay's second ship, the *Lady Charlotte*, was of 400 tons; his third, the *Lady Prevost*, of 230; and his fourth, the *Hunter*, of 180 tons. On the American side the *Caledonia*, like the *Hunter*, was of 180 tons, and the largest schooner, the *Ariel*, of 112. The other schooners and sloops on both sides were of from 70 to 95 tons apiece.

The two American brigs and the British ship were completed in August. Until their completion the British squadron was superior in force, and Barclay kept up a close blockade of the harbour of Erie, where there was a bar having on it less than seven feet of water. This bar prevented the British from going in, but it also prevented the two American brigs from getting out so long as the enemy was off the harbour. Finally Barclay, early in August, was obliged to be away for a couple of days; and Perry by great exertions managed to get the two brigs across the bar without their guns, which were put in later.[1] Soon afterwards the *Detroit* joined Barclay's squadron, and the captains made ready for battle.

Barclay's squadron was so inferior in force that he would not have been justified in risking action if it could have been avoided. But there was no alternative. The control of Lake Erie virtually decided the control of the disputed territory around the Detroit River. Moreover, Barclay was so short of provisions that he had to bring matters to a head. On September 10th, 1813, the two squadrons came together.

Perry had nine vessels, the brigs *Lawrence*, *Niagara*, and *Caledonia*, the schooners *Ariel*, *Scorpion*, *Somers*, *Porcupine*, and *Tigress*, and the sloop *Trippe*. Their total tonnage was 1671, and their total crews amounted to 532 men; but sickness had been so prevalent that only about 416 were fit for duty. In his vessels fifty-four guns were mounted, fourteen of which were on pivots. In the action his broadside weight of metal was 896 pounds; 288 of which were thrown from long-guns. The *Lawrence* and

[1] Cooper, ii. 389.

Niagara were large men-of-war brigs, armed in the usual manner with eighteen 32-pr. carronades, and two long 12's apiece. The smaller vessels, in addition to two or three light carronades, carried long 32's, 24's, and 12's. Barclay's squadron consisted of six vessels, the ships *Detroit* and *Queen Charlotte*, the brig *Hunter*, the schooners *Lady Prevost*, and *Chippeway*, and the sloop *Little Belt*. The aggregate tonnage was 1460; the aggregate of the crews summed up

CAPTAIN OLIVER HAZARD PERRY, U.S.N.

(From S. Freeman's engraving, after the portrait by J. W. Jarvis.)

to about 440 men.[1] The total number of guns was sixty-three, five being on pivots. The total broadside weight was 459 pounds, of which 195 were from long guns; for many of Barclay's guns were of very small calibre, including long 2's, 4's, and 6's, and 12-pr. carronades.

[1] James (vi. 250, ed. 1837) puts the numerical strength of Barclay's command at only 345 men, including 80 Canadians, and 240 soldiers of the Newfoundland and 41st regiments.—W. L. C.

The difference in number of men between the two squadrons was not very material. Both had scratch crews, made up of regular seamen, of lake seamen, of British regulars, and a few Indians in Barclay's squadron, and American militia and a few negroes in Perry's. In tonnage Perry was superior by just about what would be indicated by the possession of three extra schooners. The decisive difference was in the armament. In weight of broadside the superiority of the Americans in long-gun metal was nearly as three to two, and in carronade metal it was greater than two to one. The ship *Detroit* mounted chiefly long guns, and was on the whole probably rather superior to either of Perry's big brigs. The *Queen Charlotte* was greatly inferior to either. The smaller vessels lacked the long guns which made the small American vessels formidable. In smooth water and at a distance the long guns of Perry's smaller vessels gave his squadron a very marked advantage ; in a brisk breeze his two big brigs should have been almost a match for the entire British squadron.

When, at daylight on September 10th, Perry discovered Barclay's squadron he was at anchor at Put-In Bay. As soon as the ships were made out, Perry got under way and bore down toward them, having the weather gage. Barclay lay to in close column, the *Chippeway* ahead, followed by the *Detroit*, the *Hunter*, the *Queen Charlotte*, the *Lady Prevost*, and the *Little Belt*.[1] Perry went down with the wind off his port beam, and made the attack in column ahead obliquely. The *Erie* and *Scorpion* led the line a little ahead, and on the weather bow, of Perry's ship the *Lawrence*. Next came the *Caledonia*, and after her the *Lawrence's* twin sister, the *Niagara*, under Captain Jesse D. Elliott, whom Perry had superseded, and who showed by his actions that he felt no particular zeal in helping Perry to gain glory. The *Niagara* was followed by the *Somers*, the *Porcupine*, the *Tigress*, and the *Trippe* in that order.[2]

The winds were light and baffling, and, as the American ships came down, they formed a straggling and irregular line which

---

[1] The British vessels were commanded as follows : *Chippeway*, Master's Mate J. Campbell ; *Detroit*, Commander Robert Heriot Barclay ; *Hunter*, Lieutenant George Bignell ; *Queen Charlotte*, Commander Robert Finnis (acting); *Lady Prevost*, Lieutenant Edward Wise Buchan. The commander of the *Little Belt* is unnamed in Barclay's letter of September 12th to Yeo.—W. L. C.

[2] Letters of Captain Barclay and Lieutenant Inglis, Sept. 12th and 10th, 1813 ; of Captain Perry, Sept. 11th, 12th, and 13th. Lossing gives some valuable matter ; so does Ward in his ' Naval Tactics,' and James in his ' Naval Occurrences.'

approached at an angle of about fifteen degrees to the line of Barclay's squadron, which was in much better and more compact order. At a quarter to twelve the *Detroit* opened the action with her long 24's. Her first shot fell short; her second crashed through the *Lawrence;* whereupon the *Scorpion* replied with her long 32. Ten minutes after the *Detroit* had first fired, the *Lawrence*, which had shifted her port bow-chaser into the place of one of the carronades on her starboard side, opened with both her long 12's. At noon she tried her carronades, but the shot fell short. Shortly afterwards the action became general on both sides, though the rearmost American vessels were still so far away that they were themselves not exposed to any danger at all, and only the longest guns occasionally reached. The *Lawrence* was steadily nearing Barclay's line, Perry making every effort to close; but it was half an hour after the *Detroit* had opened before the *Lawrence* got to the close quarters necessary for the effective use of her carronades. Throughout this half-hour Barclay's leading ships had concentrated their fire on Perry's vessel, and so the *Lawrence* had suffered a good deal; though the schooners *Scorpion* and *Ariel* had been pounding away with their long guns to help her.

For some time, therefore, the action at the head of the line was in favour of the British. The sides of the *Detroit* were dotted with marks of shot that did not penetrate, partly because of the long range, partly because the Americans in this action seemed to show a tendency to overload their carronades. There was a carronade in the *Scorpion* which upset down the hatchway as soon as it got hot; and one of the long guns on the *Ariel* burst. On the other side, the *Detroit* had her own difficulties. There were no locks for her guns, thanks to the hurry with which she had been prepared, and they had to be discharged by flashing pistols at the touch-holes. Nevertheless, Barclay fought her to perfection, and the trained artillerists among his seamen and soldiers aimed the guns so well that Perry had his hands full. The *Caledonia* came down beside the *Lawrence*, helping to divert the attention of the *Hunter* and the *Queen Charlotte* from her. But Elliott handled the *Niagara* poorly. He did not follow Perry to close quarters, but engaged the *Queen Charlotte* at a distance which rendered the carronades of both vessels useless. In fact, the only effective fighting at the rear of the lines was that done by the four American gun-vessels astern of the *Niagara*. Each of these had a long 32 or 24, of which, on such smooth seas, she could make good use against the *Lady Prevost, Queen Charlotte*, and *Hunter*; the latter having an absurd armament of little guns which threw a broadside of thirty pounds all told. Both Commander Finnis, of the *Queen Charlotte*, and his first lieutenant, Thomas Stokoe, were killed early in the action. Her next in command, the Canadian lieutenant Irvine, finding that he could make no effective answer to the long guns of the schooners, drew forward and joined in the attack on the *Lawrence* at close quarters. The *Niagara* was left practically without any antagonist, and, at the end of the line, the fight became one at long range between the *Somers, Tigress, Porcupine*, and *Trippe* on the one side, and the *Lady Prevost*, and *Little Belt* on the other. The *Lady Prevost's* armament consisted chiefly of 12-pr. carronades. She made a noble fight, but such an armament at long range in smooth water was utterly useless against the heavy guns of the schooners. Her commander, Lieutenant Buchan, and her first lieutenant, Francis Rolette, were both seriously wounded, and she was greatly cut up, and began to fall to leeward.

The fight at the head of the line was waged with bloody obstinacy between the *Scorpion, Ariel, Lawrence*, and *Chesapeake* on the one hand, and the *Caledonia, Detroit, Queen Charlotte*, and *Chippeway* on the other. Instead of pairing in couples, the ships on each side seemed to choose the largest opponents as special targets. The Americans concentrated their fire on the *Queen Charlotte*, and *Detroit;* while the British devoted their attention mainly to the *Lawrence*, which had already suffered severely while working down to get within range of her carronades. The *Queen Charlotte* was soon almost disabled. The *Detroit* was also pounded practically to a standstill, suffering especially from the raking fire of the gun-boats. Barclay was fighting her himself with the utmost gallantry; but he was so badly wounded that he was at last obliged to quit the deck. His first Lieutenant, John Garland, was also wounded mortally; but Lieutenant George Inglis, to whom the command was turned over, continued the fight as gamely as ever.

Meanwhile the *Lawrence* was knocked to pieces by the combined fires of her adversaries. Of the one hundred and three men who had been fit for duty when she began the action, eighty-three were killed or wounded. As the vessel was so shallow, the ward-room, which was used as the cockpit into which the wounded were taken, was mainly above water, and the shots came through it continually. Many of the wounded were killed or maimed while under the hands of the surgeons.   The first lieutenant, Yarnall, was hit three times, but refused to leave the deck, and fought the ship to the last.   The only other lieutenant on board, Brooks, of the marines, was mortally wounded.   Every brace and bowline was shot away, and the hull was so riddled that it looked like a sieve.   One by one the guns on the engaged side were dismounted, while the men were shot down until they could not man even the guns that were left. However, the slaughter of four-fifths of his crew before his eyes did not daunt Perry in the least.   When there were no men left to serve the last three or four guns, he called down through the skylight for one of the surgeon's assistants.   The call was repeated and obeyed, until all those officers had been used up.   Then he shouted down, " Can any of the wounded pull a rope ? " and three or four of them hobbled up on deck to help him lay the last guns.   Finally, Perry himself was left with only the purser and chaplain, and by their aid he fired a final shot ; and, immediately afterwards, the gun which he had used, the only one left, was disabled.

Meanwhile Mr. Turner in the *Caledonia*, having put his helm up, had passed the *Lawrence* and run into the British line, where he engaged at half pistol-shot distance, though his little brig was absolutely without quarters.

Perry's vessel lay an unmanageable hulk on the water, while the shot ripped through her sides, and there was not a gun that could be fired in return ; but Perry had not the slightest intention of giving up the fight.   He had gone into the battle flying on his flag Lawrence's dying words, " Don't give up the ship " ; and he intended to live up to the text.   The *Niagara* was at that time a quarter of a mile to windward of the *Lawrence* on her port-beam. She was steering for the head of Barclay's line, and was almost uninjured, having taken very little part in the combat, and never having been within a distance that rendered her carronades of any use. Perry instantly decided to shift his broad pennant to her.   Leaping into a boat with his brother and four seamen, he rowed to the fresh brig, having literally been hammered out of the *Lawrence* by the pounding which he had received for two hours and a half.   As soon as he reached the *Niagara*, he sent Elliott astern to hurry up the three rearmost schooners ; for the sloop *Trippe*, on her own account, had steered straight for the British line, and was very near the *Caledonia*.   The *Lawrence*, having but fourteen sound men left, struck her colours ; but the action began again before possession could be taken of her, and she drifted astern out of the fight. At a quarter to three the schooners had closed, and Perry bore up to break Barclay's line, the powerful brig to which he had shifted his broad pennant being practically unharmed, as indeed were his rearmost gun-vessels.

The British ships had fought till they could fight no longer. The two smallest, the *Chippeway* and *Little Belt*, were not much damaged; but the other four were too disabled either to fight or to manœuvre effectively so as to oppose fresh antagonists. However, they answered as best they could, with great guns and musketry, as the *Niagara* stood down and broke the British line, firing her port battery into the *Chippeway*, *Little Belt*, and *Lady Prevost*, and her starboard battery into the *Detroit*, *Queen Charlotte*, and *Hunter*, raking on both sides. The *Detroit* and *Charlotte* had been so cut up aloft, almost every brace and stay being shot away, that they could not tack, and tried to wear; but they fell foul of one another, and the *Niagara* luffed athwart their bows, firing uninterruptedly, while, under their sterns, the *Caledonia* and the schooners stationed themselves so close that some of their grape-shot, passing over the British vessels, rattled through Perry's spars. The *Lady Prevost* had sagged to leeward, an unmanageable wreck. Barclay had done everything in the power of man to do. The first and second in command of every one of his six vessels had been either killed or wounded; and at three o'clock his flag was struck. The *Chippeway* and *Little Belt* tried to escape, but were overtaken and brought-to by the *Trippe* and the *Scorpion*, the commander of the latter, Mr. Stephen Champlin, firing the last shot of the battle, as he had likewise fired the first on the American side.

None of the American ships had suffered severely, excepting the *Lawrence*, to whose share over two-thirds of the total loss had fallen. In breaking the line, however, the *Niagara* had suffered somewhat; and the *Caledonia*, *Ariel*, *Scorpion*, and *Trippe* had come in for some of the pounding. All told, twenty-seven men had been killed and ninety-six wounded, three mortally. The British loss amounted to forty-one killed and ninety-four wounded, chiefly in the *Detroit* and *Queen Charlotte*. Barclay's letter is a model of its kind for generosity and manliness, stating matters precisely as they were. He needed no justification, for the mere recital of the facts was proof enough of his gallantry and skill. In his letter he stated, " Captain Perry has behaved in the most humane and attentive manner, not only to myself and officers, but to all the wounded." [1]

The victory was decisive, giving the Americans complete control of the upper lakes; and it was very important in its effects, putting an end to any 'effort to wrest from them the supremacy on the western frontier. Perry and the American shipwrights are entitled to high praise for the energy and forethought with which they prepared the squadron. Moreover, Perry showed the most determined courage and great fertility in resource, which enabled him not merely to destroy, but also to annihilate his enemy; and he deserved the credit he received. Both sides displayed the same dogged courage; but, on the whole, Barclay and his captains unquestionably showed superior skill in the actual fighting. The disposition of the American line was such that it was brought into action by fragments. Captain Elliott did not fight the *Niagara* well; and four of the American gunboats were kept so far astern as to prevent their being of much use at first, so that the brunt of the action fell on the *Lawrence*, even during the early part of the action, when the fighting was at long range and her carronades were useless. Perry, towards the end, showed ability to use his force to the best advantage, and his own ship was faultlessly handled and fought; but some of his captains did not support him, nor one another, as they should have done. Whether through his fault or through his misfortune, he failed to get from them the full co-operation which he should have received.

Barclay's dispositions, on the contrary, were faultless; and the British captains supported one another, so that the disparity in damage done was not equal to the disparity in force. Barclay could not arrange his ships so as to be superior to his antagonists. In any circumstances, whether in rough water or in smooth, the Americans were the more formidable in force. All that he could do he did. Perry, in making his attack, had shown the same headlong energy as he had previously shown in preparing his squadron, and he behaved with that indomitable determination not to be beaten, than which, after all, there is no greater merit in any fighter, afloat or ashore.

---

[1] Lieutenant Robert Heriot Barclay had his Commander's commission confirmed on November 19th, 1813, ere news of the disaster reached the Admiralty. He was tried at Portsmouth for the loss of his flotilla on September 16th, 1814, and was "most fully and honourably acquitted." He was posted on October 14th, 1824, and died on May 12th, 1837.—W. L. C.

The superior force of the Americans had been brought into action in such a manner that the head of the line was crushed by the inferior force opposed ; but, when literally hammered out of his own ship, Perry had brought up her powerful twin sister, and overwhelmed the shattered hostile squadron, pushing the victory with such energy that all the opposing ships were captured.   In other words, Providence, as so often before, declared in . favour of the heavier battalions, when those battalions were handled with energy and resolution.   The victory was due to heavy metal, as in many another sea fight between far greater forces.   Like the victories of La Hougue and of Camperdown, waged between huge armadas, this combat between the little lake flotillas shows, what certainly ought not to need showing, that energy and forethought in preparing a superior force, and energy and courage in using it, will ensure victory if the skill and bravery on both sides be equal, or even if there be a slight advantage in skill on the part of the enemy.

The destruction of Barclay's squadron left the Americans un-disputed masters of the upper lakes ; but exactly as they had begun their career by a cutting-out expedition, which enabled them to acquire the nucleus of their squadron, so now they, in their turn, suffered by a couple of cutting-out expeditions, in which the British performed, at their expense, two really brilliant feats, though on a small scale.   Neither feat was of weight enough to interfere with the American supremacy, but both exploits reflected great credit on the victors, and caused much mortification to the vanquished.

In July 1814 Captain Arthur Sinclair, U.S.N., sailed into Lake Huron with five of Perry's smaller vessels.   He attacked the fort at Macinaw, but was repulsed, and then destroyed the British block-house on the Nattagawassa, together with an armed schooner ;[1] but the crew of the schooner, under Lieutenant Miller Worsley, R.N., escaped up the river.   Sinclair then departed for Lake Erie, leaving the *Scorpion*, under Lieutenant Turner, and the *Tigress*, under sailing-master Champlin, to keep a watch on the river.   The two commanders grew very careless, and paid the penalty ; for the Indians brought word to the British that the two American vessels were in the habit of stationing themselves far apart, and it was at once resolved to attempt their capture.   Accordingly, the effort was made with four boats, one manned by twenty seamen, under Lieutenant Miller Worsley, the other three by seventy-two soldiers,

---

[1] This schooner was the *Nancy*, belonging to the North-West Company.—W. L. C.

under Lieutenants Bulger, Armstrong, and Raderhurst, of the army. Two light guns accompanied the expedition. After twenty-four hours' search the party discovered one vessel, the *Tigress*, late on the evening of September 3rd. It was very dark, and the British were not detected until they had come within fifty yards. Champlin at once fired his long-gun at them; but, before it could be reloaded, the four boats had run him on board, two on the starboard and two on the port side. The gunboat had no boarding nets, and the assailants outnumbered the crew by more than three to one, but there was a sharp struggle before she was carried. Of the twenty-eight men on board her, three were killed and five wounded, including Champlin himself, whose hurt was very severe. Of the assailants, the loss was still heavier, for it included two killed and a dozen wounded, one of whom was Lieutenant Bulger. The latter showed himself prompt to recognise courage in others, in addition to exhibiting it by his own acts. In his letter he wrote, " The defence of this vessel did credit to her officers, who were all severely wounded." [1]

Forty-eight hours afterwards the *Scorpion* rejoined her consort, entirely ignorant of what had occurred. She anchored two miles from the *Tigress*, and, in the dawn, the latter, with the American ensign and pennant still flying, ran her on board. The first notice her crew of thirty men had was a volley which killed two, and wounded two others ; and she was carried without resistance. No one had time even to seize his arms.[2]

This was an exceedingly creditable and plucky enterprise. At almost the same time an even more daring cutting-out expedition took place at the foot of Lake Erie. The three American schooners, *Ohio*, *Somers*, and *Porcupine*, each with thirty men, under Lieutenant Conkling, were anchored at the outlet of the lake to flank the works at Port Erie. Several British vessels [3] were lying off the fort, in the Ontario waters, and their officers determined to make an effort to carry the American gunboats by surprise. On the night of August 12th Commander Alexander Dobbs and Lieutenant Copleston Radcliffe, with seventy-five seamen and Marines,

---

[1] Letter of Lieut. A. H. Bulger, Sept. 7th, 1814.

[2] For these services Lieutenant Miller Worsley was made a Commander on July 13th, 1815. He died, still in that rank, on May 2nd, 1835.—W. L. C.

[3] Including the *Charwell*, Commander Alexander Dobbs, *Netley*, Lieutenant Copleston Radcliffe, and *Star*.—W. L. C.

made the attempt.[1]   Aided by some militia, they carried a gig
and five bateaux twenty-eight miles overland to Lake Erie, launched
them, and rowed toward the gunboats.   At about midnight the
look-out in the *Somers* discovered and hailed them.   They answered,
"provision boat," which deceived the officer on deck, as such
boats were passing and repassing every night.   In another moment
they drifted across his hawser, cut his cables and ran him
on board.   The two men on deck were shot down, and, before
the others could get up, the schooner was captured.   In another
moment the British boats were alongside the *Ohio*, Lieutenant
Conkling's own vessel.   The sound of the firing had awakened his
people, and, disordered though they were, they attempted resistance,
and there was a moment's sharp struggle; but Conkling himself,
and the only other officer on board, sailing-master Cally, together
with five seamen, were shot or cut down, and Dobbs carried the
gunboat sword in hand.   Lieutenant Radcliffe was killed, however,
and seven British seamen and Marines were killed or wounded.
Dobbs then drifted down stream with his two prizes, the *Porcupine* being too demoralised to interfere.   It was a very bold and
successful enterprise, reflecting the utmost credit on the victors.[2]

At the beginning of the war the Americans had the supremacy on
Lake Champlain, possessing two little sloops, each mounting eleven
small guns, and six row-galleys, mounting one gun each, under the
command of Lieutenant Sidney Smith.   On June 3rd, 1813, Smith
took his two sloops to the Sorrel River, the outlet of the lake, where
he saw three British row-galleys, each mounting one long-gun.   The
wind was aft, and he imprudently chased the row-galleys down the
river to within sight of the first British fort.   The river was narrow,
and the infantry at the fort promptly came to the assistance of the
galleys, and began to fire on the sloops from both banks.   The
sloops responded with grape, and tried to beat back up the stream,
but the current was so strong and the wind so light that no headway could be made.   The row-galleys turned and began to fire with
their long 24's, while the light guns of the sloops could not reach

---

[1] James, in his 'Naval Occurrences,' gives the best account of this expedition; the
American historians touch very lightly on it; precisely as, after the first year of the
war, the British authorities ceased to publish official accounts of their defeats.

[2] Alexander Dobbs, born in 1784, was a Commander of February 14th, 1814, and
was posted on August 12th, 1819.   He died at Milan in 1827.—W. L. C.

them in return. After three hours' manœuvring and firing, a shot from one of the galleys struck the *Eagle* under her starboard quarter and ripped out a whole plank. She sank at once, but in such shoal water that all her men got ashore. The *Growler* continued the fight alone, but, her forestay and main-boom being shot away, she became unmanageable, ran ashore, and was captured. Of the 112 men on board the two sloops, twenty were

CAPTAIN THOMAS MACDONOUGH, U.S.N.

(From S. Freeman's engraving, after the portrait by J. W. Jarvis.)

killed or wounded and the rest captured. No one was touched in the galleys, but three of the British soldiers ashore were wounded by grape.[1]

Captain Thomas Macdonough was in command on the lake from that time onwards, and he set to work to build some new sloops. Until this was done there was nothing to interfere with the British. They re-christened the captured *Growler* and *Eagle*, *Chubb* and

---

[1] Letter of Major Taylor (British) to General Stone, June 3rd, 1813.

Finch, and with these and three row-galleys conveyed an expedition of about one thousand British troops, under Colonel Murray, which destroyed all the barracks and stores at Plattsburg and at Saranac on the last day of July. Three days later Macdonough completed three sloops [1] which, with his six row-galleys, restored to him the command of the lake. Nothing more was done during 1813.

In 1814, however, Lake Champlain became the scene of the greatest naval battle of the war. In August a British army of eleven thousand men, under Sir George Prevost, undertook the invasion of New York by advancing along the bank of Lake Champlain. He got as far as the Saranac River, where the Americans had thrown up extensive earthworks. To cover Prevost's flank it was necessary that the British squadron on the lake should be able to overcome the American squadron. This squadron was put under the command of Captain George Downie. Both Downie and Macdonough were forced to build and equip their vessels with the utmost speed; and the two squadrons [2] were both very deficient in stores, etc., some of the guns of each being without any locks, so that they had to be fired by means of pistols flashed at the touch-holes. Captain Macdonough took the lake a couple of days before his antagonists, and came to anchor in Plattsburg Bay. Captain Downie moved out of Sorrel River on September 8th; and on the morning of the 11th sailed into Plattsburg Harbour to the attack. [3]

[1] *President*, 12; *Preble*, 7; and *Montgomery*, 9.—W. L. C.

[2] The squadrons engaged in the action on Lake Champlain, September 11, 1814:—

BRITISH.			AMERICAN.		
Ships.	Guns.	Commanders.	Ships.	Guns.	Commanders.
Confiance . .	37	Commander George Downie.	*Saratoga* . .	26	Captain Thomas Macdonough.
Linnet . . .	16	,, Daniel Pring.	*Eagle* . . .	20	,, Robert Henley.
Chubb . . .	11	Lieutenant James M'Ghie.	*Ticonderoga* .	17	Lieut.-Com. Stephen Cassin.
Finch . . .	11	,, William Hicks.	*Preble* . . .	7	

12 gunboats or row-galleys, mounting 17 guns and carronades in all. — 10 gunboats or row-galleys, mounting 16 guns and carronades in all.

—W. L. C.

[3] Official letters of Prevost, Macdonough, and Pring. Admiral Codrington's 'Memoirs,' i. 322. Letter of Midshipman Lea, *Naval Chronicle*, xxxii. 272. Cooper: both his 'History,' and especially his two articles in *Putnam's Magazine*. James's. 'History' and 'Naval Occurrences.' The various articles in *Niles's Register* for September and October 1814. Captain J. H. Ward's 'Manual of Naval Tactics.' Lossing's 'Field-book of the War of 1812,' i. 868, quoting Admiral Paulding. Navy Dept. MSS.: Letters of Macdonough before the battle; Log-book of the *Surprise* (*Eagle*), etc. Roosevelt's 'Naval War,' 147 376. American State Papers, xiv. 572.

The largest vessel of Downie's squadron was the ship *Confiance*. She was frigate built, of about 1200 tons' burden, and carried on her main deck thirty long 24's. On her poop were two 32-pr. carronades, and on her top-gallant forecastle were four 32-pr. carronades and a long 24 on a pivot. Thanks to having a furnace, she was able to employ hot shot in the battle. His next vessel was the *Linnet*, a brig of 350 tons, mounting sixteen long 12's. The *Chubb* and the *Finch* were of about 110 tons each, carrying eleven light guns apiece. There were also twelve row-galleys of from 40 to 70 tons each. They carried seventeen guns, long 24's and 18's, and 32-pr. carronades. The crews aggregated from nine hundred to one thousand.[1] In all there were sixteen vessels, of about 2400 tons' total burden, with a total of ninety-two guns, throwing a broadside of 1192 pounds, 660 of which were from long-guns, and 532 from carronades.

Macdonough had one heavy corvette, the *Saratoga*, of 734 tons, carrying eight long 24-pounders, and six 42-pr., and twelve 32-pr. carronades; a large brig, the *Eagle*, of about 500 tons, carrying eight long 18's and twelve 32-pr. carronades; a schooner, the *Ticonderoga*,[2] about the size of the *Linnet*, carrying eight long 12's, four long 18's, and five 32-pr. carronades; a sloop, the *Preble*, mounting seven light guns, and ten row-galleys of about the same size as the British, and mounting sixteen guns— 24's, 18's, and 12's. His aggregate of crews amounted to less than nine hundred men.[3] His fourteen vessels were of about 2200 tons, with eighty-six guns, throwing a broadside of 1194 pounds, only 480 of which were from long-guns. In tonnage, number of men in crew, number of guns, and weight of metal in broadside, there was no great difference; but Downie possessed one marked advantage, for most of his pieces were long-guns, whereas the weight of the American broadside was from carronades. In ordinary circumstances this made his flotilla much the stronger. Even under the conditions in accordance with which the battle was fought, the range was so long that the carronades could not be used with proper efficiency. Downie was almost as much superior in strength to

---

[1] James (vi. 346, ed. 1837), I know not upon what authority, puts the total of the British crews at 537; and he publishes a statement, which appears to be misleading, of the comparative forces engaged.—W. L. C.

[2] She had been a steamer, but her machinery continually got out of order, and she was changed to a schooner.

[5] James puts the American force at 950 men.— W. L. C.

Macdonough as Chauncey had been to Yeo on Lake Ontario in the summer of 1813, the difference in armament of the two squadrons being very similar in each case. Macdonough, having the weaker force, chose his position with such skill, and exercised such careful forethought, that he more than neutralised the material superiority of his opponents.

Both the squadrons were makeshifts. The row-galleys on both sides were manned chiefly by soldiers. The larger vessels, however, were manned mainly by sailors from the regular navies, British and American. The crews were gathered hastily, and had little training while on the lake, so that they betrayed various shortcomings, especially as artillerists, except in the *Confiance*, where Macdonough, and in the *Linnet*, where Pring, had the men at the highest point of efficiency. The armaments of the ships were of the most haphazard description, carronades and long-guns of different calibres being all jumbled together. The vessels were of every kind and rig. The Americans had a ship, a brig, a schooner, a sloop, and two kinds of row-galleys. The British possessed a ship, a brig, two sloops, and two kinds of row-galleys. It would have been exceedingly difficult for either squadron to undertake any kind of manoeuvring in any kind of weather, as no two craft were alike in speed or handiness. Indeed, in a seaway, the frigate-built *Confiance* would have been a match for Macdonough's whole squadron, and the *Saratoga*, a heavy corvette, for all Downie's squadron except the *Confiance*. In point of fighting capacity the men who manned the two squadrons were about equal, for though some of the British accounts accuse certain of the British row-galleys of cowardice in the fight, the exhibition was probably due to the disheartening circumstances of seeing the big vessels fail, which, of course, insured the repulse of the open galleys. In some circumstances an engagement on the lake would have been very much to Downie's advantage, and would have enabled him to make good use of his superiority in force ; but Macdonough, a very cool and competent commander, had the advantage of the defensive, and utilised it to the full. All he had to do was to hold Downie in check, whereas Downie had to win a decisive victory if the invasion was to be a success.

Accordingly, Macdonough decided to await the attack at anchor in Plattsburg Bay, which is deep, and which opens to the southward. The lake being long and narrow, and running north and south, the winds usually blow up or down it, while the current sets northward toward the outlet. All the vessels were flat and shallow, and beat to windward with difficulty. In September, there are often sudden and furious gales which make it risky for any squadron to lie outside the bay until the wind suits; whereas, inside the bay, the breezes are apt to be light and baffling. A wind which would enable Downie to come down the lake would render it difficult for him to beat up the bay; and Macdonough made his arrangements accordingly. He moored his vessels in a north and south line, out of range of the shore batteries, and just south of the outlet of the Saranac. The head of his line was so close to shore as to render it very difficult to turn it. To the south a flank attack was prevented by a shoal, on which was a small island containing a hospital, and mounting one 6-pounder gun. The *Eagle* lay to the north: then came the *Saratoga*, the *Ticonderoga*, and the *Preble*, all at anchor, while the galleys, under their sweeps, formed a second line forty yards back. By this arrangement it was rendered impossible for Downie to double the line, or to anchor completely out of reach of the American carronades; and his attack had to be made by standing in bows on. Macdonough realised thoroughly that he had to deal with a foe of superior physical force, and of great courage and seamanship, and he made every preparation possible. Nothing was left to chance. Not only were his vessels provided with springs, but also with anchors to be used astern in any emergency, so that they might shift their broadsides when necessary. If one battery was knocked to pieces he intended to use the other. Macdonough further prepared the *Saratoga* by laying a kedge broad off on either bow, with a hawser and preventer hawser, hanging in bights under water, leading from each quarter to the kedge on that side.

The morning of September 11th opened with a light breeze from the north-east, and Downie[1] weighed anchor at daylight, and came down the lake with the wind nearly aft, while Macdonough's sailors watched the upper sails of the British ships across the narrow strip of land which formed the outer edge of the bay. When he had opened the bay, Downie hove to with his four larger vessels, and waited until the row-galleys came up.

At about half-past eight[2] the British squadron stood gallantly

---

[1] Downie, it should be explained, was not ready, and weighed only at the urgent solicitation of General Sir George Prevost, who desired his co-operation.—W. L. C.

[2] According to the times in the British accounts, Downie filled and made sail at 7.40 A.M. *See* Pring's letter of September 12th to Yeo.—W. L. C.

in on the starboard tack, in line abreast. The *Chubb* stood to the
north, while next came the *Linnet*, both heading for the *Eagle*,
which they expected to weather, while the *Confiance* was to be
laid athwart the hawse of the *Saratoga*, and the *Finch* and the
row-galleys were to engage the *Ticonderoga* and the *Preble*, with the
American row-galleys behind them. There were a few minutes of
perfect quiet as the distance between the two squadrons lessened,
the men waiting under great nervous tension for the moment of
action. Then the *Eagle* fired her long 18's, but prematurely, for
the shots fell short. Soon afterwards the *Linnet*, in her turn, fired
her long 12's at the *Saratoga*, but these shots also fell short, except
one that struck a hencoop which happened to be on board Macdonough's vessel. There was a gamecock inside, and when the
coop was knocked to pieces he jumped up, clapped his wings, and
crowed lustily. To the nervously-expectant sailors it seemed a
good omen. They laughed and cheered, and, immediately afterwards,
Macdonough himself fired one of his long 24's. His aim was good,
and the ball ranged the length of the *Confiance*, killing and wounding
several men. All the American long-guns opened, and those of
the British galleys replied.

The *Chubb* and the *Linnet* escaped nearly unscratched, and
anchored on the *Eagle's* beam, for both the *Saratoga* and the *Eagle*
devoted their attention chiefly to the *Confiance*. The latter frigate
stood steadily in without replying to the American fire, but she was
terribly cut up, losing both her port bow anchors ; and she suffered
much in her hull. She ported her helm, and came to while still
about four hundred yards from the *Saratoga*. Downie came to
anchor in grand style, making everything tight, and then delivered
a well aimed and terribly destructive broadside into the *Saratoga*.
Two or three of the British galleys took part in the attack on
the head of the American line, where there were also five or six
of the American row-galleys. Meanwhile the *Finch*, under her
sweeps, led the remaining British row-galleys to the attack of
the *Ticonderoga*, where the four or five weakest of the American
row-galleys were also stationed.

At the foot of the line the British effort was to turn the American
flank. At first the fighting was at long range, but gradually the
assailants closed. On both sides there was great variety in the
individual behaviour of the galleys, some being handled with the
utmost courage, and others rather timidly, as was not unnatural, for

the men in them were not used to their work, nor to act with one another; and the attack of each depended upon who its commander happened to be. Moreover, as they were open boats, it was easy to inflict very heavy slaughter among the closely-crowded crews. The British galleys which took part in the attack on the *Ticonderoga* and the *Preble* were under the command of Lieutenant Christopher James Bell, and were well handled. Two or three of them hung back, as did those at the head of the line, where it was impossible to expect them to make head against the *Saratoga* and the *Eagle ;* but where Bell himself led them, they followed him with the utmost determination. About an hour after the discharge of the first gun, the *Finch* got close to the *Ticonderoga*, only to be completely crippled by the broadsides of the latter. Half her crew were killed or wounded; and she drifted helplessly away, grounding near Crab Island, where she surrendered to the patients in the hospital. At about the same time the *Preble*, on the American side, was forced out of line by the British gunboats, and drifted ashore out of the fight. The American gunboats in that part of the line also gave way. Two or three of the British row-galleys had already been so roughly handled by the long-guns of the *Ticonderoga* that they made no further effort to come within effective range, so that, at the foot of the line, the fight became one between the *Ticonderoga*, under Lieutenant-Commander Stephen Cassin, on the one side, and the remaining British gunboats, under Lieutenant Bell, on the other. Bell's attack was most resolute, and the defence of the American schooner was equally obstinate. Cassin walked the quarterdeck, paying no heed to the balls singing round him, while he scanned the movements of the galleys, and directed his guns to be loaded with canister and bags of bullets when the British tried to board. He was well seconded by his officers, especially by a young midshipman named Hiram Paulding. When Paulding found that the matches of his division were defective, he fired his guns by flashing pistols at the touch-holes during the remainder of the fight. Bell's galleys were pushed to within a boat-hook's length of the schooner; but her fire was so heavy that they could not get alongside, and one by one they drew off, so crippled by the slaughter that they could hardly man the oars.

At the head of the line the advantage had been with the British. The *Chubb*, however, was too light for the company she was in, and speedily suffered the fate of the *Preble* and the *Finch*, being driven out

of the line. Her cable, bowsprit, and main-boom were shot away,
and, when she drifted inside the American ships, she was taken possession of by a midshipman from the *Saratoga*. The *Linnet*, which
was remarkably well handled by her captain, Daniel Pring, paid no
attention to the American gunboats, directing her whole fire against
the *Eagle*. The *Eagle* was a much heavier vessel, but she was also
partially engaged with the *Confiance ;* and, moreover, the *Linnet*
was fought with the utmost courage and skill. After keeping up a
heavy fire for a long time, the *Eagle's* springs were shot away, and
she hung in the wind, unable to answer the *Linnet* with a single
shot. Accordingly, she cut her cables, started home her topsails,
and ran down between, and in shore of, the *Saratoga* and *Ticonderoga*, where she again came to anchor and opened fire on the
Confiance. The *Linnet* was then able to give her undivided attention
to the American row-galleys. After she had driven them off she
sprang her broadside so as to rake the *Saratoga*.

The *Saratoga* had already suffered heavily. The first broadside
of the *Confiance's* double-shotted long 24's had crashed into her hull
with a shock which threw half her people on the deck, knocking
down many, and either killing or crippling them. Her first lieutenant,
Peter Gamble, was among the slain, being killed just as he knelt
down to sight the bow-gun. Macdonough himself worked like a
tiger in pointing and handling his favourite piece. While bending
over to sight it the spanker-boom above his head was cut in two by
a round shot. It fell on him, and knocked him senseless for two or
three minutes. Leaping to his feet, he again returned to the gun.
Immediately afterwards a round shot took off the head of the captain
of the gun, and drove it into Macdonough's face with such force as
to knock him to the other side of the deck.

The broadsides of the *Confiance*, however, grew steadily less
effective. Her guns had been levelled to point-blank range at first,
but the quoins were loosened by the successive broadsides, and, as
they were not properly replaced, her shot kept going higher and
higher so as to pass over the enemy. Very soon after the beginning
of the action the gallant Downie was slain, a shot from the
Saratoga throwing one of the long 24's off its carriage against his
right groin. His death was instantaneous, though the skin was not
broken.

No ships could bear the brunt of such a battle without suffering.
After a few minutes, the fire from both the *Confiance* and the

Saratoga began to decrease. One by one the guns were disabled, and the lack of complete training among the crews showed itself in the way in which each side helped to disable its own battery. The American sailors overloaded their carronades, cramming their guns until the last shot reached the muzzle. The British on board the *Confiance* made an even worse showing. They became demoralised by the confusion and slaughter, and spoiled one or two of the guns by ramming the wadding and round shot into them without any powder, or by putting in two cartridges of powder and no shot. When, however, the *Linnet* was able to devote herself exclusively to the *Saratoga*, the latter began to get rather more than she wanted. Macdonough had his hands full, with the frigate on his beam, and the brig raking him. Twice the *Saratoga* was set on fire by the hot shot of the *Confiance;* one by one her long-guns were disabled by the enemy's fire; and her carronades either suffered from the same cause, or else were rendered useless by over-charging. At last only one carronade was left in the starboard battery; and on firing it the gun flew off the carriage and fell down the main hatch. This left the *Saratoga* without a single gun which she could fire, and, though the *Confiance* had been almost as roughly handled, the British ship still had a few port guns that could be used. On both sides the unengaged batteries, the starboard battery of the *Confiance* and the port battery of the *Saratoga*, were practically unharmed.

The British victory would now have been secure had not Macdonough provided in advance the means for meeting just such an emergency.

The anchor suspended astern of the *Saratoga* was let go, and the men hauled in on the hawser that led to the starboard quarter, bringing the ship's stern up over the kedge. The ship then rode by the kedge, and by a hawser that had been bent to a bight in the stream cable. In that position she was exposed to a raking fire from the *Linnet,* and suffered much from the accuracy of Pring's long 12's. By hauling on the line, however, the ship was at length got so far round that the aftermost gun of the port broadside bore on the *Confiance*. The men had been sent forward to keep them as much out of harm's way as possible. Enough were now called back to man the piece, and they at once began a brisk and accurate fire. Again the crew roused on the line until the next gun bore, and it, too, was manned, and opened with effect on the *Confiance*. Then the ship hung, and would go no farther round. But Macdonough was not at the end of his resources. The hawser leading from the port quarter was got forward under the bows, and passed aft to the starboard quarter. The *Saratoga* gradually yielded to the strain, and, a minute later, her whole port battery opened with fatal effect. The *Confiance*, meanwhile, had also attempted to round. The springs of the British ships were on the starboard side, and so, of course, could not be shot away as the *Eagle's* were; but as the *Confiance* had nothing but springs to rely on, her efforts did little beyond forcing her forward; and she hung with her head to the wind. She could not stand the pounding of the fresh battery. Over half her crew were killed or wounded; all but three or four of the guns on the engaged side were dismounted; her stout masts looked like bundles of splinters; and her sails were in shreds and tatters. Nothing more could be done, and the *Confiance* struck about two hours after she had fired her first broadside. Without pausing a minute the *Saratoga* again hauled on her starboard hawser till her broadside was sprung to bear on the *Linnet*, and the ship and brig began a brisk single fight; for the *Eagle*, in her then berth, could not fire at the *Linnet*, and the *Ticonderoga* was driving off the British galleys. The shattered and disabled state of the *Linnet's* masts, sails and yards rendered it utterly hopeless for Pring to try to escape by cutting his cable; and most men would have surrendered at once. But Pring kept up a most gallant fight with his greatly superior foe, hoping that some of the gunboats would come and tow him off. Meanwhile he had despatched to the *Confiance* a lieutenant, who returned with news of Downie's death. The British gunboats had been driven half a mile off, and were evidently in no state to render aid to any one; so, after having maintained the fight single-handed for fifteen minutes, until, from the number of shot between wind and water, the lower deck was flooded, the plucky little brig hauled down her colours, and the fight ended a little over two hours and a half after the first gun had been fired. Not one of the American vessels had a mast that would bear canvas, and the captured British vessels were in a sinking condition.

The British row-galleys had drifted to leeward, and they now pulled slowly off. The American row-galleys were in no position to interfere with their retreat, which was not molested.

The battle had been bloody and destructive. The *Confiance* had

been struck in the hull one hundred and five, and the *Saratoga*
fifty-five times; about two hundred men were killed or wounded
on the American side, and over three hundred on the British.[1]
This does not include those who were merely knocked down, or
bruised, or grazed by flying splinters; indeed, an officer of the *Confiance* reported that at the close of the action there were not five men
in her who were unhurt. Macdonough appreciated the gallantry
of his adversaries, and at once returned the British officers their
swords; and Pring, the senior British officer left, expressed in his
official letter his acknowledgment of the generosity, courtesy, and
humanity with which Macdonough had treated himself and his men.
Pring, and Cassin of the *Ticonderoga*, shared with Macdonough the
honour of the day.

This lake fight decided the fate of the invasion of Sir George
Prevost,[2] who retired at once with his army. Macdonough had
performed a most notable feat, one which, on the whole, surpassed
that of any other captain of either navy in this war. The consequences of the victory were very great, for it had a decisive effect
upon the negotiations for peace which were then being carried on
between the American and the British commissioners at Ghent. The
Duke of Wellington, who had been pressed to take command of
the British army in Canada, advised against any prolongation of the
war, if it could be terminated on the basis of each nation being left in
the position which it had held before the struggle, giving this advice
on the ground that the failure of the British to obtain control of the
lakes rendered it impossible to expect any decisive triumph of the
British arms.[3] Indeed, in the war of 1812, the control of the lakes
was the determining factor in the situation on the Canadian border,

---

[1] The *Confiance* had 41 killed and about 60 wounded; the *Linnet*, 10 killed and
14 wounded; the *Chubb*, 6 killed and 16 wounded; and the *Finch*, 2 wounded. There
were further losses in the gunboats.—W. L. C.

[2] Prevost's failure to co-operate with the squadron, as he had undertaken to do,
was largely responsible for the disaster. Sir James Lucas Yeo preferred certain
charges against him in consequence; but Prevost died before he could be brought
before a court-martial. *See* Mems. of C.M. on Pring and others, August 28th, 1815.
—W. L. C.

[3] Wellington's Dispatches, xii. 224; Supplementary Dispatches, i. 426, and ix. 438.
See Adams, viii. 102–112, for this battle, and ix. 36–41, for its effects on the
negotiations for peace.

In his letter of November 9th, written after the receipt of the news of the battle
of Lake Champlain, Wellington advises the Cabinet that they "have no right, from
the state of the war, to demand any concession of territory from America," and gives
as the main reason, "the want of the naval superiority on the lakes."

for at that time the frontier between the two countries nowhere passed through any thickly-settled regions, except in the immediate neighbourhood of great bodies of water; and the military operations that were undertaken had to be conducted with this condition in view.

The inability of America in any way to interrupt the British blockade of her coast was now to bear fruit in the disgrace of the loss of the national capital. Of course, so long as the British possessed absolute control of the sea, they could take the offensive whenever and wherever they wished, and could choose their own point of attack, while the American government never knew what point to defend. From Maryland to Georgia the militia were under arms literally by the hundred thousand, and they were less efficient than one-tenth the number of regulars. While in the field they suffered greatly from disease, so that there was much loss of life, although there was hardly any fighting; and on the few occasions when it was possible to gather them soon enough to oppose them to a British raiding party, they naturally showed themselves utterly incompetent to stand against trained regulars. The loss of life and the waste of wealth by the employment of these militia in the southern states, though they were hardly ever used in battle, offset many times over the expense that would have been incurred by building a fighting fleet sufficient to prevent a blockade, and therefore to obviate all the damage which it cost during the two years when it was in force—damage which the privateers only partially avenged, and in no way averted.

Vice-Admiral Sir Alexander F. I. Cochrane had succeeded to the command of the British fleet on the coast of North America in the summer of 1814. Rear-Admiral George Cockburn was in command in the Chesapeake, whither Cochrane himself sailed in August, together with a fleet of transports containing a small British army under Major-General Robert Ross. At about the same time Cochrane had issued a general order to the British blockading squadrons, instructing them to destroy and lay waste the towns and districts which they could successfully assail, sparing only the lives of the unarmed inhabitants. This was done in alleged retaliation for the conduct of a party of American soldiers on the Canadian boundary, who had wantonly destroyed the little town of Newark; although the destruction of Newark had been promptly avenged by the destruc-

tion of Buffalo and one or two other small American towns, while
the officer who had ordered Newark to be destroyed had been court-
martialled for his conduct.   A curious feature of Cochrane's order,
which was, of course, grossly improper, was that it applied only to
the Navy; and Ross showed by his actions how strongly he disapproved of it, for though the Navy did a great deal of plundering
and burning, in accordance with the instructions given, Ross's

CAPTAIN JOSHUA BARNEY, U.S.N.
(*From the portrait by Wood.*)

troops at first paid scrupulous heed to the rights of the citizens,
and in no way interfered with private property.[1]

The first duty of the fleet was to get rid of Captain Joshua
Barney's flotilla of gunboats.   This flotilla had indulged in several
indecisive long-range skirmishes with various ships of the blockading
squadron, and it was now forced to put into the Patuxent, where
it was burned when Ross advanced on Washington.   Barney's

[1] Adams, viii. 126.

flotilla-men then joined the motley forces gathered to defend the capital city, and offered a striking contrast in their behaviour on the field of battle to the rabble of militia around them, who fled while the sailors fought.[1]

About the middle of August Cochrane and Ross were ready for action. On the 20th Ross's troops were disembarked on the Maryland shore, some fifty miles distant from Washington; Cockburn proceeding up the Patuxent[2] on the Maryland side. On the 23rd they definitely made up their minds to attack Washington first and Baltimore later. Meanwhile a British squadron, composed of the frigates *Seahorse*, 38, Captain James Alexander Gordon (1), and *Euryalus*, 36, Captain Charles Napier (2), with four bombs and rocket ships, moved up the Potomac. In addition Captain Sir Peter Parker (2), in the *Menelaus*, 38, was sent to create a diversion above Baltimore; but he happened to meet a party of militia, who fought well, for when he landed at Bellair to attack them, on August 30th, he was himself killed and his party beaten back, with a loss of forty-one men.[3]

Ross and Cockburn moved against Washington, and, on August 24th, encountered a huddle of seven thousand American militia at Bladensburg. It could not be called an army. A few companies were in uniform. The rest were clad as they would have been clad in the fields, except that they had muskets. They were under two or three worthless generals, one named Winder being in supreme command; and various members of the cabinet, notably Monroe, accompanied President Madison in riding or driving aimlessly about among

[1] 'Biographical Memoir of the late Commodore Joshua Barney,' p. 315.

[2] Rear-Admiral Cockburn had under his orders the armed boats and tenders of the fleet, having on board Royal Marines under Capt. John Robyns, and Royal Marine Artillery under Captain James H. Harrison. The boats were under the general superintendence of Captain John Wainwright (2), of the *Tonnant*, and were in three divisions, commanded as follows: I. Commanders Thomas Ball Sulivan and William Stanhope Badcock; II. Commanders Rowland Money and Kenelm Somerville; III. Commander Robert Ramsay. Following the boats, so far as the depth of water permitted, were the *Severn*, 40, Captain Joseph Nourse, *Hebrus*, 42, Captain Edmund Palmer, and *Manly*, 12, Commander Vincent Newton; but the frigates could not get higher than Benedict, whence their Captains, with their boats, proceeded to join Cockburn.—W. L. C.

[3] Sir Peter Parker (2), Bart., was eldest son of Vice-Admiral Christopher Parker (2), and was born in 1786. He was a Captain of October 22nd, 1805, and, in 1811, had succeeded to the Baronetcy of his grandfather, Admiral of the Fleet Sir Peter Parker (1). In the affair at Bellair, near Baltimore, 14 British were killed, including, besides Parker, Midshipman John T. Sandes; and 27 were wounded, including Lieutenants Benjamin George Benyon and George Poe, R.M.—W. L. C.

the troops. Not a third of Ross's little army was engaged,[1] for the militia fled too quickly to allow the main body of the assailants to get into action. As they were running off the field, however, Barney appeared, with his sailors from the flotilla, also on the run, but in the opposite direction. He had with him about four hundred and fifty seamen and marines, the latter being under their own officer, Captain Miller; and he also had a battery of five guns. It was a sufficiently trying situation, for Barney's force was hopelessly

SIR JAMES ALEXANDER GORDON (1), G.C.B., ADMIRAL OF THE FLEET.

(*From Blood's engraving, after a portrait painted about 1813, when Gordon was a Post-Captain.*)

outnumbered by the victorious troops whose attack he was advancing to meet through a throng of fugitive militia; but the sailors and marines were of excellent stuff, and were as little daunted by the flight of their friends as by the advance of their foes. Again and

[1] In the action at Bladensburg the British army lost 64 killed and 185 wounded. The Navy lost only 1 killed and 6 wounded. Among the naval officers present were Rear-Admiral George Cockburn, Captain Edmund Palmer, Lieutenant James Scott (2), of the *Albion*, Midshipman Arthur Wakefield, Lieutenant John Lawrence, R.M.A., and Lieutenant Athelstan Stephens, R.M.—W. L. C.

again the sailors repulsed the troops who attacked them in front.
They were then outflanked, and retired, after half an hour's fighting,
a hundred of their men having been killed or wounded. Both
Barney and Miller were wounded and captured, together with the
guns. One of the British officers, writing afterwards of the battle,
spoke with the utmost admiration of Barney's men. " Not only
did they serve their guns with a quickness and precision that
astonished their assailants, but they stood till some of them were
actually bayoneted with fuses in their hands ; nor was it till their
leader was wounded and taken, and they saw themselves deserted
on all sides by the soldiers, that they left the field." [1] The victorious
British showed every attention to Barney and his men, treating
them, as Barney said, " as if they were brothers." [2]

As Ross and Cockburn led their troops into Washington they
were fired on from a house, Ross's horse being killed. They then
proceeded to burn the Capitol and the White House, together with
various other public buildings.[3] Next day the work of destruction
was completed,[4] a few private buildings sharing the same fate, while
Cockburn took particular pleasure in destroying one of the news-
paper offices, as he seemed much to resent the criticism of himself
in the American press. Having completed their work, Ross and
Cockburn marched back to the coast, leaving behind them most of
their wounded to be cared for by the Americans.

Whatever discredit attached to the burning and plundering of
Washington attached to both Ross and Cockburn, though Ross
evidently disliked the work as much as Cockburn enjoyed it. It was
only an incident in the general destruction undertaken by Cochrane's
orders. Washington was burned just as, along the shores of the
Chesapeake, hamlets and private houses were burned. The pretext
was that this was done to avenge the destruction of the public
buildings at York, and of the town of Newark, in the American
descents upon Canada. The public buildings at York, however,
were but partially destroyed by stragglers, whose work was at once
checked by the American officers in command. The burning of
Newark had been promptly repudiated by the American government,

---

[1] Gleig's 'Subaltern,' p. 68.   [2] Barney's report, Aug. 29th, 1814.

[3] Letters of Cockburn, Aug. 27th, and Ross, Aug. 30th; Ingersoll, ii. 188; James's
'Military Occurrences,' ii. 495; Am. State Papers, Military Affairs, i. 550; Niles,
September 1814.

[4] The Americans themselves destroyed the *Argus*, 22, and a frigate which was
nearly ready for launching, in order to save them from capture.—W. L. C.

and, moreover, had already been amply avenged. The destruction of the public buildings at Washington was indefensible; and it was also very unwise so deeply to touch the national pride. The affair had a perceptible effect in making the country more determined to carry on the war. It is, however, nonsense to denounce the act in the language that has so often been applied to it. Cockburn and Ross undoubtedly treated the capital of the American nation in a way which justified an eager desire for revenge; but Americans should keep the full weight of their indignation for the government whose supineness and shortsightedness rendered such an outrage possible. Jomini has left on record the contemptuous surprise felt by all European military men when a state, with a population of eight million souls, allowed a handful of British soldiers to penetrate unchecked to its capital, and there destroy the public buildings. The first duty of a nation is self-defence; and nothing excuses such lack of warlike readiness as the Americans had shown. The incidents which accompanied the capture of Washington were discreditable to the British, but the capture itself was far more discreditable to the Americans.

Meanwhile Captain Gordon's little squadron[1] worked its way up the Potomac, and, on August 28th, took Alexandria, where it remained for four days, loading the vessels with whatever the warehouses contained.[2] Then the squadron began its descent of the river, which was shoal, and very difficult to navigate. Captain John Rodgers, with some of the crews of two new 44's which were building, tried to bar his way, but lacked sufficient means. Twice Rodgers attempted to destroy one of the British vessels with fireships, but failed, and once, in his turn, he repelled an attack by the British boats. The squadron also passed, without much damage, a battery of light field-pieces. On September 6th Gordon silenced and passed the last of the batteries, having taken six days to go down from Alexandria. He had lost forty-two men[3] all told, and had

---

[1] *Seahorse*, 38, Captain James Alexander Gordon; *Euryalus*, 36, Captain Charles Napier (2); *Devastation*, bomb, Commander Thomas Alexander (2); *Ætna*, bomb, Commander Richard Kenah; *Meteor*, bomb, Commander Samuel Roberts; *Erebus*, rocket-vessel, Commander David Ewen Bartholomew; *Fairy*, 18, Commander Henry Loraine Baker (joined with orders, after the fall of Alexandria); and *Anna Maria*, dispatch-boat.—W. L. C.

[2] Letter of Captain Gordon, Sept. 9th, 1814.

[3] *Viz.*, 7 killed, including Lieutenant Charles Dickinson (*Fairy*), and 35 wounded, including Captain Charles Napier (2), Commander David Ewen Bartholomew, Lieutenant Reuben Paine, and Master's Mate Andrew Reid.—W. L. C.

thus concluded successfully, at a very trivial cost, a most venturesome expedition, which reflected great honour on the crews engaged in it.

The very rough handling received by Sir Peter Parker (2) put a check to the marauding of the British frigates and sloops. As soon as Gordon rejoined him Cochrane sailed from the mouth of the Potomac to the mouth of the Patapsco River, on which Baltimore stands. Formidable earthworks had been thrown up about Baltimore, however; and to guard it against attack by sea there were good forts, which were well manned by men who had at last begun to learn something. Ross advanced against the city by land, and was killed in a sharp encounter with a body of militia. The troops found the earthworks too strong to assault; the ships bombarded the forts without any effect; and then both the soldiers and the sailors [1] retired. [2] Not long afterwards Cochrane left for Halifax, [3] and the British troops for Jamaica, so that operations in the Chesapeake ceased.

During this time the British Navy had protected an expedition which overran, and held until the close of the war, a part of the Maine sea-coast, and in September, 1814, a large British force, under Rear-Admiral Edward Griffith, destroyed the American corvette *Adams*, 28, which had run up the Penobscot for refuge.

After leaving Baltimore the British prepared for a descent on New Orleans, and gathered a large fleet of line-of-battle ships, frigates and small vessels, under Vice-Admiral Sir Alexander F. I. Cochrane, convoying a still larger number of storeships and transports, containing the troops under Major-General Sir Edward Pakenham. The expedition made its appearance at the mouth of the Mississippi on December 8th. The first duty which fell to the boats of the squadron was to destroy five American gunboats which lay in the shallow bayou known as Lake Borgne. Accordingly, forty-two launches, each armed with a carronade in the bow, and

---

[1] In the attack on Baltimore, the 600 seamen who were landed were under Captain Edward Crofton, and Commanders Thomas Ball Sulivan, Rowland Money, and Robert Ramsay, and the Royal Marines under Captain John Robyns. In the affair of September 12th, when Major-General Ross fell, the Navy lost 7 killed and 48 wounded, among the latter being Captain John Robyns, R.M., Lieutenant Sampson Marshall, and Midshipman Charles Ogle (2). During a subsequent expedition up the Coan River, on October 3rd, Commander Richard Kenah, of the *Ætna*, was killed.—W. L. C.

[2] Cochrane's report, Sept. 17th, 1814.

[3] Cochrane sailed for Halifax on September 19th to make preparations for the New Orleans expedition. On the same day Rear-Admiral Cockburn departed for Bermuda; and on October 14th, Rear-Admiral Pulteney Malcolm quitted the Chesapeake for Negril Bay, Jamaica.—W. L. C.

carrying nine hundred and eighty seamen and Royal Marines all told, were sent off, under Commander Nicholas Lockyer,[1] to effect their destruction. The gunboats carried an aggregate of one hundred and eighty-two men, under the command of Lieutenant Thomas Ap Catesby Jones, U.S.N. Each was armed with one heavy long-gun, and several light pieces.[2] The attack was made on the morning of December 14th, 1814.[3] Jones had moored his five gun-vessels in a head and stern line in the channel off Malheureux Island passage, with their boarding nettings triced up, and every-thing in readiness; but the force of the current drifted his own boat and another out of line, a hundred yards down. Jones had to deal with a force five times the size of his own, and to escape he had only to run his boats on shore; but he prepared very coolly for battle.

Commander Lockyer acted as coolly as his antagonist. When he had reached a point just out of gunshot, he brought the boats to a grapnel, to let the sailors eat breakfast and get a little rest, for they had been rowing most of the time for a day and a night, and a cutting-out expedition meant murderous work. When the men were refreshed he formed the boats in open order, and they pulled gallantly on against the strong current. At ten minutes past eleven the Americans opened fire, and, for a quarter of an hour, had the firing all to themselves. Then the carronades and light guns on both sides were brought into play. Lockyer led the advance in a barge of the *Seahorse*. The nearest gunboat was that of the American commander. Accordingly, it was these two who first came to close quarters, Lockyer laying his barge alongside Lieutenant Jones's boat. An obstinate struggle ensued, but the resistance of the Americans was very fierce, and the barge was repulsed, most

---

[1] Commander Nicholas Lockyer, of the *Sophie*, 18, was assisted by Commanders Henry Montresor, of the *Manly*, and Samuel Roberts, of the *Meteor*, bomb, and each commanded a division of boats. The boats engaged were those of the *Tonnant*, *Norge*, *Bedford*, *Ramillies*, *Royal Oak*, *Armide*, *Seahorse*, *Cydnus*, *Trave*, *Sophie*, *Meteor*, *Belle Poule*, *Gorgon*, *Alceste*, and *Diomede*. A medal for the action was granted in 1847.—W. L. C.

[2] Lieutenant Jones's account gives his full force as 5 gunboats, mounting in all three long 32's, two long 24's, twenty-two long 6's, four 12-pr. carronades, two 5-in. howitzers, and twelve swivels, and having 182 men on board. He had also with him the schooner *Seahorse*, which he detached to Bay St. Louis before the attack, and the little sloop *Alligator*.—W. L. C.

[3] Letters of Captain Lockyer, Dec. 18th, 1814, and of Lieutenant Jones, March 12th, 1815.

of her crew being killed or crippled, while her gallant captain was severely, and the equally gallant Lieutenant George Pratt mortally, wounded.   Another boat, under the command of Lieutenant James Barnwell Tatnall, grappled the gunboat and was promptly sunk. But the other boats pulled steadily up, and, one after another, were laid on board the doomed vessel.   The boarding-nets were slashed through and cut away ; with furious fighting the deck was gained ; the American commander and many of his crew were killed or wounded, and the gunboat was carried.   Her guns were turned on the second boat, which was soon taken, and then the British dashed at the third, which was carried with a rush after a gallant defence, her commander, Lieutenant Robert Spedden, being badly wounded.   The next gunboat fell an easy prey, her long-gun having been dismounted by the recoil, and the fifth then hauled down her flag.   Forty-one of the Americans, and ninety-four of the British,[1] were killed or wounded.

A brigade of British sailors took part in the battles before New Orleans, and shared the disasters that there befell the British army ; but their deeds belong to military rather than to naval history.

The British Navy did not confine itself to attacks in Chesapeake Bay and at the mouth of the Mississippi.   On September 15th, 1814, the *Hermes*, 20, Captain the Hon. Henry William Percy, *Carron*, 20, Captain the Hon. Robert Churchill Spencer, and 18-gun brig-sloops *Sophie*, Commander Nicholas Lockyer, and *Childers*, Commander John Brand Umfreville, with a land force of about two hundred men, made an attack on Fort Bowyer, at Mobile Point.[2] The attack failed completely.   The carronades of the ships were unfit for such a contest, and no damage was done to the fort, while the *Hermes* grounded and was burnt, and the assailants were repulsed, losing about eighty men all told.

Early in 1815 Rear-Admiral George Cockburn began to harry the coast of Georgia.   He gathered a great deal of plunder, and did much destruction in an expedition up the St. Mary's River.   As

---

[1] The British lost 17 killed and 77 wounded, out of a total of about 980 engaged. Among the killed were Midshipmen Thomas W. Moore, John Mills, and Henry Symons ; among the wounded were Commander Nicholas Lockyer, Lieutenants William Gilbert Roberts, John Franklin, Henry Gladwell Etough, and George Pratt (mortally), and Lieutenant James Uniacke, R.M.   For the gallantry displayed, Commander Lockyer was posted on March 29th, 1815, and Commanders Henry Montresor and Samuel Roberts were similarly advanced on June 13th, following.—W. L. C.

[2] James, vi. 356 (Ed. 1837).

usual, the militia were helpless to impede his movements or relieve the threatened points.   One or two of his boat attacks failed; and the small force of American seamen which manned the little flotilla of gunboats in the shallow waters of the South Atlantic twice themselves made cutting-out expeditions, in which they captured two boats of one of his frigates, the *Hebrus*, and the tender of another, the *Severn*.[1]   These little checks, however, were merely sufficient to irritate the British; and Savannah was in an agony of well-grounded fear lest she should suffer the fate of Washington, when peace came, and Cockburn reluctantly withdrew.   A disagreeable incident occurred after the news of peace had come.   The British 20-gun sloop *Erebus*, Commander David Ewen Bartholomew, came across an American gunboat, under the command of Mr. Hurlburt, and ordered her to lie to.   The gunboat refused, whereupon the sloop gave her a broadside, and she fired her only gun, and struck.[2]   Afterwards Bartholomew apologised, and let the gunboat proceed.   His gunnery had been bad, and none of the gunboat's crew were hurt.   A few months later, on June 30th, 1815, a parallel incident, with the parties reversed, occurred in the China Seas, where the American sloop *Peacock*, 22, met the little East India Company's brig *Nautilus*, 14.[3]   The meeting will be described later.

Thus, throughout the last year of the war, the American coast had been blockaded, and harassed, and insulted by harrying parties, as well as by descents in force, from the St. John's to the Mississippi. Virginia, Maryland, Maine and Georgia had been equally powerless to repel or avenge the attacks from which they had suffered. Alexandria had been plundered and Hampton burned, the Georgia coast ravaged and part of Maine permanently held ; and only at the mouth of the Mississippi—and there, thanks solely to the genius of Andrew Jackson—had the invaders met a bloody and crushing defeat.   Moreover, the blockade was so vigorous that the shipping rotted at the wharves of the seaports, and grass grew in the business quarters of the trading towns.   Of course very swift and very lucky merchant vessels now and then got in or out, but they had to charge for their wares prices that would repay the great risk of capture ; and,

---

[1] Navy Dept. MSS., Captains' Letters, vol. 42, Nos. 100 and 130.

[2] *Ib.*, vol. 43, No. 125. *Niles's Register*, viii. 104, 118.

[3] The *Nautilus*, however, fared worse than Mr. Hurlburt's gunboat, for she lost 6 killed, and 9, including her commander, Lieutenant Charles Boyce, wounded.— W. L. C.

for an impoverished people, those prices were nearly prohibitory. The general suffering was very great, and the people, instead of realising that their own shortcomings were at fault, stormed at the administration—with very good reason, it must be confessed. The war had really done a great service; but this the people, naturally enough, failed to recognise at the moment; and the discomfort and humiliation to which they were subjected made them long for peace. For eight months the overthrow of Napoleon had left Great Britain free to put her whole strength against the United States. The result had by no means come up to her expectations, for her aggressive movements, at Plattsburg Bay and at New Orleans, had met with defeat. But the ceaseless pressure of the blockade told heavily in her favour. Every American citizen felt in his pocket and on his table the results of the presence of the British warships off the harbour mouths.

No stringency of the blockade, however, could keep the American cruisers in port. The sloops of war and the big privateers were commanded and manned by men whose trade it was to run risks and overcome dangers. Daringly and skilfully handled, they continually ran in and out of the ports, ever incurring the risk of capture, but ever doing damage for which their capture could not atone.

Thanks to their numbers, and to the fact that they only fought when they had to, the privateers did more damage than the sloops to British commerce. Like the privateers, the sloops cruised, by choice, right in the home waters of Britain, but they never went after merchantmen when there was a chance of tackling men-of-war; and the chief harrying of the British commerce was left to the men who did it for personal reasons, actuated half by love of gain and half by love of adventure.

The deeds of the commerce-destroyers in this war are very noteworthy. In spite of the fact that the stringency of the blockade of the American coast increased steadily, and of the further fact that, during the latter part of the war, the British were able to employ their whole Navy against the Americans, the ravages of the American cruisers grew more and more formidable month by month until the peace. The privateers were handled with a daring and success previously unknown. Always before this, in any contest with a European power, the British Navy had in the end been able to get the hostile privateers completely under, and to prevent any large portion of British trade from being driven into neutral bottoms.

France possessed treble the population of the United States, and she had a great fighting fleet; while her harbours were so near the English coast as to offer an excellent base of operations against British commerce. But, when the American war broke out, Britain had very nearly driven the French privateers from the ocean, and had almost entirely expelled them from British home waters. The result was that, in 1812, British commerce was safer at sea than it had been during the early period of the French war. But nothing of the kind happened in the American war. The boldness of the privateers, and the severity of their ravages, increased every year. In 1814 the privateers that put to sea were large, well-built, formidably armed, and heavily-manned vessels, of about the size of the smaller sloops of war, and faster than any other craft afloat. England was near to continental Europe, and America was divided from her by the broad Atlantic; yet no European nation ever sent her privateers so boldly into British home waters as did America.

Wherever on the ocean the British merchantmen sailed, thither the American privateers followed. Their keels furrowed the waters of the Indian Ocean and the China Seas; and they made prizes of vessels that sailed from Bombay, Madras, and Hong Kong. They swarmed in the West Indies, where they landed and burnt small towns, leaving behind them proclamations that thus they had avenged the burning of Washington. They haunted the coasts of the British colonies in Africa; they lay off the harbour of Halifax, and plundered the outgoing and incoming vessels, laughing at the ships of the line and frigates that strove to drive them off. Above all they grew ever fonder of sailing to and fro in the narrow seas over which England had for centuries claimed an unquestioned sovereignty. They cruised in the British Channel where they captured, not only merchantmen, but also small regularly armed vessels. The Irish Sea and the Irish Channel were among their favourite cruising grounds; they circled Scotland and Ireland; one of them ransomed a Scottish town. The *Chasseur* of Baltimore, commanded by Thomas Boyle, cruised for three months off the coast of England, taking prize after prize, and in derision sent in, to be posted at Lloyd's, a proclamation of blockade of the sea-coast of the United Kingdom.[1] In September 1814 the merchants of Glasgow, Liverpool, and Bristol held meetings, and complained bitterly to the British Government of the damages inflicted upon them. The

[1] Coggeshall's book is filled with incidents of this kind.

Liverpool meeting recited that some ports, particularly Milford, were under actual blockade. The merchants, manufacturers, shipowners, and underwriters of Glasgow protested that the audacity of the American privateers had become intolerable; that they harassed the British coasts; and that the success with which their enterprise had been attended was not only injurious to British commerce, but also humbling to British pride; and they added a significant comment upon the damage which had been done by " a Power whose maritime strength had hitherto been impolitically held in contempt." The rates of insurance rose to an unprecedented height. For the first time in history a rate of 13 per cent. was paid on risks to cross the Irish Channel. The Secretary of the Admiralty, Mr. Croker, was forced to admit the havoc wrought even in the Irish and Bristol Channels, and could only respond that, if the merchantmen would never sail except under the convoy of a sufficient number of men-of-war, they would be safe. Such a statement was equivalent to admission that no unguarded ship could safely go from one British port to another; and it sufficed to explain why the rate of insurance on vessels had gradually risen to double the rate which had prevailed during the great war with France.[1] On February 11th, 1815, the *Times* complained in these bitter words of the ravages of the American sloops of war and privateers: " They daily enter in among our convoys, seize prizes in sight of those that should afford protection, and if pursued ' put on their sea-wings ' and laugh at the clumsy English pursuers. To what is this owing? Cannot we build ships? . . . It must indeed be encouraging to Mr. Madison to read the logs of his cruisers. If they fight, they are sure to conquer; if they fly, they are sure to escape."

The privateers were not fitted to fight regular war-vessels. As a rule they rarely made the effort. When they did they sometimes betrayed the faults common to all irregular fighting men. Many instances could be cited where they ran away from, submitted tamely to, or made but a weak defence against, equal or even inferior forces. But such was by no means always the case. Exceptionally good commanders were able to get their crews into a condition when they were formidable foes to any man-of-war of their weight in the world; for, though naturally the discipline of a privateer was generally slack, yet the men who shipped on board her were sure to be skilful seamen, and trained to the use of arms,

[1] Adams, viii. 200.

so that, with a little drilling, they made good fighting stuff. The
larger privateers several times captured little British national vessels,
cutters and the like. On February 26th, 1815, the famous Baltimore
schooner *Chasseur*, of fourteen guns and seventy men, under Thomas
Boyle, captured in fair fight the British war-schooner *St. Lawrence*,
Lieutenant Henry Cranmer Gordon,[1] of almost exactly the same
force, after an obstinate action.[2]

Some of the bloodiest engagements of the war were between
British cutting-out parties and privateers. The two most notable
cases were those in which the two famous New York privateers, the
Prince de Neufchâtel and the *General Armstrong*, were the chief
figures. Both were large swift vessels. The latter was a brig
and the former a brigantine, and both had committed exceptionally
severe ravages on British commerce, having been unusually lucky
in the prizes they had made. As with all of these privateers, it is
difficult to get at full particulars of them, and, in some accounts, both
are called schooners. The *General Armstrong* was armed with one
heavy long-gun and eight long 9's. The *Prince de Neufchâtel*
carried 17 guns, 9's and 12's, being the larger vessel of the two.

On the 26th of September, 1814, the *General Armstrong* was lying
at anchor in the road of Fayal. Her master was Samuel Chester
Reid,[3] and she had a crew of ninety men on board. A British
squadron, composed of the *Plantagenet*, 74, Captain Robert Lloyd (2) ;
Rota, 38, Captain Philip Somerville (1) ; and *Carnation*, 18, Commander
George Bentham, hove in sight towards sundown. Experience had
taught the Americans not to trust to the neutrality of a weak Power
for protection ; and Reid warped his brig near shore, and made ready
to repel any attempt to cut her out. Soon after dark Captain Lloyd
sent in four boats. He asserted that they were only sent to find out
what the strange brig was ; but of course no such excuse was

---

[1] The *St. Lawrence* mounted twelve 12-pr. carronades and one long 9, and had,
according to James (vi. 370, ed. 1837), 51 men and boys, besides passengers, on board.
She lost 6 killed and 18 wounded. The *Chasseur* mounted eight 18-pr. carronades and
six long 9's. James, without specifying his authority, says that she lost 5 killed and
8 wounded, out of a complement of 115. O'Byrne (408), in his notice of Lieutenant
H. C. Gordon, entirely ignores the affair, and says that Gordon, after receiving his first
commission, on February 4th, 1815, never served again. I cannot find any official
report of the action.—W. L. C.

[2] Letter of Boyle, March 2nd, 1815.

[3] His father, while serving in the British Navy, had been made prisoner by the
Americans, whose cause he had subsequently joined. He had in the meantime married
a colonial lady, Rebecca Chester. The son, born in 1783, survived until 1861. He
was originally in the U.S. Navy.—W. L. C.

tenable.   Four boats, filled with armed men, would not approach
a strange vessel after nightfall merely to reconnoitre her.   At any
rate, after repeatedly warning them off, Reid fired into them, and
they withdrew.   He then anchored, with springs on his cables,
nearer shore, and made every preparation for the desperate struggle
which he knew awaited him.   Lloyd did not keep him long in
suspense.   Angered at the check he had received, he ordered seven
boats of the squadron, manned by about a hundred and eighty picked
men, to attack the privateer.   He intended the *Carnation* to accompany them, to take part in the attack; but the winds proved too
light and baffling, and the boats made the attempt alone.   Under
the command of Lieutenant William Matterface, first of the *Rota*,
they pulled in under cover of a small reef of rocks, where they lay
for some time; and, at about midnight, they advanced to the attack.
The Americans were on the alert, and, as soon as they saw the boats
rowing in through the night, they opened with the pivot-gun, and
immediately afterwards with their long 9's.   The British replied
with their boat carronades, and, pulling spiritedly on amidst a
terrific fire of musketry from both sides, laid the schooner aboard
on her bow and starboard quarter.   A murderous struggle followed.
The men-of-wars' men slashed at the nettings and tried to clamber
up on the decks, while the privateersmen shot down the assailants,
hacked at them with cutlass and tomahawk, and thrust them through
with their long pikes.   The boats on the quarter were driven off;
but on the forecastle the British cut away the nettings, and gained
the deck.   All three of the American mates were killed or disabled,
and their men were beaten back; but Reid went forward on the run,
with the men of the after division, and tumbled the boarders back
into their boats.   This put an end to the assault.   Two boats were
sunk, most of the wounded being saved as the shore was so near;
two others were captured; and the others, crippled from their losses,
and loaded with dead and disabled men, crawled back towards the
squadron.   The loss of the Americans was slight.   Two were killed
and seven wounded.   The fearful slaughter in the British boats
proved that they had done all that the most determined courage
could do.   Two-thirds of the assailants were killed or wounded.[1]

[1] The number killed was 34, including Lieutenants William Matterface and
Charles R. Norman.   The number wounded was 86, including Lieutenant Richard
Rawle, Lieutenant Thomas Park, R.M., Purser William Benge Basden, and two
Midshipmen.—W. L. C.

The brig's long 24 had been knocked off its carriage by a carronade shot, but it was replaced and the deck again cleared for action. Next day the *Carnation* came in to destroy the privateer, but was driven off by the judicious use of the long-gun. However, as soon as the wind became favourable, the *Carnation* again advanced. Further resistance being hopeless, the *General Armstrong* was scuttled and burned, and the Americans retreated to the land.[1]

The *Prince de Neufchâtel* was attacked on October 11th, 1814. She had made a very successful cruise, and had on board goods to the amount of 300,000 dollars, but had manned and sent in so many prizes that only forty of her crew were left, while thirty-seven prisoners were confined in the hold. At midday on the 11th, while off Nantucket, the British frigate *Endymion*, 40, Captain Henry Hope, discovered her and made sail in chase. Soon after nightfall it fell calm, and the frigate despatched her boats, with one hundred and eleven men, under the command of the first lieutenant, Abel Hawkins, to carry the brigantine by boarding. The latter triced up the boarding nettings, loaded her guns with grape and bullets, and made everything ready for the encounter. The rapid tide held back the boats as they drew near, but they laid the brigantine aboard, and a most desperate engagement followed. Some of the British actually cut through the nettings and reached the deck, but they were killed by the privateersmen as fast as they mounted. Once the boats were repulsed ; again they came on, but again they were beaten back ; the launch was captured, and the others pulled back to the frigate. The slaughter had been very heavy, considering the number of combatants. The victorious privateer had lost seventeen killed, and fifteen badly, and nine slightly, wounded, leaving but nine untouched. Of the British, about half were killed or wounded, including among the former Lieutenant Hawkins himself, and, in addition, the launch was taken with the twenty-eight men in her.[2] The master of the *Prince de Neufchâtel* was John Ordronaux, a New Yorker. His name caused the Captain of the *Endymion* to put him down as a Frenchman.

The commerce-destroying exploits of the American cruisers had a very distinct effect in furthering the readiness of the British to come to terms. They helped to make England willing to

[1] Letter of Captain S. C. Reid, Oct. 7th, 1814, and of Consul John B. Dabney Oct. 5th, 1814. James, vi. 349 (Ed. 1837). Letter of Captain Lloyd ; Adams, viii. 202.
[2] Coggeshall's 'History of American Privateers,' 241 ; James, vi. 362 (Ed. 1837).

accept a peace by which neither side lost or gained anything.   The great service rendered by the American commerce-destroyers in the war of 1812 must not be blinked ; but on the other hand, the lesson it teaches must not be misread.   The swift cruisers cut up the British trade terribly, and rendered it unsafe even for the British coasters to go from one port to another ; but it cannot be too often insisted that the blockading squadrons of Great Britain almost destroyed both the foreign and the coast commerce of the United States.   The commerce-destroyers of America did their part toward making the war of 1812 a draw ; but the great fighting fleets of England came near making the war a disastrous defeat for the Americans.   The people of the British seaports, especially the merchants and ship-owners, were sorely distressed by the war ; but in America whole regions were brought by the blockade into a condition of such discontent with their government, that they openly talked treason.   Moreover, the privateers, in spite of their ravages, produced no such effect on the contest as the regular vessels of the American navy.   The victories of the American warships kept up the heart of the United States as no privateer cruiser, however successful, could keep it up ; and Macdonough's triumph on Lake Champlain had more effect on the negotiations for peace than the burning and plundering in the Irish Channel.

The American sloops of war were almost or quite as swift as the privateers, and were formidable fighters to boot.   The smaller man-of-war brigs (with the exception of the *Enterprise*) were picked up at different times by British cruisers, being able neither to run nor to fight.   Of the large sloops there were by the spring of 1814 four all told, including the *Hornet*, 20, and the newly built *Wasp*, *Peacock*, and *Frolic*, 22.   These vessels were as successful in breaking the blockade as the privateers, and more success-ful in evading capture ; and each of them was a menace, not merely to the British merchantmen, but to all British armed vessels less in force than a heavy corvette or a small frigate.   Like the privateers, they cruised by preference on the seas where the British merchantmen and British armed vessels were most numerous, the immediate neighbourhood of the British Islands being a favourite haunt.

The British Admiralty had at least partially solved the problem of meeting the American frigates, by providing that the British frigates, which were usually lighter ships, should cruise in couples

or small squadrons, and should avoid encounters with American
frigates of superior force; but it made no such provision in the
case of the sloops, nor was there any evidence of endeavour to make
better the gunnery of the sloops. In consequence, the various sloop
actions with which the war closed ended as favourably for the
Americans as had the early fights in 1812. The ordinary British
sloop was the 18-gun brig. She was not so good a vessel as the
American ship-sloop carrying twenty or twenty-two guns. There
were corresponding ship-sloops in the British Navy; but no effort
was made to substitute them for the brig-sloops, nor were they so
employed as to bring them into contact with the *Wasp*, the *Hornet*,
and their fellows. Moreover, the brig-sloops proved on the whole
to be far more inferior to their opponents in skill than they were in
force. The gunnery of the Americans showed itself to the end
much better than the gunnery of the British. The former used
sights for their guns, and were trained to try to make each shot tell,
while even in Nelson's day, and still more after his death, the
British cared more for rapidity of fire than for exactness of aim.
They sought to get so close to their antagonists that the shots could
not well miss. But a badly aimed gun has infinite capacity for
missing, even at close range.

The first of the new American sloops to get to sea was the *Frolic*, 22,
so named after the prize captured by the old *Wasp* in 1812. She
cruised for a couple of months under Master-Commandant Joseph
Bainbridge, and, among other deeds, sank a large Carthagenan
privateer, nearly a hundred of her crew of Spaniards, West Indians,
and the like, being drowned. Finally, on April 20th, 1814, she was
captured after a long chase by the British 36-gun frigate *Orpheus*,
Captain Hugh Pigot (3), and the 12-gun schooner *Shelburne*, Lieutenant David Hope.[1]

The *Peacock*, 22, Captain Lewis Warrington, sailed from New
York on March 12th, 1814. On April 29th, in latitude 27° 47′ N.,
longitude 80° 7′ W., he encountered a small convoy of merchantmen under the protection of the British 18-gun brig-sloop *Epervier*,
Commander Richard Walter Wales. The *Peacock* had one hundred
and sixty-six men in crew, and carried two long 12's and twenty
32-pr. carronades, like the rest of her class. The *Epervier* had
one hundred and eighteen in crew, and carried sixteen 32-pr. and
two 18-pr. carronades. In broadside force the difference was about

---

[1] The *Frolic* was added to the Royal Navy as the *Florida*.—W. L. C.

five to four.   However, Wales hauled up to engage, while the
convoy made all sail away.

The *Peacock* came down with the wind nearly aft, while the
Epervier stood toward her close hauled.   At 10.20 A.M. they
exchanged broadsides, each using the starboard battery.   The
Epervier then eased away, and the two vessels ran off side by side,
the Englishman firing his port guns, while Warrington still used
the starboard battery, aiming at the brig's hull.   The *Epervier* did

CAPTAIN LEWIS WARRINGTON, U.S.N.
(*From Gimbrede's engraving, after the portrait by Jarvis.*)

practically no damage whatsoever, while she was heavily punished
by her adversary.   Commander Wales's crew, moreover, showed a
lack of courage such as was very unusual in the service, muttering
sullenly that the American was too heavy for them.   Half an hour
after close action had begun most of the guns on the engaged side of
the *Epervier* had been dismounted by the *Peacock's* shot, or owing to
defective breeching-bolts, or carelessness in the handling ; her hull had
been struck forty-five times ; her masts were badly wounded ; there

were five feet of water in her hold; twenty-three of her men were killed or wounded;[1] and she struck her colours. The *Peacock* had lost but two men, both slightly wounded; and there had been some trifling damage aloft; but her hull was not touched. In other words, the *Epervier* was cut to pieces, and the *Peacock* hardly scratched.[2] Warrington put a prize crew on board the captured brig, and brought her in safety to the United States, though on the way the vessels were chased by two British frigates. These Warrington succeeded in drawing after his own ship, which was very fast, and could, he was sure, outsail his pursuers. The event justified his judgment. The *Peacock* again sailed on June 4th, and cruised in the mouth of the Irish Channel, round the west and northern coast of Ireland, and finally in the Bay of Biscay. She escaped from the frigates that chased her, and captured fourteen merchantmen: a record which could have been equalled by few of the privateers, although the latter devoted themselves entirely to preying on commerce.

The *Wasp*, a sister ship of the *Peacock*, and named in honour of the old *Wasp*, left Portsmouth, Virginia, on May 1st, 1814, under the command of Captain Johnston Blakely, with a very fine crew of one hundred and seventy-three men, almost exclusively New Englanders. Her cruise, both because of her signal daring and success, and because of the tragic mystery of her end, became one of the most famous in the annals of the American navy. She slipped through the blockaders and ran right across to the mouth of the English Channel. There she remained for several weeks, burning and scuttling many ships. Finally, on June 28th, in the morning, she made out. a sail which proved to be the 18-gun British brig-sloop *Reindeer*, Commander William Manners. The *Reindeer* was armed with 24-pr. carronades and had a crew of one hundred and eighteen, so that Manners knew that he had to do with a foe who was half as heavy again as himself. But in all the British Navy, rich as it was in men who cared but little for odds of size or strength, there was no more gallant or more skilful commander than Manners, nor were there braver or better trained men than those under him. As day broke the *Reindeer* made sail for the *Wasp* with the wind

---

[1] Among the severely wounded was Lieutenant John Hackett.—W. L. C.

[2] James's 'Naval Occurrences,' 243; Navy Dept. MSS., Letters of Warrington April 29th and June 1st; American State Papers, xiv. 427; Memoirs of Admiral Codrington, i. 322.

M

nearly aft. The sky was cloudy and the light breeze barely rippled the sea, so that the vessels stood on almost even keels. All the morning they slowly drew together, each captain striving to get or to keep the weather-gage. The afternoon had well begun before the rolling drums beat to quarters, and it was three o'clock when the two sloops came into collision. The *Wasp* was running slowly off with the wind a little forward of the port beam, brailing up her mizen, while the *Reindeer* closed on her weather quarter with the flying-jib hoisted. When but sixty yards apart the British fired

CAPTAIN JOHNSTON BLAKELY, U.S.N.
(From an engraved portrait by Gimbrede.)

their shifting 12-pr. carronade, loaded with round and grape, into the *Wasp*. This was the only gun in either ship that would bear, and five times it was discharged, before, at twenty-six minutes past three, Captain Blakely, finding that the *Reindeer* was not coming on his beam, put his helm a-lee and luffed up, firing his port guns from aft forward as they bore. A biscuit could have been tossed from one vessel to the other as the two lay abreast. The heavy metal of the American was too much for the *Reindeer*. Manners himself was mortally wounded, and was hit again and again, but he would not leave his post, and continued to cheer and hearten his men. The vessels had come close together; and, putting his helm

a-weather, he ran the *Wasp* aboard on her port quarter, and called
the boarders forward to try the last desperate chance of a hand to
hand conflict.   But Blakely fought with the same courage and skill
as were shown by his antagonist, and used his greatly superior force
to the utmost advantage.   As the vessels ground together the men
hacked and thrust at one another through the open port holes.   The
Americans gathered aft to repel boarders, the marines, cutlassmen
and pikemen clustering close to the bulwarks, while the topmen
kept up a deadly fire.   Then through the smoke the British
boarders sprang, only to die or to be hurled back on their own
decks, while the *Reindeer's* Marines kept answering the American
fire.   As his men recoiled, Manners, mortally wounded, but high
of heart and unconquerable save by death, sprang, sword in hand,
into the rigging to lead them on once more; and they rallied behind him.   At that moment a ball from the *Wasp's* main-top
crashed through his head, and, with his sword closely grasped in
his right hand, he fell back dead on his own deck, while above him
the flag for which he had given his life still floated.   As he fell
Blakely passed the word to board.   With wild hurrahs the
Americans swarmed over the hammock nettings; the wreck of
the British crew was swept away by the rush; and the Captain's
Clerk, Mr. Richard Collins, the senior officer left, surrendered the
brig, just eighteen minutes after the *Wasp* had fired her first broadside.   Twenty-six of the *Wasp's* crew and sixty-seven[1] of the
Reindeer's were killed or wounded.[2]

In neither navy was any ship ever more bravely and more
skilfully fought than either the *Wasp* or the *Reindeer*, and the
defeated side showed themselves heroes indeed.   In courage,
seamanship and gunnery, there was nothing to choose between
the two combatants; and the advantage lay with the nation whose
forethought had provided the better ship.   In all these naval duels
no victorious ship, except the *Shannon*, suffered so heavy a relative
loss as the *Reindeer* inflicted on the *Wasp*, and, before accepting
defeat, the *Reindeer* herself had suffered more than any other
defeated ship, except the *Frolic*.

<hr/>

[1] The *Reindeer* lost 25 killed and 42 wounded.   Among the killed were Commander Manners and Purser John Thomas Barton; among the wounded, Lieutenant
Thomas Chambers, Master's Mate Matthew Mitchell, and Midshipman Henry Hardi-
man.   Manners was a young Commander of February 7th, 1812, and was an excellent
and idolised officer.—W. L. C.

[2] Letter of Captain Blakely, July 8th, 1814; Cooper, ii. 287; James, vi. 294 (Ed. 1837).

The *Wasp* burned her prize, and sailed into the French port of Lorient to refit.   On August 27th she sailed again, making two prizes in the first three days.   On the 1st of September she came upon a convoy of ten sail under the protection of the *Armada*, 74, bound for Gibraltar.   Confident in her speed and in the seamanship of the crew, Blakely hovered round the convoy, though chased off again and again by the two-decker, and finally cut off and captured a ship laden with iron and brass cannon, muskets, and other military stores of value.   He was then on a cruising ground traversed in every direction by British warships and merchantmen, and on the evening of the same day he made out four sail, of whom it after-wards turned out that three were cruisers, being the British ship-sloop *Tartarus*, 20, and the brig-sloops *Avon*, 18, and *Castilian*, 18. Blakely soon became convinced that three of the four were hostile vessels of war.   Nevertheless he determined to engage one of them after nightfall, hoping to sink or capture her before either of her consorts could come to her aid.   It was a very bold determination, but it was justified by the *Wasp's* efficiency as a fighting machine. Blakely had less men in crew than when he fought the *Reindeer*, but, profiting by his experience with the latter, he had taken on board her 12-pr. carronade.

The three British sloops were in chase of an American privateer schooner, while the American sloop in her turn chased them.   The privateer outsailed her pursuers, and the latter gradually drew apart until the headmost, the *Castilian*, was nine miles distant from the rearmost, the *Avon*, when, late in the afternoon, the *Wasp* began to approach the latter.   The *Avon* was under the command of Com-mander the Hon. James Arbuthnot.   She carried twenty guns, including sixteen 32-pr. carronades, a light shifting carronade, two long guns as bow-chasers, and another light long-gun as stern-chaser. Her crew numbered one hundred and seventeen.   The odds against her in point of force were thus far less than in the case of the *Reindeer*, being about what they were against the *Epervier*, or five to four in weight of broadside.   As the *Wasp* approached, the *Avon*, not desiring to encounter her single-handed, began signalling with her lanterns to her consorts ahead, and when she met with no response she fired signal shots to them.[1]

Soon after 9 P.M. the *Wasp*, steering free through the darkness,

---

[1] According to some British accounts, the night-signals and the shots were directed to the *Wasp*.   James, 297 [ed. 1837].—W. L. C.

got on the weather quarter of the *Avon*, and the vessels exchanged hails. The action began by the *Wasp* firing her 12-pr. carronade, and the *Avon* responding, first with her stern-chaser, and then with her aftermost port guns. Blakely put his helm up lest his adversary should try to escape, ran to leeward of her, fired his port broadside into her quarter, and then ranged up on her starboard beam.[1] A furious night fight followed at very short range. The *Wasp's* men did not know the name of their antagonist, but her black hull loomed clearly through the night, and aloft in her tops the clustered forms of her sailors could be seen against the sky. Four round shot struck the *Wasp's* hull, killing two men; and another man was wounded by a wad. This was all she suffered below, but aloft her rigging was a good deal cut, for the practice of the *Avon* was bad, her guns being pointed too high. The *Wasp's* fire, on the contrary, was directed with deadly precision. The *Avon's* hull was riddled through and through, until there were seven feet of water in the hold, the lower masts were wounded, and the standing and running rigging were cut to pieces. Five of the starboard guns were dismounted, and forty-two of the crew killed or wounded.[2] Less than three quarters of an hour[3] after the beginning of the action she struck her colours.

While Blakely was lowering away the boat to take possession, the *Castilian*, Commander George Lloyd (actg.), made her appearance, and soon afterwards the *Tartarus* also approached.[4] They had been recalled by the noise of the cannonade, and had come up under a press of sail. When the *Castilian* came in sight Blakely again called his men to quarters, and made ready for battle; but the appearance of the *Tartarus* forced him to relinquish the idea of fighting. Accordingly, the braces having been cut away, the *Wasp* was put before the wind until new ones could be rove. The *Castilian* followed her, but the *Avon* had begun to fire minute-guns and make signals of distress, and Commander Lloyd deemed it his duty to put back to her assistance. He accordingly returned

---

[1] Blakely's letter, Sept. 8th, 1814.

[2] The number killed was 10, including Lieutenant John Prendergast; the number wounded was 32, including Commander Arbuthnot, Lieutenant John Harvey (4), and Midshipman John Travers.—W. L C

[3] According to the British accounts, the action began at 9.26 P.M., and the *Avon* surrendered at 10.12 P.M.; but James (vi. 298, ed. 1837) shows grounds for believing that the surrender occurred at nearly 11 P.M.—W. L. C.

[4] *Niles's Register*, vi. 216.

to his consort, after firing his lee guns over the weather quarter of the *Wasp*, cutting her rigging slightly, but not touching a man, nor doing any other damage. He consoled himself by reporting that if he had been able to attack the *Wasp* she would have "fallen an easy prey" to him, and that he did not doubt that his broadside was "most destructive."[1]   The *Avon* sank soon afterwards.

James comments on this action as follows : "The gallantry of the *Avon's* crew cannot for a moment be questioned, but the gunnery of the latter appears to have been not a whit better than, to the discredit of the British Navy, had frequently before been displayed in combats of this kind.   Nor, from the specimen given by the *Castilian*, is it likely that she would have performed any better."[2] As for the *Wasp*, she had performed a most notable feat of cool daring and skilful prowess.

She next cruised southward and westward, taking and scuttling or sending in several prizes, one of much value.   On October 9th she spoke the Swedish brig *Adonis*, which had on board a couple of the officers formerly of the *Essex*, on their way to England from Brazil. This was the last that was heard of the gallant *Wasp*.   How she perished none ever knew.   All that is certain is that she was never seen again.   In all the navies of the world at that time there were no better sloop, and no braver or better captain and crew.

The blockading squadrons watched with special vigilance the harbours containing American frigates.   Three frigates cruised off Boston, where the *Constitution* lay, and four off New York, where Decatur kept the *President* ready to put to sea at the first opportunity.   The *Constitution*, always a lucky ship, managed to take advantage of a temporary absence of the three frigates that were watching her and slipped to sea.   The *President* made a similar attempt, but fared badly.

The *Peacock* and *Hornet* were lying with her, all three intending to start on a cruise for the East Indies, where they hoped to do much damage to British trade.   The blockading squadron off the port consisted of the *Majestic*, 56, Captain John Hayes, with long 32-prs. on the main-deck, and 42-pr. carronades on the spar-deck, the *Endymion*, 40, Captain Henry Hope, carrying twenty-six 24-prs. on her main-deck, and twenty-two 32-pr. carronades, and two bow-chasers on her spar-deck, with a crew of about three hundred and

---

[1] Letter of Lloyd, Sept. 2nd, 1814; Adams, viii. 190.
[2] James, vi. 299 (Ed. 1837).

fifty men; and the two 38-gun frigates *Pomone*, Captain John
Richard Lumley, and *Tenedos*, Captain Hyde Parker (3).   On
January 14th, 1815, a severe snow-storm blew them off the coast.
Hayes was sure that the *President* would take advantage of their
absence to slip out; and he shaped his course back with a view to
the course which the escaping American would be apt to take.[1]
The event justified his judgment.

The *President* had tried to put to sea in the gale, but she struck
on the bar, where she beat heavily for an hour and a half, springing
her masts and becoming so hogged and twisted that she would have
put back to port if the storm had not blown so furiously as to
render it impossible.[2]   Before daylight next morning, Sandy
Hook bearing W.N.W., fifteen leagues distant, she ran into the
British squadron, and a headlong chase followed.   During the early
part of the day, when the wind was still strong, the powerful
Majestic went better than any of the other ships, and fired occasionally at the *President* without effect.   The *Pomone* towards
noon began to gain rapidly, and would have overtaken the *President*
had she not been sent to investigate the *Tenedos*, which turned up in
an unexpected quarter, and was mistaken for another American ship.
In the afternoon the wind became light and baffling, and the *Endymion* forged to the front and gained rapidly on the *President*, which
was making a large amount of water in consequence of the injuries
which she had received while on the bar.   For three hours the ships
occasionally interchanged shots from their bow and stern chasers.
At about half-past five the *Endymion* drew up close, and began to
pour in her broadsides on the *President's* starboard quarter, where
not a gun of the latter would bear.   For half an hour the *President*
bore the battering as best she might, unable to retaliate; and she
did not like to alter her course, lest she should lessen her chance of
escape.   Moreover, Decatur expected the *Endymion* to come up
abeam.   But Captain Hope kept his position by yawing, not wishing
to forfeit his advantage.   In this he was quite right, for the
President suffered more during the half-hour when she had to endure
the unreturned fire of her opponent than during the entire remainder
of the combat.   At six o'clock Decatur found his position unbearable,

---

[1] Letters of Rear-Adm. the Hon. Sir Henry Hotham, Jan. 23rd, 1815, and Captain
Hayes, Jan. 17th, 1815.
[2] Letters of Decatur, Jan. 18th and March 6th, 1814; Report of court-martial,
April 20th, 1815.

and kept off, heading to the south.   The two frigates ran abreast, the Americans using the starboard, the British the port, battery.   Decatur tried to close with his antagonist, but the latter, being both a lighter and a swifter ship, hauled up and frustrated the attempt.   The *President* then endeavoured to dismantle the British frigate, and thus get rid of her.   In this she was successful.   The *Endymion's* sails were cut from her yards, and she fell astern, the fire gradually dying away on both sides.   The last shot was fired from the *President.*[1] Three hours afterwards, at eleven o'clock, the *Pomone* caught up with the *President*, and gave her two broadsides, which killed and wounded a considerable number of people.   The *Endymion* was out of sight astern.   Decatur did not return the fire, but surrendered, and was taken possession of by the *Tenedos.*   He delivered his sword to Captain Hayes of the *Majestic.*   In the *President* twenty-four were killed, and fifty wounded;[2] in the *Endymion* eleven were killed and fourteen wounded.   Two days afterwards, in a gale, all three of the *President's*, and two of the *Endymion's* masts went by the board, and the *Endymion*, in addition, had to throw overboard her quarter-deck and forecastle guns.

This was an important success for the British.   It was won by the vigilance of Captain Hayes, and the foresight of the British in stationing ample blockading squadrons off the harbours where the American frigates lay.   The *Endymion* was a much lighter ship than the *President*, and could not be expected to capture her, for the *President* had a hundred more men in crew, two more guns in broadside on the main-deck, and 42's instead of 32's on the spar-deck. What Captain Hope could do he did; that is, hang on the quarter of an enemy who had no choice but flight, pouring in broadsides which could not be returned, and then, when he did engage, keep up the battle as long as possible, and do as much damage as he could, before dropping out of the combat.   The relative loss is of course no criterion of the merits of the fight, because the *President* was trying to escape.   She did not attempt to return the earliest and most destructive broadsides of the *Endymion*, and afterwards devoted her attention chiefly to the effort to unrig her opponent, while part of her loss was caused by the two unreturned broadsides of the *Pomone.*

---

[1] Log of *Pomone*, 'Naval Chronicle,' xxxiii. 370.

[2] Neither Hope nor Hayes in his letter gives details of the loss suffered by the *President.*   James (vi. 365, ed. 1837), without specifying his authority, says that the *President* lost 35 killed and 70 wounded.—W. L. C.

So far as the *Endymion* is concerned, Decatur seems to have done all he could, and no severe censure could be passed on him for surrendering when attacked by a fresh frigate, with another close astern. It certainly seems, however, that it would have been worth his while to try at least a few broadsides on the *Pomone*. A lucky shot might have taken out one of her masts, and then he would have had a chance to dispose of the *Tenedos* and make good

CAPTAIN CHARLES STEWART, U.S.N.

(*After Goodman's engraving, from a portrait by Wood.*)

his escape. Of course it was not much of a chance, but there were plenty of captains in both the British and the American navies who would certainly have taken advantage of it.

After escaping from Boston, the *Constitution*, 44, Captain Charles Stewart, went to Bermuda, thence to the Bay of Biscay, and finally towards Madeira. On February 20th, 1815, the latter island bearing W.S.W. 60 leagues, she encountered two British ships, the frigate-built *Cyane*, 22, Captain Gordon Thomas Falcon, and the flush-decked *Levant*, 20, Captain the Hon. George Douglas. The *Cyane* carried twenty-two 32-pr. carronades on her main-deck, and, on her spar-deck, two long 6's, eight 18-pr. carronades, and a 12-pr. boat carronade. The *Levant* carried eighteen 32-pr. carronades, and two long 9's, together with a 12-pr. boat carronade. The *Cyane* had about 170, and the *Levant* about 130 in crew. The *Constitution* carried about 450 men.

The two ships together could not be considered as powerful as a 38-gun frigate like the *Java* or the *Guerrière*, which the *Constitution* had already captured. Nevertheless the two British Captains very gallantly, but not very discreetly, came to the conclusion to try their luck with the *Constitution*. Five years earlier two such vessels, the *Rainbow* and the *Avon*, had fought a draw with the French 40-gun frigate *Néréide*, the odds against them being just about as heavy as against the *Cyane* and *Levant;* but on this occasion the two small craft had to deal with a much more formidable antagonist than any French frigate; and nothing in their own skill, or in the events of the preceding three years of warfare with the Americans, warranted their making the experiment.

The *Constitution* came down off the wind, while the two ships hauled close to the wind to try to weather her, so as to delay action until after nightfall, when they hoped that the darkness would favour their manœuvres. The frigate came down too fast, however, and the British stripped to fighting canvas, and stood on the starboard tack, the *Levant* a cable's length ahead of the *Cyane*. The *Constitution's* long-guns would have enabled her to cut the two craft to pieces without damage to herself, as she was to windward; but this would have involved the risk of one or the other of them escaping; and she ranged up to windward of them, with the *Levant* on her port bow and the *Cyane* on her port quarter, close enough for the marines to begin firing soon after the engagement began.[1] There was a bright moon, but the smoke hung so heavily that at one time the firing ceased, the antagonists not being able to distinguish one another. There was some dexterous manœuvring, all three ships endeavouring to rake or avoid being raked, and at 6.50 P.M., just forty minutes after the beginning of the action, the *Cyane* submitted and was taken possession of.

---

[1] Letter of Captain Charles Stewart, May 20th, 1815; Log of *Constitution* Feb. 20th, 1815; 'Naval Chronicle,' xxxiii. 466; Niles, viii. 219, 363, 383.

When the prize had been manned, Stewart made sail after her consort, which had run off to leeward. Captain Douglas had only gone out of the combat to refit, however, and, as soon as he had rove new braces, he hauled to the wind and stood back in search of his consort, an act of loyal gallantry which should not be forgotten. At 8.50 P.M.[1] he met the huge frigate, and passed under her battery, the *Constitution* and *Levant* going in opposite directions and exchanging broadsides. Finding that the *Cyane* had surrendered, and it being, of course, utterly impossible for a ship of his force to fight the *Constitution*, Douglas crowded all sail to escape, but was overtaken and captured half an hour afterwards. Of the 302 men on board the British ships, 41 were killed or wounded :[2] of the 451 men on board the *Constitution*, 15 were killed or wounded, and she was hulled eleven times, more often than by either the *Guerrière* or the *Java*. She was of such superior force that only a very real inferiority of skill on her part would have enabled her enemies to make it a drawn combat. As a matter of fact both sides fought well ; but the *Constitution* captured her foes without suffering any material loss or damage. The gallantry of the two British Captains was conspicuous, but they did not show good judgment in engaging, for, as has been said, there was nothing in their experience to justify the belief that their conduct would result otherwise than it did, that is, in an easy victory for their antagonist.[3]

Stewart took his prizes to the Cape de Verde Islands, and anchored in Porto Praya on March 10th. A hundred of the prisoners were landed to help fit out a brig which was taken as a cartel. Next day the weather was thick and foggy, with fresh breezes, and at noon the upper canvas of a large vessel was suddenly made out, just above the fog bank, sailing towards the harbour. Immediately afterwards the canvas of two other ships was discovered, and it became evident that all three were heavy frigates. In fact they were the very three ships which had blockaded the *Constitution* off Boston : the *Leander*, 50, Captain Sir George Ralph Collier, K.C.B. ; the *Newcastle*, 50, Captain Lord George

[1] The time given in the British accounts is 8.30 P.M., and the time of striking at 10.30 P.M.—W. L. C.

[2] The *Levant* had 6 killed and 16 wounded ; the *Cyane*, 6 killed and 13 wounded. —W. L. C.

[3] Captains Douglas and Falcon were tried on board the *Akbar*, at Halifax, on June 28th, 1815, for the loss of their ships, and were most honourably acquitted.— W. L. C.

Stuart; and the *Acasta*, 40, Captain Alexander Robert Kerr.[1] Captain Stewart knew that the neutrality of the port would not save him, and that there was not a minute to lose if he wished to escape. As it was, only the perfect training of his officers and men enabled him to get out. Signalling to his prizes to follow him, he cut his cables, and, in less than ten minutes from the time when the first frigate was seen, all three vessels were standing out of the harbour, the *Levant* being commanded by Lieutenant Hoffman, and the *Cyane* by Lieutenant Ballard. The prisoners on shore promptly manned a Portuguese battery and delivered a furious, but ill-directed fire at the retreating *Constitution*, *Levant*, and *Cyane*. They stood out of the harbour in that order on the port tack, all to windward of the British squadron. The Americans made out the force of the strangers correctly, and the *Acasta* discerned the force of the Americans with equal clearness; but the *Leander* and *Newcastle* mistook the two sloops for American frigates—an error, by the way, which the American Captain Rodgers had once committed in regard to a couple of British ships which he encountered, a sloop and a little 12-pr. frigate.

The British ships made all sail in chase, the *Newcastle* and *Leander* on the *Constitution's* lee quarter, and the *Acasta* well to windward of them. In an hour the *Cyane* had fallen so far astern and to leeward that Captain Stewart signalled to Hoffman to tack lest he should be cut off. Hoffman did so, and escaped unmolested, no British ship following him. He took his prize safely to the United States. Half an hour later the *Newcastle* opened on the *Constitution*, but the shot fell short. Though so close, the commanders of the two 50-gun ships still apparently mistook the *Levant*, which was a low flush-decked sloop, for an American frigate. At three o'clock she had sagged so as to be in the same position as that from which the *Cyane* had just been rescued. Accordingly, Captain Stewart signalled to her to tack. She did so, whereupon all three British ships tacked in pursuit. Such a movement is inexplicable, for, even had the *Levant* been a frigate, the rearmost 50-gun ship alone would have been enough to send after her, while the other two should not have abandoned the chase of the *Constitution*. It is said that there was a mistake in the signalling, but the blunder was never satisfactorily explained.

[1] Log of *Constitution*, March 11th, 1815; Letters of Lieut. Hoffman, April 10th, and of Lieut. Ballard, May 2nd; Marshall's 'Naval Biography,' ii. 533.

At any rate, Stewart got off in safety, and, when he learned of the peace, returned to New York.

Meanwhile Lieutenant Ballard took the *Levant* back to Porto Praya, and anchored a couple of hundred yards from a heavy battery on the shore. The event justified the wisdom of Captain Stewart in not trusting to the neutrality of the port. All three British frigates opened upon the *Levant* as soon as they got into the harbour, while the British prisoners on shore fired the guns of the battery at her. The *Levant* was at anchor, and did not resist; and the gunnery of her assailants was so bad that not a man in her was killed by the broadsides of the three heavy frigates, though she was a stationary target in smooth water. The chief effect of the fire was to damage the houses of the Portuguese town.

A week after the *President's* effort to run the blockade out of New York, the *Peacock* and *Hornet* made the same attempt, with more success. On January 22nd a strong north-westerly gale began to blow, and the two sloops at once prepared to take advantage of the heavy weather. They passed the bar by daylight under storm canvas, the British frigates lying-to in the south-east, in plain sight from the decks of the sloops. A few days out they parted company, intending to meet at Tristan d'Acunha.

The *Hornet* was then under the command of Captain James Biddle, and she had on board a crew of about one hundred and forty men.[1] She reached the island on the 23rd of March, and was about to anchor, when she made out a strange sail, which proved to be the British brig-sloop *Penguin*, 18, Commander James Dickinson (3), with a crew of one hundred and thirty-two men, she having taken on board twelve extra Marines from the *Medway*, 74. The *Hornet* carried twenty guns, all 32-pr. carronades, except two long 12's for bow-chasers. The *Penguin* carried nineteen guns: sixteen 32-pr. carronades, two long 6's as bow-chasers, and a 12-pr. carronade. The difference in force was trifling, but, such as it was, it was in favour of the Americans.

The two ships began action at 1.40 P.M., within musket-shot of one another, running on the starboard tack, the *Penguin* to wind-

---

[1] Her muster rolls, in the Treasury Department at Washington, show that when she left New York she had about 146 officers and crew all told, including 20 marines; but she had manned a prize. The same rolls show the names of 122 prisoners which she took out of the *Penguin*; and ten of the *Penguin's* crew were killed in the fight or died immediately afterwards.

ward.[1] After a quarter of an hour of close action Commander Dickinson put his helm a-weather to run his adversary aboard. Almost at the same moment he was mortally wounded, and the first lieutenant, James M'Donald, endeavoured to carry out his intentions. The *Penguin's* bowsprit came in between the *Hornet's* main and mizen rigging, but the sea was very rough, and no attempt at boarding was made. As the *Hornet* forged ahead, the *Penguin's* bowsprit

CAPTAIN JAMES BIDDLE, U.S.N.
(From Gimbrede's engraving, after the portrait by J. Wood.)

carried away her mizen shrouds, stern davits, and spanker boom, and the brig then hung on the ship's starboard quarter, so that none of the big guns could be used on either side. A British officer called out something which Biddle understood to be the word of surrender. Accordingly, he directed his marines to cease firing, and jumped on to the taffrail, but was himself at once shot and wounded

[1] Biddle's letter, March 25th, 1815; M'Donald's letter, April 6th, 1815; Vice-Adm. Tyler to Commander Dickinson, Jan. 3rd, 1815; James, vi. 498; Niles, viii. 345.

rather severely in the neck by two of the Marines on the *Penguin's* forecastle, both of whom were killed in another moment by the marines of the *Hornet*. As the ships drew apart the *Penguin's* foremast went overboard. Her hull was riddled, and most of the guns on her engaged side were dismounted, while thirty-eight of her men were killed or wounded.[1] Thereupon, she struck her colours at two minutes past two, but twenty-two minutes after the first gun had been fired. In the *Hornet* one man was killed, and ten were wounded, chiefly by musketry fire, for not a round shot struck her hull. Next day Biddle destroyed his prize.

This was the last regular action of the war. In it the British displayed their usual gallantry, but it is astonishing that their gunnery should have continued so bad. Dickinson laid down his life for the flag which he served; and when a man does that it is difficult to criticise him; but the gunnery of the *Penguin* was certainly as poor as that of any of the British ships in 1812. The *Hornet* showed the utmost efficiency in every way. There was no falling-off from her already very high standard of seamanship and gunnery.

Next day the *Peacock* joined the *Hornet*, and on April 2nd the two started for the East Indies. On the 27th of the month they made sail after what they supposed to be an Indiaman, but, when they got close, discovered, to their consternation, that she was the *Cornwallis*, 74, Captain John Bayley, bearing the flag of Rear-Admiral Sir George Burlton, K.C.B. The *Peacock*, a very fast vessel, was speedily out of danger, but the *Hornet* endured a forty-eight hours' chase.[2] By daylight of the 29th the 74 was within gunshot of the sloop, and opened fire upon her. Throughout the early part of the day the *Hornet* was several times on the very edge of capture. More than once she was within fair range of the 74's long-guns, and the latter not only used her bow-chasers but also hauled up to deliver broadsides. On each occasion Biddle gained a brief respite by lightening ship, throwing overboard by degrees all his spare spars, stores, anchors, shot, boats, ballast, and all the guns but one. The guns of the *Cornwallis* were very unskilfully served, and but three shot got home. In the afternoon the sloop was saved by a shift in the wind, which brought her to windward; and, as it

---

[1] The *Penguin* had 6 killed, including Commander Dickinson, 4 mortally wounded, and 28 otherwise wounded, including Lieutenant John Elwin, Master's Mate John Holmes Bond, and Midshipman John Noyes. James Dickinson (3) was a Commander of October 21st, 1810.—W. L. C.

[2] Biddle's letter of June 10th; Log of *Hornet*.

blew fresher and fresher, she got further ahead. When day broke
the two-decker was hull down astern, and, shortly afterwards, aban-·
doned the pursuit.

The *Peacock* rounded the Cape of Good Hope, and captured four
great Indiamen, very valuable prizes. Then on the 30th of June,
in the Straits of Sunda, she fell in with the East India Company's
cruiser *Nautilus*, a brig of not half her force.[1] The *Nautilus* informed Captain Warrington of the peace, but Warrington chose to
disbelieve the information, and ordered the brig's commander, Lieutenant Charles Boyce, I.N., to haul down his colours. This the latter
refused to do until a couple of broadsides had been exchanged, when
he surrendered, having had fifteen men killed or wounded. The
Peacock was not even scratched. There was no excuse whatsoever
for Warrington's conduct. It was on a par with that of Commander
Bartholomew, of the British sloop *Erebus*, mentioned above.

This was the last expiring sputter of the war. Peace had been
declared; and, while Warrington was cruising in the far Indian seas,
his countrymen at home were building and launching ships of the
line, and Decatur was preparing to lead a squadron against the
Moorish pirates.

The United States' Navy ended the war far stronger than it had
begun it; and in the list of the United States' vessels for 1815 there
appeared two novel engines of destruction, the forerunners of their
kind, the heralds of the revolution which, fifty years later, opened a
new era in naval warfare. In the United States' Navy List for
1815 appeared the names of the war-steamer *Fulton*, and of the
Torpedo. During the war several efforts had been made by the
Americans to destroy British vessels with torpedoes, but nothing had
been accomplished beyond making some ships wary about venturing
into good anchorage, especially in Long Island Sound. The *Fulton*,
with her clumsy central wheel concealed from shot by a double hull,
with scantling so thick that light guns could not harm her, and with,
instead of broadside batteries of light guns, two 100-pr. columbiads
on pivots, was the prototype of the modern steam ironclad.

The war had ended, and the treaty [2] left matters precisely as

---

[1] 'History of the Indian Navy,' by Charles Rathbone Low, p. 285.

[2] A convention was signed at Ghent on December 24th, 1814, but the convention
was only a compromise, which left undecided all the chief points upon which the two
countries had been at issue, and which reserved certain questions for future negotiation.
As has been seen, definite news of the peace did not reach·outlying stations until two
or three months later.—W. L. C.

they were before the war began ; yet it would be idle to say that, for either side, the war was not worth fighting. To Great Britain it was probably a necessary incident of the Napoleonic struggle, for neither the British statesmen of that day, nor the people whom they governed, realised either the power or the rights of the United States.   To America it was certainly a necessary prerequisite for attaining the dignity and self-respect of a free nation.   The war left enduring memories of glory, and courage, and love of country, which more than made up for the loss of blood.   Moreover, the war taught certain lessons which should have been, although perhaps they were not, well pondered by the statesmen of the two countries, and especially by those who had, or have, to do with shaping the national policy of either.   Nations must be prepared for war : lack of preparation, laxness in organisation, invite disasters which can be but partially repaired.   The successes of the American cruisers show that no power can afford to lull itself to sleep by the dream of invincibility.   A nation should see that its ships are of the best, and that the men who man them are trained to the highest point of efficiency.   The terrific pressure of the British blockade on the American coast, and the utter impotence of America to break it, show, what has already been shown ten thousand times, that the assumption of a simple defensive in war is ruin.   Success can only come where war is waged aggressively.   It is not enough to parry the blows of the enemy.   In order to win, the foe must himself be struck, and struck heavily.

The sea-power of the British, the unceasing pressure of the British fleet, very nearly made the struggle a victory for Great Britain ; but the triumphs of the American squadrons on the lakes, and of the frigates and sloops on the ocean, and the ruthless harrying of the British trade by the American commerce-destroyers, inflicted such severe punishment as to make the British more than willing to call the fight a draw.[1]

---

[1] The history of the Hartford Convention is proof enough of how near the United States were to disaster. The impression produced in Great Britain by the prowess of the American ships is shown in a letter from the British naval historian, William James, to George Canning, in 1827, when war was once more threatened. " One [merchant] says, ' We had better cede a point or two than go to war with the United States.' ' Yes,' says another, ' for we shall get nothing but hard knocks there ! ' ' True,' adds a third, ' and what is worse than all, our seamen are more than half afraid to meet the Americans at sea ! ' Unfortunately this depression of feeling, this cowed spirit, prevails very generally over the community, even among persons well-informed on other subjects, and who, were a British seaman to be named with a Frenchman or

The man who is anxious to learn the lessons of history aright, and not merely to distort them for the gratification of his national pride, will do well to study the differences in comparative prowess shown in the single-ship fighting of the Americans, British and French, in 1780, 1798 and 1812 respectively. Readers of this history, on turning to the single-ship contests of the war of the American Revolution, will be struck by the fact that the British ships were then markedly superior to the American; whereas the difference between the former and the French was very slight. In 1798, the year in which America had a brush with France, a great change had taken place. At that time America had been forced to make reprisals at sea against the French, and three single-ship contests took place. American ships won twice against antagonists of inferior strength; and in a third case an American frigate fought a draw with a more powerful French frigate which, some time afterwards, was captured by a British frigate no stronger than her former American antagonist. Compared with their relative position in the preceding war, the French had fallen very far behindhand, and, while the British had kept their position of primacy, the Americans, leaping forward, had passed the French, and were close behind the leaders. In 1812 the relative positions of the English and French remained unchanged; but the Americans had forged still further ahead, and were better than the British.

Of course, there had been no change of national character or aptitude for the sea during this period. The simple facts were that, in the war of the American Revolution, the American ships were manned by officers and crews who were without the training of a regular service; and so, while occasionally individual ships did exceedingly well, they often did very badly. The French navy, on the other hand, was at a high point of perfection, with excellent ships, and well-trained captains and crews. Throughout that war, in the single-ship fighting, victory normally lay with the heavier vessel, whether she was British, Dutch or French. In the war of the French Revolution all that had changed. The Revolution had destroyed the discipline of the French crews and

---

Spaniard, would scoff at the comparison." (Stapleton's Correspondence of George Canning, ii. 450.) See also Lane-Poole's 'Life of Stratford Canning,' i. 302, to show how completely both sides accepted the fact that there was to be no repetition of the grievances, in the way of impressment and search, which had caused the war.

annihilated the old school of officers; while the enthusiasm with which it inspired the men could not at sea, as it did on land, in any way take the place of the lack of years of thorough training. On the other hand, the Americans had at last established a regular war navy, and their ships were officered by men carefully trained to their profession. During the next dozen years the French, constantly beaten by the British, were unable to develop an equality of prowess with the latter; and the British, accustomed to almost invariable victory over foes who were their inferiors alike in gunnery and seamanship, neglected their own gunnery. and sank into a condition of ignorant confidence that, even without preparation, they could "pull through somehow." The small American navy meanwhile was trained by years of sea service, including much scrambling warfare with the Algerines; and the American captains, fully aware of the formidable nature of the foe whom they were to meet, drilled their crews to as near perfection as might be. In such circumstances, they distinctly outmatched their average opponents, and could be encountered on equal terms only by men like Broke and Manners.

The lesson from this is so obvious that it ought not to be necessary to point it out. There is unquestionably a great difference in fighting capacity, as there is a great difference in intelligence, between certain races. But there are a number of races, each of which is intelligent, each of which has the fighting edge. Among these races, the victory in any contest will go to the man or the nation that has earned it by thorough preparation. This preparation was absolutely necessary in the days of sailing ships; but the need for it is even greater now, if it be intended to get full benefit from the delicate and complicated mechanism of the formidable war engines of the present day. The officers must spend many years, and the men not a few, in unwearied and intelligent training, before they are fit to do all that is possible with themselves and their weapons. Those who do this, whether they be Americans or British, Frenchmen, Germans or Russians, will win the victory over those who do not.

Doubtless it helps if the sailormen—the sea mechanics, as they are now—have the sea habit to start with; and they must belong to the fighting stocks. But the great factor is the steady, intelligent training in the actual practice of their profession. Any man who has had to do with bodies of men of varied race origin is forced to realise that neither courage nor cowardice is a purely national peculiarity. In an American warship of the present day, the crews are ordinarily of mixed race origin, somewhat over half being American born ; while among the remainder there are sure to be Scandinavians, Germans, men from the British Isles, and probably others, such as French Canadians or Portuguese. But the petty officers are sure to be drawn from all classes indiscriminately, simply because merit is not confined to any one class ; and, among the officers, those whose fathers came from Germany or Ireland will be found absolutely indistinguishable from their brethren of old native American origin. The Annapolis education and the after-training have stamped the officers, and the conditions of actual sea-service in modern ships under such officers have stamped the men, with a common likeness. The differences of skill, courage, application and readiness will not be found to coincide with the differences of race.

What is true of the ships of one sea power is as true of the navies of all sea powers. No education will fit a coward, a fool or a weakling for naval life. But, as a rule, the war fleets of great nations are neither commanded nor manned by cowards, fools and weaklings ; and, among brave and intelligent men of different race-stocks, when the day of battle comes, the difference of race will be found to be as nothing when compared with differences in thorough and practical training in advance.

CHAPTER XLII.

VOYAGES AND DISCOVERIES, 1803–15.

SIR CLEMENTS R. MARKHAM, K.C.B., F.R.S.

Surveying—The office of Hydrographer—Dalrymple's successors—Barrow's services at
the Admiralty—Expedition to the Congo.

BADGE OF THE MOST HONOURABLE
ORDER OF THE BATH
(MILITARY CLASSES).

*Worn, by a G.C.B., from a red ribbon across the
right shoulder; by a K.C.B., round the neck;
by a C.B., on the left breast.*

DURING the nineteenth century the British Navy conferred inestimable benefit on the
whole civilised world by discoveries, by surveys, and by the
publication of charts. Discoveries
came first, then running surveys,
and, finally, the surveys executed
on rigorously accurate principles,
and the resulting charts and sailing directions. This work was
steadily pursued both during peace
and in war time, although the
progress was naturally more rapid
in time of peace.

The need for accurate surveys
was first felt along our own shores;
and Mr. Murdoch Mackenzie,[1] succeeding his relation, Professor
Mackenzie, was head Marine Surveyor to the Admiralty from 1771
to 1778. His charts of the coasts of England were published in
1804. His cousin, Græme Spence,[2] completed a survey of the Scilly

---

[1] Murdoch Mackenzie was a Lieut. R.N. of Aug. 5th, 1779, and retired with the
rank of Commander on Jan. 31st, 1814.—W. L. C.

[2] Græme Spence was bound apprentice for seven years, in 1773, to his cousin, to
learn surveying; and he remained as assistant to Mackenzie until 1788, when,
Mackenzie's sight failing, the work of Marine Surveyor fell into Spence's hands. He
died in 1812, aged 54. He was not a commissioned naval officer, though at one
time he had a Mate and a Midshipman under him.—W. L. C.

Islands between 1789 to 1793, and, after retiring from active sea service, was employed at the Admiralty from 1803 to 1811. Mackenzie and Græme Spence may be looked upon as the fathers of the modern naval surveying service.

But it was not until August 12th, 1795, that the Minute was signed, appointing the first Hydrographer to the Admiralty, with the duty of collecting and compiling information for the improvement of navigation. The selection fell upon Alexander Dalrymple,[1] a retired Madras civilian, who had been actively engaged for many years in collecting materials and engraving charts of coasts and ports in the East Indies, and had been, since 1779, hydrographer to the East India Company. He had published a valuable work on voyages in the Pacific, and had even been named, before Captain James Cook, to command the Transit of Venus expedition. But Dalrymple devoted his attention to the engraving of the numerous charts which he had collected, rather than to the supply of the latest information to ships; and at last the Admiralty came to the conclusion that their Hydrographer should be a naval officer. Dalrymple was asked to resign. He declined to do so, and was superseded in 1808 by Captain Thomas Hurd.[2] He died, it is said of a broken heart, in the same year, when the Admiralty bought his stock of engraved copper plates, one hundred and thirty in number.

Captain Hurd, the second Hydrographer, held that office for fifteen years, from 1808 to 1823; and he began a system of issuing regular supplies of charts to the ships on each station. Nor was active work neglected. In 1811, Captain Francis Beaufort (1), in the *Frederiksteen*, 28, surveyed the coast of Karamania; and William Henry Smyth,[3] in the face of great difficulties, and at first on his own responsibility, made pioneer surveys, between 1813 and 1824, of the Sicilian coasts, the Adriatic and Ionian Islands, and the north coast of Africa. Smyth formed a school of surveyors; and in the list of officers trained by him are such names as Frederick William Beechey, Thomas Graves (6), Henry Raper (2), and William George Skyring,[4] all well known in after years. The

---

[1] *See* Vol. IV. p. 186.

[2] Com., 1795; Capt., Ap. 29th, 1802; died Ap. 30th, 1823.—W. L. C.

[3] William Henry Smyth, born Jan. 21st, 1788; Lieut., Mar. 25th, 1813; Com., Sept. 18th, 1815; Capt., Feb. 7th, 1824; retired, 1846; retired r.-adm. 1853; retired v.-adm., 1858; retired adm. 1863; died Sept. 9th, 1865.—W. L. C.

[4] Com., Feb. 25th, 1830. Murdered while in com. of *Ætna* by natives near Cape Roxo, Dec. 23rd, 1833.

coasts of the British Isles were also re-surveyed under the auspices of Captain Hurd.

Mr. John Barrow became permanent Secretary to the Admiralty in 1804. He was out of office during the Grenville administration, but was reinstated in 1807, and held office continuously from that time until 1845, a period of thirty-eight years. He was a steady supporter of the surveys, and an ardent promoter of expeditions for discovery alike in the frigid and in the torrid zones; while his influence and persistence usually prevailed against indifference and ignorance in high quarters.

It was owing to Barrow's initiative, aided by the influence of Sir Joseph Banks, that it was resolved, in August, 1814, before the war was over, to equip an expedition to explore the lower reaches of the River Congo. The command was entrusted to an officer who had served in the East Indies and Australia, and had done good surveying work, but who had been a prisoner in France for nine years. Commander James Hingston Tuckey, this accomplished and most amiable man, commissioned the schooner *Congo* on September 28th, 1815, and sailed in company with a transport, the *Dorothy*. The expedition consisted of forty-nine officers and men, and four scientific civilians, and in July, 1815, it reached the mouth of the Congo. The exploring party, led by Commander Tuckey, went up the river for 150 miles in boats,[1] then marched round the Yellala rapids by land, and reached the wide stream above, altogether 280 miles. But in those days the sanitary precautions necessary in a deadly climate were not well understood. Commander Tuckey[2] and five of his officers[3] died of fever, and the Master brought the schooner home with the survivors.[4] This disaster seems to have checked African exploratory work for a time; and soon, as will be seen later, the attention of the Lords of the Admiralty was turned, by their Secretary, to polar discovery.

---

[1] In this expedition steamboats were used.—W. L. C.

[2] Com. Tuckey died on Oct. 4th, 1816.—W. L. C.

[3] Including Lieut. John Hawkey (Lieut. of May 5th, 1804).—W. L. C.

[4] *See* 'Nav. Chron,' xxxiv. 289, 317, 349, 514; xxxvi. 57; xxxvii. 86.—W. L. C.

CHAPTER XLIII.

CIVIL HISTORY OF THE ROYAL NAVY, 1816–1856.

Administrative officers of the Navy—Administrative reforms under Sir James Graham —Admiralty buildings—Naval expenditure—Seamen, Boys, and Royal Marines voted—Improvements in naval architecture—Typical sailing-ships of the period— The introduction of steam—Engineers—Paddle-steamers—Iron steamers—Screw-steamers—Typical steamships of the period—The beginnings of armour—Arma-ment of typical ships of the period—Varieties of guns—The beginning of rifled guns and breechloaders—Rockets—Small-arms—Revolvers—Engines—Training in gunnery—The Royal Naval College—The *personnel*—Unemployed officers—Pro-motion and retirement—Excessive age of officers—Superannuation—The Royal Marines—Continuous service men—Scarcity of seamen—Rum—The Navy List— Miscellaneous innovations—Uniform—Beards and moustaches—Seamen's clothing —Excentric costumes—Medals—The Victoria Cross—The honour of the Flag— Flogging—Excentric punishments—A happy commission—Ladies on board ship— Reduction of the rum allowance—The dining hour—Excentric characters—A naval bishop—Mast-heading.

STAR OF A G.C.B.

THE succession of the more important administrative officers of the Navy during the period 1816–1856 was as follows :—

FIRST LORD OF THE ADMIRALTY.[1]
Robert, Viscount Melville (till 1827).

LORD HIGH ADMIRAL.
May 2, 1827. H.R.H. Prince William Henry, Duke of Clarence, Admiral of the Fleet, General of Royal Marines, K.G., K.T., G.C.B., G.C.H., etc.

---

[1] For convenience of reference, the names of the Prime Ministers from 1815 to 1856 inclusive, with the dates of their accession to office, are appended : June 9, 1812, Earl of Liverpool; Apr. 24, 1827, George Canning; Sept. 5, 1827, Viscount Goderich; Jan. 25, 1828, Duke of Wellington; Nov. 22, 1830, Earl Grey; July 18, 1834, Viscount Melbourne; Dec. 26, 1834, Sir Robert Peel; Apr. 18, 1835, Viscount Melbourne; Sept. 6, 1841, Sir Robert Peel; July 6, 1846, Lord John Russell; Feb. 27, 1852, Earl of Derby; Dec. 28, 1852, Earl of Aberdeen; Feb. 10, 1855, Lord Palmerston.

FIRST LORD OF THE ADMIRALTY (revived).

Sept. 19, 1828. Robert, Viscount Melville, K.T.
Nov. 25, 1830. Rt. Hon. Sir James Robert George Graham, Bart., M.P.
June 11, 1834. George, Baron Auckland.
Sept. 19, 1835. Gilbert, Earl of Minto, G.C.B.
Sept. 8, 1841. Thomas, Earl of Haddington.
Jan. 13, 1846. Edward, Earl of Ellenborough, G.C.B.
July 13, 1846. George, Earl of Auckland, G.C.B.
Jan. 18, 1849. Rt. Hon. Sir Francis T. Baring, Bart., M.P.
Mar. 2, 1852. Algernon, Duke of Northumberland, Rear-Adm.
Jan. 5, 1853. Rt. Hon. Sir James Robert George Graham, Bart., M.P.
Mar. 8, 1855. Rt. Hon. Sir Charles Wood, Bart., M.P.

SECRETARIES OF THE ADMIRALTY.

First Secretary.

Rt. Hon. John Wilson Croker, M.P.
Nov. 29, 1830. Hon. George Elliot (3), Capt., R.N. (C.B., 1831).
Dec. 24, 1834. Rt. Hon. George R. Dawson.
Apr. 27, 1835. Charles Wood, M.P.
Oct. 4, 1839. R. More O'Ferrall, M.P.
June 9, 1841. John Parker, M.P.
Sept. 10, 1841. Hon. Sidney Herbert, M.P.
Feb. 1845. Rt. Hon. H. T. Lowry Corry, M.P.
July 13, 1846. Henry G. Ward, M.P.
May 21, 1849. John Parker, M.P.
Mar. 3, 1852. Augustus Stafford, M.P.
Jan. 6, 1853. R. Bernal Osborne, M.P.

Second Secretary.

John Barrow (Bart. 1835).
Jan. 28, 1845. William Alexander Baillie Hamilton, Capt. R.N.
May 22, 1855. Thomas Phinn.

Treasurer of the Navy.

Rt. Hon. George Rose, M.P.
Feb. 12, 1818. Rt. Hon. Frederick John Robinson (Visct. Goderich, 1827 ; Earl of Ripon, 1833).
Feb. 28, 1823. Rt. Hon. William Huskisson.
Sept. 10, 1827. Rt. Hon. Charles Grant (afterwards Lord Glenelg).
Feb. 25, 1828. Rt. Hon. W. F. Vesey Fitzgerald, F.R.S. (afterwards Lord Fitzgerald and Vesey).
Feb. 25, 1830. Rt. Hon. Thomas Frankland Lewis, F.R.S.
Dec. 13, 1830. Rt. Hon. Charles Poulet Thompson (afterwards Lord Sydenham).
Dec. 27, 1834. Rt. Hon. William, Viscount Lowther (afterwards Earl of Lonsdale).
Apr. 22, 1835. Rt. Hon. Sir Henry B. Parnell, Bart. (afterwards Lord Congleton).

Sir Henry Parnell's salary as Treasurer ceased on Sept 30, 1835, and he afterwards became Paymaster-General. The Navy Pay Office was abolished in January, 1836.

Controller of the Navy.

Sir Thomas Boulden Thompson, Bart., Vice-Adm.
Feb. 9, 1816. Sir Thomas Byam Martin, Kt., K.C.B., Rear-Adm. (Vice-Adm., 1819 ; G.C.B. and Adm. 1830).

Nov. 2, 1831. Hon. George Heneage Lawrence Dundas, C.B., Rear-Adm.[1]

DEPUTY CONTROLLER OF THE NAVY.

William Shield, Capt. R.N.

Dec. 1, 1815. Sir Thomas Byam Martin, Kt., K.C.B. (*till* 1816).

Mar. 13, 1829. Hon. Henry Legge.

Oct. 21, 1830. Hon. Robert Dundas.[1]

Patent revoked, June 9, 1832.

SURVEYORS OF THE NAVY.

Sir Robert Seppings, Kt.

June 9, 1832. William Symonds, Capt., R.N.(Kt., 1836; F.R.S., 1835; C.B., 1848).[2]

Feb. 5, 1848. Sir Baldwin Wake Walker, K.C.B., Capt. R.N. (Rear-Adm. 1858) *till 1860, when he was made Controller of the Navy.*

CHIEF ASSISTANT AND DRAUGHTSMAN TO THE SURVEYORS.

(*Office created by O. in C. of June* 17, 1839.)

July 1, 1839. John Edye.

CHIEF CONSTRUCTOR.

May 4, 1848. Isaac Watts.

COMMISSIONERS WITHOUT SPECIAL FUNCTIONS.

Feb. 9, 1816. James Bowen (1), Capt., R.N.

Jan. 13, 1819. Hon. Granville Anson Chetwynd Stapylton.

June 11, 1823. Hon. Courtenay Boyle, Capt., R.N.

Feb. 3, 1825. Hon. Robert Dundas.

Apr. 13, 1826. John Mason Lewis, Capt., R.N.[1]

CHAIRMAN OF THE COMMISSIONERS OF VICTUALLING.

John Clarke Searle, Capt., R.N.

Mar. 1822. Hon. Granville Anson Chetwynd Stapylton, Col. (afterwards Maj.-Genl.).[1]

SUPERINTENDENT OF TRANSPORTS.

Mar. 1829. Hon. Courtenay Boyle, Capt., R.N.

CONTROLLER OF THE VICTUALLING [2] (AND OF THE TRANSPORT SERVICE).

June 9, 1832. James Meek.

Dec. 18, 1850. Thomas T. Grant, F.R.S.

STOREKEEPER-GENERAL.

May 8, 1829. Robert Gambier Middleton, Capt., R.N.

June 9, 1832. Hon. Robert Dundas.[2]

ACCOUNTANT-GENERAL OF THE NAVY.

May 8, 1829. John Deas Thomson, F.R.S. (*till July*, 1829).

June 9, 1832. Sir John Thomas Briggs, Kt.[2]

Feb. 20, 1854. Sir Richard Madox Bromley, K.C.B.

PHYSICIAN-GENERAL OF THE NAVY.[2]

June 9, 1832. Sir William Burnett, M.D.

Title changed on Jan. 25, 1841, *to*

INSPECTOR-GENERAL OF NAVAL HOSPITALS AND FLEETS.

Jan. 28, 1841. Sir William Burnett, M.D.

---

[1] By 2 Will. IV., cap. 40 (June 1, 1832) the Navy and Victualling Boards, and the offices of Commissioners of the Navy and Victualling, and Controller of the Navy were abolished; and instead, five "Principal Officers" were appointed, viz.: Surveyor of the Navy, Accountant-General of the Navy, Storekeeper-General, Controller of Victualling, and Physician-General. To these departmental officers others were subsequently added. The office of Controller of the Navy remained in abeyance from June 9, 1832, until 1860, when it was revived.

[2] Office established by 2 Will. IV., cap. 40.

Title changed on Jan. 1, 1844, *to*

DIRECTOR-GENERAL OF THE MEDICAL
DEPT. OF THE NAVY.

Jan. 1, 1844. Sir William Burnett, M.D., K.C.B., R.N.
Apr. 30, 1855. Sir John Liddell, M.D., F.R.S., R.N.

COMMISSIONERS (AND, FROM 1832, SUPER-INTENDENTS) OF H.M. DOCKYARDS, ETC.

Chatham.

Sir Robert Barlow, Kt., K.C.B., Capt., R.N.
Apr. 1, 1823. Charles Cunningham, Capt., R.N. (*till May* 5, 1829).
May 9, 1829. John Mason Lewis, Capt., R.N. (resident at Sheerness).
Dec. 1831. Charles Bullen, C.B., Capt., R.N.
June 9, 1832. Sir James Alexander Gordon (1), K.C.B., Capt., R.N. (Rear-Adm. 1837). Also of Sheerness Yd.
Apr. 7, 1837. John Clavell, Capt., R.N.
Aug. 24, 1841. William Henry Shirreff, Capt., R.N. Also of Deptford Yd.
Sept. 20, 1846. Sir Thomas Bourchier, K.C.B., Capt., R.N.
May 5, 1849. Peter Richards, C.B., Capt., R.N.
June 14, 1854. Christopher Wyvill, Capt., R.N.
Mar. 23, 1856. George Goldsmith, C.B., Capt., R.N.

Portsmouth.

Hon. Sir George Grey, Bart., K.C.B., Capt., R.N.
Jan. 14, 1829. Sir Michael Seymour, K.C.B., Capt., R.N.
June 28, 1832. Sir Frederick Lewis Maitland (2), K.C.B., Rear-Adm.
July 26, 1837. Hon. Duncombe Pleydell Bouverie, Rear-Adm.
Aug. 4, 1842. Hyde Parker, C.B., Rear-Adm.
Sept. 27, 1847. William Henry Shirreff, Rear-Adm.

Dec. 15, 1847. Henry Prescott, C.B., Rear-Adm.
Oct. 1, 1852. Arthur Fanshawe, C.B., Rear-Adm.
Dec. 2, 1853. William Fanshawe Martin, Rear-Adm.

Plymouth (from 1851 *Devonport*).

Robert Fanshawe, Capt., R.N.
Dec. 12, 1815 William Shield, Capt., R.N.
May 21, 1829. Charles Bayne Hodgson Ross, C.B., Capt., R.N. (Rear-Adm. Jan. 10, 1837).
Apr. 1, 1837. Frederick Warren, Rear-Adm. (Vice-Adm. Nov. 23, 1841).
Dec. 16, 1841. Sir Samuel Pym, K.C.B., Rear-Adm.
Dec. 17, 1846. Sir John Louis, Bart., C.B., Rear-Adm. (Vice-Adm., Oct. 9, 1849).
Feb. 9, 1850. Lord John Hay, C.B., Commodore, 1st Class, (Rear-Adm. 1851).
Sept. 8, 1851. Michael Seymour (2), Commodore, 1st Class (Rear-Adm., May 27, 1854).
During his absence as Captain of the Fleet in the Baltic, there were temporarily appointed : Rear-Adm. Hon. Montagu Stopford, Mar. 28, 1854, and Rear-Adm. Henry Eden, Aug. 8, 1854.

Sheerness.

Hon. Courtenay Boyle, Capt., R.N. (*till Feb.* 1, 1822).
From Feb. 1822 *to May* 1829 *there was no Resident Commissioner at Sheerness ; and from* 1822 *to* 1834 *the Yard seems to have been superintended by the Chatham Commissioner.* See under *Chatham.*

June 24, 1834. Thomas Fortescue Kennedy, Capt., R.N.
Mar. 9, 1838. Sir John Hill, Kt., Capt., R.N.
Dec. 11, 1841. Sir Watkin Owen Pell, Kt., K.C.H., Capt., R.N.
Dec. 17, 1841. Peter Fisher (1), Capt., R.N. (died Aug. 28, 1844).
Sept. 23, 1844. Richard Arthur, C.B., Capt., R.N.
Nov. 10, 1846. David Price, Capt., R.N.
Nov. 14, 1850. Michael Seymour (2), Capt., R.N.
Sept. 29, 1851. Charles Hope, Capt., R.N.
Apr. 3, 1854. Christopher Wyvill, Capt., R.N.
June 16, 1854. John Jervis Tucker, Capt., R.N.

Gibraltar.

Isaac Wolley, Capt., R.N. (*till Jan.* 9, 1818).
June 21, 1821. M. B. Mends, R.N. (N.O. in Charge).
Oct. 26, 1829. John Slight, R.N. (N.O. in Charge).
Apr. 1, 1833. John Davidson (Clerk in Charge: died Aug. 18, 1842).
Dec. 17, 1842. Sir John Gordon Sinclair, Bart., Capt., R.N. (N.O. in Charge).
Oct. 16, 1846. Hon. George Grey (2), Capt., R.N.
Dec. 13, 1856. Frederick Warden, C.B., Capt., R.N.

Malta.

Joseph Larcom, Capt., R.N.
Jan. 10, 1818. Isaac Wolley, Capt., R.N.
June 11, 1823. John Mason Lewis, Capt., R.N.
Dec. 15, 1825. Charles Bayne Hodgson Ross, C.B., Capt., R.N.
Nov. 4, 1828. Sir Michael Seymour (1), K.C.B., Capt., R.N.
Mar. 13, 1829. Thomas Briggs, Capt., R.N. (Rear-Adm., June 27, 1832; G.C.M.G., 1833).

Jan. 6, 1838. Sir John Louis, Bart., Commodore (Rear-Adm. June 28, 1838).
Mar. 8, 1843. Sir Lucius Curtis, Bart., C.B., Rear-Adm.
Mar. 9, 1848. Edward Harvey, Rear-Adm.
Apr. 13, 1853. Houston Stewart (1), C.B., Rear-Adm.
Jan. 18, 1855. Hon. Sir Montagu Stopford, K.C.B., Rear-Adm.

Halifax.

Hon. Philip Wodehouse, Capt., R.N. (*till Aug.* 12, 1819).
On July 11, 1832, *a Naval Storekeeper and Agent Victualler was appointed to Halifax.*

Hydrographer.

Thomas Hurd, Capt., R.N.
Dec. 1, 1823. William Edward Parry, F.R.S., Capt., R.N. (actg. till Nov. 22, 1825, when he was confirmed), (Kt. 1829).
May 14, 1829. Francis Beaufort, F.R.S., Capt., R.N. (Rear-Adm. on Oct. 1, 1846, and later K.C.B.).
Jan. 29, 1855. John Washington, Capt., R.N.

CONTROLLER OF STEAM MACHINERY, AND THE PACKET SERVICE.

(*Office created by O. in C. of Apr.* 19, 1837.)

Apr. 24, 1837. Sir William Edward Parry, Capt., R.N.
Dec. 2, 1846. Alexander Ellice, Capt., R.N.

CHIEF ENGINEER, AND INSPECTOR OF STEAM MACHINERY.

Apr. 6, 1847. Thomas Lloyd, *till* 1869.

Title abolished, Feb. 4, 1869.

It may be said, speaking generally, that, with slight changes, the business of the Navy continued, until 1832, to be conducted as it had been conducted during the latter part of the long French wars ; and that in 1832, owing mainly to the reforming and constructive energy of Sir James Graham and his assistants at the Admiralty, the existing system of administration was introduced. This system has since been considerably amplified and altered to suit new conditions as they have arisen. Fresh offices and departments have been created from time to time, but few modifications of any far-reaching character were adopted between 1832 and 1856. The nature of some of Sir James's reforms will be gathered from a study of the above lists, and of the footnotes accompanying them. By way, however, of additional explanation of what was done in 1832, Sir Richard Vesey Hamilton [1] may be quoted.

"When," he says, "Lord Grey took office in 1830, and Sir James Graham was appointed First Lord, it was anticipated that the reforms advocated by Earl St. Vincent would at length be carried into effect. Various Boards of Admiralty had debated whether the subsidiary Commissioners might not with advantage be merged in the Navy Board. But this was not enough for the new Cabinet. It was determined to do away with all divided control, and, abolishing the Board of Principal Officers and Commissioners of the Navy, and the Commissioners for Victualling, and for the Care of Sick and Wounded Seamen, to concentrate the whole of the civil departments under the Admiralty itself, each branch having an individual at its head. Sir James Graham did not mature his measures without full and anxious inquiry into the organisation and working both of the civil departments and of the dockyards under them, and he had the great advantage of the counsel and assistance of Sir John Barrow, whose long and ripe knowledge of our naval administration, then for nearly thirty years—as Second Secretary and Secretary of the Admiralty—peculiarly fitted him to advise. The 'Act to amend the Laws relating to the Business of the Civil Departments of the Navy, and to make other Regulations for more effectually carrying on the Duties of the said Departments' (2 Will. IV. c. 40)—vesting in the Board of Admiralty the powers of the Commissioners of the Civil Departments—provided, in place of the numerous Controllers and Commissioners of the Navy, of Victualling, and of Transports—then located at Somerset House—for the creation of five separate and independent superintendents of departments, under the Board of Admiralty collectively, and the Lords of the Admiralty individually. These new officials were the Surveyor of the Navy, the Accountant-General, the Storekeeper-General, the Controller of Victualling and Transports, and the Physician of the Navy, whose title was altered in 1844 to that of Director-General of the Medical Department of the Navy.

"By the dispositions thus taken, the Board of Admiralty and the subsidiary departments acquired the united and flexible character they have to-day, that character which they possessed before the civil departments had attained their magnitude and semi-independence, and were yet closely in touch with the Admiralty, holding the means—when they exercised them—of controlling and supervising the business for which they were responsible. Once again that close organisation for discussion of the conduct of affairs, which fall often under the care of several branches of the adminis-

---

[1] 'Nav. Admin.,' 21.

trative machinery, had been built up. Great as was the advantage thus won, the reorganisation brought a further gain in the considerable economy that was effected through the abolition of sinecures and redundant posts, which the existence of a complex set of individual branches had involved. Sir John Briggs, Accountant-General of the Navy, prepared, in June, 1834, a statement of the reductions that had been effected in the naval departments since November, 1830, from which it appears that an economy of £253,342 had been made. But the merit of the reorganisation effected by Sir James Graham is not to be estimated by the pecuniary saving it made possible, but by the fact that it struck at the root of abuses of long and slow growth which endangered our naval efficiency. Sir John Barrow, writing in 1847, said of the new system : ' On the whole, I can venture to say with great confidence, and after the experience of fifteen years since the plan was put in operation, under half-a-dozen Boards of Admiralty, Whig and Tory, that it has been completely successful in all its parts ; and the proof of it is that no fault has been found with it, nor has any alteration of the least importance been required.' " [1]

About the year 1780, the offices of the civil departments of the Navy had been concentrated in Somerset House, where the Victualling, Navy Pay, and Transport branches were lodged on the west side. On the west terrace were the official residences of the Treasurer and Surveyor of the Navy, of the three Commissioners of the Navy Board, and of the principal officers of the Victualling Department. The homes of the civil departments of the Navy were successively removed thence to Whitehall and Spring Gardens, the Surveyor's Department in 1855, and all the rest by 1870.

The expenditure on the Navy, and the numbers of seamen and Royal Marines voted each year from 1816 to 1856, were as follows :—

Year.	Total Naval Supplies granted.	Seamen and Boys voted.	Royal Marines voted.	Total Numbers voted.	Total Numbers actually borne.
	£				
1816	13,114,345	24,000	9,000	33,000	35,196
1817	7,645,422	13,000	6,000	19,000	22,944
1818	6,547,809	14,000	6,000	20,000	23,026
1819	6,527,781	14,000	6,000	20,000	23,230
1820	6,691,345	15,000	8,000	23,000	23,985
1821	6,391,902	14,000	8,000	22,000	24,937
1822	6,480,325	13,000	8,000	21,000	23,806
1823	5,442,540	16,000	8,700	24,700	26,314
1824	5,762,893	20,000	9,000	29,000	30,502
1825	5,983,126	20,000	9,000	29,000	31,456
1826	6,135,004	21,000	9,000	30,000	32,519
1827	6,125,850	21,000	9,000	30,000	33,106
1828	6,395,965	21,000	9,000	30,000	31,818
1829	5,878,794	21,000	9,000	30,000	32,458
1830	5,594,955	20,000	9,000	29,000	31,160
1831 [1]	7,221,797	22,000	10,000	32,000	29,336
1832 [2]	5,045,827	18,000	9,000	27,000	27,328

[1] 15 months, to March 31st, 1832.   [2] April 1st to March 31st of next year.

[1] ' Autob. Mem.', 424.

Year.	Total Naval Supplies granted.	Seamen and Boys voted.	Royal Marines voted.	Total Numbers voted.	Total Numbers actually borne.
	£				
1833	4,803,647	18,000	9,000	27,000	27,701
1834	4,716,894	18,500	9,000	27,500	28,066
1835	4,434,783	17,500	9,000	26,500	26,041
1836	4,689,651	24,700	9,000	33,700	30,195
1837	4,930,736	25,165	9,000	34,165	31,289
1838	4,960,911	25,165	9,000	34,165	32,028
1839	5,532,724	25,165	9,000	34,165	34,857
1840	6,182,247	26,165 (2 mos.) 28,165 (7 mos.) 30,665 (3 mos.)	9,000	35,165 (2 mos.) 37,165 (7 mos.) 39,665 (3 mos.)	37,665
1841	6,772,969	32,500	10,500	43,000	41,389
1842	7,000,442	32,500	10,500	43,000	43,105
1843	6,579,960	28,500	10,500	39,000	40,229
1844	6,466,019	25,500	10,500	36,000	38,343
1845	7,344,363	29,500	10,500	40,000	40,084
1846	7,920,324	29,500	10,500	40,000	43,314
1847	8,068,985	29,500	11,000 (6 mos.) 12,000 (6 mos.)	40,500 (6 mos.) 41,500 (6 mos.)	44,969
1848	7,955,001	29,500	12,500 (6 mos.) 13,500 (6 mos.)	42,000 (6 mos.) 43,000 (6 mos.)	43,978
1849	7,021,724	28,000	12,000	40,000	39,535
1850	6,672,588	28,000	11,000	39,000	39,093
1851	6,543,255	28,000	11,000	39,000	38,957
1852	6,705,746	28,000 (8 mos.) 33,000 (4 mos.)	11,000 (8 mos.) 12,500 (4 mos.)	39,000 (8 mos.) 45,500 (4 mos.)	40,451
1853	7,197,804	33,000	12,500	45,500	45,885
1854	15,017,591	48,000	15,500	63,500	61,457
1855	19,590,833	54,000	16,000	70,000	67,791

From 1832 onwards the financial year was computed in Calendar instead of in Lunar months, and began on April 1st, lasting till March 31st of the following year.

During the wars with France and her allies, and with the United States, the chief British improvements in naval architecture were copied from the best of the prizes taken from the enemy, and, for many years after the peace, this plan was still largely followed. Thus, as late as 1845, there was laid down at Devonport a *Sanspareil* designed upon the lines of the ship of the same name captured from the French in 1794; although, it is true, the vessel was never actually launched as a sailing line-of-battle ship, but, while yet upon the stocks, was lengthened, converted to a screw ship of 80 guns, and launched as such in 1851. Modifications were, however, introduced by Sir Robert Seppings, who was responsible for building large ships with circular or elliptical, instead of square sterns, thereby giving them increased strength and additional stern fire; and in 1832 Sir Robert was succeeded as Surveyor by an officer who was not content to be, in any sense, an imitator, and who was really a great naval architect. This was Captain Sir William

Symonds, Kt., R.N.   In 1825, Symonds, then a Commander, was permitted by the Admiralty to construct a corvette upon his own lines.   The *Columbine*, 18, was so great a success as to earn Symonds his promotion in 1827.   Nevertheless, no further progress might have been then made had not the Duke of Portland given Symonds orders to build him a yacht.   This craft, the *Pantaloon*, was presently purchased by the Admiralty, and, being adapted as a 10-gun brig, did so extremely well that her designer was at once employed to construct the *Vernon*, 50, *Vestal*, 26, *Snake*, 16, and

CIRCULAR STERN OF H.M.S. 'ASIA,' 84, BUILT AT BOMBAY, 1824.
FLAGSHIP AT NAVARINO.

(*From an etching by E. W. Cooke, R.A.*)

other men-of-war of various classes, and was quickly made Surveyor. In that capacity, he built, in the ensuing fifteen years, no fewer than 180 vessels.   His ships owed their superior speed and stability chiefly to the improved form of their bottom, which he made much less heavy and full than had previously been usual.   They were also broader, roomier, and loftier between decks than their forerunners, and in them the sailing Navy of England undoubtedly found its highest development.   Among Symonds's greatest triumphs were the *Queen*, 110, *Vernon*, 50, and *Pique*, 40.   The solidity of his methods of construction was amply demonstrated by the last-named, which, on her first commission, while returning from Canada in 1835, under Captain the Hon. Henry John Rous, took the rocks near Point Forteau, Labrador, and ground away all her false keel,[1] and much of the outer skin of her bottom. Although she bumped heavily for eleven hours in a violent sea, and afterwards made from 14 to 36 inches of water an hour, she found her way home unaided, in spite of terrible weather; and, in twenty-one days, she reached St. Helens.[2] It is noteworthy that, during his period of office, not one of his vessels foundered, though several craft by other architects were less fortunate. Symonds also introduced a system under which the masts, yards, cross-trees, etc., of men-of-war were classified into twenty "establishments" or sizes, instead of into eighty-eight, as before; and which was so arranged that the spars became interchangeable, not only as between ship and ship of the same class, but also—though, of course, for different purposes—as between ship and ship of different classes. Particulars of a few of the most famous sailing men-of-war [3] of the time are given below.

Date of Launch.	Ship.	Guns.	Tons.	Length.		Beam.		Depth.		Designed by.
				Ft.	ins.	Ft.	ins.	Ft.	ins.	
1839	*Queen*	110	3104	204	2½	60	0½	23	9	Sir W. Symonds.
1833	*Rodney*	92	2626	205	6	54	5½	23	1	Sir R. Seppings.
1835	*Vanguard*	80	2609	190	0	57	0	23	4	Sir W. Symonds.
1842	*Cumberland*	70	2214	180	0	54	3	22	4	Sir W. Symonds.
1850	*Nankin*	50	2049	185	0	50	10	15	10½	Mr. Oliver Lang.
1845	*Raleigh*	50	1939	180	0	50	1	16	8	Mr. Fincham.
1832	*Vernon*	50	2082	176	0	52	8½	16	5	Sir W. Symonds.
1834	*Pique*	40	1633	160	0	48	10½	14	7	Sir W. Symonds.
1836	*Inconstant*	36	1422	160	1	45	5	13	7	Capt. Jno. Hayes (1).
1848	*Diamond*	28	1055	140	0	42	2	11	0½	Sir W. Symonds.
1823	*Rainbow*	28	503	113	9½	31	11¼	8	8½	Surveyor's Dept.
1843	*Eurydice*	26	921	141	3	38	10	8	9	R.-Adm. Hon. Geo. Elliot (3).
1841	*Spartan*	26	918	131	0	40	7¼	10	9	Sir W. Symonds.
1828	*Cruiser*	18	384	100	0	31	0¾	12	9½	Sir W. Rule.
1829	*Larne*	18	463	113	3	30	10½	8	0	Prof. Inman.
1837	*Modeste*	18	568	120	0	33	2½	14	2	R.-Adm. Hon. Geo. Elliot (3).
1824	*Pylades*	18	433	110	1	30	4¼	8	2	Sir R. Seppings.
1838	*Pilot*	16	485	105	0½	33	6	14	10	Sir W. Symonds.
1844	*Flying Fish*	12	445	103	1	32	4½	14	4½	Sir W. Symonds.
1831	*Pantaloon*	10	323	91	10¾	29	4¼	12	8	Sir W. Symonds.
1847	*Britomart*	8	330	93	0	29	3¾	13	5½	Sir W. Symonds.

[1] Her false keel was on a principle introduced by Mr. Oliver Lang.

[2] C.M. Sept. 22nd, 1835. *Naut. Mag.*, iv. 691, 755. *See also* model in Nav. Mus. at Greenwich, showing state of ship when docked.

[3] Models of all these are at Greenwich.

Yet, even ere Symonds and his assistants had begun to introduce the improvements which brought the sailing man-of-war to the highest pitch of perfection, the sailing man-of-war was doomed. Steam, as a means of propulsion for ships, was used for a considerable period before the Admiralty became willing to try its merits. At length, however, the famous engineer Marc Isambard Brunel persuaded their Lordships that their conservatism must give way, and that the use of steam must be countenanced in the Navy. In consequence, the *Comet*, a paddle wooden steamer of 238 tons and 90 H.P. nominal, was built at Deptford in 1822; and presently the somewhat similar vessel *Monkey*, of 212 tons and 80 H.P. nominal

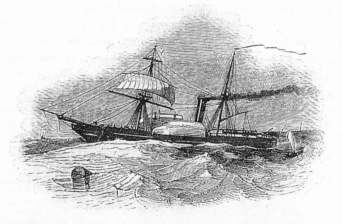

H.M.S. ‘RETRIBUTION,’ 10 GUNS, 1641 TONS (B.M.), 400 H.P. NOM.

LAUNCHED AT CHATHAM, 1844; SOLD, 1864.

(*Built of wood, after designs by Sir W. Symonds: length*, 220 *ft.: beam*, 40 *ft.* 6 *in.: depth*, 26 *ft.* 4 *in.*)

(373 I.H.P.), which had been built at Rotherhithe in 1821, was purchased for the use of the service. These, and other early steam craft, were either tugs, or what would now be called special service vessels; and the Admiralty, although it adopted them, did so half-heartedly, and with a bad grace, their construction not coming within the province of the Surveyor of the Navy, the design and building of them being left to contractors, and there being no regular corps of engineer officers to manage them. In fact, for some years, the builders were expected to hand over with the vessels the necessary engine-room staff; and, for a time, not so much as the names of the despised novelties appeared in the official Navy List.

But the new power soon forced itself into fuller recognition. In 1832, the Surveyor designed his earliest steamers.[1] Until after 1840, however, few of these were of more than 1000 tons measurement, or of very heavy armament, and all were built of wood, and had paddles as their propellers.

In the meantime, although the Admiralty, as always, was not in the van of the advance, further progress had been made. Iron lighters were built in England in the first years of the nineteenth century: the first iron steamboat was completed in 1821: as early as 1833, an iron steamboat suitable for sea service was in existence:

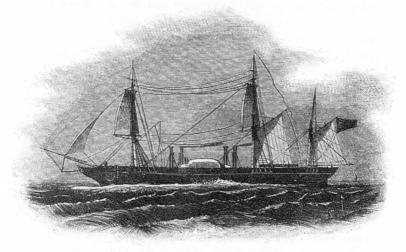

H.M.S. 'TERRIBLE,' 20 GUNS, 1847 TONS (B.M.), 800 H.P. NOM.

LAUNCHED AT DEPTFORD, 1845.

(Built of wood, after designs by Mr. Oliver Lang: length, 226 ft.: beam, 42 ft. 6 in: depth, 27 ft. Engines by Maudslay & Co.)

in 1838, an iron steamboat crossed the Atlantic, though she crossed it under sail: and in 1839, Messrs. Laird, of Birkenhead began to build iron steam warships for the East India Company. One of these, the *Nemesis*, of 660 tons, was armed with two 32-pr. pivot

---

[1] The *Nautical Magazine* of June, 1833, says: "A high-pressure steam-engine, with an improved boiler, by Mr. George Mills, of London, is now fitting for trial on board the *Falcon*, an old 10-gun brig, in the basin at Sheerness. In this engine the steam is raised by fire-tubes passing through the boiler, which is surrounded at a slight distance by a double cylinder, filled with cold water, serving as a surface condenser. The boiler will bear a pressure of at least 150 lbs. on the square inch. . . . The *Falcon* is fitted with two engines of 50 horse-power each." I cannot find any account of the trials. The boiler was, however, not adopted.

guns ; and, although she drew but five feet of water, she made the passage to India by way of the Cape of Good Hope, and subsequently, under the orders of Captain William Hutcheon Hall, R.N., rendered excellent service in China during the operations of 1841-42. The Admiralty, however, did not possess an iron steamer of any sort until 1840, when the paddle packet *Dover* was launched for it at Birkenhead. In the same year it acquired three small iron paddle gunboats ; but it hesitated for many years ere it made up its mind that, for large craft as well as for small, iron was a trustworthy material. As early, nevertheless, as 1836, Mr. John Laird had proposed to construct an iron frigate, and had prepared plans for it ; and in 1842 he actually launched an iron paddle frigate, which he offered in vain to the Government, and which he eventually sold to Mexico. At length, in 1846, the ill-fated *Birkenhead* was launched at Birkenhead for the Admiralty, and, in 1849, Napier, of Glasgow, followed with the *Simoon,* and Fairbairn, of Millwall, with the *Megæra.* All these were originally classed as steam frigates, and armed as such ; but experiments [1] made upon an iron vessel called the *Ruby* induced the authorities to fear that such craft would be torn to pieces by the effects of shot ; and the ships were consequently transformed into transports, and their armaments greatly reduced. The *Birkenhead,* of 1400 tons, was fitted with paddles ; the *Simoon,* and *Megæra* had screws.

The origin of the screw, as a means of propulsion for ships, is wrapped in some obscurity. Early in the century, one Dr. Shorter devised a plan for driving vessels through the water by means of a circular fan, but does not seem to have thought of working his propeller by steam. In 1834, Mr. (afterwards Sir) Francis Pettitt Smith, a Hendon farmer, son of the postmaster of Hythe, constructed a model which was propelled through the water by means of a submerged screw. In 1836 he took out a patent for his invention, and in 1838 he submitted his plans to the Admiralty. By that time he had associated himself with the great Swedish engineer, John Ericsson ; and the screw was applied to several small experimental craft, one of which, though only 45 feet long and 8 feet broad, towed a barque of 630 tons against a strong tide at a speed of nearly 4·5 knots, and later towed the Admiralty barge, with their Lordships on board, from Somerset House to Blackwall, and back, at an average speed of about 10 knots. Yet their Lordships, who in-

[1] *Naut. Mag.,* Sept. 1846, p. 498.

cluded Vice-Admiral Sir Charles Adam, Rear-Admiral Sir William
Parker (2), and Captain Sir Edward Thomas Troubridge, curtly
" declined to entertain the project " of fitting screws to naval vessels,
apparently under the delusion that the screw was useful only in
smooth water.   But the performances of the *Archimedes*,[1] a vessel
which, fitted with Smith's screw, made the tour of Great Britain,
and steamed to Oporto, Amsterdam, and other places, caused the
Admiralty to reconsider its decision.   In 1842, there had been laid
down for the Navy at Sheerness a sloop which was originally named
the *Ardent*.   She was ordered to be lengthened aft, to be fitted with

SCREW *versus* PADDLE.

[The trial between H.M.SS. *Rattler* and *Alecto*.]

(*From ' La Rivista Marittima.'*)

a screw, and to be renamed *Rattler*; and she was launched in April,
1843.   Her after part was of a form very unsuited to assist the work
of the propeller, yet she was so much of a success that, from the day
of her trials, the future of the screw in the Navy was assured.   The
Rattler was of 888 tons measurement, and had engines of 200 H.P.
nominal.   In 1845, she underwent some very convincing tests with
the paddle sloop *Alecto*, a vessel of 796 tons measurement and 200
H.P. nominal.   On an eighty miles' course, in a calm, the screw beat

<hr />

[1] *Naut. Mag.*, 1839, pp. 426, 430.   Her engines were by Messrs. Rennie.   *See also*
Naut. Mag., 1840, pp. 453, 529, 671, 735, 744, 812.

the paddle by 23½ minutes; on a thirty-four miles' course, in a moderate breeze, with sails set, the screw was again victorious by 13 minutes. On a sixty miles' course, against a head sea, the *Rattler* won by 40 minutes. But the most conclusive experiment of all was made when, the two vessels being fastened stern to stern, and both steaming their best, the *Rattler* towed the *Alecto* at the rate of 2½ miles an hour.[1] The form, pitch, number of blades, and other details of the screw remained, of course, to be modified in accordance with practical experience; but the general principles of the design of Smith and Ericsson have undergone but little change.

At first, already existing vessels belonging to the Navy were fitted with the screw after first having been lengthened and otherwise altered. Several very old ships of the larger classes were thus treated, among them being the *Ajax*, launched in 1809, the *Horatio*, launched in 1809, and the *Nelson*, launched in 1814. The first ship of the line to be designed, *ab initio*, for the screw was the *Agamemnon*, 80, which was laid down at Woolwich in 1849, and launched in 1852. Particulars of a few typical steam men-of-war[2] of the period 1816–1856 are given on p. 199.

Only one other radical new departure in naval construction remains to be noticed here. It was made at the very end of the period now under review, and, in 1856, when it had barely indicated its nature and significance, few can have suspected whither it was destined to lead. This departure was necessitated by the fact that the power of the gun had begun to grow greatly. Fulton, years before, had aimed at giving a steam war-vessel such impenetrable scantling as should afford complete protection to her crew in action; but he had used only wood as armour. The swift and tragic destruction, chiefly by shell-fire, of the Turkish squadron off Sinope, on November 30th, 1853, led to the building, for the purposes of the war with Russia, of vessels armoured not with wood but with iron. The credit of the invention is due to France; but, upon plans of the vessels being sent across the Channel, England, in 1855, promptly followed suit by constructing the four wooden-hulled armoured batteries, *Trusty*, *Thunder*, *Glatton* and *Meteor*, and by adding to them in 1856 the iron-hulled armoured batteries *Thunderbolt*, *Terror*, *Ætna* and *Erebus*.[3] The craft of the earlier type were of about 1540 tons measurement, 150 H.P. nominal, and a speed of 4·5 knots.

---

[1] *Naut. Mag*, 1845, p. 331.   [2] Models of all these are at Greenwich.
[3] Models of these are at Greenwich.

Date of Launch.	Ship.	Guns.	Tons. (measnt.)	H.P.N.	Speed. Kts.	Length. ft. ins.	Beam. ft. ins.	Depth. ft. ins.	Remarks.
1852	Duke of Wellington	131	3771	700	10·15	240 7	60 1	24 8	Laid down as a sailing ship. Converted for screw on stocks at Pembroke. Compt. 1100.
1853	St. Jean d'Acre	101	3199	600	11·19	238 0	55 4	24 5	Designed by the Surveyor's Dept. for the screw. Compt. 900.
1854	Orion	91	3281	600	12·5	238 0	55 9	23 4	Laid down as a sailing ship. Converted for screw on stocks at Chatham. Compt. 850.
1852	Agamemnon [1]	80	3102	600	11·0	230 0	55 6	24 6	Designed by Mr. J. Edye for the screw. Compt. 820.
1851	Sanspareil	80	2239	350	7·05	200 0	52 3	22 8	Laid down as a sailing ship. Converted for screw on stocks at Devonport. Compt. 700.
1855	Shannon [2]	51	2667	600	11·8	235 1	50 1¼		Screw. Designed by Surveyor's Dept. Blt. at Portsmouth. Compt. 560.
1853	Euryalus [3]	51	2371	400		212 0	50 2	16 9	Designed by the Surveyor's Dept. for the screw. Blt. at Chatham.
1848	Arrogant	46	1872	360	8·64	200 0	45 5½	15 1	Screw. Designed by Mr. Finchan. Blt. at Portsmouth.
1853	Tribune [4]	31	1569	300	10·41	192 0	43 0	12 11	Screw. Designed by Surveyor's Dept. Blt. at Sheerness. Compt. 300.
1849	Tiger [5]	16	1221	400		250 0	35 11¾	24 6	Paddle. Designed by Mr. J. Edye. Blt. at Chatham.
1844	Retribution	10	1641	400		220 0	40 6	26 4	Paddle. Designed by Sir W. Symonds. Blt. at Chatham.
1849	Simoom [6]	8	1980	40?	8·89	246 0	41 0		Iron screw ship. Designed and bll. by Napier at Glasgow.
1853	Himalaya [7]	6	3453	700	12·8	340 5	46 1¼	23 0	Iron screw ship. Blt. for P. & O. Co. at Blackwall. Purchased 1854.
1837	Gorgon	6	1111	320	8·5	178 0	37 6¼	15 10	Paddle. Designed by Sir W. Symonds. Blt. at Pembroke.
1834	Tartarus	4	523	136		145 0	28 4	13 0	Paddle. Designed by Sir W. Symonds. Blt. at Pembroke.
1833	Gulnare [8]	3	306	130		120 0	23 3	13 0	Paddle. Designed by Sir W. Symonds. Blt. at Deptford.
1855	Resolute [9]	2	1793	400	11·44	282 10¼	36 4¼		Iron screw ship. Blt. by Laird at Birkenhead. Purchased 1855.
1847	Caradoc	2	676	350	16·0	191 7½	26 11¾	14 0	Iron paddle sloop. Designed by Sir W. Symonds. Blt. at Blackwall.
1854	Arrow [10]	2	477	160	11·0	169 0	25 4		Screw. Designed by Surveyor's Dept. Blt. at Blackwall. Compt. 65.
1856	Albacore [11]	2	235	60		108 4	22 1		Screw. Designed by Surveyor's Dept. Blt. at W. Cowes. Compt. 36.
1843	Victoria and Albert (1) [12]	—	1034	430	15·0	200 0	33 0	22 1	Paddle royal yacht. Designed by Sir W. Symonds. Blt. at Pembroke.
1851	Victoria and Albert (2) [13]	—	2345	600	18·0	300 1	40 3½	24 6	Paddle royal yacht. Designed by Surveyor's Dept. Blt. at Pembroke.

1 The *James Watt* (1853), *Victor Emmanuel* (1855), and *Edgar* (1868) were on similar lines.
2 The *Liffey* (1856), *Topaze* (1858), *Bacchante* (1859), and *Liverpool* (1860) were on similar lines.
3 The *Imperieuse* (1852), *Chesapeake* (1855), and *Porte* (1858) were on similar lines.
4 The *Curacoa* (1854) was on similar lines.
5 The *Magicienne* (1849) was on similar lines. The *Tiger* surrendered to the Russians in May, 1854.
6 Built as a steam frigate. Transformed to a troopship.
7 Built for passenger service. Purchased as a troopship.
8 Renamed *Gleaner*, 1837. Lengthened by 18 ft., 1839.
9 Renamed *Adventure*, 1857. The *Assistance* (1855) was on similar lines. Both were troopships.
10 Built for the Russian War. The *Beagle*, *Snake*, *Lynx*, *Wrangler*, and *Viper* (all 1854) were on similar lines.
11 Built too late for the Russian War. One hundred and fifteen others were on similar lines.
12 Renamed *Osborne*, 1854.
13 Remained chief chief royal yacht till 1901.

They carried fourteen 68-prs., 95 cwt. smooth-bore muzzle-loaders, and a complement of 200 men, and were protected with 4·5 inch iron plates. The vessels of the later type were of about 1950 tons measurement, 200 H.P. nominal, and a speed of 5·5 knots. They carried each 16 guns instead of 14, but had complements and armour like the earlier batteries. The *Erebus*, which may be taken as a type of the whole class, was 186 feet 8½ inches in length and 48 feet 6 inches broad, and drew 8 feet 10 inches forward and 8 feet 11 inches aft.

The armament[1] of some of the ships which have been named as having been constructed between 1815 and 1856 was, according to the original design, which, however, in a few cases, was modified later, as follows:—

		NUMBER, NATURE, AND POSITION OF GUNS.										
		Lower Deck.			Middle Deck.			Main Deck.			Upper Deck, or Qr. Deck & F'castle.		
Date.	Ship.	No.	Prs	Weight. Cwt.	No.	Prs.	Weight. Cwt.	No.	Prs.	Weight. Cwt.	No.	Prs.	Weight. Cwt.
1852	Duke of Wellington, 131.	{10 / 26	8in. / 32	65 / 56	{30 / 6	32 / 8in.	56 / 65	38	32	42	{20 / 1	32 / 68	25 / 95
1839	Queen, 110.	{24 / 6	32 / 8in.	56 / 65	{26 / 4	32 / 8in.	56 / 65	30	32	41	{14 / 6	32 / 32	25 / 45
1853	St. Jean d'Acre, 101.	{20 / 16	8in. / 32	65 / 56	..	..		{28 / 8	32 / 8in.	56 / 65	{28 / 1	32 / 68	42 / 95
1833	Rodney, 92.	{26 / 6	32 / 8in.	56	..	..		{30 / 4	32 / 8in.	} 56	26	32	42
1854	Orion, 91.	34	8in.	65	..	..		34	32	56	{22 / 1	32 / 68	42 / 95
1835	Vanguard, 80.	{20 / 8	32 / 8in.	56 / 65	..	..		{24 / 4	32 / 8in.	50 / 65	24	32	42
1852	Agamemnon, 80.	36	8in.	65	..	..		34	32	56	{2 / 8	68 / 10in.	95 / 85
1842	Cumberland, 70.	{22 / 4	32 / 8in.	56 / 65	..	..		{26 / 2	32 / 8in.	50 / 65	16	32	42
1855	Shannon, 51.	..	..		..	..		30	8in.	65	{20 / 1	32 / 68	56 / 95
1832	Vernon, 50.	..	..		..	..		{22 / 6	32 / 8in.	56 / 65	22	32	45
1848	Arrogant, 46.	..	..		..	..		{16 / 12	32 / 8in.	56 / 65	{16 / 2	32 / 68	32 / 95
1834	Pique, 40.	..	..		..	..		..	..		..	..	
1836	Inconstant, 36.	..	..		..	..		22	32	56	14	32	25
1853	Tribune, 31.	..	..		..	..		20	32	56	{10 / 1	32 / 10in.	42 / 85
1823	Rainbow, 28.	..	..		..	..		20	32	(carr.)	{6 / 2	18 / 9	(carr.)
1848	Diamond, 28.	..	..		..	..		20	32	45	{6 / 2	32 / 8in.	25 / 56
1844	Retribution, 10.	..	..		..	..		..	..		{2 / 4 / 4	8in. / 8in. / 32	112 / 65 / 25
1849	Tiger, 16.	..	..		..	..		8	32	56	{2 / 6	10in. / 32	85 / 56
1828	Cruiser, 18.	..	..		..	..		16	32	(carr.)	2	6	
1837	Gorgon, 6.	..	..		..	..		..	..		{4 / 2	32 / 10in.	42 / 85
1847	Britomart, 8.	..	..		..	..		..	..		8	18	15
1856	Albacore, 2.	..	..		..	..		..	..		{1 / 1	68 / 32	95 / 56

Numerous guns were used in the naval service. Particulars

[1] Particulars chiefly from Off. Catal. of R. N. Museum.

of the most important of those which are mentioned above are appended : [1]—

GUN.	WEIGHT.	LENGTH.	CALIBRE.	CHARGE OF POWDER.		PATTERN.	REMARKS.
	Cwt.	Ft. in.	In.	Lbs.	oz.		
10 in.	85	9 4	10·0	12	0	Gen. Millar's [1]	For shell. Bursting charge, common shell, 6¾ lbs.
8 in.	65	9 0	8·05	10	0	Gen. Millar's	Originally for shell (51 lbs.) and plugged hollow shot (56 lbs.) only. Later as 68-prs. Bursting charge, 2 lbs. 9 oz.
68 pr.	95	10 0	8·12	16	0	Col. Dundas's	Bursting charge, for common shell, 2 lbs. 9 oz.
32 pr.	56	9 6	6·41	10	0	Sir T. Blomefield's [2]	
32 pr.	50	8 0	6·41	8	0	Dickson & Millar's	Bursting charge, for common shell, 1 lb. 5 oz.; for diaphragm, 3 oz. 2 drs.
32 pr.	50	9 0	6·375	8	0	Monk's " A "	
32 pr.	45	8 6	6·35	7	0	Monk's " B "	
32 pr.	42	8 0	6·35	6	0	Monk's " C "	
32 pr.	25	6 0	6·3	4	0	Sir T. Blomefield's	A bored-up 18-pr.
32-pr. carr.	17	4 0	6·25	2	11	Carron Co.'s	

[1] Lt.-Genl. Wm. Millar, Dir. Genl. of Art., died 1838.

[2] Genl. Sir Thos. Blomefield, Bart., Insp. of Art. from 1780 to his death in 1822.

It seems unnecessary to say anything here of the various rifled and breechloading heavy guns which began to be experimented with towards the close of the period under review. Some Lancaster guns —pieces having a twisted elliptical bore of small excentricity, in lieu of rifling, to make the projectile rotate—were used before Sebastopol by the Naval Brigade ; but they took no permanent hold in the service ; and it may be stated broadly that, until after 1856, the British Navy's weapons afloat were exclusively smooth-bore muzzle-loaders, of types not greatly differing from the guns which had been used at Trafalgar.

Incendiary rockets, the invention of Mr. (afterwards Sir) William Congreve,[2] in 1805, had been used afloat in Basque road, in 1809, and ashore, at the battle of Leipzig, in 1813. After 1815 they were considerably improved, and became valuable auxiliaries, especially in conflicts with semi-civilised peoples. The shrapnel [3] shell, also, though it originated before the Napoleonic wars, underwent great improvements after the peace.

The small-arms used in the Navy during the period underwent far greater improvement than the heavy guns. The weapon in use immediately after the conclusion of the long wars was a flint lock

[1] Chiefly from Sir H. Douglas, ' Nav. Gunnery,' ed. of 1855 ; and Off. Cat. of Mus. of Art., Woolwich.

[2] Succeeded his father, Lt.-Genl. Sir W. Congreve, Bart., as Cont. of the Royal Laboratory : was never in the regular army; died 1828.

[3] Lt.-Genl. Henry Shrapnel invented the shell bearing his name in 1792, and it was adopted in 1803. In 1814 he was granted a pension of £1200 a year. He died in 1842.

musket, which was issued in two lengths, the shorter [1] being intended for boat service. This musket, the "Brown Bess," was altered, late in the thirties, into a percussion musket. About the year 1840, the Brunswick naval rifle, the first rifle used in the service, was partially introduced. Then followed the shorter smooth-bore percussion musket of 1842, which, rifled with three grooves, was used in the Navy. In 1851, the Delvigne-Minié percussion rifle became the Army weapon, and it was subsequently adopted by the Navy, where it was not actually superseded by the Enfield [2] until after 1856. A few particulars of these muzzle-loading muskets,[3] though they were by no means the only types employed, may be welcome, and are therefore given below :—

NATURE.	CALIBRE.	LENGTH OF BARREL.	WEIGHT OF MUSKET.	REMARKS.
	In.	In.	Lbs.	
Sea service Musket, *ca.* 1825 . .	·753	37	10·13	Flint lock.
do. do. (short) . .	·753	24	8·22	Flint lock. Length complete, 56 in.
Sea service "Brown Bess" . . .	·753	36	9·4	Converted to percussion.
Brunswick naval rifle, 1840. . .	·796	33	11·34	Grooves, 2. Twist, 1 in 30 in.
S.B. Percussion Musket, 1840 (short)	·753	30	8·8	Charge, 4·5 drachms.
Percussion Musket (Converted) .	·758	30	8·75	Grooves, 3. Twist, 1 in 78 in.
Delvigne-Minié Percussion Rifle [1] .	·702	39	9·31	Grooves, 4. Twist, 1 in 78 in.

[1] Bullet, 670 grs. ; charge, 68 grs.

The old "pepper box" revolver was used early in the century ; but in 1849 Colt's, and, in 1851, Deane and Adams's muzzle-loading, chambered, percussion-capped revolvers were patented ; and these, or similar weapons, were much carried by officers during the Crimean War.

All, or very nearly all, the earlier engines used for steam propulsion in the Navy were of the side-lever type, and all the boilers were of the flue variety, working with a pressure seldom or never exceeding from 22 to 30 lbs. In 1843, tubular boilers and oscillating cylinders first received the countenance of the Admiralty, though oscillating engines had been patented as early as 1827.[4] In the first screw ships the engines were not coupled directly to the screw shaft, but were geared to it. When, however, the screw had been for a few years applied to ships of the line, it was seen that it was desirable to keep the engines, then always horizontal, as far as possible below the water-line. This led to the coupling of the engines

[1] Length complete, 4 ft. 8 in.
[2] Cal. 0·577 ; in various lengths and weights, with three or five grooves.
[3] From specimens in R. U. S. Mus., etc.
[4] By Joseph Maudslay.

immediately to the screw shaft. More revolutions were, of course, needed than had been called for under a system which multiplied them by means of cogged wheels; but the use of high-pressure steam, introduced into the Navy in 1853,[1] served to simplify the problems thus created. For some years, nevertheless, high-pressure steam found little favour among naval engineers. The firms most intimately and honourably associated with the somewhat difficult task of inducing the Lords of the Admiralty to utilise steam as it deserved, were those of Boulton and Watt, Maudslay, and Penn.

The events of the war with the United States, having pointedly directed the attention of artillery experts to the vital importance of good gunnery in the Navy, a naval gunnery school was formed tentatively at Portsmouth in 1830. The origin of this was due chiefly to the persistent appeals of General Sir Howard Douglas to the Admiralty. Sir Howard, like Captains Joseph Needham Tayler, and Sir Philip Bowes Vere Broke, R.N., had been instrumental in securing the general fitting of sights to ships' guns in the early years of the peace, and also, like Captains James Marshall, and Thomas Hastings, had long taken a wide and active interest in all that pertained to the development of artillery science. The school, which was lodged on board the *Excellent*, was entrusted to the direction of Commander (afterwards Captain) George Smith, an officer well known for his own improvements in gunnery and for his invention of paddle-box boats. In 1832, the system of gunnery instruction thus introduced was extended and permanently established on board the *Excellent*, under Captain (later Sir) Thomas Hastings, who remained in command until August, 1845, and who was then succeeded by Captain Henry Ducie Chads. In the meantime, a school, on somewhat different lines, had been established on board the *San Josef*, at Devonport, by Captain Joseph Needham Tayler, while in charge of the Ordinary there from 1838 to 1841. The present Devonport gunnery establishment is, however, a more modern institution than the Portsmouth one, and dates only from August, 1856, when Captain Richard Strode Hewlett assumed command of the *Cambridge*.

In 1836, the Royal Naval College at Portsmouth, which up to that time had been devoted to the education of "young gentlemen" for the Navy, was appropriated for the instruction of half-pay naval

---

[1] The engines of the *Malacca*, of that year, worked with steam at 60 lbs.

officers, of all ranks, in the higher branches of the science of their profession.[1]

The final cessation of the French and American wars led, of course, to the making of enormous reductions in the employed strength of the *personnel* and *matériel* of the Navy. In 1813, there were in commission 99 ships of the line, and 495 cruisers, and 140,000 seamen and Royal Marines were serving. In 1817, only 13 ships of the line and 89 cruisers were in commission, and only 19,000 seamen and Royal Marines were voted. Thus, within about four years, 121,000 seamen and Royal Marines must have been thrown out of Government employment. The majority of these, it is to be feared, fell into something very like destitution. The fate of the unemployed officers was only a trifle less unfortunate, for the number of them placed upon half-pay was naturally nearly proportionate. In 1813, there were 3285 Lieutenants ; in 1817, there were 3949 ; and very little reflection will show that if every one of the Lieutenants was employed in 1813, about 3350 must have been unemployed in 1817. This state of affairs gave rise to much misery throughout the country. The peace not merely deprived all officers of practically every chance of prize money, but also suddenly reduced the regular emoluments of upwards of 80 per cent. of them in the following proportions : Admirals, from £5 to £2 2s. ; Vice-Admirals, from £4 to £1 12s. 6d. ; Rear-Admirals, from £3 to £1 5s. ; Captains, from (in some instances) £2 3s. 10d. to 14s. 6d. ; Commanders, from 16s. 6d. to 8s. 6d., or, at best, to 10s. ; and Lieutenants to, in the vast majority of cases, as little as 5s. a day. In no case could a half-pay Lieutenant expect to receive more than 7s., a sum equal only to £127 15s. a year ; and, unless he happened to be high up on the list, the allowance available for the support of himself as a gentleman, and probably of a wife and family as well, was no more than £91 5s. per annum ; nor was there much prospect of a brighter future, or even of employment.

"So long as war lasted, there was possible promotion, at least as far as post rank, for all ; and, from 1793 to 1815, deserving officers were seldom neglected for long by those with whom lay the selection. But the very readiness of the Admiralty to reward good service during war-time, led in peace-time to considerable hardships, besides being in some instances distinctly antagonistic to the public welfare. The promotions consequent upon the happy conclusion of hostilities, brought the Captains' list up to 883, the highest point it has ever attained since a British Navy has existed. At the time when that maximum was reached—it was in 1818—the senior Captain on the list had

---

[1] *Naut. Mag.* 1836, p. 311.

held that rank for twenty-two years, a period more than long enough, consistently with the best interests of the service, to qualify for flag-rank and command. Yet twenty-two years was a very short period in comparison with the time for which officers, who at the peace were Captains of medium or junior standing, had to wait ere they attained flag-rank. The evil reached its height in 1841.[1] In the earlier part of that year, all the Captains at the head of the list were men who had held post-rank ever since the year after Trafalgar. The senior one of them, judged by the date of his commission as Captain, was about sixty-eight years of age; several were over seventy; and one, at least, was as much as seventy-eight. Yet it was from among these old gentlemen that the list of Admirals had to be recruited; for then, as now, promotion to flag-rank went by simple seniority; and, to make matters worse, there was at that time no regular scheme of retirement for officers of above the rank of Commander. The consequence was that almost all the Admirals, besides a large number of Captains, were too old to be in a condition to render effective service in their profession; and the political caricaturist was justified, a little later, in representing the typical Commander-in-Chief of the period as a gouty veteran, obliged to promenade his quarter-deck in a bath-chair. Both Sir John Chambers White, and Vice-Admiral Edward Harvey, were seventy-four when they took up the command at the Nore; Admiral Bowles was seventy-nine when he became Port-Admiral at Portsmouth; Sir David Milne was of the same age when he assumed the like office at Devonport; and, even on foreign stations, Sir Robert Stopford flew his flag at seventy-three; Sir Peter Halkett at seventy-two; Rear-Admiral Charles John Austen (1) at seventy-three; and Lord Dundonald at seventy-five. And, in spite of such facilities as existed in 1841 for the retirement of officers of less rank than that of Post-Captain, the active lists were still choked throughout with old officers, survivors of the French wars. Of this category, there were about 200 Commanders and 1450 Lieutenants who had received no promotion whatsoever for a period of twenty-six years or more. One officer had been a Commander for forty-seven years; another had been a Lieutenant for sixty years; yet another had been a Master for sixty-one years; and there was a Purser with sixty-four years' service in that rank to his credit. All these officers, however, were set down in the Navy List as being fit for duty."[2]

During the war with Russia, the Navy, all things considered, disappointed the expectations of the country; and it may well be that its comparative failure to effect brilliant results may be traced in some degree to the excessive age of many of the Flag-officers and Captains, all of whom were, of course, the products of the system which has been described. In 1854, Sir Charles Napier was sixty-eight, and Vice-Admiral James Whitley Deans Dundas was a year older; and Sir Edmund Lyons, though only a Rear-Admiral, was sixty-four, while Rear-Admiral David Price was of the same age, and Rear-Admiral Henry Ducie Chads was sixty-six. From officers of such advanced life it was perhaps unreasonable to look for the energy, activity, and mental suppleness that distinguish capable younger men.

[1] A Royal Commission to inquire into the subject of promotion and retirement had been appointed in 1838. It reported in 1840, making various recommendations, some of which were adopted, one of them being the abolition of the rank of retired rear-admiral.

[2] Author; in 'Social England,' vi. 14.

Long ere the days of the Russian War, however, the Admiralty had made repeated efforts with the object of doing something towards clearing the congested lists, reducing the age of flag-officers, and accelerating promotion.   As early as 1816, 100 of the senior Lieutenants who, owing to age and infirmities, were assumed to be incapable of further service, were permitted to accept super-annuation with the rank of commander,[1] and a pension of 8s. 6d. a day.   This arrangement was a slight extension of the very limited scheme of superannuation for Lieutenants that had been in operation for some years previously.   In 1827, for the first time, some attempt was made to reduce the active flag list.[2]   In 1830, another Order in Council [3] authorised the retirement of Lieutenants who were of suffi-cient seniority to be in the receipt of half-pay at 7s. a day.   The list of officers who took advantage of this provision soon became a long one; yet the measure thinned the lower executive ranks only to a partial extent, and, of course, left untouched the upper ranks, which were equally crowded.   A further step was taken in 1840,[4] when 50 of the senior Commanders were allowed to retire with the rank of captain, and half-pay at 10s. 6d. a day.   Still the tension remained extreme until the elaboration of a more general scheme, which was published in the *London Gazette* of September 1st, 1848, and became part of the Regulations under an Order in Council of April 24th, 1847.   This provided that the rank of retired rear-admiral [5] should be given by seniority, with pay at the rate of £1 5s. a day, to such Captains on the 14s. 6d. half-pay list as might apply for it ; and that an addition of 7s. 6d. a day should be given to applicants by seniority from the 12s. 6d. and 10s. 6d. half-pay lists of Captains of not less than twenty years' standing and fifty-five years of age, officers from both lists to be permitted to assume the title of retired rear-admiral at the period when, had they remained upon the active list, they would have obtained the flag by seniority.   The Order also gave proportionally increased pensions to the widow of the officers affected.   The great merit of this Order was that it tended to facilitate promotion, and to reduce the age of flag-officers on the active list, though, from the nature of the situation, it could not produce these results except gradually.   A still more effective Order

---

[1] O. in C., Jan. 30th, 1816.   [2] O. in C., June 30th, 1827.
[3] Nov. 1st, 1830.   [4] O. in C., Aug. 10th, 1840.
[5] Which had been abolished only a few years earlier in pursuance of the Report of 1840.

of June 25th, 1851, reduced the number of flag officers on the active list to 99, exclusive of Admirals of the Fleet; reduced the number of Captains on the active list to a permanent maximum of 350; placed the number of Commanders on the active list at 350, and the number of Lieutenants at 1200; and made various retiring arrangements accordingly. These various Orders, on December 20th, 1856, had had the salutary result of transferring to the Retired, or Reserved Half-pay Lists, 221 flag-officers, 372 captains, and 449 commanders, in addition to officers who, having been retired, had died before that date. The needful reforms had not even then been completed, but an excellent and very substantial beginning had been made with them. The number of officers then actually remaining on the active list was :

Admirals	.	.	21	Masters	. .	336	Naval Instructors [1] 51
Vice-Admirals	.		29	Mates	. .	148	Medical Officers . 617
Rear-Admirals	.		51	Engineers	. .	119	Paymasters. . 447
Captains	.	.	389	Second Masters	.	105	Officers, R.M.L.I.. 423
Commanders	.		542	Chaplains	. .	142	Officers, R.M.A. . 58
Lieutenants	.		1138				

[1] Besides those who were also Chaplains, and who are counted as such.

It should here be recalled, with regard to the Royal Marines, that a fourth, or Woolwich Division,[1] of the force had been formed in 1805,[2] and that an artillery company had, at about the same time, been added to each division ; but it should be noted that it was not until 1854 that the separate title of Royal Marine Light Infantry was conferred, and that the old artillery companies, by that time increased in number, were constituted a separate corps under the name of the Royal Marine Artillery. This corps, with headquarters at Portsmouth, was then given a strength of fourteen companies.

Continuous service for seamen in the Navy dates from the issue, on February 14th, 1853, of the report of a Committee on Manning which had been ordered on the previous July 26th, and from the consequent promulgation of an Order in Council of April 1st, 1853. The real author of the scheme as adopted was Mr. Charles Henry Pennell, then a senior clerk in the Admiralty, who, in 1867, was knighted for his services, and who died in 1898, aged ninety-three.

But, at first, seamen were almost as difficult to obtain as they had ever been. Lord Clarence Paget, writing of his appointment to the *Princess Royal*, 91, in October, 1853, says :—

" There was a scarcity, indeed almost an absence, of seamen. However, with assistance of several valuable officers who were appointed to the ship, and by dint of

---

[1] Abolished in 1870.   [2] O. in C., Aug. 15th, 1805.

handbills and touting of all sorts, we managed to enter at the average of twenty to th ity per week, such as they were. Scarcely any of them had been in a man-of-war, and consequently they were entirely ignorant of the management of great guns and muskets. . . . I had named March 1st (1854) as the earliest period I could get the ship to Spithead, but the Admiralty were so anxious to make a show, that we were forced out on February 15th; and a very pretty mess we made of it . . . But still we could not get men, men, men! I wrote and wrote to the Admiralty, stating that if they did not assist me by placing two hundred coastguards on board, I should be taken by the first Russian frigate we fell in with." [1]

Up to 1823 the daily rum allowance per man in the Navy was always half a pint, and was the cause of much drunkenness. In that year, on commissioning the *Thetis*, 46, Captain Sir John Philli-more obtained the permission of the Admiralty, subject to the con-sent of the crew, to reduce the allowance to a quarter of a pint. The innovation made the people of the *Thetis* unpopular with those of other ships, and even led to fighting; but, on the return of the *Ganges*, 84, from the Mediterranean, her crew announced that they would not suffer the *Thetis's* people to be maltreated, as the innova-tion was most beneficial. The change enabled the men to have meat every day, and to escape the two " banyan days " per week, on which no meat had formerly been served out. It also enabled them to have cocoa and tea, and gave them 2s. per month extra pay. [2]

It is unfortunately impossible, on account of lack of space, to follow here the development and history of the Packet Service, [3] the Coast Blockade, the Coastguard, the Impress Service, the Excise and Customs' Service, the Transport Service, the Signal Station Service, the Coast Volunteers, and other organisations which, during a part or the whole of the period now under review, were connected with the Royal Navy. Indeed, in a work like the present, it is extremely difficult to include even a sufficient number of the facts needful to enable the reader to follow in the broadest and most general way the gradual evolution of the fighting Navy; and, owing to the vastness and complexity of the subject, it has been found imperative to omit many details which, though they are of the

[1] Adm. Lord C. Paget, ' Autobiog.,' 79.

[2] Life of Sir B. J. Sulivan, 12.

[3] The "Falmouth Packets," first established in 1688 for the conveyance of mails all over the world, were taken over by the Admiralty in 1823, and thenceforward placed under naval officers. This arrangement continued until 1853. In the later part of the period, Falmouth was abandoned, and "Packet Stations" were established at Dover, Portpatrick, Pembroke, Liverpool, and Holyhead. Steamers began to be utilised in the service in 1830.

greatest interest, cannot be adequately illustrated outside the covers of special treatises.

Until 1814 there was, using terms in their modern sense, no official Navy List. For many years previously there had been published at intervals, on behalf of the Admiralty, lists of Flag-officers, Captains, Commanders, and Lieutenants. These, which very well printed, on the best quality of thick paper, swelled, towards the close of the long wars, to bulky volumes, which are commonly met with in red morocco bindings and with gilt edges, and which must have been very costly. They showed merely the seniority and dates of commissions of officers of the ranks in question, and gave no other information whatsoever. To supplement them, Mr. D. Steel, a publisher, of Union Row, Minories, caused to be compiled and issued periodically a pamphlet which, at its first appearance, in 1780, was entitled, ' Complete List of the Royal Navy.' This originally included nothing beyond a list of ships, with the number of their guns, the names of their commanders, and letters indicating whether the vessels were in commission, out of commission, or only in process of building. It consisted of no more than a dozen very small pages, and cost sixpence. But it quickly grew ; and as early as the end of 1781, it also gave the stations of ships in commission, and a list of men-of-war taken by or from the enemy. It next began to chronicle the names of officers of Commander's rank and upwards who from time to time perished in the service of their country. In 1782 it added the date of launch or acquirement to the other information concerning each ship, and gave lists of the Lords of the Admiralty, Commissioners of the Navy, etc., and Navy Agents. So it progressed, coming out monthly in time of war and quarterly during peace, and, at length, increasing its price to a shilling for the edition on common, and to eighteenpence for the edition on fine paper. Towards the close of the war it contained an immense mass of useful intelligence, and extended to sixty pages or upwards of closely-printed matter. It then comprised not only the information given in the earlier issues, but also lists of Flag-officers, Captains, Commanders, Lieutenants, Masters, Surgeons, and officers of the Royal Marines.

But Steel's Navy Lists, though very accurate and trustworthy, were not official; and it was not until the beginning of 1814 that any list giving the kind of information to be found in Steel was published by authority. The Navy List which was then begun, and which has been continued to the present time, seems to have been originally compiled, under Admiralty direction, by a Mr. Finlaison, and was issued by Mr. John Murray, who remained its publisher for more than seventy years. The lists contain the history of many changes, showing, for example, as they do, the gradual rise to influence of the engineer officers, who, nevertheless, were not catalogued by name in them until as late as 1852. They are, however, astonishingly reticent on other matters concerning which it seems natural to consult them. Thus, for instance, they vouchsafe no enlightenment concerning an important reform which was made in 1843, and which transmuted Masters, Paymasters (Pursers), Surgeons, Naval Instructors, and Chaplains from Warrant into Commissioned officers.

Some interesting and important Admiralty Memoranda or Orders, or Orders in Council of the period, are those of December 22nd, 1836, establishing the warrant rank of "Naval Instructor and Schoolmaster"; July 24th, 1837, regulating the rank and pay of engineer officers, and directing that they should rank "below Carpenters"; December 6th, 1838, establishing ships' libraries; and March 30th, 1839, conferring upon seamen the right to purchase tobacco at a shilling a pound—the price paid by them to this day.

The lists, moreover, enable us to follow the alterations which were made in Naval uniform. The earliest of these dates from January 1st, 1825.

"Waistcoats and knee-breeches of white kerseymere were ordered for all grades; but pantaloons of blue cloth, and half boots, were also permitted to be worn. A Master of the Fleet, and all officers of civilian status, were assigned black grips to their swords, and were directed not to have the blades blued. Physicians and Secretaries were given dress swords with rapier blades. The lapels of all these Warrant Officers' coats were to be blue, with distinguishing marks on collars and buttons. A Master of the Fleet bore on his collar, and all officers of his department bore on their buttons, three anchors, the seal of the Navy Office. Physicians bore on their collars, and all Medical officers on their buttons, an anchor with a serpent twisted round the shank and stock, the seal of the Sick and Hurt Office. Pursers bore on their collars, and all members of the accountant branch on their buttons, two anchors and cables, crossed saltire, the seal of the Victualling Office. Blue, instead of white pantaloons, were made optional for junior officers, probably with a view to save expense. Mates were given a gold button and a button-hole of gold lace on the stand-up collars of their coats, and a narrow white edge to the coat. Midshipmen were given a white turn-back as before, but their coats were not edged with white. Mates, Midshipmen, Gunners, Boatswains, and Carpenters were assigned swords similar to those of the Masters, but were not confined to weapons of any particular length. All officers were required to wear cocked hats when in full or undress, but, while at sea, might wear round black hats, with black silk bindings and bands, and black buckles, black silk or leather cockades and loops, and distinctive buttons. The cocked hat had previously been worn as individual fancy suggested; but in 1825 it was so prescribed as to be wearable ' fore and aft ' only, although, until some years later, a few perverse officers continued to have their hats so made that they could be worn ' athwart-ships.' The full-dress coats of those commissioned officers who were then of warrant rank had turned-down collars ; and their buttons bore no crown above the anchor. The officers in question, moreover, were no longer given knee-breeches. All undress coats had fall-down collars, and lapels to button across the chest ; and commissioned officers were given distinguishing stripes on their cuffs, or were rendered recognisable by their epaulettes or buttons.

"In 1827 full-dress was abolished, and knee-breeches were directed to be worn only at Drawing-Rooms. The colour of coat collars was changed from white to blue, and the collars were made to stand up. The white cuffs were given a slashing ; but the cuff rings distinctive of flag-rank were withdrawn. In 1831, full dress, with a few changes, was re-established.

"In 1833 King William altered the facings of naval uniform from white to red, and the old colour was not restored until 1843. In 1837 a uniform was first established for Engineers, who were then all warrant officers. In 1843 it was ordered that officers should be distinguished by the disposition of their buttons, executive officers being given a double-breasted, and civilian officers a single-breasted arrangement, and Masters having their buttons at regular intervals, Paymasters theirs in twos, and Surgeons theirs in threes. All special devices were withdrawn from buttons, except from those of the Engineers, which bore an engine surmounted by a crown, and were disposed in groups of four. Black-handled sword grips were thenceforth given only to Boatswains, Gunners, and Carpenters.

"In 1846 scales, or epaulettes without bullion, were made permissible to be worn on jackets at sea by Captains and Commanders ; and Mates and Second Masters were given single epaulettes, with distinguishing badges, to be worn on the right shoulder. The undress coats of executive officers were assigned pointed flaps instead of lapels, and a gold crown was ordered to be worn over the lace on caps. In 1847 scales for Captains and Commanders were abolished, and the frock-coat was established, to be worn without epaulettes, but, in the case of executive officers, with distinctive cuff rings. Caps were not allowed to be worn ashore in full or undress uniform. In 1856, the marks on the epaulettes were altered ; Mates were given shoulder-straps or scales ; Midshipmen had dirks substituted for their swords ; the cap-badge was introduced ; and mohair cap-bands took the place of gold cap-lace. At the same time the Engineers' distinctive button was withdrawn."

But, during the time, as the following extracts will show, there was more laxity than is now permitted :—

"Beards and moustaches were never seen in the navy till Crimean times. The first Captain who ever dared upon the innovation was Lord John Hay,[1] in the *Wasp ;* and, as to the hairy faces of his gig's crew he added red caps, no small sensation was created . . . The first Captain who had the temerity to invade the sacred precincts of the Admiralty with hirsute 'fixings' was Captain Moorsom,[2] of percussion shell fame, who, on his return from the Black Sea, 'repaired' to the sanctum of the First Sea Lord to report himself. . . . Admiral Sir Maurice Fitzhardinge Berkeley [3] . . . pale

---

[1] Admiral of the Fleet Lord John Hay (3) was Commander of the *Wasp,* 1852–54.

[2] Constantine Richard Moorsom, born 1792, died a Vice-Admiral on the retired list in 1861.

[3] Later Lord Fitzhardinge ; died an Admiral in 1867.

with rage and astonishment . . . was not in a condition to do more than wave the daring intruder to the door with the cutting remark : ' Horseguards next door ! ' [1]

"The late Admiral Sir Alexander Milne [2] told me of an eccentric Captain, who insisted upon all his officers wearing tall white beaver hats—even Midshipmen having to go aloft in them." [3]

During all this period, moreover, there was no established uniform for seamen; nor was anything of the kind introduced until 1857. The next extracts will show what kind of clothing was occasionally worn by men on the lower deck :—

"The Pursers' Instructions of 1824 contain a long list of the various descriptions of slop-clothing of which a stock was to be maintained, such as blue-cloth jackets, knitted worsted waistcoats, blue cloth trousers, duck trousers and frocks, shirts, stockings, hats, mitts, blankets, and black silk handkerchiefs." [4]

"The Captain of the *Vernon*, in 1840, ordered his men, on fitting out, to wear red serge frocks, with red woollen comforters ; but, when the ship had been in commission a short time, the unforeseen difficulty of keeping up the supply arose, and was eventually overcome by appropriating all the remaining red frocks to one watch, the other donning the blue, which were obtainable from the Purser. . . . In the *Blazer*, in 1845, the ship's company wore blue and white striped guernseys, with jackets. Commander Arthur Parry Eardley Wilmot, of the *Harlequin*, in 1853, dressed his gig's crew as harlequins ; and in 1854, Captain Wallace Houstoun, in the *Trincomalee*, had all his ship's company in red shirts and fancy caps." [5]

"We embarked at the King's Stairs in the Dockyard, where we found the ship's barge, with its stalwart crew dressed in white frocks and trousers, awaiting us." [6]—(*Amphitrite*, 24, Captain Thomas Rodney Eden, 1847.)

"A year or two after this my father took me to see the review of the Experimental Squadron, which was assembled at Spithead under the command of Admiral Sir Hyde Parker. Her Majesty reviewed the squadron in her yacht . . . between two lines of towering stately ships . . . with their yards manned by sailors all dressed in white." [7]

"The sailors . . . were dressed in their best clothes, or Sunday rig. . . . This consisted of a short blue jacket with double rows of large mother of pearl buttons placed very close together, white frock with wide blue jean collar worn outside the jacket, . . . and immensely wide blue cloth trousers." [8]—(*Victory*, Captain Francis Price Blackwood, 1850.)

"Very slack ideas prevailed in these times with regard to uniformity in seamen's dress. . . . Captains of ships were allowed to vary the uniform of their men almost at their pleasure. As an instance of this I may mention that the crew of the *Caledonia* were allowed to wear a Scotch bonnet with a tartan band, as in character with the ship's name." [9]—(*Caledonia*, Captain Thomas Wren Carter, 1851.)

---

[1] ' At School and at Sea,' by ' Martello Tower ' (1899), p. 230.

[2] Born 1806, died Admiral of the Fleet, 1896.

[3] ' At School and at Sea,' 147.

[4] ' Brit. Fleet,' 506 n.

[5] ' Brit. Fleet,' 507. Have we in this paragraph a clue to the origin of the term "blazer," as applied to a striped jacket ?

[6] Capt. C. Sloane-Stanley : ' Remins.,' 9.

[7] Sloane-Stanley, ' Remins.,' 11. But this was, not after 1847, but in the summer of 1845 ; and it was not Admiral Sir Hyde Parker, but Rear-Adm. Hyde Parker (3), who commanded.

[8] Sloane-Stanley, ' Remins.,' 61.

[9] Sloane-Stanley, ' Remins.,' 168.

"The Captain wore a moustache. Having commanded a ship in the Mediterranean on the Greek station, he fancied petticoat trousers for the crew."[1]—(H.M.S. *Tweed,* Captain Lord Henry John Spencer Churchill, 1827.)

In these pages it has been repeatedly mentioned that during the long wars no medals were granted except in a few cases to Flag-officers and Captains, for any service, no matter how distinguished. After a lapse, however, of upwards of thirty years, it was decided to grant medals to survivors who had participated in certain selected actions. The selection was to be made by Admirals Sir Thomas Byam Martin and Sir Thomas Bladen Capell, and Rear-Admiral Sir James Alexander Gordon, who, with Admiral Sir William Hall Gage,[2] were appointed for the purpose in accordance with the provisions of a *Gazette* notice of June 1st, 1847. It was at first intended that medals should be given only for those actions for which gold medals had previously been granted to Flag-officers and Captains, and of which a complete list is given below;[3] but the scope of the Board of Selection was afterwards extended by a notice of June 7th, 1848; and, on January 25th, 1849, it was announced that medals were ready for issue in accordance with the recommendations of the Board. It cannot be pretended that the selection was well made. The names

FLAG OFFICERS' AND CAPTAINS' GOLD MEDAL, 1794–1815.

(*On the obverse, within an oak an laurel wreath, was the recipient's name.*)

of officers who had not been present were set down as having been associated with certain actions;[4] and numerous actions which

---

[1] Sir H. Keppel, 'Life,' i. 68.

[2] Gage, for some reason, did not sign the lists which were delivered by the Board.

[3] Gold Medal actions :—

Lord Howe's victory, June 1st, 1794.
Battle of Cape St. Vincent, February 14th, 1797.
Battle of Camperdown, October 11th, 1797.
Battle of the Nile, August 1st, 1798.
Recapture of the *Hermione,* October 25th, 1799.
Battle of Trafalgar, October 21st, 1805.
Sir Richard Strachan's victory, November 4th, 1805.
Battle off San Domingo, February 6th, 1806.
Brisbane's capture of Curaçoa, January 1st, 1807.
Capture of the *Thétis* by the *Amethyst,* November, 10th, 1808.
Capture of the *Badere Zaffer* by the *Seahorse,* July 6th, 1808.

Capture of the *Furieuse* by the *Bonne Citoyenne,* July 6th, 1809.
Capture of Banda Neira, August 9th, 1810.
Hoste's victory off Lissa, March 13th, 1811.
Capture of the *Rivoli* by the *Victorious,* February 22nd, 1812.
Capture of the *Chesapeake* by the *Shannon,* June 1st, 1813.
Capture of the *Etoile* by the *Hebrus,* March 27th, 1814.
Capture of the *President* by the *Endymion,* January 15th, 1815.

[4] *E.g.,* one "L. Purver," was set down as having commanded the *Entreprenante* at Trafalgar. It should have been Lieut. Robert Benjamin Young.

might have been justly included were entirely ignored. Honour was, however, tardily done to hundreds of gallant and deserving men; and the country cleansed itself from the reproach of having been ignobly ungrateful to those who had fought so well for its liberty and its empire.

The ribbon from which this medal was ordered to be worn was white, with blue edges.

Several other naval medals were instituted during the period. The Long Service and Good Conduct (Navy) Medal was first granted in 1831. It is worn suspended from a blue white-edged ribbon. The medal for Conspicuous Gallantry (Navy) dates from 1855, and is worn from a blue ribbon which has a white stripe

NAVAL WAR SERVICE MEDAL, 1793–1815.
(Numerous clasps were granted with this.)

along its middle. Other special war-service medals were also given, in some instances with clasps, for Burmah (1824–26),[1] Burmah (1852–53),[2] the Crimea (1854–56), and the Baltic (1854–55); and there is an Arctic Medal for explorations between 1818 and 1855. In addition, the Navy shared in the general service medals which were distributed for the operations in China (1839–42), New Zealand (1845-46), and the Cape (1850–53). Certain late naval services, as, for example, the battle of Navarino and the bombardment of Acre, were rewarded with the Naval Medal, 1793–1815, with appropriate clasps.

The Victoria Cross, instituted by Royal Warrant of February 5th, 1856, is conferred for exceptional exhibitions of personal bravery and devotion in face of the enemy, and is worn by naval recipients

---

[1] Indian medal, No. 1, issued in 1851.   [2] Indian medal, No. 2.

from a ribbon of dark blue. The first investiture of it was held by
Queen Victoria in Hyde Park on June 26th, 1857; and the first naval
men to obtain the distinction were, specifying their rank at the time
of the act for which it was given :—

"Captain William Peel; Lieutenants John Edmund Commerell, Henry James
Raby, George Fiott Day, Cecil William Buckley, John Bythesea, and Hugh Talbot
Burgoyne; Mates William Nathan Wrighte Hewett, and Charles Davis Lucas; Mid-
shipman Edward St. John Daniel; Boatswains Henry Cooper, Joseph Kellaway, and
John Shepherd; Boatswain's Mates John Sullivan, and Henry Curtis; Quartermaster
William Rickard; Captain of the Mast, John Ingoueville; Seamen Joseph Trewavas,
Thomas Reeves, James Gorman, and Mark Scholefield; Lieutenant of Marines George
Dare Dowell; Corporal of Marines John Prettyjohn; and Bombardier Thomas
Wilkinson."

Two little episodes connected with the honour of the flag
occurred in 1839, and deserve a brief notice. The schooner

NAVAL LONG SERVICE AND GOOD CONDUCT MEDAL.
Instituted 1831.
Ribbon: blue, with white edges.

Spider, 6, Lieutenant John O'Reilly (1), while working up the
River Plate at night, was fired into by a French row-boat, her
leadsman being wounded. News of the affair was sent to the
senior officer on the station, Captain Thomas Herbert, of the *Calliope*, 26, who at once demanded an explanation from the French
senior officer. It was shown that the offending boat had been at
the time without an officer on board; and Herbert asked for an
inquiry into the conduct of the captain of the ship to which she
belonged, for suffering her to be officerless while on patrol duty.
The French admiral offered to write home for instructions, and, in
the meantime, volunteered to indemnify the wounded man. Herbert
refused the gratuity, answering: "The British Government can

and will reward all who suffer in its service."[1]　A suitable expression of regret was eventually accepted.

The other occurrence took place at Port Louis, Mauritius.　In the harbour there lay the British merchantman *Greenlaw*, Thomas Driver,[2] master, and the French warship *Isère*.　On Saturday, September 7th, the *Isère*, when dressing ship, hoisted at her mizen peak, uppermost, the French flag, then the flags of different nations, and under all the St. George's ensign.　Driver took upon himself to resent this, and on the following morning, having converted his telegraph flag into a French one, stopped it under his bowsprit.　A boat from the French ship went alongside him, and desired him to haul it down.　He refused.　On the 9th, two officers from the Frenchman challenged him.　Driver considered that they were not of sufficient rank to fight with him, but offered to meet a French captain with pistols.　Thereupon the French complained to the Governor, Sir W. Nicolay, and asked that Driver should not only apologise, but also make obeisance on the French quarter-deck.　After much correspondence, Driver apologised, and the obeisance was then not insisted upon.　It does not appear that the Governor obliged the French captain also to apologise; but it is satisfactory to be able to add that the incident led to the adoption, by the navies of all civilised Powers, of the principle that the flag of a friendly nation shall never be displayed on board a man-of-war of another nation in such a position as to possibly suggest that the strange flag is in any way inferior in value or dignity to the flag of the ship.[3]

Flogging continued to be a frequently-awarded punishment in the Navy, especially in ships which had been commissioned only with difficulty, and which therefore contained numerous landsmen of bad character.　There were also still many severe, if not actually brutal, Captains in the service.

" A week rarely passed at this period without some man receiving his three or four dozen lashes at the gangway.　The first time I witnessed corporal punishment I was horror-struck, and, after the first minute or so, averted my eyes to avoid the ghastly sight; but after a time I became so used to seeing what was called ' scratching a man's back,' that I could contemplate the spectacle from beginning to end without shrinking. The punishment of flogging was usually inflicted for crimes of insubordination or

---

[1] *Hants Telegraph.*

[2] Driver's bitterness may in part be attributed to the fact that he was a survivor of the old French wars—in fact, a Master, R.N., of Sept. 7th, 1809.　He returned to active service in the Navy, and died on the eve of the Crimean war.

[3] Corr. in *Naut. Mag.*, Jan. 1840.

drunkenness, more often for the latter than for the former. It was undoubtedly a severe one, as the discoloured, raw-beef-hued appearance of the victim's back attested; but I never saw any streams of blood or severe laceration of the flesh caused by any flogging I have ever witnessed; and I must have seen some hundreds in my day. That the punishment was not considered degrading by the great majority of the men I am quite certain. Indeed, the young and plucky ones used to consider it a feather in their caps to be able to undergo their flogging without uttering a cry, and advanced themselves considerably in the estimation of their shipmates if they took their 'four bag' like a man. . . . There were no cells on board ship in the time I am writing of; and offences that are now punished by confinement for ten days or so in these dreadful little dens were then expiated at the gangway in as many minutes." [1]

Punishments were sometimes as excentric as they were frequent :—

"I have seen the whole of a boat's crew spread-eagled in the rigging for two or three hours. Gags were often used." (This applies to a period subsequent to 1846.) "I have seen a troublesome man confined in a little cage made of gratings, scarcely bigger than himself, in which he could neither stand upright, scarcely sit, and not lie down. I have seen the owner of a shore boat, detected in bringing spirits alongside, hoisted up to the mainyard-arm *in his boat*, and left to dangle there for hours." [2]

But ships the commissioning of which did not involve any particular difficulties, and which were manned for the most part by people accustomed to discipline, were often, especially if commanded by first-rate officers, places in which the infliction of corporal punishment was quite exceptional. H.M.S. *Havannah*, 19, was commissioned in August, 1855, with a complement of 240 officers and men. Her commander was Captain Thomas Harvey (2), an officer as well known for his high professional attainments as for his tact and firmness. I have before me his logs and private memoranda from August, 1855, to June, 1859; and from these it appears that during the forty-seven months, only 14 men and 7 boys were flogged in the ship. The total number of lashes inflicted was, on the men, 600, and upon the boys, 336; and the greatest number awarded to any culprit was four dozen, that being the limit for such summary punishments, while the least number was 30. It is instructive to examine the causes which induced Captain Harvey to act with this severity. Of the men, 3 were punished for having been drunk and mutinous; 3 for petty theft; and 3 for having been drunk while on sentry duty; 1 had disposed of his kit and attempted to desert; 1 had drawn a knife on the sergeant of the guard; 1 had told the Master-at-Arms to "Go to hell"; 1 had used violence

---

[1] Sloane-Stanley, 'Remins.,' 283. The writer describes life in the *Albion* in 1852.

[2] 'At School and at Sea,' 214. The same book contains many other examples of excentric punishments.

and insolence to the first Lieutenant; and 1 had broken open and used a case of brandy which had been entrusted to his charge. Of the boys, 1 was flogged for stealing; 1 for drunkenness and insubordination; and 1 for disobedience and mutinous conduct; and 4 were punished for having brought infamous charges without being able to substantiate them. During the commission, which was served in the Pacific, then a very attractive station for deserters, only 37 men ran.

A few miscellaneous extracts illustrative of some social aspects of the Navy in the period under review must end the chapter.

"I was shortly ushered out of the cold into the presence of Mrs. Hunn and two charming young ladies. . . . We sailed from Portsmouth on April 12th, Mrs. Hunn and my playfellows with us. . . . On June 5th, we arrived at Madeira . . . here our Captain, his wife, children, and gig's Midshipman were entertained." [1]—(H.M.S. *Tweed*, Captain Frederick Hunn, 1824.)

"Had to attend my Captain at a court-martial which caused an unusual sensation. . . . The prisoner was Captain of the *Ariadne*. He was tried for having purchased a negro slave at Zanzibar, and taken her to sea. She mysteriously disappeared off the coast of Africa. . . . He was dismissed the service." [2]—(Portsmouth, January, 1826.)

"We sailed on the 19th from Malta, having Mrs. and Miss Duckworth, the Captain's family, Mrs. Mends, and Miss Stiloe on board." [3]

"*Powerful*, Avoli, Gulf of Adramyti; June 16th, 1840.

"You will be surprised to hear we have three ladies on board, guests of the Captain; and how they came here I must explain. You know there is an order by the Admiralty that no Captain or officer shall take his wife to sea with him; but it does not say that he may not take any other person's wife; so Mrs. —— the wife of the Captain of the ——, having got tired of staying at Malta without ever seeing her husband, came up to Smyrna; and, as he could not take her on board of his own ship, Captain Napier kindly offered to take her in his, and got two English ladies of Smyrna to accompany her for the trip." [4]

". . . there was no longer any necessity for me going to the Admiral's office every morning—the Captain, with his wife and family, having taken up their residence on board." [5]—(*Albion*, Capt. William James Hope Johnstone, in Plymouth Sound, 1850.)

"Presently the Captain came up, accompanied by his wife and daughters, who made their first appearance on deck after a considerable interval of confinement to the cabin." [6] —(*Albion*, Capt. W. J. Hope Johnstone, off Lisbon, Dec. 29th, 1850.)

"Lady ——, the Admiral's wife, who was living on board with her husband, had taken up a position in the stern gallery to see the race, and her sensitive ears were so

---

[1] Sir H. Keppel, 'Life,' i. 27, 33.

[2] Sir H. Keppel, 'Life,' i. 55, 56. But the officer in question, Captain Isham Fleming Chapman, was restored to the service, from which he did not retire until 1846.

[3] Mids. James Francis Ballard Wainwright, from the *Rodney*, Capt. Hyde Parker (3), May 27th, 1838. MS. in Author's collection.

[4] Letter of Lieut. Robt. Hilley Elliot, in 'Life of Sir C. Napier,' ii. 409.

[5] Sloane-Stanley, 'Remins.,' 114.   [6] *Ib.*, 147.

shocked by the vigorous Anglo-Saxon of our men, that she beat a hasty retreat, and made a formal complaint to her husband of the conduct of our boat's crew, which resulted in the whole boat's crew being severely punished for giving way to their feelings in the presence of a lady. The moral deduced from this in the gun-room was : That ladies have no business on board ship."[1]—(Rear-Admiral J. W. D. Dundas, in *Britannia*, at Port Mahon, May 24th, 1852.)

" It will scarcely be believed that formerly each man's daily allowance was half a pint of rum mixed with three half pints of water, in two issues, at dinner and supper; which, on the introduction of tea and cocoa into the naval dietary—perhaps in the thirties—was reduced to a quarter of a pint, one gill; and again in 1850 to half that quantity during dinner, supper grog, for very sufficient reasons, being entirely abolished."[2]

The fashionable dining hour was earlier then than now :—

" These sea dinners were usually between three and four o'clock; and, half an hour or so before the time, the squadron would bring to, main-topsail to the mast, as the saying is, and lower their lee quarter boats, and despatch their respective Captains to the scene of the banquet on board the flagship." [3]

Supper in the gun-room was at half-past six. Afterwards the seniors played cards there, and, at a certain hour, a fork was stuck into one of the overhead beams, this being a signal for the youngsters to withdraw, and leave the oldsters to their own devices. The morality of the gun-room left much to be desired. There was much drunkenness, and " orgies were of almost nightly occurrence." [4]

The Navy was still, as in the days of " Mad Montagu," a school for excentrics :—

" Just before our arrival in the Archipelago, a distressing event occurred on board a corvette, the *Hind*, commanded by Lord ———. His ship was anchored close to the Greek camp at Salamis, and almost within sight of the Turkish stronghold of Athens. He invited the Greek chiefs to an entertainment, and, being of a jovial turn, the wine passed freely. He suddenly turned up the hands to make sail, and told the Greeks that he was going to hand them over to their mortal enemies. They made a rush on deck, which was full of their armed retainers, drew their yataghans, and set to work to cut away all the ropes. The sailors were taken in a panic, and ran forward, so that the Palikari had full possession of the ship, and made a wreck of the upper deck. At length the Captain succeeded in persuading them that it was only a joke, and order was restored; but it cost him his career.[5] He was ordered home, and was never employed again. He became years afterwards equerry to the Duke of Sussex, who was very fond of him, as, indeed, were all who knew him." [6]

---

[1] Sloane-Stanley, ' Remins.,' 282.

[2] ' At School and at Sea,' p. 82. *See* p. 208 *antea*.

[3] Sloane-Stanley, ' Remins.,' 291. The C. in C. was then (1853) R.-Adm. J. W. D. Dundas.

[4] Sloane-Stanley, ' Remins.,' 141–143, 146.

[5] I think that Lord C. Paget was mistaken, and that the officer in question was Lord Henry John Spencer Churchill, who was appointed to the *Hind*, April 25th, 1823, posted August 4th, 1826, appointed to the *Tweed*, May 18th, 1827, and died in command of the *Druid*, June 3rd, 1840.

[6] Adm. Lord C. Paget, ' Autobiog.,' 10.

Nothing, perhaps, better illustrates the simple, self-sufficient, self-reliant, and withal excentric character of the typical British Captain of the period than a story, the truth of which has been questioned, although without reason.

"I have often been asked," says Admiral Sir B. J. Sulivan,[1] "if it is true that a Captain in the Royal Navy once made a Bishop of his Chaplain; and I have replied : 'Not only is it true, but the ship[2] I first served in as a Midshipman was the ship in which it took place, though I joined her afterwards.' Her last voyage had been to take an African regiment to the first Ashantee war ; and she landed some officers and men to share in the defence of Cape Coast Castle and the detached forts. On her way home she touched at St. Michael's, one of the Azores. In Roman Catholic countries, in which there were no Protestant cemeteries, their dead had to be buried in gardens. The Protestants of St. Michael's had purchased a piece of ground about half a mile outside the town, and had enclosed it by a wall. When the *Thetis* arrived, a deputation called on Sir John Phillimore, and asked him to take two petitions home for them—one to the Archbishop of Canterbury, requesting him to send a Bishop to consecrate their ground, and another to the First Lord of the Admiralty, asking him to provide a ship to take out the Bishop. Sir J. Phillimore assured them that it was quite unnecessary, because his Chaplain would consecrate it for them. They replied that it *must* be a Bishop. He then said he would give his Chaplain an acting order as Bishop. I have seen that 'acting order.' It ran as follows: 'You are hereby requested and directed to take on yourself the office of Bishop of St. Michael's, for the purpose of consecrating a Protestant cemetery; and for so doing this shall be your warrant. Given under my hand, this — day of ——, 1824. (Signed) John Phillimore, Captain; N. Royse,[3] Chaplain, H.M.S. *Thetis.*' The cemetery was thereupon consecrated with full naval honour."

The ship's band, sailors, and Marines attended; and the "Bishop," on landing, was saluted with nineteen guns.

And here is one version of the truth about the abolition of mast-heading as a punishment for "young gentlemen" :—

". . . Drummond, a promising young Guardsman, was the cause of doing away with the mast-heading of Midshipmen. . . . One day at sea, Ingestrie sent a Mid . . . to say he wished to speak to Drummond, who was playing backgammon, and delayed obeying the summons until he finished his game. When he appeared, Ingestrie told him that on board a man-of-war orders must be obeyed, and, in joke, said he would next time send him to the masthead. On which Drummond replied he would see the Captain blowed first. Ingestrie hailed the maintop and ordered a hauling-line to be sent down. . . . The story was talked about in Malta as an amusing joke . . . but Lord Brougham put the question to Lord Auckland as to an 'outrage' alleged to have been committed by a Captain in the Navy. . . . Subsequently an order was issued from the Admiralty prohibiting mastheading as a punishment."[4]—(H.M.S. *Tyne*, Captain Lord Ingestrie, 1835.)

---

[1] 'Life and Letters,' 14.

[2] *Thetis*, 46, commanded by Sir John Phillimore, 1823–26.

[3] Rev. Nathaniel T. Royse, Chaplain of Dec. 26th, 1823. He was subsequently in the *Forte* and in the *Pallas*, but served only for a few years, and then obtained a civil appointment.

[4] Sir H. Keppel, 'Life,' i. 176.

The reform, however, was more apparent than real :—

" ' Mastheading' of Marryat's sort was abolished in 1836 ; but we lived " (*ca.* 1850) " under a distinction without a difference, for it was all the same to the Midshipman, whether he was ordered up to the masthead ' till I call you down,' or to look out for whales, wrecks, or volcanoes." [1]

[1] ' At School and at Sea,' 242.

THE VICTORIA CROSS.

(*Instituted by Royal Warrant, Jan. 29th,* 1856 : *revised April 23rd,* 1881.)

Bronze : worn on a blue ribbon by the Navy, and on a red by the Army.

CHAPTER XLIV.

MILITARY HISTORY OF THE ROYAL NAVY, 1816–1856.

Commanders-in-Chief at home and abroad, 1815–1856—The Mediterranean Pirates—
Bombardment of Algier, 1816—Corsairs in the Channel—Maxwell at Bocca Tigris
—And at Pulo Leat—The slave-trade—Lumley at Mocha, 1820—Collier in the
Persian Gulf—Piracy in the West Indies—Capture of the *Zaragozana*—Action
with the *Tripoli*—Blockade of Algier—The *Naiad* at Bona, 1824—Phillimore at
Cape Coast Castle—THE FIRST BURMESE WAR, 1824–26—Affairs of Greece—
Pirates at Psara and Candia—Irby and pirates—Treaty of London—The Battle of
Navarin, 1827—Staines at Grabusa—Siege of Morea Castle—The Naval Adven-
turers—Cochrane in Chile, Brazil, and Greece—Capture of the *Esmeralda*—Sar-
torius—Napier—Battle of Cape St. Vincent—Pirates and slavers—Exploits of
Sherer, M‘Hardy, Downes, Butterfield, and Broughton—Blockade of Nanning—
Special service squadrons—Warren's prizes—Re-occupation of the Falkland Islands
—Capture of the pirate, *Panda*—Bolton's prizes—Blackwood and Chads in the
Canton river, 1834—Vassall in the strait of Malacca—The first Kaffir War—The
Racehorse at Para—Bosanquet at Mozambique, etc.—Intervention against the
Carlists—Capture of the *Joven Carolina*—Exploits of Milne—Drew in Canada—
Sandom on the Lakes—Capture of Aden—Capture of Kurrachee—THE FIRST
CHINA WAR, 1839–42—OPERATIONS ON THE COAST OF SYRIA, 1840—Bombard-
ment of St. Jean d'Acre—Disaster at Tongatabu—The squadron in Mexican
waters, 1838–39—Capture of the *Mercedita* and *Firme*—Capture of Corisco—
Exploits of Stoll, Adams, and Milne—Denman at the Gallinas—Capture of the
fleet of Cartagena—The *Southampton* at Port Natal—Keppel and the Borneo
pirates—Cochrane in the Eastern Archipelago—Services of Mundy and Brooke—
Defeat of Sooloo pirates—The *Conway* at Tamatave—WAR IN THE PARANA,
1845–46—Battle of Obligado—Operations in New Zealand, 1845–47—The Nicaragua expedition—Services against pirates and slavers—Gallantry of Tottenham
and of Lodwick—The *Felicidade*—The *Pantaloon* and a slaver—Nicolson off
Cape Treforcas—The *Siren* at Stanchio—Affair at Maranhão—The *Président* at
Anjoxa—Chinese pirates—Exploits of the *Scout* and *Columbine*—Shap'n'gtzai—
Services of E. M. Lyons and W. N. L. Lockyer—Hay and the pirates—Capture
of the *Unaio*—The pirates of the Seba river—The Moorish pirates—Case of the
Three Sisters, the *Joven Emilia*, and the *Violet*—Farquhar in the Sarebas—The
Lagos expeditions, 1851–52—THE SECOND BURMESE WAR, 1852–53—Case of the
Cuthbert Young—O'Callaghan at Shanghai—Chinese pirates, 1854–56—THE WAR
WITH RUSSIA, 1854–56—Bombardment of Odessa—The fleets in the Black Sea—
Loss of the *Tiger*—Blockade of the Danube—Death of Hyde Parker—Recon-
naissance of Sebastopol—Invasion of the Crimea—Napier to the Baltic—Cruise of
Plumridge—And of Yelverton—Reconnaissance of Kronstadt—Capture of Bomar-
sund—Operations in the White Sea—Fiasco at Petropaulovski—The Alma—The
Naval Brigade in the Crimea—Bombardment of Sebastopol—Balaclava—The

hurricane of November, 1854—Inkerman—Defence of Eupatoria—The expedition to the sea of Azof—Evacuation of the south side of Sebastopol—Russian ships destroyed—Re-embarkation of the Naval Brigade—Expedition to Kinburn—The first ironclads—Operations in the White Sea—Operations in the Pacific—Massacre at Hango Head—Torpedoes off Kronstadt—Raids in the Baltic—Attack on Sweaborg—Concluding operations—Return of the fleets—Treaty and declaration of Paris—The Review at Spithead.

STAR OF A K.C.B.

BEFORE entering upon the history of the numerous naval operations which were undertaken between 1815 and the close of the Russian War, the reader may be glad to have laid before him in convenient form the following list of the officers who held the principal commands-in-chief at home and abroad during that period. It will be useful for purposes of reference.

PORTSMOUTH.

Apr. 28, 1815. Sir Edward Thornbrough, K.C.B., Adm.

May 15, 1818. Sir George Campbell, G.C.B., Adm.

Jan. 31, 1821. Sir James Hawkins Whitshed, K.C.B., Adm.

Mar. 26, 1824. Sir George Martin, G.C.B., Adm.

Apr. 17, 1827. Hon. Sir Robert Stopford, K.C.B., Adm.

Apr. 23, 1830. Sir Thomas Foley, G.C.B., Adm.

Jan. 23, 1833. Sir Thomas Williams, G.C.B., Adm.

Mar. 28, 1836. Sir Philip Charles Calderwood Henderson Durham, G.C.B., Adm.

Apr. 19, 1839. Hon. Charles Elphinstone, Fleeming, Adm.

Nov. 22, 1839. Sir Edward Codrington, G.C.B., G.C.M.G., Adm.

Dec. 26, 1842. Sir Charles Rowley, Bart., G.C.B., Adm.

Sept. 30, 1845. Sir Charles Ogle, Bart., Adm.

Sept. 13, 1848. Hon. Sir Thomas Bladen Capell, K.C.B., Adm. .

Sept. 13, 1851. Sir Thomas Briggs, G.C.M.G., Adm.

Dec. 18, 1852. Sir Thomas John Cochrane, K.C.B., Vice-Adm.

Jan. 1, 1856. Sir George Francis Seymour, K.C.B., Vice-Adm. (Adm., May 14, 1857).

DEVONPORT.

Jan. 3, 1815. Sir John Thomas Duckworth, Bart., K.B., Adm.

Sept. 8, 1817. Viscount Exmouth, G.C.B., Adm.

Jan. 25, 1821. Hon. Sir Alexander Inglis Cochrane, K.B., Adm.

Mar. 24, 1824. Sir James Saumarez, Bart., K.B., Adm.

Apr. 17, 1827. William, Earl of Northesk, K.B., Adm.

Apr. 22, 1830. Sir Manley Dixon, K.C.B., Adm.

Apr. 27, 1833. Sir William Hargood (1), G.C.B., G.C.H., Adm.

Apr. 27, 1836. Lord Amelius Beauclerk, G.C.B., G.C.H., Adm.

Apr. 24, 1839. Sir Graham Moore, G.C.B., G.C.M.G., Adm.

Apr. 21, 1842. Sir David Milne, G.C.B., Adm.

Apr. 15, 1845. Sir John West, G.C.B., Adm.

Apr. 17, 1848. Sir William Hall Gage, Kt., K.C.B., G.C.H., Adm.

Apr. 17 1851. Sir John Acworth Ommanney, K.C.B., Adm.

May 1, 1854. Sir William Parker (2), Bart., G.C.B., Adm.

THE NORE.

1815. Sir Charles Rowley, K.C.B., Rear-Adm.

1818. Sir John Gore (2), K.C.B., Rear-Adm.

1821. Sir Benjamin Hallowell, K.C.B., Vice-Adm.

1824. Sir Robert Moorsom, K.C.B., Vice-Adm.

1827. Hon. Sir Henry Blackwood, Bart., K.C.B., Vice-Adm.

July 30, 1830. Sir John Poo Beresford, Bart., K.C.B., Vice-Adm.

July 23, 1833. Sir Richard King (2), Bart., K.C.B., Vice-Adm.

Aug. 16, 1834. Hon. Charles Elphinstone Fleeming, Vice-Adm.

Feb. 23, 1837. Sir Robert Waller Otway (1), Bart., K.C.B., Vice-Adm.

July 27, 1840. Sir Henry Digby, K.C.B., Vice-Adm. (Adm., Nov. 23, 1841).

Dec. 8, 1841. Sir Edward Brace, K.C.B., Vice-Adm.

Jan. 13, 1844. Sir John Chambers White, K.C.B., Vice-Adm.

Apr. 18, 1845. Sir Edward Durnford King, Kt., K.C.B., Vice-Adm.

May 9, 1848. Hon. George Elliot (3), C.B., Vice-Adm.

Jan. 23, 1851. Hon. Josceline Percy, C.B., Vice-Adm.

July 1, 1854. Hon. William Gordon, Vice-Adm.

THE MEDITERRANEAN.

1815. Lord Exmouth, K.C.B., Adm.

1818. Sir Thomas Francis Fremantle, G.C.B., Rear-Adm. (Vice - Adm., Aug. 12, 1819).

1820. Sir Graham Moore, K.C.B., Vice-Adm.

1823. Sir Harry Burrard Neale, Bart., G.C.B., Vice-Adm.

Nov. 1, 1826. Sir Edward Codrington, K.C.B. (G.C.B. 1827), Vice-Adm.

June, 1828. Sir Pulteney Malcolm, K.C.B., G.C.M.G. 1829, Vice-Adm.

Mar. 30, 1831. Hon. Sir Henry Hotham, G.C.B., G.C.M.G., Vice-Adm.

May 3, 1833. Sir Pulteney Malcolm, G.C.B., G.C.M.G., Vice-Adm.

Dec. 18, 1833. Sir Josias Rowley, Bart., K.C.B., G.C.M.G., Vice-Adm.

Feb. 9, 1837. Hon. Sir Robert Stopford, G.C.B., G.C.M.G., Adm.

Oct. 14, 1841. Sir Edward William Campbell Rich Owen, K.C.B., Vice-Adm.

Feb. 27, 1845. Sir William Parker (2), Bart., G.C.B., Vice-Adm.

Jan. 17, 1852. James Whitley Deans Dundas, C.B., Rear and Vice-Adm.

1854. Sir Edmund Lyons, Bart., G.C.B., Rear - Adm.[1] (Vice-Adm. Mar. 19, 1857. Lord Lyons).

NORTH AMERICA.

1815. Edward Griffith (later Colpoys), Rear-Adm.

1817. Sir David Milne, K.C.B., Rear-Adm.[2]

---

[1] With temp. rank of Admiral.

[2] Sir David Milne was appointed to North America on May 2, 1816, but had been permitted, before proceeding to his station, to take part in the Algerine expedition.

1819. Edward Griffith (later Colpoys), Rear - Adm. (Vice-Adm., July 19, 1821).

1821. William Charles Fahie, C.B., Rear-Adm.

May 18, 1824. Willoughby Thomas Lake, C.B., Rear-Adm. (Vice-Adm., May 27, 1825).

Apr. 27, 1827. Sir Charles Ogle, Bart., Rear-Adm.

Feb. 20, 1830. Sir Edward Griffith Colpoys, K.C.B., Vice-Adm.

Dec. 6, 1832. Rt. Hon. Sir George Cockburn, G.C.B., Vice-Adm.

Feb. 12, 1836. Sir Peter Halkett, Bart., Vice - Adm. (Adm., Jan. 10, 1837).

Feb. 11, 1837. Hon. Sir Charles Paget, Kt., Vice-Adm.

Mar. 22, 1839. Sir Thomas Harvey (1), K.C.B., Vice-Adm.

Aug. 17, 1841. Sir Charles Adam, K.C.B., Vice-Adm.

Dec. 27, 1844. Sir Francis William Austen (1), K.C.B., Vice-Adm.

Jan. 12, 1848. Thomas, Earl of Dundonald, G.C.B., Vice-Adm.

Jan. 13, 1851. Sir George Francis Seymour, Kt., G.C.B., Vice-Adm.

Nov. 23, 1853. Arthur Fanshawe, C.B., Rear-Adm.

Nov. 26 1856. Sir Houston Stewart, G.C.B., Rear - Adm. (Vice-Adm., July 30, 1857).

The Pacific (till 1837, "South America").

1819. Sir Thomas Masterman Hardy, K.C.B., Commodore.

1823. Sir George Eyre, K.C.B., Rear-Adm.

1826. Sir Robert Waller Otway, K.C.B., Rear-Adm.

Jan. 9, 1829. Thomas Baker, C.B. (K.C.B., 1831), Rear-Adm.

Jan. 1, 1833. Sir Michael Seymour (1), Bart., K.C.B., Rear-Adm.

Sept. 16, 1834. Sir Graham Eden Hamond, Bart., K.C.B., Rear - Adm. (Vice - Adm., Jan. 10, 1837).

Sept. 4, 1837. Charles Bayne Hodgson Ross, C.B., Rear-Adm.

May 5, 1841. Richard Thomas, Rear-Adm.

May 14, 1844. Sir George Francis Seymour, Kt., C.B., Rear-Adm.

Aug. 25, 1847. Phipps Hornby, C.B., Rear-Adm.

Aug. 21, 1850. Fairfax Moresby, C.B., Rear-Adm.

Aug. 17, 1853. David Price, Rear-Adm.

Nov. 25, 1854. Henry William Bruce, Rear-Adm.

The East Indies and China.[1]

1816. Sir Richard King (2), Bart., K.C.B., Rear-Adm.

1819. Hon. Sir Henry Blackwood, Bart., K.C.B., Rear-Adm.

1822. Charles Grant, C.B., Commodore.

1825. Sir James Brisbane, Kt., C.B., Commodore.

Dec. 13, 1825. William Hall Gage, Rear-Adm.

Dec. 20, 1828. Sir Edward William Campbell Rich Owen, K.C.B., Rear-Adm.

Dec. 16, 1831. Sir John Gore (2), K.C.B. Vice-Adm.

May 30, 1834. Hon. Sir Thomas Bladen Capell, K.C.B., Rear-Adm. (Vice - Adm., Jan. 10, 1837).

---

[1] These were not separated until 1865.

July 26, 1837. Sir Frederick Lewis Mait-
land (2), K.C.B., Rear-
Adm.
Feb. 13, 1840. Hon. George Elliot (3),
C.B., Rear-Adm.
May 12, 1841. Sir William Parker (2),
K.C.B. (G.C.B., 1842,
Bart., 1844), Rear -
Adm. (Vice - Adm.,
Nov. 23, 1841).
1844. Sir Thomas John Coch-
rane, Kt., C.B., Rear-
Adm.
June 24, 1846. Samuel Hood. Inglefield,
C.B., Rear-Adm.

Apr. 7, 1848. Sir Francis Augustus
Collier, Kt., C.B.,
Rear-Adm.
Jan. 14, 1850. Charles John Austen (1),
C.B., Rear-Adm.
Dec. 6, 1852. Hon. Sir Fleetwood
Broughton Reynolds
Pellew, Kt., C.B.,
Rear - Adm. (Vice-
Adm., Apr. 22, 1853).
Jan. 19, 1854. Sir James Stirling (1),
Kt., Rear-Adm.
Feb. 18, 1856. Sir Michael Seymour (2),
K.C.B., Rear-Adm.

During the colossal wars of which Europe was the scene
between 1793 and 1815, the Moorish pirates, and particularly
those of Algier, carried on their depredations with comparative
impunity, although both St. Vincent and Nelson checked their
insolence on more than one occasion, and the American Commodore, Stephen Decatur, read them a still sharper lesson immediately
after the conclusion of peace between Great Britain and the United
States. Much more, however, needed doing ; and in 1816, after
renewed outrages and vain negotiations, a formidable British expedition was organised to bring the Dey of Algier to reason. Its
command was entrusted to Admiral Lord Exmouth, who sailed from
Plymouth with his fleet on July 28th, and who, on arriving at
Gibraltar on August 9th, found there a Dutch squadron, the commander of which asked, and obtained, leave to co-operate with him
in the contemplated action.

On August 14th, after some delay caused by adverse winds, the
combined fleet weighed ; and on the 16th it was met by the *Prometheus*, 16, Commander William Bateman Dashwood, from Algier,
with fugitives, and with the information that part of her crew, and
the British Consul had been detained by the Moors. Having to
beat to windward for some time, the fleet did not make Cape
Cazzina until the 26th, and did not sight Algier till the early
morning of the 27th, when it was very nearly calm. Demands
for the release of Christian slaves, repayment of money which had
been recently paid for the freeing of slaves, peace with the
Netherlands, and liberation of the imprisoned British Consul,
Mr. McDonell, and the *Prometheus's* people, were at once sent

in by Lieutenant Samuel Burgess,[1] while the fleet stood on slowly with a light sea-breeze, and at length lay to about a mile from the city. In the afternoon, Burgess returned without the reply which, it had been promised, should be given in two hours. The Admiral thereupon asked by signal whether all his ships were ready, and, the affirmative flag being instantly hoisted by every vessel, he bore up to the attack with his fleet in an order which had been already prescribed. The force thus pitted against the powerful defences of Algier was as follows. The general position taken up by the various ships will be described later.

Ships.	Guns.	Killed.	Wounded.	Commanders.	First Lieutenants.	Round Shot fired.
Queen Charlotte .	100	8	131	{ Adm. Lord Exmouth, G.C.B. (B.)[1] { Capt. James Brisbane, C.B.	Peter Richards (1st).[6] Frederick Thomas Michell (2nd).[6]	4,462
Impregnable . .	98	50	160	{ R.-Adm. David Milne (B.).[2] { Capt. Edward Brace, C.B.	James Boyle Babington (1st).[6] Roger Hall (2nd).	6,730
Superb	74	8	84	Capt. Charles Ekins.[3]	Philip Thicknesse Horn.[6]	4,500
Minden	74	7	37	Capt. William Paterson.[3]	Joseph Benjamin Howell.[6]	4,710
Albion	74	3	15	Capt. John Coode.[3]	Robert Hay.[6]	4,110
Leander	50	17	118	Capt. Edward Chetham, C.B.	Thomas Sanders.[6]	3,680
Severn	40	3	34	{ Capt. Hon. Frederick William { Aylmer.[3]	James Davies.[6]	2,920
Glasgow	40	10	37	Capt. Hon. Anthony Maitland.[3]	George M'Pherson.[6]	3,000
Granicus . . .	36	16	42	Capt. William Furlong Wise.[3]	John Parson.[6]	2,800
Hebrus	36	4	15	Capt. Edmund Palmer, C.B.	{ Edward Hollingworth Dela- { fosse.[6]	2,755
Heron	18	—	—	Com. George Bentham.[4]		
Mutine	18	—	—	Com. James Mould.[4]	George Blurton.	
Prometheus . . .	16	—	—	Com. William Bateman Dashwood.	Charles Aubrey Antram.	
Britomart . . .	10	—	—	Com. Robert Riddell.	David John Dickson.	
Cordelia	10	—	—	Com. William Sargent.		
Beelzebub, bomb .	8	—	—	Com. William Kempthorne.[4]	George Pierce.	
Fury, bomb. . .	12	—	—	Com. Constantine Richard Moorsom.	William Russell (3).	
Hecla, bomb . .	12	—	—	Com. William Popham.	George Vernon Jackson.	
Infernal, bomb .	12	2	17	Com. Hon. George James Perceval.	John Foreman.	
(Explosion vessel).	—	—	—	Lieut. Richard Howell Fleming.[5]		
		128	690			

a transport, a dispatch vessel, gun-vessels, etc., with Royal Sappers and Miners, and Royal Rocket Corps.

Melampus . . .	40	3	15	{ V.-Ad. Baron Theod. Fred. van { Capellen. { Capt. A. W. De Man.		
Frederica . . .	40	—	5	Capt. J. A. van der Straaten.		
Diana	40	6	22	Capt. Petrus Ziervogel.		10,148
Amstel	40	4	6	Capt. W. A. van der Hart.		
Dageraad . . .	30	—	4	Capt. J. M. Polders.		
Eendracht . . .	18			Capt. J. F. C. Wardenburg.		

[1] Viscount Exmouth, Sept. 21st, 1816.   [4] Post-Captain, Sept. 16th, 1816.
[2] K.C.B., Sept. 21st, 1816.   [5] Commander, Sept. 17th, 1816.
[3] C.B., Sept. 21st, 1816.   [6] Commander, Sept. 16th, 1816.

The total number of guns in the Moorish batteries has been estimated at upwards of 1000, of which about 80 were on the north side, where the shoalness of the water prevented any heavy vessel from getting within range, about 220 on the mole, about 95 on the

[1] Commander, Sept. 16th, 1816.

eastern sea front, and most of the rest in batteries on heights behind the town, or in the environs. The guns were chiefly 32, 24, and 18-prs., but there were also some heavier pieces, and several enormous mortars. In addition, there were in port four 44-gun frigates, five large corvettes of from 24 to 30 guns, and between thirty and forty[1] gun and mortar boats ; and the garrison consisted of at least 40,000 men.

At 2.35 P.M. the *Queen Charlotte* anchored with springs on her cables, not more than fifty yards from the mole-head. She was lashing herself to an Algerine brig which lay fast to the pier there, when a shot was fired at her, followed by two shots aimed at other vessels which were advancing to their stations. Exmouth humanely waved to the crowds on shore to indicate that he was about to fire, and then the flagship opened, the other ships of the fleet joining in the fray as soon as their guns would bear. The general position ultimately taken up by the larger vessels was, beginning from the north, *Impregnable, Albion, Minden, Superb,* and *Queen Charlotte,* this portion of the line being roughly parallel with the external contour of the mole ; and *Leander, Severn,* and *Glasgow,* this portion lying parallel with the coast in the neighbourhood of the Fishmarket Battery. The line was continued to the southward by the Dutch frigates *Melampus, Diana,* and *Frederica,* with the *Dageraad* and *Amstel* further out, and the *Eendracht* under way. The *Hebrus* and *Granicus* had been directed to make themselves useful in situations where opportunity offered. The *Hebrus* finally took station on the *Queen Charlotte's* port quarter, and the *Granicus,* in an exposed, difficult, and highly honourable position, between the flagship and the *Superb.* The *Mutine* anchored on the port bow of the *Impregnable,* the remaining sloops keeping, for the most part, under way. The bombs stationed themselves about two thousand yards north-east of the mole ; and in their neighbourhood were the gun, mortar, and rocket boats of the fleet, fifty-five in number, under Lieutenant Frederick Thomas Michell (actg. Commander), and Lieutenants John Davies (3)[2] and Thomas Revans.[3]

The bombardment, which was of the fiercest character, rapidly made its effects felt, everything exposed to the close fire of the ships quickly tumbling into ruin. At about 4 P.M. an Algerine frigate,

---

[1] Exmouth's disp. in one place has " between 40 and 50."

[2] Commander, Oct. 8th, 1816, for this service.

[3] Commander, Oct. 16th, 1816, for this service.

which was moored across the mole, was set on fire by the crew of the flagship's barge, under Lieutenant Peter Richards ; and, a little later, she drifted out in flames, the *Queen Charlotte* shifting berth to allow her to pass. A few minutes afterwards[1] the *Impregnable* sent word that she had suffered very severely, and asked that a frigate should be despatched to divert some of the enemy's fire from her. The *Glasgow* was assigned to this service, but, owing to lack of wind, she could not carry out her mission, and, in attempting to do so, got herself terribly mauled. By about 7 P.M., however, the town, arsenal, storehouses, and vessels within the mole, were burning briskly. Between 8 and 9 P.M., further damage and consternation were caused by the explosion vessel which, under Lieutenant Richard Howell Fleming, accompanied by Commander Herbert Brace Powell, a volunteer serving in the *Impregnable*, was run on shore near the battery northward of the lighthouse, and there blown up soon after 9 P.M.

The engagement continued till about 10 o'clock, when, ammunition threatening to give out, and the hostile fire being nearly silenced, the ships, by order, began to cut their cables and springs, and, after hauling and towing, to stand out before a light air which had just sprung up. But not much before 2 A.M. on the 28th, had every vessel come to out of reach of the guns of Algier, though not beyond the bright glare which was thrown far to seaward by the blaze in the bay.[2] Immediately afterwards a very violent thunderstorm burst upon the fleet. At daylight, Exmouth renewed his demands of the previous morning ; and, at the same time, he made preparations for recommencing the bombardment; but they were needless. It was quickly made known that the terms would be acceded to. Conferences were held, at some of which Rear-Admiral Sir Charles Vinicombe Penrose, who arrived in the *Ister*, 36, on the 29th, was present; and, in the end, 1083 Christian slaves were freed, a promise was given to abolish slave making, 382,500 dollars, which had been paid by Naples and Sardinia by way of ransom, were restored, an indemnity of 3000 dollars, with an apology, was tendered to the British Consul, and peace was made with the Netherlands.[3] On

---

[1] "About sunset." Exmouth's disp.

[2] Exmouth to Croker, Aug. 28th, 1816 (*Gazette*, p. 1790). Logs, esp. of *Leander, Q. Charlotte, Impregnable* and *Superb*. Mids.' letters in *Nav. Chron.*, xxxvi. 289 and 291. Salamé, ' Narr. of Exped. to Algiers.'

[3] Exmouth to Croker, Aug. 30th and Sept. 1st, 1816. *Gazette* notice of Sept. 28th, 1816.

September 3rd, at midnight, Exmouth weighed to return home, leaving the *Prometheus* to attend upon the reinstated Consul.

The numerical losses experienced by the ships engaged will be found set forth in the table on p. 227. The officers killed in the British fleet were:

Master's Mate Thomas Howard (*Superb*); Assistant Surveyor Thomas Mends (*Albion*); Midshipmen John Hawkins (*Impregnable*), Robert C. Bowen (*Superb*), John Jardine (*Albion*), Richard Calthorp, — Lowdon, and P. G. Hanwell (*Leander*), Robert Pratt (*Granicus*), and George H. A. Pococke (*Hebrus*); Captain of Marines James Willson (*Leander*); Lieutenants of Marines George Baxter (*Leander*), and William Moore Morgan, and William Remfry (*Granicus*); and Lieutenant of Marine Artillery John James Patrick Bissett (*Infernal*).

Among the officers wounded were:

Captains Charles Ekins, and John Coode; and Lieutenants Frederick John Johnston (mortally), George Morrison King, and John Sampson Jago (actg.) (*Queen Charlotte*), Philip Thicknesse Horn, John M'Dougall (3), and George W. Gunning (actg.) (*Impregnable*), Henry Walker (1), and John Stewart Dixon (*Leander*), Edmund Williams Gilbert (*Glasgow*), Henry Augustus Perkins (*Granicus*), and John Foreman (*Infernal*).

None of the ships lost any spars, but several had their masts badly injured; and the hulls of the *Impregnable* and *Leander* were

MEDAL COMMEMORATIVE OF THE BOMBARDMENT OF ALGIER, 1816.
(*From an original, lent by H.S.H. Prince Louis of Battenberg, G.C.B., Capt. R.N.*)

very severely mauled, that of the former being said to have received 233 large shot. Estimates of the losses suffered by the Algerines put the number killed and wounded at from 4000 to nearly 7000. The principal honours granted in recognition of the victory, and some of the consequent promotions, are set forth in the table on p. 227. The behaviour of the Dutch contingent is reported to have been admirable.

It is impossible to believe that the fortifications, guns, and gunners of Algier in 1816 can have been at all up.to the European standard of that age, or even that the defences were of quality as good as those which Duckworth had had to encounter in the Dardanelles in 1807. To have placed comparatively few heavy ships, such as Exmouth had, in close conflict with first-rate works, mounting several hundred good guns, and manned by experienced gunners, would have been little short of madness. Had the defences been really as powerful as a mere paper summary of them suggests, a larger force would have been sent to reduce them. It is certain, however, that the Algerines fought with far greater skill than had been expected, that the action was an exceptionally hot one, and that the success gained was not easily won. For the manner in which the operations were conducted, Exmouth richly deserved his advancement in the peerage.

Only international considerations had prevented the adoption of much stronger measures against the piratical states of the Mediterranean. Algier had once been a British possession; and in 1816 many Englishmen were of opinion that it must again become one ere the evils of which it was the centre could be put an end to. That these views were not without some justification is evident from the fact that within a few months of Exmouth's lesson to the Algerines, the Dey had begun to restore his fortresses and to re-create his navy, and that two Tunisian pirates captured a Hamburg vessel, the *Ocean*, in the North Sea, and were chased in vain by the *Ganymede*, 26, Captain William M'Culloch. The prize was, however, eventually retaken by the *Alert*, 18, Commander John Smith (6), in May, 1817. The corsairs were then solemnly warned, and escorted clear of the Channel. " Further," says the *Plymouth Telegraph* of that day, " our government cannot go." [1]

It was at about the same time that another semi-civilised state received from Great Britain its first serious lecture on the subject of international courtesy. In 1815, Lord Amherst's famous embassy to China was decided upon. The mission, which sailed in February, 1816, was escorted by the *Alceste*, 46, Captain Murray Maxwell, C.B., and *Lyra*, 10, Commander Basil Hall. During Lord Amherst's presence on Chinese soil, Maxwell occupied part of his time in carrying out some very useful surveys. When, on November 2nd, 1816, he anchored off the island of Lin-tin, he learnt that the Ambassador had

[1] Marshall, ' Nav. Biog.,' Add. to Supp., Pt. II., 417; *Nav. Chron.*, 435, 514.

been dismissed in disgrace, and that the British Government's presents to the Emperor had been contumeliously refused.   He desired a pass to enable him to proceed up the Canton River, where he wished to effect some necessary repairs.   Insults and evasions were the sole answers vouchsafed to him, and he therefore determined to run up without permission.   At Bocca Tigris he was informed that, if he advanced, he would be instantly sunk.   This was in the evening of November 13th.   The river is there about as wide as the Thames at London, but the banks are high, and they were then guarded by works which with those on Wangtong Island, mounted 110 guns.   Above, off Chuenpee, was a line of small war junks.   As the *Alceste* did not bring to, some blank cartridges were fired at her.   Maxwell feigned to regard the firing as a salute, and, as such, returned it.   He then anchored, and, on the following morning, weighed again and passed the junks.

Immediately afterwards, both junks and forts opened with shotted guns.   Maxwell, who, owing to the lightness of the breeze, was obliged to anchor again, returned only a single shot, aimed at the Chinese admiral, and considerately fired it himself, so that, in case of the enemy demanding the man who had fired, he might take all the responsibility.   Either the shot, or the fact that the frigate had anchored, satisfied the Chinese for the moment; but when, in the evening, the *Alceste* weighed once more to run higher up, she was greeted with a heavy yet ill-directed fire from both banks.   Maxwell returned it coolly, until, getting within half pistol shot of the largest battery, he delivered an entire broadside, which silenced that work. The effect of this was that resistance presently ceased, and that, by daylight on the 15th, the *Alceste* found herself in a secure anchorage, with no one hurt, and only a couple of shot in her hull.   No further insult was offered to the flag, and all responsibility for the affair was afterwards disavowed by the Chinese authorities, who, when Maxwell reached Whampoa, congratulated him effusively.   Lord Amherst safely re-embarked in the river, and quitted it without further incident, but was unfortunately wrecked, on February 18th, 1817, on a reef near Pulo Leat, in the Strait of Gaspar.   The Ambassador was enabled to reached Batavia almost immediately.   Maxwell, having landed with the greater part of his officers and crew on Pulo Leat, there fortified himself against the Malays, who burnt the remains of the wreck on February 22nd.   In face of several attacks, he maintained himself, until, on March 3rd, he was relieved by

the Company's cruiser, *Ternate*, which conveyed the whole party
to Batavia.[1]

Such further active operations as were undertaken by the Navy,
prior to the outbreak of the first Burmese War, were all necessitated
by the depredations of pirates and slavers,[2] or by the tyranny of
petty potentates. Several of the actions are worth recalling.

In 1820, in order to obtain redress for injuries inflicted on British
subjects by the Imaum of Sanaa, in whose territories Mocha lay, an
expedition, consisting of the *Topaze*, 46, Captain John Richard
Lumley, several of the East India Company's cruisers, and a bomb
vessel, was sent by Rear-Admiral Sir Richard King (2), Bart., who
commanded on the East India station; and, although not without
serious loss, it succeeded at length in placing the relations between
the British and the local authorities on a satisfactory footing. The
expedition arrived off Mocha on December 3rd, and on the 4th, supposing the north fort to have been abandoned, Lumley attempted
to take possession and destroy it. Unfortunately, however, it
proved to be held in force, and the landing party was driven back
with considerable loss. On the 5th, negotiations took place; but the
repulse of the British led the Dolah to presume too long upon their
patience; and on the 26th, fire was opened on the north fort, which,
in a few hours, was breached, taken, and blown up. Further negotiations leading to no satisfactory results, the south fort was similarly
treated on the 30th. Thereupon the local authorities submitted;
and, on January 15th, 1821, copies of a treaty which had been
drawn up on behalf of the Company, were returned, duly signed,
to Captain Lumley. During the two bombardments, the *Topaze*
expended upwards of 3500 shot. Her loss consisted of Lieutenant
Robert Gordon Atkinson, R.M., Master's Mate C. P. Gill, Midship-

[1] Hall, 'Voyage to Corea'; Ellis, 'Journal'; Abel, 'Narrative'; M'Cleod, 'Voyage
of *Alceste*'; Mins. of C. M., Aug., 1817; Marshall, ii. 805.

[2] Slave-dealing by British subjects had been abolished by the Act of March 25th,
1807, as from January 1st, 1808. In 1811 the offence had been made punishable by
transportation for fourteen years. In 1824 it was declared to be piracy, and made
punishable with death. In 1837 the punishment was reduced to transportation for
life. France agreed in 1816 to abandon the slave trade: Spain and Portugal had
already, in 1814, agreed to abandon it north of the equator; and they formally
abandoned it altogether, the one in 1817, the other in 1823. Brazil likewise gave it
up under the treaties of 1826 and 1830. Yet the trade was secretly prosecuted. The
year 1833 saw the complete emancipation of slaves in all British colonies. The
numerous seizures of slavers were made, for the most part, under various treaties which
gave to the naval powers a right of searching for slaves, of capturing and confiscating
vessels engaged in the traffic, and of punishing participants in the illegal business.

man Francis S. Burnett, and 5 seamen and Marines killed, and 20 people, including Lieutenants William Moriarty and Charles Mayson Moncrieffe Wright, wounded.[1]

A similar expedition had been undertaken against the pirates of Ras-al-Khyma, in the Persian Gulf, in 1819, by a military force accompanied by a naval contingent under Captain Francis Augustus Collier, in the *Liverpool*, 50. The works were taken and destroyed, and all the piratical vessels in port were burnt or sunk. In these operations the *Eden*, 26, Captain Francis Erskine Loch, and *Curlew*, 18, Commander William Walpole, participated.[2]

In the West Indies, where Rear-Admiral Sir Charles Rowley commanded, piracy, often more or less intimately connected with slave trading, flourished exceedingly, the principal offenders being scoundrels of Spanish extraction. Rowley determined to put this down, if possible, and, to that end, sent the *Tyne*, 26, Captain William Mackenzie Godfrey, to cruise on the north coast of Cuba, where many of the pirates had their headquarters. Attached to the *Tyne*, as tender, was the small hired sloop, *Eliza*, mounting a 12-pr. carronade, and having on board Midshipman George White (1a), and 24 men, the whole under the command of Mr. Hugh Nurse, Mate. On September 30th, 1822, when the *Eliza* lay at anchor off Guajara, she was approached by a suspicious schooner, which proved to be the *Diableto*, 6, and a felucca, which proved to be the *Firme Union*, 5. Nurse, who had promptly prepared to slip and make sail to close, was attacked at about 8.30 P.M. by the schooner. He returned the fire from his only gun, loaded with round and grape, and mauled the enemy so severely that the felucca endeavoured to place herself between the combatants, and to shelter her friend. The manœuvres resulted in the *Eliza* and the *Firme Union* running nearly alongside one another. Nurse instantly boarded, and, in five minutes, having killed 10 of the pirates, and driven overboard most of the rest, about 27 in number, was master of the vessel. On the British side, 2 seamen were killed, and the gallant Nurse,[3] and 6 men severely wounded. On the following day an effort was made to follow the schooner, which had got away during the darkness, but, unfortunately, she could not be found.[4]

[1] Marshall, iv. Pt. II., 113; *Gazette*, 1821, pp. 939, 2029.

[2] Brenton, v. 265; *Gazette*, 1820, p. 1670.

[3] Nurse was made a Lieutenant, Dec. 5th, 1822, and a Commander, Jan. 26th, 1828. He died a Captain in 1841.

[4] Marshall, iv. Pt. II., 263; James, vi. (1837) 390.

A little later, Captain John Edward Walcott took command of the *Tyne*, and, with the *Thracian*, 18, Commander John Walter Roberts, under his orders, began a careful and systematic examination of the numerous creeks and inlets along the Old Bahama Channel. On March 28th, 1823, he learnt from an American pilot-boat that a famous pirate schooner, the *Zaragozana*, of 120 tons, and between 70 and 80 men, was in his neighbourhood. She was commanded by a desperado named Cayatano Aragonez, and mounted a long 18-pr. swivel, four long 9-prs., and eight small swivels. The leader, some of whose people had been hanged at Jamaica not long before, had caused his crew to swear never to spare an Englishman's life, and to blow up their ship rather than be taken. To set a seal upon this bloodthirsty compact, the miscreants had immediately afterwards tortured and murdered their cook, a negro belonging to Jamaica. Walcott and Roberts sighted their quarry on the 31st, off Baracoa, and, in order not to alarm her, disguised their craft as merchant vessels. Ere, however, they could get near her, the *Zaragozana* detected them, and crowded sail for the harbour of Mata. The British chased until 1.30 P.M., by which time the pirate had anchored in her port, and had moored head and stern, with her broadside across its entrance. She had also landed some men at the harbour's mouth, so that they might enfilade any attack from seaward. The British got out their boats, which, as they neared the enemy, were fired at. Undeterred, nevertheless, by the danger to which they were exposed, their crews pushed on for more than three quarters of an hour, using their carronades and musketry, and at length boarding under a storm of grape and small arms. Twenty-eight pirates, including the chief, were taken, and were subsequently hanged. Ten others were killed. The rest escaped.[1] This little action was a most heroic one, but was happily accomplished without very severe loss, only one man being killed, and five wounded, on the British side. In his report, Captain Walcott particularly praised the conduct of Lieutenant Amos Plymsell, first of the *Thracian*, who was second in command of the boats.[2]

As had been suspected at the time in England, the lesson given in 1816 to the Dey of Algier had not been sufficiently severe to be

[1] Probably, however, some of these were drowned, and, certainly sixteen of them were afterwards captured by the Governor of Baracoa.

[2] Walcott to Rowley, in Marshall, Supp., Pt. IV., 392; O'Byrne, 1234.

lasting. After allowing his subjects to commit numerous outrages on the high seas, His Highness filled up the measure of his iniquities by again violating the sanctity of the British Consulate, and by seizing the persons of two consular servants. To remonstrate against these proceedings, the *Naiad*, 46, Captain the Hon. Sir Robert Cavendish Spencer, accompanied by the *Cameleon*, 12, Commander James Ryder Burton, was sent to Algier, off which place she arrived in January, 1824. He found in the harbour two Spanish vessels, which had been recently captured by one of the Dey's cruisers. Spencer added a demand for the release of their crews to the other claims which he had been instructed to make against the Moorish government; but, getting no satisfactory reply, he took on board the British Consul and his family, and, on the 31st, worked out of the bay. While the *Naiad* and *Cameleon* were still beating out, the latter sighted to windward a sail, which presently proved to be the Algerine corvette *Tripoli*, 20, the same which had captured the Spanish vessels. The *Naiad*, hoisting her colours, fired a shot across the stranger's bows. The stranger replied with a shot directed at the *Naiad*. Both British vessels at once went in chase, endeavouring especially to cut off the corsair from the mole. The *Naiad* was the better sailer, and, at length, passed ahead of the *Tripoli*, firing into her and reducing her to a wreck. The *Cameleon* was then close under the enemy's lee, and had suffered somewhat from the shot of the *Naiad*, as well as from the broadsides of the pirate. Spencer, deeming that he had sufficiently punished the foe, stood out to sea, and made the signal of recall to the *Cameleon*. Burton, however, chose to disregard it, and, after some manoeuvring, most gallantly ran the Algerine on board, and, at the head of his men, only 45 all told in number, drove her 150 people below. He was then about to take the *Tripoli* in tow, when Spencer, who had wore round, passed within hail, and ordered him to abandon the prize.

The *Tripoli* was, of course, a thoroughly beaten ship when she was boarded. The disparity of numbers opposed to him might well, nevertheless, have deterred Burton from risking a hand to hand conflict; and high credit must be assigned to him for his bravery. He was deservedly promoted on February 23rd following.

After this affair the Algerian coast was for some time blockaded by the ships of Vice-Admiral Sir Harry Burrard Neale; and, during the blockade, the *Naiad's* boats, under Lieutenants Michael

Quin,[1] Thomas Dilke, and George Evans, very creditably destroyed an Algerine brig of war under the fortress of Bona, on the night of May 23rd, 1824. The brig was pierced for 16 guns, and was moored head and stern, protected by a 40-gun battery only eighty feet from her, but her guns, and probably most of her people, were in the defences on shore, where were also about 400 soldiers. Nevertheless, the vessel was burnt as she lay, and the assailants got off with nothing worse than a few contusions.[2]

A squadron was afterwards assembled with the object of once more bombarding Algier; but the Dey gave way in time; and, when His Highness had signified his readiness to come to terms, Sir Harry Burrard Neale left Sir Robert Cavendish Spencer to make final arrangements and to conclude the treaty.

In the course of the same year disturbances broke out on the West Coast of Africa; and the *Thetis*, 46, Captain Sir John Phillimore, C.B., was despatched to Cape Coast Castle, with a detachment of the Royal African Corps, and supplies. From July 4th to July 11th, 1824, when the enemy was finally defeated, the people of the *Thetis*, and of the *Swinger*, 12, co-operated in the defence of the place against the Ashantees. Among the officers who chiefly distinguished themselves during the operations were Lieutenants Andrew Drew and William Cotesworth, the former of whom was promoted on October 19th following.[3]

Irritation at the presence and growing power of the British in India; hatred of foreigners; ignorance of Britain's resources; and greed of the wealth to be obtained by the plunder of British factories, were the impelling causes which brought about the first Burmese war. Numerous aggressions had been committed upon the frontier of the East India Company's territories; and at the beginning of 1824 it was decided to suffer such insults no longer, but to attack the offenders. Two divisions of troops were accordingly embarked, one at Calcutta and the other at Madras, and placed under the orders of General Sir Archibald Campbell; and the assistance of the Navy was sought. The squadron in East Indian waters was then under the command of Commodore Charles Grant, C.B., who directed the *Larne*, 20, Commander Frederick Marryat, and the *Sophie*, 18, Commander George Frederick

---

[1] Promoted, Oct. 5th, 1824.

[2] Spencer to Neale, May 24th, 1824, in *Gazette*.

[3] Marshall, Supp., Pt. I., 249; O'Byrne, 232, 306.

Ryves (2), to accompany the expedition. At Marryat's request, the little paddle steamer *Diana*, the first ever seen in India, was purchased, and added to the force.

Most of the transports made their rendezvous at Port Cornwallis, in the Andaman Islands, by May 2nd. The *Liffey*, 50, Commodore Grant, *Slaney*, 20, Commander Charles Mitchell, and four of the Company's cruisers under Captain Henry Hardy, (Bombay Marine), together with numerous small craft, also joined at various times. On May 5th the expedition proceeded, a division under Brigadier Michael M'Creagh, escorted by the *Slaney*, being presently detached against Cheduba Island, another detachment, under Major Wahab, going to Negrais, and the main body anchoring within the bar of the Rangoon River on May 10th. The total strength of the military force embarked at the beginning of the campaign was 8701 officers and men, of whom 4077 were British.

At that time the numerous waterways were practically the only roads existing in Burmah; and the chief waterway in the country to be attacked was the Irawadi, of which the Rangoon river forms one of the mouths. Rangoon itself is about twenty-eight miles from the sea, the stream opposite it having a maximum width of about 700 yards. The town was fortified by means of palisades and embankments; and near the river gate was a battery of fourteen guns. Just before the arrival of the expedition the governor had thrown the British residents into prison.

On May 11th, the *Larne*, followed by the *Liffey*, led the way up the river; and, at about 2 P.M., the squadron anchored abreast of the battery, which fired a few ill-directed shot at the *Liffey*, but was silenced in a few minutes. While preparations were being made to land troops, the battery again opened, and was again easily reduced to silence. The troops were then landed, and the town, which had been deserted, was occupied without the slightest resistance. Marshall believes that the British flag was first hoisted in Rangoon by Lieutenant Samuel Thornton, of the *Liffey*. On May 16th, a party of troops, accompanied by the boats of the *Liffey*, under Lieutenant James Wilkinson, attacked and carried three stockaded posts higher up the river, near Kemmendale, with a loss to the Navy of Wilkinson and nine men wounded, and to the army of two killed and nine wounded.

The facility with which these operations were carried out seems

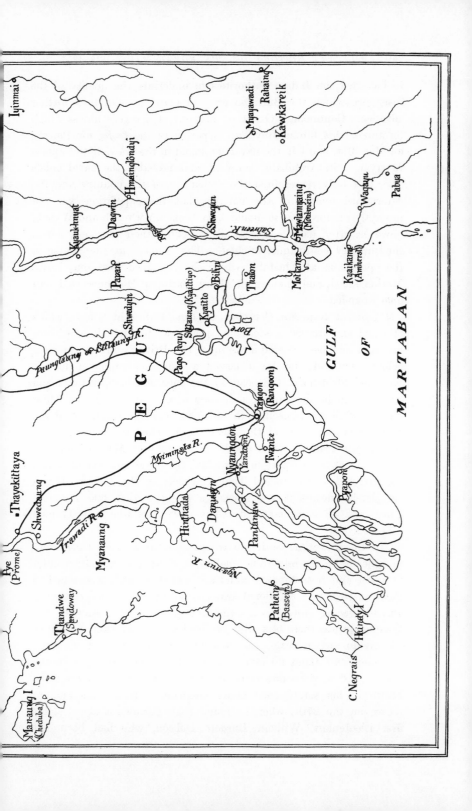

to have led the Indian authorities to underrate the quality of the resistance which the Burmese were prepared to offer to a further advance. Commodore Grant, on account of a severe illness which terminated his life on July 25th, departed in the *Liffey* for Penang on May 31st, and left the naval command in the Irawadi to Captain Marryat. Sir Archibald Campbell, and probably the naval chiefs also, had fully represented the difficulties of the country and the determined temper of the natives ; but the expedition was not promptly reinforced as it should have been. M'Creagh and Wahab, however, after having successfully executed their missions, joined the military commander-in-chief. The *Slaney*, in the course of the operations at Cheduba, where she remained, lost one Royal Marine killed, and Lieutenant Henry Bathurst Matthews and four men wounded.

While at Rangoon, Campbell, on June 10th, sent a force which attacked and carried a stockaded post near Kemmendine, whence fire-rafts had been floated down upon the British craft in the river below. On July 1st he dispersed a Burmese command in the same neighbourhood, the boats of the squadron co-operating ; and on July 8th he despatched a division against the enemy at Kummeroot, while he himself, with 800 men, and the assistance of the small craft and boats of the squadron, attacked the same body of the enemy from the river above Kemmendine. Marryat was too ill to take an active part in this affair, the naval conduct of which he entrusted to Lieutenant Thomas Fraser, of the *Larne*. It was completely successful, ten stockades being carried, 800 Burmese killed, and 38 guns captured. The naval loss was only 11 men wounded.

In the meantime both the troops and the seamen had begun to suffer very severely from cholera, and other diseases incidental to a wet and hot climate ; and the *Sophie* had been despatched to Calcutta to obtain additional seamen by entering or impressment, and to procure stores ; while the Burmese leaders, conscious that the climate was their best ally, refrained for a space from hostilities on any important scale, and concentrated the bulk of their army at Donoobew, about 60 miles north of Rangoon. Marryat, in the *Larne*, had to drop down the river on July 13th, to recruit the health of his sorely tried ship's company ; but he was able to return on the 27th, when he found that, during his absence, his first Lieutenant, William Burdett Dobson, who had been left behind, had led a useful reconnaissance up Puzendown Creek. The same officer subsequently captured thirty-five deeply-laden cargo boats.

In August an expedition mainly military, but accompanied by a few gunboats, was detached from Rangoon to Tenasserim, where it presently captured and occupied Tavoy and Mergui; but for some time, owing to the immense difficulties of the country and climate, the operations in the direction of Ava made very little progress. Continual fighting, however, went on. Campbell and Marryat made a successful raid up the Syriam river in the first week in August; and in the second week of the same month a composite force sent up the Dalla river under Lieut.-Colonel H. M. Kelly and Lieutenant Thomas Fraser, R.N., behaved magnificently, in spite of the cowardice of the Bengali boatmen who formed part of the crews of the small craft. Among the naval officers who most distinguished themselves were Lieutenant Fraser, and Messrs. Robert Atherton, John Duffill, George Winsor, and John Henry Norcock. Late in the month the Dalla natives reoccupied some of their positions, and, on September 2nd, were attacked by Marryat, with two mortar-boats and several gunboats, and Major Richard Lacy Evans, of the Madras army. That night a strong stockade which commanded the creek leading up to Thontai, the capital of the province of Dalla, was captured; but three days afterwards the Burmese, perceiving the importance of the position, made a desperate effort to retake it, with about 1800 men and a number of large war boats. The people on shore, and the *Kitty*, gun brig, were very sorely pressed, when Marryat, with a division of boats, relieved them, and drove off the enemy. In these affairs Lieutenant Thomas Fraser, Messrs. Henry Hodder, John Duffill, and Alexander Cranley, R.N., and Robert Crawfurd, Bombay Marine, gained honourable mention for their conduct, and Marryat evoked the highest praise from Evans.

By that time sickness had made frightful ravages ashore as well as afloat. The European part of the army fit for service did not exceed 1500 men; about 750 British soldiers had died of disease; the *Sophie*, 18, which returned to Rangoon on September 4th, had buried a quarter of her crew; and scurvy and other maladies were so rampant in the *Larne* that only 27 of her original crew remained, and Marryat had to obtain permission to take her to Penang to recruit the health of the survivors. He left behind him Lieutenant William Burdett Dobson, and a few men, in charge of the armed transport *Satellite*.

The death of Commodore Grant left Captain Thomas Coe, then of the *Tees*, 26, senior officer on the East India station. Coe assumed command of the *Liffey*, and promoted Marryat into the *Tees*. After Marryat's departure, Commander Henry Ducie Chads, in the *Arachne*, 18, who arrived off the bar on September 11th, took naval command in the Rangoon river. The *Arachne* had been sent from England to relieve the *Sophie*; but, looking to the state of affairs, Chads, who found her at Rangoon, took the responsibility of ordering her to remain.

Operations were renewed on September 19th, when Sir Archibald Campbell began a movement up the river upon a place called Panlang. The expedition, which was entrusted to Brig.-General Hugh Fraser and Commander Chads, returned to Rangoon on the 27th, having defeated the enemy, taken several stockades, and captured a number of guns. The transport *Satellite*, the steamer *Diana*, all the boats of the *Arachne* and *Sophie*, and many small craft, co-operated in these proceedings; and Fraser's dispatch made special mention of Chads, Lieutenants Charles Keele, and John Bazely (3), and Messrs. Stephen Joshua Lett, and George Winsor, R.N. The little steamer rendered great assistance.

Another joint expedition, under Chads and Major Thomas Evans, captured Than-ta-Bain, about thirty miles from Rangoon, on October 7th. Among the naval officers mentioned for their services on that occasion were Lieutenants Augustus Henry Kellett, George Goldfinch (actg.), and William Burdett Dobson, and Mr. George Winsor, of the *Sophie*, who had charge of the *Diana*. Yet another joint expedition was despatched, under Lieut.-Colonel Henry Godwin and Lieutenant Charles Keele, R.N., against Martaban, a strong place at the mouth of the Salween, a hundred miles eastward of Rangoon. Martaban was reached on October 27th, and Keele at once destroyed about thirty of the enemy's war boats. On the 30th, the stockade was very gallantly stormed, Keele being one of the first to enter it. The total British loss was only 7 (including 2 seamen) killed and 14 (including 4 seamen) wounded; but the success was of great importance, for, with Martaban, 16 guns, 600 smaller firearms, huge quantities of ammunition, a powder factory, and various stores fell into British hands, and the H. E. I. Co.'s gun-vessel *Phaeton*, which had put into Martaban by mistake, and had been seized, was retaken. Her crew was found in irons. Her commander had been carried prisoner to Ava. In addition to Lieutenant Keele, Lieutenant John Bazely (3), and Mr. Lett, R.N., were highly praised in dispatches.

By the fall of Martaban, the previous capture of Tavoy and Mergui, and the subsequent submission of Yeh and other places, control was obtained of the whole coast of Tenasserim, with its valuable hinterland. Large stores of grain also became accessible.

Little was done during November; but, in the course of that month, the health of the troops and seamen in the Rangoon river greatly improved. The temporary relaxation of British activity may have suggested to the enemy that the moment was favourable for a grand attack on the positions which had been won by the invaders; for, towards the end of the month, the main Burmese army, which, as has been already noticed, had concentrated at Donoobew, descended the river, heralding its approach by floating down scores of fire-rafts and masses of blazing timber. Commander George Frederick Ryves (2), who, in the *Sophie*, was stationed near Kemmendine, pluckily kept his post, and disposed of many of these dangers as they arrived abreast of him; but the risks of the situation induced Richard E. Goodridge, of the Company's cruiser *Teignmouth*, to slip his cable, and to move down stream, until he was ordered back by Ryves. The great attack on Kemmendine was made on December 1st. At the moment Ryves was senior naval officer, Chads having led a reconnoitring party to Pegu and being still absent. Ryves made what he held to be the best dispositions, and, though he had to take station below the threatened point, co-operated with the army, until the return of Chads, on the morning of December 2nd. In the interval, fighting was furious, and the fort was sorely pressed, when there came up the river to its assistance Lieutenant Kellett and Midshipman Valentine Pickey, followed soon afterwards by Midshipman William Coyde. These had with them boats and men detached by Chads within a few minutes of his arrival at Rangoon. The timely reinforcement probably saved Kemmendine. In the afternoon, Chads also moved up the *Sophie* and three gunboats, and ordered the *Satellite*, under Dobson, with some men from the *Arachne*, to support the defence on the Dalla side, where the enemy had been observed to be throwing up works. On the 3rd, the Burmese in the river pressed their attack with more determination than ever, and succeeded in setting fire to the *Teignmouth*, which however, was not seriously damaged. More reinforcements were sent up by Chads; and, that night, Ryves, putting the whole of his available European force into boats under Kellett, ordered a dash to be made at the Burmese flotilla. The attack was made in the early morning of the 4th, when the moon had set. The Burmese remained steady until the British were within pistol shot, and then fled. Kellett drove ashore some of their rearmost boats, and Lieutenant Goldfinch took one craft bearing a flag, six others being also captured. The pursuit could not be continued for more than three or four miles, as Kellett had a strong force of the enemy up a creek in his rear.

This valuable service was performed without loss. The naval officers concerned in it were, besides Kellett, Lieutenant George Goldfinch, and Midshipmen Valentine Pickey, William Coyde, Charles Kittoe Scott, and —— Murray. Messrs. William Lindquist and George Boscawen, of the Bombay Marine, were also present. The situation was further relieved by the operations of Chads in the Puzendown creek against the Burmese left and rear on the night of December 5th; by the work of the *Satellite* at Dalla; and by the exertions of Kellett, with the *Diana*, in the Panlang branch of the river. The enemy persisted in his attack on the 6th, when Chads sent his mortar vessels up to Kemmendine, where they were most useful; and on the 7th, many fire-rafts and large boats were sent down against the shipping, though without effect. Not, however, until nearly noon on the 7th, when the Burmese had become very bold, were the enemy's positions subjected to a general assault by the army. They were then carried, and their defenders were routed. Chads sent every available man from the *Arachne* to reinforce Ryves, and to enable him to intercept the retreat; but the fugitives were too quick for the British. It is calculated that during the week ending December 7th, they lost 5000 men. The loss on the part of the army was 26 killed, and 252 wounded.

On the following night, a successful combined assault was made on the Burmese corps on the Dalla side of the river, Chads, Kellett, and Mr. Archibald Reed, R.N., co-operating, aided by the fire of the *Satellite*. On that occasion, five of the naval brigade were wounded.

The Burmese soon reassembled; and they renewed their attacks on December 13th. Early in the morning of the next day, moreover, some of their emissaries managed to set fire to, and burn down, about one-fourth of the town of Rangoon. On the 15th, therefore, Chads sent a detachment under Kellett up the Lyne branch of the river. The expedition consisted of the *Diana*, towing the H. E. I. Co.'s cruiser *Prince of Wales*, and the pinnaces of the *Arachne* and *Sophie*; and it captured three large war boats, and about forty small craft, many with useful cargoes, besides destroying numerous fire-rafts. At the same time, Sir Archibald Campbell, with 1300 infantry, stormed the Burmese stockades in the same direction, and gained a most brilliant victory over 20,000 of the enemy. The naval brigade had no one hurt.

During the remainder of the month, naval reconnoitring parties went in several directions, destroying stores and rafts; the army was reinforced from Bengal, Madras and Ceylon; the *Larne* returned from Calcutta; and about twenty additional gunboats arrived from Chittagong. It was the turning point in the war. From that time the Burmese stood mainly on the defensive, and almost entirely evacuated the country below Donoobew; while many of them, realising that they would not be harmed by the invaders, returned to their homes within the occupied territory, and afforded no small assistance, especially to the commissariat.

It was decided to begin the advance towards Ava, the capital, early in 1825; and, in preparation for this, Sir Archibald Campbell, who could not, of course, afford to leave any obstruction in his rear, sent a combined expedition, which gallantly captured the old Portuguese fort and the stockaded pagoda of Syriam. The naval contingent, of 48 officers and men, was headed by Lieutenant Charles Keele, who was the first person into the works at the pagoda.

As land carriage was almost unobtainable, the advance had to be made on lines parallel with the river Irawadi, and to be accompanied by a flotilla. Captain Thomas Alexander (2), in the *Alligator*, arrived at Rangoon on January 22nd, and, being Chads's senior, assumed the naval command. Under his direction, Chads, with the *Satellite*, *Prince of Wales*, *Diana*, 15 row gunboats, 7 boats of the squadron, and various canoes, co-operated with Lieut.-Colonel Henry Godwin in securing control of the Lyne branch of the river, and in taking and destroying, on February 5th, the stockaded position of Than-ta-bain, commanding its banks; and Lieutenants Kellett and Keele also cleared the Panlang branch. In these operations 4 seamen were wounded, and 1 seaman was drowned. Thus free communication between the Rangoon river and the main stream of the Irawadi was assured. Upon the return of the expedition, the regular advance commenced on February 13th, Commander Ryves being left in charge at Rangoon, and the forward movement being made by way of the Panlang branch.

The naval flotilla accompanying the army, under the command of Captain Alexander, consisted of the *Diana*, *Satellite*, two mortar-boats, six gun-vessels, thirty armed row boats, all the boats of the squadron in the Rangoon river, and about sixty launches, flats, and canoes, with, embarked in them, all the disposable officers and men of the *Alligator*, *Arachne*, and *Sophie*, and a brigade of troops under Brig.-General Willoughby Cotton, about 1160 strong. Parallel with and a little in the rear of this, moved the main army of about 2500 men. A third division, under Major Robert Henry Sale, with the co-operation of the *Larne* and *Mercury*, was detached with directions to attack Bassein, on the western coast, and then to join the main force at Donoobew. A force of about 3800 men was left at Rangoon, under Brigadier Michael M'Creagh. From Rangoon, Ava is 600 miles distant up the Irawadi. Alexander's flotilla sailed on February 16th, the Bassein flotilla on the 17th.

On the 19th, a stockade at Panlang was carried; and the *Satellite* was left to protect the post, which was also garrisoned. On March 6th, the river flotilla sighted the pagoda of Donoobew; and the place was soon afterwards summoned; but in vain. A first attack was made on the morning of March 7th, and, with the support of the boats, a stockade was carried, though a second work beat off Cotton with heavy loss, the result of the failure being that, on the 8th, the vanguard of the expedition dropped down to Youngyoun, nine miles below Donoobew. In the affair, the naval loss was 2 killed and 13 wounded. Sir Archibald Campbell pressed on with the main force to support the marine column, and on the 25th, took up a position close to the main stockade. There was some fighting, especially on the 27th; but, the Burmese general, Bandoola, having been killed on April 1st by a shell, his troops fled, and Donoobew was easily taken possession of on April 2nd.

On April 3rd, Sir Archibald Campbell, always in communication with the marine column, advanced towards Prome; and at Suwarrah, on the 12th, he was joined by Brigadier M'Creagh. The neighbourhood of Prome was reached on the 24th, and, as there was no resistance, the place was taken possession of on the day

following. A hundred guns were found mounted in the stockades.
The rainy season then commencing, the army went into cantonments.

In the meantime, Major Sale's division, 780 men strong,
accompanied by the *Larne*, Commander Frederick Marryat,[1] and
Mercury. (Bombay Marine), Drummond Anderson, commander,
had attacked Bassein. The expedition had arrived off the mouth
of the Bassein river on February 24th, and on the 26th, had
advanced, and had been fired at from two stockades, which had
been abandoned on the fire being returned.   On March 3rd, the
ships had anchored within three miles of the town, which, it was
found, had been destroyed. Sale pushed up the river for about
130 miles ; but, as the enemy always fled before him, he returned
to Bassein on the 23rd, having lost but 2 wounded. Commander
Marryat subsequently received the surrender of Thingang, and
Lieutenant Thomas Fraser, that of Pumkayi.   The result was
that the enemy no longer owned a port between Cape Negrais and
Tenasserim.

During the wet weather, the army lay nearly inactive at Prome ;
nor did the Navy do much in the Irawadi.   On May 1st, however,
Lieutenant James Wilkinson, while on a reconnoitring expedition
up the river, captured eight large war boats, without having a man
hurt, although he performed the service under a fire from about
500 muskets.   After the occupation of Prome, Captain Chads
returned to Rangoon; Marryat, transferred to the *Tees*, 26, in
April, went also to Rangoon, and quitted the Rangoon river in
May ; Ryves was invalided; Lieutenant Edward Blanckley,[2] of
the *Alligator*, was given command of the *Sophie*, and soon afterwards left the station; and the only ships then remaining at
Rangoon were the *Alligator* and *Arachne*.   Between that town and
Prome a chain of gunboats kept communications open, and insured
the prompt forwarding of provisions and stores to the front.

The campaign of 1825 was not resumed until late in the year ;
for, although a Burmese leader named Memia-Boo, with an army of
nearly 20,000 men, had advanced to Meaday, and threatened Prome,
an armistice was arranged, and negotiations were entered into.   In
the meanwhile, Captain Sir James Brisbane, Kt., C.B., of the
Boadicea, 46, which he had left at Rangoon, joined the headquarters
of the army, bringing with him his ship's boats.   Eventually the

[1] Posted, July 25th, 1825.
[2] Confirmed as Com., Dec. 10th, 1825.

court of Ava declined all terms; and the armistice ceased on November 3rd.

The first episode of the renewed hostilities was an unfortunate defeat for the British. Lieut.-Colonel Robert M'Dowall, of the Madras Army, while attempting, on November 15th, to dislodge a large force of the enemy from a position 48 miles N.E. of Prome, was driven back, he himself and 53 men being killed, and 110 wounded. The Burmese, with 50,000 men, then surrounded Prome; though they received a check on November 25th, when they attacked Padoung-mew, on the west bank of the river, and were repulsed by a small force which was much assisted by part of the flotilla under Kellett.[1]

While Sir Archibald Campbell was getting ready to strike in return, Captain Alexander died, on November 7th., and was succeeded in the command of the *Alligator* by Chads. On the 14th, the *Champion*, 18, Commander John Fitzgerald Studdert, arrived at Rangoon.

On December 1st, Sir Colin moved out in the direction of Meaday, while Brisbane and the flotilla began action with the enemy entrenched on Nepadee ridge. The advance was steadily continued from day to day, the flotilla capturing numerous boats, and the army driving all before it. Commander John Francis Dawson,[2] of the *Arachne*, fell in the fighting of December 2nd, and was succeeded in his command by Lieutenant Andrew Baird,[3] of the *Boadicea*.

When Meaday was sighted, on December 17th, it was found to have been evacuated. Sir Archibald pressed on, and arrived before Melloone on December 29th. There he agreed to another armistice, in order that negotiations might be again entered upon. Immediately after a treaty of peace had been signed on January 3rd., Brisbane fell ill, and was obliged to proceed to Pulo Penang. This gallant officer, who never wholly recovered his health, died in New South Wales on December 19th, 1826, when he was on his way to the west coast of South America, with his broad pennant in the *Warspite*, 76. His departure from the Irawadi, caused the command there to revert to Captain Chads.

Unfortunately, the signature of the treaty of peace did not end the war. The engagements entered into at Melloone were neither

---

[1] Com., July 25th, 1825.   [2] Com., Nov. 7th, 1825.
[3] Confd. as Com., May 25th, 1826.

ratified nor observed by the court of Ava; and hostilities were renewed on January 19th, 1826, when the British opened a bombardment of Melloone, which the Burmese had undertaken to evacuate. In the course of the same day, the town was assaulted and taken, the assailants losing only 9 killed and 35 wounded. In this affair the naval officers employed were Captain Chads, Lieutenants Joseph Grote, and William Smith (5),[1] and Mates or Midshipmen Valentine Pickey,[2] Sydenham Wilde,[3] William Hayhurst Hall,[3] George Sumner Hand, George Wyke, Stephen Joshua Lett,[4] and William Coyde.

Even the lesson thus taught at Melloone did not convince the Burmese of the propriety of conceding British demands. A chief picturesquely known as Nie-Wooh-Breen, or the King of Hell, took up a strong and threatening position in the town of Pagahm-mew, with 16,000 men. The enemy once more tried to negotiate, and so to gain time; but Sir Archibald advanced without delay, and, on February 9th, defeated the King of Hell with great slaughter, and took his city, losing but 2 killed and 15 wounded. This convinced the court of Ava of the necessity of surrendering. A sum of 25 lacs of rupees was handed over at Yandaboo, only 45 miles from the capital, as an earnest of good faith; and, after little more than a fortnight's discussion, a definitive treaty was signed on February 24th. By this instrument Burmah agreed —

To abstain from all future interference with the principality of Assam, and with Cachar, etc.: if required, to recognise Ghumbir Singh as rajah of Manipur: to cede to Great Britain in perpetuity Arakan, Ramri, Cheduba, Sandoway, Yeu, Tavoy, Mergui, and Tenasserim: to receive a British resident at Ava: to depute a minister to reside at Calcutta: to reciprocate the privileges granted to Burmese vessels in British ports: to enter into a commercial treaty: and to pay an indemnity of one crore (10,000,000) of rupees.

On March 8th, the troops were re-embarked; and by May 6th, the whole force, having returned to Rangoon, had been broken up. The thanks of both Houses of Parliament were most deservedly voted to Sir James Brisbane, and the officers, seamen, and Marines engaged under his orders, as well, of course, as to the army; and the gratitude of the country was further evinced by the conferring of the C.B. on Captains Henry Ducie Chads, and Frederick Marryat, and Commander George Frederick Ryves (2). There were also

[1] Com., July 22nd, 1826.　　　[3] Lieut., Dec. 23rd, 1826.
[2] Lieut., June 22nd, 1826.　　　[4] Lieut., Dec. 26th, 1826.

numerous promotions; and in addition, both the Admiralty and
the East India Company expressed their approbation of the zeal
and gallantry displayed by the naval contingent. It had, indeed,
been a most arduous and difficult conquest; and one, be it remembered, which could scarcely have been effected by any Power not
possessed of command of the sea, and of officers and men expert
in the various problems of river warfare.[1]

The officers and men of the Navy engaged in this war received
no medal whatsoever until 1851, the general Naval Medal, 1793–

ADMIRAL SIR ROBERT WALLER OTWAY (1), BART., G.C.B.

(From J. W. Cook's engraving after a family miniature.)

1815, being, it must be supposed, considered to be too great a
reward for services of the kind. In 1851, however, upon the issue
of the medal known as "India, No. 1," that decoration, with clasp
for "Ava," was distributed to the surviving officers and men who
had served during the Burmese war in the following of H.M.
ships: *Alligator, Arachne, Boadicea, Champion, Larne, Liffey,
Sophie, Slaney, Tamar* and *Tees.*

[1] James, vi. 420–470; Marshall, 'Narr. of Nav. Ops. in Ava' (1830), where are
the disps.; Snodgrass; H. H. Wilson's Coll. (Calcutta, 1827).

Turkish oppression, and a revival of national spirit among the Greeks, provoked a general rebellion of the Greek provinces of the Turkish Empire, which broke out about the year 1821, and which soon led to frightful exhibitions of savagery by both sides. In western Europe, and especially in Great Britain, popular feeling was, upon the whole, much in favour of the patriots; and the governments were strongly pressed to intervene, and even to assist in driving the Mahometans altogether out of Europe. The contest grew more and more bloodthirsty as it progressed; and it was but natural, looking to the nature of the warfare, that the Levant became the scene of continual piracy and rapine, as well as of the more legitimate operations of hostile races. During the tenure of the Mediterranean command by Vice-Admiral Sir Harry Burrard Neale, this condition of affairs more than once demanded and received the active attention of British naval officers on the spot. Thus, for example, on April 9th and 10th, 1826, Commander George James Hope Johnstone, of the *Alacrity*, 10, found it his duty to send his boats, under Lieutenant Richard Shepheard Triscott, to destroy three Greek piratical vessels near the island of Psara. Triscott and 3 seamen were severely wounded, and Lieutenant John Wheatley was badly burnt; but, on the other hand, 40 of the pirates were killed, and 70 were made prisoners in a tower under which their vessels had sought protection.[1] On June 18th, 1826, two Greek misticoes, which had plundered a Maltese vessel, were followed into a passage between Candia and some outlying rocks by the *Sibylle*, 48, Captain Sir John Pechell. The position was defended by the crews of several other misticoes, which it was endeavoured to cut out. In the warmly fought affair that followed, Midshipman J. M. Knox and 12 men were killed outright, and 4 officers (1 mortally), and 27 men were wounded.[2] Similarly, on January 3rd, 1827, Commander the Hon. Charles Leonard Irby, of the *Pelican*, 18, falling in with a piratical schooner, the *Aphrodite*, 4, in the gulf of Kalamata captured her. On March 2nd following, the obstinacy of a Turkish skipper, who refused to bring to and be examined, caused Irby to mistake him for a pirate, and to send boats, which took and destroyed his vessel, killing 2 and wounding 4 of her crew. In this affair, Lieutenants Henry Smith (2), who was badly injured, and Daniel F. Grant, who was also wounded, distinguished themselves. The total British loss

[1] Marshall, iv., Pt. II., 352.   [2] *U.S. Journal*, 1841, 332.

was 2 killed, and 7 (2 mortally) wounded. On June 13th, Irby was actually obliged to open fire on the Greek town of Scardamoula, in order to obtain the restitution of plundered property which lay there, the governor being, apparently, in league with the pirates. Two days later, the *Pelican's* boats destroyed a pirate vessel at Petalidion.[1]

The commercial inconveniences consequent upon such a state of things, the sanguinary character of the contest, and the barbarities of the Turks, led, in 1826,[2] to the signature at St. Petersburg of a protocol on the affairs of Greece; and, in the following year,[3] to the conclusion of the Treaty of London, the parties to which were Great Britain, France, and Russia, and the objects of which were the pacification of Greece, the suppression of piracy and anarchy in the Archipelago, and, more immediately, the enforcement of an armistice between the belligerents, to give opportunity for the opening of negotiations. In December, 1826, Vice-Admiral Sir Edward Codrington was appointed to supersede Sir Harry Burrard Neale in the Mediterranean; and the new Commander-in-Chief, who reached his station in February, instructed his Captains on September 8th, 1827,[4] that the intentions of the Powers had been formally signified both to Turkey and to Greece; that Greece had agreed to an armistice, while Turkey had not; and that, as a result, it became his duty to see that supplies of men and arms destined against Greece should be intercepted. The work of interception, he pointed out, must be carried out with caution, and must not degenerate into hostilities, unless, indeed, the Turks should persist in endeavouring to force passages prohibited to them by the allies. At the same time, firmness was to be employed; and, if absolutely necessary, the prescribed policy was to be enforced by means of cannon. This declaration, to the tenor of which the Turks were no strangers,[5] and the manner in which the British commanders carried out the instructions, induced the Turks, on September 25th, to verbally accede to an armistice by land and sea.

At that time there lay in the port of Navarin a Turco-Egyptian

---

[1] Marshall, iii., Pt. II., 6; O'Byrne, 1202.

[2] April 4th. Text in 'Codrington,' 501.

[3] July 6th. Text in 'Codrington,' 502. Addit. secret article in 'Codrington,' 505.

[4] Letter in James, vi. 473. It was compiled after receipt of instructions agreed upon on July 12th by the plenipotentiaries. These are in 'Codrington,' 508.

[5] Codrington to Turkish Admiral, Sept. 19th, 1827; Codrington to Ibrahim Pasha Sept. 21st, 1827.

fleet[1] of some force : and, as the objects of this were suspected, it was closely watched by Codrington. Navarin harbour, in Messenia, is a spacious bay which opens to the westward, but the mouth of which, except to the south-west, is almost completely filled by the island of Sphagia.[2] The passage is there about half a mile broad, and, in 1827, was flanked, on the south, by a citadel, behind which lay the Turco-Egyptian army 40,000 strong, and on the north, by the island, by batteries.

It should be mentioned here that the French Rear-Admiral, Henri de Rigny, with a squadron, had joined Codrington, off Navarin, on September 21st, and that a Russian squadron, under Rear-Admiral Count Heiden, joined on October 13th, when Sir Edward, who on the 14th formally assumed command of the combined forces, was off Zante. The constitution of the allied fleets will be set forth later.

On the day following the conclusion of the verbal agreement above mentioned, Codrington and de Rigny were preparing to put to sea, when there came off to the British flagship, *Asia,* a messenger from Ibrahim Pasha, who commanded the Turco-Egyptian fleet and the Egyptian troops in the Morea, with word to the effect that his master, having received intelligence that Lord Cochrane[3] had made a descent upon Patras, requested to be allowed to send a sufficient force to frustrate his lordship's plans. Codrington returned a decided negative, and asked whether Ibrahim did not consider himself bound by the agreement. The messenger, on leaving, answered that, unless he should return within an hour, Codrington was to understand that the agreement of the 25th was still in force ; and, as the man did not return, Codrington and de Rigny put to sea at sunset, leaving the *Dartmouth,* 32, to watch the Turco-Egyptian fleet.

On October 2nd, the *Dartmouth* communicated to the Admirals, who were in the offing, that a strong detachment of the Turks and Egyptians had weighed and was standing towards Patras. The blockading force obliged this division to put back to the southward of Zante ; and, on the 3rd, when 15 more Turkish ships had joined, and a further attempt was made to proceed, the allied commanders made representations which induced the whole to steer for Navarin.

---

[1] This had left Alexandria on Aug. 6th, and had reached Navarin on Sept. 9th.

[2] The ancient Sphacteria.

[3] Afterwards Admiral Lord Dundonald, then in the service of the Greek patriots.

Again the *Dartmouth* was left on watch; and again, on the 4th, she had to report that some vessels had sailed for Patras. The *Asia*, 84, with the *Dartmouth* and *Talbot*, 28, assisting her, interfered with their purpose; though it is possible that Ibrahim's intentions were frustrated rather by the state of the weather than by the appearance, and warning guns, of the British ships. In any case, the allies were unable to prevent the Turco-Egyptians from once more entering Navarin; although it had been determined that the vessels which had issued thence should, if possible, be cut off from the port, and obliged to make for Alexandria.

These events indicated that it was useless for the allies to confide in the word of the Turks and Egyptians. On the other hand, they induced Ibrahim, on his return to Navarin, to disembark the troops who had been designed for operations at Patras; and these troops at once began to perpetrate the most terrible barbarities in the Morea, neither women nor children being spared. The three admirals considered it to be their duty not only to see that Ibrahim should keep his word, but also, so far as might be, to put moral pressure upon him to stop the atrocities. They decided that a blockade of Navarin throughout the winter would be difficult, expensive, and perhaps useless; and that, upon the whole, the best way of effecting their objects, and the objects of the civilised Powers, would be for them to take their squadrons into Navarin Bay, and there anchor them in such a position as to make it hopeless for the Turco-Egyptian fleet to attempt to disobey them, and dangerous for the Turco-Egyptian troops to further violate the convention. Ibrahim's ships were moored in a semicircle in the bay, so that no anchorage save a central one remained for the allies. The arrangement had been adopted at the suggestion of certain French volunteer officers who were in some of the Egyptian vessels. The larger ships and frigates formed the Turco-Egyptian inner line, and the smaller craft were disposed beyond them so as to command the intervals between them. On October 18th, therefore, Sir Edward Codrington issued the following instructions :—

"It appears that the Egyptian ships in which the French officers are embarked, are those most to the south-east. It is therefore my wish that his Excellency Rear-Admiral Chevalier de Rigny should place his squadron abreast of them. As the next in succession appears to be a ship of the line with a flag at the main, I propose placing the *Asia* abreast of her, with the *Genoa* and *Albion* next to the *Asia*; and I wish that his Excellency Rear-Admiral Count Heiden will have the goodness to place his squadron next in succession to the British ships of the line. The Russian frigates in this case can occupy the Turkish ships next in succession to the Russian ships of the line; the English frigates forming alongside such Turkish vessels as may be on the western side of the harbour abreast of the British ships of the line; and the French frigates forming in the same manner, so as to occupy the Turkish frigates, etc., abreast of the French ships of the line. If time permits, before any hostility is committed by the Turkish fleet, the ships are to moor with springs on the ring of each anchor. No gun is to be fired from the combined fleet without a signal being made for that purpose, unless shot be fired from any of the Turkish ships; in which case the ships so firing are to be destroyed immediately. The corvettes and the brigs are, under the

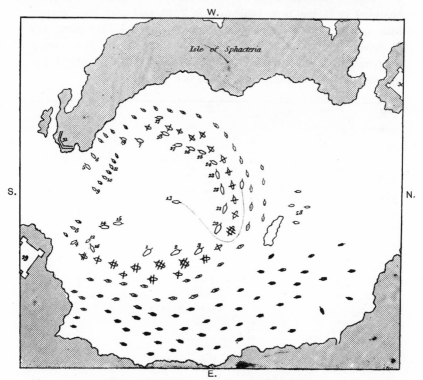

W.

S.   N.

E.

PLAN OF THE BAY OF NAVARIN, OCT. 20TH, 1827.

(*Chiefly from a plan by Lieut. John Harvey Boteler, H.M.S. Albion.*)

For reference numbers 1 to 27, see the table on p. 256.

28. Three Tunisian frigates, and a brig.	30. Old Navarin.
29. Town and citadel of Navarin.	31. Batteries.

direction of Captain Fellowes, of the *Dartmouth*, to remove the fire-vessels into such a position as will prevent their being able to injure any of the combined fleet. In case of a regular battle ensuing, and creating any of that confusion which must naturally arise from it, it is to be observed that, in the words of Nelson, 'No Captain can do very wrong who places his ship alongside that of an enemy.'"

The exact strength of the Turco-Egyptian fleet is, strange to say, a matter of some doubt. According to a statement of the

Secretary to the Capitan Bey, it consisted of 65 sail, including two
84's, one 76, four double-banked 64's, fifteen 48-gun frigates, 26
corvettes, 12 brigs, and 5 fire-vessels; and this statement is
probably correct : but Codrington sets its total strength at 89 sail,
besides 41 transports, and makes it to have comprised 3 ships of
the line, 4 double-banked frigates, 13 other frigates, 30 corvettes,
28 brigs, 6 fire-brigs, and 5 schooners. The number of guns
mounted in it has been estimated at 2240, and may have been a
little greater. The combined fleet, which mounted 1276 guns, was
as follows, the names of the commanding officers, and the number
of men killed and wounded in the battle of October 20th, being
inserted against each ship for convenience of reference :—

		Ships.	No. on Plan, p.255.	Guns.	Commanders.	Killed.	Wounded.
Starboard or Weather Line.	British.	*Asia*	1	84	Vice-Adm. Sir Edward Codrington . . } Capt. Edward Curzon . . . . }	19	57
		Genoa	2	76	Capt. Walter Bathurst . . .	26	33
		Albion	3	74	Capt. John Acworth Ommanney . . .	10	50
		Glasgow . .	6	50	Capt. Hon. James Ashley Maude . .	—	2
		Cambrian . .	5	48	Capt. Gawen William Hamilton, C.B. .	1	1
		Dartmouth .	4	42	Capt. Thomas Fellowes, C.B. . . .	6	8
		Talbot . . .	7	28	Capt. Hon. Frederick Spencer . . .	6	17
		Rose . . .	8	18	Com. Lewis Davies [1]	3	15
		Mosquito . .	10	10	Com. George Bohm Martin [2] . . .	2	4
		Brisk . . .	11	10	Com. Hon. William Anson	1	3
		Philomel . .	9	10	Com. Viscount Ingestrie [3]	1	7
		Hind, cutter .	12	6	Lieut. John Robb	5	9
	French.	*Scipion*. . . .	14	80	Capt. Milius	2	21
		Trident . . .	15	74	Capt. Morice	—	7
		Breslau . . .	13	84	Capt. Botherel de La Bretonnière .	—	15
		Sirène	16	60	R.-Adm. Henri de Rigny . . . . } Capt. Robert . . . . . . }	23	42
		Armide. . . .	17	42	Capt. Hugon	14	25
		Alcyone . . .	18	10	Com. Turpin	1	10
		Daphne. . .	19	6	Com. Férétrier	2	5
Port Line.	Russian.	*Azof*	20	74	R.-Adm. Count de Heiden . . . . } Capt. Lazaref . . . . . . }	24	67
		Gangoot . . .	21	84	Capt. Avinof	14	37
		Yezekeyeel . .	22	74	Capt. Svinkin	13	18
		Alexander Nevski	23	74	Capt. Bogdanovich	5	7
		Constantin .	25	44	Capt. Hrooschof	—	1
		Provornyi. . .	24	42	Com. Epanchin (2)	3	4
		Elena . . .	26	44	Com. Epanchin (1)	—	5
		Castor . . .	27	32	Com. Sitin	—	—

[1] Posted Oct. 21st, 1827.   [2] Posted Apr. 19th, 1828.   [3] Posted Oct. 22nd, 1827.

For particulars of the Russian ships I am indebted to the naval General Staff at St. Petersburg.

The state of the wind did not allow of the bay being entered
before October 20th. On that day, the weather being fine, and the
wind from S.W., the combined squadrons stood towards Navarin
early in the afternoon. To give no cause for feelings of jealousy,
the Commander-in-Chief had determined that the order of sailing
should be the order of battle; and the fleet went in, the British
and French forming the weather, or starboard, and the Russians,
the lee line. At the mouth of the harbour a boat from the shore

came alongside the *Asia*, the leading ship, with a message to the
effect that, as Ibrahim Pasha had not given any order or permission
for the allies to enter, it was requested that they would again put
to sea.   Codrington's reply was : " I am come not to receive orders,
but to give them ; and, if any shot be fired at the allied fleet, the
Turkish fleet shall be destroyed."

The *Asia* pursued her way, and dropped anchor close alongside
a ship of the line, instantly mooring with 30 fathoms on each
cable near the flagship of the Capitan Bey.   The *Genoa* came next,
and was about to place her bow towards the bow of the *Asia*, when
she was hailed by the Vice-Admiral, and desired to anchor with her
head in the same direction as that of the flag-ship.   This she did,
placing herself near another ship of the line.   The *Albion* followed,

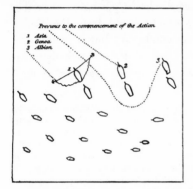 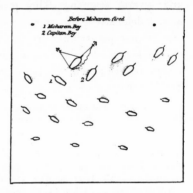

and took station close to a double-banked frigate.   In the general
plan, all the ships are represented as in their proper places ;
but the action had begun, and had continued for between twenty
and thirty minutes, ere the sternmost of the French, or the headmost of the Russian ships, had anchored ; and nearly two hours
elapsed before the *Cambrian*, *Glasgow*, and *Constantin* were able
to take up their positions, the wind being very light.   Codrington
entered cleared for action; but his lower-deck ports were not
hauled flat against the ship's sides, but were kept square, as at
sea in fine weather.   This arrangement, and the fact that he did
not anchor his ships by the stern, but ordered springs on the
ring of each anchor, indicated a certain readiness to engage, yet
no necessary intention of becoming the assailant.   At the same
time, it must be admitted that the entry of the allies could scarcely
be interpreted save as a provocation to hostilities.

Codrington's orders were in process of being carried out; and the leading ships had anchored, some of them even having furled their sails, and the *Asia's* band having been called on deck, when musketry fire broke out in the direction of the *Dartmouth.* Some of that frigate's boats had been sent to the fireships on the right of the entrance to request that those craft would move further away from the stations taken up by the allies. This, of course, was scarcely a politic measure, seeing that the new-comers, and not the vessels already in the bay, were obviously the cause of any crowding that might be objectionable. The despatch of the boats was, moreover, a measure likely to be misunderstood ; and, in fact, the Turks, supposing that force was about to be employed, opened fire and killed Lieutenant George William Howe Fitzroy, and several seamen. This produced what Codrington described as a "defensive" fire from the *Dartmouth,* and from the *Sirène.* Up to that point musketry only was employed ; but at length one of the Egyptian ships fired a round shot at the French flag-ship, which replied ; and so, very quickly, the action became general. Says Codrington :—

"The *Asia,* although placed alongside the ship of the Capitan Bey, was even nearer to that of Moharem Bey, the commander of the Egyptian ships; and, since his ships did not fire at the *Asia,* although the action was begun to windward, neither did the *Asia* fire at her. The latter, indeed, sent a message ' that he would not fire at all'; and therefore no hostility took place betwixt our two ships for some time after the *Asia* had returned the fire of the Capitan Bey. In the meantime, however, our excellent pilot, Mr. Peter Mitchell, who went to interpret to Moharem my desire to avoid bloodshed, was killed by his people in our boat alongside. Whether with or without his orders I know not; but his ship soon afterwards fired into the *Asia,* and was consequently effectually destroyed by the *Asia's* fire, sharing the same fate as his brother admiral on the starboard side, and falling to leeward a mere wreck. These ships being out of the way, the *Asia* became exposed to a raking fire from vessels in the second and third line, which carried away her mizen mast by the board, disabled some of her guns, and killed or wounded some of her crew. This narration of the proceedings of the *Asia* would probably be equally applicable to most of the other ships of the fleet. The manner in which the *Genoa* and *Albion* took their stations was beautiful; and the conduct of my brother Admirals, Count Heiden, and the Chevalier de Rigny, throughout, was admirable and highly exemplary. Captain Fellowes executed the part allotted to him perfectly, and, with the able assistance of his little but brave detachment, saved the *Sirène* from being burnt by the fire-vessels. And the *Cambrian, Glasgow,* and *Talbot,* following the fine example of Captain Hugon, of the *Armide,* who was opposed to the leading frigate of that line, effectually destroyed their opponents, and also silenced the batteries. This bloody and destructive battle was continued with unabated fury for four hours; and the scene of wreck and devastation which presented itself at its termination was such as has been seldom before witnessed. As each ship of our opponents became effectually disabled, such of her crew as could escape from her endeavoured to set her on fire; and it is wonderful how we avoided the effects of their successive and awful explosions."

So thick was the smoke in the bay that the Russian ships, as they entered, had great difficulty in finding their way, and in distinguishing friend from foe. The *Armide*, going to her station, found the *Talbot* pressed by three ships of the enemy, and skilfully interposed herself between the *Talbot* and her chief adversary while the British cheered lustily.[1] The *Armide*, in turn, was saved by the *Rose* from an attack by a Turkish fire-ship; and the *Sirène*, as stated in the dispatch, was similarly saved by the *Dartmouth*. The little *Hind*, cutter, tender to the *Asia*, had been detached, and returned as the squadron was entering the bay. Without orders, Lieutenant Robb took her into the *mêlée*, and fought her most gallantly and effectively. The Turks behaved with the utmost bravery and determination, but, having allowed

the allies to enter without opposing them, their fate was sealed. Either they ought not to have resisted at all, or, upon seeing their boat return from the advancing *Asia* with an unsatisfactory answer to the message of Ibrahim Pasha, they should have instantly opened fire from every gun on land and water that would bear. In the latter event, they would undoubtedly have derived immense advantage from their horse-shoe formation, and from the presence of their fire-ships just within the mouth of the bay. Nor can it be urged that they were unprepared. The ships were all at quarters, and the guns had their tompions out, and were loaded

---

[1] "Our work was now easy enough, for by this time the Russian frigates got to their stations, and hammered away. One of them, however, in passing our stern, sent several shot into us, and killed the old signalman; whereupon Captain Spencer ordered Grey" (Mids. Hon. Geo. (2)) "and me, his two aides-de-camp, to go on board and remonstrate. We found, I regret to say, that several of the officers were quite drunk, and the captain not much better." Otway's 'Adm. Lord Clarence E. Paget,' 15.

nearly to the muzzles with shot and scrap iron. Owing to their lack of decision and promptitude, they lost a ship of the line, three double-banked frigates, nine other frigates, twenty-two corvettes, nineteen brigs, a schooner, and five fire-ships, and, probably, 4000 men,[1] without causing any proportionate degree of damage to the allies. Codrington, in his General Order of October 24th, overrated the amount of destruction wrought, and expressed his belief that " one frigate and fifteen smaller vessels " were all that remained in a condition ever again to put to sea. He was mistaken, doubtless owing to the fact that when he was in the bay several vessels which were afterwards saved, appeared to be burnt or bilged. When the *Pelican*, 18, reconnoitred the scene on November 17th, she found there 29 sail at anchor,[2] including a ship of the line and four frigates much shattered, besides a *rasé*, two frigates, five corvettes, eleven brigs, and five schooners ready for immediate service. These may not all have been in the bay on October 20th; but the particulars serve to confirm the general truth of all accounts save the one in Codrington's General Order. All agree that the destruction was less than is there stated.

The ships of the combined squadrons nearly all suffered considerably in hull as well as aloft. The number of killed and wounded has been already set forth. In the British squadron among the officers killed were Captain Walter Bathurst,[3] of the *Genoa*, Lieutenant George William Howe Fitzroy, Master William Smith, of the *Genoa*, Captains (R.M.) George Augustus Bell, and Cornelius James Stevens, and Lieutenant (R.M.) Philip James Sturgeon. Among the severely wounded was Commander John Norman Campbell,[4] second in command of the *Albion*. The practice of appointing Commanders as " second Captains " to large ships was then quite new; and therefore it may be of interest to add that Commander Robert Lambert Baynes[5] served in the *Asia*, and Commander Richard Dickinson,[6] in the *Genoa*, in that capacity. All the Commanders and all the first Lieutenants of ships engaged were promoted in consequence of the action. All

---

[1] Chevalier: ' Mar. Franç. de 1815 à 1870,' 48.
[2] Marshall, Supp., Pt. II. 332.
[3] Capt. of Oct. 24th, 1799. He was 63 at the time of his death.
[4] Posted Oct. 22nd, 1827.
[5] Posted July 8th, 1828.
[6] Posted May 13th, 1828.

the Captains and Commanders who had not previously held the
C.B. were given that honour; and Codrington himself was made
a G.C.B. In addition, France, Russia, and Greece showered decora-
tions upon the victors. Yet a large body of public opinion in
England condemned the Vice-Admiral's behaviour as rash, useless,
and impolitic; and the battle was officially alluded to as an "un-
toward event." Vice-Admiral Sir John Gore (2) was sent out to Sir
Edward with a long list of queries from the Admiralty and the
Foreign Office; Ministers, from their places in Parliament, charged
the Commander-in-Chief with inattention or disobedience to orders;
and at length, after the lapse of some months, Sir Edward was
recalled, as Brenton says, either as a sacrifice to the Opposition,
or as a peace offering to the Sublime Porte: perhaps as both. The
specific cause assigned for his removal had, however, no reference

COMMEMORATIVE MEDAL OF THE BATTLE OF NAVARIN.
(From an original, kindly lent by H.S.H. Captain Prince Louis of Battenberg, G.C.B., R.N.)

to Navarin, but arose out of other circumstances which need not
here be entered into. Suffice it to say that Codrington was in no
way to blame.[1]

Before he returned to England, he was able to strike a most
important blow for the suppression of Greek piracy in the Mediterranean. The island of Grabusa, which had been taken by the
Greeks from the Turks, lies off the western end of Crete, and,
being an almost inaccessible fortified rock, with a good though
small anchorage, formed a most admirable headquarters for the
light vessels in which the freebooters chiefly pursued their trade.

On January 31st, 1828, by the Commander-in-Chief's direction,
Commodore Sir Thomas Staines, K.C.B., in the *Isis*, 50, anchored
off Grabusa, with the *Cambrian*, 48, Captain Gawen William Hamil-

---

[1] Bourchier, 'Codrington,' ii. *passim*; James (1837), vi. 471; Brenton, ii. 610;
Gazette, 1827, 2320, etc.

ton, *Rattlesnake*, 28, Captain the Hon. Charles Orlando Bridgman, *Zebra*, 18, Commander Charles Cotton (2), *Cameleon*, 10, and two French corvettes, and found 14 Greek vessels lying in the port, with an Austrian ship, and an Ionian merchantman, their prizes. Staines demanded the surrender of all these, and, receiving no satisfactory reply, fired into, and destroyed most of them. There was no resistance. Unfortunately, while the British ships were retiring, the *Isis* and the *Cambrian* fouled one another in the narrow channel; and the latter, paying off on the wrong tack, presently fell broadside on to a reef of rocks, where she was lost. Her people were saved; but Commander Cotton, of the *Zebra*, exerted himself so violently and continuously on the occasion as to bring on brain fever, from which he died. The court-martial fully exonerated Captain Hamilton.[1]

The destruction of the Turco-Egyptian fleet had had the effect of reducing the Porte to a condition of powerlessness at sea, but had made very little immediate difference to the lamentable state of affairs on land, where Ibrahim Pasha continued his career of violence and devastation in the Morea. This led France, in the summer of 1828, to send a small army to Greece; and eventually, Ibrahim was obliged to depart to Egypt. Turkey's hands were full, she being at war with Russia; and her positions in the south of Greece surrendered one after another, until only Morea Castle remained. In the siege of it the French were assisted by Captain Edmund Lyons, of the *Blonde*, 46, and Captain the Hon. Frederick Spencer, of the *Talbot*, 28, both of whom served with a naval brigade in the trenches until the capitulation of the place on November 1st, 1828.

Mention has been made above of the interference of Lord Cochrane in the affairs of Greece. Cochrane was then no longer in the British Navy. In the summer of 1814 he had been convicted of complicity in a sordid scheme of conspiracy and fraud, and had in consequence been imprisoned, fined, deprived of his naval rank, his Knighthood of the Bath, and his seat in Parliament.[2] Years afterwards, doubts began to be entertained as to the justice of his sentence; and, these having grown, his name was reinstated in its proper place in the Navy List in 1830, he became a Vice-Admiral in 1841, and, finally, the Order of the Bath was restored to him in 1847. During the fifteen years or more when he lay under the

---

[1] Marshall, Supp., Pt. II. 451; Bourchier, 'Codrington,' ii. 188; Mins. of C. M.
[2] 'Autobiog. of a Seaman,' ii. 317, etc.

imputation of disgrace, his marvellous energy and love of adventure led him to adopt the career of a sailor of fortune, and won for him, in that capacity, a fame such as has hardly been won by any other seamen in the whole course of history.[1] The story, of course, does not in strictness belong to the annals of the British Navy; but it is so closely connected with them, and it reflects so much honour and glory upon the profession which produced the hero, that a very brief summary of it naturally finds a place here.

In 1817, Lord Cochrane accepted the request of the revolutionary government of Chile to assume command of its scanty naval force in the struggle against Spain. After having partially superintended the equipment of a war-steamer which was building in London for the revolutionists, he landed at Valparaiso in November, 1818. General O'Higgins was Supreme Director of the infant republic, and Admiral Blanco Encalada commanded the little fleet, which consisted of a captured Spanish frigate, a couple of ex-Indiamen, the ex-British sloop *Hecate*, 18, renamed *Galvarino*, and two other sloops or corvettes. Cochrane was at once made "Vice-Admiral of Chile, and Commander-in-Chief of the Naval Forces of the Republic." Blanco most sensibly and patriotically assented to this arrangement, in spite of the opposition which was at first offered to it by Commander Martin George Guise,[2] R.N., and Lieutenant John Tooker Spry,[3] R.N., who had already taken service with the Chilians. The new chief hoisted his flag, on December 22nd, in the *O'Higgins*, 50 (ex-Spanish frigate *Maria Isabel*), and at once began a most extraordinary series of successes. It is not possible here to follow him through his difficulties and dangers. It will suffice to say that in spite of jealousy, treachery, mutiny, no pay, bad ships, and short-ness of supplies and ammunition, he drove the Spanish navy from the South Pacific, and was instrumental in perfecting the liberation not only of Chile, but also of Peru. In the course of his anti-Spanish campaigns, which lasted until 1823, Cochrane's most wonderful exploit was the capture of the Spanish frigate *Esmeralda*, 40, in 1820.

In November of that year, the *Esmeralda* lay under the batteries

---

[1] "He was at this time, in the estimation of the Old World and the New, the greatest man afloat. He was tall and thin, of powerful build, with close-cut red hair." Keppel, i. 36.

[2] Com. R.N. of Mar. 29th, 1815. He eventually became a vice-admiral in the Peruvian service.

[3] Lieut. R.N. of July 17th, 1813.

of Callao, protected by no fewer than 300 guns mounted on shore, and manned by a good and large crew, which slept every night at quarters.   Outside her anchorage was a strong boom, with chain moorings ; near her were some armed blockships, and, covering the whole, were twenty-seven gunboats.   On the evening of November 5th, Cochrane, who had with him off the port the *O'Higgins, Independencia*, and *Lautaro*, issued a proclamation to his men, and called for volunteers.   The narrative of what followed is given in Cochrane's own words :—

"A hundred and sixty seamen and eighty marines were selected, and, after dark, were placed in fourteen boats alongside the flag-ship, each man, armed with cutlass and pistol, being, for distinction's sake, dressed in white, with a blue band on the left arm. The Spaniards, I expected, would be off their guard, as, by way of ruse, the other ships had been sent out of the bay under the charge of Captain Foster, as though in pursuit of some vessels in the offing—so that the Spaniards would consider themselves safe from attack for that night.

"At ten o'clock all was in readiness, the boats being formed in two divisions, the first commanded by my flag-captain, Crosbie, and the second by Captain Guise—my boat leading.   The strictest silence, and the exclusive use of cutlasses were enjoined ; so that, as the oars were muffled, and the night dark, the enemy had not the least suspicion of impending attack.

"It was just upon midnight when we neared the small opening left in the boom, our plan being well-nigh frustrated by the vigilance of a guard-boat, upon which my launch had luckily stumbled.   The challenge was given, upon which, in an undertone, I threatened the occupants of the boat with instant death if they made the least alarm.   No reply was made to the threat, and in a few minutes our gallant fellows were alongside the frigate in line, boarding at several points simultaneously.

"The Spaniards were taken completely by surprise—the whole, with the exception of the sentries, being asleep at their quarters—and great was the havoc made amongst them by the Chileno cutlasses while they were recovering themselves.   Retreating to the forecastle, they there made a gallant stand, and it was not until the third charge that the position was carried.   The fight was for a short time renewed on the quarterdeck, where the Spanish marines fell to a man, the rest of the enemy leaping overboard and into the hold to escape slaughter.

"On boarding the ship by the main chains, I was knocked back by the butt end of the sentry's musket, and, falling on a thole pin of the boat, it entered my back near the spine, inflicting a severe injury, which caused me many years of subsequent suffering. Immediately regaining my footing, I reascended the side, and, when on deck, was shot through the thigh; but binding a handkerchief tightly round the wound, managed, though with great difficulty, to direct the contest to its close.

"The whole affair, from beginning to end, occupied only a quarter of an hour, our loss being eleven killed and thirty wounded, whilst that of the Spaniards was a hundred and sixty, many of whom fell under the cutlasses of the Chilenos before they could stand to their arms.   Greater bravery I never saw displayed than that of our gallant fellows.   Before boarding, the duties of all had been appointed, and a party was told off to take possession of the tops.   We had not been on deck a minute, when I hailed the foretop, and was instantly answered by our own men, an equally prompt answer being returned from the frigate's maintop.   No British man-of-war's crew could have excelled this minute attention to orders.

"The uproar speedily alarmed the garrison, who, hastening to their guns, opened fire on their own frigate, thus paying us the compliment of having taken it; though, even in this case, their own men must still have been on board, so that firing on them was a wanton proceeding, as several Spaniards were killed or wounded by the shot of the fortress; and amongst the wounded was Captain Coig, the commander of the *Esmeralda*, who, after he was made prisoner, received a severe contusion by a shot from his own party."

Cochrane had intended, after carrying the *Esmeralda*, to capture every ship near her, and had given orders to that effect; but, after his disablement, Captain Guise took upon himself to cut the cables of the prize; and nothing then remained but to loose her top-sails, and to move out. The unwounded prisoners numbered 200, among them being a Spanish flag-officer, who had his flag flying in the frigate. Cochrane was so little popular in the British service that Captain Thomas Searle, of the *Hyperion*, 42, which lay close by, sternly repressed all signs of admiration by those in his ship at the spectacle of this magnificent exploit. On the other hand, the officers of the U.S. frigate *Macedonian* quietly wished success to Cochrane's boats as they passed in, and expressly refrained from calling attention to them by hailing. The *Hyperion* had hailed each one separately. Among the officers who took part in the attack were Lieutenants Esmonde, Morgell, Bell and Robertson; but, as Cochrane's account does not give their Christian names, it is almost impossible to identify them, or to decide whether, as is most probable, they had served previously as British naval officers.

In consequence mainly of the thankless and treacherous manner in which he was treated, Cochrane quitted the service of Chile and Peru, and entered that of Dom Pedro, who had then embarked upon the struggle which resulted in the separation of Brazil from Portugal. He reached Rio de Janeiro in March, 1822; found the new government with only the skeleton of a small fleet; rapidly organised a squadron; and gained some remarkable successes, which practically freed the Brazilian coasts from the presence of Portuguese men-of-war. But again, owing no doubt in part to his quarrelsome nature, Cochrane failed to obtain generous treatment at the hands of his employers; and he indignantly left Brazil in 1825. It must be admitted that he had had very much to put up with, that he had served the young empire with single-hearted devotion, and that, upon the whole, his brilliant adventures in South America cost him much more than he ever received from the governments whose cause he espoused to such good effect.[1] Dom Pedro conferred upon him

---

[1] 'Narr. of Services in Chile, Peru, and Brazil,' 2 vols., 1859.

the title of Marques de Maranhaõ. Among the English-named
officers who served with him in Brazil were David Jowett, James
Wallace,[1] Thomas Sackville Crosbie,[2] W. Jackson, James Shepherd,[3]
S. E. Clewley, Francis Clare, G. March, W. Jannary, George Man-
son,[4] Leonard Coming, Francis Drummond, Joseph Fitzcosten,
C. Rose, and J. Pascoe Grenfell, who subsequently rose to flag-rank
in Brazil. I regret that I cannot identify the majority of these.
Lord Cochrane, after a period of rest in England, served the cause
of Greece for about twelve months in the years 1827–28; but his
exploits in the Levant were tame in comparison with those in South
America.

Cochrane was by far the greatest of the British sailors of fortune
who, after the conclusion of twenty years of war with France, found
congenial work as the mercenaries of foreign governments, or of
revolutionary movements abroad; but the number of officers who
thus kept their swords from wholly rusting is much larger than is
commonly suspected. Two only, however, besides Cochrane, need
special mention here, in connection with what has been written
above. These are Admiral of the Fleet Sir George Rose Sartorius,
who, in 1832, when a Post-Captain of eighteen years' standing,
assumed command, as Admiral, of the fleet of Dom Pedro, of
Portugal. His name was, in consequence, struck from the Navy
List, though it was restored in 1836. He received for his services
the title of Viconde de Piedade. He was succeeded in his
appointment in 1833 by Captain Charles Napier (2), C.B., one at
least of whose exploits almost rivalled those of Cochrane, and
must be described.

Into the nature of the constitutional quarrel between Dom Pedro
and Dom Miguel it is unnecessary to enter. When in April, 1833,
Napier left England to command the naval forces of the former, he
was accompanied by Commander James Wilkinson, Lieutenant
Henry Frederick Peake, Master Edward John Phillips Pearn, and
Lieutenant Charles Elers Napier, all of the Royal Navy. To evade
the provisions of the Foreign Enlistment Act, each one assumed an

[1] Qy., Lieut. R.N. of Oct. 24th, 1807?
[2] Lieut. R.N. of Feb. 1st, 1815.
[3] Killed in the war between Brazil and Buenos Ayres, 1827. On the side of Buenos
Ayres in that campaign were many English-named officers, including Admiral Brown,
Captains Drummond (perhaps the Francis Drummond of the text), and Granville, Lieut.
Ford, and Mids. Attwell and Hall.
[4] Qy., Lieut. R.N. of Oct. 18th, 1802?

alias, Napier himself becoming Carlos de Ponza.[1] On June 8th,
Napier received his commission as Vice-Admiral and Commander-in-
Chief of the Portuguese Navy; and on the 11th, he hoisted his flag
in the *Rainha de Portugal,* 46, in Oporto Road. Wilkinson was given
the posts of Commodore, and Captain of the Fleet, with his pennant
in the *Rainha de Portugal* ; Peake obtained command of the *Donna
Maria,* 42 ; Pearn was made Master of the Fleet; and young Napier,
with Commander's rank, became Aide-de-camp to the Vice-Admiral.
Besides the *Rainha de Portugal* and the *Donna Maria,* the Pedroite
squadron included the *Dom Pedro,* 50, Captain Goble,[2] the *Villa
Flor,* 18, Commander Ruxton, and the *Portuense,* 20, besides a few
steam tugs and transports. The Miguelite force was considerably
stronger, comprising as it did two vessels of the line, a 56-gun ship,
a 50-gun frigate, three corvettes, and several brigs, all ready for sea
in the Tagus. Moreover, Napier's ships were in bad order, the
crews being "half-naked and undisciplined." Nevertheless, after
some expeditions along the coast, the Vice-Admiral put to sea from
Lagos on July 2nd, in quest of the enemy, and, on the following
morning, sighted him, though, owing to various causes, he was not
able to engage him until the 5th. The battle was fought off Cape
St. Vincent. After a brief but very hot short-range action, the
Rainha de Portugal, 46, boarded and carried the *Não Rainha,* 74 ;
and the *Donna Maria,* 42, treated the *Principessa Reale,* 56, in a
similar manner. The *Dom João,* 74, the *Martino de Freitas,* 50,
and a 22-gun corvette were also taken. It was a remarkable victory ;
yet, since nearly the whole of the officers and men of the prizes subsequently joined and fought for the Pedroite cause, it is possible that,
as Miguelites, they fought half-heartedly, though, at the same time,
they lost heavily. Napier, who was rewarded with the title of Conde
de Cabo São Vincente, remained at the head of the Portuguese navy
after the collapse of Dom Miguel, until October, 1834, when he
resigned, and, shortly afterwards, returned to England.[3] His name
had been removed from the Navy List, but was restored to it as
from March 9th, 1836.

After the Battle of Navarin, the Navy took no part in any operations on a large scale until after the outbreak of the first China War

---

[1] *See* Vol. V., pp. 522–23.

[2] Qy., Thomas Goble, a Lieut. R.N. of Dec. 24th, 1805? He was killed on
July 5th, 1833.

[3] 'Life and Corr. of Napier,' i. 168, etc.; War in Portugal' (2 vols., 1836).

in 1839; yet never was it wholly idle for long. Pirates, slavers, truculent semi-savages, and European revolutionists gave it plenty to do in several directions; and there is much to be said concerning its services in the eleven years 1828–1838, although the period was practically one of peace.

Lieutenant Joseph Sherer,[1] who was appointed to the *Monkey* on the West Indies station in October, 1828, and transferred to the *Nimble*, 5, in August, 1829, was one of those who made for themselves enviable names at that time. In the *Monkey*, a vessel of only 75 tons, mounting one long 12-pr. on a pivot, and carrying but 26 men, he made prize, in April, 1829, of the Spanish schooner *Josepha*, carrying one 12-pr. gun, a crew of 21 men, and 207 slaves; and, on June 27th following, after a 35 minutes' action, of the brig *Midas*, of 360 tons, mounting four long 18-prs. and four medium 12-prs., with a crew of more than 50 men, of whom 1 was killed and 3 were wounded. In her 400 slaves were captured. In the *Nimble*, in November, 1829, Sherer took the *Gallito*, of one 9-pr., with 16 hands and 136 slaves on board. He was, in consequence, made a Commander, as from December 30th, 1829.[2]

The terror equally of pirates and of slavers in the West Indies was Lieutenant John Bunch Bonnemaison M'Hardy, who, while acting in the *Icarus*, 10, Commander John George Graham, previous to the receipt of his commission, had participated, under Lieutenant Charles Croker, on August 20th, 1824, in the capture, off Havana, of the pirate schooner *Diableto*, 6, with a complement of 55 men. The British boats employed had only 34 all told in them. On January 1st, 1828, M'Hardy was given command of the schooner *Pickle*, 3, manned by 30 men and 6 boys. In her, on June 6th, 1829, he fell in with the famous slaver *Boladora*, mounting two long 18's and two long 12's, and having 60 men, besides armed negroes, on board. A good account of what happened, written by an officer of the *Pickle*, will be found in the *Nautical Magazine*. It will be sufficient here to say that, after a close and severe action lasting 80 minutes, in which the enemy lost 10 killed and 14 wounded, the little schooner, which herself had 1 killed and 10 (3 mortally) wounded, was successful. In this gallant affair, Mate William Newton Fowell behaved with much credit.

---

[1] A Lieut. of 1822; had served with Lyon in the *Hecla*. He was posted in 1841 and died in that rank.

[2] O'Byrne, 1060; Marshall, iv. Pt. II. 348.

M'Hardy was promoted to be Commander on December 20th following.[1]

Two other distinguished officers of the same stamp were Lieutenant Henry Downes, and Mate Edward Harris Butterfield. These officers, and Mate Thomas Philip Le Hardy, were detached, in 1829, on a cruise in the *Black Joke*, of one long 18-pr. and 34 men, then tender to the *Sibylle*, 48, Commodore Francis Augustus Collier, on the West Coast of Africa. This little craft is credited with having captured no fewer than 21 slavers, with upwards of 7000 slaves in them. Among them was the Spanish brig *Providencia*, of 14 guns and 80 men; the Brazilian brig *Vengador*, of 8 guns and 645 slaves; the Buenos Aires privateer *Presidente*, of 7 guns and 97 men, which, with her prizes, the *Hossey*, 6, and *Marianna*, 2, was boarded and carried after a close running fight of ten hours; and the Spanish brig *Almirante*, 14 (ten 18's and four long 9's), with 80 men and 460 slaves. The last was carried after an eleven hours' chase with sweeps, and an eighty minutes' severe action, in which the enemy had 15 killed and 13 wounded, and the British, 3 killed and 7 wounded. For this most dashing exploit, Downes and Le Hardy were promoted, and Butterfield, who had passed his examination in 1827, was placed on the Admiralty list, and appointed, in January, 1830, first Lieutenant of the *Primrose*, 18.[2] The *Black Joke* continued her successful career, under Lieutenant William Ramsay,[3] and, on April 25th, 1831, boarded and carried the large armed Spanish slaver *Marinerito*, of 5 guns and 77 officers and men, off the Calabar River, losing 1 killed and 7 wounded.

The *Primrose*, which, under Commander Thomas Saville Griffinhoofe, had already distinguished herself on the same station, was, in September, 1830, commanded by Commander William Broughton. On the 7th of that month she encountered the exceptionally powerful slaver *Veloz Pasajero*,[4] which mounted 20 heavy guns, had a crew of 180 desperadoes, and carried 555 slaves between decks. In the hand to hand conflict which followed, Butterfield again signalised himself, and, when Broughton had been badly hurt, succeeded to

---

[1] O'Byrne, 698; *Naut. Mag.*, iii. 649.

[2] *Gazette*, 1829, 710; O'Byrne, 156, 646. Downes was made a Com. May 2nd, 1829, and Le Hardy, a Lieut. on the same day.

[3] Com., Aug. 15th, 1831.

[4] Keppel met her skipper, José Antonio Barbozo, still in command of a slaver, in 1838, and describes him as handsome and intelligent-looking. He had lost an arm in the action with the *Primrose*. Keppel, i. 239.

the command.   The enemy did not surrender until she had lost 46 killed and 20 wounded, and caused a loss to the British of 3 killed and 13 wounded.   In 1831 Butterfield commissioned the *Brisk*, 3, and in her captured the slaver *Prueba*, with 313 slaves on board.   For his gallantry he was made a Commander on March 7th, 1832, that being the earliest possible date at which, under the regulations, he was eligible for promotion.[1]

In the summer of 1832, boat parties from the *Magicienne*, 24, Captain James Hanway Plumridge, under Lieutenants Frederick Hutton and the Hon. Henry Keppel, rendered useful service in the rivers of the Malay peninsula by preventing the passage of supplies by water to the Rajah of Nanning, who, for nearly two years previously, had been at war with the East India Company.   The blockade assisted in bringing the war to a satisfactory conclusion.[2]

In 1831–32, the course of events on the continent of Europe necessitated the employment of two special squadrons in foreign waters.   The situation created in Portugal by the war between Dom Pedro and Dom Miguel, and the resultant interference with British trade, led to the considerable strengthening of the force which, under Rear-Admiral William Parker, in the *Asia*, 84, Captain Peter Richards, lay in, or cruised off, the Tagus.   Several of the reinforcing ships were drawn from an Experimental Squadron which, under Vice-Admiral Sir Pulteney Malcolm, was organised in 1832, chiefly in order to try the rates of sailing of various new types of vessels.   Towards the end of 1832, the insistance of Holland in defying the great Powers with regard to the Belgian question, and the active interference of Louis Philippe on behalf of his son-in-law, King Leopold, who was also a cousin of King William IV., induced Great Britain to join with France in declaring a blockade of the ports of Holland, and an embargo on Dutch shipping, the King of the Netherlands having precipitated matters by ordering British and French vessels to quit his ports within three days.   The French contingent of the blockading fleet was under the orders successively of Rear-Admirals Ducrest de Villeneuve, and de Mackau ; the British was commanded by Sir Pulteney Malcolm, and consisted largely of vessels of the Experimental Squadron.   Towards the end of the blockade, which practically ceased with the capture of the citadel of

---

[1] Marshall, iv. Pt. II. 476 ; O'Byrne, 130, 156 ; *Gazette*, 1830, 2451.   Broughton was posted Nov. 22nd, 1831.

[2] Keppel, i. 134.

Antwerp by the French on December 23rd, 1832, Malcolm's fleet was made up of the—

Donegal, 74 (flag), Captain John Dick; *Malabar,* 74, Captain the Hon. Josceline Percy; *Revenge,* 78, Captain Donald Hugh Mackay; *Spartiate,* 74, Captain Robert Tait; *Talavera,* 74, Captain Thomas Brown; *Southampton,* 52, Commander John Milligan Laws (actg. Captain); *Vernon,* 50, Captain Sir Francis Augustus Collier; *Castor,* 36, Captain Lord John Hay (1); *Stag,* 46, Captain Nicholas Lockyer; *Conway,* 28, Captain Henry Eden (1); *Volage,* 28, Captain Lord Colchester; *Childers,* 18,

H.R.H. PRINCE WILLIAM HENRY, DUKE OF CLARENCE,

ADMIRAL OF THE FLEET, LORD HIGH ADMIRAL.

(Later H.M. King William IV.)

From a mezzotint by W. Ward, junr., after the painting by A. Vivell.

Commander Robert Deans (2); *Rover,* 18, Commander Sir George Young (5), Bart.; *Scout,* 18, Commander William Hargood (2); *Dee,* 4, steamer, Commander Robert Oliver (2); *Rhadamanthus,* 4, steamer, Commander George Evans; *Larne,* 18, Commander William Sidney Smith (2); *Snake,* 16, Commander William Robertson (2); and *Satellite,* 10, Commander Robert Smart.

All such ships as were detained appear to have been afterwards liberated.

Among the actions with slavers in 1832, none were more gallant than those which were fought on the West Indies station by the *Speedwell*, 5, Lieutenant William Warren, which captured, on April 6th, the *Planeta*, on June 3rd, the *Aquila*, and on June 25th, the *Indagadera*, the three having on board about 1000 slaves. The *Aquila*, brig, which was of more than three times the tonnage of the *Speedwell*, and which had a crew of 70 men on board, fought doggedly for an hour within pistol-range ere she struck. Warren was promoted for these exploits.[1]

In the course of the same year, the *Clio*, 18, Commander John James Onslow, was detached by Rear-Admiral Sir Thomas Baker (1), commanding on the South America station, to reclaim possession of the Maluinas, or Falkland Islands, which lapse of time had encouraged the Buenos Aireans and others to regard as wholly abandoned. Onslow arrived at Port Egmont in December, 1832, formally exercised the rights of sovereignty, surveyed the coasts, and ejected a Buenos Aires garrison and the war schooner *Sarandi*, which he found at Port Louis, East Falkland. The reoccupation created some excitement and diplomatic correspondence; but, of course, it was persisted in.[2]

In May, 1833, the *Curlew*, 10, Commander Henry Dundas Trotter, happened to call at the little frequented port of Antonio, Prince's Island, on the African coast. He there learned that a suspicious craft, resembling the pirate schooner *Panda*, had recently quitted the anchorage. In the previous autumn, the *Panda* had captured the valuable American brig *Mexican*, Butman, master, and had rifled her on the high seas. The *Curlew* went in search of her, and, on June 4th, tracked her to the river Nazareth. Trotter manned and armed three of his boats, and, at the head of forty men, boarded and captured her, though not until she had been abandoned by her people. These scoundrels were taken prisoners by Passall, the chief of the district, who, however, refused to give them up. In endeavouring to force him to do so, Trotter lost the *Panda*, which was blown up by an accidental explosion of loose powder. This catastrophe cost the lives of the Purser, and the Gunner of the *Curlew*, and of two seamen and a boy. Many delays occurred; but, ultimately, several members of the pirate crew were laid hands on, and sent in the *Savage*, 10, Lieutenant Robert Loney, to Massachusetts,

[1] Jamaica *Courant*, Aug. 2nd, 1832; O'Byrne, 1253.
[2] *Naut. Mag.*, ii. 614; O'Byrne, 838.

where they were tried.   On June 11th, 1835, Pedro Gibert, the
Panda's master, and four of his seamen, were deservedly executed at
Boston.   The capture of Gibert and some others was due to the
courage and resource of Mate Henry James Matson, of the *Curlew*,
who was in consequence promoted.   Trotter received the thanks of
the Admiralty, and of the President of the United States.[1]

Lieutenant Charles Bolton, who, for twenty months following
February 24th, 1833, was in command of the *Nimble*, 5, on the West
Indies station, was another distinguished captor of slavers.   He took
six heavy vessels, having on board a total of 1902 negroes.   One of
his toughest opponents was the *Joaquina*, which did not surrender
until she had had her master and 2 men killed, and was in a sinking
condition.[2]

So far as the Navy was concerned, the most important event of
1834 was the brush which occurred in the Canton River in the
autumn of that year.   A few months earlier, five ports, including
Canton, had been formally thrown open by China to the general
trade of all nations.   Soon after noon on September 7th, H.M.S.
Imogene, 28, Captain Price Blackwood,[3] and *Andromache*, 28,
Captain Henry Ducie Chads, which had business up the river,
weighed from below Chuenpee Point to proceed through the narrow
passage known as Bocca Tigris, or the Bogue.   A stir was at once
perceived among some war junks lying in Anson Bay, and in the
neighbourhood of the forts on Chuenpee and Tycock-tow Points.
After blank cartridges had been fired, the forts opened with shot,
which, however, fell short, or astern of the ships.   The junks
crowded into the shallow recesses of Anson Bay.   Just as the
frigates got within range of the foe at the Bogue, the wind shifted
to north.   The *Andromache* then stood towards Anunghoy Fort,
the eastern one, on one tack, while the *Imogene* stood towards
Wangtung Fort, the western one, on the other.   The latter ship
waited until Wangtung had fired several shots, and then replied.
The *Andromache* returned the fire of Anunghoy with evident effect.
The forts were soon silenced ; but they reopened whenever the
British ceased firing for a minute or two.   The *Imogene* received
several shots ; but the Chinese practice was bad ; and, although the
passage lasted for nearly an hour and three-quarters, the British

---

[1] O'Byrne, 742; *Naut. Mag.*, iv. 499; vi. 1, 179.
[2] O'Byrne, 96 ; *Naut. Mag.*, iii. 122.
[3] Later Lord Dufferin.

sustained very little damage. The two frigates, while continuously tacking, exposed themselves so much to be raked that they ought to have been sunk; and a tender, the *Louisa*, which accompanied them, her commander sitting under an umbrella on deck, and manœuvring her with great coolness, had most marvellous escapes. Owing to the state of the wind, the ships anchored below Tiger Island, where they were kept by calms or baffling airs until the afternoon of the

ADMIRAL SIR HENRY DUCIE CHADS, G.C.B.
(*From a drawing made about* 1857, *when Sir Henry was a Rear-Admiral.*)

9th. The Chinese occupied the interval in improving their defences; but, when the frigates, with a fair breeze, again got under way, and were fired at, they returned the fire so much more warmly, closely, and rapidly than on the first occasion, that the forts were almost knocked into ruins, many of their defenders perishing. The British had but 2 seamen killed, and 6 or 7 wounded. There, for the time, the quarrel ended; and presently the ships anchored below the second bar, off Seecheetow. Explanations were made, and officials were disavowed ; and so matters rested until the reckoning of five years later.[1]

In the course of the same year, 1834, the pirates in the Straits of Malacca were dealt several severe blows by Commander Spencer Lambart Hunter Vassall, of the *Harrier*, 18, who, after two serious conflicts, succeeded in destroying the piratical settlements at Pulo Arroa and Pulo Sujee.[2] He may be regarded as the beginner of a work which, later, was taken up more systematically by Henry Ducie Chads and Henry Keppel.

During the first Kaffir War, 1834–35, the *Wolf*, 18, was able to render useful assistance to the military forces ; and her commander, Commander Edward Stanley, received, in consequence, the public thanks of Sir Benjamin D'Urban, governor of the Cape.

The *Buzzard*, 10, Lieutenant Jeremiah M'Namara, signalised herself early in 1835 by the capture, after a forty-five minutes' action, of a large Spanish slave brig, the *Formidable*, losing 2 men, but, on the other hand, killing 7. The horrors of the middle passage are well illustrated by the fact that ere the prize could be carried into Sierra Leone, 307 slaves, out of 707 originally in her, perished from disease and misery.[3] Another important capture was effected on April 8th, off Little Cayman, by the schooner *Skipjack*, 5, Lieutenant Sydney Henry Ussher. This was the *Martha*, a craft nearly three times as big as the *Skipjack*, and carrying six Congreve 18's, and two long 12-prs., with a crew of 62 all told. The engagement between the two vessels lasted for two hours and a half, and was followed by an intermittent running action lasting five hours more. The prize lost 1 of her crew killed and 8 wounded ; the *Skipjack*, only 1 wounded. The *Martha* had originally taken 790 slaves on board at Loango. When she met the *Skipjack*, forty-three days later, but 460 survived ; and of those, 13 were killed in the action.[4]

In the summer of 1835, during a local insurrection at Para, Brazil, the *Racehorse*, 18, Commander Sir James Everard Home, Bart., co-operated with a Brazilian flotilla in the siege of the town, and was on several days in action with its batteries. On one occasion, Mates Baldwin Arden Wake, and Byron Drury landed at night, and assisted in bringing off 220 fugitives from the midst of the insurgents, thus saving them from massacre.

[1] O'Byrne, 183, etc.; *Naut. Mag.*, iv. 247.
[2] App. to Crt. of Admlty., Mar. 2nd, 1838; O'Byrne, 1227.
[3] *Naut. Mag.*, iv. 312.
[4] *Naut. Mag.*, iv. 439.

Two excellent pieces of service were done in 1836 by Lieutenant Charles John Bosanquet, commanding the *Leveret*, 10, on the Cape station. Reaching Mozambique, in September, he found the place in a state of insurrection, and all the Portuguese authorities under arrest. Landing at night with his ship's company, and securing the support of a few well-affected people, he took the insurgents by surprise, seized an 84-gun battery, obtained possession of the custom house and government offices, and, within three days, restored tranquillity, and re-established the ascendency of the Queen of Portugal. Three months later he chased for 800 miles, and ultimately captured by boarding, the slaver *Diogenes*, mounting five 24-prs., and having 70 people on board: The prize was at that time within musket-shot of the battery above alluded to, and also of a Portuguese frigate.[1]

In 1836, another Experimental Squadron was organised, and entrusted to the command of Rear-Admiral Sir Charles Paget. The cruise which followed was to a large extent devoted to testing the qualities of some of the vessels newly constructed after the plans of Sir William Symonds, and Captain John Hayes (2). Towards the latter part of the year, and again in May, 1837, the irreconcilable attitude of the Carlists on the north coast of Spain, and especially at San Sebastian and Bilbao, led to British intervention. Supplies were prevented from reaching them by sea; and the work of a British volunteer legion, which was assisting the Government, was supported. In these operations, which were conducted under the orders of Commodore Lord John Hay (1) (successively of the *Castor*, 36, *Phœnix*, 4, steamer, and *North Star*, 28), the *Pique*, 36, Captain the Hon. Henry John Rous, *Castor*, *Ringdove*, 16, Commander William Frederick Lapidge, and *Salamander*, 4, steamer, Commander Sidney Colpoys Dacres, were the vessels most actively engaged. On one occasion the *Pique* and *Castor* had a considerable force of seamen and Marines serving on shore; and on another, the Carlist lines were shelled. In the eastern seas, between May and October, the boats of the *Andromache*, 28, Captain Henry Ducie Chads, did some good work towards the repression of Malay piracy. On the West Coast of Africa, on July 22nd, 1836, Mate Samuel Otway Wooldridge, who had been lent from the *Thalia* to the *Buzzard*, distinguished himself by boarding and taking, with only 5 men, the Portuguese slaver *Joven Carolina*, of two guns and 33 men,

[1] O'Byrne, 99.

and having on board 422 slaves. He was deservedly promoted on February 6th, 1837.

The year 1837 witnessed the capture of numerous other slavers. In the West Indies, the *Snake*, 16, Commander Alexander Milne, was particularly successful, making prize, on November 23rd, of the Portuguese brigantine *Arrogante*, with 406 negroes, and on December 5th, of the Spanish schooner *Matilda*, with 529. The *Scout*, 18, Commander Robert Craigie, on January 11th, took a Portuguese vessel having no fewer than 576 slaves on board. The ill-starred rebellion in Canada did not afford much work for the Navy; but it enabled a naval officer, Commander Andrew Drew, who happened to be upon the spot, to distinguish himself greatly. On December 29th, 1837, Drew most daringly cut out from under Fort Schlosser, on the American side of the Niagara, the American steamer *Carolina*, which was being useful to the rebels, and sent her in flames over the great Falls. For this exploit he was thanked by the Governor and two Houses of Upper Canada, and appointed commodore of the provincial marine. In that capacity, with his broad pennant in the hired armed steamer *Colborne*, he commanded on Lake Erie from October, 1838, till August, 1839. The Commodore of H.M. ships on the Lakes in 1838 was Captain Williams Sandom, of the *Niagara*, 20, who was able to save the towns of Brockville and Prescott from destruction. When the latter town was attacked, on November 13th, 1838, Sandom's force, aiding the troops, was instrumental in driving back the rebels, and forcing them to surrender.[1]

The year 1839 saw the addition of the important strategical position of Aden added to the possessions of the British crown. For some time there had been disputes; but in January, 1838, the local Sultan had been prevailed upon to agree to make certain territorial concessions. The Abdella tribe, however, ultimately declined to carry out its written promise to hand over the town of Aden to the British; and at length it declared war, by opening fire upon the H. E. I. Co.'s corvette, *Coote*, and her boats. In the meantime, Rear-Admiral Sir Frederick Lewis Maitland (2), Commander-in-Chief in the East Indies, had despatched an expedition under Captain Henry Smith (2), of the *Volage*, 28, in support of the claims of his country. That expedition arrived off Aden on January 16th, 1839, and, on the same evening, Smith received from the

[1] *Gazette*, 1838, p. 2975.

Political Agent a' letter setting forth what had taken place, and requesting him to take measures for the immediate capture and occupation of the place. The Agent, Captain J. B. Haines, I.N., had taken refuge on board the *Coote*. Smith then had with him H.M.S. *Cruiser*, 16, Commander Richard Henry King, the H. E. I. Co.'s cruisers *Coote*, and *Mahé*, a mortar boat, and the transports *Lowjee Family*, *Ann Crichton*, and *Ernaad*, with troops from India, under Major Baillie.

"On the morning of the 18th," says Captain Smith in his dispatch, "I weighed with the squadron, to proceed to the front of the town, which I reached in the afternoon, in company with the *Cruiser*, towing a mortar boat, and the *Mahé*, schooner. On standing in towards the island of Seerah,[1] a fire was opened on the ship, with musketry and several large guns, when I commenced a partial attack. The *Coote*, corvette, and transports, not having come up, I anchored for the night. On the morning of the 18th, the whole force having arrived, I made the signal to prepare to attack, and the troops to be held in readiness for landing in two divisions. At half-past nine the *Volage* anchored with a spring on her small bower cable, in four fathoms of water, at about 300 yards' distance from the lower battery on the island of Seerah. At the same time the *Mahé* took up her position to the southward of the island. On standing in the enemy opened a fire of great guns and musketry on us; but, the ship being laid so close to the shore, the guns on the heights were rendered useless, their shot passing over us. At ten o'clock the *Cruiser* anchored, and was of essential service in destroying the flank of the battery. During this period a heavy firing was kept up; but, in a short time, two of the guns in the lower battery were dismounted, and most of the people were driven from the remainder. They, however, took shelter behind the ruins of the battery, and kept up an incessant fire of musketry on the ships; and, although the lower battery was almost knocked to pieces, still we had great difficulty in dislodging the men. At this period I directed the fire to be opened on the round tower and batteries on the heights, which were filled with men armed with matchlocks; and in the course of one hour I had the satisfaction to see this tower, though 60 feet high, and strongly built, a mass of ruins. At 11 o'clock the *Coote* anchored with the second division of the troops to the southward of the island, and opened her fire upon the town. Finding the fire had not ceased from the lower battery, I directed the *Mahé*, schooner, to proceed to the end of it, and endeavour to drive out the men from behind it by musketry. This service was performed by her commander, Lieutenant Daniels, in a most gallant manner, but I regret to say that Mr. Nesbitt, midshipman, was severely wounded.

"The fire having now almost entirely ceased, I gave directions for the boats of both divisions to land. Lieutenant Dobree,[2] who had charge of the first division, Mr. Rundle,[3] Mate, and a quartermaster of this ship, were the first on shore, and made for a 68-pounder, which had been fired at us several times; when a matchlock was fired at the quartermaster by a man behind the gun, who was immediately cut down by him; and the first British flag was planted by Mr. Rundle. So completely were the enemy driven from all points, with the exception of the island, by the fire of the ships, that the whole of the troops landed with the loss of only two men killed and wounded.

---

[1] Sirah, opposite the town.
[2] Thomas Peter Dobree, promoted for this service, May 1st, 1839.
[3] Joseph Sparkhall Rundle, Lieut. for this service, May 1st, 1839.

"A partial firing was kept up from the island, when I directed Lieutenant Dobree, who had returned, with two Mates, Messrs. Stewart[1] and Rundle, with a party of seamen, and Lieutenant Ayles[2] with the Marines, amounting altogether to 50, to land and take possession of it. This was gallantly accomplished, the party ascending the heights, spiking and dismounting the guns, taking the flag which had been flying from the tower, and making prisoners of 139 armed Arabs, who were conducted from the island to the main by the party, and given over into the charge of Major Osborne. In an attempt to disarm the prisoners, made by the military, they made a most formidable resistance; and I regret to say that many lives were lost on both sides. Mr. Nesbitt, a midshipman of the *Mahé*, was the only person hurt on board the squadron: on the part of the military, 16 were killed and wounded, most of them dangerously; and one sergeant has since died."

Captain Smith mentions in his dispatch that he believed the place to have been held by more than 1000 men. Their loss is unknown, but amounted certainly to upwards of 50. The guns captured in the town and defences were 33 in number, 25 being in battery; and they included one brass 89-pr., one brass 85-pr., one brass 68-pr., one brass 32-pr., and four 18-prs., the rest being small.[3] As only 114 matchlocks were taken, it is tolerably clear that the Arabs made as good a resistance as could be expected. The post, which was afterwards formally purchased by the East India Company, was even then important as a station on the overland route to India. As a coaling port, especially since the opening of the Suez Canal, it has become immensely valuable to the Navy, as well as to the mercantile marine.

Early in the same year the troubles with Afghanistan and Persia, and the refusal of Colonel Pottinger's demand for a passage through the territory of Scind for the army under Sir John Keane, led to a slight outbreak of hostilities on the shores of the Persian Gulf and the Arabian Sea. On February 2nd and 3rd, in the course of the operations, Kurrachee was captured by a naval force under Rear-Admiral Sir Frederick Lewis Maitland (2), in conjunction with troops from India. The ships chiefly engaged were the *Wellesley*, 74 (flag), Captain Thomas Maitland, and the *Algerine*, 10, Commander William Sidney Thomas. One of the results of this action was the signature of the Treaty of Hyderabad.

The next work of the Navy was of a much more arduous character.

For several years prior to 1820 India had exported opium to China, where the drug was admitted, subject to a fixed duty. In

[1] Robert Arthur Stewart, Lieut. for this service, May 1st, 1839; Com., 1845.
[2] Lieut. John George Augustus Ayles, R.M.
[3] *Gazette*, 1839, 669; *Naut. Mag.*, 1839, 351.

1820, however, the Chinese Government issued a proclamation against the trade, which thenceforth became illicit, although it continued to flourish, thanks largely to the willingness of most of the mandarins to accept bribes, and to the fact that not a few of them were personally interested in the traffic. In 1837 stricter measures were adopted by the government; and foreign ships were ordered to quit the coasts of China, and foreign merchants to leave Canton and proceed to Macao, which then, as now, was Portuguese territory. To enforce these orders, one Lin was ultimately appointed governor of Canton; but not until December 3rd, 1838, did the Chinese authorities begin to take such active measures as brought them into conflict with their western neighbours. On that day they seized some smuggled opium; and, a little later, they expelled from Canton the British merchant to whose warehouse the opium was being carried. Riots and recriminations followed; Captain Charles Elliot, R.N., Chief Superintendent of British Trade in China, had to intervene; the river traffic was impeded; and when, on February 26th, 1839, the Chinese police executed in front of the foreign hongs a native accused of opium dealing, all the consuls in the city struck their flags, and H.M.S. *Larne*, the only British man-of-war in port, though then about to depart for India, was detained at the request of the merchants. In March, Lin required that all opium on board ships in the river should be surrendered; and, pending compliance with his demand, he suspended the issue of passports, and of permits to foreigners to move beyond the limits of the factories. On March 24th, Captain Elliot, who had been to Macao, returned to Canton, and hoisted the British flag over his quarters in the British factory. He was subjected to some indignities by the Chinese authorities; yet, in the interests of justice, he made arrangements that all opium then in the river in British bottoms should be given up. Many thousands of chests had been thus surrendered, when, owing to new demands and insolent conduct on the part of Lin, delivery was suspended by Elliot's direction. The Chinese appeared to give way, and the surrender of opium went on as before; but, in the middle of May, Lin's attitude and military preparations became so threatening that Elliot formally warned British subjects that Canton was no longer a place in which they could reside with safety or honour, and that they would do wisely to withdraw at once. On May 23rd, by which date 20,283 chests of opium had been handed over, Elliot

himself left Canton for Macao ; and on the 30th, he despatched
from Macao to Suez a fast clipper with news of what had occurred.
The opium, which had been collected at Chunhow, and which was
said to be worth £2,500,000, was presently destroyed by order of
Commissioner Lin.[1]

After the abandonment of Canton, the harbour of Hong Kong
became the chief rendezvous for British shipping in China.　Lin,
however, erected batteries to command the anchorage, and occupied
the Kowloon peninsula on the north side of the harbour ; while,
on the other hand, the idle seamen got into trouble on shore.　In
spite of the situation thus created, Hong Kong became daily more
and more a British centre, owing to the fact that the hostility of
the Chinese soon made it impossible for British residents to remain
at Macao, except at the risk of compromising the Portuguese
authorities there.　Captain Elliot removed from Macao to Hong
Kong on August 23rd, and, though the town was not formally
ceded until 1841, it was thenceforward practically British.　Provocation and outrage continued ; and when, on August 30th,
H.M.S. *Volage*, 22, Captain Henry Smith (2), reached Macao, and at
once proceeded to Hong Kong, her arrival was extremely welcome.
On September 4th, the refusal of the Chinese at Kowloon to permit
the transit of provisions across the harbour obliged Captain Smith,
in concert with Mr. James Douglas,[2] of the *Cambridge*, formerly
of the H.E.I. Co.'s marine, to employ his boats to drive off a
squadron of war-junks, and so to open a passage for the supplies.
Further outrageous action induced Elliot to call upon Smith to
proclaim a blockade[3] of the port of Canton as from September 11th.
Negotiations were subsequently entered into ; but Elliot displayed
such unwise weakness that the Chinese were only encouraged to
persist in their implacable attitude.　At length, the *Hyacinth*, 18,
Commander William Warren, having joined the *Volage*, Elliot
stiffened himself so far as to inform the Chinese, on October 28th,
that if the British shipping lying below the Bogue were subjected
to more of certain annoyances which had become intolerable, re-
taliatory measures would be adopted.　The Chinese admiral, Kwan,
returned first a temporising and then an insulting answer, and on

---

[1] Ouchterlony's 'Chinese War,' 1–20.

[2] Afterwards Sir James Douglas.　The *Cambridge* was purchased by the Chinese
government ere regular hostilities began.

[3] This was afterwards relaxed.

November 3rd got under way with twenty-nine junks, evidently intending to attack. Smith made a further fruitless attempt to negotiate, and then, with the *Volage* and *Hyacinth*, opened fire, and in a short time won a success which would have been much more complete than it was, but for the interference of Elliot, who, when three junks had been sunk and as many more driven ashore, procured a cessation of the firing, alleging his desire to spare the lives of the Chinese. Kwan, on returning to Canton, was thus able to boast that he had been victorious; and he was rewarded accordingly.

During the winter and spring, little or nothing was done on the spot by the British, although the Chinese continued to collect troops, to build and arm forts, and to excite their people against the foreigners. But at home and in India preparations were made for hostile action on a larger scale than had been possible when two small vessels only were available. Rear-Admiral Sir Frederick Lewis Maitland (2), K.C.B., Commander-in-Chief in the East Indies, would, in the ordinary course, have commanded the expedition; but he died on December 30th, 1839; and the direction of affairs then passed temporarily to the surviving senior officer on the station, Captain Sir James John Gordon Bremer. Rear-Admiral the Hon. George Elliot (3), C.B., and Captain Charles Elliot were appointed royal commissioners to deal with the Chinese Government, the former having also the command afloat; and, early in May, 1840, a squadron, having on board about 3600 infantry,[1] and some royal artillery and engineers, was assembled at Singapore, where, however, Rear-Admiral Elliot had not yet appeared.

In June the squadron [2] proceeded, and, on the 21st, halted off the Great Ladrones to communicate with Macao. There Bremer declared a blockade of the Canton river, to begin on June 28th, and thence he went on to the northern harbour of Chusan, where lay a few war junks. He entered unopposed; but the local authorities, pleading lack of power to treat, refused to surrender the island. Accordingly, at 2 P.M. on July 5th, fire was opened upon the defences of Tinghae, and upon the junks; and in a few minutes the enemy was silenced, and the junks were driven ashore or

---

[1] Including H.M. 18th, 26th, and 49th Regts., the whole military force being under Col. Burrell, 18th Regt.

[2] Then consisting of *Wellesley*, 74; *Alligator*, 28; *Conway*, 28; *Larne*, 20; *Algerine*, 10; *Rattlesnake*, 6; the two H.E.I. Co.'s steamers *Atalanta*, and *Madagascar*, and 26 transports and storeships. Other vessels joined soon afterwards.

reduced to wrecks. In this affair the *Wellesley*, 74, Commodore Sir
James John Gordon Bremer, Captain Thomas Maitland, *Conway*,
28, Captain Charles Ramsay Drinkwater Bethune, and *Algerine*, 10,
Lieutenant Thomas Henry Mason, took the leading parts.[1] The
town and island were then occupied, after some resistance had been
offered. Ere the fighting was quite over, Rear-Admiral Elliot, in
the *Melville*, 74, Captain the Hon. Richard Saunders Dundas,
arrived on the scene to assume command. In his eagerness to
participate, he ran ashore his ship, then in tow of the H.E.I. Co.'s
steamer *Atalanta*; and subsequently he had to hoist his flag in the
Wellesley, leaving the *Blenheim*, 74, Captain Sir Humphrey Fleming
Senhouse, which joined soon afterwards, to heave down the *Melville*,
and to assist in repairing her.

In the meantime, letters addressed by Lord Palmerston to the
advisers of the Emperor were sent in to Chinhae, at the mouth of
the Ningpo river, and to Amoy. At Chinhae the communication
was examined by the local mandarins, and returned as being of a
nature too insulting for transmission. At Amoy, on July 3rd, the
mandarins, besides refusing to receive the message, fired treacherously on an unarmed boat of the *Blonde*; whereupon Captain
Thomas Bourchier, of that frigate, opened a heavy fire, and did not
desist until he had reduced to silence all the works on shore.
Then, leaving on the beach a copy of the letter, attached to a
bamboo, he rejoined the squadron. A blockade of the Ningpo river
and of the coast northward to the Yangtsekiang was soon afterwards proclaimed; and the Rear-Admiral, with several vessels,[2]
departed to the Gulf of Petchili to negotiate. During the period of
inactivity that followed, disease ravaged the troops at Chusan, there
being, between July 13th and December 31st, no fewer than
5329 admissions to hospital, and 448 deaths there among the
Europeans alone. It would have been wiser to employ the force
to impress the Chinese with a full sense of British power; for the
negotiations were prolonged, and, even while they continued, the
Chinese committed further outrages, which were never properly
resented and punished. The *Algerine* had on one occasion to defend

---

[1] Among the officers commended in Bremer's dispatch were Captains Bethune,
Maitland, and Aug. Leop. Kuper (actg. of *Alligator*, 28); Commanders Henry Wells
Giffard (*Cruiser*), and John Venour Fletcher (*Wellesley*); Lieut. Thos. Hy. Mason;
Master Wm. Brodie (comdg. trooper *Rattlesnake*, 28); Mate C. E. Hodgkinson (comdg.
schooner *Young Hebe*); and Capt. Samuel Burdon Ellis, R.M.—*Gazette*, 1840, p. 2991.

[2] Including *Wellesley*, *Blonde*, *Pylades*, *Volage*, and *Modeste*.

herself against a Chinese battery at Chapoo ; Midshipman Harvey, and a seaman of the *Conway* lost their lives in a foraging expedition at the western end of Tsungming ;[1] and on August 6th, an unprovoked attack, made upon a clergyman in Casilha Bay, near Macao, brought about decided action by Captain Henry Smith (2), of the *Druid*, 44, who, with the *Hyacinth*, 20, *Larne*, 20, *Louisa*, cutter, *Enterprize*, steamer, and boats containing 120 Marines under Lieutenant William Robert Maxwell, R.M., 80 seamen under Lieutenant George Goldsmith, and 180 Bengal volunteers, under Major Mee, assaulted and captured the Chinese works behind Macao, spiking seventeen guns, sinking two junks, and having only four of his people wounded.

At Amoy, also, where Commander Augustus Leopold Kuper, of the *Alligator*, 28, maintained a blockade, the threatening attitude of a large fleet of war-junks, led to the destruction of several of them, and to other reprisals. But Kuper had to abandon an attempt, which he made, to force the passage between Kolangso and Amoy harbour ; and consequently the Chinese were left with the conviction that they had won an important success. Nowhere were they made to feel that they were dealing with foes who were vastly their superiors. Nowhere were they crushingly and convincingly defeated. A truce, however, was concluded on November 6th, 1840. As early as the 21st of the same month it was violated by the Chinese, who, upon the appearance of the steamer *Queen*, Actg. Master William Warden, with a white flag, off the Bogue Forts, fired upon her boat. Warden retaliated with his 68-prs., and then rejoined the Rear-Admiral, who was in the *Melville*, 74, at Macao. The outrage should have been promptly and very severely punished by the Commander-in-Chief : but both the Elliots, in their dealings with the Chinese, who wanted only to gain time, continued to betray most regrettable weakness ; and it must have been with a sense of relief that on November 29th, the British merchants learnt that the Rear-Admiral, on account of sudden and severe illness, had resigned his command into the stronger hands of Commodore Sir James John Gordon Bremer. Rear-Admiral Elliot quitted Chusan in the *Volage*, on December 7th, 1840, and returned to England.

Negotiations between Captain Elliot and the Chinese commissioner, Keeshen, dragged on until the end of the year. Elliot,

[1] Since called Harvey Point.

in the *Wellesley*, lay at Lintin, near the forts of Chuenpee and the Bogue, which were almost daily strengthened.   The expeditionary force also, at this time, was increased, notably by the arrival of seven companies of the 37th Madras Native Infantry, and of the new H.E.I. Co.'s iron steamer *Nemesis*, Master William Hutcheon Hall,[1] R.N., "a vessel," says Ouchterlony, "destined to be very conspicuous in all the most important achievèments of the war."

At length even Captain Elliot realised that he was being trifled with, and made a laughing-stock of by the Chinese ; and it was determined to attack the approaches to Canton.   On the morning of January 7th, 1841, therefore, about 1400 Royal Marines, and troops, under Major Pratt, of the 26th Regiment, having been landed two miles south of Chuenpee fort, pushed on against that work, while the *Calliope, Larne, Hyacinth, Queen,* and *Nemesis* dropped anchor abreast of the batteries, and opened fire.   The fort was soon rushed, a landing-party from the squadron entering almost at the same moment from the sea-front ; and the enemy was driven away with terrible loss.   On the British side the total casualties in this affair were 38 wounded.   Simultaneously, Captain James Scott, with the *Samarang, Druid, Modeste,* and *Columbine,* proceeded a little further up the river, and hotly bombarded the fort of Tycocktow, on the right, or south bank, for an hour.   He then landed Marines and small-arms men, and, with some little difficulty, cleared and occupied the works at the point of the bayonet and cutlass.   In the assault, Lieutenant James Paterson Bower, of the *Samarang,* was among the wounded.

That day the *Nemesis*, shallow of draught, well-armed, and ably handled, did wonders.   After shelling Chuenpee at close range, and pouring grape into the embrasures of the fort, she pushed

---

[1] William Hutcheon Hall had entered the Navy in 1811, and was a Master of May 30th, 1823.   One of the first British officers to make a thorough study of steam, he was given command of the *Nemesis* in November 1839, and, in consequence of his brilliant services in her, the Admiralty procured an Order in Council to enable it to make him a Lieutenant on January 8th, 1841.   The Admiralty later obtained power to enable him to count his time in the *Nemesis* as if it had been served in one of H.M. ships, and made him a Commander, June 10, 1843; and a Captain, October 22nd, 1844. He was the inventor of Hall's patent anchor, and of iron bilge tanks.   In 1847 he was elected an F.R.S.   His career, exceptional though it was, indicates that sometimes at least the Admiralty is willing to depart from the rules of red-tape rather than neglect true merit.   He was made a Rear-Adm. in 1863, and a K.C.B. in 1867.   In 1869 he retired, and died in 1878.

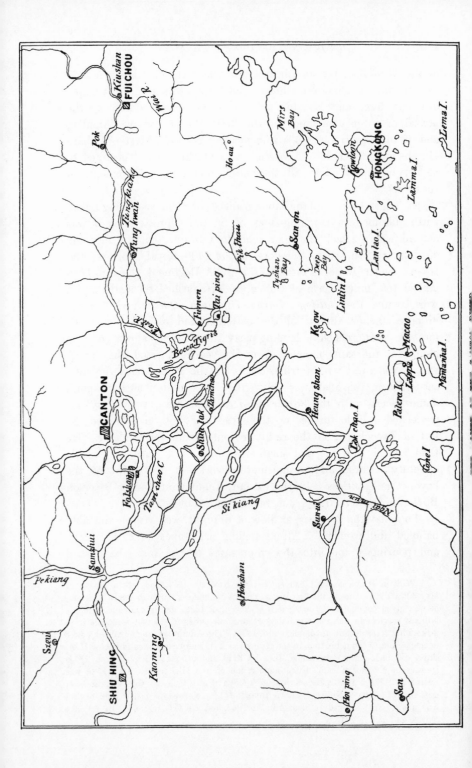

on over the shallows into Anson's Bay, and there attacked eleven war junks at anchor. Her first rocket directed at these set fire to one of the largest, which presently blew up with all on board ; and, aided by boats from the squadron, Hall soon destroyed all the others.

The works were dismantled, the guns, 97 in number, disabled, and the buildings and stores burnt. On the 8th, the fleet, led by the *Blenheim*, 74, Captain Sir Humphrey Fleming Senhouse, advanced to attack the Bogue forts ; but, when the vessels got almost within range of Anunghoy, they were met by a Chinese emissary, bearing a request for a suspension of hostilities ; and once more, accordingly, Captain Elliot, as High Commissioner, began negotiations. He should have first razed to the ground the forts between him and Canton. On January 20th, nevertheless, he was able to announce that he had concluded a preliminary arrangement, in virtue of which Hong Kong was to be ceded in perpetuity to Great Britain, an indemnity of $6,000,000 was to be paid in instalments, and official intercourse and trade were to be reopened. Hong Kong was formally taken possession of on the 26th, under a royal salute ; and the island of Chusan, at about the same time, was evacuated. On January 27th, Elliot proceeded in the *Nemesis* to a point near Whampoa, and resumed the conferences, which, he reported, were going on "satisfactorily," though he also declared that British merchants and others must not yet think of returning to Canton, save at their own risk. More meetings, and more procrastination followed. The Chinese, while parleying, brought up fresh troops, and mounted more guns hour by hour. At length Elliot lost patience, and sent the *Nemesis* to demand an instant ratification of the treaty. Hall failed to get it ; and hostilities were forthwith recommenced.

On February 20th, Bremer, who had fallen down the river after January 8th, again pushed up with the fleet to the neighbourhood of Anunghoy ; and, on the 23rd, the *Nemesis*, aided by boats from the *Calliope*, *Samarang*, *Herald*, and *Alligator*, the whole under Captain Thomas Herbert, broke up a force which was endeavouring to obstruct a channel at the back of Anunghoy, carried a masked battery and field-work, and spiked about 80 guns, without the loss of a man. Of the Chinese about 30 fell.

" Up to the present time," says Ouchterlony, " the ordinary passage by which vessels of any considerable burden entered the Canton River was that between the islands of

VESSELS OF THE ROYAL NAVY, AND OF THE HON. EAST INDIA COMPANY'S
SERVICE, ENGAGED IN THE OPERATIONS IN CHINA, 1839–42.

Ships.	Guns.	Commanders.	Remarks.
H.M. Ships:—			
*Algerine. . . .	10	Lieut. Thos. Hy. Mason.	Com. June 8th, 1841. From Oct. 10th, 1841, Lieut. Wm. Heriot Maitland.
*Alligator . . .	26	Com. Aug. Leop. Kuper (actg. Capt.).	Later, Com. Pat. Jno. Blake (actg. Capt.). From Jan. 14th, 1841, Com. (and Capt.) Sam. Perkins Pritchard.
*Apollo, trp. s. . .	46	Com. Chas. Frederick.	
*Belleisle, trp. s. .	72	Capt. Jno. Kingcome.	
Bentinck, surv. .	10	Lieut. Rich. Collinson.	Com. June 18th, 1841. See Plover.
*Blenheim . . .	72	Capt. Sir Humph. Fleming Sen-house, Kt.	Died in com. June 14th, 1841, Capt. Thos. Herbert (K.C.B. Oct. 14th, 1841). See
*Blonde	42	Capt. Thos. Bourchier.	C.B. June 29th, 1841. [Calliope.
Cambrian . . .	36	Capt. Hy. Ducie Chads, C.B.	
*Calliope	26	Capt. Thos. Herbert.	From June 14th, 1841, Capt. Aug. Leop. Kuper (C.B. Jan. 21st, 1842).
*Childers	16	Com. Edw. Pellew Halsted.	
*Clio	16	Com. Edw. Norwich Troubridge (actg. Capt.).	
*Columbine . . .	16	Lieut. Thos. Jordaine Clarke (actg. Com.).	Com. June 3rd, 1840; Capt. June 8th, 1841, From Oct. 16th, 1841, Com. Wm. Hy. Anderson Morshead.
*Conway	26	Capt. Ch. Ramsay Drinkwater Bethune.	C.B. July 29th, 1841.
*Cornwallis . . .	72	R.-Ad. Sir Wm. Parker (2), K.C.B. Capt. Peter Richards.	See Wellesley.
*Cruiser	16	Com. Hy. Wells Giffard.	Capt. June 8th, 1841. From Oct. 16th, 1841, Com. Jos. Pearse.
*Dido	18	Capt. Hon. Henry Keppel.	
*Druid	44	Capt. Hy. Smith (2), C.B.	
*Endymion . . .	44	Capt. Hon. Fredk. Wm. Grey.	
*Harlequin . . .	16	Com. Lord Fras. Jno. Russell.	
*Hazard	18	Com. Chas. Bell.	
*Herald	26	Capt. Joseph Nias.	C.B. June 29th, 1841.
*Hyacinth . . .	18	Com. Wm. Warren.	Capt. May 6th, 1841. From Aug. 14th, 1841, Com. Geo. Goldsmith.
*Jupiter, trp. s. . .	—	Master Robt. Fulton.	Later, Master Geo. B. Hoffmeister.
*Larne	18	Com. Aug. Leop. Kuper.	From Jan. 17th, 1840, Capt. Pat. Jno. Blake.
Louisa, tender . .	—	Mate Thos. Carmichael.	Lieut. June 8th, 1841. Wrecked, 1841.
*Melville	72	R.-Ad. Hon. George Elliot (3), C.B. Capt. Hon. Rich. Saunders Dundas.	During earlier operations.
*Modeste	18	Com. Harry Eyres.	Capt. May 6th, 1841; C.B. Oct. 14th, 1841. Later, Com. Rundle Burges Watson.
*Nimrod	20	Com. Chas. Anstruther Barlow.	Capt. June 8th, 1841; C.B. Oct. 14th, 1841. Later, Com. Jos. Pearse. Later, Com. Fredk. Hy. Hastings Glasse.
*North Star . . .	26	Capt. Sir Jas. Everard Home, Bt.	
Pelican . . .	18	Com. Chas. Geo. Elers Napier.	Capt. Nov. 1st, 1841.
*Plover, surv. . .	—	Com. Rich. Collinson.	
*Pylades	18	Com. Talavera Vernon Anson.	Capt. June 8th, 1841. Later, Com. Louis Symonds Tindal.
*Rattlesnake, trp. s.	28	Master William Brodie.	Died in com. Later, Master Jas. Sprent.
*Samarang . . .	26	Capt. Jas. Scott.	C.B. June 29th, 1841.
*Sapphire, trp. s. .	28	Master Geo. Wm. Nembhard.	
*Starling, surv. cutt.	6	Lieut. Hy. Kellett.	Com. May 6th, 1841.
*Sulphur, surv. . .	8	Com. Edward Belcher.	Capt. May 6th, 1841; C.B. Oct. 14th, 1841.
*Vixen, padd. . .	6	Com. Hy. Boyes.	
*Volage	26	Capt. Hy. Smith (2).	From June 30th, 1840, Com. Geo. Aug. Elliot (actg. Capt.). Later, Capt. Wm. Warren, and, on Aug. 30th, 1841, Capt. Sir Wm. Dickson, Bart.
*Wanderer . . .	16	Com. Edw. Norwich Troubridge.	Later, Com. Steph. Grenville Fremantle.
*Wellesley . . .	72	R.-Ad. Sir Fredk. Lewis Maitland (2), K.C.B. Capt. Thos. Maitland.	From Jan. 17th, 1840, Commod. Sir J. J. G. Bremer, Kt., C.B., with Capt. Maitland. Later, flag of R.-Adm. Sir Wm. Parker (2), (V.-Adm. Nov. 23rd, 1841).
Young Hebe, tender	—	Mate Rich. Robt. Quin.	Later, Lieut. Wm. Cotterell Wood.
H. E. I. Co.'s ships:—			
Atalanta. . . .			
Auckland, str. . .	—	Com. R. Ethersey, I.N.	
Aurora			
Enterprise . . .			
Madagascar, str. .	—	Capt. Dicey, I.N.	Burnt by accident, 1842.
Medusa, str. . .	—	Lieut. W. H. Hewitt, I.N.	
Nemesis, str. . .	2	Master Wm. Hutcheon Hall, R.N.	Lieut. Jan. 8th, 1841.
Phlegethon, str. .	4	Lieut. Jas. Johnstone M'Cleverty, R.N.	
Pluto, str. . . .	—	Lieut. Jno. Tudor, R.N.	
Proserpine, str. .	—	Com. Jno. Jas. Hough, R.N.	
Queen, str. . . .	2	Actg. Master Wm. Warden, R.N.	
Sesostris, str. . .	4	Com. H. A. Ormsby, I.N.	
Tenasserim, str. .	—	Actg. Master A. P. Wall, R.N.	

* Medals were granted to these ships.

North and South Wangtung and the peak of Anunghoy[1]; but it had been for some time known that a safe channel also existed to the westward; and no pains had been spared to render the latter as difficult and dangerous as possible by bringing the fire of two formidable batteries, of 45 and 40 guns, to bear upon it : the one constructed on the western extremity of North Wangtung, the other on the opposite or right bank the river. From Anunghoy a strong chain had been carried, right across the eastern passage, to a rocky point near a formidable battery which had for years existed on the eastern tongue of North Wangtung, where its end was made fast, the chain being held up to within a few feet of the water by means of a line of rafts."

But the Chinese had omitted to occupy the lower island lying within point-blank range of North Wangtung, to the southward; and there, on the night of February 25th, with the assistance of some seamen, three howitzers were mounted in a sandbag battery. At daybreak on the following morning they opened fire upon the works on North Wangtung. Several hours elapsed, owing to a calm, ere the fleet was able to move up, yet in the interval the Chinese artillery failed to do any harm to the howitzers, or their gunners. At 11 A.M., however, the *Blenheim* and *Queen* anchored abreast of the large battery of Anunghoy, and the *Melville*, passing ahead, brought up with her port bow guns bearing on the eastern battery of Wangtung. By noon, the action on the eastern side of the river was general. The *Wellesley*, *Druid*, and *Modeste* in the meantime entered the western channel, and engaged the battery on North Wangtung, and a fort and camp on the opposite bank; while the *Calliope*, *Herald*, *Samarang*, and *Alligator* pressed on to the northward of the Chinese defences, firing their starboard broadsides into the lower Wangtung battery as they passed. After about an hour's cannonade, Captain Sir Humphrey Fleming Senhouse, with 300 seamen and Royal Marines, landed under Anunghoy, and carried the works without much trouble. The Chinese admiral, Kwan, was killed there. North Wangtung was similarly carried by the troops, and many prisoners were taken; and at 4 P.M., when the *Nemesis*, with some of the *Wellesley's* boats, was sent against the fort and camp on the Tycocktow side, those positions were abandoned, and occupied without resistance. The works there and at Anunghoy were destroyed; but the North Wangtung works were garrisoned, though the Chinese guns, being almost useless, were disabled and thrown into the water.

While part of the squadron remained at the Bogue, an advanced division,[2] under Captain Thomas Herbert, of the *Calliope*, moved

[1] *See* map, p. 286.
[2] *Calliope, Nemesis, Madagascar, Modeste, Herald, Alligator* and *Sulphur.*

up with some boats from the *Wellesley*, and, on February 27th, attacked the enemy's position at Second Bar, near Whampoa, where a floating boom had been thrown across the river, flanked on one side by an entrenched camp containing 2000 troops, and on the other by the guns of the *Cambridge*, the old H. E. I. Co.'s vessel, which had been purchased by the Chinese before the outbreak of war. The raft was cut through; the enemy was driven off with heavy loss; and the *Cambridge* was boarded, captured, and blown up. Herbert afterwards anchored in Whampoa reach. On March 2nd, the *Sulphur*, with some boats, proceeded, took a masked battery on the N.E. end of Whampoa island, and occupied Howqua's fort.[1] The *Sulphur*, with the *Herald, Alligator*, and *Modeste*, then anchored in the stream between that fort and Napier island. On the 3rd there was another brief suspension of hostilities. It was at about that time that Major-General Sir Hugh Gough arrived from Madras to take command of the military part of the expedition.

By March 7th, Captain Elliot realised that he was again being trifled with; and the armistice was declared to be at an end. Between then and the 18th, all the enemy's works on the river banks, as far as the factories at Canton, and along the deep-water branch passage known as the Macao channel, were, one after another, taken and destroyed. Many junks also were burnt or scuttled. Yet, in the whole of the operations, no one on the British side was killed in action, and but one man died of his wounds. The Royal Marines employed were commanded by Captain Anthony Blaxland Stransham,[2] who was wounded by an explosion on the 17th, and was mentioned in dispatches for his gallantry. In these affairs, especially in some which took place on the 12th and 13th in the Broadway, a western passage between Macao and Whampoa, the *Nemesis* rendered very valuable service. She, and the boats which she had in tow, were responsible for the capture and destruction of no fewer than 105 guns, and the burning of nine junks. Lieutenant Hall displayed energy and resource beyond praise.

On March 20th, Captain Elliot announced that yet another armistice had been concluded with the imperial commissioner Yang, who had succeeded Keeshen. In consequence of this, all the

---

[1] Also called Howqua's Folly.

[2] Died General Sir A. B. Stransham, G.C.B., in Oct. 1900, aged 95.

fleet, except some light craft of Captain Herbert's division, returned
to Hong Kong, where Sir Hugh Gough busied himself in the
reorganisation of his small force, which was sadly depleted by
sickness, and by the recall of the Bengal volunteers. A little
later the *Melville* and *Samarang* sailed for England, and the
Madagascar and *Queen*, the latter bearing Bremer's broad pennant,
went provisionally to Calcutta, where plans for further operations
were discussed. Indeed, it was evident that the troubles were still
only at their commencement. The edicts of the Chinese Emperor
breathed increasing animosity; fresh defences were thrown up at
Chusan, Chinhae, and Amoy; and near Chusan Mr. Stead, master
of the transport *Pestonjee*, was barbarously murdered by villagers
and soldiers who had been promised a reward for the head of any
British subject. At Canton, however, the situation seemed for the
moment to have quieted down, so much so that many merchants
returned to their hongs; and Captain Elliot himself took up
temporary residence. But, upon getting trustworthy news of
Mr. Stead's murder, Elliot sent the *Columbine* to Chusan to
demand redress. That vessel had to return without having been
allowed to communicate. She could only report that huge preparations for war were going forward at Tinhae. Elliot was at that
time back at Hong Kong. When he returned to Canton on
May 11th, he not only discovered unmistakable signs that the
Chinese had negotiated only to gain time, but also was at last
persuaded that further parley was worse than useless, and that
Great Britain must unhesitatingly put forth her strength if she
would convince the enemy of the necessity of submission and
improved behaviour. He regained Hong Kong without delay,
and, on May 19th, induced the Commander-in-Chief to cause the
whole of the British forces, except the *Druid* and the small
garrisons of Hong Kong and North Wangtung, to be moved above
the Bogue, which was passed on the 20th.

Herbert was still at anchor off the factories. On the 21st Senhouse took the *Blenheim* into the Macao passage, and anchored her,
as a kind of base, six miles below Canton. During the day the
British subjects remaining in the city quitted it, at Elliot's desire.
That night, from the creeks above Shaming, a flotilla of fire-rafts
was let loose upon the *Louisa*, cutter, and *Aurora*, schooner, which
had just received on board the last of the fugitive merchants; and,
at the same time, the batteries, from Shaming to the Creek factory,

opened, the *Louisa* and *Aurora* escaping to the mouth of the Macao passage only because of the enemy's wretched aim. The boats of the *Herald*, coming from Napier's Reach, towed the fire-rafts clear; the *Modeste*, *Pylades*, and *Algerine*, from the Macao passage, ran in and engaged some of the batteries; and the *Nemesis* steamed close in to the large battery at Shaming, and was there for some time in difficulties under a heavy fire, her bow gun being temporarily disabled, her rudder being jammed, and a rocket hanging in a tube, and in its explosion badly burning Lieutenant Hall. But the Marines, firing into the embrasures, disconcerted the Chinese gunners; and, at length, the *Nemesis* was again in full fighting trim. She had been struck in many places, but her casualties were quite trifling, and at dawn, having silenced the Shaming battery, she pushed on, with the boats of the squadron in tow, and destroyed a flotilla of 39 war junks and boats. In the interval, first the mob and then the Chinese soldiery pillaged and gutted the factories. It was, of course, necessary to effect a land-ing in force in order to check the work of destruction. Captain Edward Belcher, of the *Sulphur*, was sent to find a suitable point for disembarkation. He reported in favour of a creek to the west-ward of the city, whence there was no serious obstacle to the pass-age of troops and guns to some forts crowning several eminences on the north-west. Upon the fall of these forts, it would be possible to establish a battery which should command the town, and bring it to reason. Belcher, during his absence, destroyed 28 war junks and row boats; and he brought back with him a number of decked craft, which proved most serviceable for the business of disembarkation.

On Her Majesty's birthday, May 24th, a royal salute having first been fired, the troops were landed in two divisions, and, after a preparatory cannonade, the four forts on the heights were carried at the point of the bayonet. A naval brigade, under Captain Thomas Bourchier, participated in the assault, and, after the storming, suffered somewhat severely from a heavy fire which burst out all along the northern ramparts of Canton. All the captured works, however, were held, in spite of a temporary failure of the ammuni-tion supply; and, in the course of the following day, fifteen guns and howitzers were got into position before the walls. Just as the batteries were ready to open on the 27th, it was announced that the enemy had proposed terms, which Captain Elliot had accepted. It was stipulated that, upon the withdrawal of all imperial [1] troops to a distance of upwards of sixty miles from the city, and the payment within one week of $6,000,000, and of an indemnity for damage to British property, the British forces should retire without the Bogue, and restore all the captured forts, which, however, were not to be rearmed pending a final settlement. It was not a wise arrangement. Canton had not been occupied, and the provincial mandarins had not been humiliated as they deserved after their long course of treachery and duplicity. The British flag should have been hoisted above the city ere any terms were listened to. But Elliot believed that Gough had not sufficient force to hold the place; and so, as soon as the Chinese had carried out their share of the undertaking, the expedition fell down the river. During the armistice, however, the enemy to the west of the city attacked the British in such force that a catastrophe was only averted by the unhoped-for intervention of two companies of Royal Marines. On the following day, in spite of Gough's remonstrances and threats, a still more formidable attack was imminent, until the local authorities, at the last moment, dispersed their soldiery. Thus, although the Chinese had lost heavily [2] in the various engagements, it was open to them to pretend that they had not suffered any decisive reverse. This was a dangerous possibility; and it should never have been left to them. It precluded, indeed, all immediate prospect of a satisfactory settlement. Nor, in any case, was Canton China.

The expedition retired to Hong Kong, where, within a few days of its arrival, it had to regret the death, by fever, of Captain Sir Humphrey Fleming Senhouse, who, in the absence of Bremer elsewhere on the station, had most ably conducted the naval portion of the operations in the river. His body was buried at Macao.

Captain Elliot's management of political affairs had long since failed to give satisfaction at home. A new era opened when he was recalled, and superseded by Colonel Sir Henry Pottinger, who left England in May, in company with Rear-Admiral Sir William Parker (2), who had been appointed to fill the vacancy in the East Indies and China command occasioned by the death of Sir Frederick

---

[1] As distinct from provincial.

[2] The British loss in the entire operations was less than 130 killed, wounded, and missing. The Chinese probably lost in all about 1200 men.

Lewis Maitland (2). The two new heads reached Macao road on board the H.E.I. Co.'s steam frigate *Sesostris* on August 3rd, 1841. In the interim Elliot had made arrangements for the government of Hong Kong, and had adjusted certain claims for indemnity; the *Conway* and *Calliope* had been despatched, one to England and the other to Calcutta, with the bulk of the Canton ransom money; and Gough's force had been strengthened by the arrival of a battalion of the 55th Regiment. Two bad typhoons had occasioned much damage to the transports and men-of-war; and, during one of them, on July 21st, Elliot, with Bremer, who had returned to China in the *Queen* with the powers of joint plenipotentiary, had been wrecked in the *Louisa*, cutter, between Macao and Hong Kong on a piratical island, whence they had escaped only upon undertaking to pay $3000 for their liberation.

Parker, Gough, and Pottinger were men who were not to be contented with half measures. It was determined to strike a blow, as soon as possible, to the northward; and by August 20th the fleet [1] and 21 transports, having on board about 2700 troops,[2] with field guns and rocket tubes, being ready for sea, headed for Amoy. Pottinger accompanied the expedition, after having declined to open negotiations with the provincial governments, and completed the organisation of the administration of Hong Kong. On August 24th, Amoy and the neighbouring fortified island of Kolangsoo were reconnoitred; and, on the following day, the strong Chinese works were bombarded, the *Wellesley* and *Blenheim* being laid alongside the big shore batteries, the *Druid*, *Blonde*, and light craft dealing with Kolangsoo, and the steamers landing troops and destroying junks. It does not appear that even the broadsides of the two 74's made much impression on the batteries, which were admirably constructed; but, when the troops assaulted, there was but little resistance; and, on the 26th, Amoy itself was occupied, having been abandoned in the darkness. The chief loss on this occasion was due to the *Sesostris* having towed under water a boat full of troops. The Amoy batteries were dismantled, and about 500 guns destroyed; and the place was evacuated, a garrison, however, being left at Kolangsoo. On September 4th, the expedition proceeded for Chusan; but its progress was so impeded by fogs and baffling winds

---

[1] *Wellesley* (flag), *Blenheim*, *Druid*, *Blonde*, *Modeste*, *Pylades*, *Columbine*, *Cruiser*, *Algerine*, *Rattlesnake*, *Queen*, *Sesostris*, *Nemesis*, and *Phlegethon*.

[2] Including 18th, 49th, and 55th, and part of the 26th British regiments.

that great part of it did not make the rendezvous until towards the end of the month. As elsewhere, the Chinese had immensely strengthened their defences, and near Tinghae upwards of 200 guns were in battery; but the whole line of works was so laid out as to be capable of being easily turned. On October 1st, therefore, while the attention· of the enemy was occupied by the ships, the troops were landed on the Chinese right; and, with some little loss, they presently carried some heights which dominated the whole position. The forts were then stormed, and Tinghae fell, not, unfortunately, before the Royal Marines and the 18th Regiment had had a number of men hit. After the capture the *Nemesis* and *Phlegethon* steamed round the island of Chusan in order to intercept escaping junks or boats. Tinghae was garrisoned, and the expedition[1] moved on to the mouth of the Ningpo river and to the city of Chinhae.

When, on October 9th, a reconnaissance was made, the estuary was found to be strongly fortified, and the channel blocked with a double row of piles, backed by a moored line of junks and gunboats. On the 10th, the position was attacked, the army being landed to operate on the right bank, and a naval force disembarking on the left. The latter, after a preliminary cannonade from the squadron, captured Chinhae without much difficulty. On the other side of the stream, the Chinese were caught between two columns; and something very much like a massacre took place ere the troops could be induced to cease firing. Chinhae was held; and, on the 13th, when a flotilla of light craft pushed up to Ningpo, that important city was found to have been evacuated. It promised to form a good winter headquarters for the expedition, and was occupied as such.

In the meantime, the Chinese in the Canton river having committed infractions of the treaty of the previous May, Captain Joseph Nias, of the *Herald*, senior naval officer at Hong Kong, took a small force up the river, razed North Wangtung fort to the ground, sank or burnt a number of junks, and shot a few persons whom he believed to have been guilty of treacherous conduct. This was in October; but, upon the withdrawal of Nias, the Chinese at once began to build pile barriers across both the Macao passage and the Junk river, and to construct new batteries. It was at about the same time that the transport *Nerbudda*, proceeding northward with camp-followers and a few men of the 55th Regiment, was driven

---

[1] The ships then present were: *Wellesley, Blenheim, Blonde, Jupiter, Columbine, Bentinck, Rattlesnake, Modeste, Nemesis, Queen, Phlegethon, Sesostris,* and *Cruiser.*

in a leaky condition into a bay on the coast of Formosa, and there basely abandoned by her European crew and passengers, who made off in some of the boats, after having destroyed the others and all the ammunition that was not taken away. The fugitives reached Hong Kong, where Nias made a prisoner of the dastardly master of the transport. The *Nimrod* was then despatched to the scene of the wreck; but she arrived too late. The wretched Indian passengers, having been obliged to drift ashore on rafts and planks, had there been seized by the savage inhabitants, and killed or made prisoners. Ultimately, indeed, almost all of them were murdered, though a few, after the conclusion of peace, were sent to Amoy and handed over to the British.

The only further offensive operations of the expedition ere the close of 1841 were at Tsekee, Yuyao, and neighbouring places on the Ningpo river, where, in December, the *Sesostris*, *Nemesis*, and *Phlegethon* assisted the troops in the capture and destruction of several small Chinese works; but the tone of the Imperial edicts, and the general attitude of the mandarins during the winter, indicated that the campaign was still far from an end. Piracy, too, was a source of much trouble, especially in the vicinity of Amoy, where, on one occasion, a boat of the *Druid*, Captain Henry Smith (2), C.B., lost several men by the sudden blowing up of a large junk at the moment of boarding.

The active renewal of the campaign in the early spring of 1842 was the work of the Chinese. Gough was at Chusan conferring with Sir William Parker when, early in the morning of March 10th, large bodies of the enemy made a most determined attack on Ningpo. The west gate was successfully defended, but the south gate was forced, and the city was entered by the foe. The Chinese were, however, met in the streets, and driven back, while, in the river, the *Modeste*, *Sesostris*, *Columbine*, and *Queen* dispersed some troops which endeavoured to fire across the stream, and towed aside or destroyed some fire-rafts which were sent down from above. The attack was repulsed with great slaughter, though the British did not have a man killed.

On the same day, and at the same time, an attempt was made to surprise Chinhae, where Colonel Schoedde, of the 55th Regiment, commanded; but the Chinese were easily driven back, and the fire-rafts, which, there as at Ningpo, were floated down the stream, were dealt with by the boats of the *Blonde* and *Hyacinth*. Chusan was to have been attacked at about the same date, but news of the project reached Parker, who sent the *Nemesis* to Taishan, where the Chinese, who had gathered for the adventure, were dispersed, and several junks were burnt.

Sir Hugh Gough at once returned to Ningpo, and, learning that there was still a large Chinese army in the neighbourhood, marched out on March 13th with about 900 men of all arms, and with the *Sesostris* on his flank. It was found, however, that this particular army had retired beyond reach. A second army, under General Yang, was known, however, to be at Tsekee, across the river; and, Sir William Parker, with several additional ships, and bluejackets and Marines, having arrived at Ningpo on March 14th, an expeditionary force was embarked [1] on the following morning, and landed four miles from Yang's position on the heights of Segaon, behind Tsekee. With the troops was a naval brigade under Captain Thomas Bourchier. Parker also was with Gough. After some stubborn fighting, a complete and, happily, a not very expensive victory was won, the Navy's casualties numbering only fifteen. Of the enemy, at least 450 fell. It was the most decided advantage which had as yet been gained by the British since the occupation of Chusan, where, by the way, a fresh attempt to burn the shipping by means of fire-rafts was defeated on April 14th by some of the boats of the *Cornwallis, Nemesis, Jupiter, Hyacinth, Starling, Phlegethon,* and *Bentinck.*

It had been the desire of the Commanders-in-Chief to follow up their success by an attack on Hangchowfoo, capital of the province of Che-kiang; but deficient means of supply, and difficulties of navigation prevented such a stroke from being dealt; and it was finally resolved instead to proceed to Chapoo. Not, however, until May 6th was the expedition able to leave Chinhae; and, although the distance to be traversed did not exceed sixty miles, the fleet did not, as a whole, make its rendezvous until May 16th. In 1840 the *Algerine,* Lieutenant Thomas Henry Mason, had paid a flying visit to the port, had been fired upon, and had silenced the battery which had annoyed her. She had then had occasion to notice the coolness and stubbornness with which the local Tartar gunners fought their pieces. Chapoo still had a Tartar garrison, which occupied the N.W. corner

---

[1] On this occasion there were employed the *Phlegethon, Modeste, Nemesis, Queen, Hyacinth, Columbine, Sesostris,* and boats of *Cornwallis* and *Blonde,* with about 350 seamen and Marines in the landing-party.

of the city proper, and which, as will be seen, fully maintained its reputation for tenacity. The town was reconnoitred on the 17th; and on the 18th all the troops were landed, to the N.E. of Chapoo, in two columns, one, on the right, to pass round the rear of the enemy, who had taken up a position on the cliffs to the N.E. of the town, the other, on the left, to flank the Chinese entrenchments. A third landing-party, formed of seamen and Marines,[1] was put ashore nearer to the town, and nearly due east of it. The steamers in the anchorage co-operated by shelling the Chinese. The advance of the two British columns, went on without serious opposition until it had cut off from the city about 350 Tartar troops who had held a position on the extreme right of the enemy's line. These troops quietly threw themselves into a joss house, and waited until both the British columns, and the naval brigade on the attacking left had unsuspectingly passed by them. They might then have escaped, had they not been accidentally discovered by a small detached party under Hall, of the *Nemesis*. The Tartars opened a spirited fire upon the few seamen and soldiers.[2] It was pluckily returned until the arrival on the scene of a reinforcing company of the 18th Regiment; and then an assault was made. But the British were repelled by the defenders. Other reinforcements arrived, a field-piece was turned upon the building, and part of the wall was blown in by means of a 50 lb. charge of powder; yet the Tartars fought on with as much determination as ever, though a second breach was made, and their stronghold was set on fire. When, at length, after more than three hours' desperate struggle, the place was carried, only sixty of the defenders remained alive, and of them many were wounded. The occupation of Chapoo itself was effected with but small difficulty.

Hangchowfoo was still considered to be unapproachable; and the expeditionary force re-embarked on May 28th. The fleet headed northward, it having been determined to deal a series of blows against the important cities at the mouth, and along the banks, of the Yangtsekiang. It was a wise decision : for never has China been thoroughly intimidated by attacks, no matter how successful, against her coast towns only. After various delays the fleet anchored off Woosung on June 13th.

---

[1] From *Cornwallis, Starling, Modeste, Bentinck, Blonde, Sesostris, Columbine,* and *Algerine*. A few officers and men of *Nemesis, Phlegethon,* and *Jupiter* were also landed.

[2] Chiefly of the 18th and 49th Regiments, about thirty in all.

Woosung lies not only near the mouth of the main Yangtse-kiang, but also near that of another large river, the Woosung, twelve miles further up which is the town of Shanghai. Shanghai, besides being an important naval station, had a great trade with Nanking, the capital; and the Commanders-in-Chief felt that it was most desirable to occupy it. It was, however, necessary first to force the defences at the mouth of the Woosung river. The water in front of these was sounded and buoyed on June 14th and 15th by Commanders Richard Collinson, and Henry Kellett; and, on June 16th, the works on both sides of the river were bombarded by the warships, while the transports, with the troops on board, lay four miles out in the stream. On the north or Woosung bank of the river there was simply a line of armed ramparts, terminating, after an upward course of about three miles, in the small fort of Powshan. There were no flanking defences. On the south side there was an old masonry fort, supplemented by a line of incomplete earthen batteries. Only the first discharge of the enemy's guns, delivered as the ships were anchoring, produced much effect. A Marine officer, and two men in the *Blonde* were killed by it; and a leadsman in the *Phlegethon* lost both his legs, while several vessels were hulled. After two hours' firing, towards the close of which the Chinese guns were nearly silent, detachments of seamen and Marines were landed, and all the works, except Powshan, were cleared and occupied ere any of the troops were disembarked. Powshan was soon afterwards evacuated; so that the whole of the success, such as it was, was won by the Navy alone.[1] Few Chinese were killed; and the greater part of the 200 or 250 guns captured were unmounted or useless. The British loss was 3 killed and 20 wounded.

"Among the curiosities," says Ouchterlony, "found at Woosung, were two junks, fitted each with four paddlewheels about five feet in diameter, worked by two cranks fitted on axles placed athwart in the fore and aft parts of the vessel. They were clumsy enough, but nevertheless useful craft for transporting troops on smooth water."

The Chinese had, in fact, adopted, independently or otherwise, a device very similar to the one which had been employed by Sir Charles Napier (2), twelve years earlier, to move his frigate, the *Galatea*, during calms.

[1] Ships engaged: *Cornwallis, Phlegethon, Modeste, Nemesis, Blonde, Sesostris, Columbine, Jupiter, Algerine, Medusa, North Star, Pluto, Clio,* and *Tenasserim.*

On the evening of the engagement the *Dido*, 20, anchored off the town, with a convoy of transports having on board 2500 additional men from India. Part of the whole force was at once directed against Shanghai, one column marching along the left bank of the Woosung river, and another going up in light craft,[1] and in steamers towing them. Parker and Gough accompanied the latter in the *Medusa*. A battery, half-way, opened on a reconnoitring vessel, but was evacuated as soon as the main body of the flotilla approached it. The only real difficulty encountered on the way up to within half a mile of Shanghai was occasioned by the grounding of the *Sesostris*, which lost her rudder. Just below the town, at a right-angled bend of the river, was a low-lying 18-gun battery, which, if it had been properly manned, would have occasioned serious loss to the vessels, and would have needed a landing-party to capture it by taking it in flank. It was, however, easily silenced by a few broadsides from the men-of-war, not a man in which was hurt. On June 18th, when the 18th Regiment reached the north gate of the town, only a few matchlocks were discharged at it, ere the place was hastily abandoned. On the 20th, Lieutenant Hall, in the *Nemesis*, pushed fully sixty miles further up the river in search of a channel to the city of Soochowfoo. Finding no signs of it, he returned at a moment when, as subsequently appeared, his smoke was visible from the walls, and when, but little ahead of him, was a fleet of fugitive junks laden with sycee silver from Shanghai treasury.

Shanghai was evacuated on June 23rd, and the troops and vessels fell back to Woosung. The expedition into the Yangtsekiang proper was then promptly organised. The European troops which took part in it were the 18th, 26th, 49th, 55th, and 98th Regiments, with some Royal Artillery and Engineers, the whole being under Sir Hugh Gough, Major-Generals Lord Saltoun, Schoedde, and Bartley, Colonel Montgomerie, R.A., and Captain Pears, R.E. Besides about forty transports, the following vessels of the Royal Navy and H.E.I. Co.'s marine participated :—

> H.M.S. *Cornwallis, Blonde, Calliope, North Star, Dido, Modeste, Endymion, Clio, Columbine, Algerine, Belleisle, Apollo, Sapphire, Jupiter, Rattlesnake, Plover, Starling,* and *Vixen,* paddle.
> H.E.I. Co.'s *Sesostris, Auckland, Queen, Tenasserim, Nemesis, Phlegethon, Pluto, Proserpine,* and *Medusa*—all paddle steamers.

---

[1] *North Star, Modeste, Clio,* and *Columbine.*

The entire fighting force included about 9000 troops and Marines, and 3000 seamen.

After the *Plover* and *Starling*, convoyed by a steamer, had made some soundings in the river, the general upward movement was begun on July 6th. Progress was slow, owing to the strong current and the difficulties of navigation, but no serious opposition was offered[1] until, on July 19th, the fleet anchored safely abreast of Chingkiang, the gate, as it were, of the far-reaching Grand Canal, and, as it has been called, " the very lungs " of China;—the portal, moreover, of Nanking, and the chief port of the Yangtsekiang. In the stream, opposite the town, lies Golden Island ; across the river, at the mouth of the northward prolongation of the Grand Canal, is Kwangchow. At first it appeared that Chingkiang was not to be defended, and, indeed, that there were no Chinese troops in its neighbourhood ; but on the 20th, some fire-rafts, which proved perfectly harmless, were dropped down upon the fleet; and a reconnaissance showed that two large entrenched camps occupied a low range of hills to the southward. On the 21st, nevertheless, the troops were landed, without interference, to right and left of the city, which was supposed to have been evacuated. The first brigade, under Lord Saltoun, advanced against the entrenched camps in the rear of the city, and drove their defenders out of them. In the meantime, Schoedde on the west, and Bartley on the east, attacked the city itself. Both brigades encountered steady and unexpected opposition almost as soon as they had landed. Schoedde, who was partially covered by the 68-prs. of the *Auckland*, carried the nearest bastion by escalade ; but had to fight his way thence step by step onwards until he reached some gates, which he opened, so admitting the rest of his column. The Tartar defenders not only fought stubbornly in their positions, but also charged most gallantly. Schoedde, however, at length pushed his way across to within distance of the east gate, which, after three hours' struggle, still barred Bartley's progress. A little later, Bartley's brigade forced its way in, and joined hands with Schoedde's. With Bartley were Sir Hugh Gough, Sir William Parker, and a small naval brigade under Captain Peter Richards, and Commander Rundle Burges Watson ; and, co-operating with him, in the mouth of the Grand Canal, were two boats of the *Blonde*,

---

[1] The *Pluto*, *Nemesis*, and *Modeste* were fired at on various occasions; but the enemy made no stand.

under Lieutenant Edward Crouch, and Midshipmen William Leigh Lambert, Robert Jenkins, and Henry Thomas Lyon. These boats had on board four field-pieces and howitzers belonging to the artillery ; and Crouch had been directed to land them at some favourable spot. Close to the east gate, the boats were suddenly saluted with an extremely hot fire from the lofty city wall. Crouch and Lyon, besides no fewer than 26 other people, were soon wounded ; and, as the guns could not be sufficiently elevated to clear the top of the wall, the crews wisely abandoned their boats and sought cover among the buildings on the further bank. At much risk to themselves, they reassembled ; and they were at length relieved by some boats of the *Cornwallis*, under Lieutenant James Stoddart. All this had, of course, taken place before the forcing of the east gate. Stoddart, with his boats, and some of the *Blonde's* people, as also a small party from the *Modeste*, under Master John T. Forster, then assisted the brigade under Captain Richards [1] and Commander Watson ; and a portion of the little force independently escaladed the wall just as the east gate was blown open by the head of Bartley's column. The first man up the ladder, a Marine, was killed, and Watson [2] was wounded. Among other naval officers who distinguished themselves during the day were Captain Granville George Loch, who fell ten years later in Burmah, and who acted as volunteer aide-de-camp to Gough, and Lieutenants James Fitzjames (wounded), and George Henry Hodgson.

Even after the gates had been taken, there was still a considerable amount of fighting in the streets and among the houses. When further resistance was hopeless, many of the Tartar defenders of the city deliberately slew their wives and children, and then committed suicide. Their general, Hailing, burnt himself, with all his papers, in his house.

The material and moral effects of this blow, dealt at a spot about 150 miles from the sea, against the best of the Tartar troops, upon the most important waterways of China, and within a short distance of one of the capitals of the empire, were immense ; and, within a month of the fall of Chingkiang, it became apparent that the long-continued campaign had at length produced its desired results upon the minds of the Emperor and his advisers. In the meantime, however, preparations were made for a further advance to Nanking,

---

[1] C.B. December 24th, 1842.

[2] Capt. December 23rd ; C.B. December 24th, 1842.

the passage towards which had been reconnoitred by the *Plover* ; and, on July 29th, Saltoun's and Bartley's brigades were re-embarked, Schoedde's being left in cantonments just without the city.

Ere anything further could be done, some mandarins sought out Sir Henry Pottinger with news that Eleepoo, an imperial High Commissioner, was on his way from Soochowfoo to treat for peace. Pottinger declined to stop operations before the arrival of the Commissioner with full powers to conclude an instant settlement; and on August 1st and 2nd, the *Cornwallis* and some other ships quitted Chingkiang, anchoring on the 5th off the northern angle of the walls of Nanking. The rest of the fleet, and the transports, all reached the same neighbourhood by the 8th. No opposition was experienced on the way up ; and over the capital flew a white flag.

THE CHINA MEDAL, 1840–42.
Ribbon : crimson, with yellow edges.

Upon receiving trustworthy assurances that Eleepoo was close at hand, Pottinger consented to stay active operations; but, on the 9th, finding that he was again being trifled with, Pottinger consulted with Parker and Gough for an immediate attack. The *Cornwallis* was moved into a position more advantageous for using her heavy broadside; the *Blonde* was towed up a creek, whence she could breach the walls preparatory to an assault ; and the army was actually landed, and encamped. All this induced the Chinese to give way. On the 13th they again begged for delay; on the 18th, negotiations were so far advanced that Pottinger informed Parker and Gough that hostile movements might be suspended ; and on the 20th, the Chinese plenipotentiaries were received in a friendly manner on board the *Cornwallis*. Pottinger returned the visit on the 24th, in company with the two Commanders-in-Chief; another interview took place on the 26th within the city ; and on the 29th, the treaty of Nanking was signed in the cabin of the *Cornwallis*. It was arranged that China was to pay an indemnity of $21,000,000 ; that Canton, Amoy, Foochow, Ningpo and Shanghai were to be thrown open to British merchants under just and regular tariff regulations ; that consuls should be appointed to reside at each of those ports ; that Hong Kong should be ceded in perpetuity to Great Britain ; that all British prisoners in China should be unconditionally released ; that Chinese who had held intercourse with the British should be amnestied ; and that Kolangsoo and Chusan should be held until the indemnity should be paid and the ports opened.

Thus, after almost exactly three years' hostilities, was peace restored.   The course of the war proved that, in dealing with China, sternness and firmness must be consistently employed ; that Chinese dilatoriness can be cured only by persistent pressure ; and that Chinese policy can be but little coerced save by blows dealt at the very gates of the seats of government.

Among the honours granted in return for services rendered by the Navy during the war may be mentioned the following :—

> Vice-Admiral Sir William Parker, Bart., to be G.C.B., Dec. 2nd, 1842.
> Captain Thomas Herbert, to be K.C.B., Oct. 14th, 1841.
> Captain Thomas Bourchier, to be K.C.B., Dec. 24th, 1842.
> Captain the Hon. Richard Saunders Dundas, to be C.B., June 29th, 1841.
> Captain James Scott, to be C.B., June 29th, 1841.
> Captain Charles Ramsay Drinkwater Bethune, to be C.B. June 29th, 1841.
> Captain Joseph Nias, to be C.B., June 29th, 1841.
> Captain Thomas Maitland, to be C.B., June 29th, 1841.
> Captain Edward Belcher, to be C.B., Oct. 14th, 1841.
> Captain William Warren, to be C.B., Oct. 14th, 1841.
> Captain Harry Eyres, to be C.B., Oct. 14th, 1841.
> Captain Charles Anstruther Barlow, to be C.B., Oct. 14th, 1841.
> Captain Augustus Leopold Kuper, to be C.B., Jan. 21st, 1842.
> Captain the Hon. Frederick William Grey, to be C.B., Jan. 21st, 1842.
> Captain Peter Richards, to be C.B., Jan. 21st, 1842.
> Captain Sir James Everard Home, Bart., to be C.B., Jan. 21st, 1842.
> Captain Henry Kellett, to be C.B., Jan. 21st, 1842.
> Captain Rundle Burges Watson, to be C.B., Jan. 21st, 1842.
> Captain William Henry Anderson Morshead, to be C.B., Jan. 21st, 1842.
> Captain Richard Collinson, to be C.B., Jan. 21st, 1842.
> Brev. Lieut.-Col. Samuel Burdon Ellis, R.M., to be C.B., Dec. 24th, 1842.

In 1839–42, apart from the Chinese War, which has just been described, and from the Syrian operations, which will be described presently, there were several small affairs in which the fleet had a share.

At the time of the French operations in Mexico, and the capture of San Juan de Ulloa and Vera Cruz by Rear-Admiral Baudin, in 1838–39, British interests on the coast were looked after by the following squadron, viz. : *Cornwallis*, 74, Vice-Admiral the Hon. Sir Charles Paget, Captain Sir Richard Grant; *Edinburgh*, 74, Captain William Honyman Henderson ; *Madagascar*, 46, Captain Provo William Parry Wallis ; *Pique*, 36, Captain Edward Boxer; *Andromache*, 28, Captain Robert Lambert Baynes; *Vestal*, 26, Captain Thomas Wren Carter; *Rover*, 18, Commander Thomas Matthew Charles Symonds ; *Modeste*, 18, Commander Harry Eyres ; *Racehorse*, 18, Commander Henry William Craufurd ; *Snake*, 16, Commander Alexander Milne ; and *Ringdove*, 16, Commander (actg.) the Hon. Keith Stewart (2).   While lying off Sacrificios, on January 19th, 1839, during a northerly gale, the *Madagascar* had occasion to send a cutter, with her Gunner and seventeen men, to pick up her pinnace, which had broken adrift.   Both boats were, unfortunately, swamped by a heavy sea, and eleven of the men were drowned, the Gunner and the rest saving themselves only with the greatest difficulty.[1]

Among the minor actions of these years should be mentioned the capture, in 1839, by the *Crocodile*, 26, Captain Alexander Milne, on the West Indies station, of the Spanish slaver *Mercedita* ; and the cutting out, by the boats of the *Dolphin*, 3, Lieutenant Edward Littlehales, of the Brazilian slaver *Firme*, off Whydah, on May 30th, 1841.   This last affair was a particularly brilliant one.   Mate Augustus Charles Murray in the gig, with five men, and Second-Master John Fletcher Rees in the cutter, with eight men, pulled hard for two hours and a half, engaged the *Firme*, a brigantine of 170 tons, and, after a twenty minutes' struggle, boarded and took her, losing, however, 2 killed and 3 wounded.   For his gallantry Murray, who was twice wounded, was promoted.[2]   In the meantime, in charge of another prize slaver, the little schooner *Dores*, only sixty feet in length, he made a most adventurous voyage from near Accra to Sierra Leone, with a crew of two men and two boys. He suffered great hardships of all kinds, met with terrible weather, lost one of his people, and did not succeed in making his port until after he had struggled with every sort of difficulty for no fewer than

---

[1] *Naut. Mag.*, 1839, 309, 314.
[2] *Gazette*, 1841, p. 2688.   Promd. Lieut., Oct. 1st, 1841.   Rees was also promd. to be Master, Dec. 21st, 1841.

146 days. The voyage was then ordinarily done in ten days. The *Wolverine,* 16, Commander William Tucker (3),[1] was another vessel that was most active in the repression of the slave trade. She not only made several prizes, but also, in 1840, captured the island of Corisco by assault, and destroyed the slave factories there established. On this occasion the storming party, originally 40 in number, led by Lieutenant Henry Dumaresq, lost 10 killed and wounded. Mention should also be made of Lieutenant John Luke Richard Stoll, who, in the *Bonetta,* 3, in about twenty-six months, ending May, 1840, took nine slavers, three of which, of superior force, were captured fifty miles up the Congo, and one of which, after a smart resistance, was cut out of the river Pongos; and of Commander John Adams, of the *Acorn,* 16, who, among other prizes, took, on July 6th, 1841, the notorious piratical slaver *Gabriel,* and, during his commission, caused the condemnation of about 3300 tons of shipping. One of the best slaver captures of 1841 was that of the Spanish schooner *Segundo Rosario,* which, with 284 slaves on board, was taken on January 27th, on the West Indies station, by the *Cleopatra,* 26, Captain Alexander Milne.

In 1840, Sir R. Doherty, governor of Sierra Leone, learnt that Prince Mauna, son of King Siacca of the Gallinas, a group of islands at the mouth of the Gallinas river, about 160 miles from Sierra Leone, had detained two British subjects for a pretended debt. He ordered Mauna to surrender them to Commander the Hon. Joseph Denman, of the *Wanderer,* 12, senior naval officer on that part of the coast, on pain of having every building in the Gallinas levelled with the ground. Denman not only recovered the prisoners, but also induced Siacca to agree to a treaty in virtue of which the British forces destroyed all the factories of Spanish slave traders within his dominions, and liberated the slaves in them. These measures were strongly approved by the home government, and Denman was posted on August 23rd, 1841, as soon, that is, as the full reports of his proceedings had been received in London. The Spanish slave dealers, however, were not equally satisfied; and they began suit for immense damages. The matter was not settled until 1848, when, after long litigation, a jury in the Court of Exchequer rendered a verdict in Denman's favour.[2]

Early in 1842 a young naval officer had an exceptional opportunity

---

[1] Posted, Oct. 26th, 1840.
[2] O'Byrne, 278; *Naut. Mag.,* 1848, p. 163.

for demonstrating his self-reliance, his determination, and his fitness for a responsible post in difficult circumstances. Cartagena, always one of the most turbulent states [1] of what is now the Republic of Colombia, was at that time little better than a piratical oligarchy. On February 6th, 1842, the British brig *Jane and Sarah,* and a sloop, the *Little William,* at anchor in the Cartagenan harbour of Sapote, were seized and plundered by five Cartagenan vessels of war under the orders of one General Carmona, and their crews and passengers, including a Colonel Gregg, were thrown into prison. The British consul at Cartagena endeavoured in vain to obtain the release of these unfortunate people. He then communicated with H.M. brig *Charybdis,* 6, Lieutenant Michael de Courcy (3), which was stationed off the coast. De Courcy arrived off the port of Cartagena, where the Cartagenan war vessels then lay, and at once sent on board the commodore's corvette a demand for the liberation of the British subjects. The commodore was insulting and contemptuous, and refused to receive de Courcy's letter. The Cartagenans, moreover, had by that time shot Colonel Gregg. Upon the return of his officer, de Courcy instantly entered the port. In spite of her nominal rating, his brig had on board only one long gun and two carronades, with a complement of 55 all told. The Cartagenan flotilla, on the other hand, included, besides the commodore's corvette, a brig and three schooners. As the *Charybdis* passed up to an anchorage, she was fired into by the corvette. De Courcy replied with the greatest steadiness and spirit; and, in a short time, the corvette struck, having lost her commodore and 25 men killed. Scarcely had the prize been taken possession of when the brig and schooners came down and furiously attacked the *Charybdis*; but the British gunnery quickly sank the brig, whereupon the schooners surrendered. The whole action occupied less than an hour; and, at its conclusion, de Courcy, instead of withdrawing, anchored proudly in the enemy's port, there to await the decision of his Commander-in-Chief concerning his captures.

It cannot, of course, be supposed that the seamen of one of the ruffianly South American states of that day were worthy opponents for British bluejackets, or that their vessels were well found; yet the victory was obtained against forces numerically much superior; and the loss suffered by the corvette indicates that the people fought stubbornly. De Courcy's conduct was approved of, both by the

---

[1] There was a separatist revolt in Cartagena as recently as 1899–1900.

Commander-in-Chief and by the Admiralty; and the gallant Lieutenant was deservedly promoted.[1]

For many years previous to 1838 there had been a few British settlers at Port Natal[2]; but, although the Cape government then sent up a small military force as a garrison for the district, it withdrew it again in 1839. Thereupon the Boers, who had determined to put their ally, Panda, on the throne of Zululand, and so secure peace in that quarter, turned their eyes upon what they presently called the Republic of Natalia. Numbers of them migrated from the inner parts of Cape Colony to the seaboard; and, pretending to have formed an independent state, they asked the British government to recognise Natalia as such. The request was refused; and, fresh native disturbances having broken out, and having threatened to set the borders of Cape Colony in a blaze, the Governor sent up a detachment of the 27th Regiment to re-garrison Natal and to keep order. The Boers resisted, and at length defeated the troops, and blockaded them in their fort at Durban. It was then that Richard King, a colonist, made his famous ten days' ride to Grahamstown in search of succour. The result of his appeal was that, reinforcements having been collected from Capetown and Algoa Bay, H.M.S. *Southampton*, 50, Captain Thomas Ogle, accompanied by the *Conch*, schooner, William Bell, master, appeared off Port Natal on the night of June 24th, 1842, with part of the 25th and 27th Regiments on board. On the two following days the frigate forced the entrance to the port, and landed the troops. The Boers fled, and, being followed up, submitted to Colonel Cloete on July 5th at Pietermaritzburg. In May, 1843, Natal was formally annexed to the British Crown.

The causes leading up to the employment of the Navy on the coast of Syria in 1840 may now be glanced at.

On September 14th, 1829, the Ottoman Porte had unwillingly signed the treaty of Adrianople with Russia; and, early in the following year, she had been obliged to recognise the independence of Greece, and to see the suzerainty of Algier pass from her to France. During many centuries the Sultan had experienced no harder blows from fortune; and during many centuries he had never been less able to resist the attacks and aggressions of foreign or

---

[1] Com., Feb. 12th, 1842. *Naut. Mag.*, 1842, p. 358. De Courcy was posted Sept. 6th, 1852, and obtained flag-rank on Oct. 10th, 1867. *Vide* F.O.'s list.

[2] The inlet on which stands Durban.

nominally dependent states; for, in 1826, he had abolished his ancient corps of Janissaries, and begun to reorganise his military system; and, amid the troubles and distractions of the succeeding years, he had not had opportunity to provide himself with a new army.

It was while he was still thus almost powerless that Mehemet Ali, his greatest vassal, bethought himself of seizing the moment for casting off allegiance and winning the independence of Egypt. Mehemet Ali had a good army, trained by ex-officers of the French Empire, plenty of arms and supplies, and a fleet which, though manned chiefly by fellahs, who were no match for the best European seamen, was well built, after French designs, and officered, to a large extent, by Frenchmen. Sultan Mahmoud had no naval force so effective.

In 1832, accordingly, Ibrahim Pasha, son of Mehemet Ali, invaded Syria, and gained striking and repeated victories, until the Sultan, fearful of losing Constantinople itself, called in the aid of the Russians, who landed an army in Anatolia, and induced Ibrahim to stay his advance. Great Britain and France thereupon put pressure upon Mahmoud to patch up a settlement[1] with his rebellious vassal; and the Sultan, convinced for the moment that Russia was his only friend, threw himself into the arms of the Tsar by signing the treaty of Unkiar-Skelessi, and determined to await a more favourable occasion for reducing Egypt to full obedience.

But Egypt was not content to wait. Fresh difficulties soon arose between the Porte and Mehemet Ali. This time, while Great Britain, as well as Russia, supported Turkey, France gave encouragement to Egypt. Hostilities recommenced; and, on June 29th, 1839, the Turkish army was badly defeated at Nesib. On July 1st Mahmoud died, leaving the throne to Abdul Medjid, a boy of sixteen. To increase the already serious troubles of Turkey, its main fleet, sent to sea to watch the movements of the Egyptians, deserted in a body, and joined the rebels at Alexandria. It was felt in London that, in order to prevent Abdul from becoming a mere dependent of Russia, some countenance must be shown him in his misfortunes; and, in consequence, negotiations on the subject were opened with France, the result being that an Anglo-French fleet of observation, under Admiral Sir Robert Stopford and Rear-Admiral Lalande, was presently anchored in Besika Bay. But France would

---

[1] Signed at Konieh, May 4th, 1833.

go no further; and when, on July 15th, 1840, Great Britain, Austria, Russia, and Prussia, by treaty, signed at London, engaged with the Sultan to bring his vassal to reason, France not only held aloof, but also assumed a sulky and threatening attitude, making vast preparations by land and sea, as if to oppose the Powers, and bringing Europe within measurable distance of a general war. Happily France was ultimately so wise as to reconsider her position, and, ere the end of the following year, to rejoin the European concert.[1]

In the meanwhile the four Powers offered Mehemet Ali that if, within a given time, he would evacuate Arabia, Syria, Crete, and other possessions of the Porte which he had occupied, and would make certain additional concessions, he should be made hereditary viceroy of Egypt, and might hold St. Jean d'Acre and some other territories during his life. If not, he would be deprived of all his dominions; and the four Powers would execute the sentence. He was allowed ten days wherein to make up his mind upon some of the proposals, and ten days more wherein to decide as to the rest of them.

The ultimatum appears to have been delivered on August 9th, at Alexandria, where the *Cyclops*, 6, paddle, Captain Horatio Thomas Austin, was directed to await the return of a reply. In the harbour lay the Egyptian fleet, and the Turkish squadron which had deserted. Mehemet Ali declared on the 16th that what he had won by the sword he would maintain by the sword, and that he would not withdraw his troops at the bidding of anyone; yet, further grace having been formally allowed him, it was not deemed fair to commence active operations so long as any part of the term of grace remained unexpired; and the *Cyclops* stayed on at Alexandria to afford to the last a *locus penitentiæ* to the hot-headed viceroy. In the meantime, however, Admiral Sir Robert Stopford, Commander-in-Chief in the Mediterranean, wrote on August 8th, from the *Princess Charlotte*, 104, off Mytilene, to Captain Charles Napier (2), C.B., of the *Powerful*, 84, who was off the coast of Karamania, directing him to hoist a broad (blue) pennant as Commodore of the third class, and, taking under his orders, besides the *Powerful*, the *Ganges*, 84, *Thunderer*, 84, *Edinburgh*, 72, *Castor*, 36, and *Gorgon*, 6, paddle, to proceed to Beyrout.[2] Napier received the dispatch on August 10th, and, two days later, anchored before the town.

Beyrout was chosen because it was on the flank of the Egyptian

[1] By her adherence to the treaty of July 15th, 1841.   [2] Napier, 'Napier,' ii. 7.

advance; because it was the best port in the neighbourhood of the Lebanon, the semi-independent inhabitants of which, under their own chief, the Emir Beschir, had recently rebelled against Mehemet Ali; and because it was hoped to support and utilise the mountaineers against the invader. Beyrout itself, however, was occupied by about 11,000 men of the Egyptian army, and by about 4000 Turkish soldiers, who had been landed from the deserting fleet. In military command was Suleiman Pasha,[1] a very capable French renegade, who had served under the first Napoleon. His camp lay outside, and to the northward of, the town, the seaward defences of which, consisting chiefly of three forts, were too old to be of any serious value. Stopford, with the major part of the Mediterranean fleet, remained for the time in the neighbourhood of the Dardanelles, firstly as a protection to Constantinople against a *coup de main* by Mehemet Ali, secondly as a guard against possible French interference, and thirdly as convoy for a Turkish squadron of men-of-war and transports, which was assembling to proceed to Cyprus and Syria under Captain Baldwin Wake Walker, R.N., who had taken service as an admiral with Turkey. It had been determined among the Powers that the naval part of the task of carrying out the decision of the signatories should be entrusted to Great Britain and Austria-Hungary; and, accordingly, a small but well-found Austrian division presently joined Stopford, and put itself under his orders. (*See* table, p. 312.)

The brief campaign which followed was a remarkable illustration of the military importance of command of the sea. On shore was a triumphant and, upon the whole, formidable army of 70,000 or 80,000 men, pressing northwards. At Alexandria was a large but by no means efficient Egyptian fleet, which, had the sea been open to it, could have accompanied the left wing of the advancing army, protected it, and supplied it. But the sea was not open to it. The less numerous yet much more efficient fleet under Stopford not only terrorised the Egyptians into remaining under the forts of Alexandria, or captured such vessels as ventured out, but also struck blow after blow on the flank of Mehemet Ali's communications, landed and supported troops there, and, in less than two months, so imperilled the conquering army of Egypt that the rebellious viceroy was glad to make terms.

---

[1] Originally the general was Abbas Pasha; but Suleiman succeeded him ere actual hostilities began.

Ships.	Guns.	Commanders.	Ships.	Guns.	Commanders.
Asia . . .	84	Capt. Wm. Fisher.	*Princess Char-lotte.* . . .	104	Adm. Hon. Sir Robt. Stopford, G.C.B., G.C.M.G.
Bellerophon . .	80	Capt. Chas. Jno. Austen (1).			Capt. Arthur Fanshawe.
Benbow . . .	72	Capt. Houston Stewart.			
Cambridge . .	78	Capt. Edw. Barnard.	*Revenge* . . .	76	Capt. Hon. Wm. Waldegrave (2).
Carysfort. . .	26	Capt. Hy. Byam Martin.			
Castor. . . .	36	Capt. Edw. Collier.	*Rodney* . . .	92	Capt. Sir Thos. Mansell(1), Kt.
Cyclops, padd. .	6	Capt. Horatio Thos. Austin.	*Stromboli*, padd..	4	Com. Woodford Jno. Williams.
Daphne . . .	18	Capt. Jno. Windham Dalling.			
Dido	18	Capt. Lewis Davies, C.B.	*Talbot*. . . .	26	Capt. Hy. Jno. Codrington.
Edinburgh . .	72	Capt. Wm. Wilmott Henderson.	*Thunderer* . .	84	Capt. Maur. Fredk. Fitzhardinge Berkeley.
Ganges . . .	84	Capt. Barrington Reynolds, C.B.	*Vesuvius*, padd..	4	Com. Thos. Henderson.
			Vanguard . .	80	Capt. Sir David Dunn, Kt.
Gorgon, padd. .	6	Capt. Wm. Honyman Henderson.	*Wasp*	16	Com. Geo. Mansel.
			Zebra	16	Com. Jas. Jno. Stopford.
Hastings . . .	72	Capt. Jno. Lawrence.			
Hazard . . .	18	Com. Hon. Chas. Gilbert Jno. Brydone Elliot.	Austrian :*		
			Medea . . .	48	R.-Adm. Franz Baron Bandiera.
Hecate, padd. .	6	Com. Jas. Hamilton Ward.			Com. Johann von Buratovich.
Hydra, padd. .	6	Com. Robt. Spencer Robinson.	*Guerriera* . .	49	Capt. H.I.H. Archduke Friedrich.
Implacable . .	74	Capt. Edward Harvey.	*Lipsia* . . .	20	Lieut. Peter Madalena.
Magicienne . .	24	Capt. Fredk. Thos. Michell.	*Clemenza* . .	21	Lieut. Peter Logotetti.
Medea, padd.. .	4	Com. Fredk. Warden.	*Veneto* . . .	17	Lieut. Augustin Milonopulo.
Phœnix, padd. .	4	Com. Robt. Fanshawe Stopford.	*Montecuccoli* .	17	Sec. Lieut. Ludwig von Kudriafsky.
Pique	36	Capt. Edw. Boxer.	*Maria Anna,* str. . . .	6	Sec. Lieut. Peter Manessi.
Powerful. . .	84	Commod. Chas. Napier (2), C.B.	*Arethusa*, schr.	12	Sec. Lieut. Anton Basilisco.

And the Turkish ships, an 84, bearing the flag of R.-Ad. Baldwin Wake Walker (Capt. R.N.); and a cutter, 8, captured from the Egyptians, etc.

* Here, Captain = Linienschiffs-Capitän; Commander = Fregatten-Capitän; Lieutenant = Corvetten-Capitän : Second Lieutenant = Linienschiffs-Lieutenant   For the names of these officers I am indebted to Capt. Leopold Freiherr v. Jedina, Imp. and Roy. Aust, Hung. Navy.

Napier, as has been said, anchored off Beyrout on August 12th. He placed his ships in such positions as best to cover the seaward forts and the Egyptian camp. He also opened communications with the governor of the place, with the commander of the revolted Turkish troops, who were supposed to be anxious to return to their allegiance, with the British consul in the town, and with the Emir Beschir, chief of the Lebanon. But, as the twenty days' grace had not expired, he did not feel at liberty to take decided action, although, more than once, he unwisely made threats that he would do so, and thus, perhaps, by non-performance of them, encouraged resistance. He did, however, detain several vessels that were proceeding up the coast with supplies, and, among others, a fine Egyptian frigate, armed *en flûte*, and bound for Scanderoon. She was taken by the *Castor*. A general blockade of Syria and Egypt was also declared. Napier utilised the days of delay by making reconnaissances in the *Gorgon* at various points where it seemed possible to land troops, and by visiting Walker Bay, who was then at Cyprus. He was joined, off Beyrout, by the *Magicienne*, 24, paddle, on August 19th, the *Wasp*, 16, on August 30th, the *Revenge*, 76, on August 31st, and

later by the *Benbow*, 72,[1] *Pique*, 36, etc., ere, on September 7th, the
Cyclops arrived with definite news of the rejection of the ultimatum,
and heralded the approach of the main body of the allied fleets,[2]
which appeared on September 9th. On September 1st, too, there
reached Beyrout a small British force of artillery and engineers
under Colonel Sir Charles Felix Smith, R.E., who was ill at the
time, and who was unable, for several weeks afterwards, to assume,
as had been intended, the command of the shore operations.

Napier had always a great repugnance to serving under anyone's
orders;[3] and he knew, of course, that on the arrival of Stopford,
that distinguished officer would be supreme afloat. Recollecting
with pleasure his own military experiences in the Peninsula, and,
later, in Portugal, where he did the work of general as well as of
admiral, and taking advantage of Smith's illness, he came to the
extraordinary decision that, rather than be a junior afloat, he would,
if possible, be in supreme command ashore; and, with that end in
view, he induced Stopford to allow him provisionally to take Smith's
place, "as no enemy was likely to be met with "[4] where he was
going. Stopford, perhaps. was not sorry to get rid of his brave, but
excitable and excentric subordinate.[5] Napier, on the other hand, had

---

[1] With arms for the Lebanon people, etc.

[2] The *Implacable*, 74, and *Asia*, 84, being, however, left before Alexandria.

[3] Napier, 'Napier,' ii. 26, 32.

[4] Stopford to Napier, Sept. 8th. (This date is in Napier. It seems to be an error
for 9th, but I have failed to see the original.)

[5] A curious picture of Napier at the time is furnished by an extract from the journal,
dated Dec. 11th, 1840, of Lieutenant Robert Hilley Elliot, then of the *Powerful*: "He
is," says Elliot, "by no means a great weight, perhaps fourteen stone, about my own
weight, but stouter and broader built; stoops from a wound in his neck; walks lame
from another in his leg; turns out one of his feet; and has a most slouching, slovenly
gait, a large round face with black bushy eyebrows, a double chin, scraggy grey
uncurled whiskers, and thin hair; wears a superfluity of shirt collar, and small neck-
handkerchief, always bedaubed with snuff, which he takes in immense quantities;
usually has his trousers far too short, and wears the ugliest pair of old shoes he can
find; and altogether takes so little pride in his dress that, I believe, you might
substitute a green or black coat for his uniform one, without his being a bit the wiser.
Still, he makes all of us conform to strict uniform. This a correct portrait of him;
but mind, you are not to laugh at him, for I do think he is one of the greatest
characters of the day; and many is the person who has come on board just to have a
sight of such a rum old fellow. He is by no means a pleasant officer to serve under;
but one must forgive much for the honour of being commanded by such a character.
His high, honourable principles and gentlemanly feelings are beyond dispute; yet he
is snappish and irritable at times; but shines particularly at the head of his own table,
which is always well found, and no want of wine." His granddaughter, Mrs. Safford,
tells me, moreover, that she recollects Sir Charles, when upwards of seventy, insisting
upon wearing a very "loud" print shirt, the pattern upon which consisted of small
figures of ballet girls, in black.—W. L. C.

no idea of going where there was no enemy, and had very vivid dreams of again distinguishing himself as a soldier. So well did he play his cards that he was permitted to land immediately after the arrival of the Commander-in-Chief. He remained on shore for a month, and, as will be seen, rendered good service.

By the morning of September 9th, thirty-three British, Austrian, and Turkish warships, besides French and American neutrals, and numerous transports, were visible from Beyrout; and in the afternoon all of them lay at anchor before the town. That evening the Turkish troops and British Marines [1] were put on board steamers, and, on the following morning, were moved in an ostentatious manner to the southward, the Egyptians marching along the coast to prevent them from disembarking, and being occasionally shelled by the ships. But as soon as the sea-breeze fairly set in, the landing force was rapidly carried to D'jounie Bay, about nine miles to the northward, and there put ashore without opposition, the *Powerful*, *Revenge*, *Thunderer*, *Pique*, *Castor*, *Carysfort*, *Daphne*, *Wasp*, and three Turkish vessels being at hand to protect it in case of need. Napier's [2] composite army, consisting ultimately of British, Austrians, Turks, and local natives, entrenched itself. It lay in a good position, as the only road between it and Beyrout passed round a projecting point two miles south of the camp, and was completely exposed to the guns of the *Revenge*, which anchored off it. During these and the following days, Beyrout was frequently bombarded by the fleet, and its walls and defences were demolished; but no serious effort was made to take the town, as the army was not then ready to occupy it.

The first serious fighting of the campaign occurred on September 11th at D'jebel (otherwise Gebail), a small fort or castle to the northward, whither the *Carysfort*, *Dido*, and *Cyclops* were detached, under Captain Henry Byam Martin, with a landing-party of 220 Marines and 150 armed mountaineers. The position, which was held by 300 Albanians in Egyptian pay, was bombarded by the ships for about an hour; and then 100 of the Marines, under Captain Charles Robinson, R.M., and as many natives, were put ashore to storm it. Unfortunately the gallant Marines, when within thirty yards of the fort, came unexpectedly upon a crenelled outwork, which had a deep ditch in front of it, and which was completely screened from the

---

[1] Under Lt.-Col. William Walker, R.M.

[2] Lieut. Stephen Bradley, of the *Powerful*, went with Napier as aide-de-camp.

ships; and they were received with so deadly a musketry fire that five of the party were killed, and eighteen wounded. Robinson, after vainly trying to find another way into the fort, had no option but to withdraw. As the party, which was accompanied by Captain Horatio Thomas Austin, was retiring, it was perceived that a British flag had been left behind, flying from a garden wall where it had been placed as a signal. Lieutenant Sidney Grenfell, and a seaman named Macdonald, of the *Cyclops*, volunteered to return and rescue it; and, amid cheers from the ships, safely accomplished their purpose. In spite of their temporary success, the Albanians abandoned the place during the following night; and it was immediately occupied,[1] whereupon large numbers of natives flocked to it to obtain arms. On September 15th, the *Hastings*, *Carysfort*, and *Cyclops* captured Batroun without much trouble. On the 17th, under direction of Captain Edward Collier, Caiffa, and, on the 24th, Tyre (otherwise Tsour), were similarly taken, no loss being suffered by the *Castor* and *Pique*, the only two British ships employed. But an attack upon Tortosa, on September 26th, by the *Benbow*, *Carysfort*, *Zebra*, and landing-parties, was disastrous and unsuccessful, though it brought credit to many engaged, and especially to Lieutenants Edward Philips Charlewood,[2] and Lewis Maitland,[3] and Midshipmen John Charles Dalrymple Hay, and William Houston Stewart, who showed great gallantry. The attacking boats ran upon a reef under fire, and could not be got off until eight of their people had been killed and eighteen wounded.[4]

Ere this, Stopford had more than once shown an inclination to recall Napier to the legitimate work of a naval officer, and to leave the conduct of the army in the capable hands of Selim Pasha, Omar Bey,[5] General Jochmus, and Lieut.-Colonel William Walker, R.M. But Napier always over-persuaded his good-natured chief, and, after winning a little action on the Nahr-el-Kelb on September 24th, and taking 400 prisoners, dined on the following day with Sir Robert, and induced him to entrust his subordinate with the direction of an attack on Sidon by land and sea, the Commodore promising to do the business, and to return within forty-eight hours. For this

---

[1] Napier, 'Napier,' ii. 37, 38, 42.
[2] Com. Nov. 5th, 1840.
[3] Com. Feb. 15th, 1841.
[4] Elliot's journal in 'Napier.'
[5] Later, as Pasha, commanding the Turkish army on the Danube, etc., in the war of 1854–5.

expedition the *Thunderer, Gorgon, Cyclops, Wasp, Stromboli, Hydra, Guerriera* (Austrian), and *Gulfideh* (Turkish) were told off, with a landing force of 750 British Marines under Captains Arthur Morrison, R.M., and James Whylock, R.M., 100 Austrians, and 500 Turks.

Sidon was protected by a moderately strong fort and citadel, and a line of wall, held by 2700 men. It was the main depôt for the southern division of the Egyptian army, and was full of stores and ammunition. Having been in vain summoned, it was bombarded by the ships for about half an hour. Captain Horatio Thomas Austin then landed with the Turks, but was so hotly received that it was clear that the spirit of the garrison had not been shaken. The bombardment was therefore renewed for a time; and, when the wall had been breached, Napier himself, at the head of part of the Marines, tried to storm it. He failed; but succeeded in breaking in at another point, whence, skirting the eastern wall as far as the upper gate, which he burst open, he seized the citadel. At about the same time Captain W. H. Henderson, of the *Gorgon*, had made a successful assault elsewhere. Upon the whole, the slaughter was not heavy, nor were the losses on the attacking side very serious.[1] The whole garrison was captured; and half of it was embarked, and so speedily despatched, that it reached Stopford off Beyrout the same evening. Napier rejoined the Admiral off D'jounie well within the stipulated forty-eight hours. There were numerous acts of individual gallantry, Midshipman James Hunt,[2] of the *Stromboli*, and Midshipman Domenico Chinca,[3] of the *Guerriera*, being especially mentioned for the rivalry which each displayed to be the first to plant the colours of his nation on the walls. The bravery of Mate Arthur Cumming (*Cyclops*), was also noticed in dispatches, where, too, the services of Captains Henderson and Austin, Commanders R. S. Robinson, W. J. Williams, and G. Mansel,[4] and Captains (R.M.) Morrison and Whylock met with various meeds of praise.

During all this time there was frequent firing at Beyrout, though, for the reasons already given, no attempt was made to occupy the place. On October 2nd, however, an Egyptian deserter who reached the *Hastings*, reported that the commander ashore had laid a train

---

[1] The only British officer killed was Lieut. Charles Francis Hockin.
[2] Lieut. Aug. 12th, 1841.   [3] Chinca was successful.
[4] Posted as from Sept. 28th, 1840.

across a bridge to the eastern fort, where lay a great quantity of
powder, and was ready to blow it up at any moment. The man
offered to guide a party to cut the train and seize the ammunition;
and Commander Henry Worth, upon volunteering for the hazardous
service, found no lack of men to join him. He pulled in in a boat of
the *Hastings*, covered by the launch and pinnace of the *Edinburgh*,
and, landing on the bridge in face of a heavy musketry fire, cut
the train, re-embarked again, again landed, forced a way into the
fort, thence threw sixty or seventy barrels of powder into the sea,
and brought away twenty others. Later in the day, he made a
second attempt and brought away some more. It was a most
brilliant exploit, which, in after times, would have won a Victoria
Cross. Nor, all things considered, was the loss severe. Midshipman —— Luscombe, of the *Hastings*, was killed, and three seamen
and the Egyptian guide were wounded.[1]

A little later it was determined by the Admiral and Commodore
to capture Beyrout by a concerted movement. On October 8th,
part of Napier's troops, under General Jochmus, occupied Kornet
Sherouan (otherwise Ornagacuan[2]), with a view to the commencement of a movement for intercepting the retreat of Suleiman Pasha.
Napier himself went to Kornet Sherouan, on the following day,
after having written overnight to quiet Sir Robert Stopford's
apprehensions concerning his subordinate's rashness. The *Princess
Charlotte* returned from D'jounie to Beyrout; two other vessels took
up their station ready to land troops in St. George's Bay; and the
Bellerophon lay near the mouth of the Dog River with orders to
prepare to cover the retreat of the army. The enemy attacked,
with some temporary success, but was driven back. On October 10th,
deterred by the movements threatening their rear, the Egyptians
evacuated Beyrout; and Napier received from Stopford notes
apprising him that Sir Charles Felix Smith had at length arrived to
take command of the army, and ordering the Commodore to retire.
Instead of retiring, Napier advanced, attacking the enemy in front
with a force led by Master Edward John Phillips Pearn,[3] and
endeavouring to turn his right with a smaller force under Lieutenant
Robert Duncan[4] (*Powerful*). Napier found not Suleiman but Ibrahim
Pasha himself in his front; both movements were checked; and,

---

[1] Elliot's journal in ' Napier.'   [2] So wrongly called in Napier's disps.
[3] Who had been with Napier in Portugal. *See* p. 266, *antea.*
[4] Com. Nov. 4th, 1840.

when reinforcements were sent for, Izzet Pasha, who had been left at Kornet Sherouan, declined to send them. At that difficult moment the situation was undoubtedly saved by the mad and infectious bravery of the Commodore, who led his staff on what was practically a forlorn hope, carried the first position in his front, and then, literally driving his troops onwards, rushed the next position, turned Ibrahim out pell-mell, took 700 prisoners, and so won the battle of Boharsef. His victory probably saved him from being brought before a court-martial for direct and deliberate disobedience to orders. In spite of his victory, there should have been a court of inquiry, if nothing further. But Stopford, one of the most kind-hearted and forgiving of men, wrote a letter of generous praise to his subordinate, and declined to assert himself in any way. Napier then returned to his duties afloat. Next day part of the Egyptian army surrendered, Suleiman, however, getting away with 300 horse.

Napier had already reconnoitred St. Jean d'Acre, and had been fired at. He reconnoitred again in the early days of October, going thither in a steamer, and sounding in front of the works, which were very strong towards the sea, and mounted 130 guns, and about 30 mortars. The fortress had been in the occupation of the Egyptians since 1837, and it had since been continually strengthened; but it was still far from what Ibrahim Pasha's engineers had intended to make it. Sir Robert Stopford, if we may believe the accounts of Napier and Elliot, showed some unwillingness to attack it without orders; but at length there came definite instructions from the Admiralty; and, in accordance with them, on October 31st, the fleet, which still lay off Beyrout, was directed to take on board a large force of troops, and to prepare for sea. On the same evening it sailed, the ships, British, Austrian and Turkish, including eight of the line, five frigates, five steamers, and two brigs.[1]

The steamers—which, it should be noted, first convincingly demonstrated their great utility in this war—preceded the squadron, and summoned Acre to surrender. The rest of the expedition, detained by light winds, did not anchor off the place until the evening of November 2nd. "The town," says Elliot, "is low, standing on an angle presenting two faces to the sea, both walled

---

[1] *Princess Charlotte, Powerful, Thunderer, Bellerophon, Revenge, Benbow, Edinburgh, Pique, Castor, Carysfort, Talbot, Hazard, Phœnix, Wasp,* and three Austrian and three Turkish vessels.

and covered with cannon—in one place a double tier." After
further soundings had been made under cover of the darkness, it
was decided that it would be difficult to take the ships close enough
in to breach the walls within a reasonable time. It was therefore
determined to open a general bombardment of the town.

On the morning of the 3rd, the breeze was so light that nothing
could be done until about ten o'clock, when, a wind springing up,
the ships weighed, and stood for their assigned stations. Stopford
kept his flag flying in the *Princess Charlotte*, but went on board
the *Phœnix*, so as to be able better to superintend operations, and
to move to any point where his presence might be desirable. The
Powerful led in, and was followed in order by the *Princess Charlotte*,
Thunderer, *Bellerophon*, and *Revenge*. Behind this first division
came the second, led by the Turkish admiral (Captain Baldwin
Wake Walker, R.N.), and consisting of that gallant officer's own
ship, followed by the *Benbow*, *Edinburgh*, *Pique*, *Castor*, *Hazard*,
Carysfort, *Talbot*, *Wasp*, and the three Austrian and two remaining
Turkish vessels. The first division made its slow way to the
western, and the second to the southern face of the fortress. The
positions taken up by the various ships will be seen on reference
to the plan overleaf. They did not, for the most part, reach them
until two o'clock.

The advance was greeted with a few dropping shots from the
batteries; but no reply was made until the ships were near their
assigned stations, and about to anchor by the stern with another
anchor ahead. The fire then became general, and, within a few
minutes, waxed furious. The smoke began to hang even before the
ships actually anchored; and thus the defenders, who had wrongly
supposed that their enemy would not venture inside the shoal, were
deceived as to the exact stations of the ships, and gave their guns
too great an elevation. This fact materially lessened the damage
and loss suffered by the fleet, and caused most of the shot that
found billets to take effect aloft. Indeed, so confident were the
Egyptians that Stopford would lie outside the shoal that, says
Elliot, they had " built up the lower part of the embrasures with
stones and sandbags for protection ; so that they could not depress "
their guns " again, and were so enveloped in their own smoke,
as well as ours blowing right in their faces, that they scarcely ever
got a sight of us, and never knew where they fired." [1]

[1] Napier, ' Napier,' ii. 95, 116.

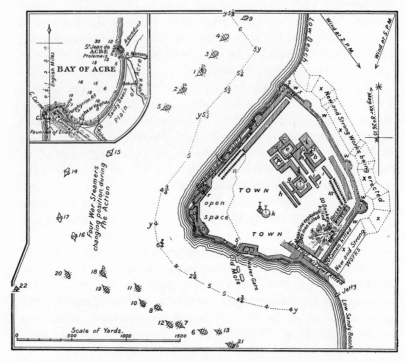

BOMBARDMENT OF ST. JEAN D'ACRE, NOVEMBER 3RD, 1840.

(From the chart by Mr. J. C. Brettell, sometime Engineer-in-Chief to Mehemet Ali.)

REFERENCES TO THE PLAN.

SHIPS.

1. *Princess Charlotte.*	9. *Pique.*	16. *Stromboli.*
2. *Powerful.*	10. *Carysfort.*	17. *Vesuvius.*
3. *Thunderer.*	11. *Talbot.*	18. *Medea* (Aust.).
4. *Bellerophon.*	12. *Hazard.*	19. *Guerriera* (Aust.).
5. *Revenge.*	13. *Wasp.*	20. *Lipsia* (Aust.).
6. *Benbow.*	14. *Gorgon.*	21. Turkish 84 (flag).
7. *Edinburgh.*	15. *Phœnix.*	22. Turkish cutter.
8. *Castor.*		

a. Harem.	*h.* Bazaar.	*q.* Unfinished work.
b. Castle.	*iii.* Stores.	*rr.* Observation towers.
c. Abdallah Pasha's harem.	*k.* Mosque.	*ss.* Mortar batteries.
d. Governor's divan.	*l.* Fortified khan.	*tt.* Traverses.
e. Hospital.	*m.* 45 brass field-pieces.	*ww.* Outer ditch.
f. Accountant-general's divan.	*n.* 47 brass field-pieces.	*xx.* Glacis.
g. Mosque.	*o.* Half-moon battery.	*yy.* Soundings.
	p. High battery.	

The Allies had midshipmen at their mast-heads to direct and correct the aim, and, whenever the smoke grew too thick, desisted for a short time. Yet the bombardment went on with very little relaxation for nearly three hours. A most frightful explosion then flung half the town into the air, and shook every ship to her keel, the concussion knocking down the seamen at their guns half a mile away. The grand magazine had blown up, killing, it is believed, upwards of 1200 people, and absolutely wrecking a space of about 60,000 square yards. This awful catastrophe sounded the fate of the town, the firing from which thereafter weakened, though a few guns were gallantly worked until the last. Towards sunset Stopford signalled to discontinue the action. Napier, however, who already, in consequence of a shift of wind, had taken up a position different from the one assigned to the *Powerful* in the original plan of attack, was, as usual, a law unto himself, and persisted with an intermittent fire until the Flag-Lieutenant brought him orders to withdraw. He then had to get a steamer to tow him out of gunshot. His action on this occasion brought on unpleasant friction with the Commander-in-Chief, and led the Commodore to demand a court-martial, which was very properly refused.

The Egyptian loss was heavy, even leaving out that caused by the explosion. About three hundred people were killed in the batteries, and nearly all the guns on the sea face were disabled. The fleet suffered very little except aloft, and had but 14 British,[1] and 4 Turks killed, and 42[2] wounded. The result would have been very different, and probably very disastrous, if the Egyptians had not blocked up their embrasures, and made false assumptions as to the probable positions of the ships, and if the explosion of the main magazine had not deprived them of most of their powder. On the day after the action, a smaller accidental explosion killed a number of Turks and a Marine, and wounded Captain Edward Collier, of the *Castor*, and the Chaplain of the *Princess Charlotte*.

Soon after midnight Captain Walker observed that the enemy was evacuating the town, and sent word to that effect to Stopford and Napier. Early on the 4th, therefore, the troops, and some Austrian marines were landed, and, uniting with 5000 men who had marched down from Beyrout, took quiet possession of the place, and detached a strong force in pursuit of the Egyptians, who fled to

[1] Including Lieutenant G. B. Le Mesurier (*Talbot*).
[2] Including Com. Francis Decimus Hastings (*Edinburgh*), posted Nov. 4, 1840.

the southward. The *Pique*, joined presently by the *Stromboli*, was left off the fortress, which was garrisoned by Sir Charles Smith with 3000 Turks, and 250 Marines under Lieut.-Colonel Walker; and it was determined to detach Napier to take command off Alexandria. After watering at Beyrout, he quitted that port for the purpose on November 15th, and, on the 21st, joined the *Rodney*, *Revenge*, *Vanguard*, *Cambridge*, *Carysfort*, and *Medea* on his station. There, with characteristic independence, and without any official authority, he entered into negotiations with Mehemet Ali, first using as his emissary Captain Sir Thomas Mansell, of the *Rodney*, an old friend of the Pasha's, and then himself entering Alexandria in the *Medea*, and meeting Mehemet. The result was that on November 27th a convention was signed, in virtue of which it was engaged that Ibrahim Pasha should evacuate Syria, and that, contingent upon the guarantee to Mehemet of the hereditary government of Egypt, the Ottoman fleet should be restored. Napier, even before the convention was actually signed, wrote to the Admiralty a letter beginning: "I do not know whether I have done right or not in settling the Eastern question,"[1] and, to his wife, "You have seen me a Lord High Admiral, a Commodore, and a General. I have now turned a Negotiator, and have made peace with Mahomet Ali. . . . I shall either be hung by the Government, or made a Bishop."[2] On November 28th, a gale drove the squadron from off Alexandria, and ultimately caused several ships, including the *Powerful*, to seek shelter, in a more or less disabled condition, in Marmorice Bay, where, on December 9th, Stopford, in the *Princess Charlotte*, also dropped anchor. This gale, on December 2nd, caused the wreck, off Mount Carmel, of the *Zebra*, 16, Commander Robert Fanshawe Stopford, and the loss of several of her people.

The Porte, the British Ambassador at Constantinople, Sir Robert Stopford, and Sir Charles Smith, all disapproved strongly of Napier's action, and denied his right to take such a course; but the four Powers had already, on November 14th, made up their minds that, if he should prove tractable, Mehemet Ali should be dealt with much as Napier had dealt with him; and ultimately the Convention, with slight modifications, was ratified, Napier, who had just previously been made a Commodore of the first (red) class, getting a K.C.B. dated December 4th, 1840, and, later, being

[1] To Minto: Nov. 26th.   [2] To Mrs. Napier, Nov. 26th.

thanked by Lord Palmerston for his management of affairs at
Alexandria, whither he was sent to see to the carrying out of the
Convention, with his broad pennant in the *Carysfort.*

Among the numerous honours and promotions conferred upon
naval officers in respect of their services during the Syrian campaign
of 1840 may be mentioned :—

To be K.C.B., Captain Charles Napier (2), C.B.

To be C.B., Captains Sir Baldwin Wake Walker (Hon.) ; Charles John Austen (1) ;
Hon. William Waldegrave (2) ; Maurice Frederick Fitzhardinge Berkeley ; Edward
Collier ; William Wilmott Henderson ; Arthur Fanshawe ; Houston Stewart ; Edward
Boxer ; Henry Byam Martin ; Henry John Codrington ; William Honyman
Henderson ; Horatio Thomas Austin ; and Lieut.-Col. William Walker, R.M.

In addition, ten Commanders were posted, and three noted for
promotion upon becoming qualified ; and great numbers of Lieutenants and Mates were advanced a step in rank.

In the course of 1840, in more distant seas, a bloody and
disastrous affair had, meantime, occurred at Tongatabu, one of the
Friendly Islands. A war was raging between the native Christians
and the rest of the islanders, and, to assist the former, Commander
Walter Croker, of the *Favourite*, 18, landed on June 24th with 90
officers, seamen and Marines, and joined a body of 1500 natives in
the attack on a fastness five miles from the coast. In the act of
storming, the natives deserted ; and the British, having suffered very
heavily, were obliged to retire. Croker was killed ; and the first
Lieutenant, Robert John Wallace Dunlop, was desperately wounded.
The second Lieutenant, Edward Pelham Brenton von Donop, who
succeeded to the command, not only carried off Croker's body under
a terrible fire, but also, finding that the colours had been left behind
during the retreat, returned with one man, and rescued them.[1] At
a later date his gallantry would have won him the Victoria Cross.

The good work which was done for the suppression of piracy on
the coasts of Borneo, and in the Eastern Archipelago, in 1843 and
the following years, was undertaken chiefly at the suggestion of that
distinguished pioneer and administrator, James Brooke. Brooke
had been in the East India Company's service, had fought in the
Burmese War, had been wounded, and had returned to England.
He had subsequently again visited the Eastern Archipelago, and,
having satisfied himself that much might be done there towards
developing the enormous resources of the islands, had once more

[1] O'Byrne, 316, 1231.

gone home, had purchased a 142-ton yacht, the *Royalist*, and, proceeding to Sarawak, in Borneo, had induced the Rajah Muda Hassim to entrust him with the government of the province, which he afterwards acquired as his own. In January, 1843, Captain the Hon. Henry Keppel, of the *Dido*, 18, became senior naval officer in the Straits Settlements. On March 17th, being then at Singapore,

ADMIRAL OF THE FLEET THE HON. SIR HENRY KEPPEL, G.C.B., D.C.L.

(From an engraving by D. J. Pound, after a photograph by Mayall, taken about 1863, when Sir Henry was a Rear-Admiral.)

Keppel met Brooke at dinner, and, as he says, " was initiated into the mysteries, depths and horrors of pirates in the ways of the Malay Peninsula."[1] After much discussion, the two men agreed that the only way in which to strike at the root of the evil would be to destroy the piratical strongholds in the interior of Borneo, and not to allow them again to prepare and send forth their fleets of prahus.

[1] 'Sailor's Life,' i. 289.

On May 1st, therefore, Keppel embarked Brooke, and sailed for Borneo. On the 8th, he detached three of his boats, under Lieutenant Frederick Wilmot Horton, to cruise among the islands to the northward; and these, guided by Brooke, defeated six prahus, some or all of which belonged to the Rajah of Rhio. The boats rejoined the *Dido* in the Morataba river, just below the town of Sarawak.[1] From Sarawak, Keppel sent one of Brooke's Sarawak-built boats, the *Jolly Bachelor*, armed with a brass 6-pr., and a volunteer crew under Lieutenant James Hunt, to cruise off Cape Datu, but on no account to land. Hunt, however, did land on May 20th to cook his provisions, and then hauled the boat out to her grapnel near some rocks for the night, with her people, twenty-two all told, on board. At 3 A.M. on the 21st, he was attacked by two large prahus. After a close and hot fight, one, in a sinking condition, was taken. The other, helped by a third which came to her assistance, got away, but with heavy loss. Each of these prahus carried two guns, and about fifty men. Hunt, who might well have been censured for his disobedience, received instead the thanks of the Commander-in-Chief and of the Admiralty.[2]

Having received from the Rajah Muda Hassim a formal complaint concerning the depredations of the pirates of Sarebas and Sakarran, Keppel and Brooke completed their preparations. The ship's boats, and others, were manned and armed; the *Dido* was anchored about two miles inside the entrance of the Sarebas river,[3] and, early in June, the flotilla pressed up towards the stronghold of the Sarebas pirates. In the *Dido's* gig were Keppel and Brooke; in the second gig, Lieutenant Edmund Hall Gunnell; in the pinnace, Lieutenant Frederick Wilmot Horton, with Mate William Luke Partridge, Assistant-Surgeon John Simpson, M.D.,[4] and Midshipman Ramsay Henry Hallowes; in the first cutter, Midshipman Edward Henry Hughes d'Aeth; in the second cutter, Master James Edward Elliott, and Midshipman Robert Jenkins; and in the *Jolly Bachelor*, Lieutenant William Tottenham, and Midshipman Henry Wandesford Comber. The *Dido* supplied eighty officers and men, and, in addition, there were numerous volunteers, and native auxiliaries.

On June 11th, a sudden turn of the river brought the expedition

---

[1] Then called Kuching. The name was altered in July, 1844.
[2] 'Sailor's Life,' i. 304; O'Byrne, 555.
[3] About 50 miles N.E. of Sarawak.
[4] Died soon after at Singapore.

opposite to a battery of brass guns, fronted by a barrier of stakes. There were other batteries further up. D'Aeth, in the first cutter, and Keppel, in the gig, found a way through almost simultaneously, and, rushing up the incline, D'Aeth captured the first battery before it had time to fire its guns a second time. He had only three people wounded. The neighbouring town of Paddi was thereupon burnt, and the flying enemy was pursued up the river towards Lyai by Horton and Brooke, who were presently followed by Keppel. Desultory firing continued during the night, and on the 12th, the Malays asked for a truce and a conference. The upshot was that they agreed to abandon piracy if their lives were spared.

On the 14th, Pakoo,[1] where there was little resistance, suffered the same fate as Paddi. On the 17th, while the expedition was on its way to Rembas,[2] another stronghold, it encountered a very formidable barrier of stakes; but the obstacle was cut through, and Rembas was also burnt.[3] In all these operations it does not appear that more than eight people in all were hurt on the side of the attacking force. The loss of the pirates was very heavy.

Keppel, being ordered to another part of the station, was unable, at that time, further to carry out his plans. After his departure two traders, the *Anna* and the *Young Queen*, belonging to, and accompanied by, the Hon. James Erskine Murray,[4] had occasion to enter the River Cote, and anchor off Tongarron. There, on February 16th, 1844, they were treacherously attacked by masked batteries and gunboats, and, slipping their cables, began an almost hopeless attempt to fight their way out. After thirty-six hours' continuous fighting, they sustained a final and very bloody action at the mouth of the Cote, and so got away, yet not until they had lost Murray and two others killed, and five people wounded.[5] At about the same time the boats of the *Wanderer*, 16, Commander George Henry Seymour, and *Harlequin*, 16, Commander the Hon. George Fowler Hastings, attacked some piratical settlements[6] on the coast of Sumatra, and inflicted considerable damage, though they suffered some loss. The Dutch East Indian authorities sent more than one expedition against

---

[1] Up a lower branch of the Sarebas.

[2] Up yet another branch of the Sarebas.

[3] 'Sailor's Life,' i. 311–321.   Singapore *Free Press*.   *Naut. Mag.*, 1843, 759; 1844, 174.

[4] Born 1810; a Scots advocate, 3rd son of 7th Baron Elibank.

[5] *Hong Kong Gazette.*

[6] *e.g.*, at Murdoo, and Qualloo Battoo.

the freebooters; and, on June 3rd and 4th, 1844, Captain Sir
Edward Belcher, C.B., of the *Samarang*, 26, assisted by Lieutenants
Henry William Baugh, and Thomas Heard, taught a severe lesson to
some pirates off Gillolo, who attacked them while they were making
observations on shore, and who wounded Belcher and a Marine.[1]
But the Malays and Dyaks became bolder, in spite of such half
measures as were taken against them ; and it was not too soon that,
on July 29th, Keppel, in the *Dido*, again entered the River Morataba,
on his way up to Sarawak.

It was determined first to proceed against the pirates of Sakarran,
who had not been chastised on the previous occasion. The *Dido*
was this time aided by the H.E.I. Co.'s steamer *Phlegethon*. On
August 7th, the two vessels were in sight of the fortifications of
Patusen, on the Batang Lupar. The *Dido* despatched four boats,
besides the *Jolly Bachelor*, which she officered and manned. The
Phlegethon sent four boats. The *Dido's* contingent numbered eighty-
six all told, including Lieutenants Charles Francis Wade, and Edward
Winterton Turnour, Master Robert Calder Allen, Mate Edward Henry
Hughes d'Aeth, acting-Mate Robert Jenkins, Midshipman C——
Johnson, and Assistant-Surgeon Robert Beith. The forts, of which
there were five, were shelled by the *Phlegethon*, and then stormed
with great gallantry, the only British loss being one man killed and
two men wounded. No fewer than sixty-four brass guns, besides iron
ones, were found in the place, which was looted and burnt. Hundreds
of prahus were also destroyed. On the same afternoon, a stockaded
post up the river Grahan was evacuated and occupied. Thus a very
serious blow was dealt at a chief who, for twenty years, had been a
leading patron of pirates, but who now found himself without war-
boats, guns, ammunition, or shelter for his followers.

A day or two later the force was divided, Turnour going up the
Undop river, d'Aeth up the Lupar, and Wade and Brooke up the
Sakarran; but, learning that much opposition was in preparation,
Keppel recalled the boats from the Lupar and Sakarran, in order to
concentrate for an attack upon Seriff Muller, a chief possessing a
town about twenty miles up the Undop, on which stream Turnour,
assisted by Master Allen and Mate Comber, had already captured a
couple of stockades. Progress in the Undop was slow and tedious,
there being regular barriers as well as felled trees to be cut through.
On the morning of August 11th, Wade, who had Brooke with him,

[1] Letter in *Naut. Mag.*, 1844, 666.

joined, and by 8 A.M. the last barrier below Seriff Muller's position was cut through. The town, however, was not defended, and the place was plundered and burnt. It was ascertained that the enemy had retired twenty-five miles further up the Undop, and the tedious progress was resumed, only five or six miles, however, being covered before night, during which d'Aeth's command rejoined, and completed the strength of the expedition. The attack on Seriff Muller was made on the 14th. Part of the position had been taken, and the force was temporarily halted, when Keppel and Wade, exploring the jungle with but seven men, suddenly discovered in a creek a number of boats filled with pirates. The officers had each a double-barrelled gun, and Wade impetuously fired and dashed in. He was presently followed by more men, but he could not wait for them to collect in strength, and, pressing on, in spite of Keppel's efforts to check him, was struck by two balls, one of which was fatal. The gallant fellow had himself brought up a prayer-book "in case of accident." That night Keppel read from it Wade's funeral service. On the 15th, the expedition returned to the *Phlegethon*.

On August 17th, the boats started again on an expedition to Karangan, one of the Sakarran strongholds. The native auxiliaries, who were ahead, came into action with the pirates on the 19th, and maintained a bloody flight amid a crowd of boats and rafts in the river; until the arrival of Keppel and Brooke, and of the second gig, containing a rocket tube worked by Master Robert Calder Allen, drove the foe first behind their barriers, and then in general retreat. The losses of the native allies were extremely heavy, owing to the temerity of their leader; and among the killed, 31 in number, was Mr. Steward, a school-fellow and life-long friend of Brooke. Karangan itself was taken without opposition; and on the 20th, the expedition again dropped down to the *Phlegethon*. On the 22nd, off Patusen, that vessel was joined by the boats of the *Samarang*, 26, Captain Sir Edward Belcher, which, upon the strength of reports that Keppel was in serious difficulties, had pushed up to his assistance. They had moved no less than 120 miles in about thirty hours.[1] On August 23rd, the entire force was once more at Sarawak.

It was on returning from this commission that Captain Keppel, finding, upon reaching Portsmouth, that his wife, whom he had not seen for four years, was at Droxford, only thirteen miles away, and that the *Dido* was ordered round to Sheerness to pay off,

[1] 'Sailor's Life,' ii. 18; 'Exped. to Borneo' (Lond. 1846), *passim*.

changed clothes with his Master, Robert Calder Allen, and made that officer personate him, and take the ship to the mouth of the Thames, Keppel himself picking up his wife, driving with her across country in a yellow post-chaise, and, at Sheerness, making a clean breast of his delinquency to the Captain Superintendent, William Henry Shirreff, thanks to whose countenance he was able again to change clothes with Allen, after a three days' absence, apparently without raising any suspicion in the mind of the Commander-in-Chief, Vice-Admiral Sir John Chambers White, K.C.B.[1] The officers in those days did not themselves always observe such strict discipline as they pretended to enforce. But it was an age in which, it is to be feared, the entire service had reached its lowest level of efficiency and keenness. Slackness and indifference, indeed, must have prevailed to an extraordinary extent, not only afloat, but also at the Admiralty, where ships on foreign stations were at times absolutely forgotten by the officials, and so reduced to serious straits. For example, at about the end of 1844, the *Royalist*, 10, reached Singapore from Port Essington, with the following strange story. In a period of twelve months she had lost three commanding officers: Lieutenant Philip Chetwode, and acting Lieutenants Gerald Kingsley and Eudo Wells, and, no official communication whatsoever having reached the brig for upwards of a year and a half, the acting Second Master had been obliged to promote himself to keep the pennant flying, and then, in sheer desperation, had gone to Singapore without orders, both his masts being sprung, and all his gear so dilapidated as to be practically useless.[2] Lieutenant Graham Ogle had been appointed to the *Royalist* in April, 1844, but seems to have been unable to discover her whereabouts, and to have waited resignedly for several months at Hong Kong, in hopes that she would turn up. Mr. Charles Parkinson, the acting Second Master, was not confirmed in his self-given rank.

In 1845 the pirates of the Eastern Archipelago were taught another severe lesson. Rear-Admiral Sir Thomas John Cochrane, after having had various conferences with Mr. Brooke, took the greater part of his squadron to the mouth of the Brunei river, where he anchored on August 6th, and whence, with the *Vixen*, steamer, Commander George Giffard, *Nemesis* (H.E.I. Co.'s steamer), and *Pluto*, steamer, Lieutenant Frederick Lane, a party of 150 Marines, and three or four armed pinnaces, he went up to Brunei to demand

---

[1] 'Sailor's Life,' ii. 28.   [2] *Naut. Mag.*, 1845, 221.

the surrender of a chief named Panquera Usof, who had behaved ill in the matter of some slaves. As Usof did not appear, his house was bombarded and destroyed on August 11th, and a landing party of Marines brought off twenty-one brass guns, and destroyed a powder magazine.

Cochrane then moved round to Malluda Bay, where he arrived on August 17th, and, assembling his Captains, communicated to them his plans for an attack on the pirate chief Seriff Osman, whose head-quarters were in one of the rivers at the head of the opening. Pursuant to these plans, the assigned small-arm men and Marines of the squadron were transferred to the steamers on the morning of the 18th ; and these, with the *Cruiser*, 16, *Wolverine*, 16, and some gunboats in tow, moved up as far as the depth of water would permit. When, the *Pluto* having grounded in her efforts to find a further passage, it became evident that such large craft could not be employed, the Rear-Admiral, whose flag was temporarily in the *Vixen*, ordered Captain Charles Talbot, of the *Vestal*, 26, to put what men he could into the boats, and to proceed. About 340 bluejackets and 200 Marines were accordingly embarked as follows :—

In command: Captain Charles Talbot, *Vestal*.
Second in command: Com. Edward Gennys Fanshawe, *Cruiser*.
In command of landing party: Com. Henry Lyster, *Agincourt*.
Second: Com. Wm. Jno. Cavendish Clifford (*Wolverine*).
Adjutant: Lieut. Jas. Aylmer Dorset Paynter (*Agincourt*).
Commanding Royal Marines: Capt. Saml. Hawkins, R.M.
Marine officers: Lieuts. And. Jno. Buckingham Hambly, Hy. Chas. Penrose Dyer, Jno. Wm. Alex. Kennedy, and Wm. Mansell Mansell, R.M.
Boats of *Agincourt* (4), *Vestal* (3), *Dædalus* (3), *Vixen* (2), *Cruiser* (2), *Wolverine* (2), *Pluto*, and *Nemesis*, under Lieutenants Marcus Lowther, John Reid, Geo. Morritt, Crawford Aitcheson Denham Pasco, Geo. Granville Randolph, Jas. Willcox, Mortimer Harley Rodney, Henry Shank Hillyar, and Thos. Heard (*Samarang*); Mates Phil. Wm. May, John Milward Reeves, Chas. Hy Young, Geo. Durbin, Chas. Nolloth, Edward Frederick Dent, and Leonard Gibbard, etc.

The boats started up against a strong breeze, and met with so many difficulties that they were obliged to anchor below the bar to wait for the tide. They crossed it, however, soon after 10 P.M., and re-anchored for the night. At 7 A.M. on August 19th, they weighed again, Captain Talbot presently going ahead to reconnoitre, and rejoining five miles up the river with the information that the next bend would see the boats in front of the enemy's batteries and stockade, and that below the works a large boom had been thrown across the stream. The launch and second barge of the *Agincourt*, the barge of the *Vestal*, and the launch of the *Dædalus* were then ordered up in line abreast, to anchor by the stern when close to the boom, and to keep up a fire, while the cutters of the *Wolverine*, *Dædalus*, and *Nemesis* were to clear away the boom, supported by the *Vixen's* and *Vestal's* pinnaces, the rest of the boats forming a reserve. Ere these instructions could be fully carried out, a flag of truce was shown from the fort, whereupon Talbot directed the boats to anchor, and demanded unconditional surrender in half an hour. A messenger brought a request from Osman for a parley ; but Talbot refused any concessions, and moved several of his boats up to the boom, the three cutters under Lyster's direction at once beginning to attempt to clear it. Another flag of truce brought news that if a parley were agreed to, two of the boats might go inside the boom ; but Talbot's only reply was that the half hour was nearly up, and that, if Osman did not surrender, action would commence.

No sooner had this flag withdrawn than the batteries opened on the boats, which instantly answered with their 12-pr. carronades, but did not seem to make much impression. When the firing had gone on for about twenty minutes, Lieutenant Paynter obtained permission to land and try the effect of rockets. These materially assisted in disconcerting the defenders ; yet, as the boom still held, the boats could not advance. This necessitated the issue of an order for the guns to husband their ammunition. Not until nearly an hour had elapsed did one end of the boom give way. Then the boats went through with a cheer. This was enough for the pirates, who made but little further resistance, and soon abandoned their works, which were found to be extremely strong. The chief battery, little more than two hundred yards above the boom, mounted one 18-pr., two 12-prs., three 9-prs., and two 6-prs. ; a floating battery of three long 18-prs. enfiladed the boom ; and, for the first half hour or more, the pirates fired splendidly. The loss on the British side was 6 killed, and 15, including 2 mortally, wounded. Mate Leonard Gibbard, of the *Wolverine*, did not long survive his injuries, and Lieutenant Thomas Heard, and Second Master R. E. Pym, acting, of the *Vestal*, were also among the wounded. A party under Commander George Giffard, of the *Vixen*, afterwards destroyed the town, and brought off a number of brass guns.[1]

The proved utility of the boom at Malluda Bay, and of other booms which, about the same time, had been encountered in the course of the operations in New Zealand, led, in the summer of 1846, to the making of a series of experiments at Portsmouth with somewhat similar obstructions, chiefly in order to determine how best they might be destroyed. Although it was then demonstrated

---

[1] *Naut. Mag.*, 1846, 16; *Gazette*, 1845, p. 6534.

that the explosion of charges in immediate contact with them was the most satisfactory method, and although, supposing gunpowder to be insufficient, gun-cotton was already then available, it having been introduced as a serviceable explosive by C. F. Schönbein in 1845, it does not appear that provision was made in the Navy, until many years afterwards, for the supply of charges and fuses proper for the purpose.

Operations against the Borneo pirates were resumed in the summer of 1846, when the frightful atrocities committed by the Sultan of Brunei against allies of the British called for notice. Rear-Admiral Sir Thomas John Cochrane determined to ascend the river to Brunei, and to deal with the Sultan, Omar Ali Suffudee, at his own door. Having, therefore, transferred his flag from the *Agincourt*, 72, to the steamer *Spiteful*, Commander William Maitland, he took in tow the *Hazard*, 18, Commander Francis Philip Egerton, and the *Royalist*, Commander Graham Ogle, and, preceded by the H.E.I. Co.'s steamer *Phlegethon*, Commander R. L. Ross, I.N., started up the Cherimon river on July 7th, accompanied by Mr. Brooke, some gunboats, and the boats, manned and armed, of several ships, including the *Agincourt*, *Iris*, 26, and *Ringdove*, 16. Two batteries near the mouth of the river were neither completed nor garrisoned, and were not then interfered with. The town lay only about nine miles up the stream; but the channel presented so many difficulties that the *Hazard* had to be left aground on the bar, and the rest of the force was unable to cross it until the morning of the 8th.

Just below Pulo Bungore five forts were discovered, "admirably placed," as Cochrane says, " for denying a passage beyond them." When the *Phlegethon* was not far from them, the first of the batteries opened a spirited fire, which was promptly returned, while the boats, commanded by Captain George Rodney Mundy, of the *Iris*, 26, and Lieutenant George Edwin Patey, first of the *Agincourt*, cast off from the steamer, formed in line, made good use of their guns, and, as soon as the enemy's fire had slackened, pushed in and gained the bank. The people instantly rushed the steep ascent to the fort; but the work was promptly abandoned. As Cochrane was anxious to proceed, he allowed Mundy time only to spike the guns, throw them over the walls, and blow up the magazine; and then, having given his men their dinners, he weighed again and engaged the next batteries, which were supported by musketry from the woods on one side of the river. At that point the *Spiteful* narrowly escaped running ashore, and might have suffered heavily, had not the *Phlegethon* made excellent practice, not only with her own guns, but also with a battery of field guns which had been placed in her bows, and with rocket tubes posted on her bridge—all under the direction of Lieutenant James Alymer Dorset Paynter, of the *Agincourt*. The result of this was that the Malays fled without waiting to be attacked by the landing parties; and the works, and heights commanding the town were presently occupied by the Marines, under Captain Samuel Hawkins, R.M. Numerous brass and iron guns, some being 68-prs., were captured, and many of them were ultimately embarked. There were in all five batteries; and, had the enemy stuck to them, a very effective defence might have been made. The losses on the side of the attack were not heavy, only two men being killed and seven wounded. That evening Mundy destroyed all five forts. In his account of the affair, Cochrane specially commends the conduct of Lieutenants Patey[1] and Paynter,[1] Captain Hawkins, R.M., Master James Edward Elliott (*Agincourt*), and Commander Ross, I.N.

Ascertaining that the Sultan had fled, and believing that he might be captured, the Commander-in-Chief despatched Mundy, with the gunboats, 150 Marines, some seamen, and some rocket tubes, in pursuit of the fugitive. In the meantime he destroyed the guns in the unfinished forts near the mouth of the river on the islands of Cherimon and Coin Arrang.

Mundy moved up the river on July 10th, accompanied by Mr. Brooke in his capacity as her Majesty's agent. He was absent altogether for six days, and destroyed several magazines, besides capturing more guns; but he failed to find his quarry. He had to make his way through most difficult swampy country, amid continuous heavy rain, yet, in spite of the terrible discomforts, his force behaved admirably. He mentions with approval the conduct, in very trying circumstances, of Lieutenants George Edwin Patey, Nicholas Vansittart, George Lowcay Norcock, Charles Sydney Dunbar, Edward Edwin Morgan, Edward Morrell Mathews, Leopold George Heath, Charles Frankland Newland, and Francis Beaufort Quin; Captain Samuel Hawkins, R.M.; Mate John Milward Reeves, and other officers.[2]

Cochrane, upon quitting the coast of Borneo, left Mundy, with

---

[1] Com., July 8th, 1846. [2] *Gazette*, 1846, pp. 3438, 3441, 3444.

the *Iris,* and the H.E.I. Co.'s steamer *Phlegethon,* to take further necessary measures against the Malays.   On August 18th, followed by the boats of the two vessels, and by 400 native allies in thirty war prahus, Mundy, accompanied by Brooke, crossed the bar of the Mambacoot river to proceed against Hadji Samon, a powerful partisan of Omar Ali Saffudee, who had a stronghold up the stream.   After about three hours' hard pulling, the boats began to be incommoded by huge rafts which were sent down from above; and, a little later, came upon a line of bamboo stakes supporting an immense boom which had been burst, apparently by the force of freshets.   Within eighty yards of these defences was a fort, which opened fire as soon as the head of the flotilla came in sight of it.   A hot action ensued; and in ten minutes Lieutenant Alexander Little pushed in and rushed the fort, only to find that the swivel guns with which it had been armed had been carried off into the jungle.   The work, however, was destroyed, and the ammunition in it was blown up. A short distance further on a prahu was captured, though her crew escaped.   In the afternoon, some miles higher, a masked battery opened on the boats.   Its fire was speedily silenced, and the enemy driven off.   An hour later the force bivouacked for the night, and, early on the 19th, Hadji Samon's last position was bombarded and captured, the chief, unfortunately, getting away into the jungle, though probably with hardly a companion.   That night the boats returned to the ships, having lost, in the course of the expedition, only 1 killed and 14 wounded, eight of the latter being native allies.[1] The Congreve rockets, on this and other occasions, greatly impressed the native mind.

On July 31st, a large prahu, fitted for sixty oars, and mounting a long 12-pr. and two 6-pr. brass swivels, was captured by the boats of the *Phlegethon,* off the mouth of the Tampassuk river. Discoveries made at the time of the capture of this prize led to the destruction of the town of Tampassuk, and of all the prahus in its vicinity, by Captain Peter M'Quhae, of the *Dædalus,* and a force of 250 seamen and Marines.   They also induced the despatch of an expedition against the town of Pandassan, under Captain Mundy, who took with him 150 seamen and 40 Marines, besides some Javanese under Commander Ross, I.N.   With the force were also Lieutenants Leopold George Heath, and George Lowcay Norcock, R.N., and Lieutenant George Gardiner Alexander, R.M.A.

[1] Mundy's letter in *Naut. Mag.,* 1847, 259.

The enemy retreated skirmishing, and the town, with the prahus belonging to it, was burnt.

On August 3rd, 1846, the *Iris* sighted three large prahus, and ordered the *Ringdove*, 16, Commander Sir William Legge George Hoste, Bart., and *Royalist*, brig, Lieutenant John Reid, to go in chase. Reid got within range of the fugitives, but, having a reef in his way, lowered his gigs, under Mate Francis Beaufort Quin,[1] and Midshipman Edward Hood Lingard Ray. Quin drove ashore and destroyed one prahu, and then went to the assistance of Ray, whose most formidable opponent had faced about, threatening to board him. Ray, however, judiciously kept at long range, and was already getting the better of his adversary when Quin arrived and ended the conflict. The affair was most gallantly managed, and the pirates, ere their craft was taken, lost heavily. The third prahu got away.

The desperate character of these pirates is indicated by the fact that, a little later, the crew of a captured prahu, while lying alongside the *Ringdove*, rose, killed or wounded all the British on board,[2] and made off, only however to be subsequently sunk.

One of the results of British action in Borneo was a treaty, whereby the Sultan ceded the island of Labuan, of which Brooke was appointed the first governor. This treaty was ratified at Brunei on May 28th, 1847. To lend solemnity to the affair, the H.E.I. Co.'s steamer *Nemesis*, Captain Wallage, I.N., which conveyed Brooke to Brunei for the purpose, took thither also Commander Charles Conrad Grey, of the *Columbine*, 16, and Lieutenant David M'Dowall Gordon, acting Commander of the brig *Royalist*. While absent upon this service, the *Nemesis*, then carrying Brooke and Grey from Brunei to Labuan, and having a cutter of the *Columbine* in tow, came upon a fleet of Balanini or Sooloo pirates in chase of a prahu, off Pilong Pilongan. By 1 P.M. the pirate vessels, eleven in number, having quitted the chase, lay anchored to await attack along a sandy beach, with their heads, which were protected by musket-proof planks, to the sea, their sterns, which were made fast by warps ashore, in the surf, and a hawser passed from boat to boat. As the steamer approached, the pirates opened fire on her; and a hot action

---

[1] He had been promoted to be Lieut. on June 6th, 1846, but had not received his commission.

[2] One of the miscreants also thrust a spear through one of the *Ringdove's* ports, and mortally wounded the Master.

followed at a range of two hundred yards, the *Nemesis* being in only two fathoms, and rolling heavily in a ground swell.

After a two hours' engagement the enemy's fire nearly ceased, and his prahus were seen to be much damaged. Commander Grey, taking the *Columbine's* cutter and two boats of the *Nemesis*, then made a dash at the left of the pirate position, while the steamer poured in grape and canister on the right and centre. The Sooloos thereupon cast loose the hawser which held their prahus together; and some of them pulled away to the eastward as fast as the damaged state of their craft would allow, leaving, however, two prahus in possession of the British. The *Nemesis* pursued, and successively drove six more prahus ashore, where they were temporarily abandoned. She continued to chase the remaining three; and, while Grey was securing his two prizes, five out of six of the abandoned boats were remanned, refloated, and very pluckily brought down to attack Grey's party. This manœuvre obliged the *Nemesis* to return, and, as she did so, the sixth prahu on the beach was remanned, and escaped with the three to the eastward. Grey and his boats were roughly handled ere the *Nemesis* relieved the pressure. She captured two, and Grey one of the five, the other two getting away in the rapidly increasing darkness. The enemy, whose strength was at least 500 men, lost, probably, between 80 and 100 killed, and twice as many wounded; and ten brass and five iron guns were taken from them. The British loss was 1 killed, and 7 (2 mortally) wounded.[1]

During these years naval operations of a more regular character had to be undertaken in another quarter of the world. They led up to a gallant little action, the great merits of which have never, perhaps, been properly appreciated. Indeed, I find it omitted altogether from one well-known book which professes to deal with the active work of the Navy during the period.

In most parts of South America the shaking off of Spanish rule in the second and third decades of the nineteenth century was followed by a period of active unrest which often became positive anarchy. In the Argentine, Don Juan Manuel de Rosas at length obtained almost unlimited power, and then turned his attention to the subjugation of the neighbouring republic of Banda Oriental, now Uruguay, and of its capital, Montevideo. A renegade Uruguayan, Oribe, assisted by Rosas, overran the Banda Oriental, laid

[1] *Naut. Mag.*, 1847, 602.

siege to Montevideo, and defeated Riviera, the Uruguayan leader. His cruelties, however, caused the foreign residents, who were perhaps unwisely encouraged by the British consul, and by Commodore John Brett Purvis, to resist his entry into the city; and the siege continued, the Argentine naval commander, Commodore Brown,[1] an Irishman, co-operating, by blockading the place with a corvette, two brigs, and seven small craft. French as well as British interests were seriously affected by this action. On the score of there being a great number of British subjects in Montevideo, Purvis declined to allow the blockade, or to permit any firing upon the city from seaward; but later, the Argentines, by seizing British property, and by their provocative action and non-observance of treaty engagements, so exasperated the British senior officer, then Sir Thomas Sabine Pasley, that Rosas was summoned to withdraw his troops. Upon his refusal, in August 1845, Brown's squadron was captured, and in part handed over to the Montevideans; Colonia was cleared of the enemy; and it was determined forcibly to re-open the navigation of the Parana, which had been blocked by the dictator. First, however, a small British force, consisting of the *Gorgon*, 6, paddle, *Philomel*, 8, *Dolphin*, 3, and *Fanny*, schooner, was sent up the Uruguay River as far as Paysandu, to facilitate the escape of such foreigners as might be hiding there. This preliminary expedition was cleverly navigated up and down by Commander Bartholomew James Sulivan, of the *Philomel*, and is interesting as having been undertaken in concert not only with a French force, but also with a motley flotilla which was commanded by the famous Giuseppe Garibaldi, who was then in the service of Montevideo. In the meantime, Rosas concentrated his opposition at Punta Obligado, on the Parana, about sixty miles below Rosario. Rear-Admiral Samuel Hood Inglefield, C.B., was at that time the British, and Rear-Admiral Lainé, the French Commander-in-Chief on the station; and those officers, in interpreting the orders of their respective governments, went, it is now notorious, somewhat beyond

---

[1] Known in Argentine history as Almirante Guillermo (William) Brown, born at Foxford, co. Mayo, June 22nd, 1777; died March 3rd, 1857, at Buenos Aires, where, in the public cemetery, there is a monument to his memory. His name has been given to one of the administrative divisions of the province of Buenos Aires, and to an Argentine battleship, launched in 1880. He commanded the revolutionary navy in the War of Independence in 1814; and in the war with Brazil, 1826–28, he commanded the improvised navy of Buenos Aires. (Letter to the Author from H. E. Don Florencio L. Dominguez, Argentine Minister in London, Feb. 4th, 1901.)

the intention of their instructions, though it can scarcely be doubted
that their vigorous measures were, upon the whole, beneficial alike
to South America and to civilisation generally.

The little international squadron told off for forcing the passage
of the Parana was as follows :—

	VESSELS.	GUNS.	TONS.	COMMANDERS.	Nov. 20.	
					K.	W.
British	*Gorgon*, padd..	6	1111	Capt. Chas. Hotham	0	3
	Firebrand, padd. .	6	1190	Capt. Jas. Hope	1	1
	Philomel . . .	8	428	Com. Bart. Jas. Sulivan . . .	1	6
	Comus	18	492	Com. Ed. Aug. Inglefield (actg.).	2	2
	Dolphin . . .	3	318	Lieut. Reginald Thos. Jno. Levinge	5	14
	¹*Fanny*, sch. . .	1	..	Lieut. Astley Cooper Key . .	0	1
French	¹*San Martin* . .	8	200	Capt. François Thomas Tréhouart	10	25
	Fulton, padd. . .	2	650	Lieut. Mazères	1	6
	Expéditive. . .	16	..	Lieut. Miniac	2	4
	Pandour . . .	10	..	Lieut. Duparc.	2	10
	¹*Procida*	4	..	Lieut. de La Rivière	0	0

¹ Taken from Commod. Brown.

The largest of the above drew nearly seventeen feet of water, and
there were but seventeen and three-quarter feet in the shallowest
parts of the river that had to be traversed in going up. All the
British vessels were short of their peace allowance of powder and
shot : not one of them had a rocket on board ; there were only three
field-pieces, without a single shrapnel shell for any of them ; and
but 70 British Marines, under Captain Thomas Hurdle, R.M., accompanied the expedition. Looking to the nature of the opposition to
be encountered, it is marvellous that a great disaster did not follow.
Rosas had caused to be moored across the river, with their heads
up stream, twenty-four large hulks, which were held together by
three chain cables. On the right bank, four batteries, all with good,
and two with great command, covered this formidable obstruction.
Nos. 1 and 2 were below the boom ; Nos. 3 and 4 above it.[1] No. 1
mounted one long brass 36-pr., one long brass 32-pr., four long brass
24-prs., and a rocket-tube. No. 2 mounted two long brass 32-prs.,
one long brass 24-pr., and three long iron 18-prs. At the rear of
these, posted in a wood, were four field-pieces. No. 3 mounted two
long brass 18-prs., two long iron 18-prs., and four field-pieces ; and
No. 4 mounted seven short 18-prs. Above the other end of the
boom, near the left bank, were two gunboats, each mounting one

[1] See plan, p. 340.

gun, and the schooner *Republicano*, which turned a broadside of six guns towards the hulks.   The river is there about half a mile broad. Near its centre, below the barrier, several fireships lay ready ; and the enemy, who was in strength, had carefully marked his distances, so as to be able to fire with the greatest possible effect.

The expedition started from off Martin Garcia on November 8th, 1845, but made slow progress.   On the way up the people were repeatedly landed for exercise and practice.   Of a certain ship's company, it was discovered that not one man had been taught to use a musket.[1]   On November 18th, the force anchored two miles below Obligado ; and that night Commander Sulivan, and Lieutenant Mazères stole up the river in their boats, and sounded close to the boom and batteries.   On the 19th, the position was further re-connoitred, and plans were made for the attack.   Sulivan was given charge of the left division, consisting of the *Philomel*, *Expéditive*, *Fanny*, and *Procida*.   Tréhouart himself took command of the right or heavier division, consisting of the *San Martin*, *Comus*, *Pandour*, and *Dolphin ;* and the steamers *Gorgon*, *Firebrand*, and *Fulton* remained in reserve under Hotham.

On the morning of the 20th, the left division weighed, and moved up past the right division, which had lain overnight nearer to the enemy.   As it reached a point abreast of him, Levinge, in the *Dolphin*, without waiting for the rest of his division, weighed, and ran up the middle of the stream, thereby diverting much of the enemy's attention from Sulivan's force, which, owing to light breeze and strong current, made but slow progress.   Battery No. 1 opened at 9.50 A.M., the first shot cutting away the ensign halliards of the *Philomel*, which, as she advanced, returning the salute, soon began to be badly knocked about.   Indeed, owing to damages received aloft, she ultimately had to anchor about three hundred yards short of her assigned position in front of the batteries.   The *Fanny* anchored near her.   The *Expéditive* and *Procida*, in trying to get their broadsides to bear, were swept a little down stream ere they brought up.   Of the right division, the *Dolphin* pushed on alone, and at length anchored within six hundred yards of every gun of the enemy.   For a quarter of an hour she was the most advanced vessel.   Then Tréhouart, in the *San Martin*, went gallantly ahead of her, and sensibly relieved her from the worst of the fire.   His anchor was let go for him by a shot which cut the stoppers ; but, by

[1] Sulivan, 72.

that time, he was very nearly in his assigned position. The *Comus*, following the *San Martin*, got well up, but, while trying to spring her broadside, was swept back to a less effective station. Nor was the *Pandour* able to afford much assistance to Tréhouart, who, in his small brig, occupied a post worthy of a vessel of eight times the force, and maintained it nobly. On her port beam, well within six hundred yards of her, were batteries 1, 2, and 3; on her port

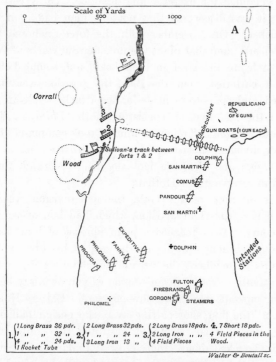

THE BATTLE OF OBLIGADO, 1845.

(*From "Life and Letters of Sir B. J. Sulivan," by kind permission of Mr. John Murray.*)

bow at little greater range were the almost raking guns of battery 4; and from nearly ahead she was raked by the *Republicano* and gunboats. In a short time she was entirely disabled, all her guns that could be brought to bear being put out of action; yet, even when her cable was shot away and she began to drift, Tréhouart[1] brought her up again, and kept his station. Ere the other vessels succeeded in diverting from him some of the storm of shot to which

---

[1] Chevalier says that when the *San Martin* drifted, Tréhouart transferred his pennant to, and pushed forward again in, the *Expéditive*.

he had been exposed, and in partially silencing the batteries, the plucky Frenchman had lost an enormous proportion of his crew of one hundred men.

At 10.50 A.M. the enemy let loose ten fire-vessels, which, however, drifted past the allies without doing any harm. The light wind still prevented the sailing craft from stationing themselves exactly as had been intended; but the arrival on the scene of the three steamers, and the aid which was at once rendered to the *San Martin* by the *Fulton*, afforded compensation. The idea had been to keep the steamers in the rear until the chain should have been cut, as it was feared that their machinery would be quickly damaged if they should be long exposed to a heavy fire. But Tréhouart's necessity, and the devotion of Mazères when his senior officer appealed to him, upset all plans. Eventually the *Fulton* made her way quite close to the obstruction.

At 11.30 the crew of the *Republicano* deserted her in the gunboats, and, having set her on fire, went to reinforce battery No. 4, which, lying high, was almost intact. No. 3 was then nearly silent, and the field-guns had been withdrawn from it to the wood. Nos. 1 and 2 had had some guns silenced, but fired steadily with the remainder, and called up fresh guns' crews time after time. At about noon, a slightly strengthening breeze enabled the sailing craft to weigh, and move nearer to the defences. At 12.15 the *Republicano* blew up. Still, however, the obstruction remained unbroken; and, as the *San Martin* and *Dolphin* had not a boat that would float, and could not, therefore, attempt to cut the chain, Captain Hope, of the *Firebrand*, volunteered to do that needful but terribly dangerous piece of work. He took three boats, and, having picked up armourers from the *Dolphin*, pulled for a point in the boom about sixteen hulks, and 500 yards, distant from the batteries. One party, under Hope himself, attacked the chain cables that crossed the deck of one of the hulks; the other two parties, under Lieutenant William Henry Webb, Mate Frederick Falkiner Nicholson (*Dolphin*), and Midshipman John Edmund Commerell, severed the riding-cables of three craft. Although a furious and concentrated fire was poured upon the boom, no one, strange to say, was touched by it; and, in four minutes, the three craft swung round in the current, leaving a gap nearly a hundred yards wide.

The *Fulton*, although she had already fired away all her shot and shell, passed through at once; and she was presently followed by the

Gorgon and *Firebrand*, which then, for the first time, got under fire. They were fresh and almost untouched when, from above the boom, they began to rake the batteries. Hotham assembled the armed boats of the squadron near the *Gorgon*, and, after a brief period of natural indecision, landed 180 British seamen, 145 Royal Marines, and a small detachment of French seamen. The enemy was still well posted in the wood, and of unknown but certainly great strength; and battery No. 4 was continuing its fire. A disembarkation was rapidly effected on the beach below battery No. 2 : five guns in that were spiked by Sulivan, who entered it alone; and No. 1, which had been recently abandoned, was occupied by parties under Sulivan, and Lieutenants Astley Cooper Key, and George Henry Richards (*Philomel*). These detachments were at once fired at by small-arm men hidden in the trees not fifty yards away; but the enemy was silenced or driven off ere the Marines, under Captain Hurdle, could get up. All was then practically over.[1] Only batteries 1, 2 and 3 were disabled by nightfall : the flag of Rosas then still waved over No. 4; and there was some firing in the woods near that battery. On the following day, No. 4 was entered, and dismantled without resistance.

The losses suffered by each ship engaged will be found set forth in the table on p. 338. On the British side, the officers killed were Lieutenant Charles John Brickdale (*Comus*), and Clerk George Andrews (*Dolphin*). Among the wounded were Lieutenant Charles Francis Doyle[2] (*Philomel*) (mortally), Lieutenant Astley Cooper Key (*Fanny*), Second Master Richard Henry Warren (*Dolphin*), Assistant Surgeon John Gallagher (*Dolphin*), and Assistant Clerk T—— Ellstob (*Dolphin*).[3]

In consequence of this action, Hotham was made a K.C.B., and Hope a C.B.; Sulivan was posted; and Lieutenants Inglefield, Levinge, Richards, Doyle, and Key were made Commanders. But no medal was ever granted for the affair, which, indeed, was practically disavowed, when Lord Aberdeen, a little later, returned the

---

[1] The little resistance that was offered ashore may be attributed to the fact that Rosas hoped to entrap the squadron further up the river. There were also numerous desertions.

[2] He had nearly recovered, when, having been accidentally given five grains of morphine, he vomited so violently that his wound reopened, necessitating a fresh operation under which he sank.

[3] Disps.; Sulivan, 71; Chevalier, 123; Mackinnon, 'Steam Warfare in the Parana.'

captured guns with an apology, after having said in public that Great Britain had no right to force Rosas to open the rivers. Very different was the view taken in France. The guns which fell to the French are still to be seen in Paris: Tréhouart was made a rear-admiral; and *Tréhouart* and *Obligado* were adopted as ship-names by the French navy.

After the action, Hope, with three boats, gallantly pursued up the river the schooner *Chacabuco*, 3, and another vessel mounting two guns. Hotham, anxious for the issue of the business, sent the *Firebrand* and additional boats in support; but, fortunately, Hope, who had but forty men with him, delayed making an attack; and the enemy, despairing of saving her, themselves blew up their schooner, whose crew of two hundred took refuge on shore near Rosario.

The squadron advanced slowly up the Parana; and part of it reached Corrientes on January 20th, 1846, without serious adventure. Hotham himself, in the French steamer *Fulton*, went as far as Asuncion, the capital of Paraguay. In the meantime, the *Dolphin* and *Fanny* had gone down to Montevideo for a convoy of sixty merchantmen, which was to be brought up the river; and Rosas, determined, if possible, both to keep in the ships that had already gone up, and to keep out all others, had assembled about 2000 men, with a dozen heavy field-guns, on the flat summits of the cliffs of San Lorenzo, fifteen or twenty miles north of Rosario. These cliffs are four miles long, and the channel, for the whole of that distance, passes within a quarter of a mile of them. Nevertheless, assisted by the *Firebrand, Dolphin, Fanny*, and French corvette *Coquette*, the convoy from below passed up, no one being killed, and only two men in the *Firebrand*[1] being wounded, although one of the merchantmen had as many as thirty-four shots in her, and the *Firebrand* received two-and-twenty. Less formidable batteries, near Tonneloro, had already been run the gauntlet of; and both these, and those at Lorenzo, had to be passed by the *Alecto*, 5, paddle, Commander Francis William Austen (2), which, with mails and rockets from England, followed the convoy, and overtook it at Baxada de Santa Fé. At about the same time the French steamer *Gassendi* joined the force in the upper waters, without having been attacked on

---

[1] She was in charge of that part of the river, and remained below the batteries until some days later, when, going up to Baxada, she was hulled eight times, and had a man killed.

her way.   She brought orders for the *Philomel* to return to Monte-video.

By that time the works at San Lorenzo had been strengthened; and when, on the evening of April 2nd, the *Philomel* ran past them, she only escaped severe damage by keeping within a cable's length of the cliffs, so that the shot passed over her.

The batteries were again passed under fire, on April 6th, by the *Alecto*; on April 21st by the *Lizard*; and on May 11th by the *Harpy*, 1, paddle, Lieutenant Edward Halhed Beauchamp; these vessels being employed in keeping up communications.   The *Alecto* had occasion to tow three heavily-laden schooners past Tonneloro against a three-knot current and a head wind.   For twenty minutes she was almost stationary under a hail of projectiles from seven 18-prs.; and seventy-five minutes elapsed ere she was able to get out of range; yet her Commander was the only man in her who was wounded.   The *Lizard*, paddle, Lieutenant Henry Manby Tylden, on her way up, was subjected to a hot fire from the San Lorenzo works for very nearly two hours, and was riddled from stem to stern, losing Clerk Charles Barnes, Master's Assistant —— Webb,[1] and two men killed; and four wounded.

During all this time the return convoy was being assembled and got ready in the upper reaches of the great river.   It ultimately consisted of 110 sail of merchantmen; and towards the middle of May it made rendezvous at Baxada de Santa Fé, where, on the 16th, it was joined by Hotham from Corrientes.   A scheme occurred to Lieutenant Lauchlan Bellingham Mackinnon, of the *Alecto*, whereby the passage of the huge fleet past the batteries of San Lorenzo might be facilitated; and this scheme, after examination, was accepted by Hotham.   In pursuance of it, Mackinnon secretly, and chiefly by night, placed a masked rocket battery upon a scrub-covered island which lay opposite the most formidable part of the batteries.   He was ably assisted by Lieutenant Charles Loudon Barnard, R.M.A., Boatswain Hamm, Mr. Baker, a pilot, twelve Marine Artillerymen, and eleven seamen.   In the works opposite, twenty-eight guns were counted.   On June 4th there was a fair wind, and the convoy, escorted by the *Gorgon*, *Firebrand*, *Dolphin*, *Fanny*, *Lizard*, *Harpy* and *Alecto*, as well as by several French men-of-war, passed down, the *Gorgon*, *Fulton*, and *Alecto* leading, and engaging the batteries as they got within range.   At a pre-

---

[1] Eldest son of Lieut. Alex. Webb, R.N. (1815), who died in 1847.

arranged moment, Mackinnon's party, the presence of which had
been totally unsuspected by the enemy, discharged a flight of rockets
with great effect, and, at the same time, hoisted a British flag on
the island. A hot rocket fire was kept up; and so disconcerting did
this prove to be that, strange to say, the entire convoy was enabled
to make the passage without the loss of a single man.[1] Mackinnon
and his gallant comrades thereupon pulled off safely in their boat,
and rejoined the squadron below the works.[2]

There was little further resistance; and although the allies afterwards relieved Montevideo from an attack by some of the friends
of Rosas, and, for a time, occupied the city, the difficulties at issue
thenceforward became the subject rather of diplomatic negotiations
than of active measures. Many of the advantages which had been
gained were, unfortunately, sacrificed or neutralised by the terms of
the settlement; but, in spite of the rather unhandsome manner in
which the services of the Navy on this most creditable expedition
were treated by the Government, it must be admitted that seldom
have British officers, bluejackets, and Marines deserved better of
their country.

In 1810 a very able and enlightened ruler, Radama I., had arisen
in Madagascar. He did there something of the work which Charlemagne did in Germany and Gaul, Egbert in Saxon Britain, and
Peter the Great in Russia. Unhappily, he died in 1828, and his
power was thereupon usurped by one of his wives, a woman
superstitious, ignorant, despotic, and cruel. Under Radama, European influences had been encouraged: under his successor, the
policy of the government was one of "Madagascar for the Malagasy
savages;" and in 1845, this worthless woman, Queen Ranavalona I.,
endeavoured to force the European traders resident in her dominions
to become her naturalised subjects. This project was, of course,
strongly opposed by Great Britain and France, the two nations most
immediately concerned; and, accordingly, the *Conway*, 28, Captain
William Kelly, met the French ships *Zélée* and *Berceau*, in Tamatave road; and their commanders did their best to induce the
Queen, by pacific representations, to adopt a less objectionable
policy. She was intractable, and on June 15th, after the Tamatave

---

[1] Four merchantmen, however, ran aground, and had to be burnt to save them
from capture.

[2] Disps. (Hotham's are very meagre) and *Gazette*, 1846, pp. 815, 861, 3210, 3255,
etc.; Mackinnon; Sulivan (till he went home). Chevalier says nothing about events
subsequent to the battle of Obligado.

forts had been bombarded, a party of 350 men, under one of the French captains and Lieutenant Albert Heseltine, landed and advanced under a smart fire against some of the native works. A battery was captured and its guns were spiked, and another outwork was stormed. This had been supposed to be the main fort; but, as soon as it was occupied, it was perceived that the main fort was a far more formidable casemated circular building beyond, mounting about thirty guns. The outwork was held for more than half an hour, and a hot musketry fire was maintained from its summit; but the force had no guns wherewith to breach the fort, and, as the men were falling fast, the position was at length abandoned. While it was being held, a ludicrous and rather childish quarrel broke out between the allies. A flag-staff standing on the main fort was shot through, and fell outwards between the fort and the outwork. Two British seamen, and a midshipman and two or three Frenchmen made a rush after the fallen flag, and began a fierce struggle for it under a heavy fire. They were about to settle the dispute by the arbitration of the cutlass, when Lieutenant John James Kennedy, leapt down among the combatants, and with his knife cut the flag in twain, giving half to each party. Kennedy was subsequently wounded. Several public buildings, and much of the town, were burnt by the fire of the men-of-war, which are said to have made excellent practice; and on the following day another landing-party brought off such European property as remained. The wounded were all saved, but the killed had to be abandoned, and their heads were derisively exposed on the beach by the Hovas, stuck on the ends of pikes. It was not an entirely satisfactory demonstration, seeing that it cost the British 4 killed and 11 wounded, and the French 17 killed, including three officers, and 43 wounded, and since its success was by no means convincing. In fact, for many years afterwards, European influence in the island was scarcely able to make itself felt at all.

At about the same time a far finer native race than the Malagasy came into active opposition with the forces of civilisation, and began a series of struggles which, though very protracted and very regrettable, ended, twenty or thirty years later, in the loyal and contented adhesion of the people to the British crown.

The early days of the settlement of the great colony of New Zealand, and especially of the north island, which has as its original inhabitants a race of people who are as intelligent as they are warlike, were not without grave troubles. The first governor, Captain William Hobson, R.N.,[1] placated the natives for a season by entering with them into the treaty of Waitangi, whereby, in return for their acknowledgment of the Queen's supremacy, they were guaranteed the exclusive possession of their lands so long as they might wish to retain them, while they conceded to the crown the exclusive right of pre-emption of any lands which might come into the market. Dying at his post on September 10th, 1842, Hobson was succeeded by another naval officer, Captain Robert FitzRoy,[2] who, however, did not reach the colony until a year later. His period of office was very stormy. Natives who had foolishly traded off fine tracts of country for a few blankets and guns, realised that they had been swindled, and were anxious to regain their patrimony ; and there were serious disputes. Before FitzRoy's arrival there was a lamentable massacre of white settlers at Wairu. This was followed by two futile and unpatriotic attempts of the New Zealand Company's agents to obtain a share in the government; and then came a rebellion of the natives, and the capture by the chief, Heki, of Russell, or, as it was called in Maori, Karorarika. This was on March 10th, 1845. In aiding a detachment of the 96th regiment to defend the station, a party from the *Hazard*, 18, lost 6 men killed and 8 people wounded, including among the latter her captain, Commander David Robertson.

The victorious Heki pressed his advantage, and began to threaten Auckland.[3] At that date, New Zealand was within the limits of the East India station; and the small naval force on the coasts was supplied by ships detached thither from the command of Rear-Admiral Sir Thomas John Cochrane, Kt., C.B. The senior officer was at first Commander Frederick Patten, of the *Osprey*, 12, who, however, was presently superseded by Captain Sir Everard Home, Bart., of the *North Star*, 26. Home supplied a small brigade which, in company with a slender military force, attacked Heki's pah, or stronghold. Unfortunately, the British had no guns ; and, although Lieutenant Charles Randle Egerton did good work with his rocket party, he failed to set the place on fire. During the engagement, a sortie and flank attack, made by Heki's brother Kawiti, caused much loss of life, and led indirectly to the withdrawal of the expedition.

---

[1] Posted July 9th, 1828.

[2] The meteorologist; posted Dec. 3rd, 1834; died a retired vice-adm., Apr. 30th, 1865.

[3] A map of part of the North Island of New Zealand will be found, illustrating the more important operations of 1860–64, in the next volume of this History.

Military reinforcements having reached the island, a new attack on the pah was begun under the command of Colonel Despard. Four 6-prs. were employed against the defences during the last week of June, but they produced little effect. On June 30th, the *Hazard's* people, by incredible exertion, dragged a 32-pr. a distance of 15 miles from the sloop, and opened with it from a commanding hill, yet failed to make a breach. After a sortie had been repulsed, Despard ventured to attempt to storm. A most gallant struggle ensued; but the assailants were at length driven back with terrible loss, among the mortally wounded being Lieutenant George Phillpotts, of the *Hazard*. On July 10th, nevertheless, it was found that Heki had abandoned his strong position and retired into the bush.

Immediately afterwards, Kawiti began the construction of a much more formidable pah called Ruapekapeka, or the Bat's Nest. It was a wonderful work, with ravelins, bastions, palisades, ditches, bomb-proofs, and wells; and within it were a 12-pr. and a 3-pr. It stood on a ridge of hill, the sides of which were perpendicular in several places; and it lay fourteen miles inland from the head of the river Kawakawa, surrounded by dense forest. By that time, Home had been superseded as senior naval officer; but, before his supersession, he prepared the plans which were carried out by his successor, Captain Charles Graham,[1] of the *Castor*, 36.

In December, 1845, Graham landed at the head of about 340 officers, seamen and Marines from the *Castor*, *Racehorse*, 18, Commander George James Hay,[2] *North Star*, *Calliope*, 28, Captain Edward Stanley, and the H.E.I. Co.'s ship *Elphinstone*, to assist Despard and detachments of the 58th and 99th regiments in the reduction of Ruapekapeka. The naval brigade took up two 32-prs., and there were other guns. Home was left with a party to hold a pah comparatively near the river's mouth; and the rest of the force, after three weeks of indefatigable labour and exertion, amid torrential rains, posted a battery, shelled and rocketed the fortress, and, on January 11th, 1846, taking advantage, it has been asserted, of the fact that the Christians among the defenders were engaged at divine service, stormed and captured the pah, after a four hours' determined struggle. The Navy's loss in the fight was 9 men killed, and a Midshipman and 17 men wounded. Among the officers favourably

---

[1] C.B., July 27th, 1846.
[2] Posted, Jan. 11th; C.B., July 27th, 1846.

mentioned were Lieutenants Robert Jocelyn Otway,[1] first of the
Castor, Maxwell Falcon,[1] also of the *Castor*, Arthur Robert Henry,
of the *Racehorse*, and Charles Randle Egerton,[1] and Alfred John
Curtis, of the *North Star*.[2] Kawiti fled, and ultimately surrendered
himself on board the steamer *Driver*, Commander Courtenay Osborn
Hayes.

Having quieted the northern end of the island, FitzRoy turned
his attention to the southern part of it, where the chiefs Te
Rauperaha and Rangehaieta were on the war path. The first of
these was at length captured in his bed, in a stockade at Taupo, on
July 23rd, 1846, by a party of seamen and Marines from the *Calliope*,
under Captain Edward Stanley, co-operating with Major Lurt, of
the 29th regiment. Rangehaieta was attacked in his stronghold,
and, being driven from it, retreated from position to position, until
he realised the folly of remaining in arms. Desultory hostilities
with other chiefs, especially in the Wanganui district, continued
until 1847; but, ere that time, the British forces in the island had
been so much strengthened, and the natives had suffered so greatly,
that the more influential chiefs had gladly accepted the terms of
peace offered them by Captain George Grey,[3] of the 83rd Foot,
FitzRoy's successor in the governorship. In the later operations,
besides some of the officers already mentioned, Commander John
Cochrane Hoseason, of the *Inflexible*, steamer, and Commander
Francis Philip Egerton, then commanding the *Hazard*, took part.
Their seamen and Marines rendered great assistance to the
troops.

In 1847-8, as on numerous other occasions, the unstable condition
of some of the Central American republics led to the perpetration of
outrages on British subjects, and to the interposition of British
naval officers in order to secure redress. An important case of the
kind happened in Nicaragua early in 1848. A certain Colonel Salas,
of the Nicaraguan army, had carried off two British subjects from
San Juan de Nicaragua; whereupon the British Consul-General at
Bluefields had asked the Commander-in-Chief on the station to
afford support and protection for British interests. Rear-Admiral
Charles John Austen promptly sent to Bluefields the *Alarm*, 26,
Captain Granville George Loch, and the *Vixen*, 6, paddle, Commander

---

[1] Com., Jan. 11th, 1846.   [2] *Gazette*, 1846, pp. 2346, 2348.
[3] K.C.B., 1848; afterwards Govr. of the Cape, and in 1877-91 Premier of New
Zealand.

Alfred Phillips Ryder, which arrived in the first week of February, and anchored at the mouth of the river. It was understood that the offending Colonel Salas, whom it was intended to bring to reason or chastise, held a fort at a place called Serapaqui, thirty miles up the river, which has a very rapid current. The fort lay on a sharp bluff about fifty feet above the water, at the head of a reach a mile and a half long, lined on both sides with thick woods. Its rear was protected by impenetrable forests ; it was believed to be strongly held, and the only possible landing-place from which it could be entered was above and in rear of it; so that the batteries had to be passed against a five-knot stream ere the landing-place could be even sighted.

Captain Loch, having under him Commander Ryder, Lieutenant Robert Anthony Edward Scott, first of the *Vixen*, Lieutenant George Agar Ellis Ridge, and other officers, put 260 men, including some of the 38th Regiment, into twelve boats, and, with great cheerfulness and resolution, set about pulling up the river, in which he soon encountered most difficult rapids and falls. The people worked by day and rested by night ; and, after seventy-two hours of rowing, towing, lifting, and punting, arrived within a short distance of Serapaqui on February 11th.

On the following morning Loch and Ryder, while proceeding in their gigs to endeavour to communicate with Salas, were fired at, first by two heavy guns at the fort, and then by musketry from both sides of the river. It was, of course, useless to make further efforts for a peaceable solution ; and an attack was at once ordered, the two gigs leading, and being pretty closely followed by some of the lighter boats. Progress was terribly slow, the current being stronger the higher the boats went. From both banks, moreover, the concealed enemy maintained a hot musketry fire, which killed two people, and wounded several, including Midshipman Nicholas Edward Brook Turner. It is extraordinary that more were not hurt, seeing that some of the boats were riddled with bullets, and that nearly all were delayed by having one or more oars smashed by shot. It took them, indeed, one hour and forty minutes to pull sufficiently high up to be able to drop down to the landing-place already mentioned. But when, led by Loch, the men landed and charged with a cheer, the Nicaraguans broke and fled within ten minutes. Denis Burke, a stoker of the *Vixen*, was one of the first ashore, and had the distinction of taking the enemy's colours, for which the British flag was soon substituted. When the pursuit had continued for about thirty minutes, Loch recalled his people, and employed them in disabling the guns, in throwing them and the captured arms into the river, and in burning the fort and stockades. The party was then re-embarked, and taken back to the ships. This little expedition was admirably managed, and deservedly brought a C.B. to Captain Loch,[1] and promotion to Commander Ryder[2] and Lieutenant Scott.[3]

After the China War of 1839-42, the duty of the British Navy in the China seas was chiefly restricted[4] to the protection of legitimate trade; and at each of the five treaty ports a consul was established, with a man-of-war to support his authority. Unfortunately, although opium was contraband in China, Indian policy required that consuls and Captains should display a benevolent blindness to those engaged in the traffic in it, and, if such were British subjects, should protect them in their persons and property. As China officially discouraged the opium trade, and, indeed, nearly all import trade with Europeans, while unofficial China craved for opium and welcomed many other exotic products, and while, at the same time, India did all that lay in its power to sell its goods, contraband as well as legal, a very difficult and dangerous situation was created.

In 1843-44 the outrages of alleged pirates upon British trade carried in Chinese bottoms led some of the consuls to direct the attention of their naval colleagues to the importance of putting a stop to the depredations. In consequence, several junks were captured, and their crews handed over to the Chinese authorities at Amoy and in the Min. While Keying remained Imperial Commissioner, no remonstrance was offered; but when Seu succeeded him, strong objections were made against foreign naval interference; the upshot being that on May 18th, 1844, by direct order of the ministry in London, Rear-Admiral Sir Thomas John Cochrane directed that the ships of her Majesty and the H.E.I. Co. should

---

[1] May 30th, 1848.

[2] Posted May 2nd, 1848.

[3] Com., July 28th, 1848.

[4] Although, in April, 1847, owing to the helpless condition of the Chinese Government and its apparent inability to carry out its engagements, a British force, which included the *Espiègle*, 12, Commander Thomas Pickering Thompson, and the *Pluto*, steamer, Lieutenant Frederick Lowe, with troops, was obliged to adopt summary measures in the Canton river, and to attack (April 3rd), capture (April 5th), and destroy (April 26th), the Bogue Forts: work which was accomplished without serious difficulty.

not in future interfere with Chinese craft, unless on absolutely unimpeachable evidence of their having molested some British vessel or subject. The order was amended on March 8th, 1845; but only with a view to make its meaning clearer and more stringent. Naval action was thereby deterred; and, on the other hand, piracy correspondingly increased. The Chinese traders in despair hired armed Portuguese lorchas to accompany their fleets; and, for a time, it was only when a convoy thus protected had been attacked, and the deposition of the European master of the lorcha was obtainable, that naval officers thought themselves justified in making prize of piratical junks, unless, of course, they had themselves actually witnessed a piratical act.

When Cochrane, after completing his term of command, returned to England, he represented that the Navy's hands were unwisely hampered by the order; which, however, was not repealed until 1849, when Rear-Admiral Sir Francis Augustus Collier held command on the East India station.

In the interval, a few pirates only were taken and condemned. On May 31st, 1848, the *Scout*, 14, Commander Frederick Erskine Johnston, while on her way to Foo-chow in search of such delinquents, sighted and chased two piratical junks near Chimmo Island. The smaller of the two, carrying 32 men and a 2-pr., with numerous gingals, was taken without difficulty. The larger made a three hours' running fight, and then got into shoal water, whither she was followed by two boats under Lieutenant John James Stephen Josling. These pulled alongside under a heavy fire, which killed a seaman, and wounded Josling, a Midshipman, and four men; nor was the prize taken possession of until the *Scout* had managed to close her, and until Johnston, and three more men, had been wounded. This junk mounted four 6-prs., and had an immense assortment of gingals and matchlocks. Soon after her capture she went down; and only 36 of her crew, which had originally numbered 120, were secured. In this case the evidence satisfied the Chinese authorities at Amoy; and the prisoners were condemned.[1]

There would have been many more captures but for the stringency of the order; for the coast literally swarmed with pirates. In the early morning of August 24th, 1848, the British brig *Hector*, which had nearly driven ashore in a gale near Amoy, was brought out from among a crowd of pirate boats by the gig of the *Colum-*

---

[1] Hay, 'Suppression of Piracy' (1889), 9; *China Mail*.

bine, 16, Commander John Charles Dalrymple Hay, under Hay himself, and Lieutenant Henry Thomas Lyon; but, as no attack had been actually made, and as the order was still unrepealed, no measures could be taken to destroy the freebooters.

This particular pirate fleet afterwards ran down to Bias Bay, a few miles north-east of Hong Kong, where its leader, Shap'n'gtzai, had his dockyard. The scoundrel obtained his European supplies through the village of Wongmakok, on the south side of Hong Kong island. On February 25th, 1849, Captain d'Acosta, R.E., and Lieutenant Dwyer, Ceylon Rifles, while out for a walk, near Wongmakok, were murdered, as ultimately appeared, by Chuiapoo, the second in command of the pirate fleet in Bias Bay. Some of these pirates afterwards assassinated Captain d'Amaral, governor of Macao. They seem to have been emboldened by an unpleasant incident which had previously occurred at Macao between the governor, and Captain the Hon. Henry Keppel, of the *Mæander*, in connection with the imprisonment and forcible release of a too zealous British missionary named Summers.[1]

In the spring of 1849 the main pirate fleet, consisting of more than seventy sail, under Shap'n'gtzai, made its rendezvous at Tienpakh, and ravaged commerce and the coast from Macao to the Gulf of Tongking; while another part of it, forty sail strong, under Chuiapoo, made its headquarters in Bias Bay, and preyed upon the trade between Hong Kong and Amoy. The daring of the outlaws was surprising.

On May 30th, Commander John Cochrane Hoseason, of the steamer *Inflexible*, being sent to examine the Lemma islands in search of pirates who had recently raided Hong Kong harbour, was fired at by the enemy as he approached; but his superior gunnery silenced the junks; and his boats; under Lieutenant William Everard Alphonso Gordon, brought out eight of them. The *Pilot*, 16, Commander Edmund Moubray Lyons, was another cruiser which, having sound evidence whereon to act, was able to do useful service against the scourge.

On May 13th, 1849, Lyons chased six pirate junks, and, with his boats, captured and destroyed two. On May 25th, he destroyed a third, and two days later, a fourth. On June 2nd a fifth, and on the 3rd the sixth fell to him. A little later, three more of Chuiapoo's

---

[1] Jurien de La Gravière, in *Revue des Deux Mondes*; Hay, 'Suppression of Piracy'; Keppel, 'A Sailor's Life,' ii. 116.

squadron having been reported against, he went in chase, and, on the 25th, destroyed one in Red Bay, and another off the Lamyat islands. All these affairs cost him only three people wounded. In consequence, Chuiapoo, with his division, returned to Bias Bay.

On July 28th the ruffians cut out a salt boat from Hong Kong harbour; and at about the same time, several vessels which had sailed from Hong Kong for Singapore were reported missing. The *Medea*, steamer, Lieutenant William Nicholas Love Lockyer (actg. Commander), was therefore sent down the coast by Captain Edward Norwich Troubridge, senior officer in China, to make inquiries.

Reaching Tienpakh, on September 7th, Lockyer found the inner harbour crowded with fifty heavily armed junks, the town deserted by the mandarin for fear of the pirates, and upwards of a hundred trading junks held for ransom. Lockyer went in in his gig, and boarded a pirate, in which he was entertained at tea, and, it would appear, given some useful information, by one Aku, the clever mistress of an American master named J. B. Endicott, as to the situation. He had not, however, sufficient facts on which to act, and he prepared to resume his voyage; but, presently meeting a trader which complained that her consort, with British goods on board, had been seized by the pirates within, he returned, manned and armed his boats, and proceeded to search for the prize containing the British property. Five junks fired at him, whereupon he attacked and boarded, and, within half an hour, made himself master of all five, losing, however, one man killed, and nine people wounded. As the main body of the fleet then got under way as if to cut off his boats, he burnt his prizes, and withdrew to his ship. She drew too much water to be able to enter the harbour; and the boats were obviously not strong enough to contend with so numerous a force.[1]

Lockyer failed to gain news of the ships which he had been detached in search of, and, having gone back to Hong Kong, was sent thence to Whampoa to relieve the *Columbine*. There he saw six junks which he had noticed at Tienpakh, and informed against them; but the Chinese authorities allowed them to weigh and make off. When at length, on September 28th, the Chinese despatched five war junks after the fugitives, the pirates captured the admiral and his entire squadron, massacred the crews, and roasted the mandarins and officers alive.

[1] Lockyer to Troubridge, Sept. 8th, 1849; Hay, 'Suppression of Piracy.'

In the meantime Troubridge had put Lieutenant William Mould, of the *Amazon*, and some seamen and Marines, into the trading steamer *Canton*,[1] Charles Jamieson, master, and had sent him on further search for the missing vessels. On September 9th, the *Canton* had captured a pirate junk, and released a vessel which had been captured by her. Later on the same day, Mould had boarded a sugar junk, which had just been released by Shap'n'gtzai on payment of 1100 dollars' ransom. That night, he had passed through a mass of junks which he had afterwards ascertained to be the pirate fleet. Early on the 10th, the *Canton* had entered Tien-pakh, and, her boats having been fired at by three junks at anchor there, she had entered the port, burnt the junks, killed many of the pirates, and taken 11 prisoners, who reported that Shap'n'gtzai had sailed on the previous evening. Mould had followed, first to Nowchow, and then to Hoihow, in Hainan, where he had learnt of an engagement between the pirates and the Chinese admiral Hwang. After destroying two more junks off Mamee, the *Canton* had returned to Hong Kong on September 15th, and Mould and his people had rejoined the *Amazon*.

The *Columbine*, and the *Phlegethon*, of the H.E.I. Co.'s service, were with the *Amazon* when the *Canton* returned. Troubridge had just been ordered to Singapore, and, leaving Hay as senior officer on the spot, he desired him to carry out certain instructions. In pursuance of these, Hay searched various ports along the coast, and then ran over to Macao, and put himself into communication with the United States' Commodore Geisinger, who was there in the *Plymouth*. One of Geisinger's officers, Lieutenant Thomas Jefferson Page,[2] had captured two pirate junks which had seized American cargoes ; and, as the Portuguese at Macao would not receive the prizes, Geisinger desired that the pirates should be tried in the Admiralty Court at Hong Kong. He therefore handed over the junks to Hay, who obtained the approval of Governor Samuel George Bonham ; whereupon the trial took place on October 4th.

At the trial full information came out as to the history and proceedings of Shap'n'gtzai, otherwise Chang-shih-wu-tz, who had lived in Hong Kong, under British protection, until 1846, and of Chuiapoo, otherwise Tzeeapo, who also had lived in Victoria as a

[1] Of the P. & O. Co.
[2] Afterwards an admiral in the Argentine service.

barber and a collector of facts which might be useful to him in his murderous profession. Just before the trial, Shap'n'gtzai had attacked and murdered a rival pirate and his people, and had then opened negotiations with the Chinese government with a view to entering the Chinese navy with his officers and fleet, and clearing the seas of other freebooters. Happily, the terms demanded were too high; and Shap'n'gtzai had to settle with the requirements of justice in another manner.[1]

On September 27th, 1849, Governor Bonham informed Hay that Chuiapoo was ravaging the coast about ninety miles to the eastward of Hong Kong. No other vessel being ready, Hay went in chase with the *Columbine* only. On the night of the 28th, fourteen pirate junks were observed leaving Tysami, which was in flames. Followed and closed, they refused to heave to, and showed a desire to fight. The *Columbine* anticipated them by pouring three broadsides into their leader, and then, the breeze having fallen, had to manœuvre by means of her sweeps. After a brisk action, the pirates made off early in the morning of the 29th, pursued by the sloop. In the chase, three junks, which had suffered more than the rest, were abandoned, their crews being distributed among the remaining eleven. Towards noon, the *Canton* was seen approaching. She had been chartered by an American, Mr. Watkins, to search for a missing ship; and, with Watkins's cordial consent, her master, Mr. Jamieson, gallantly steamed for the pirates. They were, however, too strong for him, and all he could ultimately do was to endeavour to tow the *Columbine* into action, but, receiving a shot through his steam chest, he could not accomplish even that. The *Columbine* herself grounded while trying to follow one of the pirates, and had to be towed off, but, when still aground, she sent her pinnace, cutter and gig, under Lieutenant James Henry Bridges, who was accompanied by Mr. Watkins, after the fugitive. These boarded and carried her after a desperate struggle. Seeing one of the pirates running below with a lighted joss-stick, as if to blow up the magazine, Midshipman Charles Ramsay Goddard dashed after him, but, ere he could come up with him, the fellow fired the powder. The explosion so seriously injured the brave Midshipman that he died next day. Besides him, three men were killed, and six wounded in the attack.[2]

---

[1] *China Mail*, Oct. 4th, Oct. 11th, 1849.
[2] Hay to Collier, Sept. 30th, 1849; *Hong Kong Register*, Oct. 2nd, 1849; *China Mail*, Oct. 4th, 1849.

The *Canton* towed the *Columbine* to the entrance of Bias Bay, and then proceeded with the wounded to Hong Kong, where she handed Hay's dispatch to the Commander-in-Chief, who happened to be there. Sir Francis Augustus Collier instantly ordered the *Fury*, steamer, 6, Commander James Willcox, with a strong detachment of seamen and Marines under Lieutenant William Garnham Luard, of the flagship *Hastings*, to go to the assistance of the *Columbine*. She joined her very early on October 1st, and, as soon as the light served, towed her to the mouth of Fanlokong creek.[1] The *Columbine* anchored off the mouth of this; and Hay, sounding in his boat, piloted the *Fury* up it, and soon discovered fifteen junks in line, which opened fire at about 10 A.M. The *Fury* replied smartly, and, in about three quarters of an hour, silenced the flotilla. The boats of both ships were then sent in, and by 4.30 P.M., under cover of an occasional shell, destroyed twenty-three pirate vessels, three new junks on the stocks, and many stores in the Typoon dockyard, capturing also more than two hundred guns. Although the *Fury's* hull was penetrated in thirty-two places, but one of her people was wounded. Such was the end of the remains of Chuiapoo's division.[2]

On the return to Hong Kong of the *Columbine* and *Fury*, Sir George Augustus Collier desired Hay to take measures for dealing in a like manner with Shap'n'gtzai's fleet, to the westward. The *Fury*, and the H.E.I. Co.'s steamer *Phlegethon*, Commander G. T. Niblett, I.N., were put under his orders, and he was allowed a free hand.

The little command left Hong Kong on October 8th, and worked along to Hoihow, where, meeting admiral Hwang, Hay and Willcox accompanied that officer to Kiungchau, the capital of Hainan, to see Governor Ho, in order to obtain permission for Hwang to co-operate. Permission was readily granted for Hwang and his staff to embark in the *Fury*; and it was arranged that Hwang's junks, if they could not keep up with the British, were to make rendezvous at Guiechau island. The moral effect of this association was good, though its fighting value was nothing, seeing that the junks were not sighted again.

Shap'n'gtzai was followed to Pakhoi, thence to Chukshan, and

---

[1] An arm of Bias Bay.

[2] Hay to Collier, Oct. 2nd, 1849; Hong Kong letter of Oct. 30th, in *Times*; *Friend of China*, Oct. 29th, 1849; *Times*, Dec. 22nd, 1849.

thence, still further to the westward, into waters for which there were then neither charts nor sailing directions. The pirate had hidden himself inside the bar in the Cua Keum, or Cua Cam, one of the three mouths of the Red River, or Sangwa, which then formed the boundary between China and Cochin China. From this mouth numerous creeks extend into the other mouths, the Cua Nam Trou and the Cua Tray ; and all the mouths run into one long, deep lagoon, which discharges over the bar into the sea. Ten miles up the Cua Keum is the town of Haiphong, then Cochin Chinese, and not, as now, French. Shap'n'gtzai had threatened that place in order to obtain supplies, so that the local authorities wished well to the British.

The squadron pushed slowly up through the archipelago of the estuary; and, on October 18th, at Gowtosham, found a suspicious junk, which the *Phlegethon* destroyed, and from which a couple of prisoners were taken. One of these revealed that the pirates were twelve miles away among the islands, and that the destroyed junk had been their look-out vessel. On the 19th, Hay, with Willcox, Hwang, and an interpreter, reconnoitred, and satisfied himself that the pirates were in the Cua Keum, and were preparing to attack Haiphong. On the 20th, he saw them over the islands, and, after vain attempts to find a channel to them, fell in with a fisherman who volunteered to point one out. As the squadron approached,

"it was seen," says Hay, "that twenty-seven of the fleet were anchored inshore of the banks and islands which lay opposite to the Cua Keum. They were anchored in a line slightly concave to the sea and river mouth, and extended about a mile and a half, with their heads to the north, and springs on their cables. The flagship, of 42 guns, was twelfth from the van, and the other twenty-six seemed able to show nine guns on the broadside. Two hundred and sixty-four guns were therefore bearing on the narrow entrance. They were anchored in close order, and there was no room or more to anchor in line at that anchorage. The islands and mud flats were too wide to make it possible to shell them from outside. They were too strong to be attacked with the *Phlegethon* and boats alone, and when the estuary in which they were anchored was entered by the squadron, it was too narrow to make it practicable to take advantage of accurate fire from a distance."

At about 4.30 on October 20th, Hay, who was in the *Phlegethon*, led in, followed by the *Fury*, which had the *Columbine* in tow. As soon as the *Phlegethon* was inside the bar, the pirates opened fire. Unfortunately for the enemy, the tide, which had just begun to ebb, swung the pirates so that they lay in a bow and quarter line, with their heads to the north-west, and their broadsides bearing across one another's sterns. Ere they could correct this, the attackers seized the opportunity of placing themselves in positions of comparative immunity. The *Columbine* anchored about six hundred yards from the flagship's quarter; the *Phlegethon* engaged and destroyed the two rear ships, the only ones whose guns bore upon the *Columbine*; and the *Fury* dealt with the van. When Hay had destroyed the two ships mentioned, he went in his boat to the *Fury*, which, he found, had destroyed the four van ships, and was engaging the next vessel, to the great delight of admiral Hwang. Hay then rowed on to the *Columbine*. As he went, the pirate flagship blew up, and her hull began to drift down towards the sloop, until Niblett pushed in with the *Phlegethon*, and towed the *Columbine* out of danger. By nightfall all the twenty-seven junks were entirely destroyed; but Shap'n'gtzai had saved himself; and the island between Cua Keum and Cua Nam Trou was full of fugitives, while, in a creek two miles higher up were numerous pirate ships that had not been able to find anchorage on the scene of the action; and still other vessels were in the Cua Tray. Nowhere, however, were more than nine lying together. After service on Sunday the 21st, the *Phlegethon*, with the *Columbine's* boats, went into the Cua Tray; the paddle-box boats of the *Fury*, under Lieutenant George Hancock, entered one of the creeks opening from the Cua Keum; and the *Fury* and *Columbine* remained to blockade the river at the point of junction of the various channels. In the Cua Tray, twenty craft were destroyed; Hancock accounted for nine; in all, thirty were taken or sunk that day. On the 22nd the Chinese authorities from Haiphong arrived to take possession of the wrecks, the guns, and the fugitives on the islands, and to express their gratitude.[1] Lieutenant George Edward Serocold Pearce Serocold, of the *Columbine*, seems to have been the only person hurt on the British side in the action.

On the 23rd the squadron sailed, the *Phlegethon* being subsequently detached with news to Tienpakh, and the other two vessels, after having called at various places, anchoring at Hong Kong on November 1st, to find that the Commander-in-Chief, Sir Francis Augustus Collier, had died three days before. He had, only just before his death, cancelled the mischievous order of March 8th, 1845.

---

[1] *Naut. Mag.*, 1852 (Hay's remarks), 63, 138; Hay, 'Supp. of Piracy,' etc. (1889); B. Scott, 'Account of Dest. of Fleets,' etc. (1851); *Times*, Jan. 22nd, 1850; Hay to Collier, Oct. 23rd, 1849.

For their services on these occasions Commanders Edmund Moubray Lyons,[1] John Charles Dalrymple Hay,[2] and James Willcox[3] were posted; Lieutenants George Hancock,[4] and James Henry Bridges[5] were made Commanders; and Mates Ennis Chambers,[6] Francis Arden Close,[7] and Douglas Walker[8] were made Lieutenants.

The operations were exceedingly well-conducted throughout; and, although it cannot be pretended that the pirates, when once they were brought to bay, were formidable or even worthy opponents for British warships, it is impossible to withhold admiration for the manner in which, in defiance of the difficulties raised by the ministry at home, the naval officers in China not only hunted down and destroyed the freebooters, but also gained from the local representatives of the United States, Portugal, China, and Cochin China the aid and support without which they would have been seriously crippled in their proceedings.

Piracy was also rife in many other quarters during this period. The Moorish pirates, whose outrages have been mentioned so often in these pages, continued their depredations well into the second half of the nineteenth century; and they perpetrated outrages not only in the Mediterranean but also in the Atlantic, where, on one particular occasion, a piratical flotilla of several vessels was known to be cruising off Cape St. Vincent, though it does not appear that it was ever caught. A band of Moorish pirates was, however, severely chastised by the *Fantôme*, 16, Commander Sir Frederick William Erskine Nicolson, Bart. The freebooters had captured a British merchant brig, the *Ruth*, and Nicolson was sent from Gibraltar in pursuit. Finding his enemies off Cape Treforcas on May 12th, 1846, in possession of the brig, which was aground under cover of a large force drawn up on the beach, he manned and armed his boats, and sent his Master, Francis Herbert Niblett, with one party, to get the prize off, while he, with another party, occupied the attention of the Moors, and eventually drove them from the shore. The brig, with her valuable cargo, was recovered, and very many of the pirates were slain; but the enterprise cost the life of Midshipman Richard Boys, and the wounding of eight people, including the first Lieutenant, John Sanderson (2).[9] In this affair every officer of

---

[1] Oct. 4th, 1849.
[2] Jan. 20th, 1850.
[3] April 10th, 1850.
[4] Jan. 24th, 1850.
[5] Aug. 3rd, 1850.
[6] Jan. 15th, 1850.
[7] May 20th, 1850.
[8] Sept. 2nd, 1850.
[9] Letter in *Naut. Mag.*, 1846, p. 373; O'Byrne pp. 817, 1025.

the *Fantôme* was engaged, including the Surgeon and the Clerk. Nicolson was posted as from the day of the action, and Sanderson was made Commander as from the same date.

Later in the same year, the boats of the *Siren*, 16, Commander Harry Edmund Edgell, under Lieutenant Edmund Moubray Lyons, captured four piratical craft, with sixty men, near the Turkish island of Stanchio.[1]

On October 31st, 1848, the merchant brig, *Three Sisters*, left Gibraltar with a cargo for Malta. Two days later, while becalmed off Cape Treforcas, she was attacked by several armed and strongly-manned pulling boats from the Riff coast of Marocco. The master of the brig, unable to offer any resistance, ordered his crew into the boat and abandoned the vessel, making for the open sea, and being fired at as he went. The *Three Sisters* was towed by her captors into a neighbouring bay. The fugitives were picked up by another British brig, and carried back to Gibraltar. On the same evening the steam sloop *Polyphemus*, Commander James Johnstone M'Cleverty, started thence on a punitive expedition, and, on the following morning early, ran into Al Khoyamich bay, cruising onwards towards Cape Treforcas. On the morning of November 8th, upon opening Point Calla Tremontana, she sighted the prize ashore below some precipices and ravines which were crowded with armed men, who commanded both the *Three Sisters* and their own boats, seven in number. There were at least five hundred of them. As the *Polyphemus* neared the brig the pirates fired at her, and she returned the compliment with grape, canister, and musketry, driving the foe to more secure positions. Lieutenant Alan Henry Gardner volunteered to go in the cutter, with a hawser, weigh the brig's anchor, and take her in tow. He successfully carried out his plan; but, ere it could be completed, the pirates got a 6-pr. or 9-pr. gun into a position where the sloop could not effectively reply to it, and, supporting it with musketry, wounded Lieutenant Edward Frodsham Noel K. Wasey, and two seamen. In the cutter only one man was hit.

M'Cleverty, perhaps rightly, refrained from landing to burn the pirates' boats, as he feared lest he could not carry out the service without incurring serious loss. It was, however, unfortunate that he could not read the offenders a severer lesson, for they were soon again at their old trade.

[1] *Naut. Mag.*, 1846, 551.

In 1851 they captured the Spanish vessel *Joven Emilia*; and on October 5th of the same year, a murderous act of piracy, committed by some of them in Botoya bay on the brigantine *Violet*, caused the governor of Gibraltar to send to the spot the *Janus*, 4, paddle, Lieutenant Richard Ashmore Powell. Powell departed on October 17th, arrived off the Riff coast on the following day, and, though seeing nothing of the *Violet*, found the *Joven Emilia*, high on the beach, entirely stripped. He manned his boats and proceeded to the wreck, where he dispersed a body of Moors, and destroyed some of their boats. On the 19th, off Cape Treforcas, the ribs of the *Violet* were discovered on the beach ; and, as the Bedouins in the neighbourhood fired at the steamer, the *Janus's* boats were again manned and armed, and a landing was effected with the object of destroying the enemy's coasters. Unhappily the pirates were in too great force for the small party to be able to deal with them. The people, after a brisk fight, had to retire with a loss of eight wounded, including Lieutenant Powell, who, however, was solaced for his hurt by being soon afterwards made a Commander.[1] There was much talk at Gibraltar of avenging this check, and of sending an overpowering expedition against the marauders, accompanied by the *Arethusa* and *Dauntless*; but although the *Janus*, escorted by the *Dragon*, 6, paddle, Captain Henry Wells Giffard, returned early in the following year to survey the scene of the disaster, and was again fired at by the Moors, it does not appear that any adequate reprisals were ever carried out against the offenders.

The good work done among the pirates of the Borneo seas by Keppel, Cochrane, Mundy, Rajah Brooke, and others, in 1845–47 had had the effect of greatly reducing the number of outrages on harmless traders and peaceable natives, but had not put a complete stop to them ; and in the summer of 1849 advantage was taken of the fact that many pirates were known to be then at sea, to despatch against them an expedition under Commander Arthur Farquhar, of the *Albatross*, 16, who had with him the *Royalist*, the H.E.I. Co.'s steamer *Nemesis*, the steam-tender *Ranee*, and a native flotilla under Rajah Brooke. The force first took up a position across the mouth of the Sarebas river, which was threatened with a visit from the freebooters; but on June 30th, learning that some pirates had attacked Palo, and gone thence into the Si Maring river, not far

[1] Nov. 4th, 1851.

from him, Farquhar made preparations for action. On the evening of the 31st the enemy was reported to be approaching, and the squadron got under way, the *Nemesis* proceeding to seaward to cut off fugitives, and the rest of the vessels bearing down upon the foe. Seeing the British tactics the pirates then made for the Kaluka river, but were opposed by boats under Lieutenants Arthur Wilms-hurst, and Henry Bryan Everest. This led to a running action along the coast, and, as darkness had fallen, it was extremely difficult to distinguish friends from foes. Numerous prahus, however, were sunk, the crew of one of them, while in the water, being fearfully cut up by the paddles of the *Nemesis*. In the small hours of July 1st Farquhar sent off the *Ranee* with dispatches for Brooke, who was then in the Kaluka, and himself entered the Sarebas river to prevent the escape of any of the pirates by the Rembas branch. Dawn showed the bay to be a tangle of wreckage. On the left bank of the river more than seventy prahus were ashore; and it was calculated that of 120 which had been in the Si Maring, fully eighty, with nearly 1200 Malays, had been destroyed. On the British side only a few slight injuries were received. Farquhar [1] afterwards burnt other prahus and some villages in the Sarebas, and yet others in the Rejang, and taught a lesson so severe and wholesome that it was not forgotten for many years. Nevertheless, the operations were adversely criticised in some quarters at home, and were freely, though falsely, supposed to have been dictated by considerations wholly personal to Sir James Brooke, whose conduct was never done full justice to until long afterwards.

It is impossible to find space here for mention of all the other gallant deeds that were done at about this time by the officers and men of vessels cruising for the repression of piracy and the slave trade. Something, however, must be said concerning a few of these exploits.

On August 13th, 1844, being off Fish Bay, on the West Coast of Africa, in a four-oared gig, with but one spare hand, Mate John Francis Tottenham, of the *Hyacinth*, 18, Commander Francis Scott, pursued, and ultimately drove ashore, a Brazilian slave brig of 200 tons, carrying two 4-prs., and a well-armed crew of eighteen, four of whom were wounded by the fire from Tottenham's musket. For this service, Tottenham was made a Lieutenant on December 27th following.[2]

---

[1] Posted, Oct. 27th, 1849.   [2] *Gazette*, 1844, pp. 5315–6.

On January 12th, 1845, Lieutenant John Lodwick, first of the steam sloop *Growler*, Commander Claude Henry Mason Buckle, while away cruising in the pinnace on the African coast, fell in with a suspicious felucca, which, on seeing the boat, hove to, though she might have escaped easily. When the pinnace was within thirty yards of the stranger, a whole tier of musket barrels was thrust over the bulwarks. Lodwick cheered on his men to board, and the felucca, as she opened fire, filled and went off. Lodwick replied with a round shot and 180 balls in a bag; but his enemy was too strong for him. Two of his men were shot dead; Lodwick himself and two others were severely wounded; six oars were smashed; and the pursuit had to be abandoned, the damaged and crippled boat being picked up by the *Growler* as she stood towards Gallinas. The felucca, which was afterwards overhauled and captured by a steamer, had the reputation of being one of the fastest craft on the coast, and had a crew of seventy English, French, and American scoundrels, with an English commander. Lodwick, for his bravery, was promoted on May 1st, 1845.

On February 27th, 1845, the *Wasp*, 16, Commander Sydney Henry Ussher, was cruising near Lagos, when she sighted a strange sail, and sent Lieutenant Robert Douglas Stupart in a boat in pursuit. In the evening the stranger was come up with, and found to be the Brazilian slave schooner *Felicidade*, with a crew of twenty-eight men. All of these, except the master and one other man, were transferred to the *Wasp*, and Stupart, with a Midshipman and fifteen seamen, remained in charge. On March 1st the boats of the *Felicidade* captured another prize, the *Echo*, with 430 slaves on board. Stupart shifted to her, leaving the Midshipman (Mr. Harmer), and eight men in the *Felicidade*; and both vessels then headed for Sierra Leone, where they were to have been condemned. They unfortunately separated, and, most of the *Echo's* people having been transferred to the *Felicidade*, there was a rising which resulted in the murder of all the Englishmen in the latter vessel, and the recapture of the slaver. She was, however, again taken on March 6th by the *Star*, 6, Commander Robert John Wallace Dunlop, who, suspecting that there had been foul play, took the pirates to Ascension, and put Lieutenant John Wilson [1] (6) in charge of the prize to carry her to Sierra Leone. On the voyage thither, the *Felicidade* encountered a heavy squall, which threw her

[1] A Lieut. of Feb. 22nd, 1843.

on her beam ends and left her water-logged, so much so, indeed, that the people had literally to huddle together on the gunwale. They had no boat, and could not get at their provisions, though they repeatedly endeavoured to dive for them. In these straits they made a small raft, and embarked, ten persons in all, for a two hundred mile voyage, without rudder, oar, or compass, and with scarcely any provisions and no water. This was on March 16th. They supported themselves by catching rain water in their little sail, and by capturing four of the numerous sharks which continually accompanied them; but they were not rescued until April 5th, when they were picked up in sight of land by the *Cygnet*, 6, Commander Henry Layton. Five of the unfortunates died; but Wilson and four seamen survived and recovered their strength.

On May 26th, 1845, after a two days' chase, the *Pantaloon*, 10, Commander Edmund Wilson, being then close to Lagos, came up with a large slave ship. Owing to a calm, the British sloop could not approach within about two miles. Wilson, therefore, hoisted out his cutter and two whale boats, which he placed under the command of his first Lieutenant, Lewis de Teissier Prevost, his Master, John Thomas Crout, and his Boatswain, Mr. Pasco. About thirty seamen and Marines formed the attacking party, which, as it neared the slaver, was exposed to a heavy fire of round, grape, and canister. This was replied to with musketry. The boats were half an hour under fire ere they could get alongside. Prevost and Pasco boarded on the starboard, and Crout from the cutter on the port. Crout actually leapt through a gun port as the gun was being discharged through it, and his seconder was blown into the water by the blast, but was soon up again. There was a most desperate hand to hand fight on deck, and the slavers were not overpowered until they had lost 7 killed and as many wounded. The prize was a polacca-rigged craft of 450 tons, carrying four 12-prs. and about fifty people, and she was a pirate as well as a slaver. The British loss was 2 killed or fatally injured, and 6, including Crout and Pasco, wounded. Prevost was promoted on August 30th following.[1] Unfortunately there was in those days no means for adequately rewarding the gallantry of officers like Crout and Pasco.

At about the beginning of the year 1846 an extraordinary affair happened at Maranhão, in northern Brazil. The *Alert*, 6, Commander Charles John Bosanquet, having captured a Brazilian

[1] *Naut. Mag.*, 1845, p. 611; O'Byrne, 925.

slaver, containing between seventy and eighty slaves, off Cabinda, despatched her, under Mate Edward Frodsham Noel K. Wasey, to Sierra Leone, for adjudication.   By continuous bad weather she was driven to Maranhão, where she arrived with seven feet of water in the hold, and in a sinking condition.   While Wasey was on shore endeavouring to obtain protection for the slaves until he could procure another vessel, a party of brigands, disguised as Brazilian soldiers, visited the prize, and invited crew and slaves to land, as the water was washing over the decks.   The crew, having no orders to stir, refused ; but the slaves were taken ashore, and were never afterwards recovered.[1]   In consequence of the manner in which he had managed his water-logged craft, Wasey was promoted on March 10th, 1846, to be Lieutenant.

Difficulties with Arab chiefs concerning the slave traffic between Madagascar and the mainland summoned the *President*, 50, Captain William Pearce Stanley, bearing the flag of Rear-Admiral James Richard Dacres (2) to the neighbourhood in 1847, and ultimately led to an attack by her boats on a stockaded position at Anjoxa. The fighting, however, was not of a very serious description.

On July 22nd, 1847, the *Waterwitch*, 10, Commander Thomas Francis Birch, having the *Rapid*, 10, Commander Edward Dixon, in company, captured the Brazilian slave brigantine, *Romeo Primero*, and subsequently sent her, under Lieutenant Walter George Mansfield, with four seamen, to St. Helena for adjudication. Mansfield found himself obliged to bear up for Sierra Leone, and, on August 11th, four of the slaver crew rose on him and his men. Mansfield, though wounded in nine places, succeeded in preserving the prize, but lost one of his people in the struggle.   On September 1st he entered port.   On his recovery he was deservedly promoted.[2]

In the following year, Lieutenant Francis James d'Aguilar, of the *Grecian*, 16, Commander Louis Symonds Tindal, defeated an attempt, somewhat similar to that made at Maranhão in 1846, to retake a prize slaver at Bahia.   In this case, however, the people from the shore employed force, and had to be repelled by musketry fire, losing 10 killed and 30 wounded.   D'Aguilar's prize crew consisted of 10 men only, and the officer and most of his people were wounded.

In 1848, the *Bonetta*, 3, Lieutenant Frederick Edwyn Forbes,

[1] *Naut. Standard*, 1846.   [2] Com. Dec. 31st, 1847.

did some specially good service on the west coast of Africa, capturing the *Phoco-foo*, the *Tragas Millas*, the *Andorimha*, the *Alert*, the *Louiza*, and other slavers, within a short period.

In 1849, the officer who afterwards became Admiral Sir William Graham gained his first commission owing to the manner in which he distinguished himself on the occasion of the capture of the armed slaver *Unaio* by the boats of the steam-sloop *Hydra*, 6, Commander Grey Skipwith, on the south-east coast of America. In December of the same year, on the west coast of Africa, Commodore Arthur Fanshawe, C.B., of the *Centaur*, 6, steamer, detached his Captain, Claude Henry Mason Buckle, in the *Teazer*, 2, steamer, Lieutenant Jasper Henry Selwyn, with the French steamer, *Rubis*, 2, on a very successful expedition against the black pirates in the river Seba. Unhappily the affair cost the life of Lieutenant John Crocket, R.M.A.

In the course of 1851, Coçioco, a usurping king of Lagos, then one of the chief centres of the slave trade, became troublesome and intractable. After having peaceably received Mr. Beecroft, British Consul at Fernando Po, and the British naval officers on the station, he had refused to promise, on behalf of himself and his subjects, not to favour the illicit traffic, and had also forbidden the boats of the men-of-war to proceed up the river to his town. Mr. Beecroft determined to seek another interview with the king; and, in order that Coçioco should be under no misapprehension concerning the seriousness and solemnity of the British demands, he arranged that the armed boats of the squadron should accompany the mission under a flag of truce. Accordingly, a channel over the bar was surveyed by the Masters of the *Waterwitch*, 8, Commander Alan Henry Gardner, and the *Bloodhound*, iron paddle steamer; and at daylight on November 25th, 1851, the *Bloodhound*, with a white flag, preceded by Mr. Beecroft in the *Harlequin's* gig, and followed by the armed flotilla, started up the river. The boats engaged were :—

From *Philomel*, 8, Commander Thomas George Forbes (senior officer); whaler, under Com. Forbes; pinnace, with 12-pr. carr., under Lieut. George Bell Williams; cutter; and second whaler.

From *Harlequin*, 12, Commander Arthur Parry Eardley Wilmot; gig, with Mr. Beecroft, under Com. Wilmot; pinnace, under Lieut. Charles Fenton Fletcher Boughey; cutter; and two whalers.

From *Volcano*, 5, paddle, Commander Robert Coote; whaler, under Com. Coote; paddle-box boat, under Lieut. John Milward Reeve; second paddle-box boat, under Lieut. Charles Aylmer Pembroke Vallancey Robinson; cutter.

From *Niger*, 14, screw, Commander Leopold George Heath; gig, under Com. Heath; pinnace, under Lieut. Montagu Buccleuch Dunn; three cutters; whaleboat.
From *Waterwitch*, 8; whaler, under Com. Gardner; pinnace, under Lieut. William Graham; cutter; whaler.
In all, 23 boats, with 250 officers, seamen, and Marines.

At the bar the force was saluted with musketry fire, of which, however, no notice was taken, the flag of truce being kept flying. Within a mile and a half of the town, the *Bloodhound* grounded; but the boats kept on in line, until they were fired at from both guns and musketry on shore. At length the boats replied with shrapnel and solid shot, while the *Niger*, from below the bar, threw some shells at the position whence the first fire had proceeded. For nearly an hour the fire continued; and then the boats dashed in simultaneously to an assigned landing-place, where their crews disembarked, and, leaving about ninety officers and men as a guard on the beach, fought their way into the town. Their progress was most hotly disputed, especially after they had entered the narrow streets; and, as the number of natives opposed to them was at least five thousand, the attackers suffered severely. Forbes fired as many houses as he could; and, despairing of being able to accomplish more, retreated in good order, and re-embarked. That night he refloated the *Bloodhound*, and, on the following morning, returned to the squadron. In this affair, which, though costly and ineffective, was most bravely conducted, the two Mates of the *Niger*, John George Fitzherbert Dyer, and Henry Hyde Hall, were killed, and ten people were badly wounded, numerous others being hit by spent balls, etc.[1] The *Niger* took the wounded to Sierra Leone, and communicated with Commodore Henry William Bruce, who, while engaged in organising a further expedition, ordered the *Harlequin* to remain near Lagos to prevent Coçioco from interfering with the missionary establishment at Badagry, which he had previously harried, and which had given shelter to Akitoye, the legitimate king of Lagos.

Commodore Bruce procured the co-operation of Akitoye, and nearly five hundred of his followers, who took up a position near the intended scene of action; and he intrusted the carrying out of his plans to Captain Lewis Tobias Jones, of the *Samson*, 6, paddle, and Captain Henry Lyster, of his own flagship, the *Penelope*, 16, paddle. The craft employed in the operations were the *Bloodhound*,

[1] Forbes to Bruce; *Naut. Mag.*, 1852, p. 109.

the *Teazer*, 3, screw, the *Sealark*, 8, Commander Edward Southwell Sotheby, and the boats of the *Penelope, Samson, Volcano,* and *Waterwitch.* The *Bloodhound* was commanded by Lieutenant Russell Patey, and the *Teazer* by Lieutenant Charles Tayler Leckie; and the boats were under Commanders Robert Coote, Alan Henry Gardner, and Charles Farrel Hillyar. The resistance that was met with indicated how hopeless had been the chances of success upon the occasion of the first attack, and how unwise Commodore Bruce, or the officer immediately responsible, had been to permit a comparatively weak expedition to ascend to the town, even though it bore a flag of truce at its head.

The squadron arrived at the mouth of the river on December 23rd, 1851. On the 24th, Captain Jones landed below the town, and met Mr. Beecroft, and Akitoye. The 25th, being Christmas day, was spent quietly, except that the enemy amused himself by firing at the ships, which were well out of range. On the 26th, part of the force moved up the river under a brisk fire; but, before anything could be accomplished, both the *Bloodhound* and the *Teazer*, each of which had with her a division of boats, unfortunately grounded. As the *Bloodhound*, which was in advance, was greatly imperilled, Lieutenant Thomas Saumarez (2), with the boats of the *Samson,* and some Marines under Lieutenant Edward McArthur, R.M.A., was despatched to attempt a landing and to spike the guns which most annoyed the little steamer. He made a most gallant effort, but, being at length wounded in three places, and having Midshipman Thomas Richards killed, and 10 of his people badly hit, he was obliged to give the order to retire. That day little more could be done beyond preventing the enemy from sending their boats against the stranded *Bloodhound.* In the meantime an even more vigorous effort was made to relieve the *Teazer* from the fire of the most troublesome of the guns on shore. A considerable landing force was sent in; and, although received on touching the beach with a point-blank discharge from about 1500 muskets, the officers and men pushed steadily on, and captured the stockade whence the annoyance had proceeded. Captain Lyster led this attack, and among those with him who more specially distinguished themselves were Lieutenant John Corbett, and Assistant Surgeons Michael Walling, and Robert Sproule, M.D. (acting). Corbett had the honour of spiking the guns.

Scarcely had this success been won ere it was perceived that the enemy had got round to the rear of the attacking party, and had seized a boat, which they were dragging off to place her under 'cover of some still uncaptured guns. There was a slight confusion in re-embarking; and, taking advantage of it, the blacks rushed forth from the woods on all sides, and poured in a heavy fire at pistol range. Midshipman F. R. Fletcher, and many men were killed, and more were wounded. To make matters worse, some stupid or disaffected Kroomen in the *Victoria,* a boat belonging to Mr. Beecroft, the consul, let go her anchor without orders, and brought her up under the very hottest of the fire. Lyster and Corbett went back to her to discover what had happened, and the former ordered the cable to be slipped; but, as it was a chain-cable, the end of which was clenched to the boat's bottom, it could not so easily be got rid of. With the greatest coolness and gallantry, Corbett leant over the bows, and at length cut the cable with a cold chisel, receiving, how-ever, as he did so, five new wounds, in addition to one which he had previously received on shore. Thus the *Victoria* was saved, and carried off to the *Teazer.* Lyster, while leaving her to get into his own boat, was hit in the back. The fire continued so hot, and so many of his people had by that time fallen, that he judged it imprudent then to make further efforts to retake the captured boat; but another party, under Mate James Bower Balfour, and Gunner H. A. Dewar, presently succeeded in putting a rocket into her magazine and blowing her up. At sunset, after great exertions, the *Teazer* was got off and anchored out of gunshot.

This rescue of the *Teazer* was a most costly affair. Fifteen officers and men of the squadron were killed or mortally wounded, including Midshipman F. R. Fletcher, and Master's Assistant H. M. Gillham, and no fewer than 63 people were wounded, in-cluding Captain Lyster, Commander Hillyar, Lieutenant Corbett, and Lieutenant John William Collman Williams, R.M. In addition to the medical officers already mentioned, Surgeon Richard Carpenter, and Assistant-Surgeon John Barclay, M.D., rendered most valuable and devoted services to the wounded in very difficult circumstances.

Soon after 7 A.M. on the 27th, the *Teazer* steamed up towards the still grounded *Bloodhound,* accompanied by her flotilla of boats. Captain Jones, who was in the *Bloodhound,* ordered the boats which were with her to make a diversion, and indicated to the *Teazer* the position in which he desired her to anchor. She anchored there at 8.10 A.M. A general attack on the town was soon afterwards begun, the rocket boats, under Lieutenant Edward Marshall, making splendid practice, firing numerous houses, and at length blowing up a magazine.

Up to that time Cŏote's and Gardner's divisions of boats had not moved to the scene of action. Coote arrived at 10.30 A.M., and Gardner at 1.45 P.M. An hour later, Coote, with some gunboats and a rocket boat, was sent forward to fire a few rounds at Coçioco's house; and then, feeling that the place was as good as in his possession, Captain Jones sent in to demand a capitulation. It was Saturday afternoon. The chief was therefore allowed until Monday morning to think over his position. On the Sunday, however, Coçioco abandoned the town and fled to the woods; and Akitoye, having come up the river, was formally installed as king in such buildings as had escaped destruction. Only a small British party, under Coote, was that day landed. On Monday, the 29th, Gardner landed with Coote and a larger party, which embarked or destroyed fifty-two guns of one kind or another.

Captain Jones, in his dispatch to the Commodore, specially mentioned Captain Lyster, Commander Hillyar,[1] Lieutenants Edward Marshall,[2] Frederick Dampier Rich, John Corbett,[2] and Thomas Saumarez (2); Gunner J. Cook, of the *Samson*; Boatswain's Mate Charles Blofield; George Yule, R.M.A.; Surgeon Samuel Donnelly; Paymaster Thomas Hockings; and Clerk Robert Henry Bullen,[3] than whom " no lieutenant could have done better."[4]

It may be added that, in 1861, Docemo, a subsequent king of Lagos, ceded the island and port to Great Britain, receiving in return a pension of £1000 a year until his death in 1885.

The provisions of the treaty of Yandaboo have already been summarised in this volume.[5] It will be recollected that in that instrument Burmah engaged, in 1826, to receive a British resident at the court of Ava. No resident was actually sent until 1830. For seven years after that date the Burmese Government behaved in a more or less unsatisfactory manner; and, on April 16th, 1837, Tharrawaddy, having seized the crown, repudiated the treaty, and obliged the resident, who was not properly supported by the Indian Government, to withdraw, leaving an assistant in charge. A new resident was appointed in 1838; but he was not received; and, in 1840, the establishment at Ava was broken up, the only British

---

[1] Posted, Feb. 20th, 1852.
[2] Com., Feb. 20th, 1852.
[3] Paymaster, Feb. 20th, 1852.
[4] Bruce to Admiralty; Jones to Bruce.
[5] *See* p. 249.

representative remaining in Burmah being a Rangoon merchant, who took charge of letters, etc. The long-suffering of the British emboldened the Burmese, who presently began to commit various tyrannical acts. Two, perpetrated in 1851, brought matters to a crisis. A master of a British ship was illegally detained at Rangoon on a wholly baseless charge of having drowned his pilot, and was obliged to purchase his freedom; and another master was similarly detained on a charge of having murdered one of his crew, who had, in fact, died at sea.[1] These masters, naturally and properly indignant, forced the Indian government to take action; and in November, 1851, H.M.S. *Fox*, 42, screw, Commodore George Robert Lambert, Commander John Walter Tarleton, with the H. E. I. Co.'s steamer *Tenasserim*, sailed from Calcutta to inquire into the situation. Ere they anchored off Rangoon on November 25th, they were joined by H.M.S. *Serpent*, 12, Commander William Garnham Luard, and by the H. E. I. Co.'s steamer *Proserpine*.

Lambert, on his arrival, was informed of numerous additional acts of oppression which had been committed by the governor of Rangoon. The Commodore sent to India for additional instructions, and, in the meantime, demanded the dismissal of the governor, who, on his part, assembled large forces, and armed a Burmese warship, the *Yathunah-gee-mhon*,[2] the property of the king. Outrages continued in the town; but on January 1st, 1852, the King sent a pacific message to the Commodore, and promised that the governor should be superseded. During this period the force in the river was strengthened by the arrival of H.M.S. *Hermes*, 6, paddle, Commander Edmund Gardiner Fishbourne, and of the H. E. I. Co.'s steamer *Phlegethon*. The Burmese promises were not carried out. Fishbourne, who was sent ashore with some officers to deliver a letter, was insulted; and, it being evident that hostilities were intended, all British subjects in Rangoon were embarked, all British merchantmen in the river were towed to positions of safety, and the *Yathunah-gee-mhon* was taken possession of. Interview followed interview, and threat followed threat. On January 8th, Lambert was told that he would be attacked if any of his ships attempted to move down the river; and on the 9th, in consequence, he sent a number of merchantmen to sea under escort, ordered

---

[1] The facts are set forth in 'Recent Operations at Rangoon and Martaban,' by Rev. T. T. Baker, R.N., H.M.S. *Fox* (1852).

[2] *I.e.*, "precious, sleek, excellent sailing ship." Baker.

the *Proserpine* to Calcutta with dispatches, and declared a blockade
of Rangoon, Bassein, and Martaban.[1] Below the town was the
Dunnoo stockade. On January 10th, the *Fox* was towed into
position abreast of it, and a little later the frigate was fired at from
the work. The fire was, of course, returned; the stockade was
twice silenced; and several war boats were destroyed. That day
the *Hermes* also was fired at from another stockade. By the
morning of the 12th, Lambert had withdrawn his force to the
mouth of the river, and despatched the *Phlegethon* to Martaban.
He received a letter full of fresh promises contingent upon the
restoration of the *Yathunah-gee-mhon*; but by that time, as he felt,
the matter had passed out of his hands, and, on the following day, he
himself departed in the *Hermes* to take counsel with the Indian
government.

Lambert returned on January 26th, having been unsuccessful in
seeing Lord Dalhousie, who was at Simla. In his absence a few
troops had reached Moulmein in the *Tenasserim* and *Proserpine*,
which had been sent for them; and most of the blockading vessels
had been threatened. On January 31st, having received dispatches
from Calcutta by the H. E. I. Co.'s steamer *Fire Queen*, Lambert
caused that vessel to tow the *Fox* up towards Rangoon. On the
way the frigate was fired at from a stockade, and one of her people
was wounded. The *Fox* retaliated, but did not stop, and, late in
the afternoon, anchored off the Hastings shoal below the town.
The *Fire Queen*, on her way back, was fired at from more than
one point. The *Tenasserim* also, proceeding to join the Commodore,
was similarly treated. Lambert then sent Lieutenant William
Spratt (actg.) to the town with a letter enclosing the ultimatum of
the Indian government. Getting no satisfactory reply, Lambert
caused the *Tenasserim* to tow him back to the river's mouth, and
reported to Calcutta what had happened. On his way down he was
not fired at.

These preliminary movements and negotiations are recounted
chiefly in order to show with how much patience both Lambert and
the Indian government behaved in their dealings with authorities
who were everywhere hostile. The *Serpent*, in the Bassein river,
had been fired at on January 18th, and had not replied. On
February 4th, on her way to Negrais island, she was again fired
at, off Pagoda Point, from a stockade, which Luard thereupon

---

[1] For a sketch map of the scene of operations, *see* p. 239, *antea.*

destroyed; and on the 5th, the Burmese at Negrais brought upon their stockade a similar fate. But in no case did the British commence action, and in no case did they interfere in any way with private property. At length, on February 20th, the *Fire Queen* brought dispatches which intimated that a large military force would be embarked in the following month for Burmah at Madras and Calcutta; that Rangoon, Martaban, and, in certain eventualities, Bassein, were to be seized and held as bases for the contemplated operations; and that, if the Burmese authorities should not speedily come to reason, their country must be conquered and annexed to India.[1] Late, but not too late, the Indian government adopted a firm and dignified attitude. It afforded, however, a last chance to the King for saving his position. A subsidiary dispatch, received by Lambert on February 26th by the H. E. I. Co.'s steamer *Enterprise*, while imposing new and more arduous conditions, declared that if these were complied with by April 1st, Burmah would yet be spared. But the enemy continued to concentrate troops, and maintained an increasingly provocative attitude.

On April 1st, 1852, therefore, Rear-Admiral Charles John Austen (1), C.B., Commander-in-Chief in the East Indies, anchored off the mouth of the Rangoon river, the vessels of the Royal Navy then assembled there being the *Rattler* (temporary flag), *Fox*, *Hermes*, *Salamander*, *Serpent*, and a gunboat, in addition to a number of vessels of the Indian marine. On the following day arrived a contingent of transports from Bengal, bringing troops under Lieut.-General Godwin, C.B., military commander-in-chief; and on April 7th came the contingent from Madras. The total number of troops, European and Indian, thus collected was 5767, inclusive of the 18th, 51st, and a battalion of the 80th British regiments, with eight guns and eight howitzers.

Without waiting for the junction of the Madras contingent, Godwin at once despatched the H. E. I. Co.'s steamer *Proserpine* to Rangoon to ascertain whether any reply to the ultimatum had been received from Ava. She was fired at from stockades on both banks of the stream, and was only extricated by the excellent management of her commander, Mr. Brooking, who did not return until he had inflicted serious damage upon his assailants. The military commander-in-chief promptly took up the Burmese challenge. On April 3rd, the British left the Rangoon river, appearing next day before Martaban,

[1] Outline in Baker, 30.

which they attacked on the 5th.   The place was held by 5000 men ;
but in an hour and a half, during which time it was bombarded by
the ships, it was stormed by the troops, with a loss of only 50 men
wounded.   No one on the side of the attack was killed.   H.M. ships
engaged were the *Rattler, Hermes,* and *Salamander.*   After the
place had been garrisoned, the expedition returned to the Rangoon
river,[1] where, in the interim, Commodore Lambert, with H.M.S.
Fox and *Serpent,* and the H. E. I. Co.'s steamers *Tenasserim* and
Phlegethon, had been equally active.   He had proceeded up the
river on April 4th, and on the 5th, detailing the *Serpent* and
Phlegethon, under Commander Luard, to attack the Da Sylva
stockade, had devoted his own attention to two other works near
Dunnoo.   By the evening all three had been bombarded, and
destroyed by landing parties of seamen and Marines, which were
re-embarked without casualty.[2]

The general combined advance on Rangoon began on Saturday,
April 10th, all the ships, by the evening of that day, being anchored
below the Hastings shoal.   On the following morning, the shoal was
crossed ; and fire was at once opened on the H. E. I. Co.'s steamers
Feroze, Mozuffer, and *Sesostris,* which took up positions between
series of stockades on each bank.   They replied briskly, and, in
about an hour, blew up the magazine of a work which mounted
nine 18-prs., with the result of permanently silencing those guns.
Ere that time the *Fox* also had both broadsides engaged ; and her
boats presently landed some seamen and Marines, and a company of
the 18th Regiment.   This party, covered by the frigate, gallantly
stormed two stockades at Dalla, opposite Rangoon, and carried them
with a loss of only one man wounded.   The *Serpent* and *Phlegethon*
then passed the captured works, and anchored above Kemmendine,
to deal with the war-boats there assembled, and to prevent fire-
rafts from being sent down stream[3] ; while parties from the *Fox*
and *Rattler* stormed, carried, and burnt a third stockade on the
Dalla side.

Early on April 12th, the troops were landed near Rangoon,[4]
without opposition from the enemy ; and the Dagon Pagoda battery

---

[1] Godwin's disp. of April 6th.

[2] Lambert to Austen, April 6th.

[3] In executing this service the *Serpent,* in an encounter with a strong stockade,
had Asst.-Surgeon Chas. Sproull, and 7 men wounded.

[4] The city of that day was a mile and a quarter from the river, the city of the
previous war having been destroyed.

was shelled occasionally.   Late in the day a magazine in it blew up. As the troops advanced they were attacked from the jungle, and suffered much loss ere they carried the White House stockade.   On the 13th, desultory shelling of the town and stockades was continued, and several fires broke out in consequence ; but the storming of the town had to be postponed, owing to the heavy guns not having reached the army ; and, amid terrible heat, Godwin held his position until the morning of the 14th.

At 5 A.M. the whole force was put in motion.   The guns were dragged into position by about 120 seamen, under Lieutenant John William Dorville, of the *Fox*, in spite of a heavy fire from the Great Pagoda, and the pieces on the city walls ; and, at 11 A.M., after the eastern entrance of the Pagoda had been steadily battered, a storming party under Lieut.-Colonel Coote carried the position, the fugitives from which, as they fled by the southern and western gates, were mowed down by the guns of the ships.   The success was complete, Rangoon falling, and the works at Kemmendine being abandoned and destroyed.   Nor was it very costly ; for the army lost only 17 killed and 132 wounded.   As for the Navy, it suffered very little from the fire of the enemy, though it was terribly scourged by cholera.   Among the officers specially mentioned in the dispatches were Commanders Fishbourne, and Luard, Lieutenants George William Rice, and Dorville, Chaplain Thomas Turner Baker, who died of cholera, Surgeon John Moolenburgh Minter, and Assistant-Surgeon Thomas Seccombe.[1]

On the following day, April 15th, a determined attack was made by the enemy upon the little garrison at Martaban, but was easily repelled.   Another attack was made on May 26th, when the boats of the *Feroze* rendered good service in driving back the foe.   A less formidable attempt upon the post was made two nights later.[2]   The enemy did not, upon the whole, fight as well as in the campaign of 1826.   In fact, there appears to have been a strong Burmese party which was quite ready to accept a British annexation of their country as the price of liberation from tyranny and evil government.

On May 17th General Godwin and Commodore Lambert, with a force which included the Royal Marines, and some seamen of the *Fox*, embarked at Rangoon in the *Tenasserim*, *Sesostris*, and *Mozuffer*, and proceeded to the entrance of the Bassein river, where they were

---

[1] Austen to Dalhousie, April 16th ; and disps. of Godwin.   Baker, 61–78.
[2] 'Madras Art. Records,' Aug. 1852.

joined by the *Pluto*. On the 19th they ascended the river, and, in the afternoon, anchored abreast of the town of the same name. On both sides of the stream there were large stockades; but a strong party was at once landed, the pagoda was carried, and a mud fort, in which the Burmese defended themselves with obstinacy, was attacked. It was at length stormed by a detachment, mainly military, which was accompanied by Lieutenant George William Rice, R.N. The chief stockade on the opposite side of the river was then carried by a party under Commander C. D. Campbell, I.N., after a hot struggle. Among the wounded were Lieutenant Rice, and Lieutenant John Elliott, R.M. The total British loss in the operations at Bassein was 3 killed and 31 wounded.

It was determined next to attack Pegu; and with that object, Commander Tarleton, with the *Phlegethon*, her boats, and those of the *Fox*, conveying 230 troops, left Rangoon on June 3rd, and moved up the river, accompanied on the banks by a small contingent of friendly natives. On the 4th, as the expedition advanced, it was greeted with musketry fire from the Pegu side, whereupon Tarleton landed with the *Fox's* people, and, being joined by Commander G. T. Niblett, I.N., with men from the *Phlegethon*, obliged the enemy to retire from point to point. When, however, he was returning to his boats, he was galled by a smart fire from gingals and muskets; and, as he was loath to leave the Burmese in the belief that he was retreating, he obtained the services of a guide, led his people over a causeway which crossed the ditch, entered the city of Pegu, and forced the enemy to take refuge in the pagoda. While he was thus employed, Mate Henry Robert Douglas M'Murdo, who had been left in charge of the boats, was attacked, but, succoured by the troops, succeeded in getting all his craft to the other side of the river. The whole expedition was resting, in preparation for a further advance, when the Burmese from the pagoda moved out in force as if to assault. Making no longer delay, the British rushed at them, and carried the pagoda without further casualty. The day's work was accomplished with a loss of but 1 killed and 3 wounded. As soon as the defensive works had been destroyed, the expedition returned to Rangoon.

By that time certain military critics on the spot had begun to look askance on these raids into the enemy's country, believing, as they did, that such movements prevented the Burmese from concentrating their forces, and so tended to deprive the army of an oppor-

tunity, when it should be ready to do so, of striking a crushing and
decisive blow.   Commodore Lambert, however, seems to have considered that, under guise of making a reconnaissance alcng the
Irawadi, the naval force might still find opportunities of doing
useful service.   He therefore ordered Commander Tarleton to take
under his orders the *Medusa, Proserpine, Phlegethon, Pluto,* and
Mahanuddy, and to ascertain the numbers and position of the
enemy up the river.   The flotilla proceeded on July 6th.   At
Konnoughee, twenty-five miles below Prome, it fired at an armed
party on the banks, and was heavily fired at in return, two people
being wounded.   On the night of the 7th the command anchored off
Meaoung.

Early on the following morning it weighed again, and moved on
until within sight of a strongly fortified position near Akouktoung,
which was held by about ten thousand Burmese under Bundoola, in
order to block the approach to Prome and the capital.   Tarleton was
then entering what was known as the left or western channel of
the river, the channel which alone is usually navigable except at the
rainy season ; but, discovering from his native pilots that the eastern
or shallower channel was then possible, he turned off as soon as
the enemy fired at him, and was delighted to find that he had two
fathoms of water where he had expected to get little more than as
many feet.   There he despatched ahead the *Proserpine,* instructing
Commander Brooking, I.N., to do his best to overtake a small
Burmese steamer [1] which, he heard, had passed up only the day
before ; and, upon surveying his position, he realised that the entire
Burmese army, concentrated in the place which he had turned, was
in his rear, and that nothing lay between him and Prome.   The
temptation was too great to be resisted.   He pushed on, and by
daylight on July 9th was off the city.

There being no troops in the place, Tarleton disabled and sank
the iron guns belonging to the works, and embarked the brass ones.
In the afternoon the *Medusa* reconnoitred ten miles further up; and
it became practically certain that there were no obstacles of any
sort between the expedition and the capital, Ava, which could have
been reached within four days.   Being, however, without orders to
capture the metropolis, and, perhaps, being influenced by the talk of
the military critics already alluded to, Tarleton contented himself
with remaining for twenty-four hours at Prome, and then returning.

---

[1] She was not caught.

As he re-entered the main stream, Bundoola was observed to be in motion, as if intending to follow the steamers. The British opened fire on the Burmese troops and boats, between forty and fifty of the latter being taken or destroyed, and several valuable trophies captured. After nine days' absence, the flotilla rejoined without further adventure. Its casualties were insignificant. Lieutenant John Elliott, R.M., was wounded severely, and two other people, including Assistant Surgeon Frederick Morgan, were slightly hit.

In August and September reinforcements and fresh supplies were sent from India with a view to preparing for the general advance of what was styled the Army of Ava. In the interim, the *Zenobia*, and the schooner *Pegu* did some useful work above Martaban by dispersing a body of Burmese at Ketturhee, and destroying a stockade and village.[1] The operations were completed on September 2nd. A few days earlier, Commander Charles Frederick Alexander Shadwell, of the *Sphinx*, had gone up in the *Nemesis* to relieve Commander Tarleton,[2] who had previously been senior naval officer in the Irawadi ; and a few days later, the *Hastings*, 72, bearing Rear-Admiral Austen's flag, was towed by the *Rattler* to the Hastings shoal, and anchored off Rangoon.[3]

Towards the end of September, previous to which the Rear-Admiral had made a personal reconnaissance up the Irawadi in the *Pluto*, the forward movement began. Several of the steamers grounded, and there was much delay. On October 7th, off the island of Shouk Shay Khune, there occurred another misfortune, in the death of Rear-Admiral Austen,[4] who, still in the *Pluto*, had been taken ill on the night of the 5th, and who, being seventy-three years of age, had not sufficient strength to resist the attack.

From that island, which is not more than ten miles below Prome, the flotilla started again at daybreak on October 9th. Commodore George Robert Lambert, who had succeeded to the chief command, had his broad pennant in the *Fire Queen* ; and the other vessels of war employed, all belonging to the H.E.I. Co., were the *Enterprise*, *Mahanuddy*, *Sesostris*, *Medusa*, *Nemesis*, *Proserpine*, and *Phlegethon*, accompanied by boats of H.M. ships *Winchester*, *Hastings*, *Fox*, and *Sphinx*, under Captain George Granville Loch, C.B., Commanders

---

[1] *Moulmein Times.*
[2] Posted Sept. 27th, 1852.
[3] Laurie, *Pegu*, 51. She left again for Madras on Oct. 29th.
[4] His body was ultimately sent home in the *Rattler*.

Charles Frederick Alexander Shadwell, and Edward Bridges Rice, and Lieutenants George William Rice, Henry Shank Hillyar, Richard Bulkeley Pearse, Charles Doyle Buckley Kennedy, William Brace Mason, and William Henry Edye.

As soon as the vessels neared the city, the enemy opened fire upon them from a couple of guns, supported by musketry. Returning the fire, the steamers anchored; and some of the boats, under Captain Loch, were sent closer in, to clear the banks with shell and canister. A native gun, which was brought into action abreast of the *Fire Queen,* was dismounted when it had fired but one shot; and, soon afterwards, some of the troops were landed without difficulty, the rest being put ashore on the next morning, when, with a detachment of seamen and two 24-pr. howitzers under Commander Edward Bridges Rice, they easily captured the city. In the squadron, but four people were wounded, two of them being natives of India. The army's loss was almost equally trifling.[1]

At about that time a valuable reinforcement of light river steamers belonging to the H.E.I. Co. reached the scene of operations. Of these, one, the *Lord William Bentinck,* was sent on a reconnaissance to Pegu, and the others the *Nerbudda* and *Damooda,* carried up additional troops to Prome. Soon afterwards, Bundoola, having been ordered to report himself in disgrace at Ava, preferred to take his chances as a prisoner with the British, and, upon surrendering himself, was put on board the *Sesostris,* which was acting as depôt and guardship off Prome. Before any further movement of importance was attempted, Commander Shadwell, and the military post at Shouk Shay Khune, assisted by native allies, beat off a Burmese attack with great spirit; and other small bodies of the enemy were defeated at a place called the White Pagoda, at Akouktoung, and at a stockade opposite Prome.[2]

Pegu, after its capture in June, had been evacuated, as General Godwin did not consider that he had strength enough wherewith to hold it at that time. The next move was one for its recapture; and by the middle of November, a force was ready to proceed thither.

---

[1] Lambert to Govt. of India, Oct. 11th; Godwin to the same, Oct. 12th, 1852; Laurie, 77 *et seq.*

[2] At the White Pagoda, near Prome, on Nov. 1st, Capt. Loch, Com. Frederick Beauchamp Paget Seymour, and Lieuts. Henry Shank Hillyar, and Richard Bulkeley Pearse led the naval brigade. One man was wounded. At Akouktoung, on Nov. 4th, the same officers were present. Opposite Prome, on Nov. 11th, when Loch again commanded, the enemy abandoned their strong work at the first sign of attack.

This quitted Rangoon on the 19th in the *Mahanuddy*, *Nerbudda*, *Damooda*, and *Lord William Bentinck*, the army being under Brigadier Malcolm M'Neil, the naval arrangements being under Commander Shadwell, and the General himself accompanying the expedition. The neighbourhood of Pegu was reached on the evening of the 20th, and, upon the city being reconnoitred, it was found to be held by about four thousand men, with a stockade in their front. On the following morning, under fire from the steamers and boats, a landing was effected, Commander Rowley Lambert, of the *Fox*, superintending the operation so far as the guns were concerned, and Commander Frederick Beauchamp Paget Seymour, as a volunteer, placing himself at the disposal of the General. In the advance, the troops had to encounter a smart fire; but, having refreshed under cover of a wood, they presently charged across the moat, and drove the defenders into the pagoda, whence they were driven further with but slight resistance. The army lost in this affair 6 killed and 31 wounded; the Navy happily escaped without casualty. Besides the officers already mentioned, Lieutenants William Brace Mason, and John Hawley Glover, Mate Charles Ashwell Boteler Pocock, and Assistant Surgeon John Felix Johnson, besides several of the H.E.I. Co.'s naval officers, distinguished themselves.[1] A garrison of 430 men was left at Pegu, and the rest of the expedition returned to Rangoon.

Scarcely had the General departed ere Pegu began to suffer serious annoyance from the enemy, who, early in December, invested it more or less closely, and cut up a convoy of supplies which had been sent thither. On the 8th, therefore, Commodore Lambert despatched from Rangoon seven boats from the *Sphinx*, *Fox*, and *Mozuffer*, under Commander Shadwell, with, in all, 133 officers and men, to endeavour to open communications with Major Hill, who commanded the beleaguered garrison. On the 9th, news of a somewhat more serious nature arrived at Rangoon, and decided General Godwin to forward in addition 200 European troops in the *Nerbudda*, with some armed boats under Commander Rowley Lambert. In the meantime, Shadwell, on approaching Pegu on December 10th, was met with a very heavy fire, and obliged to retreat, having lost in a short time 4 men killed, and 28 people wounded, including Mate Charles Ashwell Boteler Pocock, and Midshipman Edgar Cookson. Returning, Shadwell met the

[1] Laurie, 100, 466.

Nerbudda; and, not knowing what force of Burmese might be at Pegu, he brought her back with him to Rangoon. Godwin at once determined to go himself to the threatened point; and before 10 P.M. on the 11th, Captain Tarleton, with 1050 troops in boats of the *Fox, Sphinx, Mozuffer, Berenice,* and *Fire Queen,* started for Pegu, being followed next morning by the *Mahanuddy* and *Nerbudda,* with Godwin and 400 additional Europeans. Among the naval officers with the expedition were Commanders Lambert, and Shadwell, and Lieutenant William Brace Mason.

On the morning of December 13th, Godwin having in the meanwhile caught up Tarleton, a landing of part of the force was effected five miles below Pegu, and half a mile from the first stockade, and the rest of the troops were put ashore early on the 14th, an advance following immediately, and being accompanied by Shadwell, with two boat guns and 75 men to drag them. Later in the day, when the enemy threatened some straggling camp followers on the river bank, Tarleton landed his whole available force, and drove off the foe. He was also obliged to put the *Nerbudda* ashore to repair damages caused by her having grounded on a stake. His position, in short, was an anxious one, until, at 2 P.M., he learnt of the success of the advanced force. The Navy had one man mortally wounded.[1]

General Godwin followed up the enemy, but without displaying great activity or persistence. By proclamation of December 30th, 1852, the province of Pegu was annexed to the Empire, and any immediate intention of effecting further conquests in Burmah was formally abandoned. The annexation was made public at Rangoon on January 20th.

It remained to expel from the new province such Burmese forces as were still in arms there. Much of that work was done by the land forces alone, but the Navy co-operated on several occasions. With the Martaban expedition, for example, which set out from Rangoon on January 4th, 1853, went Commodore George Robert Lambert, with his broad pennant in the *Sphinx.* A more exclusively naval adventure was undertaken by Shadwell, with the object of settling scores with a robber chieftain who oppressed the inhabitants of a district south of Bassein and westward of Rangoon; but this force, which was absent from Rangoon from December 24th, 1852, to the morning of January 1st, 1853, saw no fighting.

[1] Godwin of Dec. 15th; Tarleton of Dec. 16th; Lambert of Dec. 18th.

Unfortunately, although the war was over, one of these subsequent expeditions ended in a most regrettable disaster, in which the naval service suffered severely. In the neighbourhood of Donnabew was a notorious robber named Nya Myat Toon, against whom it became advisable to adopt stern measures. His stronghold lay about twenty-five miles from Rangoon. At the beginning of February, 1853, Captain George Granville Loch, C.B., with 25 naval officers, 185 seamen, and 62 Marines,[1] and Major Minchin, with 300 of the 67th Bengal Native Infantry, accompanied by two 3-prs. from the *Phlegethon*, were despatched from Rangoon against the freebooter, and landed near Donnabew on the 2nd.

On the 3rd the force marched along a jungle path, and encamped for the night in a deserted valley, where it was occasionally disturbed by distant shots. On the morning of February 4th, it proceeded about five miles further along the path, which terminated abruptly at a broad nullah, the lofty opposite side of which was entrenched and fortified. Suddenly, ere the people, who had been marching two or three abreast, could deploy, or bring up the guns which were in the rear, a most murderous fire was opened by the concealed enemy. Lieutenant Charles Doyle Buckley Kennedy, of the *Fox*, was among the first to be shot down. The gallant Loch led his men to the attack, and made two unsuccessful efforts to cross the nullah and storm the work. Heading a third attempt, he was mortally hit. Lieutenant Rowley Lambert, son of the Commodore, then assumed command, and led two more hopeless rushes, receiving four balls through his clothes, yet remaining unhurt. It quickly became apparent that the force must either retreat or be annihilated; and a retreat, therefore, was ordered along the narrow path by which the advance had been made. Most of the bearers and guides had fled, the dead could not be moved, the guns had to be spiked and abandoned; and, followed by an unrelenting fire, the party, its rear manfully covered by the grenadier company of the 67th, drew off as best it could, dragging with it its many wounded, and toiling under a broiling sun without water. It did not reach Donnabew, and the *Phlegethon*, until twelve hours had elapsed. Loch died on the 6th.[2] The Navy lost in all 7 killed and 52 wounded, and the troops, 5 killed and 18 wounded. Among the officers wounded were Lieutenant James Henry Bushnell, and

---

[1] From the *Fox, Winchester, and Sphinx.*
[2] Loch was born in 1813, and was a Capt. of Aug. 26th, 1841.

Mates Hugh Alan Hinde, and William Charles Fahie Wilson, of the *Winchester*, and Lieutenant John Hawley Glover, of the *Sphinx*. Lieutenant Horatio Nelson, of the *Winchester*, was mentioned by Lambert among the officers and men who were of special assistance in most trying circumstances.[1]

The catastrophe was due to overweening confidence, and contempt for a desperate enemy, resulting in neglect of proper precautions.[2]   In the breaking up of Nya Myat Toon's followers, a work which was afterwards accomplished by Brigadier-General Sir John Cheape, the Navy had little share, although Captain Tarleton, with a small party, was present with the expedition.

The war ended without the conclusion of the usual treaty of peace between the nations which had been engaged; and not until 1862 were ordinary relations resumed between the courts of Ava and London.

The honours granted to the Navy for its services during the arduous campaign were few, and were delayed.   On December 5th, 1853, Commodore George Robert Lambert was made a K.C.B., and Captains John Walter Tarleton, and Charles Frederick Alexander Shadwell[3] were given the C.B.   Rowley Lambert had been deservedly made a Commander on February 7th, 1853.   On February 25th, Lieutenants John William Dorville, Henry Shank Hillyar, and George William Rice (who died on March 18th following); Mates Hugh Alan Hinde, and Charles Ashwell Boteler Pocock; Second Master Richard Sturgess; and Assistant Surgeons Thomas Seccombe, Henry Slade and John Felix Johnson, had also received promotion.[4]

It has not been possible, in the course of this narrative, to devote much space to the work done during the war by the officers and men of the Indian Navy; but it should be added here that they rendered the most valuable services, and always willingly and loyally co-operated with the Royal Navy.

In these years there were almost innumerable actions between H.M. ships and Chinese pirates.   The conflicts were generally very

[1] Laurie, 226, and Disps.; *Friend of India*, Feb. 24th, 1853.

[2] Gen. Godwin later ordered that, in all combined naval and military expeditions, the senior military officer should have command, no matter the rank of the senior naval officer present. The questions thus raised were not fully decided until many years afterwards.

[3] Posted Feb. 7th, 1853.

[4] *Gazette*, Feb. 28th.

bloody, at least on one side ; for the pirates knew full well that, if captured alive and handed over to the Chinese authorities, they could expect no mercy, and might look forward to torture as well as to death. Several of the conflicts, moreover, cost the loss of valuable lives on the British side.

One of the most important occurred off Namquan (lat. 27° 15' ; long. 120° 20') in 1853.

On May 5th of that year, Commander Arthur Mellersh, of the *Rattler*, 6, screw, who was then at Amoy, was informed that a fleet of pirates was at anchor near Namquan, and had not only captured a valuable convoy of junks, but also fired at and driven off the British schooner *Spec*, which had formed the escort. Mellersh at once coaled, and proceeded on the following morning to the mouth of the River Min. Bad weather prevented him from gaining further information before the 10th, when Second-Master Alfred O. West reconnoitred in a cutter, picked up the *Spec*, and ascertained that the pirates were still at Namquan, waiting for their prizes to be ransomed. On the 11th, under cover of a fog, which lifted as she approached, the *Rattler* suddenly steamed right into the enemy's fleet. The Chinese cut their cables in panic ; but, finding that the set of the tide prevented them from escaping from the harbour, they prepared for close action, and, as soon as the sloop fired a gun, opened their broadsides upon her. There were seven junks and a lorcha, *No.* 19 ; and they pluckily bore up with intent to board. A shell from the *Rattler's* 8-in. gun, fired by Lieutenant George Adolphus Pidcock, blew up the pirate admiral, also sinking a craft alongside of him ; whereupon all the other vessels, except the lorcha, ran for the shore and beached themselves. The lorcha ceased firing, and impudently hoisted Portuguese and French colours.

Most of the fugitives who gained the shore were promptly slaughtered by the waiting villagers. The *Rattler's* boats were then lowered under Commander John William Dorville,[1] Second-Master West, and Mates Robert Elliot and James Willcox, to take possession of the abandoned vessels ; the cutter, however, under Lieutenant

---

[1] Dorville, who had previously been first Lieutenant of the *Rattler*, had been promoted on the previous Feb. 25th, but was still doing duty in the sloop. He was the author of an interesting book, 'Cruising in Many Waters.' He retired, as a captain, in 1867, and died in 1894 a retired admiral. Some of his earlier services are recorded in the *Friend of China*, Mar. 5th, 1853.

Pidcock, dashing off in separate pursuit of a body of pirates who, having seized a peaceful junk and murdered her crew, were pushing up the river in her and another craft in order to escape. Unhappily, when he got up with the enemy and boarded, his small force was overpowered, he and two men being killed, and the rest of his crew driven off. Assisted by the country people, the survivors at length regained the *Rattler*, and told their tale. Dorville, West, and Willcox instantly started in search of the junks in the river, but had to return owing to the darkness; nor was a further search, made on the following morning, any more successful. From one of the burnt junks one hundred and seventy pounds of silver were recovered. Four of the other junks were taken to Foochow, and the lorcha was handed over to the Portuguese at Macao. This affray cost the British an officer and two men killed, and seven people wounded. On the other hand, it cost the pirates the loss of eight vessels, no fewer than 84 guns,[1] and probably 500 lives. Willcox was deservedly made a Lieutenant on January 19th, 1854.

It was in the same year that the British Navy first came into intimate contact with the Ti-ping rebels, in whose repression it later took an active share. On March 19th, 1853, after a siege of eleven days only, the Ti-pings captured Nankin, the ancient capital of China, and thereby placed themselves in a position of such political importance as to induce Sir George Bonham, H.M. Plenipotentiary, to visit Nankin in order to ascertain the nature, principles, and objects of the victorious revolutionists. Accordingly, he embarked in the paddle sloop *Hermes*, 6, Commander Edmund Gardiner Fishbourne, and, after having been fired at in error by some Ti-ping forts at Chinkiangfoo, reached Nankin at the end of April, had friendly communications with the rebel leaders, and arranged that Great Britain should preserve a neutral attitude with regard to China's internal commotions.[2]

As early as 1854, however, the Navy came into hostile collision, if not with the Ti-pings themselves, at least with the troops opposed to them. An ambitious "house boy" named Aling, employed by one of the foreign merchants at Shanghai, raised a force, proclaimed himself general, and, allying himself with the rebels, seized the walled Chinese city of Shanghai which lies alongside of the foreign settlement on the Yangtsekiang,

---

[1] *Friend of China*, and disps., which Dorville brought home.
[2] Fishbourne: 'Impressions of China.'

but on the other side of the Yangkingpang creek. In rear of the foreign settlement was a race-course; in rear of the walled city were forts held by imperial troops who had been sent to oppose Aling; and between the forts and the race-course were rice-marshes, swamps and alluvial ground. The imperial troops got out of hand, and some of them assaulted an English gentleman and lady on the race-course on April 3rd. The braves were, however, dispersed by some unarmed British and American seamen who happened to be ashore on liberty. This exasperated the troops, who, it was rumoured, intended, by way of revenge, to loot and burn the foreign settlement in the course of the following night; where-upon the merchants ashore asked for assistance, and the war-ships in harbour, H.M.S. *Encounter*, 14, screw, Captain George William Douglas O'Callaghan, and *Grecian*, 12, Commander the Hon. George Disney Keane, with the U.S. corvette *Plymouth*, Captain John Kelly, landed a party which quickly mastered the small fort lying nearest to the settlement, and killed, wounded, or captured a number of Chinamen. The Captains then ordered the imperial troops to evacuate the remaining forts by 3 P.M. on April 4th. It was felt that the enemy would not willingly comply; and prepara-tions were made for compelling him to do so, it being arranged that Kelly, in virtue of his seniority, should command the attacking force of seamen, marines, and volunteers from among the foreign residents. Before the hour at which the ultimatum was to expire, the force, with guns, was ready in position before the forts. At 3 precisely, as the Chinese had not budged, the word was given, and a 12-pr. shrapnel shell was fired at the nearest work. The enemy made little stand, most of them fleeing at once. After sending in one more shell, the attackers charged. The imperialists succeeded in firing only one of their heavy guns; but that one killed three people and wounded several, while the storming party was tempor-arily checked at the ditch. Lieutenant Roderick Dew,[1] however, quickly pulled down a bamboo house, bridged the chasm at the rear of the works, and led the way across. This decided the matter. Upwards of 300 Chinamen were killed; the position was occupied; and on the following day a body of coolies destroyed the whole of the forts.[2] On this occasion there was very cordial good-feeling and co-operation between the British and United States navies. The

---

[1] Prom. for this service, June 16th, 1854. He was slightly wounded.
[2] Disps.: R.-Ad. Beardslee, U.S.N., in *Harper's Mag.*

pleasant nature of the comradeship, which was destined to become still more pronounced, especially in Chinese waters, may be gathered from the fact that, a seaman of the *Encounter* having lost his arm during the firing of a salute on July 4th, 1854, the anniversary of American Independence, the officers and men of the U.S.S. *Susquehanna* and *Vandalia* spontaneously subscribed for him the large sum of £283.[1]

It would be almost impossible to find space, in a work like the present, for accounts of all the affairs, small and great, which took place between Her Majesty's ships and pirates or slavers in the period under review. In spite of the distractions caused by the war with Russia, the Navy was as active as ever in 1854–56 in striving for the repression of these freebooters.

In November, 1854, the boats of the *Winchester*, 50, Captain Thomas Wilson (2), (flag of Rear-Admiral Sir James Stirling), *Encounter*, 14, screw, Captain George William Douglas O'Callaghan, and *Spartan*, 26, Captain Sir William Legge George Hoste, Bart., were repeatedly thus engaged in the Macao River. On the 2nd of that month, the boats of the *Winchester* and *Spartan* destroyed some junks in Tymmoon Bay; on the following day the boats of all three vessels were similarly employed off Tyloo; and, on the 13th of the month, parties from the same ships, and from the *Barracouta*, 6, paddle, Captain George Parker (2), and *Styx*, 6, paddle, Commander Frederick Woollcombe, carried a battery, and destroyed more junks in Coulan Bay.

On June 25th, 1855, the *Racehorse*, 14, Commander Edward King Barnard, while working up the coast between Amoy and Foochow, discovered and chased a piratical flotilla. On the following morning, one of the junks, mounting 6 guns, was boarded by the sloop's cutter, and burnt. In the afternoon other junks were engaged by the boats, one being burnt and another taken. A captured lorcha also was retaken, and towed to Amoy. The *Racehorse* then went again in search of the pirates; and on July 4th, made prize of a junk without much resistance, and later sent all her boats in chase of a much larger one. In the chase, the sloop's gig drew ahead, and pulled gallantly alongside. She was then overwhelmed with a shower of stink-pots, some of which blew up the ammunition in her. All her people were hurled into the water; but they were picked up by the cutter, seven out of the

---

[1] *Boston Post*, Nov. 4th, 1854.

nine, however, being badly wounded. While the pirates were rejoicing at their temporary success, the stern of their vessel was nearly blown out by the bow gun in the pinnace, which had got up in the confusion unobserved. This junk was run ashore by her people to prevent her from sinking, and was then captured and burnt. Very many pirates were killed or drowned, and most of the survivors were taken prisoners either by the victors or by the villagers on shore. Of the *Racehorse's* people, two of the unfortunate crew of the gig subsequently died of their injuries.

In some of these operations for the repression of piracy there was further active and cordial co-operation between the British and the American forces on the China station. On May 28th, 1855, the boats of the *Rattler*, 11, screw, Commander William Abdy Fellowes, had destroyed some piratical junks at Samchow; but the lesson was lost on the Chinese; and, late in July, a lorcha and three trading junks, though under convoy of an armed steamer called the *Eaglet*, were cut off, and carried into a fortified bay near Coulan. Commander Fellowes, being appealed to, and having reconnoitred the place, went to Hong Kong, and invited the assistance of the U.S. steam frigate *Powhatan*. This was gladly granted; and, on August 3rd, the *Rattler*, with three boats from the *Powhatan* under Lieutenants Pegram and Rolando, U.S.N., and with the *Eaglet* in company, left the harbour. Early on the 4th the expedition steamed into the bay in which the pirates had taken refuge. A lorcha, which had lain at anchor high up, got under way as if to escape, and was chased by the *Rattler's* pinnace, having on board Lieutenants Charles Joseph Wrey, and Thomas Harpur Greer, and Mate George Gordon Lomax, and by the *Powhatan's* cutter. The boats had, unfortunately, got beyond recall, when the main body of the pirate flotilla, numbering, with prizes, 36 sail, was observed at anchor further up the passage whence the lorcha had started. The Chinese did not move until the *Eaglet* had begun to fire rockets and her 32-pr., and until the remaining boats of the expedition rounded a point and showed themselves. The pirates then weighed in a hurry and made off in a mass, yawing to fire, but being badly mauled by the boats' howitzers. The American launches, in which were a number of British Marines, presently overtook two of the rearmost and largest of the junks, and carried them, after a hard struggle, by boarding. Other junks were also carried, Boatswain James, of the *Rattler*, in that ship's whaleboat, with five seamen and a few Marines, specially distinguishing himself, and all the boats behaving most gallantly. Fellowes himself managed to secure the flag of the pirate leader, who was shot by a British Marine.

Up to that time there had been no loss worth mentioning. But when the *Rattler's* first cutter, under Paymaster Richard Brownsdon, upon running alongside a large junk, received a number of stinkpots, her crew, to escape the fumes, had to jump overboard. Two of the people were speared while in the water, and a third was drowned. Another junk blew up after she had been taken, and all on board her, including Fellowes and Rolando, were thrown into the water, three of her captors being killed outright. All the larger junks were secured; but, owing partly to the time taken in securing them, and partly to the absence of the pinnace and cutter in pursuit of the lorcha, sixteen of the smaller ones got away. Ten junks, one having, with other guns, a 68-pr., and four others having 32, 24, and 12-prs. were destroyed. Two lorchas and seven junks that had been captured by the pirates were retaken; but two of these could not be brought away, and had to be burnt. About 500 pirates were killed, and about 1000 made prisoners, while 200 guns, large and small, were taken. The total casualties were: *Rattler*, 4 killed, 7 wounded; *Powhatan*, 2 killed, 10 (2 mortally) wounded.[1]

On August 18th and 19th, 1855, the *Bittern*, 12, Commander Edward Westby Vansittart, engaged a piratical squadron off Leotung, and burnt some junks; and on September 18th, off Sheipoo, in company with the hired armed vessel *Paoushun*, she attacked twenty-two heavily armed junks, and destroyed the whole of them, killing, it was asserted, no fewer than 1200 pirates. The Chinese vessels were prepared, and had all their guns trained on the narrow channel through which the sloop had to approach them. Nevertheless, the British losses were comparatively slight. The *Bittern's* Master, Mr. Charles Turner, was killed on board the *Paoushun*, and 19 people were wounded. Commander Vansittart was deservedly posted, and Lieutenant George Augustus Cooke Brooker, who was wounded, was made a Commander, on January 9th, 1856.

Piracy had long since ceased to be the recognised national pursuit of the North African states, but was still practised occasionally by the semi-nomadic Arabs along the southern Mediterranean littoral.

[1] Disps.: *China Mail.*

On June 20th, 1854, the merchant brig *Cuthbert Young*, of South
Shields, was captured and plundered by piratical boats about ten
miles N.W. of Cape Tres Forcas, on the Riff coast.   The master and
some of the crew escaped to Gibraltar.   Captain the Hon. George
Grey, (2) naval officer in charge there, ordered the *Prometheus*, 5,
paddle, Commander Edward Bridges Rice, which arrived there on
the 25th, to proceed at once to the scene of the outrage.   Rice
anchored on the 26th off Alhucemas, learnt from the Spanish
governor of other and similar enormities having been committed,
and, proceeding, discovered the *Cuthbert Young* at 4 P.M. at anchor
in an inlet about eleven miles S.W. of Cape Tres Forcas.   As he
approached he was fired upon with musketry from the neighbouring
rocks.   Lieutenant Eugene Gustave Francis Guidoboni Visconti,
and a party of seamen, nevertheless, made a hawser fast to the brig,
and hove up her anchor; and at 6 P.M. the *Prometheus* backed out
with the vessel in tow, the sloop keeping up a brisk fire with grape,
canister, shell, and small-arms.   In his dispatch, Commander Rice
mentions with approval the conduct of Lieutenants Visconti, and
William Henry Edye, and says that he had but one man wounded.
He does not, however, say what loss was inflicted upon the pirates,[1]
who continued for many years afterwards to pursue their depredations.   In August, 1856, a large body of them near Melilla actually
defeated with heavy loss a Prussian landing-party from the *Danzig*, 12,
which sought to chastise them ; and wounded its leader, Admiral
Prince Adalbert.

The slave trade, until long after the middle of the nineteenth
century, continued to flourish, in spite of the very numerous captures
made by H.M. cruisers.   The profits of the traffic, like those of
blockade-running during the civil war in America, were so large that
a single successful venture often, it is said, more than repaid an
owner for the loss of two ships.   Moreover, the slavers had powerful
sympathisers on both sides of the Atlantic.

The *Cormorant*, 6, screw, Commander Herbert Schomberg,
which was commissioned in 1849 for service on the south-east coast
of America, cruised most successfully against these craft.   In the
summer of 1850, after having captured and destroyed the famous
slaver *Rival* in the Rio Frio by means of her boats under Lieutenant
Charles Maxwell Luckraft, and having quitted the river under a
sharp musketry fire from the banks, the sloop headed for the bay

---

[1] Rice to Admlty., June 28th.

of Paranagua. On June 29th she passed, and exchanged civilities with, a 14-gun fort at the entrance, and proceeded upwards, for about fifteen miles, towards an island which was a known headquarters of the forbidden trade. Off it lay several large vessels. The *Cormorant* steamed as close to them as possible, anchored with a spring on her cable, and despatched two cutters and a gig, under Lieutenants Luckraft, and Herbert Philip de Kantzow, Midshipman Cecil W—— Buckley, and Assistant-Surgeon William Ellis Hambly, to overhaul the suspicious craft ; whereupon two peaceable ships, which were present, weighed, and, in a marked manner, separated themselves from the others. The boats boarded and took possession of a ship [1] and two brigs,[2] which were brought out and anchored under the sloop's bow. A brigantine, which otherwise would also have been taken, was sunk by her people. Not until July 1st was the *Cormorant* able to weigh with her prizes in order to quit the bay. When she did so, her progress was challenged by the firing of an unshotted gun from the fort already mentioned. Schomberg eased and then stopped his engines ; but the fort soon began firing in earnest. The *Cormorant* went to quarters, and presently proceeded at full speed, towing the three slavers, and, as she passed, firing her starboard guns at close range into the Brazilian work. She was obliged to anchor inside the bar, where she burnt the two brigs. Later in the day, when the water rose, she went to sea. In this affair she received five shots in her hull, and had one man killed and two people wounded. Schomberg's action was fully approved, by Brazil as well as by Great Britain.

This taking of slave ships out of Brazilian ports [3] was a measure which, until shortly before this time, had not been recognised as lawful, and which had first been put in force in that year by Lieutenant John Crawshaw Bailey, commanding the *Sharpshooter*, 4, screw. On June 23rd, 1849, he had carried off the slaver *Polka* from under a battery at Macahe, and, though fired at, had escaped without casualty.

The *Vestal*, 26, Captain Cospatrick Baillie Hamilton, was another vigilant and successful cruiser. In 1852, she was refitting in Havana, when a fine slave schooner, the *Venus*, slipped out of port during the night. At dawn, Hamilton, who was heartily cheered by a

---

[1] The *Campadora*, ex-*Lucy Ann*, of Greenpoint.
[2] The *Donna Anna*, and *Serea*, noted slavers.
[3] This right was asserted by the Aberdeen Act, of 1845.

friendly American man-of-war that lay near him, went out with extraordinary promptitude, chased the *Venus* through the perils of a tornado to within the Bahama reefs, brought her to by means of a well-directed shot impelled by an extra charge of powder, and captured her. Two other slavers were then seen among the reefs. The *Vestal* could not follow them, owing to her considerable draught of water; but Hamilton, holding a pistol at the head of the master of the *Venus*, obliged that worthy to steer his own craft, with a British crew on board, after the other vessels, and so took both of them. This piece of service was mentioned in Parliament, and Hamilton was rightly praised for his quickness and resource.

Off the West African coast good work was done by the *Alert*, 8, Commander Hugh Dunlop, especially in the river Pongos at the end of 1849; by the *Phœnix*, 6, screw, Commander George Wodehouse; and by the *Pluto*, 3, screw, Lieutenant William Kynaston Jolliffe. On April 13th, 1850, the *Phœnix* chased a slaver, which, on being pressed, turned and ran her on board, reducing her to a perfect wreck aloft. The sloop, however, lowered a boat, which took possession of the enemy. The *Phœnix* took eight other slavers at about the same time. The *Pluto*, on February 14th, 1850, took the American slaver *Anne D. Richardson*, in spite of ingenious arrangements which had been made to mislead the British as to her real character.

In 1850, the natives about the mouth of the Benin river were guilty of numerous acts of piracy; and, early in 1851, the *Jackal*, paddle, tender to the *Tortoise*, 12, visited the locality, with Consul Beecroft on board, in order to make remonstrances, and, if possible, arrange matters peaceably. While this vessel was going to and returning from Warree, one hundred miles up the river, a factory near the mouth of the stream was attacked by the people of Bonbee and Battary. Beecroft sent, therefore, for a larger man-of-war; and, on March 23rd, the *Archer*, 14, screw, Commander James Newburgh Strange, anchored off the bar, and, having left two of her boats and twenty men under Lieutenant Norman Bernard Bedingfeld of the *Jackal*, departed to pick up another of her boats which she had left off Lagos. She returned on the 26th, and, on the 27th, joined the *Jackal* off Factory Isle. That afternoon Strange and Bedingfeld, in their gigs, reconnoitred Bonbee, and were fired at. On the 28th, the place was attacked by five boats of the *Archer* and three of the *Jackal*, containing ninety-two officers and men, including fourteen Kroomen. Lieutenant George Agar Ellis Ridge led in in the *Archer's* pinnace under a heavy musketry fire. Below the town were three guns on shore and five canoes, each mounting a 3-pr. swivel ; but these made little serious opposition, and the place was taken without loss on the side of the attack. On the 29th another town was taken, and, as the first had been, was destroyed. Again there were no casualties. Further operations were happily rendered unnecessary by the submission of the offenders.

In 1852, the *Dolphin*, 3, Lieutenant Henry Temple, had an interesting encounter with negro pirates or slavers in the river Congo. On June 19th, an American brig, the *Mary Adeline*, grounded on attempting to pass up. The British brigantine tried in vain to get her off that day, and, on the following morning, discovered that the stranded vessel was surrounded by canoes full of armed natives, who eventually fired into and tried to board her. The *Dolphin* sent a boat's gun, with ammunition, to the brig, and herself opened fire with shot and shell, driving off the canoes, and clearing the beach of about three thousand persons who were assembled there. In the evening, the *Firefly*, 4, paddle, Commander George Alexander Seymour, arrived. On the 21st, the natives again attacked, and were dispersed ; and on the evening of the 22nd, the *Mary Adeline*, having been lightened, was at length heaved off.

On March 11th, 1853, in consequence of the detention of a British subject at Medina, on the Sierra Leone river, by the chief, who was, moreover, suspected of complicity in the slave trade, the *Teazer*, 3, screw, tender to the *Penelope*, towing the boats of the *Linnet*, 8, Commander Henry Need, with Need and Lieutenant Frederic Dampier Rich in command, proceeded to the Bullom shore. A party was landed and marched up to the town. Need asked for the release of the prisoner, which was refused. He then retired ; and, half an hour later, the *Teazer* and boats opened fire with such good effect that the place was presently abandoned. After some little further negotiation, the chief, Kelch Moodah, gave way. On April 30th following, Need took three of the *Linnet's* boats up the Pongos river, and, on the next day, captured the Spanish slave brig *Bellona* and a slave schooner.

An expedition undertaken in 1853 by a party from the *Thetis*, 38, Captain Augustus Leopold Kuper, C.B., against some troublesome Indians in Vancouver's Island, was well managed and useful, but of little intrinsic importance.

The most serious and protracted naval operations of the period under review—those consequent on the outbreak of war with Russia in 1854—have now to be described. First, however, it will be well to say something concerning the situation which led to that outbreak.

In 1851 the Ottoman Porte appointed a mixed commission for the purpose of examining into the long-existing differences between the Latin and the Greek Churches as to the possession of the Holy Places in Palestine. The commission ultimately decided in favour of the Latin claims; and Russia, ever a staunch champion of Orthodoxy, promptly protested. The difficulties which thus arose revived in the minds of Russian statesmen the idea of cutting up the Turkish Empire and annexing as Russia's share a large and rich portion which should include Constantinople; and it seemed to the Emperor Nicholas that the moment was favourable for the pursuit of the project. Austria was bound to him by ties of gratitude: Germany, and especially Prussia, suffered still from the effects of the revolutionary crisis of 1848; and France was not free from domestic preoccupations. Great Britain remained to be reckoned with; but the Tsar believed that he could arrive at a satisfactory understanding with London. So soon, however, as his plans became known to the cabinet of St. James's, co-operation and countenance were plainly denied him; nor did he meet with better success in Paris. Nevertheless, he was unwilling to abandon a project, the realisation of which appeared both glorious and facile. A bold stroke, he considered, might serve him as well as an alliance. He decided to act ere the Powers should agree upon a line of common action, and, if possible, to confront and confound their opposition with his accomplished triumph. On May 5th, 1853, therefore, Prince Menschikoff, at Constantinople, demanded "substantial and permanent guarantees on behalf of the Orthodox Church," and required that every Orthodox subject of the Sultan should be placed forthwith under the protection of the Tsar. For the Porte, to submit was to surrender its independence. On May 18th, diplomatic relations between the two countries were broken off; and three days later the Sultan was informed that Russia purposed to occupy the Danubian Principalities until such time as the Ottoman government should see fit to accept Menschikoff's ultimatum in its entirety.

The British fleet in the Mediterranean was then commanded by

Vice-Admiral James Whitley Deans Dundas, C.B., who had his flag in the *Britannia*, 120, Captain Thomas Wren Carter. It was at once ordered to assemble at Malta; and it was very soon afterwards directed to proceed thence to Besika Bay,[1] where it should have found awaiting it a French squadron under Vice-Admiral de Lassusse, who, on March 23rd, had left Toulon, in the first instance, for Salamis. Lassusse, unfortunately, underrated the seriousness of the political situation, and, instead of using his steamers to tow his sailing ships to the rendezvous, began to make his way slowly thither under sail only. His late arrival, at a moment when neither Great Britain nor France wholly trusted the good faith of the other, created so bad an impression that he was immediately recalled, and superseded by Vice-Admiral Ferdinand Alphonse Hamelin. The allied fleets, when at length they had joined one another in Besika Bay, consisted of seven British and nine French ships of the line, and eight British and four French frigates, besides smaller vessels. Neither of the flagships was a steamer; and in large steamers, indeed, the British contingent was then woefully deficient. The French, however, had with their squadron the powerful screw 90-gun ship *Napoléon*, which made herself exceedingly useful when, on October 22nd, at the invitation of the ambassadors at Constantinople, the fleet began to move up the Dardanelles.

The Russians had entered the Danubian Principalities at the end of July; and the Sultan, Abdul Medjid, had been forced by Turkish public opinion to declare war on October 4th. Operations began at once; and, in view of the possibility that, with a fair wind, the Russian fleet from Sebastopol might hazard a sudden raid upon Constantinople, the allied fleets at the end of October entered the Bosphorus, and anchored off Beikos, opposite Therapia. In the meantime, the ambassadors of Great Britain, France, and Prussia, meeting at Vienna under the presidency of the Austrian minister of foreign affairs, tried in vain to bring about a good understanding between Russia and the Porte. Austria and Prussia effectually baulked the efforts of the other Powers to secure fair play for Turkey; and the Tsar was led to suppose that, so long as Austria and Prussia inclined in his favour, Great Britain and France would hesitate ere they took an active part in the quarrel. Indeed, the work of the conference at Vienna seemed at one moment to

---

[1] It sailed on June 8th, and arrived on the 13th. Besika Bay is on the coast of Asia Minor, between Lemnos and Tenedos.

promise Russia the attainment of her objects ; for it was instrumental in stopping the victorious advance of Omar Pacha upon
Bucharest. At that time the Porte deemed it advisable to send
supplies by sea to its troops in Asia Minor. The business of conveying these was entrusted to Vice-Admiral Osman Pacha, and a
sailing squadron consisting of one 60-gun ship, six frigates,[1] three
corvettes,[2] and two small craft. The vessels were, for the most
part, weakly armed, ill-manned, and in indifferent order ; and they
were quite unfit to attempt any operation which might expose them
to attack by a division of the well-equipped Russian fleet from
Sebastopol. As it happened, the Russian commanders in the
Black Sea had been specially directed to prevent the shipping of
supplies to Asia Minor.

Osman put to sea in the course of November, and, soon afterwards, anchored off Sinope. Vice-Admiral Nakhimoff,[3] apprised of
his presence there, despatched from Sebastopol three vessels, which
reconnoitred the Ottoman squadron, ventured well within range of
the feeble batteries which defended the roadstead, and then returned
with all speed. Osman should have been warned of his danger by
the appearance and behaviour of the hostile scouts, and should have
sought refuge elsewhere ; but, trusting to the protection which he
supposed to be afforded him by the presence of the allied fleets in
the neighbourhood, he remained where he was. Unfortunately for
him, Dundas and Hamelin had orders only to defend Constantinople
against an attack from seaward, and to prevent a Russian disembarkation anywhere in its vicinity. They had no authority to act
as convoy to Osman ; and, unless they convoyed him, they could
not protect him. On November 30th, Nakhimoff appeared before
Sinope with six ships of the line, two frigates, and three steamers.
He had left four other frigates in the offing, and had stationed fast
dispatch vessels at intervals in the direction of the Bosphorus, so
as to gain speedy news of any movement on the part of the allies.
Summoned to surrender to superior forces, Osman answered with
a broadside. In the action which followed, the Turks fought with
most dogged bravery ; but their very determination rendered their
destruction the more complete. Few of their inferior guns could

[1] Two of 52, one of 50, one of 44, one of 38, and one of 36 guns.

[2] Two of 24, and one of 22 guns.

[3] Paul Stepanovitch Nakhimoff (1803–1855), sailed round the world with Lazareff
in 1820, fought at Navarin, and died at Sebastopol of a wound received in the defence
of the place.

penetrate the stout scantling of the Russian ships of the line; and the gallant Ottoman squadron, while doing very little damage to the enemy, was annihilated. Nearly all the officers and men perished with their ships. A hundred or so gained the shore by swimming, and about as many were taken, among the latter being Osman, who was mortally wounded.

The disaster of Sinope startled Europe, discredited the Vienna conference, which had restrained Turkey but had failed to hold back Russia, and, by exasperating public opinion, precipitated the active interference of Great Britain and France. Their fleets were at once directed to enter the Black Sea, and to prevent any further enterprise of the Russian navy against the Ottoman flag; and it was decided that any Russian men-of-war which should refuse, when encountered, to return to their ports should be forcibly dealt with. The paddle frigate *Retribution*, 28, Captain the Hon. James Robert Drummond, was despatched to Sebastopol to communicate this decision to the Russian authorities. It was foggy when she arrived off the fortress; but Drummond, reducing speed and sounding carefully, pushed on; and, when the fog lifted, the Russians were astonished to find him at anchor in the centre of their harbour. They declined to receive his message until after he had shifted his berth to a point out of range of the sea batteries. He therefore weighed, and, while picking up a new anchorage, contrived, with the assistance of his very efficient officers, to make a most useful plan of the defences. The episode deserves to be remembered. When there is any danger of the outbreak of war, no military port should be left open as Sebastopol was. Look-out vessels and guard-boats should render all unsignalled approach impossible; for an unscrupulous power might easily find it to its advantage suddenly to begin hostilities during a fog, and to win an initial success by blowing up in their own harbour half-a-dozen ships of its negligent enemy.

The allied fleets entered the Black Sea on January 3rd, 1854, and proceeded to Sinope, where the wreckage of Osman's squadron was still visible in the shallows. From Sinope two divisions, one [1] under Rear-Admiral Sir Edmund Lyons, and the other under Rear-Admiral Lebarbier de Tinan, convoyed to the coast of Asia Minor a number of Turkish steamers laden with the needed troops and

---

[1] *Agamemnon*, 91, screw (flag), Capt. Thomas Matthew Charles Symonds; *Sans Pareil*, 70, screw, Capt. Sidney Colpoys Dacres, and two steam frigates.

supplies for the garrisons there ; and Trebizond, Batoum and Fort
St. Nicholas were successively visited. The divisions then returned
to Sinope, whence the body of the allied fleets withdrew presently
to the Bosphorus, only the steamships being left to show the flags
in the Black Sea, where, in the opinion of Dundas and Hamelin,
it was unwise to expose sailing vessels unnecessarily at such a
season of the year. A little later, when Greece betrayed an inclination to interfere in the quarrel between Russia and the Porte,
Lebarbier de Tinan left Beikos and assumed command in the
Archipelago.

Since the beginning of the year there had been fighting on the
Danube, where, at length, the Turks had been driven back. The
Russians had 180,000 men in the field : and it was rapidly becoming
clear that Omar Pacha, in spite of the bravery of his troops, could
not withstand them. On February 27th, accordingly, Great Britain
and France summoned Russia to evacuate the invaded Principalities,
declaring that a refusal would be considered a *casus belli*. The
Tsar declined to obey; and, on March 24th, the fleets in the
Bosphorus unmoored, and headed for the Bulgarian coast, arriving
off Kavarna, near the village of Baltchick, on the 26th. They were
thus stationed in order to be of assistance to the retreating Turks.
War had been regarded for some weeks as quite inevitable, when,
on March 27th, it was formally declared against Russia by Great
Britain and France, the two Powers immediately afterwards concluding with the Porte a treaty of alliance offensive and defensive.
The news of the declaration reached Dundas on April 9th, and
Hamelin on April 14th. Before the latter date the *Furious*, 16,
paddle, Captain William Loring, had been sent to Odessa [1] to bring
away the British consul ; and her boat, on leaving the Russian
coast, had been fired at by the forts on April 6th.[2] In the meantime, troops had begun to be despatched eastward; and on April 17th,
the first detachments (French) [3] reached Gallipoli, which, lying at
the eastern end of the Dardanelles, had been selected as a suitable
base for operations which were to have as their first object the
defence of Adrianople and Constantinople. Dundas and Hamelin
moved at once from Kavarna Bay to Odessa, before which, on

---

[1] Odessa was already informally blockaded by the *Retribution*, 28, paddle, Capt.
Hon. James Robert Drummond, and *Niger*, 14, screw, Com. Leopold George Heath.

[2] Disp. of Hamelin, Apr. 10th.

[3] Escorted by a squadron under Vice-Admiral Bruat, from Toulon.

April 20th, they anchored in positions as close to the town as the shallowness of the water would permit them to take up. The *Furious's* boat, when fired at by the batteries, had been flying a flag of truce. General Osten Sacken, governor of Odessa, declined to make reparation or satisfactory explanation ; and, in consequence, it was decided by the Admirals to bombard the place.

The situation of Odessa has been compared with that of Brighton. The line of cliffs, however, upon which the town stands, has a slight inward curve, and forms a shallow bay with a radius of about three miles. The cliffs face N.E., and towards the north they fall away into low sandy mounds and flat steppes. Stretching out from below them, at the S.E. end of the town, is the long fortified Quarantine Mole, with a lighthouse at its extremity. Within the mole lay many ships of all nations. Orders were given that these should be respected as much as possible. The military port was protected by another pier known as the Imperial Mole. The attacking force was as follows :—

	Ships.	Guns.	Commanders.
British	*Samson*, padd. . . .	6	Capt. Lewis Tobias Jones.
	Furious, padd. . .	16	Capt. William Loring.
	Terrible, padd. . .	21	Capt. James Johnstone McCleverty.
	Tiger, padd. . .	16	Capt. Henry Wells Giffard.
	Retribution, padd. .	28	Capt. Hon. James Robert Drummond.
	Arethusa . . .	50	Capt. William Robert Mends.
French	*Vauban*	20	Capt. de Poucques d'Herbinghem.
	Descartes	20	Capt. Darricau.
	Mogador	28	Capt. Warnier de Wailly.

Rocket boats, with 24-pr. rockets, one from each ship in the offing.

The rest of the allied fleets lay off the town at a distance of about three and a half miles, the *Sans Pareil*, 70, screw, Captain Sidney Colpoys Dacres, and the *Highflyer*, 21, screw, Captain John Moore (4), being, however, kept ready as a reserve.

At 5 A.M. on April 22nd, signal was made for the steamers and boats in the above list to attack the works on and near the Imperial Mole, which protected the military port. The *Samson*,[1] *Tiger*, *Vauban*, and *Descartes*, forming a first division, led in, and opened a fire which was at once returned. The four vessels circled off the forts at a range of about 2000 yards, but, it would appear, effected

---

[1] The name is uniformly misspelt *Sampson* in the Navy Lists.

little damage. On the other hand, the *Vauban* was set on fire by red-hot shot from the batteries, and was obliged to retire temporarily from the action. Thereupon,[1] the *Furious, Terrible, Retribution,* and *Mogador* were ordered to join the three ships which remained engaged ; and presently both divisions anchored, in hopes of bettering their practice. A great improvement was at once apparent; and; ere long, a red-hot shot from the *Terrible* blew up a magazine on the Imperial Mole, and caused great devastation. The *Vauban,* having extinguished the fire, soon rejoined her consorts. Several ships in the military port burst into flames, and were ultimately destroyed ; and, in the confusion, most of the British and French merchantmen which had lain within the Quarantine Mole escaped and put to sea. The rocket-boats did much damage to the storehouses in the dockyard, and burnt most of them. They also, assisted by the steamers, drove off a Russian field-battery which had suddenly opened upon them at close range from behind the shelter of some sheds on the low shore. To make a diversion, the *Arethusa,* late in the action, engaged the south side of the Quarantine Mole, and fought it under sail until she was recalled. The bombardment continued until 5.30 P.M., when, as it was desired to spare the town, which was then threatened by the advancing flames, the order was given to cease fire. The French appear to have lost no men, except in the *Vauban,* where 2 were killed and 1 was wounded: the *Terrible,* which was much cheered on her return to the fleet, had 2 killed and 5 wounded : the *Retribution* had 3 wounded : and the *Samson* had 5 wounded. Captain McCleverty remained throughout on the paddle-box of his frigate, which received twelve shot in her hull.

The allied squadrons put to sea, and, after having reconnoitred Eupatoria on April 28th, appeared on the following day before Sebastopol. Ten ships of the line, eight frigates or corvettes, and five steamers were seen at anchor in the road ; and four other ships of the line, besides small craft, were distinguished in the harbour, basins, and docks. The Russians made no sign of movement.

In the early days of May a British and a French division, under Sir Edmund Lyons and Commodore Vicomte de Chabannes respectively, were detached to the eastern shores of the Black Sea. The force consisted of the French auxiliary screw ship of the line *Charlemagne,* 90, and the steam frigates *Mogador* and *Vauban,* and

---

[1] At 7 A.M.

of the *Agamemnon*, 91 (flag), Captain Thomas Matthew Charles Symonds; *Samson*, 6, Captain Lewis Tobias Jones; and *High-flyer*, 21, Captain John Moore (4). All along the eastern coast were Russian military stations, most of which served merely as posts to keep in check the still unconquered tribes of the then recently occupied territory in the neighbourhood. In the majority of cases, the authority of the Russian garrisons extended very little beyond the range of their guns; and the places, in consequence, had to be fed and supplied by way of the sea. The declaration of war by Great Britain and France had, however, closed the sea to Russian transports, and had been quickly followed by the evacuation and destruction of all the stations except Anapa, Soujak Kaleh, and Redout Kaleh. Of those three posts, the two first were too strong for attack by Sir Edmund Lyons's little squadron. Enquiries at Soukhoum Kaleh, which had been already abandoned, showed that the Russians desired to preserve Redout Kaleh as long as possible as a doorway for supplies to their force at Kutais. Lyons therefore left Soukhoum Kaleh on the morning of May 18th.

"As we passed Redout Kaleh," he says, "we observed a body of about 1000 infantry under arms, and that the few guns on the sea defences were manned. If we had opened our broadsides we could have obliged the enemy to retire; but he would, no doubt, have returned to occupy the place on our disappearing, and I, therefore, went on with the squadron as fast as possible to Chourouksoo, in hopes of inducing the General commanding there to aid me with a sufficient number to occupy and maintain the place. . . . He sent an express to Selim Pacha . . . who placed at my disposal a battalion of 300 infantry and three field-pieces, which were immediately embarked. . . . At 4 p.m." (on May 19th) "the squadron reappeared off Redout Kaleh, where the troops were disembarked, under cover of the steam-vessels, about two miles from the batteries, and at the same time a summons was sent to the commander of the Russian forces . . . under a flag of truce, and in charge of Lieutenant Maxse.[1] . . . After a delay of nearly half-an-hour, Lieutenant Maxse left the shore without an answer; and consequently the *Agamemnon* and *Charlemagne* stood in, as close as the depth of water would permit, and opened their fire on the quarter occupied by the Russian troops, as well as on the sea defences, which tried an ineffectual fire on the boats. The enemy soon retired out of reach of the ships' guns, and the Turkish troops, advancing along the beach, took possession of the batteries, when the firing ceased."[2]

The retreating enemy set fire to the magazines, storehouses, and commercial town, as well as to the neighbouring villages of Poti and Agysoo. The allies, therefore, were left with only the military quarter to occupy. This was quickly made defensible, and was then left in charge of the Turks, for whose support the *Samson* was

[1] Frederick Augustus Maxse, Lieut. of May 14th, 1852; Com. March 10th, 1855; died an adm. on the retd. list 1900.

[2] Lyons to Dundas, May 21st.

detached. While on the coast the combined divisions captured two Russian brigs bound for Kertch, with men and munitions from some of the abandoned fortresses. Among the officers who rendered good service upon the occasion, Sir Edmund Lyons particularly mentions Lieutenant William Rue Rolland,[1] first of the *Agamemnon*, who superintended the embarkation and disembarkation of the troops.

In the course of this expedition, Lyons and de Chabannes had several conferences with the Circassian leaders, and with the representative of the famous patriot Schamyl; and the people along the coast were armed and were encouraged to co-operate with the allies. Unfortunately the Circassians were disunited, and the Turks were unpopular among them; so that little good was effected by the negotiations. The detached forces rejoined the fleets off Kavarna on May 28th.

In the meantime, the main part of the combined fleets had cruised, chiefly off Sebastopol, returning to Kavarna on May 20th. The ships had had few difficulties to contend with, except such as arose from the state of the weather. They had, however, been seriously hampered by thick and persistent fogs, and had, on several occasions, narrowly escaped damage by collision; and fog was actually responsible for the loss of one vessel, the *Tiger*.

The *Tiger*, 16, Captain Henry Wells Giffard, with the *Niger*, 14, Commander Leopold George Heath, and *Vesuvius*, 6, Commander Richard Ashmore Powell, had been detached on May 11th to cruise off Odessa. Almost immediately she became separated from her consorts, owing to the fog. Said Mr. Henry Jones Domville, her Surgeon:

"On the morning of the 12th, at 6 A.M., I was awoke by the crash of the ship going ashore; and, when the dense fog cleared a little, we found ourselves about five miles S.E. of Odessa. Guns were fired to attract the attention of the other steamers, but without avail. About 9 o'clock the guns from the shore commenced firing. In less than ten minutes the *Tiger* was on fire in two places, and the Captain and others were frightfully wounded. We could only use one gun, the others having been thrown overboard, or removed, to lighten the ship. I performed four amputations before I left the ship, which I did almost the last, in care of the wounded. Poor Captain Giffard lost his left leg, and has a severe wound in his right. My knowledge of French proved a great blessing; for some of the Russian officers understood it; and I was able to send into the town for medicines, etc. . . . A Midshipman who lost both his legs and is a relative and namesake of the Captain, died on the beach, and one man on the road. . . ."

It should be added that, immediately after having struck, the

[1] Com. Nov. 13th, 1854.

Tiger got out her boats, and laid out anchors astern, in addition to lightening herself; and that she was practically defenceless when, upon discovering her position, the Russians opened upon her from the heights at short range with field-pieces. She therefore had no course but to surrender. Before surrendering, the survivors endeavoured to burn their ship. The enemy treated the people very well, and gave them permission to remove their effects; but, upon the appearance, a few hours later, of the *Niger* and *Vesuvius*, the Russians, fearing lest the vessel might be recovered, reopened fire upon her, and succeeded in blowing her up. In trying to prevent this, the *Niger* had three men slightly wounded. Captain Giffard died of his wounds, and was buried at Odessa with military honours on June 2nd. Fatal injuries were also received by Midshipman George Giffard, two seamen, and a second-class boy; and three other persons were wounded.

On June 1st, Vice-Admiral Dundas blockaded the mouths of the Danube. This was the first sound strategical move of the allied commanders in the Black Sea. The attack on Odessa had been merely a punitive operation, involving a certain amount of loss to the enemy, but not striking at his vitals. The raid to the eastward was faultily conceived, seeing that most of the garrisons had been withdrawn safely before it was attempted, and that it was not preceded, as it should have been, by a rigorous blockade of such ports as Sebastopol and Kertch, whither, in view of the smallness of the allied forces on the coast, many of the fugitive Russians were able to make their way by sea, and whence those who remained at Anapa and Soujak Kaleh still had a chance of drawing occasional supplies. The blockade, on the other hand, of the Danube mouths, threatened the communications of the Russians who had been advancing southwards, and who were already held in check before Silistria by Omar Pacha at Shumla.

By the end of May about 32,000 French troops, under Marshal Saint Arnaud, and about 18,000 British, under Lord Raglan, had been disembarked at Gallipoli. As has been explained, that place had been selected for their concentration on account of its proximity to Adrianople and Constantinople; but, by the end of May, those cities were no longer in danger of sudden attack, and the armies at Gallipoli were, in consequence, useless in that quarter. Raglan and Saint Arnaud came to the conclusion that they could be best employed if they were transferred to Varna; and, at the request of those officers, Dundas and Hamelin took measures to facilitate the carrying out of the movement. The ships of the line were retained off Kavarna to cover the projected landing, and to protect the base, while the steam frigates of the two squadrons were despatched to the neighbourhood of Sebastopol to watch the motions of the Russian fleet, and to prevent interference from that quarter.

The blockade of the Danube led to several small encounters

ADMIRAL SIR JAMES WHITLEY DEANS DUNDAS, G.C.B.

(From an engraving by W. J. Edwards, after a photograph.)

between British vessels and forces of the enemy. On June 2nd, for example, the *Niger*, 14, screw, Commander Leopold George Heath, was able materially to annoy the Russians on Lake Adjalieh ; and, towards the end of June, the works in the Sulina mouth were bombarded, and partially destroyed, by the *Firebrand*, 6, paddle, Captain Hyde Parker (4), and *Vesuvius*, 6, paddle, Commander Richard Ashmore Powell. It was then supposed that the Russians had almost entirely abandoned the vicinity. On July 7th, Captain

Parker pulled up the stream in his gig, followed by a second boat belonging to his own ship, and by a third containing Commander Powell. He seems to have believed that no enemy was near; but he was nevertheless fired on from a stockade. Having put back, he again advanced with the other boats, and, landing, pluckily led an attack, in the course of which he was shot through the heart. Powell, succeeding to the command, easily drove off the enemy. Parker, who was much regretted, was but thirty years of age. On July 17th, boats from the *Vesuvius*, and the *Spitfire*, 5, paddle, Commander Thomas Abel Bremage Spratt, went up to the scene of Parker's death, destroying all the stockades. They then pushed on to the town of Sulina, which they burnt, leaving only the church and the lighthouse.

On June 11th, the *Furious, Terrible,* and *Descartes*, all commanded as before, appeared off Sebastopol and discovered in the road twelve ships of the line, four sailing frigates, two steam frigates, and various small craft. Certain vessels which had been noticed on the occasion of previous visits seemed to be absent; and, as it was imagined that the missing craft might have proceeded to the Gulf of Perekop, the division went northward in search of them. On the return of the allies, some days later, the Russians made an ingenious but unsuccessful effort to lead the three frigates into a trap, and to cut them off, but declined action so soon as it appeared that the nature and object of the ruse were detected. Several days afterwards the division again offered battle to a superior Russian squadron of six steamers off Cape Khersonese, but without result.[1] It was observed, during the cruise, that the enemy had organised an excellent look-out service along the coast, and noted and reported every movement of the frigates; and it became evident that it would be difficult, if not impossible, to take the Russians by surprise.

The transfer of the army to Varna was effected without much difficulty. One French division marched overland; other divisions made their way to Constantinople and embarked there for their destination, going on board the squadron of Vice-Admiral Bruat, which, towards the end of June, anchored off Kavarna, and thenceforward became part of Vice-Admiral Hamelin's command. All the British troops were carried round in hired transports, under the convoy of Dundas's squadron, which was thus left unencumbered,

---

[1] Letter from the *Terrible's* Engineer, in Nolan's 'Hist. of the War,' I. 262.

and ready for action on the voyage. It was, of course, much more costly to employ merchantmen than to utilise the men-of-war as troopships; but the troops profited by having more room, and somewhat greater comfort; and the naval officers and seamen enjoyed the immense advantage of having nothing to distract their attention from the fulfilment of their proper duties.

No sooner had the allied armies been assembled at Varna than they learnt that the Russian Marshal Paskievich had unexpectedly raised the siege of Silistria, and had retired, leaving free the right bank of the Danube. Thus the troops once more found themselves in a position where they could be of little immediate use. Yet, although the Russians were withdrawing from the Turkish provinces in Europe, the Tsar showed no inclination to treat. The question then arose whether the allies should remain in Turkey, so as to protect it against renewed invasion, or should adopt a bolder policy, and carry the war into the enemy's country, so directing, instead of merely waiting upon, the course of events. It was not deemed wise to attempt to follow up the retreating foe; for south-western Russia had already been the grave of a far greater force than Great Britain and France were prepared to throw into it in the summer of 1854; and it would take many months to collect the troops and transport necessary for a successful advance inland to the north-east. On the other hand, the allies were supreme afloat; and operations supported by the fleets promised comparatively easy victories. Moreover, at Sebastopol, a well-fortified base, lay a strong Russian fleet which, so long as it was "potential," was a continual source of anxiety to Turkey and her friends. One of the Russian steam-frigates, the *Vladimir*, indeed, as late as July, made a daring cruise from Sebastopol, sank several Turkish vessels off the Asiatic coast, and towed back with her two others. It was considerations such as these which led the military leaders to decide upon the invasion of the Crimea. Dundas himself was opposed to the project; but the authorities in London and Paris adopted the proposals of the generals; and on July 6th orders were received that the invasion should be undertaken. Vast preparations of all kinds had to be made; and on July 24th, Vice-Admirals Dundas and Bruat put to sea with a considerable force to reconnoitre the coasts of the Crimea, and to determine at what point or points the disembarkation of the troops should be effected. The squadron was accompanied by Generals Brown and Canrobert, representing respectively Raglan

and Saint Arnaud, and by several engineer and artillery officers
from both armies.

On July 25th, the military commission went on board the
Fury, 6, paddle, Commander Edward Tatham, in which Sir Edmund
Lyons hoisted his flag, and, escorted by the French steamer *Cacique*,
14, approached the Crimean coast, the squadron remaining in the

VICE-ADMIRAL EDMUND, LORD LYONS, BART., G.C.B., D.C.L.

(*From an engraving by D. J. Pound, after a photograph by Kilburn.*)

offing. On the following day, the shore, from Eupatoria to Cape
Khersonese, was very carefully examined, special attention being paid
to the beach near the mouths of the Alma and the Katcha, and
numerous soundings being made in order to discover how much
protection to the disembarking forces could be afforded by men-of-
war of deep draught. The reconnoitring ships were ultimately
joined by the *Terrible ;* and, when off Sebastopol, excited some
movement among the ships in the road. These seemed about to
weigh and proceed in chase; but they ceased their preparations so

soon as they noticed the presence of the combined squadrons. The commission returned to Varna in the *Agamemnon,* which re-anchored off Baltchick on July 28th. Dundas and Bruat showed themselves on the south coast of the Crimea, and their steamers entered the bays of Balaclava and Kaffa in order to confuse and deceive the enemy; but the whole squadron returned to Kavarna on the night of the 30th. During its absence, Odessa had been reconnoitred and alarmed.

Up to the beginning of July, the general health of the expedition had been satisfactory. Cholera had then begun to show itself, not only in the camps and hospitals on shore, but also in many of the transports which were then arriving almost daily from France. Marshal Saint Arnaud appears not only to have failed to cope with the danger when it manifested itself, but also to have courted it by sending troops in the hottest season of the year to the pestilent district of the Dobrudscha. Thousands of these were brought back in a dying condition by the French war steamers, which were despatched to their assistance; and thus the fleets became seriously infected. In one day, August 10th, sixty-two seamen died in the *Ville de Paris,* 120, and the *Montebello,* 120; but, up to that date, the British squadron had been comparatively exempt from the scourge; and Vice-Admiral Dundas, in hope of checking its progress, took all his ships to sea on August 12th.

"On the morning of August 14th the crews were tolerably healthy: before the close of that day more than 50 seamen of the *Britannia* were no more. Within three days 112 men of that ship were consigned to the deep. . . . The Admiral returned with the fleet to Baltchick Bay, and removed the remaining sick to the *Apollo* troop-ship, Captain Johnson.[1] . . . The ships of the squadron were cleansed and fumigated, and thenceforward the cholera disappeared from on board. Up to August 25th, when the disease may be said to have ceased, the French fleet must have lost more than a thousand seamen. The flag-ships of the allied fleets had been anchored close together; and in those vessels the mortality greatly exceeded that of the others. The *Ville de Paris* lost 140 men, the *Montebello* 230, the *Britannia* had a total loss of 120; of the other ships, the greatest mortality was in the *Trafalgar, Albion,* and *Furious.*"[2]

The plan of the allied generals, if plan it may be called, was to disembark an army on the shores of the Crimea under the protection of the combined fleets; to march upon Sebastopol, beating or driving back the troops encountered on the way; to seize the place; and to

---

[1] The *Apollo,* 8, was nominally a storeship, and was commanded by Master George Johnson.

[2] 'British Fleet in the Black Sea,' by Maj.-Genl. Wm. Brereton, C.B. (Privately printed, 1856).

embark again.   The idea, in other words, was to carry Sebastopol by a *coup de main*, which was to be executed with extreme rapidity and vigour.   But the plan was based neither upon knowledge nor upon reason.   " A total want of information existed, either as to the military strength of the enemy in the Crimea, or of the land defences of Sebastopol.   All that was known with certainty was derived from the fleets after their repeated reconnaissances of the harbour, that the sea defences were enormously strong, and that the Russian fleet amounted to sixteen sail of the line, eleven war steam-frigates . . . and other vessels of war." [1]   Some time before, moreover, Saint Arnaud had expressed his opinion that, safely to carry out the proposed operation, the allies should have 100,000 men.   In August they had not half that number.   In addition, only half of the British battering train had arrived ; no part of the French siege artillery had reached Varna ; and, while the British were short of means of land transport, the French were totally deficient in proper means of transport for troops by sea.

Certainly Dundas, and apparently Hamelin also, fully realised the difficulties and risks of the project.   Each represented to the generals that it was intended to land upon a stretch of coast possessing no good ports, and that the fleets would lie exposed to the mercy of the first of the storms of autumn ; that the victualling and supplying of the army would be much hampered by this lack of good ports, and by the dangers of navigation in the late season of the year ; and that, should the army meet with serious reverses, it would be impossible to disembark it in face of the enemy, without making disastrous sacrifices.   Yet the naval chiefs co-operated loyally with their military colleagues ; and when, on August 26th, at a council of war, it was formally determined to set out at once upon the expedition, Dundas stated that the fleet was fully prepared to convey the army to, and land it at, whatsoever point should have been determined on for the disembarkation.

Dundas, unfortunately, was hardly the officer for a position of so much hard work and responsibility.   In 1854 he had been for fifty-five years in the Navy, and, previous to his advancement to flag-rank, he had been a Post-Captain for thirty-four years.   Of honour-able and kindly nature, but only of moderate energy and ability, he had been enabled by family and political influences to obtain the Mediterranean command when, at a time of profound peace, he had

[1] Brereton, 8.

sought for congenial occupation for an inadventurous old age. But he had an active and capable second in Sir Edmund Lyons. Nevertheless, the work of transportation, though it was accomplished with success, was done in a bungling and foolhardy manner. The French army began its embarkation on August 31st, and completed it on September 2nd. On September 3rd, when Hamelin was ready to sail, the British were still unprepared. The French, in consequence, waited until the 5th, when fourteen of their sailing vessels, absolutely unconvoyed, put to sea in advance. Until the 8th, those ships were entirely without protection, and would have been an easy prey to any brace of roving Russian steam-frigates. The mass of the fleets and transports did not leave Baltchick Bay until September 7th. The French embarked about 28,000 men; the British about 24,000. Says Brereton,

"Transports sufficient for the latter were available; but the French army [1] had necessarily to be embarked on board the line of battle ships of that nation, each of which received from 1800 to 2000 soldiers in addition to its crew, amounting to from 800 to 1000 seamen. So crowded, indeed, were the line of battle ships of our allies, that, had the Russian fleet, at any time of the voyage from Varna, quitted their harbour, the contest must have been sustained by the English ships, of which only one line of battle ship, the *Agamemnon*, was a steamer,[2] for the *Sans Pareil*, though nominally a screw vessel, was too defective in her machinery to have been depended upon. Not a gun could have been fired from the French line of battle ships; in fact, their decks were so crowded that it was difficult even to an individual to make his way through the dense masses of soldiers upon them. It has, indeed, been subsequently made known that the Russian Admiral urged Menschikoff to be permitted to engage the allied fleets upon their voyage. The English naval Commander-in-Chief was fully alive to the disadvantage he was under, and often remarked: 'If the Russians have the spirit of mosquitoes, they will now leave their harbour and try the issue.' The convoy amounted to several hundred transports, full of troops, without means of defence, and depending upon the war vessels for protection." [3]

The point originally selected for the disembarkation of the army was the mouth of the little river Katcha. On the voyage thither a signal was made from the French flag-ship to the effect that Marshal Saint Arnaud, who was very unwell, desired to confer with Lord Raglan and Vice-Admiral Dundas, who, in consequence, proceeded in the *Caradoc*, 2, paddle, Lieutenant Samuel Hoskins Derriman, to the *Ville de Paris*. While Raglan, who had lost a leg, remained alongside, Dundas visited the Marshal, who was too ill to speak, but who pointed to an unsigned paper, which the Vice-Admiral read.

[1] Or, more accurately, the greater part of it; for the French disposed of three steam and forty-nine sailing merchantmen.

[2] There were, of course, numerous steam frigates and tugs, etc.

[3] Brereton, 9.

This paper represented that a landing at the Katcha would be too hazardous, as the British press and Parliament had made known to the enemy that it had been fixed upon as the point of disembarkation, and as the Russians were doubtless well prepared there. The paper went on to say that the season was too advanced for a siege of Sebastopol. Dundas took it to Raglan, in whose presence there was much discussion, but who declined to alter the decision at which he had arrived at Varna. He, however, agreed that the coast between Eupatoria and Sebastopol should be again reconnoitred with a view to determining whether a better point than Katcha could be found for the landing.[1] Accordingly, while the fleet and transports anchored in twenty-two fathoms of water, out of sight of land, the *Caradoc*, and the *Primauguet*, 8, escorted by some steamers under Sir Edmund Lyons, took on board Lord Raglan, and representatives of the staffs of both armies, sighted Cape Khersonese on September 10th, and thence proceeded to the northward. Little change seemed to have been made in the situation at Sebastopol; but camps had been established near the mouths of the Katcha and Alma, and elsewhere; and, after careful survey and discussion, it was decided that the landing place should be Old Fort, an open beach about twelve miles south of Eupatoria, which was flanked by lagoons, and which could be swept by the fire of the ships. It was also decided to occupy Eupatoria, and to garrison it with 2000 Turks, and two infantry battalions, one British and one French.

In pursuance of these plans, the fleets and transports proceeded. On the 11th, and again early on the 12th, the French contingent dropped entirely out of sight; but the whole force anchored off Eupatoria on the 12th and 13th. The place, which was not defensible, was at once summoned, and, surrendering, was taken possession of.[2] On the 14th and following days the troops and the Marines were landed without opposition, under cover of the guns of the ships, and within sight of Sebastopol; and, while the disembarkation was in progress, a division of frigates,[3] with troops on board, was sent to the mouth of the Katcha to deter the Russians from advancing northward. A camp there was shelled, and its occupants were forced to withdraw out of range. The advance southward

---

[1] Brereton, 12.

[2] It was placed under the command of Capt. Thomas Saumarez Brock, R.N., and was held until after the fall of Sebastopol.

[3] *Samson, Fury, Vesuvius,* and some French steamers.

along the coast began at once, the fleets keeping simultaneously within sight and range.

Long ere this there had been active naval operations in other quarters, to which attention must be temporarily directed.

As soon as war became imminent, the governments of Great Britain and France resolved to take action in the Baltic. France had sent to the Levant nearly all her immediately available ships, under Vice-Admirals Hamelin and Bruat, and Rear-Admirals Lebarbier de Tinan, Charner, and Bouët-Willaumez ; and some time elapsed ere she could fit for sea another fleet, the command of which was given to Vice-Admiral Parseval-Deschènes. Great Britain had wider resources, and, as early as March 11th, 1854, was able to despatch from Spithead the following fleet :

Ships.	Guns.	Commanders.	Tons.	H.P.N.	Crew.
Duke of Wellington, scr. . . .	131	V.-Ad. Sir Charles Napier (2), K.C.B R.-Ad. Michael Seymour (2), Capt. of Capt. George Thomas Gordon. [Fleet.	3700	780	1100
Edinburgh, scr.	60	R.-Ad. Henry Ducie Chads, C.B. (B). Capt. Richard Strode Hewlett.	1772	450	660
Leopard, padd.	18	R.-Ad. James Hanway Plumridge (W). Capt. George Giffard.	1412	560	280
Princess Royal, scr..	91	Capt. Lord Clarence Edward Paget.	3129	400	850
Royal George, scr.	120	Capt. Henry John Codrington, C.B.	2616	400	990
St. Jean d'Acre, scr..	101	Capt. Hon. Henry Keppel.	3400	600	900
Hogue, scr.	60	Capt. William Ramsay.	1750	450	660
Ajax, scr.	60	Capt. Frederick Warden.	1761	450	500
Blenheim, scr.	60	Capt. Hon. Frederick Thomas Pelham.	1747	450	600
Impérieuse, scr.	51	Capt. Rundle Burges Watson, C.B.	2347	360	530
Arrogant, scr.	46	Capt. Hastings Reginald Yelverton.	1872	360	450
Amphion, scr.	34	Capt. Astley Cooper Key.	1471	300	320
Tribune, scr.	31	Capt. Hon. Swinfen Thomas Carnegie.	1570	300	300
Valorous, padd.	16	Capt. Claude Henry Mason Buckle.	1255	400	220
Dragon, padd.	6	Capt. James Willcox.	1270	560	220

Previous to the departure of this fleet, the Masters of each ship proceeded to the Baltic in the steam sloop *Hecla*, 6, Captain William Hutcheon Hall, leaving Hull on February 19th, and rejoining Sir Charles, off Dover, with a mass of most valuable intelligence.[1]

Never before had a large force, composed exclusively of steam-vessels, quitted England on a hostile mission. Large additions, of sailing as well as of steam-vessels, were subsequently made to the command.

Although there was no excuse for the inefficient condition [2] in which this by no means very powerful fleet left England, there were excellent reasons for its despatch with the utmost speed ; for it had become known that in January the Russian fleet in the Gulf of

---

[1] Disp. of Com.

[2] *See*, for example, 'Autob. of Lord C. Paget,' 78; Napier, 224; Sulivan, 120, etc., etc.

Finland had been increased to 27 sail of the line, and that, in addition, it included 8 or 10 frigates, 7 corvettes and brigs, 9 paddle-steamers, 15 schooners and luggers, and 50 or 60 gunboats. On March 10th, 18 of the ships of the line were at Cronstadt; and gigantic efforts were being made to get some of the best of them to Sweaborg [1] through the ice. Napier's fleet made rendezvous on March 19th in Wingo Sound, on the Swedish coast, whence the Commander-in-Chief paid a visit to the King of Denmark. From Wingo Sound the ships sailed on March 23rd with a northerly wind, and, on the 27th, anchored off Kiel, having passed through the Belt without pilots, and having been joined on the way by Rear-Admiral

ADMIRAL THE RT. HON. SIR ASTLEY COOPER KEY, G.C.B., F.R.S.

Armar Lowry Corry (W), in the sailing line of battle ship *Neptune*, 120, Captain Frederick Hutton, with two other vessels of the line.

Napier's instructions from the Foreign Office will be found set forth in the 'Baltic Campaign.' [2]   He was to take care that no Russian ship should pass by him into the North Sea; to turn his attention to the Aland Islands; not to engage on any desperate venture; if called upon, to protect Danish and Swedish territory from attack by Russia; and to look into Reval and other fortified places. It appeared to him that Kjöge Bay, near Copenhagen, was the best position from which, without dividing his fleet, he might watch both the Belts and the Sound, and thither, therefore, he proceeded, arriving on April 1st. On the 4th, after he received from London news of the declaration of war, he made the following much criticised signal to his command :—

"Lads, war is declared with a numerous and bold enemy. Should they meet us

---

[1] Napier, ii. 223, 224. The Russians believed that Cronstadt would be first attacked, and that the forts there would repel the ships, whereupon the fresh vessels at Sweaborg would be able to complete their discomfiture.

[2] P. 51 *et seq.*

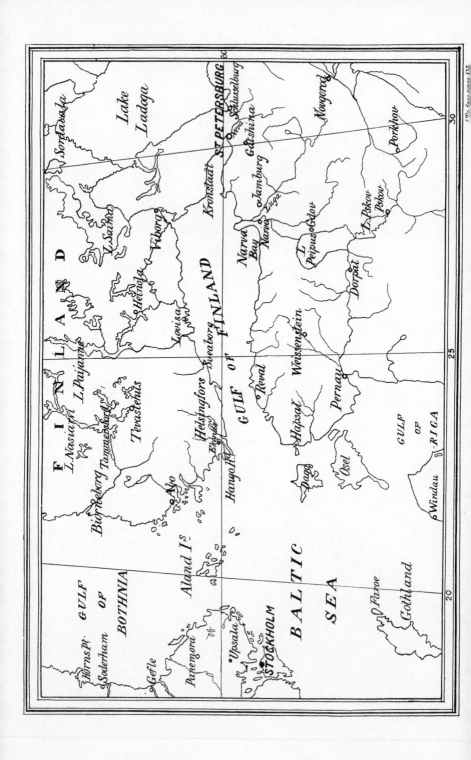

and offer battle, you know how to dispose of them. Should they remain in port, we must try and get at them. Success depends upon the quickness and precision of your firing. Also, lads, sharpen your cutlasses, and the day is your own!"

At that period France was represented in the Baltic by only a single vessel, the screw line of battle ship *Austerlitz*, 100, Captain Laurencin.[1] Some of the British frigates, and such small craft as were available, were immediately detached to blockade Riga, Libau, and other hostile ports, and to form a chain between Bornholm and the south shore of the Baltic, in order to intercept the enemy's trade; and a flying squadron of steamers, under Rear-Admiral Plumridge, was sent to reconnoitre the entrance to the Gulf of Finland. The Commander-in-Chief's hands were, however, somewhat tied by the fact that both troops and gunboats had been refused to him, and that he was already in strained relations with the Admiralty, in consequence of some expression which he had made use of at a dinner at the Reform Club before his departure; of the warmth with which he had criticised the inefficient manning of the fleet; and of the manner in which he had resented what he conceived to be the Board's rude treatment of him.

The fleet weighed from Kjöge Bay on April 12th, and took up its cruising ground off Gottska Sandö[2] on the 15th. Plumridge having rejoined, the eight battleships, *Duke of Wellington, Edinburgh, St. Jean d'Acre, Princess Royal, Cressy*, 80, screw, Captain Richard Laird Warren, *Hogue, Royal George*, and *Cæsar*, 91, screw, Captain John Robb, with several frigates, proceeded on the 16th towards Hangö and Sweaborg, while the rest of the fleet was entrusted to Rear-Admiral Corry, and left behind. But the prevalence of fog unnerved the Commander-in-Chief,[3] who presently returned to his former cruising ground, instead of pushing on at once to the neighbourhood of Helsingfors. It should be borne in mind that the Admiralty at that time refused to allow local pilots for the fleet, although, as Napier urged, it would have been more costly to lose one ship than to employ a great number of pilots. It may be remembered, too, that Napier was then an old man, very different from the Napier of the days when Ponza was captured. It may even be supposed that Napier already knew, in substance, the

---

[1] She did not, however, join Napier till May 1st. *Vide infra.*

[2] A small island not marked on the accompanying map, but lying near the "e." of "Baltic Sea."

[3] Otway, 'Paget,' 91.

views which were held at the Admiralty, and which were expressed by Sir James Graham, who, writing on April 10th,[1] said :—

" I rely on your prudence in not knocking your head against stone walls prematurely, or without the certainty of a great success, or the fair prospect of attaining some most important object worthy of the risk and of the loss, which, when you attack fortresses with ships, are serious and inevitable."

Nevertheless it looks as if Napier's return may possibly have deprived his country of the advantage and glory of the capture of part of the Russian fleet at the beginning of the war ; for it has never been satisfactorily established whether, at that time, the enemy's force lay outside or inside Helsingfors. Giffard, Plumridge's Flag-Captain, had seen it, at a distance, and believed that it was outside. And while Captain Bartholomew James Sulivan, of the *Lightning*, 3, paddle, reported that one native had told him that the Russians were inside, he also reported that another native had informed him that they had failed to get in through the ice at the harbour's mouth.[2] If the Russians were indeed outside, Napier might have taken or destroyed them. He afterwards took the fleet into Elgsnabben, about forty miles from Stockholm, where the *Austerlitz* joined on May 1st. When, on May 5th, the fleet weighed from Elgsnabben, the Gulf of Finland was entirely free from ice, and there was no further chance of catching the Russians outside their ports. Napier returned off Gottska Sandö, where, as far as can be judged, his presence was useless ; and Rear-Admiral Plumridge, with a division of paddle-vessels, was despatched to harass the enemy in the Gulf of Bothnia, where, although he acted in pursuance of definite orders from home, his wholesale destruction of property unfortunately alienated the inoffensive and perfectly friendly inhabitants. The *Amphion*, 34, screw, Captain Astley Cooper Key, *Conflict*,[3] 8, screw, Captain Arthur Cumming, and other craft, meanwhile blockaded the Gulf of Riga, where the former frigate distinguished herself by capturing a number of merchant vessels under batteries.

Plumridge, in the *Leopard*, 18, paddle, Captain George Giffard, with the *Vulture*, 6, paddle, Captain Frederick Henry Hastings Glasse, *Odin*, 16, paddle, Captain Francis Scott, and *Valorous*, 16,

---

[1] Letter received on Ap. 19th, Napier, 238.

[2] Otway, ' Paget,' 92 : Sulivan, 136.

[3] The *Amphion* and *Conflict* captured Libau, on May 10th, without firing a shot, and took all the shipping in the port. On April 18th, the *Conflict* had lost her Captain, John Foote, who had been drowned, with four men, in his gig, off Memel.

paddle, Captain Claude Henry Mason Buckle, after destroying vessels and storehouses, etc., at Brahestad and Uleaborg, and capturing several gunboats, sent the boats of the *Vulture* and *Odin*, on June 7th, into Gamla Carleby, where there was a building yard, to summon the authorities to deliver up all the property there belonging to the Russian government. The demand was refused; and the officer who had made it was in the act of retiring to the ships, when fire was opened upon him from muskets and field-pieces, and several of his people were killed and wounded. As the frigates drew too much water to be able to approach, nine of their boats, manned and armed, carrying 180 officers and men, under Lieutenant Charles Arthur Wise, were sent in in the evening with the object of teaching the enemy a lesson. The Russians, however, had made the best use of the interval, and, collecting regular troops, had posted them in favourable positions among the houses. When near the shore, the British boats were suddenly surprised by a withering fire from both guns and small arms, and quickly suffered considerable loss. A prompt reply was made; but the enemy was so concealed as to be almost invisible, and, after an hour's hot action, it was found necessary to withdraw. The attacking force was obliged to leave a boat, with its gun and crew,[1] in the hands of the foe, and, in addition, lost twenty-six officers and men killed and wounded.[2] The failure was due to ignorance of the Russian strength, and to an exaggerated estimate of the importance of the destruction of a few stores. Operations of the kind should never be attempted without adequate knowledge, and due consideration of the price that may have to be paid to attain a given result.

Other vessels made raids of the same kind, but with less disastrous results. On May 19th, Captain Hastings Reginald Yelverton, in the *Arrogant*, 46, screw, with the *Hecla*, 6, paddle, Captain William Hutcheon Hall, while examining the channel near Teverminne, was fired at from behind a sandbank, but easily dispersed the enemy. He then learnt that at Eckness, eight miles to the northward, lay three large merchantmen with cargoes on board. On the following morning, the two vessels, the *Hecla* leading, cautiously felt their way thither through narrow and intricate passages, and, while going up, were met by a fire from five field-guns and a

---

[1] This boat, under Mate Nathaniel James Morphy, had 25 men on board.

[2] Including Lieutenant Edward Murray Winter Carrington, Mate Charles Frederick Herman Montagu, and Mids. —— Athorpe, killed.

mortar. The *Arrogant*, though she ran aground, finally dismounted two, and the *Hecla* three of these, the latter being brought off. Pushing on to Eckness, the two Captains came in view of their quarry. While Yelverton engaged the defences and troops, the *Hecla* ran alongside the only one of the merchantmen that was afloat, and, taking her in tow, carried her off. On their return, the ships were met by the *Dauntless*, 33, screw, Captain Alfred Phillips Ryder, which had been sent up to ascertain the cause of the firing ; but her assistance was not required. They rejoined the fleet on May 21st, off Hango Head. In this affair, the *Arrogant* had 2 killed and 4 wounded ; and the *Hecla*, 5 wounded, including Captain Hall, and Lieutenant Offley Malcolm Crewe Read. Lieutenant Henry Vachell Haggard, in addition to the officers already named, was specially mentioned as having distinguished himself.[1]

Two days later, on May 22nd, the *Dragon*, 6, paddle, Captain James Willcox, was ordered to try the effect of her guns on Fort Gustafvard, an island work, mounting 31 guns, south-east of Hango Head, the neighbourhood of which had previously been partially examined and buoyed by Captain Bartholomew James Sulivan. The *Dragon* opened at a distance of about 1600 yards, and made excellent practice ; but the enemy soon got the range of her. She should not have been sent in alone to engage so powerful a fort, and presently the Vice-Admiral ordered her to be supported by the *Magicienne*, 16, paddle, Captain Thomas Fisher, and *Basilisk*, 6, paddle, Commander the Hon. Francis Egerton ; but ere both of them could be got into position by Captain Sulivan, who had the placing of them, the signal of recall was made. The *Dragon* had one man killed and another wounded, and, besides many shot in her hull, received one close to her shell-room under water. On the same day the *Hecla* fired a few rounds into a fort hard by mounting 11 guns, but sustained no damage. These attacks were ill-judged and useless. If made at all, they should have been made at long range, and by overwhelming force. Says Sulivan :—

"I had advised 2200 yards, and it was entirely his" (George Biddlecombe, Master of the Fleet's) "own doing that the distance was altered. The poor chief is really too shaky, nervous, and borne down by responsibility, to have such a charge on him. He has no plans or system ; but the impulse of the moment alone guides him ; and I trust we may have no serious thing to do, requiring careful plans and system."[2]

Nevertheless, the lesson seems to have made no great impres-

[1] Yelverton to Napier : Napier to Admlty., May 20th : Sulivan, 160. [2] Sulivan, 158.

sion upon Napier. In the early days of June, Bomarsund, the chief fortress in the Aland Islands, was reconnoitred by Captain Sulivan, the surveyor, in the *Lightning*, 3, paddle, with the *Driver*, 6, paddle, Commander the Hon. Arthur Auckland Leopold Pedro Cochrane, and was found to be immensely strong.[1] Sulivan believed that " an attack by ships would be attended by a loss and risk too great to warrant the attempt, unless aided by a sufficient land-force to assist, first carrying the tower[2] by assault or by regular approaches." This view was practically the one which was ultimately adopted and acted upon ; but not, as will be seen, until an ineffectual attack had been made by ships only.

In the meantime Vice-Admiral Parseval-Deschènes had quitted France on April 20th with eight sailing ships of the line, six sailing frigates, and three steamers, having on board 2500 men belonging to the marine infantry and artillery ; but he was unable to join Napier, who was then in Baro Sound, until June 13th. The combined fleets, including all craft which had then assembled, anchored together in the Sound, as follows :—

	BRITISH.	Guns.		FRENCH.	Guns.
Screw	Duke of Wellington	131	Sailing	Inflexible	90 [1]
	St. Jean d'Acre	101		Duguesclin	90 [2]
	Princess Royal	91		Tage	100
	Royal George	120		Hercule	100
	James Watt	91		Jemmapes	100
	Nile	91		Breslau	90
	Cæsar	91		Duperré	80
	Majestic	91		Trident	80
	Cressy	80		Sémillante	60
	Edinburgh	60		Andromaque	60
	Blenheim	60		Vengeance	60
	Hogue	60		Poursuivante	50
	Ajax	60		Virginie	50
Sailing	Neptune	120		Zénobie	50
	St. George	120	Steam	Austerlitz	100 [3]
	Prince Regent	90		Darien	14
	Monarch	84		Phlégéthon	10 [3]
	Boscawen	70		Lucifer	6
	Cumberland	70		Souffleur	6
Paddle	Penelope	16		Milan	4 [3]
	Magicienne	16			
	Basilisk	6			
	Driver	6			
	Porcupine	3			
	Pigmy	3			
	Lightning, surv.	3			
	Alban, surv.	4			
	Belleisle, hosp.	6			

[1] Flag of V.-Ad. Parseval-Deschènes.
[2] Flag of R.-Ad. Pénaud.
[3] Preceded V.-Ad. Parseval-Deschènes.

Note. Napier mentions only seven sail of the line, omitting the *Breslau*, which seems to have joined a little later than the rest.

[1] 'Baltic Campaign,' 333.
[2] *i.e.*, the principal work, probably. The large fort mounted 92 guns in casemates. There were also, however, three ' towers,' each pierced for 24 guns. Sulivan, 169.

On June 21st, the *Hecla*, *Odin*, and *Valorous*, of Rear-Admiral Plumridge's squadron, were sent in, in spite of what had already happened, to shell the main fort at Bomarsund. They succeeded in burning part of the wooden roof of the building; but as that existed only to keep off snow in winter, the damage done was incommensurate with the value of the shot and shell expended. Below the wooden roof the top of the work was bomb-proof. The ships left off firing for want of shell, and retired with five men wounded. It was on that occasion that Mate Charles David Lucas, of the *Hecla*, flung overboard a live shell that fell on deck. He was deservedly promoted to be a Lieutenant, as from the day of the attack, for his bravery, and, later, became one of the first recipients of the Victoria Cross. On the same day, Plumridge rejoined Napier.

The next movement of the fleets was towards Cronstadt. On June 22nd, Rear-Admiral Corry, with nine sail of the line, a frigate,[1] and five or six steamers, was left to blockade Sweaborg, while Napier and Parseval-Deschènes, with twelve screw, and six sailing line of battle ships, and nine smaller steam-vessels, weighed to reconnoitre the great Baltic stronghold.

From the 24th to the 26th the allied fleets lay at anchor off Seskar Island, near the eastern end of the Gulf of Finland. On the latter day, while the larger ships remained about eight miles off Tolboukin lighthouse, Captain Bartholomew James Sulivan was given charge of a flying squadron of three steamers,[2] which went in to observe the Russian fleet and batteries, Captain Rundle Burges Watson, in the *Impérieuse*, with the *Arrogant* and *Desperate*, keeping near at hand as a support. On the following day Sulivan was joined by the French steamer *Phlégéthon*.

"There are," wrote Sulivan, "only sixteen sail of the line, and a heavy frigate, ready outside, and one in the basin. There are three more, as block-ships, to the north-east, not rigged, and, and, beyond them, to the north-east, three frigates ready for sea, and two frigates and one corvette block-ship. There is also one two-decker in dock. . . . They have also in line this evening thirteen heavy gunboats. . . . Their ships look rather slummy in their appearance; and, as they cannot evidently make up more than seventeen or eighteen sail of the line, it is impossible for them to come out. Our English screw-ships alone could destroy them. They are all placed to resist an attack, and evidently think of nothing else. The channel is certainly formidable, and quite impregnable."[3]

[1] Besides two French frigates.

[2] *Lightning*, Capt. B. J. Sulivan; *Magicienne*, Capt. Thomas Fisher; and *Bulldog*, Capt. William King Hall.

[3] Sulivan, 189.

Napier's conclusions, as given to Sir James Graham, were :—

"Any attack on Cronstadt by ships is entirely impracticable. In going in to the south the batteries are most formidable—all constructed of solid masonry ; they are three and four-deckers of stone instead of wood, and ships going in would be raked by them the moment they came under fire, and would be sunk before they reached the ships, which are placed with their broadsides bearing also on the passage. . . . I now turn to the north side of Cronstadt. That is certainly the weakest point. A landing might be made on the island of any number of men, and the town besieged : but you must expect the Russians will always outnumber you. If you fail, your army would be lost; and, if you succeed, it would probably be starved during the long winter. I presume, therefore, that will not be thought of. It may, however, be bombarded."

Upon the whole, it was wisely decided not to attempt anything of importance against Cronstadt; and it was determined, though not perhaps with equal wisdom, to make an attack upon the Aland Islands.

During that period, and for some time afterwards, the usefulness of the British fleet in the Baltic was seriously hampered not only by Napier's age and moral timidity, but also by the relative immobility of the French contingent, which, so far as its fighting ships were concerned, consisted almost exclusively of sailing vessels. On the one hand, it was deemed advisable, in the interests of international good feeling, that the French should, if possible, be given a share in every adventure. Indeed, Parseval-Deschènes said that if there should be any action while he and his fleet were out of the way, " all the paving-stones in Paris would not be enough to throw at his head." [1] On the other hand, all movements were delayed by the necessity which existed for towing the great French sailing ships of the line. Never, perhaps, was the immense importance of homogeneity in a fleet more clearly illustrated. Cholera had broken out on board the ships, and, as the waters in the neighbourhood of Cronstadt were supposed to be " pestiferous," [2] the fleets withdrew to Baro Sound, westward of Sweaborg, where they anchored on July 6th. There they waited, while Rear-Admiral Plumridge, with a slightly reinforced squadron, blockaded Bomarsund; and while 10,000 French troops, under General Baraguay d'Hilliers, in British and French transports, were sent northwards, to be employed in the projected operations. This corps sailed from off Calais on July 22nd. On July 18th, the combined fleets moved from Baro Sound towards Ledsund, which was reached on the 21st. There, by August 5th, all transports, with troops, munitions and stores, had

[1] Sulivan, 193.   [2] Napier, ii. 268.

assembled; and, Baraguay d'Hilliers, who had preceded his command, having already reconnoitred Bomarsund, all was ready for the attack.

The Aland Islands consist of a group of 280 rocks and islets, about 200 of which are uninhabited. They enclose a perfect labyrinth of channels most difficult to navigate. The islands had been Swedish until 1809, when they had been taken by Russia, which, to protect its conquest, had erected on the largest of the islands, commanding Lumpar Bay, in the strait separating Aland from Presto, the strong fortress of Bomarsund. The fortress itself, in 1854, formed the segment of a circle, having a chord about a quarter of a mile in length, and presenting to the roadstead a casemated battery of 120 guns, in two tiers. The system of defence was made complete by a series of works commencing on the heights behind, the chief work on the north being Fort Nottich, and the chief one on the west being Fort Tzee, each mounting 14 guns. To the southwest was an unfinished new fort, and, nearly south of it, on Tranvik Point, was a 7-gun battery. The works were continued across the water, on a chain of islets, to Presto, where stood another 14-gun fort, nearly north-west of the main fortress, and somewhat less than a mile distant from it.[1] All the forts were of granite, with guns in two tiers; and they were held by about 2500 men. The plan on the opposite page will further explain the nature of the position.

The ordinary channel, leading from the fleets' anchorage at Ledsund to Lumpar Bay, was commanded by the fire of the Russians; but by the exertions of Captain Sulivan, of the *Lightning*, and of Commander Henry Charles Otter, of the *Alban*, an uncommanded channel between Lumpar and Ango Islands was discovered and surveyed; and on July 28th the squadron of Rear-Admiral Chads[2] was taken through the sinuous and difficult passage, without the use of buoys or marks. Other vessels, both French and British, passed up later.

On August 6th, the fortress was reconnoitred within 600 yards. On the 8th, near the southern extremity of Tranvik Point, the French army[3] under the protection of the guns of the *Edinburgh* and *Duperré*, was landed, while a battalion of Royal Marines, and 90 British sappers and miners under Brig.-General Jones, with 2000

---

[1] 'Baltic Campaign,' 338: Sulivan, 222: Chevalier, 233.

[2] *Edinburgh, Hogue, Amphion, Blenheim, Ajax.*

[3] Reinforced by 2000 French marines.

French Marines, were simultaneously disembarked at a point about
two miles north of the fortress. On the same day the 7-gun battery
near the southern landing-place was attacked and destroyed by the
Amphion and *Phlégéthon*, Napier, with his flag temporarily in the
Bulldog, watching the operations. The landing of three short 32-pr.
naval guns, four field-guns from the ships, and a rocket tube, on the

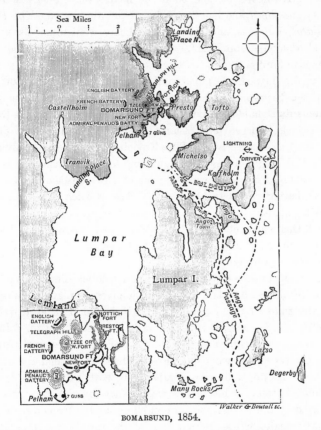

BOMARSUND, 1854.

(*From ‘Life and Letters of Sir B. J. Sulivan,’ by kind permission of Mr. John Murray.*)

10th, was superintended by Rear-Admiral Chads, whose people had
to drag them for four miles and a half over execrable ground to the
point which had been selected as the site for the British battery (see
plan). In this arduous work, Captains George Ramsay (*Euryalus*),
and Richard Strode Hewlett (*Edinburgh*), and Commander George
William Preedy (*Duke of Wellington*), specially distinguished them-

selves. The French, on Tranvik Point, had fifty horses to help drag their guns (four long 16-prs., and four 13-inch mortars) to their station, 450 yards west of Fort Tzee.

On the 10th, while passing the fortress, the *Penelope*, 16, paddle, Captain James Crawford Caffin, went ashore under the enemy's fire, and had to throw her guns overboard ere, much mauled by the enemy's red-hot shot, she could be floated off. She was struck twenty-one times, and had 2 men killed and 3 wounded. The *Hecla*, *Gladiator*, *Valorous*, and *Pigmy*, with boats, went to her assistance, and also suffered somewhat. Happily no blame was attributed to Captain Caffin.[1]

On the 11th more guns were landed from the fleet, and sent up to the British battery, in charge of parties of 200 men under Lieutenants Donald M'Leod Mackenzie (*Edinburgh*), Thomas Davies (2) (*Hogue*), George Henry Clarke (*Blenheim*), and Walter James Pollard (*Ajax*) respectively. The French battery, being ready early on the 13th, began firing without waiting for the British; and on the same evening Fort Tzee was abandoned. In consequence, General Jones's battery[2] was turned against Fort Nottich. It opened on the 15th at 950 yards, and breached the place in eight hours. Nottich then surrendered. The British naval loss was only 1 killed and 1 wounded. The enemy had 6 killed and 7 wounded: and 125 prisoners were taken.

In the meantime Captain the Hon. Frederick Thomas Pelham, of the *Blenheim*, had landed a 10-inch pivot gun, and mounted it amid the ruins of the 7-gun battery which had been destroyed on the 8th. He[3] made excellent practice against the main fortress, and, though he occupied a position of some danger, escaped without loss. On the 16th, when the French had established themselves on Presto Island, and were nearly ready with the whole of their breaching battery, a heavy fire was opened by Pelham, who was supported by the French mortars on shore, by the French squadron, and occasionally by the 10-inch guns of the *Edinburgh*, *Ajax*, *Arrogant*, *Amphion*, *Valorous*, *Sphinx*, and *Driver*. No great amount of

---

[1] For an account of the origin of the mishap, see Sulivan, 225.

[2] The battery was manned by seamen and Marine artillerymen under Capt. William Ramsay, Com. George William Preedy, Lieuts. Leveson Eliot Henry Somerset, George Foster Burgess, and Morgan Singer, Capts. (R.M.) Henry Edward Delacombe, Thomas Dudley Fosbroke, William Lawrence Sayer, and Peter Brames Nolloth (Brev Maj.), etc.

[3] With Capt. Pelham were Lieut. Francis Arden Close, and (actg.) Mate Leveson Wildman, both of whom were favourably mentioned.

damage was done to the fortress ; but the officer in command, General Bodisco, perceived that his position was desperate; and, at about mid-day, he exhibited a white flag. Captain William King Hall, of the *Bulldog*, and Commander de Surville, Parseval-Deschènes's aide-de-camp, with two of the French general's staff, were sent ashore to parley, and, as a result, it was agreed that the garrison should lay down its arms. The capitulation of Bomarsund was immediately followed by the surrender of the fort of Presto. Prisoners to the number of 2255 were taken, and were divided between the allies, the British share being sent at once to Ledsund, whence they were conducted to the Downs by Commodore the Hon. Frederick William Grey, C.B., of the *Hannibal*, 90, screw.[1] The dispatches announcing the success were carried home by Napier's Flag-Lieutenant, John de Courcy Andrew Agnew, who was, in consequence, made a Commander on August 23rd. Among other promotions immediately consequent on the capture of Bomarsund were those of Commanders the Hon. Arthur Auckland Leopold Pedro Cochrane and Henry Charles Otter, to be Captains, and of Lieutenants Donald M'Leod Mackenzie, George Henry Clarke, Thomas Davies (2), and Francis Arden Close, to be Commanders. Bomarsund was destroyed, after Sweden had refused to accept it.[2] Subsequent movements on the part of the fleets caused the Russians to blow up their fortifications at Hango.[3]

Directions were despatched to Napier on August 29th, and to Parseval-Deschènes on August 30th, ordering a retirement from the Baltic. Napier had previously sent the *Odin, Alban, Gorgon*, and *Driver* to reconnoitre Abo ; and, as he considered that it might be successfully attacked, he asked the French Vice-Admiral to join him in the enterprise. The latter, however, refused, on account of the badness of the weather. Reval, Sweaborg, and Hango were also reconnoitred. With respect to Sweaborg, Brig.-General Jones thought that it might be taken by combined sea and land operations, while the French General Niel was of opinion that the fleets alone could render it untenable in less than two hours.[4] On September 12th, Napier received from home a dispatch which allowed him a certain amount of discretion as to the time of withdrawal; and he at once met Vice-Admiral Parseval-Deschenes, and Rear-

[1] Napier to Admlty., Aug. 11th, Aug. 16th (2): *Naut. Mag.*, 1854, 498: Napier, ii. 282: Sulivan, 223.

[2] Napier, 291 : 'Baltic Campaign,' 395.

[3] Sulivan, 246.

[4] 'Baltic Campaign,' 419.

Admirals Penaud, Chads, and Seymour,[1] in order to discuss the idea of undertaking further operations. It was then decided unanimously that, owing to the lateness of the season, nothing could that year be attempted against Sweaborg or any fortified Baltic port, save at great risk. On September 17th, by which date some of the French ships had begun to go home, Napier received a further dispatch, asking for opinions on General Niel's plan for attacking Sweaborg with ships alone. Parseval-Deschènes saw no reason to modify his views, and declined to attend further councils of war ; and, although Napier again reconnoitred Sweaborg on September 23rd, and sent home a report [2] which was intended to facilitate operations in 1855, he did not attack. Towards the end of the month Parseval-Deschènes [3] went home. Napier himself still remained, chiefly off Nargen ; but, on September 27th, he sent part of the fleet, under Plumridge, to Kiel.

British expectations had not been satisfied by the work of the Baltic fleet in 1854. Napier was, perhaps, a weak officer in his old age, and may have been blameworthy ; but the Admiralty of that day was far weaker, in that it allowed itself to be forced by disappointed public opinion into inviting the Commander-in-Chief, at that late period, to undertake a venture which he and his colleagues had declared to be unfeasible a month earlier. On October 4th, there was sent to him a dispatch recommending him to choose a day and opportunity for an attack on Sweaborg, and containing the following passages :—

" You anticipate an attack by the Russian fleet, if many of your vessels are crippled or destroyed. We are always reminded that the Russians are most unwilling to navigate the Gulf of Finland in line-of-battle ships when autumn has commenced ; and Cronstadt is always locked up by ice fourteen days before Sweaborg is closed. The attack, therefore, on Sweaborg might be made towards the end of October, with least danger of attack from the Cronstadt portion of the Russian fleet. . . . This order is founded on your own last report. The final decision must rest entirely on yourself. If the attack on Sweaborg, in present circumstances, be desperate, it must on no account be undertaken by you. If, calculating the ordinary chances of war, and on full consideration of the strength of the enemy's fortress and fleets, you shall be of opinion that Sweaborg can be laid in ruins, it will be your duty, with the concurrence of the French Admiral, not to omit the opportunity."

The responsibility was thus left to Napier. The Admiralty had

---

[1] Rear-Adms. Plumridge, and Henry Byam Martin, C.B. (who had succeeded R.-Adm. Corry), were at the time absent on detached service.

[2] Napier, 303.

[3] His first service had been in the *Bucentaure,* at Trafalgar. On Dec. 2nd, 1854, he was raised to the rank of Admiral.

been induced to send him the order, partly by popular clamour, and partly by the receipt of an unfounded report that Sebastopol had fallen before an attack by the Black Sea fleet. Plumridge had been told to hurry back; Parseval-Deschènes had been directed to postpone his departure; when, on October 9th, having learnt that Sebastopol had not fallen, the Admiralty ordered Napier not to attack Sweaborg. It is scarcely surprising that the Commander-in-Chief lost his temper.[1] Having quitted Nargen on October 19th, he reached Kiel on the 22nd, leaving only a few ships to the northward under Captain Rundle Burges Watson, of the *Impérieuse;* but not until December 4th, when there was danger of its being frozen in, was the fleet ordered to be wholly withdrawn for the winter. On December 16th, Napier anchored at Spithead, and on the 18th he had a stormy interview with Sir James Graham. He was immediately, and rather curtly, directed to strike his flag; nor did he succeed in obtaining any public inquiry into his conduct. By way of protest he refused promotion to the highest class of the Bath.[2]

Such was the first year's campaign in the Baltic. Beyond the destruction of Bomarsund, and the blockade of Russian ports, it effected little or nothing. The fiasco may be attributed to three principal causes—causes which also influenced the results elsewhere. Firstly, the officers then available for responsible commands were, almost without exception, far too old to sustain the anxieties and fatigues of naval warfare under steam, without rapidly losing their efficiency. Secondly, there was at headquarters a conspicuous lack of information concerning the enemy's dispositions. And thirdly, even had the enemy's dispositions been fully known to the Admiralty, the fleet was materially incapable of doing the peculiar kind of work which the situation demanded. The commands of Napier and Parseval-Deschènes in the north, and of Dundas and Hamelin in the south, were made up mainly of craft of the heaviest draught and armament, and largely of sailing ships with necessarily limited

---

[1] See his letters of Oct. 10th and 27th to the Admiralty.

[2] Napier to Sir Chas. Wood, July 5th, 1855: to H.R.H. Prince Albert, of the same date. Lord Palmerston, speaking on the Navy Estimates, 1855, took a view different from that of Graham. "In my opinion," said he, "it is only due to him (Napier) to say that nothing has occurred in the course of the last year which, in the slightest degree, diminishes the high character which he has attained in the service of his country. . . . He secured the country against all the evils which might have arisen if the Baltic fleet of Russia had been permitted to quit its ports and scour the sea . . . .'

powers of manœuvring in narrow waters. In the first year of
the war, neither Great Britain nor France was able to employ
light-draught steam gunboats, and bomb or mortar vessels, because
neither Power possessed anything of the sort. Yet such vessels were
absolutely requisite for effective operations in the bays, and among
the islands, of the Baltic, and in the shallow outlying parts of the
Black Sea. In the following years hundreds of craft of the kind
were hurriedly and wastefully built or purchased. Scores of them,
nevertheless, were not ready until long after they had ceased to
be pressingly needed. Had there been less ignorance at headquarters, and had the allied navies been fully prepared for any work
which might have been thrust upon them, it is certain that the
struggle would have been far briefer, far less costly, and far more
decisive than it actually was.

On yet two other scenes of action there were operations of some
importance during the summer of 1854.

Almost immediately after the outbreak of war, Captain Erasmus
Ommanney, in the *Eurydice*, 26, was despatched to the White Sea,
with the *Miranda*, 14, screw, Captain Edmund Moubray Lyons,
and the *Brisk*, 14, screw, Commander Frederick Beauchamp Paget
Seymour. The object in view was a blockade of the Russian ports ;
but, in order as much as possible to spare British and French
property in neutral bottoms, the blockade was not regularly enforced
until August 1st. In the meantime, however, several Russian
merchantmen were captured, and a certain amount of damage was
done. Archangel was considered to be too strong for attack by so
small a force ; but on July 18th, while the *Miranda* and *Brisk* were
rounding Solovetskoi island, it was perceived that troops with
artillery were stationed in the woods there. A shot was fired to
dislodge them, and they returned it. At midnight the vessels
anchored off Solovetskoi monastery, where next morning it was seen
that the enemy was throwing up batteries. After unavailing
negotiations, the ships weighed at 8.20 A.M., and soon afterwards
opened fire. A smart action followed, the Russians replying from
a battery, from two towers of the monastery, and, with small-arms,
from the beach. By 11.20 A.M. the enemy began to desert his
positions ; but he returned later, only to be again driven away.
Fire, however, continued until 6 P.M., by which time red-hot shot,
shell, and musketry had silenced all opposition. The British loss
appears to have been but one killed and one wounded. On July 31st

a landing was effected on Shayley island, where the public buildings were burnt, and nine guns were taken or destroyed.

On August 23rd, Master George Williams, of the *Miranda*, buoyed the passage up to Kola; and Lyons then took his ship off the town, and anchored her at 6.30 A.M. in five fathoms. The place, in spite of its lonely and remote situation, was fortified, and contained large storehouses. Lieutenant Cecil William Buckley, under a flag of truce, went to demand a surrender; and very early on the 24th, no answer having been returned, the *Miranda* opened fire, the Russians briskly replying.

"The guns," says Lyons in his dispatch, "were shortly dismounted, and the battery reduced to ruins; but, although our shells burst well into the loopholed houses and stockades, an obstinate fire of musketry was kept up from various parts of the town. This allowed me no alternative; and I was obliged to destroy it. It was soon in flames from our shell and red-hot shot, and burned furiously, being fanned by a fresh breeze. The ship, at this time, became critically situated. The violence of the tide caused her to drag the bower and stream anchors, and the two kedges laid out to spring her broadside; and, the passage being too narrow for her to swing, she grounded at less than three hundred yards from the burning town, fragments from which were blown on board. However, by keeping the sails, rigging and decks well wetted until the ship was hove off, no bad consequences ensued."

During part of the action, a landing-party under Lieutenant John Francis Campbell Mackenzie, and actg. Mate Charles William Manthorp, rendered admirable service on shore. By 7.30 A.M. on the 24th, the work of destruction was complete.[1] In the early autumn the squadron returned to England.

In the China and Japan seas, at the beginning of the war, the Russian Rear-Admiral Poutiatin had under his orders the *Pallas*, 60, *Aurora*, 44, and *Dwina*, 12. The British force on the station was under Rear-Admiral David Price, and consisted of the *President*, 50 (flag), Captain Richard Burridge, *Pique*, 40, Captain Sir Frederick William Erskine Nicolson, Bart., *Amphitrite*, 24, Captain Charles Frederick, *Trincomalee*, 24, Captain Wallace Houstoun, and *Virago*, 6, paddle, Commander Edward Marshall. The French Rear-Admiral Febvrier-Despointes had at his disposal the *Forte*, 60 (flag), *Eurydice*, 30, *Artémise*, 30, and *Obligado*, 18. Poutiatin was, of course, helpless at sea against such a force; and therefore he sent the *Pallas* far up the river Amur, and utilised her people in reinforcing the weak garrisons on the littoral. The *Aurora* and *Dwina* took refuge in Petropaulovski, on the peninsula of Kamt-

[1] Officer's letter in Tyrrell's 'History,' i. 201.

chatka, a post against which it was foreseen that the allies would robably attempt operations.

Price and Febvrier-Despointes, after having detached the *Amphitrite*, *Artémise*, and *Trincomalee* to cruise for the protection of trade off the coasts of California, went in search of the Russians, and, on August 28th, sighted the shores of Kamtchatka. On the following day they entered Avalska Bay, at the head of which lies Petropaulovski. The Russians had worked very energetically at the defences of the roadstead. They had supplemented the pre-existing fort with numerous well-placed works, and had stationed the *Aurora* behind a sand spit,[1] where she could not be reached so long as the batteries remained unreduced. Yet, although the position was immensely and obviously formidable, the allied commanders underrated its strength. Their appearance was received with shots from the defences; and they returned the fire, but from too great a distance for it to be effective. On August 30th, they drew nearer in, and were beginning action, when Price, an officer too old, perhaps, for his work, but with a distinguished record, lost his head in the most unaccountable way, and, retiring to his cabin, shot himself. The direction of the British contingent devolved upon Nicolson; but the shocking event naturally led to the suspension of operations until the following morning, when the attack was resumed. On the 31st, at 8 A.M. the *President*, *Pique*, and *Forte* took up positions and opened fire on the nearest of the defences—three batteries mounting respectively three, five, and eleven guns. With the assistance of a landing-party from the *Virago*, the 3-gun battery, on the right, was silenced, its pieces were spiked, and the gun-carriages and platforms were destroyed; but, upon the *Aurora* disembarking 200 men to retake the battery, the *Virago's* party was withdrawn to the sloop. Later in the day the five-gun and the eleven-gun battery were silenced; but, in the night, the works were all repaired.

On September 2nd the body of Rear-Admiral Price was taken in the *Virago* to Tarinski Bay for burial. During her absence, the sloop picked up three American seamen, deserters from whalers. These men volunteered certain information—whether deliberately treacherous or merely mistaken will never be known—and, in consequence of this, it was decided at a council of war to attempt a landing with the object of seizing the town and taking the batteries

[1] On the spit was an 11-gun battery.

in reverse. Accordingly, at about 8 A.M. on September 4th, a body
of 700 seamen and Marines, under Captains Burridge and de La
Grandière (*Eurydice*), was disembarked on a low part of the
peninsula, after two protecting batteries, one of five and the other
of seven guns, had been silenced by the fire of the *President*,[1] *Forte*,
and *Virago*. Above the landing-place rose a wooded hill. The
Russians who held it were driven back; one of the two batteries,
which had been abandoned, was rendered useless; and the hill was
carried, though with difficulty. But, on endeavouring to advance
along the summit, which was covered with brushwood and brambles,
the expeditionary force, under the guidance of one of the American
deserters, became a target for Russian sharpshooters who were
almost invisible, and whose fire was very deadly. There were many
casualties. In heading a charge against the concealed foe, Captain
Charles Allan Parker, R.M., fell dead. It was presently seen that
to persist was to compromise the safety of the column; and a
retreat to the shore was ordered. It was carried on in much
confusion. In the course of it there were further losses, many of
which were occasioned by the very rough nature of the ground over
which the withdrawal had to be carried out. Ere their ships could
be regained, 107 British and 101 French had been killed or wounded,
among the killed being Captain Parker, R.M., and among the
wounded Lieutenants Alleyne Bland, Edward Henry Howard, George
Palmer (3), and William George Hepburn Morgan; Lieutenants
(R.M.) Edward Gough M'Callum and William Henry Clements;
Mate George Robinson (3), and Midshipman Louis Chichester.
The survivors returned on board at 10.45 A.M., and the ships at
once hauled out of range to attend to the wounded and to repair
damages.[2]

The unfortunate issue of this attack seems to have resulted as
much from the thoughtless rashness of the gallant leaders as from
their unwise confidence in the word of men who were confessedly
deserters. The spot chosen for a landing was one of the worst that
could have been selected, seeing that it was commanded by a hill,
and that, upon occupying the hill, the landing party ceased to be
covered by the fire of the ships. Nor, in all probability, would any
landing have been attempted, had the allied commanders had proper

---

[1] While the *President* was thus engaged, a Russian shot killed or wounded the
entire crew of one of her main-deck guns.

[2] Disps.: Off.'s letter in *Naut. Mag.*, 1855, 50; Tyrrell, i. 360; Chevalier, 240.

information concerning the strength and dispositions of the enemy. It must; however, be added that, in spite of the difficulties in their way, both British and French behaved with great bravery.

The combined squadrons, while in the neighbourhood, captured and burnt a Russian transport, the *Sitka,* 10, and took a small schooner, the *Avatska,* laden with stores. They quitted the coast on September 7th.

All the remaining naval operations of the year 1854 took place in the Black Sea.

The disembarkation of the allied armies at Eupatoria has already been described. On September 19th, flanked by the fleets, the expeditionary corps began its march along the coast to the south ward. At 11 A.M. the greater part of the fleet anchored off the mouth of the river Alma. At about 5 o'clock the army halted on the banks of the river Bulganak in order to bivouac for the night. A strong Russian force was then known to be posted upon the left bank of the Alma; and it was determined to attack it on the following morning. An officer who was in the *Rodney* with the fleet off the mouth of the Alma writes :—

" On grassy heights to the southward, we saw a Russian army encamped. To the north there was a range of low hills, the two eminences being separated by an extensive plain about four miles in width, which was occupied by a large force of the enemy's artillery and cavalry, who crossed the ravine, at the foot of their position, in which ran the little river." [1]

The Navy was able to take but very little share in the battle of the Alma,[2] which was fought on September 20th. The ships had previously made some endeavour to shell the rear of the left of the Russian position; but the range was too great for much result to be produced. They afforded, however, great assistance, by landing parties for the succour and removal of the wounded after the action—a work which lasted for three days. Dundas detached for the purpose all the boats of the fleet, nearly all his surgeons, and 600 seamen and Royal Marines.

It would have been the desire of one at least of the allied Admirals [3] to proceed, immediately after the battle, to the entrance

---

[1] ' At School and at Sea,' 324.

[2] Lieut. Samuel Hoskins Derriman, commanding the *Caradoc,* was attached to Lord Raglan's staff during the action ; and Lieut. Henry Carr Glyn, of the *Britannia,* was also present officially with the army.

[3] Dundas had this wish. Hamelin believed that the fleets could not enter until Fort Constantine should have been taken. Brereton, 17 ; Chevalier, 191.

of the harbour of Sebastopol, and, if possible, to force it; but the
fleets formed the only base for the forces which had been landed ;
and it was considered undesirable to separate them from it. As
soon as the Russians perceived that the advance along the coast
had not been checked, they took prompt measures to render the
mouth of their port impassable. On the night of September 22nd,
Captain Lewis Tobias Jones, C.B., of the *Samson*, 6, paddle, which,
with the *Terrible*, reconnoitred the place, reported to Dundas that,
outside the boom which lay between Fort Constantine and Fort
Alexander, the enemy had moored five ships of the line and two
frigates. These appeared to be connected with one another by
chains and cables, and were so disposed as not to mask the guns of
the works. Between the second and third vessels, counting from
the southern, or Fort Alexander, end of the line, a narrow passage
was perceived to have been left for entrance or exit; and thus,
although it could be seen that the whole of the Russian Black Sea
fleet was still in port, it was made evident that the enemy had not
entirely relinquished the idea of making a sally. The intention probably was to take advantage of any opportunity that might offer for
attempting a dash at some of the numerous isolated craft which
were still moving daily between Varna and the Crimea.

On September 23rd, however, when the armies, flanked by the
fleets, resumed their advance to the southward, the enemy took a
step which indicated that, in spite of the guns of Constantine and
of Alexander, and the broadsides of the ships near the boom, he
feared that his harbour might be penetrated. He sank all seven of
the vessels in the channel. The step was, upon the whole, a sound
one. By blocking the entrance as he did, he not only freed himself
from all anxiety concerning the issue of a sudden attack from seaward, but also released for the general purposes of the defence about
15,000 seamen, including many good gunners, while, at the same
time, he gained, for the armament of the new land forts which he
was erecting, an almost unlimited supply of heavy guns. Later, the
allies themselves might, no doubt, have sunk the ships near the
boom, had they so desired ; but to sink them there would, of course,
have blocked the passage as effectually as the Russians themselves
blocked it. They would hardly, therefore, have risked loss in the
effort. To gain a real success at the mouth of the harbour, the
allies would have been obliged to capture the ships near the boom,
and, instead of sinking them there, to tow them clear of the passage.

Such an operation, looking to the formidable nature of the covering forts, would scarcely have been attempted; but, so long as the vessels remained afloat, there was a bare possibility that it might be. Had it succeeded, the defensibility of Sebastopol would have been seriously impaired. The Russians, therefore, did wisely in rendering it impossible.

It had been decided by the generals at Varna to attack Sebastopol, in the first instance, from the north, and to land the necessary siege-train and supplies at the mouth of the Katcha; but it was soon found that the fire of the advanced Russian works on the north covered the ground as far as the Belbek river, only five miles south of the Katcha; and that a great disembarkation of exceedingly weighty material within so short a distance of the Russian guns would be a strategical mistake. It was therefore determined to attack Sebastopol, in the first instance, from the south; and, soon after leaving the field of the Alma, the generals struck off to the eastward in order to make the necessary turning movement. At 2 A.M. on the 24th, a message from Lord Raglan reached Dundas, who was then off the mouth of the Katcha, to the effect that the armies were about to march round the head of the harbour to the southern side of the town; and it was requested that he would detach a squadron to take possession of Balaclava, which was to be the point of disembarkation for the train and stores. Dundas at once sent off Sir Edmund Lyons, with a division of steamers, to make the desired seizure. It was at this time that Saint-Arnaud [1] was obliged to give way to the illness from which he had long suffered, and to resign his command to General Canrobert.

Lyons made for Balaclava; and it was taken possession of without much difficulty, as the troops drew near it from the north-east on the 26th.[2] The small deep bay was almost immediately filled with British transports; and when the French Rear-Admiral Charner, in the *Napoléon*, endeavoured to find an anchorage for his huge flag-ship and her convoy, he had great difficulty in doing so. It was at once seen that Balaclava harbour would not be roomy enough to serve as base for both armies. Moreover, it was at an

---

[1] Saint-Arnaud died on Sept. 29th, 1854, in his fifty-third year.

[2] This timely co-operation of the Navy with the Army was facilitated by the activity and enterprise of Lieut. Frederick Augustus Maxse, of the *Agamemnon*, who, having reached Raglan's camp on the Tchernaya on the night of the 25th with dispatches, volunteered to return at once to Lyons in the dark through a hostile country. Raglan to Newcastle, Sept. 28th. *See also* Maxse's letter of Oct. 25th in the *Times*.

inconvenient distance from the positions which had been assigned in the scheme of attack to the troops of France. A French base was, therefore, sought, and found in Kamiesh Bay, close to Cape Chersonese. Ere the end of the month much siege material had been put ashore both at Balaclava and at Kamiesh; and, on September 28th, impressed with the inadequacy of the armies for the work in hand, and relieved from much of his anxiety by the manner in which the Russians had destroyed seven of their ships, Dundas, who, with Hamelin and the bulk of both fleets, remained off the Katcha, issued an order for the formation of a naval brigade to serve ashore in the batteries. It was directed that each large ship should contribute 200 officers and men, and a contingent of lower-deck or other principal guns; and that the other war vessels should contribute in proportion. Each ship of the line sent ashore all her Marines, except a few who remained for sentry-duty, and all her best seamen-gunners, together with deck-awnings, spare canvas, spars, and half her ammunition. In all, 2400 seamen, 2000 Royal Marines, and 50 shipwrights, with 65 officers, and about 140 guns, were landed, the command being entrusted to Captain Stephen Lushington, of the *Albion*, 90. Among other officers of the brigade was Captain William Peel, of the *Diamond*, 27, whose aide-de-camp was Midshipman Evelyn Wood. The first naval camp was on a plain close to the Woronzoff Road, about two and a quarter miles from the head of the inner or Dockyard Harbour on the south side of Sebastopol. The first work of the brigade was to drag up from Balaclava guns, waggons of ammunition, and supplies, and to construct batteries and platforms for the guns. In all these labours the good humour, keenness, resourcefulness, and handiness of the seamen were so conspicuously displayed as to excite the admiration of both armies. Seldom before had the Navy had so much to do on land; and it seized the opportunity of making a new reputation for itself.

In the meantime, on October 4th, the *Sidon*, 22, paddle, Captain George Goldsmith, and the *Inflexible*, 6, paddle, Commander George Otway Popplewell, created a diversion in another part of the Black Sea by making an attack on Fort Nicolaieff; and, on November 12th, the *Tribune*, 31, screw, Captain the Hon. Swinfen Thomas Carnegie, *Highflyer*, 21, screw, Captain John Moore (4), and *Lynx*, 4, screw, supported a landing-party which destroyed a martello tower at Djemetil, near Anapa.

The cholera was not so prevalent in September and October as it had been earlier in the year in the Dobrudscha, and off Varna; but at Balaclava, afloat as well as ashore, it still caused much mortality; and, unfortunately, this was in great part due to the almost total neglect of sanitary precautions, and to the great discomfort which existed among the troops, owing to the indifferent commissariat arrangements. The defective organisation was to some extent remedied as the campaign went on; but few of the many much-needed reforms were effected until after the severe winter of 1854–5 had almost decimated the army. It had not been expected that Sebastopol would hold out for long; and no adequate provision whatsoever had been made for the prosecution of one of the most arduous and protracted sieges of modern times.

While preparations were being made for the opening of the attack on Sebastopol, there happened an affair which, though in itself trifling, was not without indirect importance, seeing that it was generally interpreted in the allied fleets as a proof of the defective character of Russian gunnery. On October 11th, an Austrian ship, laden with hay for the use of the British army, and bound from the mouth of the Katcha for Balaclava, was carried by the current so close to the entrance of Sebastopol harbour that, in order to avoid going ashore there, she was obliged to pass under the fire of the forts at a distance of not more than 1500 yards. The crew, believing that their craft must inevitably be sunk, took to the boats, and escaped, as soon as Fort Constantine opened. Presently the ship was subjected to a perfect hail of shot; but, although it is said that between 400 and 500 projectiles were aimed at her, she was struck by only four; and they did little damage. The *Beagle*, 4, screw, supported by the *Firebrand*, 6, paddle, Captain William Houston Stewart, approached the vessel as if to tow her out; whereupon the Russian fire waxed hotter than ever. The *Firebrand* was struck, and she and the *Beagle*, temporarily commanded by Second Master Alexander Fraser Boxer, did not then persist; but, some hours later, after the Austrian had gently grounded on the shore of Chersonese Bay, Captain Lewis Tobias Jones, in the *Samson*, with the *Firebrand*, *Beagle*, and French launches, towed her out in safety. While ashore, she was guarded by a detachment of French seamen from Kamiesh.[1]

The construction and arming of the first siege batteries occupied a fortnight; and it was not until October 16th that they were ready.

[1] Chevalier, 199; Dundas to Admlty., Oct. 13th.

Vice-Admiral Dundas in the interim had employed some of his steam-vessels in throwing shells at long range into several of the Russian works along the shore; but such desultory attacks had been discontinued at the request of Lord Raglan, who believed that they disquieted the army.[1] Dundas had also sent the *Leander,* 50, Captain George St. Vincent King, to Eupatoria to assist in the defence of that town. Later he sent thither as well the *Firebrand,* and the *Vesuvius,* with other vessels.

On October 15th, Vice-Admirals Dundas and Hamelin, and the Ottoman naval commander, Achmet Pacha, met on board the *Mogador,* where Hamelin had temporarily hoisted his flag, to concert measures, in response to the "urgent request" of the allied generals, for the co-operation of the fleets in the opening bombardment. Dundas was unwilling to give this co-operation. He would gladly enough have met a hostile fleet; but he was strongly of opinion that it was not the business of wooden walls to pit themselves against stone ones.

"A naval attack," says Brereton, who, as Dundas's guest at the time, had the best opportunity for knowing the Vice-Admiral's views, "must be restricted to engaging the forts at either side of the harbour. These works are of solid freestone in large blocks; and on them were mounted guns of heavy calibre, firing from casemated tiers of batteries, and batteries *en barbette* upon their summits. Moreover, they were flanked by detached works so placed as to support the stone forts. If the fleets could be expected to damage them, the reciprocal action of the batteries defending the entrance of the harbour might fairly be expected to disable the ships, sinking or destroying all, or a great number. A large and still effective Russian fleet was within the harbour. In the event of the disaster adverted to as possible, if not probable, what would be the fate of the army, should the enemy consequently become masters of the sea, and be enabled to cut off the transports daily bringing provisions to the land forces? As regarded the English Admiral, he could not fail to recollect how materially his strength had been diminished by the aid given to the English army, amounting to one-third of his crews, and one-half of his service ammunition."[2]

Chevalier, who may be assumed to reflect the views of Hamelin, says :—

"Admiral Hamelin probably shared the opinion of his colleague; but, looking to the situation in which the army was placed, and especially to the inferiority of its artillery as compared with that of the enemy, he considered that the navy, leaving ordinary rules aside, ought to neglect nothing which might facilitate the task of the troops. The Admiral also believed that, in taking such a course, he would be acting in conformity with the wishes of his officers and men. . . . The navy, which had not yet found occasion to take part in any warlike action of great importance, was animated by a lively desire to have a fighting share in the success of the expedition. The entrance to the port of Sebastopol was impassable: the action of the navy was necessarily limited; it could have no other object than to cannonade the works facing the sea; and that operation would not bring about a decisive result; but it would

---

[1] Brereton, 22.   [2] Brereton, 23.

act as a diversion; and it would oblige the enemy to man his sea batteries, and so reduce the number of artillerymen available for the manning of the works facing landwards."[1]

In short, while Dundas's unwillingness was dictated mainly by reason and prudence, Hamelin's willingness arose mainly from a deliberate determination to sacrifice prudential considerations to considerations of general tactical policy and of glory. But the appeal from the military commanders was so pressing that Dundas gave way. It was decided that the ships should be kept in movement, delivering their fire successively; and that those not in action should form a reserve. All details of the attack were discussed and decided; and, on returning to his flagship, Dundas summoned his Captains to assemble in the *Britannia*, on the morning of the 16th, to receive their final instructions. After he had given the instructions, he naturally supposed that all might be considered as definitively arranged; but, says Brereton—

"Not so; for at midnight of the same day, October 16th, Admiral Dundas received a visit from Admiral Hamelin, who, to the astonishment of the former, stated that he had been directed by General Canrobert, at whose disposal he was, to alter the plan of attack entirely, the new arrangement being that his line-of-battle ships were to anchor across the mouth of the harbour, and, from that position, to bombard the batteries. The English Admiral was requested to make a similar disposition of his squadron. Admiral Dundas at once expressed his dissent from the proposed new arrangement, strongly urged that the one so fully decided upon should be adhered to, and gave way only upon its being represented that the French Admiral was absolutely under the control of the military commander-in-chief, that in any case he must comply with the orders of that officer, and that the question resolved itself into whether he was to do so without the co-operation of the English fleet. There was but one answer to such an appeal."[2]

Chevalier indicates that one of the reasons which influenced the French in coming to the determination to engage at anchor was that the ships had lost many men by death, and many more by invaliding, and that these losses had never been made good, while, in addition, 1300 gunners and marine infantry had been landed, and guard-boats had to be manned and detached to take care of the top-gallant masts and other spars which were put overboard in preparation for action. Thus the vessels were deemed to be too short handed to be properly handled under way, or to fight both broadsides simultaneously. But Chevalier says nothing as to the sudden alteration of plans, and leaves it to be supposed that the decision to engage at anchor was the original one.[3] As for Hamelin, he says, in his dispatch of the 18th, "On the 15th, the admirals of the allied

---

[1] Chevalier, 201.   [2] Brereton, 25.   [3] Chevalier, 205, 206.

squadrons met on board the *Mogador*, and the arrangements for a general attack were made by common consent, and thereupon submitted to the generals of the land army, and most readily accepted by them."

The alteration of plans obliged Dundas to hold a new and hurried conference with his Captains. Moreover, there was delay consequent upon the necessity for bringing up vessels, many of which had to be towed, some from off the Katcha, where the bulk of both fleets had remained since the day of the Alma, and others from Kamiesh and the neighbouring bay of Kazatch. Although, therefore, the land batteries began to bombard the fortress at 6.30 A.M., it was about 1.30 P.M. ere the large ships were able to join in. Until that hour only a few small craft fired independently.

An act of distinguished daring was performed in the course of the night preceding the action. Masters William Thomas Mainprise (*Britannia*), Cornelius Thomas Augustus Noddall (*London*), and Charles Raguenau Pecco Forbes (*Samson*), in boats with muffled oars, eluded the Russian guard-boats, some of which hailed them, and took soundings close under the forts. They returned safely with very useful information.

It had been arranged among the admirals that the French should engage the works at the southern, and the British those at the northern side of the entrance to the harbour. This arrangement gave to the French ships as their object Fort Alexander, the Quarantine battery, and the adjoining works, and, to the British ships, Fort Constantine, the Telegraph batteries, and the works near them. But the majority of the ships on each side could be reached easily by the guns in the batteries on the other. Midway in the line, between the British and French fleets, but nearest to the latter, a station was assigned to the only two Turkish vessels that were able to take part. Near the centre of the channel, these vessels were the furthest removed from the forts. On the other hand, the post of honour to the northward, where the works were the most formidable, was given to the British. The French had upon the spot four steam ships of the line; and those of their vessels which had been lying at Kamiesh were much closer to the scene of action, and more readily reached it, than the British contingent, which included but two screw battleships, and most of which had to be towed from the anchorage off the Katcha. Some of the French ships, therefore, were the first to get into action; though, when they began firing, they did so at long and ineffectual ranges. Presently, however, some of them got close in, and fired at almost point-blank distance.[1] There was no wind whatsoever. All the ships adopted the usual precautions of sending down top-gallant masts, and studding-sail booms, etc., and of binding up their yards. All spare topmasts and yards were sent on board the *Vulcan.* Special precautions were adopted by many.

The vessels engaged in this first bombardment of the Sebastopol forts were as follows :—

		BRITISH.			FRENCH.
SHIPS.	GUNS.	COMMANDERS.	SHIPS.	GUNS.	COMMANDERS.
Agamemnon, scr. .	91	R.-Ad. Sir Edmund Lyons. Capt. Wm. Robert Mends.	*Charlemagne,* scr. . *Montebello,* scr. .	90 120	Capt. de Chabannes. V.-Ad. Bruat. Capt. Bassière.
Sans Pareil, scr. .	70	Capt. Sidney Colpoys Dacres.	*Friedland* . . .	120	Capt. Guérin.
Samson, padd. . .	6	Capt. Lewis Tobias Jones.	*Vauban,* 20 . . .		Capt. d'Herbinghem.
Tribune, scr. . .	31	Capt. Hon. Swinfen Thomas Carnegie.	*Ville de Paris* . .	120	V.-Ad. Hamelin. Capt. Dompierre d'Hornoy.
Terrible, padd. . .	21	Capt. James Johnstone McCleverty.	*Primauguet,* 8 . .		Capt. Reynaud.
Sphinx, padd. . .	6	Capt. Arthur Parry Eardley Wilmot.	*Valmy*	120	R.-Ad. Lugeol. Capt. Lecointe.
Lynx, scr. . . .	4	Lieut. John Proctor Luce.	*Descartes,* 20 . .		Capt. Darricau.
Albion . . . . *Firebrand,* padd., 6.	90	Com. Hy. Downing Rogers.† Capt. Wm. Houston Stewart.	*Henri IV.* . . . *Canada,* 14. . . .	100	Capt. Jehenne. Capt. Massin.
London . . . . *Niger,* scr., 14.	90	Capt. Chas. Eden Com. Leopold George Heath.	*Napoléon,* scr. . .	92	R.-Ad. Charner. Capt. Dupouy.
Arethusa . . .	50	Capt. Thomas Matthew Charles Symonds.	*Pomone,* scr. . . *Alger.*	40 80	Capt. de Saisset.
Triton, padd., 3.		Lieut. Hy. Lloyd.	*Magellan,* 14 . .		Capt. Kerdrain.
Queen . . . . *Vesuvius,* padd., 6.	116	Capt. Frederick Thomas Michell. Com. Richard Ashmore Powell.	*Marengo.* . . . *Labrador,* 14 . .	80	Capt. Martin. Capt. de Varèse.
Britannia . . .	120	V.-Ad. James Whitley Deans Dundas, C.B. R.-Ad. Hon. Montagu Stopford, Capt. of the Fleet. Capt. Thomas Wren Carter.	*Ville de Marseille* . *Panama,* 14 . . *Suffren*	80 90	Capt. Laffon-Ladébat. Capt. Goubin. Capt. Fabre Lamaurelle.
Furious, padd., 16		Capt. William Loring.	*Albatros,* 14 . .		Capt. Dubernad.
Trafalgar . . . *Retribution,* padd., 28.	120	Capt. Henry Francis Greville. Capt. Hon. Jas. Robt. Drummond.	*Bayard* . . . . *Ulloa,* 14 . . .	90	Capt. Borius. Capt. Baudais.
Vengeance . . . *Highflyer,* scr., 21 . *Rodney* . . . . *Spiteful,* padd., 6 .	84 90	Capt. Lord Edward Russell. Capt. John Moore (4). Capt. Chas. Graham. Com. Augustus Frederick Kynaston.	*Jupiter* . . . . *Chr. Colomb,* 14 .	90	Capt. Lugeol. Capt. Chevalier.
Bellerophon . . . *Cyclops,* padd., 6 .	78	Capt. Lord George Paulet. Mast. Robert Wilson Roberts.	*Jean Bart,* scr.. .	90	Capt. Touchard.
Circassian, padd. .		Actg. Sec. Mast. Edward Codrington Ball.			
Spitfire, padd., 6 .		Com. Thos. Abel Bremage Spratt.			

Besides two Turkish ships of the line.

Note. The large vessels bracketed with smaller ones were towed by, or coupled broadside to, the latter.

† In absence of Capt. Stephen Lushington, commanding Naval Brigade before Sebastopol.

[1] Corr. of *Morning Herald.*

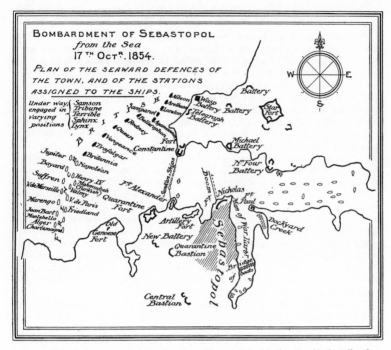

Note. Owing to circumstances, the *Queen's* actual position was that originally assigned to the *Bellerophon*, and the *Rodney's* was that originally assigned to the *Queen.* Such was the arrangement at 1.30 P.M.

STRENGTH AND ARMAMENT OF THE THREE PRINCIPAL SEA-FACE BATTERIES AT
SEBASTOPOL, AS ENGAGED BY THE ALLIED FLEETS, OCTOBER 17TH, 1854.

WORKS.	MEN.	GUNS.								Of which could be trained on the ships.
		36-prs.	26-prs.	18-prs.	3-poud[1] (shell.)	1-poud[1]	½-poud[1]	5-poud[1] mortars	TOTAL.	
Quarantine Fort .	277	29	—	—	2	12	9	6	58	33
Fort Alexander .	272	11	16	4	2	19	—	4	56	17
Fort Constantine.	470	—	50	—	—	34	4	6	94	23
		40	66	4	4	65	13	16	208	73

[1] The Russian poud equals 36·11 lbs. avoird. The 3-poud shell gun threw, therefore, a projectile weighing about 108 lbs., and the 5-poud mortar a projectile weighing about 180 lbs. The 1-poud (36-pr.) and ½-poud (18 pr.) pieces were howitzers.

See Todleben, "Defence of Sebastopol"; Kinglake, "Invasion of the Crimea"; Owen, "Modern Artillery"; Douglas, "Naval Gunnery"; *R.E. Journal of Operations.*

A correspondent of the *Times*, writing on the 18th, said :—

"Yesterday morning, about daybreak, the English and French opened fire from their batteries on the south side of Sebastopol. . . . The paddle-wheel and screw frigates lashed themselves alongside the sailing line-of-battle ships, and all was got ready for the fight. The French were to occupy the right as you enter the harbour—that is, the southern side—and the English, the left, or northern side, in one line, about 1500 yards off. The French got into their places about half-past twelve o'clock, and immediately commenced a heavy fire, which was vigorously returned from the batteries. The distance, however, was certainly greater than originally contemplated, and, as far as I can ascertain, it was over 2000 yards. By degrees the English ships successively took up their stations, passing in rear of the French, and anchoring to the left. The *Agamemnon*, *Sans Pareil*, and *London* . . . however, took an inside station in advance—perhaps about 1000 yards from Fort Constantine. Nothing could be more noble than the gallant way in which the *Agamemnon* and *Sans Pareil* steamed in amid a perfect hail of cannon-balls and shells, preceded by a little tug-steamer, the *Circassian*, commanded by Mr. Ball. This little bit of a cockleshell, which looked as if she might have been arrested by a fowling-piece, deliberately felt the way for the large ships till her services were no longer required.

"The firing soon became terrific. At the distance of six miles the sustained sound resembled that of a locomotive at full speed, but, of course, the roar was infinitely grander. The day was a dead calm, so that the smoke hung heavily about both ships and batteries, and frequently prevented either side from seeing anything. From about two till dark (nearly six) the cannonade raged most furiously.

"Towards four o'clock, Fort Constantine, as well as some of the smaller batteries, slackened somewhat in their fire ; but towards dusk, as some of the ships began to haul out, the Russians returned to their guns, and the fire seemed as fierce as ever. There was one explosion just behind Fort Constantine, which appeared to do much damage. At dark, all the ships returned to their anchorage. The change was magical from a hot sun, mist, smoke, explosions, shot, shell, rockets, and the roar of ten thousand guns, to a still, cool, brilliant, starlit sky, looking down upon a glassy sea, reflecting in long tremulous lines the lights at the mast-heads of the ships returning amid profound silence."

Another correspondent,[1] writing a little later, thus describes the slight effect produced :—

"We passed close by the forts of Sebastopol. We were quite within range (though the enemy never attempted to fire), and therefore with our glasses we could see every chink and cranny in the fortresses, which we had ample time to survey. Every fort towards the sea—those of Alexander, and Paul on the south side, and Nicholas, and Constantine on the north—was perfectly covered from the base to the summit with shot marks. In this there was no difference between those attacked by the English or French, except that Fort Constantine, to the north, had two of the casemated ports knocked into one. It was at the spot where the *Agamemnon* had been moored, and where her whole broadside had been concentrated with something like effect. As far as we could judge, it seemed that the amount of damage done to the batteries is literally and truly nothing. Where several shots have struck in the same place, the granite is splintered and broken away to the depth of about a foot, or even less. Where only one or two balls have struck, there are mere whitish marks, as if the spot had been dabbed with flour.

"To restore these forts to their original look would, of course, be expensive, because unnecessary. As forts, they are as strong as if a shot had never been fired against

[1] Writing to the *Morning Herald*.

them. A very small amount of money would repair the actual damage done to the cornices below the embrasures. The spots on the walls below the embrasures are not worth notice, for a few inches of stone make little difference in a fort where the walls are fourteen, and in some parts eighteen feet thick. . . . Owing to the shallowness of the water, no vessel, French or English, was enabled to approach nearer than 750 yards. The great majority . . . were 1000 and 1200 yards off."

The position of the Russian batteries on the north and south sides of the harbour-mouth is indicated in the plan on p. 441. The armament of the principal works is there also set forth.

Vice-Admiral Dundas's dispatch concerning the engagement is very meagre. It declares briefly that the *Agamemnon, Sans Pareil, Samson, Tribune, Sphinx,* and *Lynx,* and the *Albion, London,* and *Arethusa,* towed respectively by the *Firebrand, Niger,* and *Triton,* " engaged Fort Constantine and the batteries to the northward "; and that the other sailing ships, with a steamer lashed on the port side of each, " gradually took up their positions, as nearly as possible as marked on the plan " appended to the letter; that the action lasted from about half-past one to half-past six P.M.; that the British ships had lost 44 killed and 266 wounded; and that—

"The ships, masts, yards, and rigging are more or less damaged, principally by shells and hot shot. The *Albion* has suffered much in hull and masts; the *Rodney* in her masts, she having tailed on the reef, from which she was got off by the great exertions of Commander Kynaston, of the *Spiteful,* whose crew and vessel were necessarily exposed in performing this action; but, with the exception of the *Albion* and *Arethusa,* which ships I send to Constantinople to be repaired, I hope to be able to make my squadron serviceable in twenty-four hours."

The dispatch also praises the ability and zeal of Rear-Admirals Sir Edmund Lyons, and the Hon. Montagu Stopford, and of the officers and men engaged, and bears witness to the gallantry and skill of the French, and to the manner in which Achmet Pacha did his duty. It appears from the other dispatches, from the logs, and from independent accounts which have been consulted, that the signal to weigh was made to the British squadron at 10.50 A.M., and that the *Agamemnon,* followed by the *Sans Pareil,* led in. At 1.30 P.M., the *Agamemnon,* then closing the land, opened fire from her large pivot gun upon the Wasp battery, which at once returned it, and which was presently joined by Fort Constantine. At 2 P.M. she anchored head and stern in four and three-quarter fathoms, about 750 yards from Fort Constantine, upon which her broadside was turned. Five minutes later, the *Sans Pareil* and the *London* anchored astern of her, and hotly engaged the Star Fort, and smaller works upon the heights. At 2.20 P.M., the *Albion* anchored, and took off some of the fire of the Wasp battery, subsequently tackling Fort Constantine. The *Britannia*, then about 2000 yards from the forts, and in fifteen fathoms, began action at nearly the same time; and the bombardment then soon became general. The smaller steamers, and especially the *Terrible* and the *Samson*, placed themselves inshore of the ships of the line, and behaved most gallantly. The *Arethusa*, having had her rigging cut to pieces, many shot in her hull, and 23[1] persons killed and wounded, was presently towed off by her attendant. The *Albion*, also, with 11 killed and 71 wounded, was obliged to haul out of the fight, very badly mauled.[2] Nearly at the same moment the *London*, with 4 killed and 18 wounded, retired. Lyons, however, in the *Agamemnon*, though more exposed than any other officer, did not move. At one time his second, the *Sans Pareil*, withdrew in consequence of having expended all the ammunition which it had been decided to use on the occasion; but he called up the *Bellerophon*[3] to support him, and sent to bring back the *Sans Pareil*, fighting on, and declaring, "I'm damned if I'll leave this." The *Agamemnon* had only 4 killed and 25 wounded; but, owing to her nearness to the forts, she suffered far more aloft than in her hull. She was twice on fire; and, from first to last, she was hit 240 times. The *Rodney*, for the reason mentioned in Dundas's dispatch, suffered still more severely aloft. The *Britannia*, *Trafalgar*, *Queen*,[4] and *Vengeance* were much less injured. The last ship, the *Bellerophon*, hauled off at 7 o'clock, with 5 killed and 16 wounded.

Among the killed in the British squadron were Lieutenant Parkhurst Chase (*Albion*), and Midshipmen Charles Madden (2) (*Sans Pareil*), and —— Forster (*Bellerophon*). Among the officers wounded were Captain William Houston Stewart (*Firebrand*), Commander Augustus Frederick Kynaston (*Spiteful*), Lieutenants Francis Reginald Purvis (*Spiteful*), James Bull, and Warren Hastings Anderson (*Sans Pareil*), Charles Edward Stevens (*Albion*), James William Vaughan (*Britannia*), and Thomas Lovette Gaussen (*Agamemnon*), and Master Henry Paul, Surgeon Richard Denton

---

[1] Including 5 of the *Triton's*, who were helping to serve her guns.

[2] She was thrice set on fire, and would probably have gone ashore, but for the efforts of the tugs.

[3] She was ultimately the closest ship in, and succeeded in silencing Wasp battery. Lyons signalled to her, " Well done, Bellerophon."

[4] The *Queen*, however, caught fire, as did also the *Britannia*, which last received over seventy shots in her hull.

Mason, and Paymaster Charles Augustus Thorne (all of *Albion*). The French had 212 people killed and wounded : the Turks, but one or two men hurt. The Russians admitted a loss during the day of 1100 men,[1] among the killed being the gallant Admiral Korniloff, who had been the chief organiser of the defence of the fortress.

In the meantime, the Naval Brigade ashore did excellent service.

CAPTAIN SIR WILLIAM PEEL, K.C.B., V.C.

From a lithograph by J. H. Lynch, after a photograph by Mrs. Verschoyle.

Up to October 20th, it lost 12 killed and 53 wounded.[2]   It took part in the bombardment with some naval 32-prs., a few 68's from the *Terrible*, a couple of 13-inch mortars, and half a dozen Lancaster

---

[1] A French officer, who had previously been taken prisoner, escaped, reporting that the Russians had lost 5000 killed, besides the wounded.

[2] Among the killed were Lieuts. Cavendish Bradstreet Hore Ruthven (*London*), and George Herbert Harris Greathed (*Britannia*); and, among the wounded, Capt. William Moorsom (*Firebrand*), Lieuts. John Norris Norman (*Trafalgar*), and Alfred Mitchell (*Diamond*), and Mate Thomas Thelwall Bullock (actg.) (*Trafalgar*).

guns,[1] and it also worked some of the 24-prs. of the military siege train, until those guns were disabled. On October 18th, Captain William Peel seized a live shell which, with burning fuse, fell in his battery, and flung it over the parapet. It burst before it touched the ground outside. At Lord Raglan's desire, Dundas reinforced the Brigade, after the bombardment, with 410 officers and seamen, and placed Commander Lord John Hay (3), of the *Wasp*, 14, screw, under the orders of Captain Lushington. At Eupatoria, Captain Brock, supported by the *Leander*, 50, Captain George St. Vincent King, the *Megæra*, 6, screw, Commander John Ormsby Johnson, and other vessels, held his own, though threatened, and occasionally attacked, by large bodies of cavalry, with guns.[2] The *Sidon*, 22, paddle, Captain George Goldsmith, and *Inflexible*, 6, paddle, Commander George Otway Popplewell, with the French vessels *Cacique* and *Caton*, remained in Odessa Bay, to prevent the Russians there from communicating by sea with the Crimea.[3]

The famous cavalry action at Balaclava was fought on October 25th. On the following day the Russians made a determined sortie against the division of General Sir de Lacy Evans. Their advance threatened the right Lancaster Battery, which was held by actg. Mate William Nathan Wrighte Hewett, of the *Beagle*, and a party of seamen ; and at 300 yards they poured a hot musketry fire into the work. Owing to some error, word was passed to spike the gun and to retreat. Hewett, doubting whether the order came from Captain Lushington, commanding the Brigade, not only stuck to his post, but also, aided by his men and by some soldiers, slewed his gun round in the direction of the enemy on his flank, blew away the parapet of the battery, and opened a fire which materially assisted in obliging the Russians to retreat. Hewett was at once made actg. Lieutenant, and was afterwards officially promoted as from the day of his brave action. Later, he was given the Victoria Cross.

On November 7th, Vice-Admiral Dundas proposed to Vice-Admiral Hamelin to destroy the remaining storehouses and magazines at Odessa; and preparations were being made to that end when a dispatch from England arrived, directing the naval Commander-in-Chief not to undertake any operations against

---

[1] Including two from the *Beagle*.

[2] In repelling one of these attacks, Lieut. William Henry Pym (*Firebrand*), and Mids. Lord Edward Henry Cecil (*Leander*) distinguished themselves.

[3] Dundas to Admlty., Oct. 13th, 18th and 23rd.

the enemy without the concurrence of Lord Raglan ; while on
the same day Raglan and Canrobert decided "that the presence
of steam war-vessels for the purpose of bombarding Odessa would,
under existing circumstances, be much more disadvantageous than
useful." [1] A project of Dundas's for the occupation of Kertch was
put forward at about the same time ; but could not be carried out
owing to the inability of the Generals to spare the necessary troops

SIR WILLIAM NATHAN WRIGHTE HEWETT, K.C.B., V.C., VICE-ADMIRAL.

Born 1834 ; died 1888.

for the operation. On the other hand, Dundas was urged from
home to send some of his steamers to the eastern extremity of the
Gulf of Perekop so that their guns, by sweeping the western side of
the isthmus of that name, might interfere with the passage of troops
and supplies into the Crimea by that route. The Vice-Admiral knew
that this plan was impracticable ; but, to satisfy the Admiralty, he
detached the *Spitfire*, 5, paddle, Commander Thomas Abel Bremage

[1] Parl. Paper, ordered to be printed June 11th, 1855.

Spratt, to take soundings near the head of the Gulf. Spratt, who returned on December 13th, reported that the *Spitfire*, though only a small sloop, could not approach the shore within twenty miles, and that even her boats could not approach it within four miles. He also reported that thirty miles east of the isthmus there was a bridge across a narrow part of Lake Sivatch ; and that across the bridge, not across the isthmus, lay the chief military road between Kherson and Simpheropol.

Towards noon, on December 6th, some excitement was caused by the sudden sortie from Sebastopol of the steam frigate *Vladimir*, and the steam corvette *Chersonese*. They came out by the passage which had been left through the line of sunken ships, and headed at great speed to the W.S.W., firing at the batteries on the extreme left of the French attack, and at the French look-out vessel *Mégère*. The latter was presently reinforced by the French dispatch-vessel *Dauphin*, and by the *Valorous*, 16, paddle, Captain Claude Henry Mason Buckle ; and, before those craft, the Russians turned and withdrew, after having made what was, no doubt, a useful reconnaissance.

There were no other naval movements of importance during the year 1854. On December 22nd, his three years' period of command having nearly expired, Dundas hauled down his flag as Commander-in-Chief in the Mediterranean and Black Sea, and was succeeded by Sir Edmund Lyons, whose place as second was taken by Rear-Admiral Edward Boxer, C.B. At about the same time Vice-Admiral Hamelin was succeeded by Vice-Admiral Bruat.

One unfortunate occurrence which signalised the conclusion of Vice-Admiral Dundas's command remains to be chronicled. On November 14th, 1854, a hurricane of almost unexampled violence devastated the coasts of the Crimea. In the morning the sky was clear and the sea calm, with a light land wind blowing ; but the barometer stood at 29·50. Part of the fleet still lay off the Katcha River. In Balaclava Bay, in spite of the meteorological conditions, no special measures of precaution were taken, except that the *Agamemnon* moved out. By 10 A.M. the storm, a furious blast from the S.W., was in full play. In quick succession the transports *Progress, Resolute, Wanderer, Kenilworth, Prince*, screw, *Rip van Winkle*, and other vessels, to the number of thirty-four, were lost, chiefly off Balaclava, many of their people perishing. With the *Prince*, which had on board immense supplies of winter clothing and hospital stores, there was lost Commander Benjamin Baynton, Admiralty Agent. The warships *Vesuvius* and *Ardent* suffered severely, but escaped being wrecked. The other warships in the bay were still more fortunate, and rode out the gale without great damage. The storm was at its worst for not much more than two hours, and the weather moderated in the afternoon, though a high sea still ran.

Off the Katcha, fourteen transports, of which five [1] were British, were totally lost. H.M.S. *Samson* fouled two of them, and carried away all her masts. The Turkish admiral lost two of his masts, and H.M.S. *London* was badly damaged; but comparatively few lives were sacrificed there. Off Eupatoria,[2] where the anchorage was bad, the French line-of-battle ship *Henri IV.* dragged her four anchors, or snapped their cables, and drove ashore. The *Pluton* met with the same fate. The Russians, at the height of the tempest, made an attack upon the place, but were driven off, thanks in part to the help rendered by the grounded ships, which, though almost on their beam ends and threatening to break up, gallantly opened fire. The *Pluton* became a total loss; but the *Henri IV* long remained where the waves had cast her, and was used as a fort to defend the south side of the town, while some of her guns were landed and mounted in the batteries of the place.

In the battle of Inkermann, fought on November 5th, 1854, six hundred men of the Naval Brigade were present in the field, the rest being in the batteries. The right Lancaster battery, where (actg.) Lieutenant William Nathan Wrighte Hewett commanded, on the extreme right of the left attack, and where Lancaster guns and three 68-prs. were mounted, was fiercely but vainly assaulted by the Russians. Five bluejackets, picking up the rifles of disabled soldiers, mounted the banquette, and, with extraordinary heroism and cool-ness, under a storm of bullets, kept up a rapid fire against the enemy, while other seamen below loaded and handed up fresh weapons. Two of these gallant fellows perished, but the survivors, Thomas Reeves, James Gorman, and Mark Scholefield, were deservedly given the Victoria Cross. Sir Edmund Lyons, who had been present at Balaclava on October 25th, was also present on shore at Inkermann. So, also, were Captain Sir William Peel, and

---

[1] *Pyrenees, Ganges, Rodney, Tyrone,* and *Lord Raglan.*

[2] At Eupatoria were lost the British transports *Her Majesty, Asia, Glendalough, Harbinger,* and *Georgiana.*

his aide-de-camp, Midshipman Edward St. John Daniel. They joined the officers of the Grenadier Guards, and assisted in defending the colours of that regiment when they were in danger of capture at the Sandbag Battery. Both Peel and Daniel, it should be added, won the Victoria Cross; and both deserved it on more than one occasion.

After Inkermann, the British naval camp before Sebastopol was shifted to a new site about a mile and a half more to the left, on the right bank of the upper part of the long ravine leading down to the head of the Dockyard or Inner Harbour.

From February 1st, 1855, the blockade in the Black Sea was formally renewed, all Russian ports which were not occupied by the Allies being specified, or indicated, in the *Gazette* notice announcing the fact. Ere that time Omar Pasha, with a large Turkish army, had been transported to the Crimea, and had undertaken the military management of the defence of Eupatoria. The Russians, strange to say, delayed making any determined attack upon the place until after it had been thus strengthened; and, when they did attack, they were badly defeated.

Their great effort to capture the town began in the early morning of February 17th, 1855, and ended with their retirement at about 10.15 A.M. Omar Pasha's dispatch on the subject to Lord Raglan states that, the Turkish right and centre being specially pressed, the senior British naval officer was asked to detach the *Viper* to co-operate with the French steamer *Véloce* and the Turkish steamer *Schefer* on the right; that the left was well covered by the men-of-war; and that, in addition to the *Viper*, the *Curaçoa*, *Furious*, and *Valorous* rendered useful service. The *Valorous*, from the harbour, threw her shells with great precision, and specially annoyed the Russian cavalry; the *Furious* landed a rocket party on the extreme right of the town; and this body of men, outflanking the assaulting column as it reached the glacis, greatly contributed to throwing it into confusion.[1]

The Russians still held Anapa and Soujak Kaleh, on the Circassian coast of the Black Sea; and, although they were carefully watched, no attempts on a large scale were made to dislodge them. On February 20–24th, the *Leopard*, 18, paddle, Captain George Giffard, and boats, defeated a body of Russian troops at

---

[1] Omar to Raglan : Canrobert's disp.: corr. of *Daily News*.

Anapa, captured some guns and stores, and destroyed some buildings. On March 8th, the *Viper*, 4, screw, Lieutenant Charles Arthur Lodder, and a landing-party from her, destroyed a fort, barracks, and granaries at Djemetil, hard by; and on March 13th, the *Leopard*, and *Viper*, with the *Highflyer*, 21, screw, Captain John Moore (4), and *Swallow*, Commander Frederick Augustus Buchanan Craufurd, engaged the works at Soujak Kaleh. But sufficient force to reduce those strongholds could not then be spared from before Sebastopol.

During all that time but little real progress was made towards the reduction of the great fortress. The Russians had less valid reason than ever to fear a direct naval attack : yet they appear, while somewhat underrating the capacity of their military enemies, to have strangely overrated the powers of the allied fleets; for, says one of Raglan's dispatches, on the night of February 24th they "sank three or four more ships in the harbour, as far within the booms as the first were outside of them ; and, according to the most accurate examination yesterday,[1] there are now four barriers or impediments to the entrance of the harbour—namely, two of sunken ships, and two booms." A few days later [2] they were reported to have sunk two additional ships. The new line of obstructions ran between Forts Michael and Nicholas.

The return in the spring of comparatively fine weather led to renewed activity on the part of the attack ; and, at daybreak on April 9th, a new general bombardment of the besieged town was opened. Enormous quantities of ammunition were wasted by both sides ; and the fire was kept up, with some intermissions, for twelve days, and did not wholly die out until about April 27th or 28th. Very little damage seems to have been done, however. The allied navies co-operated on several occasions. The Russians had so greatly augmented their seaward defences, especially on the commanding heights above the permanent forts, that the ships could not stand in to engage save when the nights were dark ; and, even then, as they were obliged to direct much of their fire by the aid of signal lights placed ashore, great accuracy was scarcely obtainable. On the night of April 13th, the *Valorous* had a smart brush with Forts Constantine and Alexander, and with the Quarantine Battery, and withdrew without having been struck ; and, on the night of

---

[1] The disp. is dated Feb. 27th.   [2] Disp. of Mar. 3rd.

April 22nd, the British and French flagships, *Royal Albert*, 121,[1] screw, and *Montebello*, 120, screw, also stood in, but had to desist from their intended action owing to an accident which disabled the Frenchman's machinery. Upon the whole, it was plain that, so long as the Russian fleet remained in port—and it was certain that it did not purpose to put to sea—the presence of immense naval forces off Sebastopol was almost entirely useless; and it was this fact which at length determined the despatch of an expedition to pass through the Strait of Kertch and into the Sea of Azof, where the enemy had large stores of supplies that might be reached without great difficulty, and where, in consequence, he could be more effectively annoyed. Lyons and Bruat were, almost from the first, strong partisans of this expedition. Raglan and Canrobert also believed that it would produce valuable results; but for a long time they were unwilling to spare the troops which were required to accompany it. On April 25th, however, having decided that they would attempt no important military operations before Sebastopol until on or after May 11th, they agreed with the naval chiefs to lend their co-operation; and, accordingly, on May 3rd, 12,000 troops under Generals Sir George Brown and d'Autemarre, were embarked in forty steamers, British and French. That evening the flotilla weighed and headed for Eupatoria, to deceive the Russians. In the night it altered course.

"On the 5th," writes an officer who was present, "having arrived within twenty miles of our destination, the Admiral made a general signal for Captains, with the object, as we supposed, of discussing the plan of attack; so our surprise and disappointment may be imagined when " (our Captain) "returned, looking very glum, with the intelligence that General Canrobert had received a message from Napoleon which obliged him to recall the French. Of course the English might have gone on : but it was not thought prudent to act alone."[2]

The British, therefore, returned, and anchored in Kamiesh Bay. Canrobert, there is small doubt, exaggerated the onus which was laid upon him by his instructions from Paris; and he certainly, by recalling the expedition after it had sailed, ran serious risk not only of encouraging the enemy but also of disquieting his allies. A little later, however, an Azof expedition was again allowed to set out, and was permitted to do its work without interference. It may be noted, meanwhile, that the Emperor Napoleon's message, in con-

---

[1] Lyons had transferred his flag to her on Feb. 14th, 1855. She was commanded by Captain William Robert Mends, C.B.

[2] 'At School and at Sea,' 402. *See also* Chevalier, 259.

sequence of the receipt of which the first expedition was recalled, was one of the earliest messages that passed over the then newly-laid cable to the seat of war. It may also be noted that, soon after the laying of the cable, the French military commander-in-chief, who probably felt that he could not satisfactorily do his work at the front while he was subject to hourly dictation from Paris, resigned,[1] and was succeeded by General Pélissier. Still more in naval than in military matters is it unwise for authorities at a distance to seek to direct in detail those who are on the scene of action. The late Sir Geoffrey Hornby's opinions on this point, which have been cited in a previous volume,[2] seem to be strictly in accordance with all the lessons of the past.

The new expedition included about 7000 French, 5000 Turkish, and 3500 British, with a few Sardinian[3] troops, the British being, as before, under Sir George Brown; and the fleet employed was made up of nine sail of the line, and about fifty smaller vessels, of which those named below[4] formed the British contingent. Sir Edmund Lyons and Vice-Admiral Bruat were themselves in command.

The fleet sailed from Kamiesh Bay on May 22nd, and reached a point a few miles below Kertch on the morning of May 24th, the Queen's birthday. The troops were quickly thrown ashore near Kamiesh Bournou and Cape Paulovski, while some of the lighter vessels pushed on towards Kertch and Yenikale. But the Russians did not await the attack. Taken, apparently, by surprise, they blew up their fortifications on both sides of the strait, abandoned about a hundred guns, and retired, after having destroyed three steamers, and several other heavily-armed vessels, as well as large quantities of provisions, ammunition and stores. These results were effected without loss to the Allies, and, indeed, practically without any fighting.

---

[1] May 18th. [2] *See* Vol. II., p. 340 n.

[3] Sardinia had cast in her lot with the Allies since the beginning of the year.

[4] *Royal Albert*, 121, scr. (flag); *Hannibal*, 91, scr. (flag of R.-Ad. Houston Stewart); *Algiers*, 91, scr.; *Agamemnon*, 91, scr.; *St. Jean d'Acre*, 101, scr.; *Princess Royal*, 91, scr.; *Sidon*, 22, padd.; *Valorous*, 22, padd.; *Leopard*, 18, padd.; *Tribune*, 31, scr.; *Simoon*, 8, scr.; *Furious*, 16, padd.; *Highflyer*, 21, scr.; *Terrible*, 21, padd.; *Sphinx*, 6, padd.; *Spitfire*, 5, padd.; *Gladiator*, 6, padd.; *Caradoc*, 2, padd.; *Banshee*, 2, padd.; and the following light squadron, *viz.*, *Miranda*, 15, scr.; *Vesuvius*, 6, padd.; *Curlew*, 9, scr.; *Swallow*, 9, scr.; *Stromboli*, 6, padd.; *Ardent*, 5, padd.; *Medina*, 4, padd.; *Wrangler*, 4, scr.; *Viper*, 4, scr.; *Lynx*, 4, scr.; *Recruit*, 6, padd.; *Arrow*, 4, scr.; *Snake*, 4, scr.; and *Beagle*, 4, scr.

"There was, however, an incident during the day that called forth the admiration of both fleets, and which deserves to be particularly noticed.   Lieut. McKillop, whose gun vessel, the *Snake*, was not employed, like the others, in landing troops, dashed past the forts after an enemy's steamer, and, although he soon found himself engaged not only with her but also with two others who came to her support, he persevered, and, by the cleverness and extreme rapidity of his manœuvres, prevented the escape of all three; and they were subsequently destroyed by the enemy."[1]

The *Snake* had no one hurt, although shot passed through her. Towards the end of the affair she was supported by the *Recruit*, and other craft.   Lieutenant Henry Frederick McKillop, for his gallantry, was promoted to be Commander, as from the date of his exploit, as soon as he had completed the necessary qualifying sea time.

At Kertch and Yenikale, about 12,000 tons of coal were taken by the Allies, and were of the utmost value to them.

On May 25th, Lyons and Bruat despatched into the Sea of Azof the light squadron specified in the note on p. 453, together with four [2] French steamers, the whole under Captain Edmund Moubray Lyons, of the *Miranda*, and Commander Béral de Sédaiges, of the *Lucifer*, and ordered it to take or sink as many as possible of the enemy's ships of war and merchantmen, to destroy such stores as might be useful to the Russian army, and to respect private property.

"It was," says Hamilton Williams, "like bursting into a vast treasure-house, crammed with wealth of inestimable value.   For miles along its shores stretched the countless storehouses packed with the accumulated harvests of the great corn provinces of Russia.   From them the Russian armies in the field were fed; from them the beleaguered population of Sebastopol looked for preservation from the famine which already pressed hard upon them."

Having entered the Sea of Azof, the flotilla appeared, on May 26th, before Berdiansk, where some coasting-vessels and large stores of grain were burnt.   The *Swallow* and *Wrangler* were then detached to Genitchi, to command the entrance to the Putrid Sea; and the *Curlew* was sent to cruise off the mouth of the Don, while the squadron moved towards Fort Arabat, off which it arrived on May 28th.   The work, which mounted thirty guns, engaged the Allies, who had but one man wounded, for an hour and a half, and then blew up.   The strength of the Arabat garrison, however, prevented a landing from being attempted.   While the French contingent returned to Kertch to coal there, the British portion of the flotilla, having silenced the defenders of the place, destroyed much

---

[1] Lyons to Admlty., May 26th.
[2] Later reinforced by two more.   Chevalier, 263.

THE OPERATIONS IN THE SEA OF AZOV, 1855.

stores and many vessels at Genitchi, on May 29th, thanks, chiefly, to the exertions of a landing-party under Lieutenant John Francis Campbell Mackenzie,[1] and to the personal gallantry of Lieutenants Cecil William Buckley, and Hugh Talbot Burgoyne, and Gunner John Roberts, who, to complete the work, went ashore together, and, without assistance, in presence of a considerable force of the enemy, and beyond gunshot of their ships, fired certain vessels and stores which, owing to a shift of wind, might otherwise have escaped. Each of these three officers afterwards received the Victoria Cross. In the operations at Genitchi, only one British seaman was wounded. " Since the squadron entered the Sea of Azof, four days ago," wrote Captain Lyons, in his dispatch to his father, " the enemy has lost four steamers of war,[2] 246 merchant vessels, also corn and flour magazines to the value of at least £150,000." He afterwards estimated the amount of corn destroyed at sufficient to supply 100,000 men for nearly four months.

Having informed the Commander-in-Chief that by June 2nd or 3rd he should be ready to begin operations in the shallower waters of the Gulf of the Don, Captain Lyons received, as reinforcements, the small steamers *Danube*, and *Sulina*, and twelve launches, armed with 24-pr. howitzers and rockets, from the large ships in the Strait of Kertch. These joined him at Taganrog, off which, at a distance of about eight and a half miles, he anchored in eighteen feet of water on the evening of June 1st. In the night, owing to a brisk easterly wind, the water fell three feet, and the squadron, in consequence, had to move a mile and a half further out. In the town were about 3500 troops, and the place was fairly well defended. On the 2nd it was reconnoitred by the *Recruit*, Lieutenant George Fiott Day, which, very early on the following morning, was anchored 1400 yards from the mole head. The town was then summoned by Lieutenant William Horton, who was sent in under a flag of truce; and, when the governor rejected terms, the *Recruit* opened a sharp fire, covered by which the boats, under Commander Cowper Phipps Coles, of the *Stromboli*, pulled, or were towed, towards the beach, and plied their howitzers and rockets at point-blank range against the Russians, who strove in vain to steal down under shelter of the houses, and save their storehouses from being burnt. Many stores

---

[1] Com., in consequence, as from May 29th, 1855.

[2] These had entered the Sea of Azof upon the approach of the British, and had there been destroyed by their crews.

were set fire to by the rockets; but the conflagration would have been by no means general had not Lieutenant John Francis Campbell Mackenzie, with a separate division of boats, devoted special attention to covering a four-oared gig, manned by volunteers, and containing Lieutenant Cecil William Buckley, and Boatswain Henry Cooper.[1] These officers landed repeatedly, and fired many warehouses and buildings which might otherwise have escaped.   Indeed,

CAPTAIN EDMUND MOUBRAY LYONS.
(*From Colnaghi's lithograph by J. H. Linch,* 1855.)

the blaze ultimately took even firmer hold than had been intended, and involved the destruction of great part of the town.   The attack, having effected all its objects, ceased soon after 3 P.M.   The only British loss was one man wounded.[2]

On June 5th Mariopol, and on June 6th Gheisk,[3] were taken possession of without opposition; and all government property in them was destroyed.   Similar work was done by detached vessels at

---

[1] V.C. for this service.   [2] Lyons to Lyons, June 3rd.
[3] Eisk on the map.

Temriouk and at Kiten; and the light squadron then returned to Kertch, whence the *Miranda*, Captain Edmund Moubray Lyons, went back to her station before Sebastopol. In one of the night engagements with the forts there, on June 17th, the gallant Captain of the *Miranda* was severely wounded. He was sent to hospital at Therapia, and, though he at first affected to make light of his injury, the wound cost him his life within a week. When the light squadron resumed its operations in the Sea of Azof, his place at the head of it was taken by Commander Sherard Osborn, of the *Vesuvius*.

In the interim, Vice-Admirals Lyons and Bruat had planned descents upon Soujak Kaleh and Anapa, the Russian ports on the Circassian shore of the Black Sea. Ere, however, they could complete their preparations, they learnt that both places had been evacuated and burnt, and their fortifications destroyed. All they could do was to detach Rear-Admirals Houston Stewart, and Charner along the coast to show their flags. At Anapa, the Circassians were found to be already in possession. Such few Russian guns as had not been rendered useless were thrown over the cliffs. By June 14th, the whole of the Kertch expedition, save half-a-dozen vessels and some troops that were left to guard the neighbourhood, had set out on its return to Balaclava and Kamiesh.

During this absence of the Kertch squadron from before Sebastopol, Rear-admiral Edward Boxer, C.B., died of cholera on board the *Jason*. To him was largely due the improvement which had been by that time effected in the arrangements at, and in the sanitation of, Balaclava.

He was ultimately succeeded as commander of that port by Rear-Admiral Charles Howe Fremantle, pending whose arrival the position was held by Captain Cospatrick Baillie Hamilton, of the *Diamond*, 27. In the general bombardment of Sebastopol between June 6th and 10th, and again on June 16th and 17th, the allied navies took some part from seaward, and the Brigade ashore, under Captain Stephen Lushington,[1] earned the special commendation of Lord Raglan.[2] Besides working its guns, the Brigade supplied four parties, each of 60 men, to carry scaling-ladders and wool-bags for the troops detailed to storm the Redan. Two of these

---

[1] K.C.B. July 5th, 1855. Lushington attained flag-rank on July 4th, 1855, and on July 19th was succeeded in command of the Naval Brigade by Captain the Hon. Henry Keppel, who assumed his duties two days later.

[2] In addition to Capt. Edmund Moubray Lyons (mortally wounded), the Navy afloat lost 3 killed and 13 wounded.

parties were kept in reserve. The others were sent forward, and lost 10 killed, 41 wounded, and 1 missing. Among the killed was Lieutenant Thomas Osborne Kidd, of the *Anglia*, who, after the repulse, returning to succour a wounded soldier, was shot through the breast.[1] Among the slightly wounded was the brave Captain Peel. On June 28th Lord Raglan died, and was ultimately succeeded as military commander-in-chief by General Simpson.

In the Sea of Azof, Commander Sherard Osborn still carried forward the work of destruction that had been begun so successfully by Captain Lyons. On June 22nd, the boats of the *Vesuvius* destroyed a vessel, and repulsed a body of Cossacks, at Kamieshwa; on June 24th, the vessel herself silenced some guns at Petrovski; and on June 27th, landing-parties from the *Vesuvius*, *Curlew*, and *Swallow* destroyed a convoy of wagons near Genitchi, which place was the scene of a more spirited affair on July 3rd.

On that day, Lieutenant William Nathan Wrighte Hewett, then commanding the *Beagle*, 4, screw, made a careful examination of the floating bridge which joined the town to the extremity of the long spit of Arabat, and which thus formed part of one of the military roads southward to the Crimea. Determining to destroy it, he despatched his gig, under Gunner John Hailes, and a paddle-box boat, under Midshipman Martin Tracey (*Vesuvius*), covering their approach with a hot fire directed upon the troops which lined the beach and occupied the neighbouring houses. The boats were riddled with bullets, the enemy being not more than eighty yards from the bridge hawsers, which had to be severed; and two of their people were wounded. The actual work of cutting was most coolly accomplished by a seaman, Joseph Trewavas, lent from the *Agamemnon*. This gallant fellow, who was slightly hit, was subsequently given the Victoria Cross. At about the same time, the *Weser*, 6, paddle, destroyed some stores in the neighbourhood. There was afterwards a period of bad weather, during which the squadron had to seek refuge under the spit of Berutch, to the north-east; but coaling, provisioning, and completing stores were proceeded with; and, as opportunity offered, fisheries, guard-houses, barracks, and stores on that spit, and on the spit of Arabat, were destroyed. The only remaining floating bridge between Arabat Spit and the Crimea was, during that period, burnt by the *Curlew*. From two long and

---

[1] He was bravely carried back to the trenches by Mate John Barker Barnett, the only officer with him, and two privates, but survived a very short time.

interesting dispatches from Osborn, dated respectively July 17th and July 21st, the following passages, descriptive of the operations of the week then ended, are taken :—

" A lull in the weather enabled me to put to sea on July 13th for a sweep round the Sea of Azof, the *Ardent*, *Weser*, and *Clinker* being left under the orders of Lieutenant Horton [1] to harass Genitchi and Arabat. . . . Delayed by the weather, we did not reach Berdiansk until July 15th. . . . I hoisted a flag of truce, in order, if possible, to get the women and children removed from the town; but, as that met with no reply, and the surf rendered landing extremely hazardous, I hauled it down, and the squadron commenced to fire over the town at the forage and corn-stacks behind it; and I soon had the satisfaction of seeing a fire break out exactly where it was wanted. . . . It became necessary to move into deeper water for the night; and, from our distant anchorage, the fires were seen burning throughout the night.

" On the 16th the allied squadron [2] proceeded to Fort Petrovski, between Berdiansk and Mariopol. . . . There were evident symptoms of an increase to the fortifications. . . . At 9.30 A.M., all arrangements being made, the squadron named in the margin [3] took up their positions, the light-draught gunboats taking up stations east and west of the fort, and enfilading the works in front and rear, whilst the heavier vessels formed a semicircle round the front. The heavy nature of our ordnance . . . soon not only forced the garrison to retire from the trenches, but also kept at a respectable distance the reserve force, consisting of three strong battalions of infantry, and two squadrons of cavalry. We then commenced to fire with carcasses, but, although partially successful, I was obliged to send the light boats of the squadron to complete the destruction of the fort and batteries, a duty I entrusted to Lieutenant Hubert Campion. . . . Although the enemy, from an earthwork to the rear, opened a sharp fire on our men, Lieutenant Campion completed this service in the most able and perfect manner, without the loss of one man. . . . Leaving the *Swallow* . . . to check any attempt of the enemy to reoccupy the fort . . . the rest of the squadron proceeded to destroy great quantities of forage, and some most extensive fisheries, situated upon the White House Spit, and about the mouth of the river Berda." . . .

" On July 17th, in consequence of information received of extensive depôts of corn and forage existing at a town called Glofira,[4] upon the Asiatic coast, near Gheisk, I proceeded there with the squadron. . . . The *Vesuvius* and *Swallow* were obliged to anchor some distance off shore. I therefore sent Commander Rowley Lambert (*Curlew*), with the gunboats *Fancy*, *Grinder*, *Boxer*, *Cracker*, *Jasper*, *Wrangler*, and boats of *Vesuvius* and *Swallow*. . . . Lambert found Glofira and its neighbourhood swarming with cavalry. . . . He therefore very properly confined his operations to destroying, upon Glofira Spit, some very extensive corn and fish stores. . . . From Glofira, I next proceeded to the Crooked Spit, in the Gulf of Azof, the French squadron parting

---

[1] Lieut. William Horton, promtd. Com. Aug. 18th, 1855.

[2] It included the two French steam sloops *Milan* and *Mouette*, under Capt. de Cintre, who put himself, though senior officer, at Osborn's disposal. Lyons to Admlty., July 30th.

[3] *Vesuvius*, 6, padd., Com. Sherard Osborn; *Curlew*, 9, scr., Com. Rowley Lambert; *Swallow*, 9, scr., Com. Frederick Augustus Buchanan Craufurd; *Fancy*, scr. g.b., Lieut. Charles Gerveys Grylls; *Grinder*, scr. g.b., Lieut. Francis Trevor Hamilton; *Boxer*, scr. g.b., Lieut. Samuel Philip Townsend; *Cracker*, scr. g.b., Lieut. Joseph Henry Marryat; *Wrangler*, 4, scr., Lieut. Hugh Talbot Burgoyne; *Jasper*, scr. g.b., Joseph Samuel Hudson; and *Beagle*, 4, scr., Lieut. William Nathan Wrighte Hewett.

[4] Properly Glafirovka.

company to harass the enemy in the neighbourhood of Kamieshwa and Obitochna. The squadron reached Crooked Spit the same day (July 18th); and I immediately ordered Commander Craufurd, in the *Swallow*, supported by the gunboats *Grinder*, *Boxer* and *Cracker*, and the boats of *Vesuvius*, *Curlew*, and *Fancy*, under Lieutenants Grylls, Rowley and Sulivan,[1] to . . . clear the spit . . . and destroy the great fishing establishments situated upon it. Commander Craufurd executed this service with great vigour. . . . While this service was being executed, I reconnoitred the mouth of the river Mious, fifteen miles west of Taganrog, in H.M.S. *Jasper*. . . . The shallow nature of the coast would not allow us to approach within a mile and three-quarters of what in the chart is marked Fort Temenos. . . . I returned to the same place, accompanied by the boats of H.M.S. *Vesuvius* and *Curlew*, and H.M. gunboats *Cracker*, *Boxer*, and *Jasper*. . . . When we got to Fort Temenos, and the usual Cossack picket had been driven off, I and Commander Lambert proceeded at once with the light boats into the river. When there, and immediately under Fort Temenos, which stands upon a steep escarp of eighty feet, we found ourselves looked down upon by a large body of both horse and foot, lining the ditch and parapet of the work. Landing on the opposite bank, at good rifle-shot distance, one boat's crew, under Lieutenant Rowley,[2] was sent to destroy a collection of launches and a fishery, whilst a careful and steady fire of Minié rifles kept the Russians from advancing upon us. Assuring ourselves of the non-existence of any object worth hazarding so small a force any further for, we returned to the vessels, passing within pistol-shot of the Russian ambuscade. . . . The gig of the *Grinder*, under Lieutenant Hamilton, had a narrow escape upon the same day from a similar ambuscade, at a place called Kirpe, ten miles east of Mariopol. . . . On July 19th, I reconnoitred Taganrog in the *Jasper* gunboat. A new battery was being constructed on the heights near the hospital, but, although two shots were thrown into it, it did not reply. . . . To put a stop . . . to all traffic . . . and to harass the enemy in this neighbourhood, I have ordered Commander Craufurd to remain in the Gulf of Azof with two gunboats." . . .

On July 20th, the *Beagle*, which had been detached, rejoined Sherard Osborn, and reported that a landing-party from her had destroyed further stores and granaries in the neighbourhood. A few days later, the *Jasper*, screw gunboat, Lieutenant Joseph Samuel Hudson, having grounded on the Krivaia, was, perhaps somewhat hastily, abandoned and blown up. She was the only craft that was lost during the whole of the Azof operations, although these did not cease until some time after the fall of Sebastopol. Before the end of July, the *Ardent* wrought fresh destruction at Genitchi, where the enemy had built new storehouses ; and Sherard Osborn, with his flotilla, paid another visit to Berdiansk. On August 5th, he reappeared off Taganrog, and captured some guns ; on August 6–7th, he destroyed barracks and stores at Petrushena ; on August 23rd,[3] having returned to Genitchi, his ships shelled the camp and trenches there ; on that day and the following, in spite of a brisk fire from the enemy, he wrecked some stores at Kiril and Gorelia ; on August

---

[1] This was Lieut. George Lydiard Sulivan (*Vesuvius*).

[2] Lieut. Charles John Rowley (*Curlew*).

[3] Sherard Osborn was posted on Aug. 18th, 1855.

27th, he repulsed the Russians, and did new damage, at Genitchi and at Kiril ; and on August 30–31st, while the *Weser* and *Cracker* destroyed a bridge and government buildings in the bay of Arabat, the *Wrangler* and the boats of the *Vesuvius* burnt some depôts of supplies at Mariopol, losing however, as prisoners, two officers ; and the *Grinder* made a reconnaissance of Taganrog under fire.   On September 13th, the *Cracker's* boats destroyed the fishing establishments and forage stores at Perebond.

Towards the end of September, operations in a new direction were undertaken, the Azof flotilla lending its co-operation to a somewhat similar force under Captain Robert Hall, of the *Miranda*, 15, screw, senior officer in the Strait of Kertch.   This latter flotilla consisted, besides the *Miranda*, of the *Lynx*, 4, screw, *Arrow*, 4, screw, *Snake*, 4, screw, *Harpy*, 1, paddle, and *Sulina*, together with the French gunboats *Mitraille, Alerte, Alarme, Bourrasque, Rafale, Mutine, Stridente*, and *Meurtrière*, under Commandant Bouet ; and it had on board three companies of the 71st British regiment, and six companies of French infantry.   On the peninsula of Taman, to the east of the Strait of Kertch, the enemy had built at Taman and Fanagoria (Fanagorinsk) barracks capable of sheltering a large number of men, the idea apparently being to assemble a small army there at the approach of winter, with a view to crossing the strait upon the ice, and falling upon Kertch.   Leaving that place, the expedition arrived opposite Taman at about 11 A.M. on September 24th, and disembarked the troops under cover of the fire of the vessels without accident.   Taman was observed to have been abandoned.   The force then advanced to Fanagoria, where the fort and buildings were occupied.   They contained sixty-two pieces of artillery, all of which were rendered unserviceable.   In the meantime a body of about six hundred Cossacks assembled, only, however, to be scattered by shells from the ships.   In the following night the same force attempted a surprise, but found the Allies alert, and so retired.   All useful stores were sent across to Kertch, the rest, with all public buildings, being destroyed.

To make a diversion, and to harass and check the enemy at Temriouk, Sherard Osborn's Azof flotilla entered Temriouk Lake on the morning of September 24th, and was joined by the French steamers *Milan, Caton*, and *Fulton*.   The town could not be reached, even by the boats, owing to the extreme shallowness of the water ; but a body of 2000 troops was detained in Temriouk, and prevented from moving towards Taman; and a bridge, across which it might have advanced, was burnt.

On October 9th, Sherard Osborn set out on a series of fresh raids. He was, however, temporarily without most of his smaller gunboats, which had been withdrawn by Lord Lyons to assist in the operations against Kinburn. On the night of October 10th, a boat belonging to the *Weser* stole up the Salgir river, burnt some stacks of corn and forage, and got away without loss, though heavily fired upon by Cossacks. On October 15th at Crooked Spit, and on October 18th at White House Spit, the *Recruit*, under fire, did much damage among boats and fishing establishments. On October 20th, at Crooked Spit, the *Ardent* destroyed more boats, and dispersed a body of cavalry. On October 24th a landing-party, supported by the *Vesuvius*, wrecked some rifle-pits and small vessels at Bieloserai Spit, and scattered a weak force of troops. And on the same day, at Mariopol, the *Recruit* wrought further destruction.

At about that time the gunboats which had been temporarily detached to share in the Kinburn expedition rejoined Sherard Osborn, who, late in the evening of November 3rd, anchored with his whole force, in sixteen feet of water, off Gheisk-Liman, with designs against the enormous stores of corn, forage and fuel which he knew to be in the neighbourhood. He took all available men out of the *Vesuvius*, which he left in the offing; and he drew strong parties from the *Weser*, *Curlew*, and *Ardent*, which remained in charge of Lieutenant John Francis Ross (*Weser*), who had orders to close in on the north side of Gheisk, and to be prepared to cooperate. With the boats in tow of the *Recruit*, Lieutenant George Fiott Day, *Boxer*, Lieutenant Samuel Philip Townsend, *Cracker*, Lieutenant Joseph Henry Marryat, *Clinker*, Lieutenant Joseph Samuel Hudson, and *Grinder*, Lieutenant Francis Trevor Hamilton, Sherard Osborn departed at dawn on November 4th, and, at 6.30 A.M., appeared off Vodina, three miles north of Glofira. Commander John James Kennedy (*Curlew*), covered by the gun-vessels, was sent in with the boats, and, landing, soon set fire to numerous stores. He retired safely, just as a force of Cossacks rode up. Glofira was next attacked. Since it had been visited in the previous July it had been much strengthened, and larger supplies than ever had been accumulated there. While the *Recruit*, *Grinder*, *Boxer*, and *Cracker* opened on the entrenchments with shrapnel, and on the cornstacks with carcasses, some boats under Kennedy, towed in by the *Clinker*, endeavoured to outflank the defences; but not until Lieutenants George Fiott Day, and Hubert Campion, supported by a howitzer boat and two rocket boats, had been landed with seamen and Marines, and had executed a very gallant charge, were the defenders dislodged from their works, and driven back, and all the stores set in flames. This landing-party re-embarked with but one man wounded. By that time, Lieutenant Ross and the vessels off Gheisk were seen to be engaged. They succeeded in keeping off the enemy while Commander Kennedy burnt additional stores. During the night, the fires extended over a front of two miles.

Early on November 6th, Sherard Osborn, with the gunboats and boats, entered the Liman, the gunboats, thanks to the skill of actg. Master George David Perry (*Vesuvius*), and Second Master William Hennessey Parker (*Recruit*), were anchored as far in as possible at the east end of Gheisk, near which stores were stacked along a front of four miles. Covered by the gunboats, four separate parties were landed, respectively commanded by (1) Lieutenants George Fiott Day, and Samuel Philip Townsend; (2) Commander John James Kennedy, with Lieutenants Francis Trevor Hamilton, Hubert Campion, Joseph Henry Marryat, and Richard Charles Mayne (actg.); (3) Lieutenants Augustus Chetham Strode, and Joseph Samuel Hudson; and (4, from the *Weser's* division) Lieutenants John Francis Ross, and Gover Rose Miall. Each party met with some slight resistance; but each accomplished its object; and, by 2 P.M., the entire force was re-embarked, having lost only 6 men wounded. Sherard Osborn then burnt some stores at Glofira that had escaped the conflagration of the 4th, and returned to the *Vesuvius*. He says [1] :—

"I despair of being able to convey to you any idea of the extraordinary quantity of corn, rye, hay, wood, and other supplies so necessary for the existence of Russian armies, both in the Caucasus and in the Crimea, which it has been our good fortune to destroy. . . . During these proceedings we never had more than 200 men engaged. The enemy had, from the concurrent testimony of Lieuts. Ross and Strode, and from my own observation, from 3000 to 4000 men in Gheisk alone."

This was practically the end of the operations in the Sea of Azof. Among the honours and promotions consequent upon the good work done there may be mentioned :—

To be C.B., Captain Sherard Osborn (Feb. 4th, 1856).
To be Captain, Commander Sherard Osborn (Aug. 18th, 1855).
    „   „   Commander Rowley Lambert (Sept. 29th, 1855).

------

[1] Osborn to Lyons, Nov. 7th.

To be Captain, Commander John James Kennedy (Feb. 1st, 1856).
,,　　,,　　Commander Cowper Phipps Coles (Feb. 27th, 1856).
,,　　,,　　Commander Frederick Augustus Buchanan Craufurd (May 10th, 1856).
To be Commander, Lieutenant John Francis Campbell Mackenzie (May 29th, 1855).
,,　　,,　　Lieutenant William Horton (Aug. 18th, 1855).
,,　　,,　　Lieutenant Joseph Henry Marryat (Nov. 5th, 1855).
,,　　,,　　Lieutenant George Fiott Day (Nov. 19th, 1855).
,,　　,,　　Lieutenant Hubert Campion (Dec. 7th, 1855).
,,　　,,　　Lieutenant William Cecil Buckley (Feb. 27th, 1856).
,,　　,,　　Lieutenants John Francis Ross, Augustus Chetham Strode, Charles Gerveys Grylls, and Hugh Talbot Burgoyne (May 10th, 1856).

In addition, seven or eight Victoria Crosses were won in the course of the expeditions to Kertch and the Sea of Azof.

In England, the work done by Lyons and Sherard Osborn was the subject of some unfavourable criticism on the part of certain excellent people who professed to believe that hostilities could best be carried on by sparing the enemy as much as possible. Tenderness in war is, unfortunately, no better than a very refined form of cruelty. It leads to a prolongation of resistance, and so to increased sacrifice of life and treasure on both sides. Moreover, it encourages false hopes. When war has once been entered upon, it should be carried forward, like every other work that is to be performed economically and effectively, with energy, thoroughness, and unbending sternness. Even when such a policy upon occasions involves hardship to individuals who are not directly offensive, it still tends to effect its object, which is an early attainment of a definite result. No doubt, much private property, and some civilian lives were incidentally destroyed by the Azof flotilla. On the other hand, the work of that flotilla, while it deprived the Russian army of many of its most necessary supplies, and so crippled the military power of the Tsar, also inclined the coast populations most ardently to desire peace. In 1855 the Russian people had still less nominal influence than they have now upon the policy of their rulers; yet, in despotisms as well as in constitutional lands, the people have ever been the supreme arbiters; and that which they have willed with determination has almost invariably been the policy which the government has ultimately deemed it wise to pursue. It is foolish, therefore, to pretend that war is made upon governments and not upon peoples, and that distinction ought to be made between the two. Humanity and civilisation demand that women and children should not be wilfully or directly exposed to the actual ravages of shot and shell; but they demand also that women and children, as well as men and actual fighters, should be made to feel the general pressure of war as acutely as possible; for the sooner the majority of a people agree that the situation has become intolerable, the sooner submission and peace will come.

Before Sebastopol, the Naval Brigade ashore, and the fleet afloat continued to afford grateful support to the allied armies. From July 16th to July 19th, there was some bombardment of the forts from seaward, and again from August 6th to August 9th. In the trenches there was hot work almost continuously. There were almost daily alarms of intended sorties; and Captain the Hon. Henry Keppel, with his aide-de-camp, Lieutenant Prince Victor of Hohenlohe-Langenburg,[1] was kept fully employed. On August 17th, the day after the battle of the Tchernaya, a general bombardment was opened with the object of covering some advance of the French approaches. The Russians replied with their usual spirit, and, besides disabling two of the naval guns, killed Commander Lacon Ussher Hammet, of the *Albion*, and 6 others, and wounded 16.

On August 27th, in the course of Lord Stratford de Redcliffe's visit to the Crimea, several naval officers, including Rear-Admirals Sir Edmund Lyons, and Houston Stewart, were invested with the insignia of the Bath, as evidence of Her Majesty's approval of their conduct at the front. The recipients had been nominated on the previous July 5th, on which occasion more naval appointments to, and promotions in, the Most Honourable Order had been made than on any one date since the enlargement of the Order in 1815. The number of naval G.C.B.s thus conferred in a single *Gazette* was four; of K.C.B.s, twelve; and of C.B.s, no fewer than forty-five. Among the G.C.B.s were Vice-Admiral Sir James Whitley Deans Dundas, and Rear-Admiral Sir Edmund Lyons; among the K.C.B.s, Rear-Admirals Houston Stewart, Hon. Montagu Stopford, Henry Ducie Chads, Michael Seymour (2), Henry Byam Martin, and Stephen Lushington; and among the C.B.s, Captains Frederick Thomas Michell, Lord George Paulet, Lord Edward Russell, Sydney Colpoys Dacres, Thomas Matthew Charles Symonds, George St. Vincent King, Hastings Reginald Yelverton, Bartholomew James

---

[1] Afterwards Admiral Count Gleichen. "He shod his own horses, and, I think, was sorry when the war was over." Keppel, ii. 291.

Sulivan, George Giffard, John Moore (4), William Peel, Astley Cooper Key, William Moorsom, William Robert Mends, William Houston Stewart, Lord John Hay (3), and Richard Ashmore Powell. In addition, a K.C.B. and two C.B.s were given to officers of the Royal Marines.

Towards the end of August, the Russians manifested an intention of preparing for the abandonment of the south side of Sebastopol. This circumstance was probably not without its influence upon the engineer and artillery officers of the allied armies; and they eventually induced the military commanders-in-chief to order that a general bombardment of the place should be begun on Wednesday, September 5th, kept up for three days, and followed by a vigorous assault upon the Malakoff and the Great Redan, close to which the trenches had by that time been pushed. Accordingly, a heavy fire was opened at daylight on the appointed day, and was continued, with but short periods of partial intermission, until the morning of the 8th. On the evening of the 5th, a Russian two-decker, moored off the dockyard sheers, burst into flame; and, during the night, she was completely destroyed. On the 7th, another Russian two-decker was burnt. At noon on the 8th, the French troops successfully stormed the Malakoff. The British attack, made a little later on the Great Redan, was bloodily repulsed, chiefly because it was made in insufficient force, and because the approaches had not been carried so close to that work as to the Malakoff. French assaults on the Central Bastion, and on the Little Redan of Careening Bay, were also repulsed. But the key to the entire position had been taken; and the Russian commander-in-chief, at about 8 P.M., began to withdraw quietly from the south side of the fortress which he had so long and so well defended. At midnight some British soldiers crept into the Redan, and found it abandoned. A little later fires broke out in the town, followed by terrible explosions. At 5.30 A.M. on the 9th, two of the southern forts were blown up. By 7 A.M. the last of the Russian troops had crossed to the north of the harbour, and the bridge of boats over which they had passed had been dragged after them. Daylight showed that all the men-of-war in the harbour, save one frigate and two small steamers, had been sunk or destroyed. Even these three were destroyed by the Russians on the 10th or 11th. It had been intended that the fleets should take part in the final bombardment; but they were prevented by a strong N.W. gale from weighing to do so. Says General Sir James Simpson, in his dispatch of September 9th :—

" The boisterous weather rendered it altogether impossible for the Admirals to fulfil their intention of bringing the broadsides of the allied fleets to bear upon the Quarantine batteries; but an excellent effect was produced by the animated and well-directed fire of their mortar-vessels, those of Her Majesty being under the direction of Captain Willcox,[1] of the *Odin*, and Captain Digby,[2] of the Royal Marine Artillery. . . . The Naval Brigade, under the command of Captain the Hon. Henry Keppel, aided by Captain Moorsom[3] and many gallant officers and seamen, who have served the guns from the commencement of the siege, merit my warmest thanks. The prompt, hearty, and efficacious co-operation of Her Majesty's Navy, commanded by Rear-Admiral Sir Edmund Lyons, ably seconded by Sir Houston Stewart, has contributed most materially to the success of our undertaking."

The dispatch of Rear-Admiral Sir Edmund Lyons, dated September 10th, adds very little to the information given in the above extracts. Captain James Willcox reported :—[4]

". . . Acting in pursuance of your directions, and in conjunction with Capt. Bachm, commanding four French mortar-vessels you did me the honour of placing under my command, a fire was kept up till 7 P.M. against the Quarantine Fort and outworks, as well as upon Fort Alexander and the upper bastions (where, near to the latter place, a large number of the enemy's reserve were posted), keeping their fire so completely under that only a few shot and shell were returned, and but few fired into the French batteries and works before us. A small number of carcasses were also successfully thrown into the town and upper bastions, which produced a conflagration of some extent. . . . I am glad of the opportunity of bringing to your notice the indefatigable and zealous conduct of Mr. H. K. Leet,[5] Mate in charge of the *Firm*, who, from being the senior officer of the mortar-vessels, has always ably carried out my instructions; and I am happy to bear testimony to the praiseworthy conduct of Messrs. J. B. Creagh,[6] T. L. Pearson,[7] H. W. Brent,[8] A. F. Hurt,[9] and Henry Vaughan,[10] Mates in charge of the other mortar-vessels. I have also great pleasure in stating that no casualty occurred, and that neither the mortars or vessels were at all damaged by the heavy firing."

The mortar-vessels were stationed for this service in Streletska, or Arrow, Bay. Captain George Stephen Digby, R.M.A., in his report,[11] made favourable notice of the ability displayed by First Lieutenants (R.M.) Edward Henderson Starr, Henry Hewett, Francis Worgan Festing, William Pitman, and Joshua Rowland Brookes.

[1] Capt. James Willcox was made a C.B., Feb. 4th, 1856.
[2] Capt. George Stephen Digby, R.M.A.
[3] Capt. William Moorsom, C.B.
[4] Willcox to Lyons, Sept. 8th.
[5] Henry Knox Leet, Lieut. Sept. 22nd, 1855.
[6] John Brasier Creagh, Lieut. Sept. 22nd, 1855.
[7] Thomas Livingstone Pearson, Lieut. Jan. 5th, 1856.
[8] Harry Woodfall Brent, Lieut. Jan. 5th, 1856.
[9] Albert Frederick Hurt, Lieut. June 23rd, 1856.
[10] Henry Vaughan, Lieut. Feb. 22nd, 1856.
[11] Digby to Lyons, Sept. 8th.

The Russian ships destroyed from first to last at Sebastopol were stated to have been as follows :—

Sailing ships of the line : five 120's, eight 84's, one 80.
Sailing frigates : four 60's.
Sailing corvettes and brigs : three 20's, two 18's.
Sailing vessels, miscellaneous : eighty-two, including sixty-four gunboats.
Steam-vessels : six large, including the *Vladimir* and *Bessarabia*, and six smaller.
    The above mounted about 2200 guns.

By September 19th, the Naval Brigade had been re-embarked. Such of the Royal Marines as had been landed were re-embarked early in the following mouth. A little later, nearly all the magnificent naval works, including the docks, at Sebastopol, were destroyed. A British naval officer who examined them in the interval wrote :—

" Walking round the edge of Dockyard Creek, we soon came to the docks. We arrived suddenly among the wonders of Sebastopol; and all that we had heard of the glories of the place faded away before the magnificent reality. First of all we inspected a dock where ships of the largest size were hauled up out of the water, or launched again, by means of a cradle, placed on a tram-road. This is the work of the Englishman, Upton. Then we came to the intended government foundry, whose walls were rising to the height of ten feet, over a space of nearly twelve acres. Part of this was obtained by cutting away the spur of a mountain. The remainder of the hill was upheld by a freestone wall, every stone beautifully squared and fitted, to the height of 350 feet. . . . We then went to see the famous docks. These consist of a series of locks, like canal locks, the upper end being twenty feet higher than the entrance lock, which is even with the level of the sea. The upper end has three locks abreast. Then comes a compartment equal in area to three ; then again three more, the middle one of which is entered by three other locks from the harbour; making altogether nine chambers, as it were, and the large space in the middle. These are all dry, but can be filled with water pumped into them by two steam engines. Each chamber is 270 feet long, 60 feet wide, and contains from 25 to 37 feet of water at pleasure. A large ship can be floated into an upper lock ; all the water can then be let off, and the ship left in her cradle as dry as if on shore. The docks, with their magnificent masonry casings of gigantic granite blocks, steam-engines, and iron gates, with the aqueducts for bringing down water from the Tchernaya, cost £20,000,000 sterling." [1]

After the occupation of the south side of Sebastopol and the complete destruction of the Russian fleet, the allied navies in the Black Sea were left at liberty to strike a blow at some other part of the coast. It was not, however, until after a council of war held on September 30th that the naval and military commanders-in-chief determined to make an attack upon Kinburn.

The fortress of Kinburn occupies the western extremity of a spit which forms the southern boundary of a considerable basin known as the Liman of the Dnieper. Into this basin, in addition

[1] *Naut. Mag.*, 1855, 606.

to the Dnieper, flow the united streams of the rivers Bug and Ingul; and, at the junction of the Bug and Ingul, at some distance from the sea, stands the important naval arsenal of Nicolaief, while near the mouth of the Dnieper is Kherson, one of the richest of the commercial centres of Russia. The narrow channel into the Liman passes between the fortress of Otchakof on the north, and the fortress of Kinburn on the south, but lies closer to the latter than to the former. Consequently, the possession of Kinburn by the Allies would completely close the navigation of the Bug and Dnieper. It would also menace the communications and rear of the large Russian army which was still in the Crimea.

In 1855, the defences at Kinburn consisted of a citadel of masonry, with earthen parapets, washed in some places by the sea and in others by the waters of a deep ditch, and mounting about sixty guns, some in casemates, and some in a barbette battery above. This citadel, which had an all-round command, was supported by two batteries placed at the extreme end of the spit, on a narrow strip of sand. The entire armament of the works, according to French accounts, was 80 guns and 20 mortars. Of these, 81 pieces only appear to have been in position.

The expedition, which was commanded by Admirals Lyons and Bruat, was a far more powerful one than was absolutely necessary for the contemplated work. It comprised 10 screw ships of the line, with about 80 other vessels—frigates, sloops, gunboats, mortar-boats, tenders, and transports; it had on board 4000 British, and a rather larger number of French troops; and it is remarkable as having included the three French armoured floating batteries *Tonnante, Lave,* and *Dévastation*, which, built for the attack on Sebastopol, had arrived on the scene a few days after the fall of the place. These batteries were constructed after plans which had first been advocated in 1842 by Captain Labrousse, of the French navy, and which, in 1855, were improved upon under the personal superintendence of the Emperor Napoleon. They were the earliest armoured steam-ships; and their appearance in action marks the first beginning of, perhaps, the greatest revolution which has ever been experienced in the science of naval warfare.

The fleets sailed from the neighbourhood of Sebastopol on October 6th and 7th, and arrived at a rendezvous off Odessa on the 8th. Fogs and strong S.S.W. winds prevented their appearance off Kinburn until the afternoon of the 14th. Rear-Admiral Sir

Houston Stewart then transferred his flag from the *Hannibal*, 90, screw, to the *Valorous*, 16, paddle, and, in pursuance of orders, stationed his division of steam-vessels off the entrance to the Liman, being assisted in his selection of positions by Captain Thomas Abel Bremage Spratt, of the *Spitfire*, 5, paddle. The corresponding French division was commanded by Rear-Admiral Odet Pellion. The Commander-in-Chief, with the larger vessels, anchored further out. When it became dark, the *Cracker*, gunboat, Lieutenant Joseph Henry Marryat, with two boats of the *Tribune*, and Masters Edward Wolfe Brooker[1] (additional of *Spitfire*), and Thomas Potter (*Furious*, but lent to *Valorous*), was sent to buoy the channel between the mainland and the end of the spit; and, as soon as he signalled that the operation had been effected, he was joined by the gunboats *Fancy*, Lieutenant Charles Gerveys Grylls, *Boxer*, Lieutenant Samuel Philip Townsend, and *Clinker*, Lieutenant Joseph Samuel Hudson, as well as by the French gunboats *Tirailleuse*, *Stridente*, *Meurtrière*, and *Mutine*, which together passed the forts and anchored within, so as to afford as much protection as possible to the right flank of the troops upon disembarkation taking place. The enemy fired shot, shell, and musketry at them as they went in, but caused them no damage. Sir Houston Stewart, outside, was, of course, left in some doubt as to how far the channel had been buoyed for larger ships. At 10 A.M. on the 15th, therefore, Marryat and Brooker, in the *Cracker*, most gallantly repassed the batteries under a heavier fire than before, and personally reported to the Rear-Admiral on the subject of the difficult navigation.[2] That morning the troops, under the orders of General Bazaine, and Brigadier-General the Hon. A. A. Spencer, were landed about three miles to the southward of the citadel, so as to cut off the retreat of the Russian garrison by land. In the evening the mortar-vessels tried the ranges of their mortars against the main fort. The 16th brought a brisk wind from the southward, and a heavy swell, and prevented the opening of a bombardment; but the day was well spent by the troops ashore.

At about 9.30 A.M. on the 17th, there being a fine northerly breeze, with smooth water, the French floating batteries, mortar-vessels, and gunboats, and the *Valorous*, 16, paddle, Captain

---

[1] Promtd. to be Lieut., Nov. 5th, 1855.

[2] It would appear from a passage in Sir H. Stewart's disp. of Oct. 18th, that the *Grinder*, Lieut. Francis Trevor Hamilton, went in and took the *Cracker's* place.

Claude Henry Mason Buckle, C.B. (flag of Sir Houston Stewart), *Gladiator*, 6, paddle, Captain Charles Farrel Hillyar, *Odin*, 16, paddle, Captain James Willcox, *Lynx*, 4, screw, *Arrow*, 4, screw, *Viper*, 4, screw, *Beagle*, 4, screw, *Snake*, 4, screw, and *Wrangler*, 4, screw, with the mortar-vessels *Raven*, *Magnet*, *Camel*, *Hardy*, *Flamer*, and *Firm*, took up positions off the fort, and began a destructive fire, which was pluckily returned. The *Tonnante* and her consorts, stationed at less than one thousand yards from the enemy's guns, wrought much damage, and appeared to be themselves quite invulnerable. At noon, the Russian fire having been sensibly reduced, Sir Houston Stewart, with the British vessels above named, and also with the *Furious*, 16, paddle, Captain William Loring, C.B., *Sidon*, 22, paddle, Captain George Goldsmith, *Leopard*, 18, paddle, Captain George Giffard, C.B., *Firebrand*, 6, paddle, Commander Edward Augustus Inglefield, *Stromboli*, 6, paddle, Commander Cowper Phipps Coles, and *Spiteful*, 6, paddle, Commander Francis Henry Shortt, and Rear-Admiral Odet Pellion's division, passed through the channel. Each ship, as she got within range, engaged the forts from the northward, while, at the same time, the southern and western faces of the works were engaged by Lyons[1] and Bruat, whose ships took up positions in the closest possible order, with but two feet of water under the keels of some of them. Having anchored inside, Stewart transferred his flag to the *Cracker*. The fire of such enormous forces as were brought against the defences soon produced its effect, and the Russian batteries gradually became silent, though they did not haul down their colours. Lyons, from motives of humanity, suggested to Bruat to discontinue the action; but the French commander-in-chief, prompted, perhaps, by motives as humane in reality though not in appearance, declined to cease firing until the garrison should surrender. Lyons, thereupon, ordered his own ships to discontinue; and Bruat, after pouring in a protesting broadside, also desisted. The Russian General Kokonovitch, upon being summoned, submitted; and he and his 1400 men presently marched out with the honours of war. He had lost 45 killed and 130 wounded. The British ships had but two people hurt; and even they owed their

---

[1] With Sir E. Lyons were the *Royal Albert*, 121, scr. (flag); Capt. William Robert Mends; *Algiers*, 91, scr.; *Agamemnon*, 91, scr.; *Princess Royal*, 91, scr.; *St. Jean d'Acre*, 101, scr.; *Curaçoa*, 31, scr.; *Tribune*, 31, scr.; *Sphinx*, 6, padd.; *Hannibal*, 91, scr.; *Dauntless*, 31, scr.; and *Terrible*, 21, paddle.

injuries to the bursting of a gun in the *Arrow*. On the following morning the enemy blew up their forts at Otchakof.[1]

The operations at Kinburn are remarkable not only because they witnessed the first employment of armoured vessels in modern warfare, but also because they were among the earliest operations on a large scale in which steam-vessels only were employed. Both France and Great Britain entered on the campaign against Russia believing that sailing ships of the line might still be of some use. Sailing ships, accordingly, figured in the fleets of 1854 in the Baltic as well as in the Black Sea ; but the experience of a very few months on each scene of action determined that they had ceased to be of any practical value for fighting purposes. Thus may it be said that sails and wood went out, and steam and iron came in, in 1855.

After the capture of Kinburn, a military reconnaissance was made in the direction of Kherson ; and Rear-Admirals Stewart (in the *Stromboli*), and Odet Pellion, with part of their divisions, proceeded to the mouths of the Bug and Dnieper. In the former river, on October 20th, the *Stromboli*, *Cracker*, *Spitfire*, and *Grinder* had a slight engagement with a battery. In the latter, two huge rafts of valuable timber, intended for the arsenal at Nicolaief, were captured. Kinburn was occupied by the Allies ; a division of ships, including the French floating batteries, was ordered to remain before it so long as the sea should be open ; and the rest of the expedition returned to the neighbourhood of Sebastopol, where it arrived on November 3rd. During its absence there had been a slight brush between the Allies and a Russian force near Lake Tougla on October 26th. A little later, Bruat, with part of his fleet, sailed for Toulon, where he intended to winter. On the way he was struck down, as St. Arnaud and Raglan had been, by cholera, and he died at sea on November 19th. Lyons also quitted the Black Sea, chiefly to attend a great international council of war which was held in the winter at Paris for the purpose of advising the allied governments as to what naval and military operations could most advantageously be next undertaken. The council assembled, under the presidency of the Emperor, at the Tuileries, on January 10th, 1856, its British members, in addition to Sir Edmund Lyons, being H.R.H. the Duke of Cambridge, Lord Cowley, Rear-Admiral the Hon. Richard Saunders Dundas, C.B., and Generals Sir Richard

[1] Lyons to Admlty., Oct. 18th; Stewart to Lyons, Oct. 18th; Bruat's disp., and order of the day; Chevalier, 283 ; Tyrrell, ii. 313.

Airey, and Sir Harry Jones. No conclusions were ever arrived at; for, soon after it met, events began to assume a pacific complexion, and, as early as January 16th,[1] Russia paved the way for a settlement by unconditionally accepting certain proposals which had been made by Austria as preliminaries of peace. In the interim, the allied forces in the Black Sea confined themselves to holding such positions as they had won, to repelling attacks, and to destroying captured works and public buildings. The campaign, indeed, so far as the Navy was concerned, practically ended with the occupation of Kinburn.

Before proceeding to survey the work of the Navy in 1855 in the Baltic, it may be well to glance briefly at what was done by the fleets in that year on two less important stations.

In the White Sea, a squadron, consisting of the *Mæander*, 44, Captain Thomas Baillie, *Phœnix*, 8, screw, Commander John Montagu Hayes,[2] and *Ariel*, 9, screw, Commander John Proctor Luce, with the French vessels *Cléopâtre*, 32, *Cocyte*, 6, and *Pétrel*, 4, blockaded the coasts. The British part of it quitted the Downs on May 10th, rounded the North Cape on May 31st, formally re-established the blockade on June 11th, and was joined a few days later by the French contingent. Early in July, the *Ariel*, despatched to the Gulf of Meyen, burnt a brigantine and two smaller craft, but met with no opposition. She rejoined the *Mæander* off Cross Island on July 9th. At the same time, the *Phœnix* and *Pétrel* cruised in the Gulf of Onega. Two of the *Phœnix's* boats were fired at near the village of Liamtsi, and the place was, in consequence, bombarded; but, probably, little damage was done to it. On July 12th, the *Ariel* relieved the *Phœnix* in the Gulf of Onega, and the *Phœnix* returned to the *Mæander*, off Archangel. The *Ariel* visited Kio, Solovetskoi, Sosnovia, Umba, and the Gulf of Kandalak. Near Kandalak her boats were attacked; but a landing-party drove off the enemy, and, under the fire of the sloop, the town was burnt. In this affair three seamen were wounded. On July 16th, the *Mæander* was at Kouzemen, at the mouth of the Gulf of Kandalak. A party of sixty men, under Lieutenant Hugh Maximilian Elliot, having been landed to reconnoitre, met a body of 350 armed people; but, as Captain Baillie deemed that nothing was to be gained by

---

[1] Disp. of Count Esterhazy, Jan. 16th: followed by official Russian circular of Jan. 19th.

[2] Posted, July 9th, 1855.

attacking, he re-embarked his little force. The *Phœnix*, in a brush with the enemy near Cape Kerets, had a man shot through the head. The greater part of the squadron reassembled off Archangel on July 21st.[1] The British and French commanders at first intended to spare small local craft; but when they ascertained that these were used for the conveyance of muskets up and down the coast, they changed their minds; and thenceforward they prevented even the smallest boats from moving out of port. The squadron did not quit the White Sea until October 9th.

In the Pacific, Rear-Admiral Henry William Bruce had been appointed to command in November, 1854. During the early spring of 1855, Petropaulovski was watched by the *Encounter*, 14, Captain George William Douglas O'Callagan, and *Barracouta*, 6,[2] Commander Frederick Henry Stirling; but those vessels had to keep at some distance from the town; and, on April 17th, taking advantage of snow and fog, the whole garrison of the place embarked in the men-of-war *Aurora* and *Dwina*, and four merchantmen, and escaped into the river Amur, while the civil inhabitants removed inland to the village of Avatcha. The guns were carried away or buried. Consequently, when in May the allied squadrons,[3] under Rear-Admirals Bruce and Fourichon, appeared before the fortress with the object of renewing the attack which had failed in the previous September, nothing but empty works and deserted buildings was found. Two Americans, and their French servant, alone remained to receive the visitors; and they had hoisted the American flag. The arsenals, batteries, and magazines were destroyed by the Allies; but the town was spared. A whaler, which was discovered hidden in Rakovia Harbour, was burnt, as, having neither sails nor anchors, she could not easily be taken away. While at Petropaulovski, Rear-Admiral Bruce was able to open up negotiations with the interior, and to effect the exchange of two prisoners. He and Rear-Admiral Fourichon then visited Sitka. It was not forti-

---

[1] Corr. in *Times*, and *Naut. Mag.* Disps. of Baillie, and of Guilbert, of the *Cléopâtre*.

[2] Both vessels had been detached for the purpose from the East India station by Rear-Adm. Sir Jas. Stirling, Kt.

[3] Consisting, in addition to the *Encounter* and *Barracouta*, of the *President*, 50 (flag), Capt. Richard Burridge; *Pique*, 40, Capt. Sir Frederick William Erskine Nicolson, Bart.; *Trincomalee*, 24, Capt. Wallace Houstoun; *Dido*, 18, Capt. William Henry Anderson Morshead, C.B.; *Amphitrite*, 24, Capt. Charles Frederick; and *Brisk*, 14, scr., Com. Frederick Beauchamp Paget Seymour; with the French vessels *Forte*, 60, *Alceste*, 54, *Eurydice*, 32, and *Obligado*, 18.

fied, neither did it contain any Russian men-of-war. It was, therefore, not attacked. While the *Pique, Barracouta*, and *Amphitrite* were left with Sir James Stirling to patrol the Sea of Okhotsk, the rest of the allied squadrons separated, most of the British vessels going to Vancouver Island, and most of the French to San Francisco.[1] On August 1st, the *Barracouta* overhauled the Bremen brig *Greta*, under American colours ; and, as she had on board 277 seamen, part of the crew of the Russian frigate *Diana*, which had been wrecked on the coast of Japan a few months earlier, she was sent as a prize to Hong Kong, under Lieutenant Robert Gibson. No attempt was made to follow the *Aurora* and *Dwina* into the Amur, where they were reported to be very strongly posted behind a bar on which was only 13 feet of water.

Much dissatisfaction was expressed in England at this second failure in the extreme east ; and the commanders of the *Encounter* and *Barracouta* were freely blamed for what was popularly regarded as negligence in allowing the two Russian men-of-war to escape them.[2] There was, however, no public inquiry into the circumstances ; and the Admiralty seems to have considered that both officers did their duty.

Events in the Baltic may now be followed to their conclusion without further interruption.

Vice-Admiral Sir Charles Napier had himself made it impossible that he could be again ordered to hoist his flag. It is not necessary to suppose that he was culpably to blame for his comparative inactivity in 1854, and for his resultant fall from popularity. He was an old officer, and he had undoubtedly lost much of the dash and nerve of his brilliant youth. The Admiralty, however, may be held to have made a mistake in the original appointment. On the other hand, Napier, in his correspondence and interviews with his official superiors, had betrayed so much temper that it was out of the question for the Admiralty to repeat the same mistake. The Baltic command in 1855 was, therefore, given to Rear-Admiral the Hon. Richard Saunders Dundas, C.B., who just previously had held the office of second Naval Lord ; and the fleet which was entrusted to him, instead of being composed partly of sailing and partly of steam ships, was made up wholly of steam-vessels, and was, in every other respect, much more powerful and generally serviceable than the

[1] Bruce to Admlty., June 15th; July 17th : Amer. corr. in *Ill. Lond. News.*
[2] Tyrrell, ii. 354.

Baltic fleet of 1854 had been. Moreover, there were attached to it, as will be seen, numerous small craft, mortar-vessels, and gunboats, suitable for operations in narrow and shallow waters; and it was arranged that it was ultimately to be strengthened by the addition to it of five armoured floating batteries, somewhat similar to those which, as has been already seen, the French sent to the Black Sea,

REAR-ADM. THE HON. RICHARD SAUNDERS DUNDAS, C.B.

(*Dickinson, delt. & lith.*)

and used at the reduction of Kinburn. These vessels, unfortunately, could not be got ready in time for actual employment. A list, as complete as possible, of Dundas's fleet of 1855 will be found on the following page.

The first detachment of the command weighed anchor in the Downs on March 28th, and proceeded. Great part of the rest of it sailed from Spithead on Wednesday, April 4th. The first division of the French Baltic Fleet,[1] under Rear-Admiral Pénaud, quitted

---

[1] *Tourville, Austerlitz, Duquesne, d'Assas,* and *Aigle.*

SHIPS.	GUNS.	H.P.N.	COMMANDERS.	SHIPS.	GUNS.	H.P.N.	COMMANDERS.
1 Duke of Wellington	131	700	R.-Ad. Hon. R. S. Dundas, C.B. / Commod. Hon. Fred. Thos. Pelham. / Capt. Hy. Caldwell.	1 Cruiser	17	60	Com. Hon. Geo. H. Douglas.
1 Exmouth	90	400	R.-Ad. Michael Seymour (2). / Capt. Wm. King Hall.	Harrier	17	100	„ Hy. Alex. Story.
Retribution, padd..	28	400	R.-Ad. Robt. Lambert Baynes, C.B. / Capt. Thos. Fisher.	Desperate	8	400	„ Rich. Dunning White.
Royal George	102	400	„ Hy. J. Codrington, C.B.	Conflict	8	400	„ S. S. L. Crofton
James Watt	91	600	„ George Aug. Elliot (2).	Basilisk, padd.	6	400	„
Orion	91	600	„ Jno. Elphinstone Erskine.	Driver, padd.	6	280	„ Alan Hy. Gardner.
Cæsar	90	400	„ Jno. Robb.	1 Locust, padd.	3	100	
Nile	90	500	„ Geo. Rodney Mundy.	Porcupine, padd..	3	132	
Cressy	80	400	„ Rich. Laird Warren.	Falcon.	17	100	
Colossus	80	400	„ Robt. Spencer Robinson.	Cuckoo, padd.	3	100	Lieut. Aug. Geo. Ern. Murray.
Blenheim	60	450	„ William Hutcheon Hall.	1 Princess Alice, padd..	1	120	
Hogue	60	450	„ William Ramsay.	1 Blazer, m. v..	..	60	Act.-Gunner Josiah Hunt.[2]
1 Edinburgh	60	450	„ Rich. Strode Hewlett.	1 Havock, m. v..	..	60	Boats. Thos. Foreman.[2]
Ajax	60	450	„ Fred. Warden.	1 Manly, m. v..	..	60	Act.-Boats. Jno. Bosanquet.[2]
Hawke	60	200	„ Erasmus Ommanney.	1 Surly, m. v.	..	60	
1 Cornwallis	60	200	„ Geo. Greville Wellesley.	1 Gleaner, g. b..	4	60	Mate Arch. Geo. Bogie.[2]
1 Pembroke	60	200	„ Geo. Henry Seymour.	1 Pelter, g. b.	4	60	Lieut. Wm. Fredk. Lee.[2]
1 Hastings	60	200	„ Jas. Crawford Caffin.	1 Pincher, g. b..	4	60	„ Keith Stewart ( ).[2]
Impérieuse	51	360	„ Rundle Burges Watson, C.B.	Ruby, g. b.	4	60	
1 Euryalus	51	400	„ Geo. Ramsay.	1 Badger, g. b..	4	60	Mate Wm. Hy. Cuming.[2]
1 Arrogant	47	360	„ Hastings Reg. Yelverton.	1 Snapper, g. b.	4	60	Lieut. Arth. Julian Villiers.[2]
1 Amphion	36	300	„ Astley Cooper Key.	1 Biter, g. b.	..	60	„ Warren Hastings Anderson.[2]
1 Cossack.	20	250	„ Edw. Gennys Fanshawe.	1 Dapper, g. b.	4	60	„ Hy. Jas. Grant.[2]
Pylades	21	350	„ Edward Clayton T. D'Eyncourt.	Jackdaw	..	60	
Esk	21	250	„ Thos. Fras. Birch.	1 Magpie, g. b.	2	60	„ Bedford C. T. Pim.[2]
Tartar	20	250	„ Hugh Dunlop.	1 Redwing, g. b.	..	60	Mate Wm. Greenhill Silverlock.[2]
Archer	13	202	„ Edm. Heathcote.	1 Skylark, g. b.	..	60	Lieut. Fred. Whiteford Pym.[2]
1 Magicienne, padd.	16	400	„ Nicholas Vansittart.	1 Snap, g. b.	4	60	„ Chas. Arth. Wise.[2]
1 Dragon, padd.	6	560	„ Wm. Houston Stewart.	1 Starling, g. b.	4	60	„ Shute Barrington Piers.[2]
Bulldog, padd.	6	500	Com. Alex. Crombie Gordon.	1 Stork, g. b.	4	60	„ Geo. Jno. Malcolm.[2]
1 Vulture, padd.	6	470	Capt. Fred. Hy. Hastings Glasse.	Swinger, g. b.	..	60	
Centaur, padd.	6	540	„ Wm. Jno. Cavendish Clifford.	1 Thistle, g. b.	4	60	„ David Spain.[2]
Gorgon, padd..	6	320	Com. Rich. Borough Crawford.	1 Weazel, g. b.	..	60	„ Robt. Geo. Craigie.[2]
1 Merlin, padd..	6	312	Capt. Bar. Jas. Sulivan.	1 Lark, g. b.	4	60	„ Mark Robt. Pechell.[2]
1 Geyser, padd..	6	280	Com. Roderick Dew.	1 Rocket, m. v.	..	60	Boats. Jno. Thoms.[2]
1 Lightning, padd..	3	100	Lieut. James Carter Campbell.	1 Pickle, m. v.	..	60	Act.-Boats. Rich. Jones.[2]
Firefly, padd..	4	220	Capt. Hy. Chas. Otter.	1 Mastiff, m. v.	..	60	Act.-Gunner Rich. Fowell.[2]
				1 Drake, m. v.	..	40	„ Jno. Dew.[2]
				1 Prompt, m. v.	..	60	Act.-Boats. Chas. Ford.[2]
				1 Beacon, m. v.	..	60	„ Rich. Broad.[2]
				1 Porpoise, m. v.	..	60	„ Charles Haydon.[2]
				1 Redbreast, m. v..	..	..	Act.-Gunner G. Taylor.[2]
				1 Grappler, m. v..	..	60	Act.-Boats. Thos. Hawkins.[2]
				1 Growler, m. v.	..	60	
				1 Carron, m. v.	..	..	Act.-Boats. J. Terdre.[2]
				1 Sinbad, m. v..	..	..	Act.-Gunner Hy. Wallace.[2]
				Lively, m. v..	..	60	Boats. Chas. Blofield.[2]
				1 Belleisle, trp. s.	..	..	Com. Jas. Hosken.
				1 Æolus, st. s.	..	..	
				Perseverance, trp. s.	..	360	
				1 Volcano, padd.	..	140	Mast. Rich. Cossantine Dyer.

1 Present at Sweaborg.

2 These officers commanded at the bombardment of Sweaborg. In some cases there were changes before or after that time.

Brest on April 26th, but did not effect its junction with the British until the early part of June.[1] Ere that time, the coast of Courland had been formally blockaded, and several small operations had been carried out in the Gulf of Finland, where numerous vessels belonging

1 Chevalier, 273.

to the enemy were destroyed. On May 10th, the fleet made rendez-vous off Nargen Island ; on the following day the Admirals, in the *Merlin*, reconnoitred Reval; and on May 12th, in the same vessel, escorted by the *Euryalus* and *Cossack*, they reconnoitred Sweaborg. Both Reval and Sweaborg were observed to have been greatly strengthened since the autumn of 1854. At the latter place, about sixty fresh guns had been mounted in seven new earthworks ; and in port were seen four ships of the line, three of which were dismantled, together with a frigate and two small steamers. Reval offered few inducements for attack. Any large operations against Cronstadt were ultimately felt to be out of the question in the absence of the armoured batteries. There remained only Sweaborg among im-portant places which it might be both possible and worth while to reduce. Even Sweaborg, after Dundas had looked at it, narrowly escaped being set aside as a fortress too strong to be attempted by the fleets. Sulivan, however, steadfastly declared that it might be reduced with the aid of the gun and mortar boats.

"Dundas, though very anxious to do all that was possible, felt much doubt about succeeding in this latter plan; and much influence was used in an important quarter in the fleet to convince him that it could not succeed, and that the small mortar-vessels could not safely lie at anchor under the fire of such a strong place. . . . Whilst waiting at Nargen for the arrival of the mortar-vessels, it seemed probable that the attempt would be given up, and some minor points on the coast attacked instead. On one visit to the flagship, Sulivan was told by the Admiral that he had decided not to attempt it; and it was only after using every argument to combat the adverse view, and pressing his opinion also on the French Admiral, who generally supported him, that Sulivan got Admiral Dundas to alter his decision and make up his mind to carry out the plan; but he made this condition—that Sulivan should agree to place the mortar-vessels 3300 yards from the fortress, instead of 3000, as proposed by him. It was only after the mortar-vessels had arrived, and he had consulted Captain Wemyss,[1] of the Marine Artillery, who thought that, even at that distance, the mortars would be able to cover all the fortress, that Sulivan yielded the point." [2]

Thus, the only considerable purely naval operation of the second campaign in the Baltic would, in all probability, have been never undertaken but for the advocacy of Captain Bartholomew James Sulivan. But it was not undertaken until comparatively late in the season ; and ere that many things happened.

Long before the fleets in the Baltic had reached anything like their intended strength, small-pox broke out in some of the ships ; and on May 16th, the *Duke of Wellington* had to leave Nargen for

---

[1] Capt. John Maurice Wemyss, R.M.A., Maj. in Army, Nov. 2nd, 1855, C.B. Jan. 2nd, 1857.

[2] Sulivan, 274.

Farö Sound, on the Swedish coast, in order to land her sick. To guard against any sudden dash on the part of the Russians at Cronstadt, during the absence of the flagship, the *Euryalus*, *Merlin*, and *Magicienne*, under the Captains named in the table on p. 478, were detached to cruise well to the eastward until the 19th. They were not interfered with. Indeed, the Russians never attempted to utilise their ships as fighting machines during the whole of the war. On May 26th, boats from the *Cossack*, 20, Captain Edward Gennys Fanshawe, and *Esk*, 21, Captain Thomas Francis Birch, took and destroyed some vessels off Hango Head, and met with little opposition, even from the shore. On the same day, the fleet moved up the Gulf of Finland; and on the 27th, the *Merlin* and *Magicienne* were detached to look into Viborg Bay and Björko Sound. Off Biskops Island, several small craft were taken, and the *Magicienne* captured two fine transport galliots from their convoy, a steamer, which cast them off and abandoned them on the approach of Captain Vansittart. The *Orion*, 91, Captain John Elphinstone Erskine, simultaneously reconnoitred Cronstadt; and though she lay throughout the night of the 27th within sight of about eight Russian steamships—four being very heavily armed ones—she was not attacked. A more extensive reconnaissance was made on May 31st by the fleet, headed by the *Euryalus*, *Merlin*, and *Amphion*. Admirals Dundas and Seymour, upon closing, went on board the *Merlin*, and, proceeding, anchored off the lighthouse, where they landed, and whence they obtained a fine view. In spite of the fear of infernal machines, or stationary torpedoes, the reconnaissance was renewed on June 1st, and pushed well round to the north-east side of Cronstadt.[1] The *Merlin* narrowly escaped grounding, and was for some time in difficulties within range of about twenty guns, but was not fired at. Upon rejoining the fleet, the Admirals found that the French division, under Rear-Admiral Pénaud, had just arrived. Another reconnaissance was made on June 2nd, and numerous soundings were taken; but the more Cronstadt was looked at, the less it was liked.

In the meantime the *Cossack*, which had visited the fleet off Nargen, had returned to Hango Head, with the object of landing three prisoners who had been taken in the neighbourhood in the affair of May 26th, and four other prisoners who had been captured elsewhere. She arrived off Hango in the morning of June 5th, and,

[3] See plan on p. 483.

at 11 A.M., sent in a boat with a flag of truce, under Lieutenant Louis Geneste, with orders to land the prisoners, to allow none of the ship's people to straggle from the boat, and to return without delay. Strangely enough, however, three officers' stewards were allowed to go ashore. To give them this permission implied, of course, that they might venture at least so far from the boat as to obtain supplies from any natives who might be willing to sell them. Surgeon Robert Tulloh Easton also accompanied the party. Upon reaching the beach, the boat was screened from the ship by some intervening islands. At 4.30 P.M., the boat not having returned, Captain Fanshawe sent in the first Lieutenant, John Bousquet Field, in the gig, with another flag of truce ; and, as neither craft had come back at the close of the day, the *Cossack* and *Esk* were anchored in the inner road. At about 8.30 P.M. the gig reappeared, reporting that after a long search she had found the cutter, hauled within a small jetty, and that in her were the bodies of four of her people, Edward Thompson, leading seaman, William Linn, Captain's steward, Benjamin Smith, able seaman, and James Cornwell, ordinary seaman. Captain Fanshawe ordered that the ships should weigh at 2.30 A.M. on the 6th, take up positions for covering the village and telegraph-station, and send in a demand for the return of the cutter and the missing officers and men. Before, however, the ships could weigh, the cutter was seen to be coming out, in charge of one dangerously wounded man, who, upon being brought on board, reported that, having reached the jetty, Geneste, Easton, Master's-Assistant Charles Sullivan, and the prisoners, had stepped ashore and advanced, Geneste waving the flag of truce.[1] Immediately afterwards a body of Russian soldiers, headed by an officer who spoke English, had appeared, and, after a brief and angry parley, had opened fire. No resistance had been made, and, according to the survivor, all his companions had been killed. It subsequently turned out, however, that only seven people had been killed, and that the rest, including Geneste, Sullivan, and Easton, had been taken prisoners, some in a wounded condition. Captain Fanshawe thereupon opened fire at 600 yards upon the place, and continued until a thick fog obliged him to cease and haul off.[2]

This affair made a great noise : but it is only right to recall that,

---

[1] Geneste reported that it was carried by one of the stewards.

[2] Disp. of Fanshawe, June 6th; Report of Geneste, July 8th.

on the Russian side, it was declared, firstly, that no flag of truce was seen, and secondly, that, even supposing that the boat landed and the party advanced under such a flag, the whole proceeding was irregularly conducted, and likely, therefore, to lead to such a catastrophe as actually occurred. The *Cossack* herself should have displayed a white flag during the absence of her cutter; and she ran some risk in sending in a boat at all, so long as she did not know that the Russians at Hango were willing to receive a flag of truce there. It is conceivable that it might be inconvenient and even dangerous to a defending force to allow a boat, under any pretext whatsoever, to approach a given position. Apart from all such questions, it may be asked : what were the stewards doing in the boat, and why were arms and the arms' chest taken with the party ? Neither foragers nor muskets should have been sent in in such circumstances. It was at last arranged between the belligerents that in future the Russians should receive flags of truce only at Cronstadt, Sweaborg, Reval, Libau, Windau, Tornea, and Wasa ; and it was understood on both sides that vessels desiring to communicate must hoist a white flag of large dimensions, cast anchor beyond long range, and wait until a boat from the other side should visit them to receive the message. It was further accepted, as a matter of course, that no attempts to obtain information or supplies under a flag of truce ought to be made in any circumstances. More than one British Captain of the time appears, unfortunately, though, no doubt, unintentionally, to have been far too careless of the impressions which his methods of procedure were likely to make upon a wary and suspicious enemy.[1] The business, though in many respects most regrettable, had the good effect of rendering Captain Fanshawe and other commanders more punctilious.

On June 6th and 7th, the *Magicienne*, 16, paddle, Captain Nicholas Vansittart, destroyed a couple of galliots, and dispersed some small bodies of troops in Kansiala Bay and Ravensair Inlet, and at Kiskulla.

On June 9th, a little accident which might easily have had far-reaching results happened. Rear-Admiral Pénaud, and a number of other officers, desiring to make as near a survey as possible of the defences on the north and north-east sides of Cronstadt, went on board the *Merlin*, 6, paddle, which, attended by the *Firefly*, 4,

Corr. of Prince Dolgorouki and Genl. de Berg with Dundas : Sulivan, 299.

paddle, *Dragon*, 6, paddle, and French corvette *d'Assas*, proceeded
rather further than she had gone on any previous reconnaissance.
She was fired at by a distant Russian gunboat, which probably
desired to tempt her to approach still closer in that direction. She
turned off, however, and was leisurely steaming at about two and
a half miles from the island, the *Firefly* following her, and the
Dragon and *d'Assas* keeping further out, when she exploded a small
infernal machine, or torpedo. She was not damaged; but she was

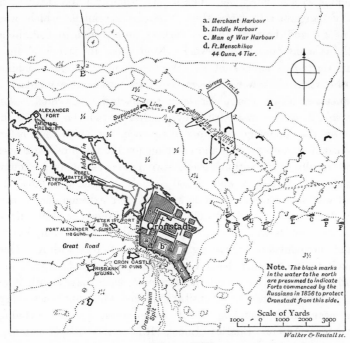

CRONSTADT, 1855.

(*From 'Life and Letters of Sir B. J. Sulivan,' by kind permission of Mr. John Murray.*)

stopped, and then went astern a little; whereupon she struck a
second torpedo, which exploded just before her starboard paddle-box,
and shook her very severely. The *Firefly*, which, already warned
off, had hauled a cable's length inside the *Merlin*, exploded a third
machine under her bow. In the *Merlin*, mess-traps, lockers, plates,
cups, glasses and bottles were smashed by the second blow, two
girders were bent or broken, and some copper was torn away; but
the vessel's complete efficiency was in no wise impaired. The
torpedoes which were thus encountered were, no doubt, of a type

2 I 2

the invention of one Jacobi. Each consisted of a cone-shaped zinc vessel, generally about 2 feet deep, and 15 inches broad, moored base upwards. At the bottom was a charge of gunpowder. In the broader end were an air-chamber and the firing apparatus. This last was a simple device whereby, upon anything impinging strongly against the periphery of the upturned base of the cone, a glass tube, containing acid, was broken in such manner as to ignite a primer placed below it and communicating with the main charge.[1] The machine worked fairly well; but it was usually far too small to be really dangerous to large ships. Several specimens which were crept for and brought to the surface were found to contain as little as eight pounds of powder. None seem to have held more than thirty-five pounds of it. Why very much larger machines of the same class were not employed in considerable numbers is a question which has never been satisfactorily answered. The *Vulture*, 6, paddle, was struck by another torpedo on June 20th; and on the following day, in consequence, the ships then before Cronstadt began sweeping and creeping for the machines with such good results that, within ˇseventy-two hours, as many as thirty-three of the torpedoes were fished up. It is astonishing that the work was done without great loss of life; for extreme carelessness was often displayed in the handling of these dangerous obstructions. Rear-Admiral Seymour, and Captain William King Hall, having found one, hauled it into their gig, and began to play with it. They took it to the Commander-in-Chief, and again played with it; and finally, carrying it on board the *Exmouth*, they played with it on the quarter-deck once more, until it exploded, knocking down everyone near, and wounding about half-a-dozen people, including Seymour, Captain Charles Louis, R.M., and Flag-Lieutenant Richard Bulkeley Pearse. The Russians, who knew better what they were about, and were more careful, were less fortunate; for a torpedo, exploding in one of their boats, killed seventeen men. Rear-Admiral Dundas himself nearly lost his sight through unwise trifling with the firing apparatus of an empty infernal machine.[2]

The repeated reconnaissances of Cronstadt had by that time showed that the place, in which lay about twenty-three sail of the line, besides numerous frigates, corvettes, and steamers, and very many gunboats, was too strong to be successfully attacked by the

---

[1] One of these machines is in the museum of H.M.S. *Excellent*, at Portsmouth.

[2] Sulivan, 301–304.

then available forces of the naval commanders-in-chief, who had not enough light-draught gun and mortar-vessels, who had no armoured batteries at all, and who could not bring their big ships within effective gunshot of the enemy. Pending, therefore, the arrival of more force, and of a decision as to the point against which the whole should be directed, numerous small expeditions were despatched against comparatively unimportant places. On June 14th, the *Basilisk*, 6, paddle, Commander Stephen Smith Lowther Crofton, appeared in Siela Sound, between Dago and Ösel, and destroyed ten boats laden with grain. On June 16th, the *Exmouth*, bearing the flag of Rear-Admiral Seymour, with the *Blenheim*, *Pincher*, and *Snap*, parted company in order to reconnoitre the mouth of the river Narva. On the 17th, they had a slight brush with the Russian batteries; and on the 18th, desiring to cut out some coasters which were seen in shore, Seymour temporarily transferred his flag to the *Snap*, and, followed by the *Blenheim* and *Pincher*, stood close in. He unexpectedly came within sight of a 14-gun sand battery, upon which he opened at about 1200 yards. A brisk engagement followed; but although the enemy suffered some loss and had a gun disabled, no material result was attained. The division rejoined the fleet, which was then off Nargen, on the 19th, and with it proceeded to Seskar, and so to nearly its old position off Cronstadt, the larger part anchoring about five miles north of the fortress, and a few vessels, in mid-channel, between the lighthouse and the mainland. There was no longer a question of attacking Cronstadt. It was only desired to observe, and to "contain" it; but more than once, in the next few weeks, while schemes for reducing Sweaborg were being matured, shots were exchanged with the forts and batteries.

On June 20th, the *Arrogant*, *Magicienne*, and *Ruby* destroyed a fort at Rotchensalm in the Gulf of Finland;[1] and, on the same day, the boats of the *Conflict* and *Desperate* destroyed five coasting sloops off Pernau, at the north point of the Gulf of Riga. Two days later, the *Amphion* had a slight engagement with batteries at Sandhamn, Storholm, and Ertholm. A more important service was performed by Commander Henry Alexander Story, of the *Harrier*, 17, which formed one of Captain Frederick Warden's division, employed in the Gulf of Bothnia. The navigation up to the town of Nystad having been previously made familiar to him by Captain Henry

---

[1] A blockade of the coast of Finland had been declared on June 15th.

Charles Otter, of the *Firefly*, Story, on June 23rd and 24th, destroyed no fewer than 47 sail, or about 20,000 tons, of the enemy's shipping in that neighbourhood, after having worked continuously in his boats for twenty-two hours. He specially mentioned in his dispatch[1] the assistance which he had received from Lieutenant William Henry Annesley. On June 27th, the *Firefly*, 4, paddle, Captain Henry Charles Otter, and *Driver*, 6, paddle, Commander Alan Henry Gardner, of the same division, destroyed two masked but unarmed batteries at Christenestad;[2] and on June 30th, in Werolax Bay, in the Gulf of Finland, the *Ruby*, gunboat, Lieutenant Henry George Hale, and boats of the *Magicienne*, 16, paddle, Captain Nicholas Vansittart, burnt or scuttled twenty-nine vessels.

On July 2nd, the *Driver*, Commander Alan Henry Gardner, with the *Harrier*, Commander Henry Alexander Story, appeared off Raumo, in the Gulf of Bothnia, and summoned the town. The burgomaster pulled out under a flag of truce, and, having agreed to give up such vessels as lay in port, recommended Gardner to pull up to the head of the bay, where he would find the sails belonging to the craft in question. The man then went back. As the vessels could not be well taken out while a flag of truce was flying, Gardner hauled his down, and sent in his boats, understanding that he was to receive the vessels and spare the town ; but, owing either to misapprehension or to treachery, the boats were greeted with a cross fire, and had to retreat with a loss of two men killed or mortally wounded, and three others severely hurt. The *Driver* covered the retirement, and then threw shot, shell, and 24-pr. rockets into the town for about an hour and a half, but, strange to say, failed to set it on fire, though it was built of wood.[3]

At about that time it was rumoured that the enemy was strengthening the entrance to the Gulf of Lovisa, some miles to the eastward of Helsingfors and Sweaborg. Thither accordingly went Captain Hastings Reginald Yelverton in the *Arrogant*, 47, screw, with the *Magicienne* and *Ruby*. On July 4th, he anchored his vessels close under Fort Swartholm, which he found to be a modernised work capable of mounting 122 guns, and having casemated barracks for 1000 men. Guns, stores, and ammunition had, however, been removed by the Russians, who had received

[1] Story to Warden, June 24th.
[2] Notes (by Otter), in *Naut. Mag.*, 1855, 465.
[3] Notes (by Otter), in *Naut. Mag.*, 1855, 470.

intelligence of the British approach. The fort and barracks were destroyed. On July 5th, Yelverton, in the *Ruby*, reconnoitred the town of Lovisa, and, with musketry and rocket fire, dispersed a body of Cossacks. Landing, he burnt the government stores and barracks in the place, but spared the town, which, nevertheless, caught fire accidentally during the following night, and was, unfortunately, reduced to ashes.[1] Yelverton went thence to Kounda Bay, where he dislodged some more Cossacks; to the mouth of the river ·Portsoiki, where he destroyed buildings and drove off a few troops; and to Transsund, off the town of Viborg, where he arrived on July 13th. In the sound he encountered, chased, and exchanged shots with a Russian man-of-war steamer. Pushing on in the *Ruby*, with the boats of the *Arrogant* and *Magicienne*, he sighted another steamer and three gunboats, but was suddenly brought up by a sunken obstruction, and, while examining it, was opened fire upon from a masked battery only about three hundred and fifty yards from him. After a short period of natural confusion, the boats pulled steadily up to the earthwork, and maintained a spirited engagement with it for upwards of an hour, but could effect nothing, as the enemy, reinforced by his steamers and gunboats, was in greatly superior force; and at length the British had to retire to the ships. While the boats were still under fire an explosion took place in the *Arrogant's* second cutter, killing Mr. Story, the Midshipman in charge of her, and half swamping the boat, which drifted under the battery. All remaining in her would probably have been killed or taken, had not George Ingoueville, one of her crew, though wounded, jumped overboard, with the painter in his hand, and towed her off. Her condition was then seen from the *Ruby*, whereupon Lieutenant George Dare Dowell, R.M.A., of the *Magicienne*, who happened to be on board, calling for volunteers, jumped into the *Ruby's* gig, was joined by Lieutenant Henry Vachell Haggard,[2] first of the *Arrogant*, and two men, and pulled off under an increasingly hot fire to the rescue. The gallant little party saved the boat and her crew; but the whole affair cost the loss of two killed and ten wounded.[3] Ingoueville, and Lieutenant Dowell received the Victoria Cross for their bravery and initiative.

While Captain Yelverton was engaged in these affairs, the

---

[1] Yelverton to Dundas, July 8th; Dundas to Admlty., recd. July 16th: Sulivan, 311.
[2] Promtd. Com. July 24th, 1855, for this service.
[3] Yelverton to Dundas.

Lightning, 3, paddle, off Bogskarin Beacon, and the *Basilisk*, 6, paddle, in Siele Sound, injured the enemy by destroying a number of salt boats. On July 17th, the *Basilisk*, in company with the *Desperate*, 8, Commander Richard Dunning White, had a smart brush with batteries and gunboats in the Gulf of Riga.

On July 19th, there began an important series of reconnaissances. Admirals Dundas and Pénaud went on board the *Merlin*, 6, paddle, Captain Bartholomew James Sulivan, and, attended by the *Amphion, Dragon*, a gunboat, and a small French screw steamer, looked into Helsingfors and Sweaborg.

"The enemy," says Sulivan,[1] "were in the act of sinking a two-decker to block the western passage, one having been sunk within a few days in the same passage. In turning to come out in one place, the French screw astern of us exploded two 'infernals,' but nearly twenty yards from her. Probably they were exploded by wires from the shore. . . . The next day we went into Reval, and had a close look at all the batteries. . . . The same evening I was off with two gunboats to examine all the shores inside the large islands of Dago and Ösel. . . . The next day, Saturday, we reached the sound inside Wormsö Island, and I tried to go to Hapsal. . . . It was too shallow about five miles off for *Merlin* to pass. . . . But . . . I got both gunboats (drawing seven feet) through. . . . There were no vessels and no defences. . . ."

On July 23rd, 24th, and 25th, the expedition examined the coasts of Dago and Ösel, and then returned to the rendezvous off Nargen, calling on the way at Odensholm. Pénaud came to the conclusion that Helsingfors, and not Sweaborg, its guardian fortress, ought to be attacked. Sulivan induced Dundas to advocate the attack on Sweaborg; and, in consequence, on July 31st, the *Merlin* was detached from the fleet to examine the place more minutely, and to buoy the approaches to it.

In the meantime, Yelverton, with his division, then consisting of the *Cossack*, 20, Captain Edward Gennys Fanshawe, as well as of the *Arrogant, Magicienne*, and *Ruby*, as before, appeared on July 21st before the recently constructed batteries of Frederikshamn, on the Finland coast, nearly midway between Viborg and Helsingfors. The British opened fire a little before 10 A.M., and for an hour and a half there was a brisk engagement. The enemy, however, having suffered heavily, eventually abandoned his guns, some of which had been dismounted. The loss on the attacking side was only three men wounded, though the ships were several times struck. Part of the town was unintentionally burnt, and the fort was much knocked about; but, having no troops with him, and there being a strong body of Russian troops in the

[1] Sulivan, 307.

immediate neighbourhood, Yelverton did not attempt a landing, and presently withdrew. He then reported that it was desirable that the island of Kotka, where, a month earlier, he had destroyed a work, should be again examined, as the enemy was active there. Dundas, therefore, reinforced him with the mortar-vessels *Prompt, Pickle, Rocket,* and *Blazer,* and with four gunboats, the latter from the division of Rear-Admiral Baynes, who lay off Cronstadt, and the former from the fleet off Nargen. These joined the *Arrogant* on July 26th, off Hogland, and at 2 P.M. the squadron anchored off Fort Rotchenholm.

" As," says Yelverton,[1] " the safety of our expedition rested chiefly on our investing, and holding the entire possession of, the fortified island of Kotka, I determined upon taking it at once. Accordingly, I anchored the mortar-vessels out of range, and, leaving two gunboats to look after them, I proceeded with the rest of the vessels to the westward of Kotka, for the purpose of destroying the bridge, so as to cut off the retreat of the garrison, and prevent their receiving reinforcements from the mainland. Captain Vansittart, of the *Magicienne,* with his accustomed zeal and activity, threaded his way at once through the shoals, and destroyed the bridge. As soon as all the vessels had anchored, so as to command the great military road leading from the fort of Hogforsholm, and also the channel dividing the island from the main, I landed all the Marines, under the command of Captain Samuel Netterville Lowder, R.M., with Lieutenant George Dare Dowell, R.M.A., and Lieutenants Henry Colton Mudge and Ponsonby Ross Holmes, R.M., who took possession without being opposed, as the garrison (no doubt apprised of our coming by the telegraphs along the coast) had very recently evacuated, leaving behind them a large amount of military stores, which have since been burnt. . . ."

Three barracks, four stores, four magazines, four guard-houses and detached buildings, six other buildings, and some workshops and supplies were destroyed, and on the 27th the squadron departed, Captain Fanshawe, with the *Cossack,* being left in charge of the island. Yelverton, in his dispatch, specially mentioned the services rendered by Masters George Giles (*Arrogant*), and George Alexander Macfarlane (*Magicienne*), in sounding and buoying the intricate channels on the coast. Indeed, the whole campaign in the Baltic was essentially a campaign of navigators and marine surveyors, at the head of whom were Captains Bartholomew James Sulivan, and Henry Charles Otter.

In the Gulf of Riga, on July 23rd, Arensburg, in the island of Ösel, was taken possession of by a landing-party from the *Archer,* 13, screw, Captain Edmund Heathcote, and *Desperate,* 8, Commander Richard Dunning White. On the 30th, the *Archer,* with the

---

[1] Yelverton to Dundas, July 28th. The expedition alluded to was the coming attack on Sweaborg.

Conflict, 8, screw, dispersed some troops, and destroyed some public buildings at Windau, on the Courland coast, just outside the limits of the gulf.   And on August 6th, the *Archer* and *Desperate*, landing a detachment near Dome Ness, destroyed a sloop and government buildings, and repulsed a body of cavalry.

In the Gulf of Bothnia, the smaller vessels of Captain Warden's division continued their activity.   On July 24th, the *Harrier*, 17, screw, Commander Henry Alexander Story, and *Cuckoo*, 3, paddle, destroyed part of the town of Raumo, and a quantity of shipping. The *Firefly*, 4, paddle, pushed further north, and on August 1st was off Korsoren beacon.   Getting out his two paddle-box boats and his gig, Otter pulled in towards Brandon, the seaport of Wasa, cut down a telegraph on a small island in Korshamn Fiord, and captured a large barque laden with tar, returning early on the following morning to his ship.   That night he carried her up, and anchored her within four hundred yards of Brandon, which was then a con-siderable shipbuilding centre.   Under cover of the *Firefly's* guns, Lieutenant John Ward (4), with the boats, went to examine the magazines and storehouses.   Otter determined to burn them, but agreed to await a favourable opportunity, the wind then blowing directly on to the town, which he had no desire to damage.   In the course of the day Lieutenant Edward Burstal[1] took another prize, a schooner, and discovered two barques and two brigs in a neigh-bouring creek.   In the evening, while a working party was trans-ferring some tar and deals to the schooner prize, a brisk musketry fire was opened upon the party, and also upon the *Firefly*, and was returned with shot and shell.   The schooner could not be brought out, and was abandoned.   A barque, however, was carried off, thanks largely to the exertions of Second Master John Augustus Bull ; and the other barque and the two brigs were destroyed.   In this affair, while the enemy had 25 killed and many hurt, the total British loss was only 2 slightly wounded.   During the continuance of unfavourable weather, Cossacks, with several guns, reinforced the town.   Not until the 8th was Otter able to attempt the destruction of the magazines and storehouses.   He then opened fire at 1500 yards, first on a 4-gun battery, which did not reply, and then on the buildings, which, by 2.30 P.M., were observed to be burning.   At about that time Lieutenant John Ward (4) volunteered to go in with a paddle-box boat, and attempt to cut

---

[1] Promtd. Com. for this service, Sept. 29th, 1855.

out the abandoned schooner; but, although he made a very
gallant effort, he had at length to retire before overwhelming
strength, happily, however, without loss. At 8 P.M., the conflagration ashore being obviously no longer in danger of extinction, Otter
closed to fire a few more rounds at the still silent battery, and
then, since his ammunition was nearly expended, began to back
out. A general and heavy fire was thereupon suddenly directed
against him. His situation, in a narrow and shallow channel where
he dared not turn, was, for more than half an hour, extremely
trying; but at length he drew slowly out of range.[1]

It has been already said that, after much discussion, Admirals
Dundas and Pénaud had decided to attack the fortress of Sweaborg,
and to spare the city of Helsingfors. The wisdom of this decision
has been often called in question. Helsingfors, besides being a very
wealthy and important place, challenged attack, in that it was
strongly fortified. If captured, it could not have been occupied,
seeing that the Allies had no troops available for the purpose; but, if
it had been bombarded and destroyed, its fate would have been a
most serious blow to the enemy; and the discomfort caused to its
large population would, no doubt, have had a salutary effect upon
such public opinion as then existed in Russia. On the other hand,
the bombardment of Sweaborg affected neither the military prestige
of the Russian government nor the pockets of influential Russians;
and, upon the whole, it was a very aimless, if not dangerous, proceeding, in view of the fact that, even had the forts been entirely
levelled with the ground, their disappearance would not have
furthered the end to the attainment of which Great Britain and
France had committed themselves. Had it been purposed, after
bombarding Sweaborg, to storm, capture and hold the works in
force; to use them for operations against Helsingfors; and to use
Helsingfors itself as a base for a military movement against Cronstadt and St. Petersburg, the attack would have justified itself.
There was, however, no scheme of this kind. Feeling in London
and Paris demanded that something striking should be done in the
Baltic; and Sweaborg appeared to offer to the Allies a magnificent
target in front of which they might make a noisy display for the
delectation of the crowd at home. It is to be feared that no considerations very much sounder dictated the course which was pursued. The attack is, however, of some interest, because, unlike the

[1] Otter to Warden, Aug. 11th, 1855.

attacks on Sebastopol, it was entirely of a naval character, and because, in spite of the huge strength of the defences, the ships did undoubtedly inflict a considerable amount of damage, while themselves escaping almost scot free.

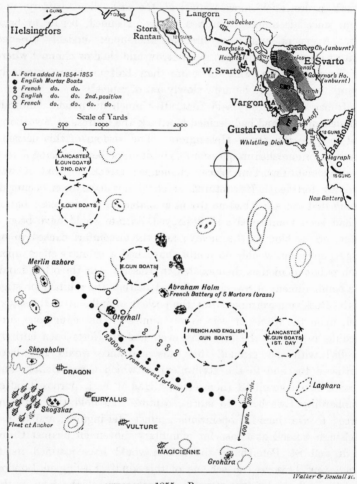

SWEABORG, 1855. PLAN OF ATTACK.

NOTE.—The shaded portions indicate the area of the conflagrations caused by the bombardment.

(From ' Life and Letters of Sir B. J. Sulivan,' by kind permission of Mr. John Murray.)

In 1855, the congeries of fortresses called Sweaborg occupied part of the group of small islands lying E.S.E. of Helsingfors, the centre of the works being about 3500 yards from the nearest part of the city. The islands are little more than large granite rocks, and the works upon them were to a large extent excavated in the solid stone. Chief among the fortified islets were Vargon, in the middle, Gustafvaard, East Svarto, West Svarto, and Lilla Svarto. These, which showed a general front towards the S.W., and most of which were interconnected by bridges, or fortified stone piers, protected the entrance to Helsingfors Bay. In two of the intervals which separated them, and which formed the passages into the bay, lay ships of the line, moored with their broadsides athwart the channel; and in the various works were upwards of 800 guns, with full garrisons to man them.

During the first few days of August, Captain Bartholomew James Sulivan, in the *Merlin*, was continuously engaged in superintending the sounding and buoying of the waters immediately about the fortress, and in making plans and marking positions for the attacking ships. On the 6th, Dundas, with the British fleet, arrived from off Nargen; and, in the evening of the same day and morning of the next, he was joined by Pénaud, with the French contingent, which included, besides ships of the line, gunboats, steamers and storeships, the sailing mortar-vessels *Tocsin*, *Fournaise*, *Trombe*, *Torche*, and *Bombe*.[1] A sufficient observing force remained, of course, near Cronstadt. The British contingent was made up of the vessels whose names are prefaced by a [1] in the table on page 478. The main attack was to be made by means of the mortar-vessels,[2] ranged along a curve on either side of the islet of Oterhall, the French occupying the centre of the line. Admiral Pénaud, soon after his arrival, began to supplement this scheme by establishing a battery of four brass 10-inch mortars on Abraham Holm, a rock about 600 yards nearer than Oterhall to the fortress; but he was unable to complete the business until the morning of the 9th. Ere that time all the mortar-vessels had been stationed in positions, 3900 yards from the batteries, whence they could easily warp into action at 3600 yards' range. This work had been done under direction of Captain Sulivan, the general management of the flotilla being then entrusted to Lieutenant the Hon. Augustus Charles Hobart, and the management of the mortar-fire being committed to Captains (R.M.A.) John Maurice Wemyss, Joseph Edward Wilson Lawrence, and George Augustus Schomberg. Behind the line of mortar-vessels were anchored the *Euryalus*, *Vulture*, *Magicienne*, and *Dragon*, as

---

[1] Each mounting two 13-in. mortars.
[2] Sixteen British and five French. The British each mounted one 12-in. mortar.

supports and supply ships; and in rear of these lay the mass of the combined fleets.   The gunboats, having been previously armed with additional guns of heavy calibre, were removed from among the ships of the line, and employed as will be shown later.   The *Stork* and *Snapper*, which were fitted with Lancaster guns, were specially entrusted to Captain Richard Strode Hewlett, of the *Edinburgh*, who had experience in the use of those weapons.

Early on the 9th, the mortar-vessels warped in to their assigned stations, and, soon after seven o'clock, began firing.   The *Stork* and *Snapper*, circling inside and to the right of the line of mortar-vessels, devoted their attention to a three-decker that lay across the channel between Gustafvaard and Bakholmen.   Inside, and to the left of the line, Commander George William Preedy, with the *Starling*, *Thistle*, *Pelter*, *Biter*, and *Badger*, circled and bombarded the western batteries; and, near Abraham Holm, the *Pincher*, *Skylark*, and *Lark*, under Captain George Ramsay, the *Vulture*, *Snap*, and *Gleaner*, under Captain Frederick Henry Hastings Glasse, and the *Dapper* and *Redwing*, under Captain Nicholas Vansittart, manœuvred in a similar manner.   Further to the N.W., ordered to keep Vargon church open of Stora Rantan, were the *Magpie* and *Weazel*, under Captain William Houston Stewart.   The *Hastings*, *Amphion*,[1] and *Cornwallis*,[2] under Captain George Greville Wellesley, of the ship last-named, were detached off the south-east end of Sandhamn to seize every opportunity of engaging the enemy there; and the *Arrogant*, *Cossack*, and *Cruiser* were sent to the westward to occupy the attention of the troops which were posted on Drumsio Island. Within a short time, the action became general in every direction.

" A rapid fire," says Dundas, " of shot and shells was kept up from the fortress for the first few hours upon the gunboats, and the ranges of the heavy batteries extended completely beyond the mortar-vessels; but the continued motion of the gunboats, and the able manner in which they were conducted by the officers who commanded them, enabled them to return the fire with great spirit, and almost with impunity, throughout the day.   About ten o'clock in the forenoon fires began first to be observed in the different buildings, and a heavy explosion took place on the island of Vargon, which was followed by a second about an hour afterwards on the island of Gustafvaard, inflicting much damage upon the defences of the enemy, and tending greatly to slacken the fire from the guns in that direction.   The advantage of the rapidity with which the fire from the mortars had been directed was apparent in the continued fresh conflagrations which spread extensively on the island of Vargon." [3]

---

[1] *Amphion* had 3 wounded.
[2] *Cornwallis* had 10 wounded.
[3] Dundas to Admlty., Aug. 13th.

The explosions alluded to, and especially the second, which was, in effect, a series of explosions lasting more than two minutes, were very severe, and are believed to have cost the enemy a large number of lives. As sunset drew near, Dundas recalled the gunboats, in consequence of the intricate nature of the navigation, and of the fact that more than one of them had grounded even in daylight. But the French battery on Abraham Holm went on with the bombardment ; and, at half-past ten, the boats of the fleet, assembled under

ADMIRAL THE RT. HON. SIR ASTLEY COOPER KEY, G.C.B., F.R.S.

(From a photo by the London Stereoscopic Co.)

Captain Henry Caldwell, began a three-hours' fire with rockets upon the fortress, causing new conflagrations and increasing the old ones. These rocket-boats, about thirty in number, were commanded by Lieutenants Leveson Eliot Henry Somerset, and Thomas Barnardiston (*Duke of Wellington*), Charles Maxwell Luckraft (*Euryalus*), Henry Bedford Woolcombe, and Cornwallis Wykeham Martin (*Arrogant*), John Binney Scott, and Francis Moubray Prattent (*Pembroke*), Robert Boyle Miller (*Vulture*), John Appleby Pritchard (*Edinburgh*), John Bousquet Field (*Cossack*), Thomas Stackhouse

(*Dragon*), Henry Bartlett King (*Magicienne*), William Naper Corne-wall, and Francis Bland Herbert (*Geyser*), Robert Cooper Tattnall, and Maxwell Fox (*Cornwallis*), John Dobrée M'Crea, and James Graham Goodenough (*Hastings*), and Armine Wodehouse, and Charles Henry Clutterbuck (*Amphion*), together with junior officers. The premature explosion of a rocket in the pinnace of the *Hastings* wounded two men; nine persons were also wounded by a somewhat similar accident in the pinnace of the *Vulture*, and there were other slight casualties, very few, however, of which were due to the enemy's fire. The boats of the *Cornwallis*, *Hastings*, and *Amphion* were employed, not against the forts, but against a frigate which lay moored in Kungs Sund. The vessel could not be burnt; but Lieu-tenant Tattnall, senior officer of these boats, was praised by Captain Wellesley for the manner in which he had carried out orders.

" At daylight on the morning of the 10th," continues Dundas, " the positions of the several mortar-vessels had been advanced within easier range, and the gunboats were again directed to engage. The three-decked ship, which had been moored by the enemy to block and defend the channel between Gustafvaard and Bakholmen, had been withdrawn during the night to a more secure position; but the fire from the batteries was increased, and the engagement was renewed with activity on both sides. Fires continued to burn without intermission within the fortress, and about noon a column of smoke, heavier and darker than any which had yet been observed, and succeeded by bright flames, gave signs that the shells had reached combustible materials in the direction of the arsenal."

The conflagration had, in fact, spread beyond the island of Vargon, and had extended to East Svarto, in its rear. During the whole night of the 10th, a heavy fire was kept up; and, upon the recall of the gunboats as before, divisions of mortar-boats again proceeded to annoy the enemy. One division, directed by Captain George Henry Seymour, of the *Pembroke*, was under the orders of Lieutenants Robert James Wynniatt, and James Carter Campbell (*Exmouth*), Charles Maxwell Luckraft (*Euryalus*), Henry Bedford Woolcombe, and Cornwallis Wykeham Martin (*Arrogant*), John Binney Scott, and Francis Moubray Prattent (*Pembroke*), and Henry Bartlett King (*Magicienne*). The other division, directed by Captain Cald-well, was under the orders of Lieutenants Leveson Eliot Henry Somerset, and Thomas Barnardiston (*Duke of Wellington*), John Appleby Pritchard, and William Hans Blake (*Edinburgh*), Robert Boyle Miller (*Vulture*), and John Bousquet Field (*Cossack*), assisted by junior officers. In the course of the night, seeing that nearly every building on Vargon had been destroyed, and that such buildings as remained standing on East Svarto were almost, if not quite, out of range, while the enemy scarcely returned the fire, the allied Admirals agreed to discontinue the action before daylight on the 11th. By that time, most of the mortars had been disabled, and two, if not three, completely split;[1] and the vents of some of the French guns employed in the attack had fused. There were, unfortunately, no spare mortars, owing to lack of prevision at home. There had, however, been singularly few casualties on the side of the attack, only one man, it is said, having actually lost his life. The British alone had expended in the bombardment about 100 tons of powder, and 1000 tons of projectiles.[2]

How much injury was inflicted on the Russians has never been exactly ascertained. Rear-Admiral Pénaud received, through a spy, a report to the effect that the dockyard, and all the government stores were completely destroyed, all the powder-magazines blown up, twenty-three vessels burnt, and 2000 men killed. Eighteen or nineteen other vessels were alleged to be severely damaged. Russian accounts make the injuries to have been of a less serious nature. However this may be, it is certain that the sea-defences of the place were little the worse for the awful fire to which they had been subjected, and that, supposing them to have still had ammunition available, they were practically as strong as ever. Captain Wellesley, who, as has been seen, had been detached on the 9th, off the south-east of Sandhamn, and who had gallantly engaged the batteries there, likewise produced no appreciable result.[3] Where there were storehouses, magazines, and government buildings, there were fires and explosions; but where there were carefully constructed forts and batteries, the Allies made little or no impression. " Still," says Chevalier, " these operations had the effect of disquieting the population, and of forcing the enemy to busy himself with continual movements of troops." It can scarcely be considered that the game, which exposed numerous costly vessels to the risks not only of red-hot shot and of shell fire, but also of intricate and imperfectly-surveyed navigation, was worth the candle. The *Merlin* herself, carrying the allied Admirals in on the evening of the 10th to view

---

[1] " It is a disgrace to our iron-founders that one old mortar of the last war stood 350 rounds, while all the others, quite new, were unfit for use, or burst, after 200 to 250." Sulivan, 340.

[2] The French mortars threw 2828 shells, and the French vessels, apart from the mortar-vessels, 1322 shells and round shot. Chevalier, 278.

[3] Wellesley to Dundas, Aug. 9th.

the damage which had been done, piled up on a rock in a position where, in full daylight, she might easily have been hulled from the shore. Happily she was got off, though not till after all firing had ceased. Captain Sulivan was in no wise to blame. On the contrary, he and Lieutenant Richard Boynton Creyke [1] were singled out for special praise in the dispatches.

The allied fleets remained in view of the scene of action until the morning of August 13th, when they sailed for Nargen, the *Merlin* and *Locust* staying behind to take up buoys and marks. A few days later, there being practically no mortars left in a serviceable condition, the mortar-vessels were sent home. At the same moment the *Sans Pareil* was taking on board fresh mortars at Woolwich; but Dundas was not kept informed of what was being done. When it became known at Whitehall that the mortar-vessels were returning, a steamer was hastily despatched to meet them, and turn them back; but ere they could be re-armed, the season was too far advanced for further operations of importance in the Baltic. As the *Times* said, a fleet costing about £30,000 a day for maintenance was reduced to impotence, and made a laughing-stock, in consequence of the Government's omission to spend at the right moment "about as much as a man of taste gives for three early Sèvres vases." The administration seems to have forgotten that ships cannot participate in big engagements without expending weapons as well as ammunition. In future naval wars, especially if they be prolonged, it will be more than ever necessary to have made arrangements beforehand for the rapid substitution of new guns for old. Moreover, nothing is more dangerous to the *moral* of a gun's crew than a well-founded suspicion that the piece has already done more work than it was intended for, and may burst, or blow its breech-block out, at the next round. Yet it is difficult to avoid using a weakened gun, when there is nothing to take its place.

From the time of the bombardment of Sweaborg until the closing of the navigation in November, the campaign in the Baltic languished; but small operations continued in various quarters. On August 10th for instance, the *Hawke*, 60, screw, and *Desperate*, 8, screw, had a brush with some batteries and gunboats near the mouth of the Dwina; and, on the 14th, the *Hawke*, and *Conflict*, 8, screw, landed parties, destroyed several vessels,

[1] Promtd. Com., Sept. 29th, 1855.

and repulsed a body of troops near Dome Ness, at the mouth of the Gulf of Riga. On August 15th, the gunboats *Jackdaw,* and *Ruby,* with the boats of the *Pylades,* 21, screw, captured four craft under fire from Russian troops in the Bight of Kossoria; and on August 16th, the *Impérieuse,* 51, screw, *Centaur,* 6, paddle, and *Bulldog,* 6, paddle, had a long-range engagement with batteries and gunboats in the vicinity of Tolboukin lighthouse, off Cronstadt. In the Gulf of Bothnia, where Rear-Admiral Baynes commanded, the *Harrier,* 17, screw, *Tartar,* 20, screw, *Cuckoo,* 3, paddle, and French *d'Assas,* sent their boats on August 17th up towards Biorneborg, burnt seventeen vessels, and obtained the surrender of a small steamer, in spite of the presence in the neighbourhood of about 2000 troops. On September 2nd, the *Porcupine,* 3, paddle, with boats of the *Tartar,* made a reconnaissance of, and exchanged fire with, the batteries at Gamla Carleby ; and on the 6th, the boats of the *Bulldog* made prize of a couple of government schooners off Biörko. But in none of these, or similar affairs, of which there were many, were there any incidents calling for special description. On September 12th, a number of ships, including the *Nile,* 90, screw, and *Arrogant,* 47, screw, participated in the destruction of some transports under fire in the Bay of Virta Nemi. On September 18th, the boats of the *Nile* boarded and burnt some vessels near Hammeliski.

On September 12th, the *Hawke, Archer, Conflict,* and *Cruiser* received the peaceful surrender of Pernau, in the Gulf of Riga; and on the 20th, the *Gorgon,* 6, paddle, and her boats, exchanged shots with the batteries at the mouth of the Dwina, where, with the *Archer, Conflict,* and *Desperate,* the *Gorgon* was again slightly engaged on September 27th. Almost the last service of the Gulf of Riga division seems to have been rendered, in the mouth of the river Rua, on October 3rd, by the *Archer* and *Desperate,* with their boats. A few small vessels and some stores were destroyed. On September 30th, the *Conflict,* belonging to the same division, having quitted the gulf, destroyed two boats and dispersed a body of Cossacks, near Libau, on the west coast of Courland. In the meantime, at the mouth of the Gulf of Finland, on September 26th, and again on October 5th, the *Blenheim,* 60, screw, with the gunboats *Snap, Stork,* and *Lark,* was employed in the vicinity of Hango, and, besides rendering useless several telegraph stations, exchanged shots with the Eckness forts. Throughout the fleet, however, at that period, there was, as Sulivan says,[1] too much of a kind of unfeeling, senseless anxiety to fire at anything, for the mere sake of firing, for notoriety, or for bringing about a pretence of a fight, and a consequent opportunity for writing a dispatch ; and, although most of the above-mentioned affairs were of a very different character, it would be possible to cite others which, besides being of a paltry nature, were perfectly useless to the cause of the Allies, and were effective only in bringing the flag into disrepute.

The fleet had begun to return to England in the latter part of September. The gunboats, in four divisions, departed on October 8th ; and only a few ships of the line and large steamers remained. Not until the middle of November did the Commander-in-Chief himself make for Kiel. After he had gone home, the last half-dozen ships were withdrawn, almost one by one, as the advance of winter rendered the blockade unnecessary. The Hon. Richard Saunders Dundas was rewarded on February 4th, 1856, with a K.C.B. At the same time the C.B. was conferred upon several of the Baltic Captains, including George Ramsay, George Henry Seymour, George Greville Wellesley, James Willcox, and Henry Caldwell. Batches of Baltic promotions were dated September 22nd and 29th, 1855 ; but many most deserving officers were then passed over, and the omissions were to some extent remedied on October 31st, 1855, and January 5th, February 21st and 22nd, and May 10th, 1856, when numerous further advancements were made.

Early in 1856,[2] Rear-Admiral Sir Richard Saunders Dundas was re-appointed to the Baltic command ; but the resumption of active operations had by that time been rendered unnecessary by the progress which had been made during the winter in the direction of peace. The Treaty of Paris was not actually signed until March 30th, nor ratified until April 27th ; but, long ere even the earlier of those dates, it had become evident that the war was over. By the final arrangement it was stipulated that all conquests made and territories occupied during the hostilities should be evacuated as promptly as possible ; that the Sublime Porte should be " admitted to participate in the advantages of the public law and concert of Europe " ; that the independence and territorial integrity of the Ottoman Empire should be respected and guaranteed

---

[1] Sulivan, 353, 354.   [2] Feb. 18th.

by all the parties to the treaty; that the Sultan should not be interfered with in the government of any of his subjects, nor in the internal administration of his dominions; that the Black Sea should be neutralised, and its ports thrown open to commerce; that Russia and Turkey should neither establish nor maintain naval arsenals in the Black Sea; that the navigation of the Danube should be regulated by an international commission; that the Russian frontier in Bessarabia should be rectified; that the principalities of Moldavia and Wallachia should continue as before under the suzerainty of the Porte, but with additional liberties; that Servia should enjoy similar advantages; and that the Russo-Turkish frontier in Asia should be settled by a commission. By special conventions annexed to the treaty, it was declared that the Sultan would continue to exercise his ancient right to prohibit foreign ships of war from entering the Bosphorus and the Darda-nelles, and that he would not permit them so to enter, except for the service of the embassies and the Danube Commission, in time of peace; that Russia and the other contracting Powers would agree and adhere to that principle; that neither Russia[1] nor Turkey would maintain in the Black Sea more than six steam-vessels (not to exceed 55 metres in length, with a tonnage of 800), and four lighter steam or sailing vessels (of not more than 200 tons apiece); and that the Aland Islands should not be fortified.

A "declaration," made, perhaps somewhat needlessly, by the plenipotentiaries at Paris, and signed on behalf of Great Britain, France, Russia, Sardinia, Turkey, Austria, and Prussia,[2] set forth formally that, so far as those Powers are concerned:—

1. Privateering is, and remains, abolished.
2. The neutral flag covers enemy's goods, with the exception of contraband of war.
3. Neutral goods, with the exception of contraband of war, are not liable to capture under enemy's flag.
4. Blockades, in order to be binding, must be effective—that is to say, maintained by a force sufficient really to prevent access to the coast of the enemy.

No indemnity was demanded from Russia; no special privileges whatsoever were secured to Great Britain and France, which, for nearly two years, had poured forth blood and treasure like water;

---

[1] Russia tore up this Convention in 1870.
[2] This declaration was subsequently adhered to by several other Powers.

and, upon the whole, it may be said that never did the unsuccessful party to a great war escape more easily. But it must be recollected that the Allies, in spite of their immense efforts, had touched only a very little of the extreme outer fringe of the huge empire of the Tsar. Sebastopol had been reduced. Not even the Crimea, however, had been conquered ; and the heart of Russia, in spite of the levelling of Bomarsund, the wreckage of buildings at Sweaborg, and the burning of stores and capture of small craft in the Sea of Azof and elsewhere, was as whole and sound as it had been before the war. The result might have been very different, and better terms might have been exacted by the Allies, had the British fleet at the commencement of hostilities been in a more efficient condition than it was, and had younger men and reformed ideas guided its action. There was a time, early in the campaign, when Sebastopol might have been seized by a *coup de main* from seaward, probably without either much expenditure or much loss of life ; nor can it be doubted that if Great Britain, previous to 1854, had properly developed her screw navy, had availed herself of existing improvements in gunnery[1] and rifle-manufacture,[2] and had devoted proper attention to the advocacy, as early as 1842, by the French Captain Labrousse, of the value of armoured vessels, she would have been a much more formidable enemy to Russia than she actually proved herself. It must not be forgotten that, but for the false conservatism of her administrators, she might, even in 1854, have possessed a great fleet of fast screw ships with well-protected machinery, and of fast and heavily armed gunboats, rifled guns of large calibre, breech-loading small-arms, and floating batteries practically impervious to Russian projectiles, even at short range. With such material at her disposal, and with men younger and more enlightened than Napier and the Dundases to lead her fleets, it is possible, nay probable, that she might have taken Cronstadt, and even St. Petersburg, early in the war, and so, by her sudden and indubitable successes, have frightened Russia into speedy submission. Perhaps the most valuable lesson of the war of 1854–55 was the importance to a naval power of being able promptly to utilise the newest and most formidable inventions that have been produced by the ingenuity of man. The lesson, unfortunately, has not been thoroughly learnt by Great Britain, even to this day. The war, however, led directly

---

[1] Rifled heavy guns had been constructed and proved useful many years earlier.

[2] The needle-gun had been the weapon of the Prussian Army since 1848.

or indirectly to many naval reforms, including the introduction of continuous service for seamen, the building of ironclads, and the development of the power of the gun.

On St. George's Day, April 23rd, 1856, in honour of the conclusion of peace, and in recognition of the work of the Navy, Queen Victoria, in the *Victoria and Albert*, reviewed at Spithead a large fleet, most of which had recently served either in the Baltic or in the Black Sea, and all of which was ready for a fresh campaign, if one had been deemed necessary. Her Majesty, in addition to her personal suite, had with her in the yacht Admiral Sir William Parker (2), Bart., G.C.B., principal A.D.C., Rear-Admiral John, Marquess Townshend, A.D.C., Rear-Admiral Sir Edmund Lyons, G.C.B., Rear-Admiral Jurien de La Gravière, representing the French Navy, and Mr. Ralph Bernal Osborne, M.P., Secretary of the Admiralty. The vessels reviewed were :—

No.		Guns.	H.P.N.
24	Ships of the line	2,029	9,650
19	Screw frigates and corvettes . .	407	5,030
18	Paddle-vessels	127	6,130
4	Armoured floating batteries . .	56	600
120	Gun-vessels and gunboats . .	274	8,700
1	Sailing frigate	44	—
2	Ammunition ships	—	—
1	Hospital ship	6	—
1	Floating factory	3	140
50	Mortar vessels and mortar floats .	50	—
240		2,996	30,250

The command afloat was held by Vice-Admiral Sir George Francis Seymour, K.C.B., Commander-in-Chief at Portsmouth, who, in the *Royal George*, 102, led the fleet past the Queen's yacht, which was anchored near the Nab. A number of French officers were entertained on board the paddle-yacht *Black Eagle*. The Peers were in the *Transit*, screw, Commander Charles Richardson Johnson; the Commons in the *Perseverance*, 2, screw, Commander John Wallace Douglas McDonald. After the review there was a sham fight, and at night the fleet was illuminated.

SIR JOHN EDMUND COMMERELL, V.C., G.C.B., ADMIRAL OF THE FLEET.

APPENDIX TO CHAPTER XLIV.

LIST OF H.M. SHIPS WRECKED, FOUNDERED, BURNT, TAKEN OR DESTROYED, 1816–1856.

(Steamers are indicated as such.)

Year.	Date.	H.M. Ship.	Guns.	Commander. [* Lost his life on the occasion.]	Remarks.
1816	Feb. 20	*Phœnix*	42	Capt. Chas. John Austen (1).	Wrecked near Smyrna.
1816	Sept. 21	*Whiting*, sch. . .	14	Lieut. Jno. Jackson (3).	Wrecked near Padstow.
1816	Nov. 4	*Comus*	32	Capt. Jas. Jno. Gordon Bremer, C.B.	Wrecked off Cape Pine, Newfoundland.
1816	,, 5	*Briseis*	10	,, George Domett.	Wrecked near Pt. Pedras, Cuba.
1816	,, 11	*Tay*	20	,, Saml. Roberts, C.B.	Wrecked in G. of Mexico.
1816	,, 16	*Bermuda* . . .	10	Com. Jno. Pakenham (2).	Wrecked near Tampico Bar.
1817	Jan. 21	*Jasper*	10	,, Thomas Carew (1).	Wrecked under Mt. Batten : 72 lost.
1817	,, 21	*Telegraph*, sch.. .	12	Lieut. Jno. Little (2).	Wrecked under Mt. Batten.
1817	Feb. 18	*Alceste*	46	Capt. Murray Maxwell, C.B.	Wrecked off Pulo Leat.
1817	Oct. 2	*Julia*	16	Com. Jenkin Jones.	Wrecked off Tristan d'Acunha : 55 lost.
1817	Dec. 8	*Martin*	18	,, Andrew Mitchell (2).	Wrecked off W. of Ireland.
1818	..	*Shark*, rec. ship .	..	Lieut. Charles Newton Hunter (actg. Com.)	Wrecked at Jamaica.
1819	June 1	*Erne*	20	Com. Timothy Scriven, C.B.	Wrecked at the C. de Verde Islands.
1819	Dec. 5	*Vigilant*, rev. cruis.	14	Lieut. Hy. Nazer.	Wrecked near Torbay.
1820	July 6	*Carron*	20	Com. John Furneaux.	Wrecked near Puri, India.
1820	Oct.	*Hardwicke*, rev. cruis.	12	Lieut. Saml. Mottley.	Wrecked in Dundrum Bay.
1821	Jan.	*Sprightly*, rev. cut.	6	..	Wrecked off Portland.
1821	Mar.	*Bermuda*, sch.. .	..	..	Foundered between Halifax and Bermuda : all lost.
1822	Apr. 21	*Confiance* . . .	18	Com. William Thomas Morgan.*	Wrecked off Mizen Head : all lost.
1822	June 20	*Drake*	10	,, Charles Adolphus Baker.*	Wrecked off Newfoundland : many lost.
1822	Dec. 14	*Racehorse* . . .	18	,, Wm. Benj. Suckling.	Wrecked on Langness, I. of Man.
1823	Dec. 12	*Arab*	18	,, Wm. Holmes (2).*	Wrecked off Belmullet, W. of Ireland : all lost.
1824	Jan. 25	*Columbine* . . .	18	,, Hon. Chas. Abbot.	Wrecked off I. of Sapienza.
1824	Feb. 23	*Delight*	10	,, Robt. Hay.*	Wrecked in a cyclone, Mauritius : all lost.
1824	Mar. 3	*Dwarf*, cut.. . .	10	Lieut. Nicholas Gould.	Wrecked on the pier, Kingstown.
1825	Aug. 1	*Fury*, disc. ship .	4	Com. Henry Parkyns Hoppner.	Bilged in Regent's Inlet, Arctic.
1825	Nov. 27	*Partridge* . . .	10	..	Stranded off the Texel.
1826	Jan. 9	*Algerine*	10	Com. Charles Wemyss (2).*	Capsized in a squall, Mediterranean : all lost.
1826	..	*Martin*	20	..	Supposed foundered off the Cape.
1826	Aug. 27	*Magpie*, sch. . .	5	..	Wrecked in Colorados Road, Cuba : nearly all lost.
1827	Jan. 14	*Nimrod*	18	Com. Saml. Sparshott.	Bilged in Holyhead Bay. (Got off and sold.)
1827	Feb. ,18	*Diamond* . . .	46	(In ordinary).	Accidentally burnt at Portsmouth.
1827	June 6	*Cynthia*, packet .	..	Lieut. John White (2).	Wrecked off Barbados.
1827	Nov.	*Hearty*, packet .	10	..	Supposed burnt at sea : all lost.
1827	..	*Redwing* . . .	18	Com. Douglas Chas. Clavering.*	Supposed foundered, W. Afr. station : all lost.
1828	Jan. 31	*Cambrian* . . .	48	Capt. Gawen Wm. Hamilton, C.B.	Wrecked off Grabusa, Mediterranean.

Year.	Date.	H.M. Ship.	Guns.	Commander. [* Lost his life on the occasion.]	Remarks.
1828	Apr. 14	*Acorn*	18	Com. Edward Gordon.*	Wrecked on Halifax station : all lost.
1828	„ 14	*Contest*, g. b. . .	12	Lieut. Edward Plaggenborg.*	Wrecked on Halifax station : all lost.
1828	May 15	*Parthian* . . .	10	Com. Hon. Geo. Fredk. Hotham.	Wrecked near Marabout Isld., Egypt.
1828	„. 17	*Union*, sch.. . . .	4	Lieut. Chas. Madden.	Wrecked off Rose Isld., W. Indies.
1828	Oct. 11	*Jasper*	10	Com. Leonard Chas. Rooke.	Wrecked off Sta. Maura.
1828	..	*Redpole*, packet .	10	..	Sunk in action with *Congress*, a pirate, off C. Frio.
1828	Dec. 18	*Kangaroo*, surv. ves.	..	Master Anth. de Mayne.	Wrecked on Jamaica station.
1828	„	*Ariel*, packet . .	6	..	Supposed lost near Sable Island.
1829	Feb. 17	*Nightingale*, sch. .	..	Lieut. Geo. Wood.	Wrecked on the Shingles.
1829	Apr. 3	*Myrtle*, packet . .	6	..	Wrecked off Nova Scotia.
1829	Nov. 29	*Success* . . .	28	..	Wrecked in Cockburn Sound.
1830	Mar. 10	*Wolf*	18	Com. Robt. Russell (3).	Wrecked off I. of Wight.
1830	Dec. 5	*Thetis*	46	Capt. Saml. Burgess.	Wrecked off Cape Frio.
1831	May	*Monkey*, sch. . .	3	..	Wrecked on Tampico Bar.
1832	..	*Recruit*, g. b. . .	10	Lieut. Thomas Hodges.*	Supposed foundered off Bermuda : all lost.
1833	Feb.	*Calypso*, packet .	6	„ Richard Peyton.*	Foundered between Halifax and England : all lost
1833	Dec.	*Thais*, packet . .	..		Supposed foundered in Atlantic : all lost.
1834	Aug. 27	*Chameleon*, rev. cut.	..	„ John Pratten.*	Run down off Dover by H.M.S. *Castor*.
1834	Dec. 4	*Nimble*, sch. . .	5	„ Charles Bolton.	Wrecked in Old Bahama Channel.
1835	Feb. 27	*Firefly*, sch. . .	3	„ Jas. Julius McDonnell.	Wrecked off British Honduras.
1835	Mar. 11	*Jackdaw*, surv. sch.	4	„ Edward Barnett.	Wrecked off Old Providence, Honduras.
1835	„ 27	*Hound*, rev. cut. .	..	„ Jno. Hasler Helby.	Wrecked in Weymouth Bay.
1835	May 19	*Challenger* . . .	28	Capt. Michael Seymour (2).	Wrecked on coast of Chile.
1836	Feb. 5	*Pike*, sch. . . .	12	Lieut. Arthur Brooking.	Wrecked on Pelican Reef, Jamaica.
1838	Jan.	*Briseis*, packet. .	6	„ John Downey.*	Supposed foundered in Atlantic : all lost.
1838	Mar. 6	*Pincher*, sch. . .	5	„ Thomas Hope (1).*	Capsized off the Owers : all lost.
1838	Apr. 12	*Rapid*	10	„ Hon. Graham Hay St. V. de Ros Kinnaird.*	Wrecked off Crete, Mediterranean.
1839	..	*Diligence*, rev. cut.	..		Wrecked on coast of Ireland : 46 lost.
1839	Nov. 28	*Tribune*	24	Capt. Chas. Hamlyn Williams.	Wrecked near Tarragona.
1840	July 28	*Buffalo*, st. ship. .		Master James Wood.	Wrecked off New Zealand.
1840	Oct.	*Talavera* . . .	72	(In Ordinary).	Accidentally burnt at Plymouth.
1840	„	*Imogene* . . .	26	(In Ordinary).	Accidentally burnt at Plymouth.
1840	Nov. 13	*Fairy*, surv. ves. .	10	Capt. Wm. Hewett.*	Wrecked off coast of Suffolk : all lost.
1840	„ 28	*Spey*, packet . .	..	Lieut Robt. Bastard James.	Wrecked on Racoon Key.
1840	Dec. 2	*Zebra*	16	Com. Robt. Fan-hawe Stopford.	Wrecked off Mt. Carmel, Levant.
1841	June	*Skipjack*, sch. . .	5	Lieut. Aug. Chas. May.	Wrecked on the Caymans.
1842	..	*Victor*	16	Com. Chas. Cooke Otway.*	Supposed foundered between Vera Cruz and Halifax : all lost.
1842	Sept. 10	*Spitfire*, steamer .	2	Lieut. Hay Erskine Shipley Winthrop.	Wrecked on Half Moon Key, Honduras.
1843	Mar. 4	*Megœra*, steamer .	2	„ Geo. Oldmixon.	Wrecked on Bare Bush Key.
1843	July 24	*Lizard*, steamer .	3	„ Chas. Jas. Postle.	Run down by French warship *Véloce*.
1845	Apr. 25	*Skylark*, packet .	4	„ Geo. Morris.	Wrecked on Kimmeridge Ledge.
1846	Mar. 11	*Osprey*	12	Com. Fredk. Patten.	Wrecked off False Hokianga, New Zealand.
1847	Feb. 3	*Thunderbolt*, steam sloop	6	„ Alexander Boyle.	Wrecked on Cape Recife, S. Africa.
1847	Aug. 29	*Snake*	16	„ Thos. Bourmaster Brown.	Wrecked in Mozambique Channel.
1847	Dec. 20	*Avenger*, steam frigate	6	Capt. Chas. Geo. Elers Napier.*	Wrecked on Sorelle Rocks, Medterranean : 246 lost.
1848	„ 21	*Mutine*	12	Com. John Jervis Palmer.	Wrecked in the Adriatic.
1848	..	*Erebus*, screw disc. ves.	3	Capt. Sir John Franklin, Kt. (d. 1847). „ James Fitzjames (d. 1848).	Abandoned in the Arctic Ice.
1848	..	*Terror*, screw disc. ves.	4	„ Francis Rawdon Moira Crozier (d. 1848).	Abandoned in the Arctic Ice.
1850	Oct. 9	*Adelaide*, tender .	..	Lieut. Jno. Lyons Macleod.	Wrecked on Banana Isld., W. Africa.
1850	Nov. 22	*Flamer*, steam g. v.	3.	Com. Jas. Aldworth St. Leger.	Wrecked on coast of Africa.
1851	May 31	*Reynard*, steam g. v.	9	„ Peter Cracroft.	Wrecked on Pratas Shoal, China Seas.
1852	Feb. 27	*Birkenhead*, steam tr. s.	..	Master Robert Salmond.*	Wrecked off Pt. Danger, S. Africa : 436 lost.
1852	..	*Investigator*, surv. ves.	3	Com. Robt. Jno. Le Mesurier McClure.	Abandoned in the Arctic Ice.

Year.	Date.	H M. Ship.	Guns.	Commander. [* Lost his life on the occasion.]	Remarks.
1854	May	*Jasper*, steam g. v.	..	Lieut. Chas. Gibbs Crawley.	Burnt in the Channel.
1854	..	*Assistance* . . .	2	Capt. Sir Edward Belcher, C.B.	Abandoned in the Arctic Ice.
1854	..	*Pioneer*, screw tender.	2	Com. Sherard Osborn.	Abandoned in the Arctic Ice.
1854	..	*Resolute*	2	Capt. Henry Kellett.	Abandoned in the Arctic Ice. Recovd. 1856.
1854	..	*Intrepid*, screw tender.	2	Com. Fras. Leop. McClintock.	Abandoned in the Arctic Ice.
1854	May 12	*Tiger*, steam frigate	16	Capt. Henry Wells Giffard.*	Grounded under batteries near Odessa: taken and sunk.
1855	July	*Jasper*, steam g. v.	2	Lieut. Joseph Saml. Hudson.	Wrecked in the Sea of Azof. Taken by Russians.
1855	..	*Bermuda*, sch. . .	3	Lieut. Wm. Cashman.	Wrecked in the W. Indies.
1855	Aug. 11	*Wolverine* . . .	12	Com. John Corbett.	Wrecked on Courtown Bank.
1856	..	*Nerbudda* . . .	12	Com. Henry Ashburton Kerr*	Supposed foundered on Cape Station about July 10th: all lost.
1856	Jan. 29	*Polyphemus*, steamer	5	..	Wrecked on coast of Jutland.

NOTE.—Particulars of the finding of the Court of Inquiry, or of the Court Martial, in most of the above cases will be found in the Parliamentary Returns, Nos. 176, and 399, of 1891 (Navy: Ships Lost otherwise than in Action). The Returns in question are, however, incomplete, and, in several cases, inaccurate, and were the subject of a correspondence between myself and Lord George Hamilton, then First Lord.

THE BALTIC MEDAL.

CHAPTER XLV.

VOYAGES AND DISCOVERIES, 1816–56.

SIR CLEMENTS R. MARKHAM, K.C.B., F.R.S.

William Scoresby—Buchan's voyage—John Ross in Baffin's Bay—Parry's first voyage
—Parry's second voyage—Parry's third voyage—F. W. Beechey—Franklin's over-
land expedition—Patriotism of Felix Booth—Discoveries of John, and J. C. Ross—
Back's search for the Rosses—Back's voyage—Scientific results of Arctic work—
Admiralty surveys—W. F. Owen—Clapperton's travels—The Niger expedition—
P. P. King—Robert FitzRoy—Basil Hall—R. Collinson—H. Kellett—Sir Edward
Belcher—F. P. Blackwood—Owen Stanley—Henry Raper—Sir Francis Beaufort
—J. C. Ross, and Crozier in the Antarctic—Franklin's last voyage—Kellett in the
Pacific—The long search for Franklin—The younger Arctic voyagers—Surveyors
in war time.

ARCTIC MEDAL.

Ribbon : white.

TWO years after
the peace,
the well-known
whaling master,
William Scoresby,
returned from the
Arctic regions
with the intelli-
gence that so open
a season had never
been known. It
was hoped that
the next season would find the Arctic seas equally clear of ice, and
Barrow made such good use of the report that it was resolved to
despatch two expeditions to the north in 1818, one to the Spitzbergen seas, and the other up Davis Strait. Thus was the era of
naval Arctic exploration happily commenced with some prospect of
continuity. Four whalers were hired, the *Dorothea*, and *Trent* for
Spitzbergen, the *Isabella*, and *Alexander* for Davis Strait. The

command of the Spitzbergen expedition was entrusted to Commander David Buchan,[1] who had previously been employed on the exploration of the interior of Newfoundland. He had Mr. Arthur Morell as his first Lieutenant. The *Trent* was commanded by Lieutenant John Franklin,[2] who had already seen hard surveying service with Flinders. Frederick William Beechey, one of Mediterranean Smyth's pupils, was his second in command, and George Back, who was destined, like Franklin and Beechey, to become a renowned Arctic explorer, was a Mate on board the vessel. It turned out to be a bad year, and Buchan was not so successful as Phipps in pushing northward. Bad weather and much danger from the ice were encountered in very unseaworthy vessels, but priceless experience of Arctic navigation was acquired.[3]

The voyage up Davis Strait was more important. The leader of this expedition was Captain John Ross,[4] an officer who had seen much service in the Baltic with Saumarez. His more distinguished nephew, James Clark Ross,[5] went with him as a Midshipman in the *Isabella.* The *Alexander* was commanded by Lieutenant William Edward Parry,[6] under whom was Lieutenant Henry Parkyns Hoppner. The two vessels, *Isabella,* and *Alexander,* passed north through Davis Strait, and sailed round Baffin's Bay, the existence of which had long been doubted. Ross thus rehabilitated the fame of the great Elizabethan navigator. The result of Ross's first voyage[7] was very important. The whalers immediately followed him into the north water of Baffin's Bay, and thus a lucrative trade was established, which continued to flourish for many years. Ross also took the deepest sounding, and brought

---

[1] Com. Ap. 13th, 1816; Capt. June 12th, 1823.—W. L. C.

[2] John Franklin (1), born 1786; entered Navy, 1800; Lieut. Feb. 11th, 1808; Com. Jan. 1st, 1821; Capt. Nov. 20th, 1822; Kt. 1829; K.C.H. 1836; took command of *Erebus* for Arctic discovery, 1845; perished in the ice, June 11th, 1847. He was a F.R.S., and a D.C.L. (Oxon.)—W. L. C.

[3] *See* 'A Voyage of Disc. towards the N. Pole,' by Capt. F. W. Beechey, 1843.—W. L. C.

[4] Born, 1777; entered Navy, 1786; Lieut. Mar. 13th, 1805; Com. Feb. 1st, 1812; Capt. Dec. 7th, 1818; died a Kt., C.B., and retired r.-adm., in 1856.—W. L. C.

[5] Born, 1800; entered Navy, 1812; Lieut. Dec. 26th, 1822; Com. Nov. 8th, 1827; Capt. Oct. 28th, 1834; died a Kt. and retired r.-adm. in 1862.—W. L. C.

[6] William Edward Parry, born 1790; entered Navy, 1803; Lieut. Jan. 6th, 1810; Com. Nov. 4th, 1820; Capt. Nov. 8th, 1821; Actg. Hydrographer, Dec. 1st, 1823; Hydrographer, Nov. 22nd, 1825, to Nov. 10th, 1826, and Nov. 2nd, 1827, to May 13th, 1829; Kt. 1829; Contr. of Steam Dept. of Navy, 1837 to 1846; F.R.S., LL.D., (Cantab.); R.-Adm. July 30th, 1852; died July 8th, 1855.—W. L. C.

[7] *See* 'A Voyage of Discovery,' 2 vols., 1819.—W. L. C.

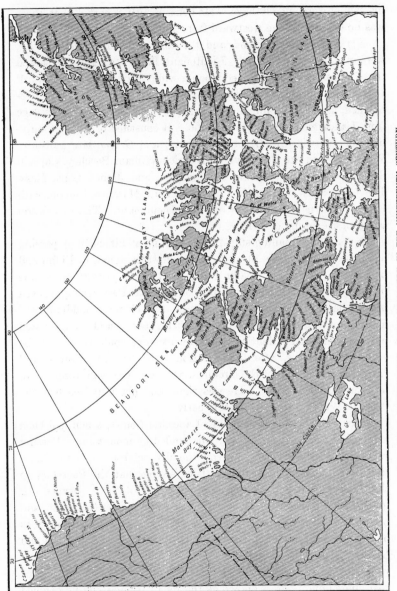

SKETCH MAP ILLUSTRATING ARCTIC DISCOVERY IN THE NINETEENTH CENTURY.

up organisms from the greatest depth, then known. But he conceived that Smith, Jones, and Lancaster Sounds, discovered and
named by Baffin at the head of the bay, or rather sea, which bears

his name, were merely bays. He consequently reported that there was no opening to the westward from Baffin's Bay.

His second in command, and the other officers of the *Isabella*, were of a different opinion. Lieutenant Parry strongly represented that Lancaster Sound opened upon a wide strait leading westward. It was, therefore, resolved that a second expedition should be despatched, under the command of Parry, to endeavour to find a passage from Lancaster Sound to the Pacific. It consisted of two strongly-built old vessels, the *Hecla*, late bomb, and *Griper*, late gun-brig. With Parry, in the *Hecla*, were Frederick William Beechey, Captain Sabine, R.A., for magnetic observations, and James Clark Ross. The *Griper* was commanded by Lieutenant Matthew Liddon, with Henry Parkyns Hoppner as his first Lieutenant. The expedition sailed in the spring of 1819.

In the days of sailing ships, there was great difficulty in passing northwards from Davis Strait to the open water, found by Baffin and by Ross, in the head of Baffin's Bay. The safe passage which was made by sticking to the land floe of Melville Bay usually caused much delay ; while an attempt to pass through the " middle pack " drifting south entailed the danger of being beset, and being drifted out again into the Atlantic. Such an attempt could very rarely be successful. Parry, after consultation with his ice masters, and careful consideration of the circumstances of the season, resolved to take the " middle pack." He was right, and his ships reached the " North Water " unprecedentedly early.

Parry sailed triumphantly into Lancaster Sound, which had been supposed by Ross to form a bay surrounded by mountains. Passing westward, he named after Barrow the channel leading in the direction which he was instructed to take, seeing that the Secretary to the Admiralty had been the chief promoter of these voyages. A great opening leading north was named Wellington Channel, and one to the south was called after the Prince Regent. Drifting floes of ice were seen, but they offered slight obstruction to the *Hecla* and *Griper*. Parry discovered islands on the northern side of his route, which he named the North Georgian group, but which have since been more appropriately known as the Parry Islands, and he reached the far western longitude of 110°. The sagacious leader saw, from the nature of the ice, that no further progress was possible, and he proceeded to establish his ships in the safe quarters of " Winter Harbour," in Melville Island.

The first time that disciplined men-of-war passed a winter in the Arctic regions is memorable for several reasons. It tested the qualities of officers and men amid very trying circumstances, and proved the adaptability of British seamen to novel and unaccustomed service. While discipline was necessarily much relaxed, no advantage was taken of that fact; and officers and men worked harmoniously together to maintain and preserve health and spirits by joining in the occupations and amusements devised by their leader. Parry's first voyage, both as regards the experience acquired during a difficult and anxious navigation, and the qualities brought out in the still more trying period of the winter, showed the immense value of such service as a training ground for officers and men.

The return of Parry's expedition in the autumn made a deep impression on the nation. The despatch of such voyages became a settled policy for fully fifteen years. The great advantages to the Navy were then clearly understood, and the most captious acknowledged that the slight outlay which secured such results was well spent.

The objects of the Arctic voyages of the nineteenth century were not the discovery of routes for commerce, but the attainment of valuable scientific results. Parry had ascertained that there could be no passage to the westward of Melville Island, owing to the impenetrable character of the polar pack. He, therefore, turned his attention in his second voyage, 1821–23, to the completion of work commenced in the eighteenth century to the north of Hudson's Bay. His ships were the *Fury* and *Hecla*, both strongly-built old bomb vessels, the former being his own ship, and the latter being under the command of the accomplished George Francis Lyon,[1] who had just returned from an African exploring journey. Parry had with him several veterans of the first voyage— Lieutenants Henry Parkyns Hoppner, and Joseph Nias; Alexander Fisher (Surgeon), and James Clark Ross; and some, such as Joseph Sherer, Francis Rawdon Moira Crozier, and Edward Joseph Bird, who then made their first acquaintance with Arctic ice, but who remained true to that fascinating branch of naval service.

In his second voyage, Parry performed the work very thoroughly, as he always did. His object was to discover an outlet leading westward, to the north of Hudson's Bay; and he succeeded, having remained out for two winters, 1821 to 1823. He traced out "Hecla

---

[1] Com. Jan. 3rd, 1821; Capt. Nov. 13th, 1823; died Oct. 1832.—W. L. C.

and Fury Strait," which opened on a previously unknown sea, and he discovered Melville Peninsula, an important feature of the north coast of America.[1] In 1824, the year after Parry's return, Lyon was sent, in the *Griper*, to attempt a voyage to Repulse Bay, but the ice was impenetrable, and he failed.

A combined effort was organised, in 1824, to complete the

REAR-ADMIRAL SIR WILLIAM EDWARD PARRY, KT., D.C.L., F.R.S.

(From the picture by Chas. Scottowe.)

[By permission of the Lords of the Admiralty.]

discovery of the northern coast of America. Parry was to make the attempt to reach the sea to the westward of Hecla and Fury Strait by way of Barrow's Strait and Prince Regent's Inlet. He commissioned the *Hecla*, while his old and tried companion Hoppner commanded the *Fury*. Many of their officers afterwards became well known in the service. There were Henry Foster,[2] whose

---

[1] 'Journal of a Second Voyage,' etc. London, 1824.—W. L. C.

[2] Henry Foster, born 1798; Com. Nov. 30th, 1827; died Feb. 3rd, 1831.

scientific attainments won him honour from the Royal Society, James Clark Ross, the leader of the famous Antarctic voyage, F. R. M. Crozier and E. J. Bird, his faithful companions in that enterprise, Joseph Sherer, so famous as the capturer of slavers, Horatio Thomas Austin, who did admirable service himself as an Arctic leader—two ships manned by men of high promise. At the same time the *Blossom* was commissioned by Commander Frederick William Beechey, whose record was a very distinguished one. As a surveyor he was the pupil of Mediterranean Smyth. He had been first Lieutenant of the *Trent* with Franklin, and of the *Hecla* in Parry's first voyage; and had done good service in the Tripoli expedition of 1822, when he explored Cyrenaica and the Greater Syrtis.[1] The *Blossom's* work included an examination of the numerous islands east of Tahiti, and an attempt to meet Parry's expedition by way of Bering Strait.

Franklin, after his command of the *Trent*, had been employed from 1819 to 1822 on a land journey to trace down the great rivers, Mackenzie and Coppermine, to the Arctic Sea, and to explore its shores. He had been accompanied by a naval Surgeon, Dr. John Richardson (2), and by two Midshipmen, Hood and George Back. The latter had served with him in the *Trent*. The story of the fearful hardships and sufferings endured by these intrepid officers is one of the most absorbing in naval annals.[2] Franklin had returned after a three years' absence, but he was allowed very little rest. His second journey to the Polar Sea was undertaken with the object of co-operating with the expeditions of Parry and Beechey.

Parry found the season in Baffin's Bay exceptionally unfavourable. He was obliged to winter at Port Bowen, on the eastern shore of Prince Regent's Inlet, where most valuable observations were taken. But, soon after the two vessels got out of winter quarters in 1825, the *Fury* was driven on shore by the ice, on the western coast, and became a wreck. Her provisions were landed on what has ever since been known as Fury Beach, and the two crews returned home in the *Hecla*. The *Blossom* discovered the north coast of America from Icy Cape, the furthest point of Captain Cook, to Cape Barrow, a distance of 126 miles. Her commission extended

---

[1] *See* 'Proceedings of the Exped. to explore the N. Coast of Africa,' by Beechey. —W. L. C.

[2] *See* Franklin's ' Narr. of a Journey to the Shores of the Polar Sea.'—W. L. C.

from 1825 to 1828, during which time Captain Beechey, besides his Arctic discovery, did most valuable surveying work in the Pacific. Meanwhile, Franklin, with his well-tried companion George Back, reached the Polar Sea by Mackenzie River, and traced the coast of the continent westward as far as Cape Turnagain. A very short gap was left between Franklin's and Beechey's farthest; and this was subsequently filled up by Dease, and Simpson, of the Hudson's Bay Company's service.

While Sir Edward Parry was employed on his second and third voyages he held the post of Hydrographer; that excellent draughtsman Michael Walker conducting the work of the department during the absence of his chief on active service. The Admiralty consented to a third period of absence, when the indefatigable explorer submitted a plan for attempting to reach the Pole from Spitzbergen, by means of two boats to be dragged over the ice on runners, while a ship remained in a harbour on the north coast of Spitzbergen as a base for their operations.

Sir Edward Parry sailed on this adventurous enterprise on board the *Hecla* in the summer of 1827, accompanied by his old Arctic comrades Foster, Crozier, Ross, and Bird. The ship was safely moored in Hecla Cove in charge of Lieutenant Foster; and Parry, with his other officers, landed the two boats on the ice of the Polar pack, and began his northward journey. With much difficulty he reached a latitude of 82° 45' N., which, for the next fifty years, continued to be the most northern point ever attained by man. But the ice-floes were drifting southward as fast as the explorers, with all their efforts, could make their way northwards. At last the hopeless struggle was abandoned, and the expedition returned home.[1] Parry retained the appointment of Hydrographer until 1829, when he was succeeded by Captain (afterwards Sir) Francis Beaufort.

During those ten years of Parry's brilliant Arctic service, Captain John Ross had been brooding over his fatal blunder in converting Lancaster Sound into a bay—a blunder which had ruined his prospects at the Admiralty. At last he persuaded a wealthy distiller named Felix Booth[2] to incur the expense of fitting out a small expedition to enable him to rehabilitate his reputation as an Arctic explorer. A small steam vessel called the *Victory* was equipped, and Captain Ross sailed for Baffin's Bay in the spring of 1829. He was

[1] 'Narr. of an Attempt to Reach the North Pole,' etc., 1828.—W. L. C.
[2] Later a baronet.

so fortunate as to secure the services, as second in command, of his nephew, James Clark Ross, whose ice experience was equalled by that of Parry alone. The second officer was old Abernethy, a very able but hard-drinking naval quartermaster, who had also served with Parry.

With mingled feelings of regret and satisfaction Captain John

REAR-ADMIRAL SIR FRANCIS BEAUFORT, K.C.B., D.C.L., F.R.S., HYDROGRAPHER
1829–1855.

(From the picture by Stephen Pearce.)

[By permission of the Lords of the Admiralty.]

Ross must have passed the open portals of Lancaster Sound which he had so confidently closed in 1818. The *Victory* was navigated down Prince Regent's Inlet for a long distance, into a large gulf with a previously undiscovered coastline to the west. The new land received the name of Boothia Felix, and the adjoining sea was called the Gulf of Boothia. The *Victory* was secured in winter quarters in Felix Harbour, the neighbourhood of which the ice never again

2 L 2

allowed her to leave. James Clark Ross made several important land journeys, discovering Boothia Isthmus, the north coast of King William Island as far as Cape Felix, and the western shore of Boothia northwards to a point in 72° N. where he found the dip of the needle to be nearly 90°. He had discovered the North Magnetic Pole.

The *Victory* had been three years fast locked in her winter quarters, and there was no prospect of her extrication from the ice. The provisions were nearly exhausted; and in the summer of 1832 the Rosses and their crew retreated northwards in the boats to Fury Beach. It was a forlorn hope. They lived through the winter on the *Fury's* provisions, but it was doubtful whether any of them would survive to return to England. A long letter from Captain Ross to Admiral Sir Thomas Byam Martin is still in existence, describing the results of the voyage, but expressing but slight hope of being rescued. In 1833 the little party of desperate men left Fury Beach in its boats, and was eventually picked up by a whaler in Barrow's Strait, and brought home safely.[1]

Great anxiety had been felt respecting the fate of the missing explorers; and Commander George Back, accompanied by Dr. King, led a search expedition down the Great Fish or Back River, the course of which he discovered to its mouth in the Polar Sea. Dr. King left a *cache* of provisions on Montreal Island, at the river's mouth, a place which afterwards became famous as the last point reached by the survivors of the Franklin expedition.[2]

The last voyage during what may be considered as the first period of modern Arctic discovery was made under the command of Captain George Back, and in compliance with the representations of the Royal Geographical Society. The object was to attain the position which Captain Lyon had vainly attempted to reach, namely, Repulse Bay, by sea. Back also was doomed to failure. He commissioned the *Terror*[3] in 1836, and secured a set of officers of exceptional ability, several of whom succeeded in winning naval laurels during their subsequent careers. The first Lieutenant, William Smyth,[4] who had served with Beechey in the *Blossom*, was the future

[1] *See* John Ross's ' Narr. of a Second Voyage in Search of a N.W. Passage,' 1835. —W. L. C.

[2] *See* Back's ' Narr. of the Arctic Land Expedition.'—W. L. C.

[3] Back had been posted on Sept. 30th, 1835.—W. L. C.

[4] Wm. Smyth was made a Com. Nov. 15th, 1837, and a Captain Dec. 25th, 1843.— W. L. C.

explorer of the Amazons, and a most accomplished draughtsman. In the *Terror*, too, were Lieutenant Owen Stanley, the well-known surveyor of Torres Strait; Archibald McMurdo, of Antarctic fame; Midshipman Graham Gore, who was afterwards among the most able of Franklin's lost heroes; and Robert John Le Mesurier McClure, the future discoverer of a north-west passage. The voyage of the *Terror* was one of exceptional hardship and suffering. Beset by the ice off Southampton Island, Back and his gallant companions were forced to winter in the drifting pack. During the winter the ice broke up, the ship was nipped and crushed between the contending floes, and more than once the destruction of all on board seemed imminent. The darkness of an Arctic night added to the horrors of their position. The *Terror* was in a sinking state when she crossed the Atlantic, and it was necessary, on reaching the Irish coast, to run her on shore in Lough Swilly, to prevent her from going down.[1]

Arctic service is arduous and difficult, but it offers admirable opportunities for gaining habits of forming quick and right decisions, and for cultivating presence of mind, and all the qualities that are needed for success in war. This is its most useful and important side. Next in value are its scientific results. Captain Sabine, R.A., accompanied the first voyages of Ross and Parry to conduct magnetic observations; and afterwards the *Griper* was commissioned by Commander Douglas Charles Clavering to take him to Spitzbergen and the east coast of Greenland to swing the seconds pendulum. It was then that the Pendulum Islands were discovered. James Clark Ross discovered the North Magnetic Pole; and Henry Foster received the Copley medal from the Royal Society for his observations for terrestrial magnetism, refraction, and velocity of sound at Port Bowen. Equally valuable results were derived from the diligently conducted investigations relating to meteorology, anthropology, biology, and botany. Geology was then in its infancy. Nor must the practical and commercial results of Arctic naval enterprise be forgotten. The whale fishery was confined to Davis Strait until Ross, in 1818, passed through Melville Bay and showed the way into the "North Water." The consequence of his voyage was that the whalers followed him, and a most lucrative fishery was established, which flourished for more than half a century. In the same way

---

[1] 'Narr. of an Exped. in H.M.S. *Terror*,' etc. Back was given the Gold Medal of the R.G.S. in 1837, and knighted in 1839.—W. L. C.

Parry's third voyage was the direct cause of the establishment of a whale fishery up Prince Regent's Inlet. Two young Lieutenants, Joseph Sherer, and James Clark Ross, were the first to kill a payable whale in that remote and ice-encumbered sea. They led the way.

The energy and public spirit at the Admiralty, which were so remarkable with regard to Arctic enterprise while Sir John Barrow's influence prevailed, was not wanting with reference to the surveying operations of our Navy, during the same period, in other parts of the world.

In August, 1821, Captain William Fitzwilliam Owen commissioned the *Leven*, 24, for the survey of the coasts of Africa. He had previously seen much service in the East Indies, and had been a prisoner at Mauritius for two years. The *Leven* had a tender called the *Barracouta*, commanded by Commander William Cutfield; and in 1822 these two vessels executed a survey of Table Bay. Captain Owen and his officers and men were entering upon most arduous work in a deadly climate, far more dangerous to life and health than service in the Arctic regions.

Departing to Delagoa Bay, the men, serving up the rivers in open boats, died in great numbers. The ships were decimated; and among the victims was Cutfield, who was succeeded by Commander Alexander Thomas Emeric Vidal, with Lieutenant Thomas Boteler as his assistant. The work was resolutely continued along the Mozambique coast, in 1823, by Sofala and Quillimane to Zanzibar and Mombasa, and was followed by the survey of the Seychelles, and Tamatave. As giving an idea of the desperate character of this service, more desperate than a hard-fought campaign, it is recorded that two-thirds of the officers of those surveying vessels fell victims, and that half the men died in seven months.

In November, 1825, Captain W. F. Owen began the survey of the west coast of Africa at Walfisch Bay, gradually working up to Sierra Leone and the Gambia. He returned home after a service of five years, having traced thirty thousand miles of coast, and prepared eighty-three charts and plans. When it is considered that no chart-room was supplied on board the *Leven*, and that she laboured under other avoidable disadvantages, the amount of work done by her officers in such a climate must be regarded as prodigious. Boteler died of fever on the coast in 1829, being then Commander of the *Hecla*, surveying vessel. Vidal also continued to work on the west coast after the return of the *Leven*; and he later surveyed the Azores on board the *Styx* from 1841 to 1845.

It is to the Navy that are due the original discoveries which eventually led to the opening up of the Soudan. The remarkable journeys of Commander Hugh Clapperton,[1] R.N., from Tripoli to Kano, near which place he died, led to the discovery of the mouth of the Niger by his servant, Richard Lander. Lieutenant William Allen (3), R.N., was the naval leader of Lander's Niger Expedition in June, 1832; but such was the deadly character of the climate that, out of 47 men, there were only 9 survivors, Allen being one. A second Niger expedition went up the river under Lieutenant Frederick Bullock.[2] A third, consisting of three steamers,[3] commanded by Captain Henry Dundas Trotter, and Commanders William Allen (3), and Bird Allen, was despatched in 1841. Fever broke out at the confluence of the Niger and Benue; 44 men died, and the expedition returned to Fernando Po in October, 1841. Among the victims was Bird Allen, an able and zealous surveyor, who had served most of his time in the West Indies.[4]

The preliminary survey of the east and west coasts of Africa was a grand work, intended to benefit not Great Britain only, but the whole civilised world. Not less beneficent in its aim, certainly not less difficult in execution, was the survey of Magellan's Strait, and of the intricate channels leading from the Gulf of Trinidad. This also was undertaken, and Commander Philip Parker King was selected for the service, commissioning the *Adventure* in 1825. A small vessel called the *Beagle* was selected as tender to the *Adventure*, under the command of Commander Pringle Stokes. King's first Lieutenant was John Clements Wickham, and he also had with him Lieutenant William George Skyring, a disciple of Mediterranean Smyth, in the *Aid*. The work was commenced in 1826, and proceeded with in the most difficult circumstances, with frequent interruptions from thick weather and gales of wind, in a rigorous climate, and amidst perilous navigation. The chart of the extraordinarily intricate

---

[1] Born 1788; was pressed into the Navy; Lieutenant, 1815; Commander, 1825; died, 1827. See 'Narr. of Travs. in North and Central Africa,' and Lander: 'Records of Capt. Clapperton's last Expedition.'—W. L. C.

[2] A Captain of 1838. See F. O. List in next vol.—W. L. C.

[3] *Albert, Wilberforce,* and *Soudan,* specially built, by Lairds, of Birkenhead, of iron.

[4] Other officers who succumbed to fever were Master George B. Harvey; Surgeon William Barrett Marshall; Asst.-Surgeons James Woodhouse, and Horatio Collman; Mate William C. Willie; and Purser Cyrus Wakeham.—W. L. C.

channels leading from the Gulf of Trinidad represents a master-piece of patient and persevering surveying by Skyring, whose memory is preserved on the great expanse of inland water which bears his name. At length, worn out by toil and overwork, Stokes, of the *Beagle*, succumbed in 1828. Skyring was put in acting command by Commander King, but Rear-Admiral Robert Waller Otway, who was at Rio, superseded this hard-worked man, and appointed his own flag-Lieutenant, Robert FitzRoy, to the *Beagle*. Captain King [1] returned to England in 1830.

FitzRoy became a very zealous surveyor. He was reappointed to the *Beagle* in 1831, but the Admiralty never repaid him for the cost of a tender which he had bought, and which was necessary for the delineation of intricate channels and inlets. It was commanded by Lieutenant Thomas Graves (6). [2] Such was the way in which the Admiralty rewarded the zeal of its officers, leaving them several thousands of pounds out of pocket, but accepting the work executed through the use of that money. This treatment did not diminish FitzRoy's zeal. "Virtue is its own reward." The *Beagle* (of 235 tons) sailed in 1831. FitzRoy was assisted by such surveyors as Wickham, and John Lort Stokes. Skyring went to the west coast of Africa in the *Ætna*, and was murdered by some natives at the Caches river, near Cape Roxo, in 1833. FitzRoy was also accompanied by the naturalist Charles Robert Darwin. [3] During this voyage the *Beagle* surveyed the west coast of Patagonia, the Falkland Islands, and the whole of the west coast of South America as far as Guayaquil and the Galapagos Islands. This was a most important service to navigation, as the Spanish charts were many miles out, not only in longitude, but also in latitude. Captain FitzRoy was a most amiable as well as a zealous officer, and a good sailor. He was afterwards Governor of New Zealand from 1843 to 1848, and commanded the *Arrogant*, steam frigate, in 1849. His last service was the foundation of our system of meteorological forecasts.

King and FitzRoy had several distinguished disciples besides Skyring. Wickham afterwards had command of the *Beagle* in 1838, surveying Swan River and part of the north coast of Australia. John Lort Stokes, who was a Midshipman with FitzRoy, also

---

[1] Born 1793; posted 1830; retired 1850.—W. L. C.

[2] See 'Narr. of a Ten Years' Voyage of Disc. round the World,' by FitzRoy and King (1841).—W. L. C.

[3] Born 1809; died 1882.

served with Wickham in Australia, succeeding him in the command
of the *Beagle* in 1841. He afterwards, from 1847 to 1853, made an
admirable survey of the west coast of New Zealand in the *Acheron*.
Graves did good service in the Archipelago on board the *Volage*.
When Captain-Superintendent of the port at Valetta, he was
assassinated by a Maltese boatman in 1856. Owen Stanley was a
still more distinguished pupil of King and FitzRoy. George Henry
Richards, and Frederick John O. Evans, future Hydrographers,
were pupils of Stokes on board the *Acheron*.

In the period of the earlier Arctic voyages and African surveys,
there was an officer who, though not himself a professed explorer or
surveyor, exercised great and beneficial influence over those who
wished to emulate the services of Parry and Owen, and, indeed, over
the whole rising naval generation. Captain Basil Hall [1] commanded
the *Lyra*, 1815–17, when he visited the Loo Choo Islands, and was
in the *Conway* on the west coast of South America from 1820 to
1823. An intelligent observer, always anxious to increase his stock
of knowledge for the good of the service, he was also imaginative
and endowed with a strong sense of humour. But his most valuable
gift was the power of imparting the results of his observations and
his ideas to others. Of his immediate disciples in the *Conway* were
Alexander Bridport Becher, the future writer on the landfall of
Columbus, and Henry Foster, the scientific Arctic explorer. But
among several generations of naval officers, the name of the author
of ' Hall's Fragments ' continued to be a " household word."

We have seen how Basil Hall's most distinguished pupil received
the Copley Medal for his scientific work in the Arctic regions. But
Foster's career was soon afterwards cut short by an untimely death.
After his return from Spitzbergen, he received command of the
Chanticleer, a barque of 237 tons ; and he had with him Collinson
and Austin, both future Arctic commanders. She proceeded to the
West Indies, and Commander Foster took a series of pendulum
observations of the highest value. He was drowned [2] in the river
Chagres, when measuring the difference of longitude between
Chagres and Panama.

Richard Collinson,[3] the pupil both of Foster and of Beechey,

---

[1] Basil Hall, born 1788; Com. 1814; Capt. 1817; died, 1844.—W. L. C.

[2] On Feb. 3rd, 1831. He was born in 1798, and was a Commander of 1827.
—W. L. C.

[3] Sir Richard Collinson, born 1811; Com. 1841; Capt. 1842; R.-Adm. 1862
V.-Adm. 1869 ; Adm. 1875; died 1883.

showed, in his Chinese service, the importance of a thorough scientific training as marine surveyor, for at least a proportion of officers in every fleet, in time of war.   Henry Kellett[1] was another example.   Receiving his training under Owen and Skyring, he was with the latter officer when he was killed on the coast of Africa.   Collinson was engaged for three years, in the *Plover* and *Young Hebe*, in the survey of the China coasts, from Chusan to Hong Kong, including Formosa ; and Kellett was equally indefatigable in the *Starling*.   Science was then, as unfortunately it is now, despised and depreciated by ignorance in high places ; but when the war broke out in China, scientific officers were found to be indispensable in the persons of Collinson and Kellett.   It was then that Sir William Parker (2) turned, for the success of his operations, to the scientific surveyors.   Collinson was appointed Surveyor to the Fleet, and it was Kellett who led the flagship up the Yangtsze Kiang to Nankin.

Sir Edward Belcher[2] was a trained surveyor : but an officer who made " a hell afloat " of every ship he ever commanded cannot be regarded as a valuable acquisition to the service.   Belcher was with Beechey in the *Blossom*, and he afterwards completed some of Owen's work on the coast of Africa, on board the *Ætna*.   He commanded the *Sulphur* in China during the first war, and from 1842 to 1847 he conducted important surveys in the *Samarang* on the coast of Borneo and in the Eastern Archipelago, as well as on the coast of Corea, and the Majico-Sima Islands.   Belcher was severely wounded in repulsing an attack by Malay pirates, in the Strait of Gilolo.   At the same time, Captain Francis Price Blackwood,[3] in the *Fly*, was at work on the Great Barrier Reef, with the *Bramble* as a tender.   This arduous service comprised the examination of dangerous reefs for a length of a thousand miles, as well as the coral reefs in Torres Strait, and one hundred and forty miles of the coast of New Guinea.   Blackwood, in 1844, erected on Raine Island a beacon, seventy feet high and thirty in diameter, as a guide for vessels passing the barrier chain.   Charles Frederick Alexander Shadwell,[4] Blackwood's first Lieutenant in the *Fly*, was an officer whose high

---

[1] Henry Kellett, born 1806 ; Com. 1841 ; Capt. 1842.

[2] Sir Edward Belcher, born 1799 ; Com. 1829 ; Capt. 1841 ; R.-Adm. 1861 ; retd. v.-adm. 1866 ; died a retd. adm. 1877.—W. L. C.

[3] Francis Price Blackwood, born 1809 ; Com. 1830 ; Capt. 1838 ; died 1854. —W. L. C.

[4] Shadwell died an Adm. in 1886, æt. 72.—W. L. C.

scientific attainments and pre-eminence as a navigator and observer were graced by amiable qualities which won the affection of all who served under him.

Owen Stanley [1] carried forward the splendid work of Blackwood and Shadwell. Commencing his surveying career with King in the *Adventure*, he was in the *Terror* with Back during her terrible experiences in Hudson's Bay. Afterwards, under Graves in the *Mastiff*, he conducted a survey up the Gulf of Lepanto in an open boat, which he hauled across the isthmus of Corinth, regaining his ship in Voula Bay. When in command of the *Britomart*, he founded the colony of Port Essington, and, in the *Rattlesnake*, he continued the surveys of New Guinea, and Torres Strait. Owen Stanley died in the midst of his work in 1850; and his grave at Sydney is near that of another devoted officer, the late Commodore James Graham Goodenough,[2] whose funeral sermon was preached by Owen Stanley's brother, the late Dean of Westminster. In recording the deeds of Blackwood, and Stanley, the less known but equally meritorious labours of Charles Bamfield Yule [3] must not be forgotten. Trained by Bullock on the English coast, and by Skyring and Vidal in the *Ætna*, Yule subsequently commanded the tender *Bramble*, under Blackwood, from 1842 to 1845, and afterwards under Owen Stanley. He beat up against the south-east trade from Cape York to Sydney, and went through most arduous service during many years, but survived it all to find a more comfortable post in the hydrographic department at home.

It naturally happened that some of the naval surveyors devoted themselves more especially to the attractive study of nautical astronomy. Thus Henry Raper (2),[4] who received his first training in the *Adventure*, under Mediterranean Smyth, published in 1843 the best existing work on the practice of navigation ; and, in a later generation, the studies of Sir C. F. A. Shadwell resulted in the useful tables which bear his name.

The great work which was done by the Navy for the benefit of navigation needed the fostering care and the firm support of an influential official at the Admiralty. Such a man was Francis

---

[1] Owen Stanley, born 1811; Com. 1839; Capt. 1844; died 1850.—W. L. C.

[2] Goodenough, when Commod. on the Australian station in the *Pearl*, died Aug. 20, 1875, of wounds received at the hands of some Polynesian islanders.—W. L. C.

[3] A Com. of 1851.—W. L. C.

[4] A Lieut. of 1823. He was for years Secretary to the Royal Astronomical Society.—W. L. C.

Beaufort (1),[1] who held the post of Hydrographer from 1829 to 1855. His difficulties in contending against and overcoming the obstruction of "their Lordships" were very great. He had a long and hard fight with dulness and ignorance. "The natural tendency of men," he philosophically remarked, "is to undervalue what they do not understand." But his firmness and never-failing tact overcame all obstacles. To him alone is due the credit of organising those invaluable surveys in all parts of the world that were executed in his time. A member of the Council of the Royal Geographical Society himself, he actively supported all the representations of that body, which were successful in the cases of Back's voyage to Hudson's Bay, and Wickham's Australian survey. Beaufort's industry was marvellous. Having already worked for three hours at home, he began office work at 9 A.M., and continued at it for eight hours. Between 1837 and 1847, he raised the expenditure in his department from £68,517 to £123,678, which is a measure of the corresponding increase in activity and in the output of valuable work.

The surveys of the Red Sea, south-east coast of Arabia, the Persian Gulf, and the coasts of India and Burma were executed by the officers of the Indian Navy.

In 1838 the time had come for the renewal of polar research, and, with Beaufort and Barrow at the Admiralty, its cause could be sure of influential advocacy. The British Association represented the urgency of a magnetic survey of the southern ocean, and it was resolved to despatch an Antarctic expedition under the command of Captain James Clark Ross. The experience of that officer as a magnetic observer was second only to that of Sabine, while he was easily first as an ice navigator. His second in command was Commander Francis Rawdon Moira Crozier,[2] who had served in all Parry's voyages except the first. Among the officers were Edward Joseph Bird,[3] who also had served under Parry, Archibald McMurdo,[4] who had been with Back in the *Terror*, Dr. Robert McCormick, R.N., who had been with Parry in his polar voyage of 1827, Dr. David Lyall, R.N., and the future illustrious botanist, Joseph Dalton

---

[1] Sir Francis Beaufort (1), born 1774; Com. 1800; Capt. 1810; retd. r.-adm. 1846; died 1857. He was an F.R.S. of 1814, and a K.C.B. (civil) of 1848.—W. L. C.

[2] Francis Rawdon Moira Crozier, Lieut. 1826; Com. 1837; Capt. 1841; died 1854.—W. L. C.

[3] Became a Rear-Adm. 1863; retired 1869; died 1881.—W. L. C.

[4] Promoted Commander, 1843.—W. L. C.

Hooker,[1] who then commenced his great life-work for the advancement of science. Two strongly-built old bomb vessels, the *Erebus* and *Terror*, were selected for the service.

Two subordinate naval officers, John Biscoe (1830–32), and Weddell (1823), had already made some important Antarctic dis-

REAR-ADMIRAL SIR JAMES CLARK ROSS, KT., D.C.L., F.R.S.

(From the picture by Stephen Pearce.)

[By permission of the Lords of the Admiralty.]

coveries, while commanding vessels owned by Messrs. Enderby. Biscoe had discovered Enderby's Land and Graham's Land to the south of the South Shetlands, and Weddell had penetrated as far south as 74° 15′ without being stopped by the ice.

Ross boldly pushed his ships into the formidable polar pack, a feat which had never before been attempted by any navigator. Captain Cook had considered it to be impenetrable. The foreign

---

[1] Sir J. D. Hooker, born 1817; Surgeon R. N., 1839; retired 1870; K.C.S.I. 1869; Pres. of Roy. Soc., 1873–78; G.C.S.I. 1897.—W. L. C.

expeditions under Dumont d'Urville, and Wilkes did not venture to do more than look at the pack. But Ross and Crozier put the bluff bows of the old *Erebus* and *Terror* straight on to the jammed-up ice on January 5th, 1841. They received some very heavy blows, but they forced their way in, and Ross's splendid audacity was rewarded. In six days he reached open water, and discovered land with a great range of mountains extending for 450 miles to the south-ward, which received the name of Victoria Land. On the 28th of January, an active volcano, 12,400 feet in height, emitting flame and smoke in great profusion, was sighted, and named Mount Erebus. Extending from the neighbourhood of this volcano for a distance of several hundreds of. miles, Ross discovered a range of perpendicular ice cliffs rising to a height of 200 feet, and forming a stupendous barrier, the great source of supply for the icebergs which encumber the southern ocean. In 1842 the daring explorer again took the pack, and had a much more terrible ex-perience. The wind freshened to a violent gale on January 19th, when both ships were surrounded. The rudder of the *Erebus* was so damaged as to be no longer of any use, and that of the *Terror* was completely destroyed, and nearly torn away from the stern post. Ross said that " throughout a period of twenty-eight hours, during any one of which there appeared to be very little hope that they would live to see another, the coolness, steady obedience, and un-tiring exertions of each individual were every way worthy of British seamen." But Ross was not to be beaten. He forced his way through this terrible pack, and once more reached and examined the marvellous ice barrier. In 1843 he surveyed the South Shetlands ; but his third attempt to force his way through the pack in March did not succeed because it was made too late in the year. After three seasons in the Antarctic ice, facing and overcoming dangers and difficulties which had daunted all his predecessors, Ross brought his ships safely home in 1843,[1] laden with a rich harvest of valuable scientific results.[2] This was a service of which the Navy may well be proud. It was a glorious peace victory.

The return of Ross, with two strong ships well adapted for ice navigation, suggested to Sir John Barrow that another voyage might be undertaken with the object of solving the geographical problem of the North-West Passage. He was warmly seconded by

---

[1] He was knighted soon after his arrival.—W. L. C.
[2] *See* ' A Voyage of Discovery in the Southern and Antarctic Seas,' 1847.—W. L. C.

Sir Francis Beaufort, and the *Erebus* and *Terror* were re-commis-
sioned. Commander James Fitzjames,[1] who had returned from the
East Indian station in the *Clio*, should have commanded the expedition, and this was the original intention. But Sir John Franklin
put in a claim, and it was considered that, if he insisted, it could
not be overlooked. He was in his sixtieth year, and was much too
old. Moreover, his experience of ice navigation was confined to a
summer cruise more than a quarter of a century before. When a
young man he had won his laurels by his two land journeys.
Captain Crozier, who was to command the *Terror* again, though a
man of great Arctic experience, was also too old. Fitzjames, the
brilliant commander of the *Erebus*, should have been the leader of
the expedition. Seldom, nevertheless, has a more able and zealous
set of officers started on a perilous service than those who sailed in
the *Erebus* and *Terror*. The flower of the Navy volunteered, among
them the most promising young officers on board the *Excellent;* and
the pick of these was chosen. There were Lieutenants Graham Gore,
who had been with Back in the *Terror*, James Walter Fairholme, of
the Niger expedition, Henry Thomas Dundas Le Vescomte, specially
selected by Sir Francis Beaufort, and George Henry Hodgson, direct
from the *Excellent*, and Mates Charles Frederick Des Vœux,[2] Robert
Orme Sargent,[2] Frederick John Hornby,[2] and Robert Thomas.[3]

The expedition sailed from England in May, 1845, all its members
full of bright hopes and ardent enthusiasm. Everything appeared
prosperous, and seemed to point to success, as the two vessels
easily passed the ordinary obstructions of Baffin's Bay, and entered
Barrow's Strait. Franklin's instructions were to make his way to
Bering Strait by working to the south and west, but he was given
the alternative of trying Wellington Channel. Without doubt,
Franklin's matured judgment was to follow the first part of his
instructions, and make for the coast of America. But we know that
the expedition proceeded up Wellington Channel, probably tempted
by the absence of ice within sight. Stopped by the impenetrable
polar pack in 77°, as Parry had been stopped to the west of Melville
Island, Franklin resolved to return. He took his ships down a
channel, never since explored, between Bathurst and Cornwallis
Islands, and brought them back to safe winter quarters at Beechey
Island, on the western side of the entrance of Wellington Channel.

---

[1] Com. 1842; Capt. 1845; died 1854.—W. L. C.
[2] Lieuts. 1846.   [3] Lieut. 1847.

This was the most remarkable voyage that has ever been made in those ice-encumbered straits and channels.

Franklin must then have resolved fully to act in accordance with his own matured views, and push southwards to the coast of America in the season of 1846. He knew that coast, and that there

CAPTAIN SIR JOHN FRANKLIN, KT., D.C.L., F.R.S.
(*From the water-colour by William Derby.*)
[By permission of the Lords of the Admiralty.]

were leads of open water along it. Accordingly the *Erebus* and *Terror* went down what is now called Peel Sound, between North Somerset and Prince of Wales' Islands, sighted the coast of King William Land, discovered by James Clark Ross, and attempted to proceed along its west coast to the shores of the continent. But there again they were met by that impenetrable polar pack which sweeps down Melville Sound and impinges on the west coast of King William Land. Franklin was obliged to winter in the pack. If he had attempted to pass down the eastern instead of the western shore, it is quite possible that he might have succeeded. But it was not then known that King William Land was an island. It was conceived to be, and was shown on the map as, a peninsula extending west from Boothia. Up to that time Franklin had conducted the enterprise with great ability and sound judgment, in accordance with existing knowledge. He had very nearly reached the American coast, and he expected to reach it in the ensuing season of 1847.

When the sun returned, Graham Gore [1] and Des Vœux made a sledge journey down the west coast of King William Land, reached Cape Herschel, and thus completed the discovery of a North-West Passage, for Cape Herschel had been reached by Simpson from the west. With this knowledge the veteran explorer went to his rest. Sir John Franklin died on June 11th, 1847. As the season advanced it was found that, short though the distance was to the American coast, the polar pack remained impenetrable. Crozier had taken command of the expedition, and Fitzjames succeeded as Captain of the *Erebus*. It became evident that they must face the horrors of a third winter, with insufficient and unwholesome food. For there can be no doubt that the preserved meats supplied by the Admiralty, through a rascally contractor named Goldner, were bad, and unfit for human consumption. The consequence was that scurvy broke out. There were many deaths both among officers and men, and the spring of 1848 found the survivors weak, debilitated, and consequently despondent. Provisions were nearly at an end. A retreat became necessary, but it was a forlorn hope. Crozier and Fitzjames did all that was possible. They resolved to make an attempt to reach help by ascending the Back or Great Fish River. Boats and sledges were prepared with great care, and stored with such provisions as remained; and in April, 1848, the doomed heroes landed near Cape Victory. A record, left in a cairn by Graham Gore in the previous year, was accidentally found. Some ink was thawed, and a brief note of what had happened was written round it by Fitzjames, and signed by the two Captains. The record was then replaced. Dragging two heavy boats on sledges, the party resumed its hopeless journey. Debilitated by illness, and much weaker than had been supposed when they left the ships, the men fell down to die as they walked along. Only a very few reached Montreal Island, at the mouth of the Great Fish River; and near that spot the last survivor succumbed, probably before the autumn of 1848 set in. Bravely and

[1] Graham Gore had been made Com. on Nov. 6th, 1846.—W. L. C.

resolutely had those gallant sailors stuck to their duty, and died
at their posts. Their end, though unspeakably sad and pathetic,
was glorious. They died to uphold the honour and prestige of their
country. Yet the loss of the Franklin expedition was one of the
greatest calamities that ever befell the British Navy.

In the same year that Franklin sailed from England, Captain
Henry Kellett commissioned the *Herald*, with the brigantine
Pandora as a tender, and proceeded to the Pacific to continue the
survey of the west coast of South America from Guayaquil to
Panama. Having completed this work, the *Herald*, accompanied
by the *Plover*, went up Bering Strait with the idea of meeting the
Franklin expedition ; and Kellett discovered the island reported by
Baron Wrangel as being off the coast of Western Siberia, and
since known as Wrangel Land. During the same period, 1842–46,
Bartholomew James Sulivan,[1] in the *Philomel*, surveyed the south-
east coast of South America, and completed the surveys of the
Falkland Islands.

No anxiety was felt for Franklin's expedition after the second
winter in 1847, except by one person. Dr. King, who had accompanied Back in his descent of the Great Fish River, made an urgent
appeal to the Government to send supplies and relief by that route
to Montreal Island. He represented that Franklin's intention was
to reach the American coast, that a retreat, if it became necessary,
must be to the Great Fish River, and that the provisions would be
exhausted in 1848, when it would be too late. Dr. King's representations were unheeded. At length, in 1848, when it was too late,
a relief expedition was tardily fitted out, consisting of two vessels,
the *Enterprise*, commanded by Sir James Clark Ross, and the
Investigator, by Captain Edward Joseph Bird. If Dr. King's urgent
appeal had been listened to in 1847 many of his gallant countrymen
might have been saved. In 1848 the time was past. Ross had
with him two officers who were destined to win laurels by future
Arctic achievement, Robert John Le Mesurier McClure, and Francis
Leopold M'Clintock. The season of 1848 was very unfavourable,
and the expedition could only get as far as Port Leopold, near the
north-east point of North Somerset. At that time the last survivors
of Franklin's expedition were perishing near Montreal Island. In
the spring of 1849, Ross, accompanied by M'Clintock, made a

[1] Bartholomew James Sulivan, born 1810; Lieut. 1830; Com. 1841; Capt. 1845;
died an Adm. and K.C.B. 1890.—W. L. C.

sledge journey along the northern coast of North Somerset, and for some distance down its western side in the right direction for ascertaining Franklin's fate. Another party visited Fury Beach. Nothing more was done, and the expedition returned. The *North Star*, with additional supplies for it, had been sent out in 1849, under the command of Master James Saunders, who had served with Back in the *Terror*. The ice prevented him from crossing Baffin's Bay, and the *North Star* wintered in Wolstenholme Sound on the Greenland coast. In the spring of 1850, Saunders landed a depôt on the south side of Barrow's Strait, and returned home.

The nation was at length thoroughly aroused. The return of Ross without any result excited the greatest anxiety, and the Admiralty was loudly called upon for vigorous action. But it was three years too late. However, the *Enterprise* and *Investigator* were recommissioned to make a search by way of Bering Strait ; while the *Plover* was ordered to winter near Cape Barrow as a depôt ship. Captain Richard Collinson, so well known for his surveying services in the China seas, received command of the *Enterprise*, while to McClure, Ross's first Lieutenant in the former voyage, was entrusted the *Investigator*. The two exploring ships were separated in passing up the Pacific. The *Enterprise* was too late in the season, and went back to winter at Hong Kong. The *Investigator* pushed onwards along the west coast of Banks Land, a name given by Parry when he sighted from Melville Island the hills behind its northern coast. The mighty polar pack which Parry had seen was pressing against the land. There was along the shore a narrow channel, due to the immense thickness of the ice, which grounded before it could be pressed upon the beach. Through this McClure forced his ship, sometimes with his yard-arms scraping against the cliffs, and running the gauntlet of many dangers. At length he succeeded in rounding the north end of Banks Island, and in reaching a haven which he appropriately named the Bay of God's Mercy. There was no possibility of extrication, for the mighty polar pack was between him and the comparative safety of the Melville Island coast. Three dreary winters, 1850–54, were passed by the much-enduring crew of the *Investigator*. McClure made a sledge journey across the heavy ice to Melville Island, and left a notice of his position. When the provisions were nearly consumed he resolved to make a desperate attempt to reach the American coast with the strongest among his crew. He was about to start on this forlorn hope, almost as hopeless as that attempted by Crozier and Fitzjames, when succour came from an unexpected quarter.

The *Enterprise* entered upon ice navigation a year after the *Investigator*, passing Bering Strait in 1851. Collinson attempted to work up the eastern side of Banks Island, and wintered in a narrow strait, whence one of his officers, Lieutenant Murray Thomas Parks, made a sledge journey to Melville Island. In the season of 1852 he returned to the American coast, and made a very remarkable voyage eastward. From his second winter quarters he might easily have made a sledge journey to Cape Victory, if he had known how much was involved in reaching that point. The season of 1853 saw Collinson making a similar voyage westward, wintering within easy reach of Cape Barrow; and in 1854 the *Enterprise* returned home. These voyages along the northern shores of America prove the correctness of Franklin's forecast respecting the success of his enterprise if he could succeed in reaching that coast.

As soon as the *Enterprise* and *Investigator* had sailed from England, active preparations were made for resuming the search by way of Baffin's Bay. Granting the necessity, felt by the Admiralty, that none but old officers, past the time for active personal exertion, should command these expeditions, no better selection could have been made than that of Captain Horatio Thomas Austin. He had served with Parry in his third voyage, was with Henry Foster in the *Chanticleer*; and, when the use of steam was introduced into the Navy, was foremost in adapting himself to the new order of things, and in 1832 commanded the *Salamander*, one of the first steamers. He had Captain Erasmus Ommanney as his second in command; and two vessels, of a little over 400 tons each, were purchased, strengthened for ice navigation, and named the *Resolute* and the *Assistance*. It was under Austin that steam power was first introduced into ice navigation. Two sharp-bowed screw steamers were provided as tenders, to tow the heavy sailing barques when necessary, and named the *Pioneer* and the *Intrepid*. The former was commanded by Lieutenant Sherard Osborn, the latter by Lieutenant John Bertie Cator. The Admiralty also thought fit to send out, independent of the naval expedition, two brigs in command of a whaling master named Penny.

After a long detention by the ice in Melville Bay, Austin's expedition reached Barrow Strait, but found it impossible to get within 300 miles of Melville Island. It wintered between Corn-wallis and Griffith Islands. Penny's brigs wintered in Assistance Harbour, near the entrance of Wellington Channel. Franklin's winter quarters at Beechey Island were discovered; but a minute and persistent search for any record, or any clue to the intentions of the leader of the expedition, entirely failed.

It was in these circumstances that Austin was left to institute the most complete search that was possible with the means at his disposal. He proved himself equal to the task in every respect except the bodily activity of youth. For the first time he inaugurated autumn sledge-travelling for laying out depôts. His next duty was to provide for the winter, and to bring his people through it in the same health and spirits as when they left England, ready for the arduous duties of the spring. Austin had all the traditions of Parry, and he was himself gifted with a remarkable talent for organisation. He was heartily seconded by the executives, and by an exceptionally able medical staff. He himself was genial and sympathetic, and the winter of 1850–51 was the happiest ever passed in the Arctic regions, the officers and men being kept in perfect health. It was a period of preparation during which Captain Austin, with the assistance of his officers, organised a scheme of sledge-travelling such as had never been contemplated by any previous expedition. He was indeed well supported. Captain Ommanney did all in his power, and was ready to lead an extended party. M'Clintock, his first Lieutenant, was himself endowed with rare gifts of perseverance, resolution, and intrepidity, as well as with great talent for the organisation of details. Lieutenant George Frederick Mecham was second only to M'Clintock; Sherard Osborn, though not equal physically to M'Clintock and Mecham, was a host in himself, imparting his enthusiasm to others, and aiding by his great ability and quick intelligence. Two young Mates, Richard Vesey Hamilton, and Walter William May, showed great promise, to bear fruit in future years. But all were equally zealous, all did their best, as naval officers generally do.

Austin had absolutely no clue except Franklin's instructions. Moreover, he was hampered by an order from the Admiralty to examine Melville Island, the one place where it was quite certain that Franklin had not been. Austin resolved to search in every direction except Wellington Channel, which he left to Penny. The extended parties were to be enabled to increase the distance searched by the help of limited and auxiliary parties; and thus nearly every soul in the expedition was employed in sledge-travelling during the spring and summer. To M'Clintock was entrusted the feat of reaching and examining Melville Island, which he performed successfully. It was a feat then quite unequalled in Arctic annals, and since only excelled by himself and Mecham. The coasts of Bathurst Island were also examined. Cape Walker had been specially mentioned in Franklin's instructions, and three extended parties were sent in that direction under Ommanney, and Lieutenants Sherard Osborn, and William Henry James Browne; while Mecham examined Cape Walker itself, and discovered Russell Island. The extended parties discovered Prince of Wales Island, and carefully searched its eastern and western coasts. Sherard Osborn reached the edge of the same heavy polar pack which had stopped the *Erebus* and *Terror* on the coast of King William Land.

Thus was Austin's work thoroughly and completely done from his position off Griffith Island. Parties had gone in every direction, pressing onwards with a resolution and endurance above all praise. Penny had searched Wellington Channel, and made it certain that the missing expedition was not to be found in that direction. Only one thing remained to be done, which was for the Admiralty to take Dr. King's advice, and cause King William Land and Montreal Island to be searched. There in fact, as M'Clintock afterwards discovered, the Franklin expedition was actually lost. But the authorities declined to do so. The positions were too distant to be reached by Austin's parties, though one of them went as far as was possible in the right direction.

Austin's expedition returned in the autumn of 1851. He had done his work well. He had preserved his people in perfect health and spirits. His was certainly the happiest, and, on the whole, the best organised expedition that ever went to the Arctic regions. He introduced a new and most effective system of ice exploration, while his arrangements for winter quarters have never been surpassed.

Austin left nothing more to be done in the direction of Barrow's Strait, so far as the Franklin search was concerned. The Admiralty thought otherwise, and was wrong. In spite of his excellent service, and the altogether unequalled character of the work done by his expedition, he was coldly received, and harassed by an unnecessary committee of inquiry. The Admiralty recommissioned the four ships, the *Assistance* and *Pioneer* to go up Wellington Channel, and

the *Resolute* and *Intrepid* to Melville Island, while the *North Star* was
to be stationed at Beechey Island as a depôt ship.   There was some
sense in the Melville Island route this time, because nothing had
been heard of the *Enterprise* and *Investigator*, and one or both
might be in need of succour.   This arrangement did not, however, originate with the Admiralty.   It was the suggestion of
Mr. Creswell, father of one of the officers of the *Investigator*.
But the expedition up Wellington Channel was entirely useless
and unnecessary, except as regards geographical exploration.

      To command this expedition the Admiralty selected Sir Edward
Belcher, who was too old for the work, and most unfit in every
other respect.   If it had searched the whole Navy, it could not
have made a worse selection.   This was notorious.   The *Intrepid*
was commanded by M'Clintock, the *Pioneer* by Sherard Osborn.
Captain Henry Kellett, of the *Resolute*, had done admirable service
in his day, but his day was past.   He was a most amiable officer,
and had the good sense to leave everything to the men who had to
do the work—M'Clintock, Mecham, Vesey Hamilton, George Strong
Nares, Richard Roche, Frederick J. Krabbé, and George Frederick
M'Dougall.   But Belcher was a serious nuisance.   He treated
Sherard Osborn shamefully, and eventually superseded him in his
command.   M'Clintock and Sherard Osborn ought, of course, to
have commanded the two branches of the expedition.   George
Henry Richards was Commander in the *Assistance*, and, besides
Sherard Osborn, May, John Hillary Allard, and other officers who
had been trained by Austin, were in the Wellington Channel
division.

      The *Assistance* and *Pioneer* went up Wellington Channel as far
as 77° N., wintering in Northumberland Inlet.

      The *Resolute* and *Intrepid* were able, in the season of 1852, to
get as far to the westward as Melville Island, and good winter
quarters were found off Dealy Isle.   In the autumn travelling,
Mecham discovered the record left by McClure, and was thus the
means of saving the officers and crew of the *Investigator*.   The
position of that ship being thus made known, it was a simple matter
to send over a party to communicate in the following spring.   The
Investigator was abandoned, McClure and his people going across
to the *Resolute*.   McClure thus discovered a North-West Passage,
for he and his *Investigators* were the only men who ever passed
from ocean to ocean by the north.

The spring travelling of 1853, based on the system inaugurated by Austin, was the most extensive on record, and has never been equalled since. M'Clintock discovered Prince Patrick Island, travelling over 1328 miles in 105 days. Mecham went over 1163 miles in 91 days. Vesey Hamilton penetrated to the northern extremity of Melville Island. Nares explored Eglinton Island. From the *Assistance*, Richards, Sherard Osborn, and May examined the

ADMIRAL SIR RICHARD VESEY HAMILTON, G.C.B.

whole northern coast of Bathurst Island; and Richards opened communication with the *Resolute*.

In the season of 1853, the *Assistance* returned down Wellington Channel for some distance, but was stopped by the ice, and had to pass a second winter. The *Resolute*, leaving Dealy Island, was also stopped, and forced to winter in the pack. In 1854, Mecham made the most remarkable Arctic journey on record to Collinson's first winter quarters. During seventy days he travelled over heavy ice at the rate of 16 miles a day on the outward journey, and of 20 miles a day on the homeward journey, and covered 1336 miles of ground. This has never since been beaten, nor even approached. The travelling parties led by these naval officers had no dogs.

In 1854, Belcher actually resolved to abandon all the four vessels, without waiting to see whether they could be extricated from the ice, and to return to England in the *North Star*. Kellett very properly refused to abandon the *Resolute* and *Intrepid* without a written order, which he received. All the people were to be crowded on board the *North Star*, but just as she was about to sail, Captain Edward Augustus Inglefield arrived with the *Phœnix* and *Talbot*. At the close of the consequent court-martial, Kellett was complimented. Belcher's sword was returned to him indeed, but in silence—a just rebuke.

The unequalled sledge-travelling of 1853 and 1854 was the outcome of Austin's admirable initiative in 1851, and was performed, with one exception, by his officers. The names of nearly all Austin's officers were afterwards honourably known in the service.

A glance at the map [1] will show the amount of discovery made by naval officers serving in the Franklin searches, and the extraordinary intricacy of the channels, straits and inlets which give shape to the great archipelago of islands to the north of the American continent. But only those who have experienced such service can realise the amount of endurance, suffering, and hardship it entails.   There is no better nursery to bring out the best and noblest traits in the character of a British seaman.

When the Arctic explorers returned in 1854, the Crimean War was imminent.   As in the China War, immediate need was felt for scientific surveyors, and the Arctic officers were to the fore in the Baltic, in the Black Sea, and especially in the Sea of Azof.   Captain Bartholomew James Sulivan, in the *Lightning*, with Frederick J. O. Evans in the *Merlin*, was at the head of the pilot and surveying services in the Baltic.   An equally distinguished officer did yeoman's service in the Black Sea.   Thomas Abel Bremage Spratt had worked at the surveys in the Mediterranean from 1832, five years after he entered the service, until 1863.   He had served under Graves in the *Mastiff* and *Beacon*; he had commanded the *Volage* in 1847 and 1848; and afterwards he had succeeded Graves in the *Spitfire*.   He was chiefly employed on the coasts of Asia Minor and the islands, and his interesting work on Crete is well known. During the Crimean War, Spratt did splendid service in the *Spitfire*. " He was the mainspring of all the operations whilst Lord Lyons held the key."

---

[1] See sketch map on p. 509.

SIR WILLIAM JAMES LLOYD WHARTON, K.C.B., F.R.S.,
RETIRED REAR-ADMIRAL.

(*Hydrographer*, 1884.)

APPENDIX TO CHAPTERS XLIII–XLV.

List of Flag-Officers Promoted from the close of the War in 1815 to the End of 1856 (Active List only).

(In continuation of the List in Vol. V, pp. 39–43.)

Name.	Born.	Lieut.	Com.	Captain.	R.-Adm.	V.-Adm.	Admiral.	Adm. of Fleet.	Remarks.	Died.
Willoughby Thomas Lake (C.B. 1815, K.C.B. 1830)	ca. 1773	22-11-1790	25-11-1794	4-1-1796	12-8-1819	22-7-1830	23-11-1841	—		18-2-1847
Charles Ogle (suc. as Bart. 1816)	24-5-1775	14-11-1793	21-5-1795	11-11-1796	12-8-1819	22-7-1830	23-11-1841	8-12-1857		16-6-1858
Henry Raper (1)	1-4-1767	22-11-1790	4-7-1794	1-2-1796	12-8-1819	22-7-1830	23-11-1841	—		5-4-1845
William Charles Fahie (C.B. 1815, K.C.B. 1825)	1763	1783	1794	2-2-1796	12-8-1819	22-7-1830				11-1-1833
George Eyre (Kt. 1812, K.C.B. 1815)		1790	1794	6-2-1796	12-8-1819	22-7-1830				15-2-1839
Robert Stuart Lambert		1791	1794	11-4-1796	12-8-1819	22-7-1830				16-9-1836
Joseph Bingham		1790	1794	20-4-1796	12-8-1819					
Robert Dudley Oliver	31-10-1766	1790	21-10-1794	30-4-1796	12-8-1819	22-7-1830	23-11-1841			
D'Arcy Preston	1765	4-11-1790	4-4-1794	13-6-1796	—	12-11-1840	23-11-1841	—	{Retd. 24-8-1819: restd. 1840.}	21-1-1847
Man Dobson	17-11-1755	23-9-1782	9-11-1795	28-6-1796	5-7-1827	22-7-1830	23-11-1841	—	{ Retd. 24-8-1819: restd. 1827. }	4-1847
Thomas Boys (1)		1784	1795	3-7-1796	12-8-1819	22-7-1830		—	Comr. etc. 1806-22.	1832
John Clarke Searle		9-10-1790	1795	13-7-1796	8-2-1822			—		1829
Charles Brisbane (Kt. 1807, K.C.B. 1815)	ca. 1769	1790	1794	27-7-1796	12-8-1819	22-7-1830		—		1829
John Talbot (K.C.B. 1815, Hon. 1831; G.C.B. 1842)		3-11-1790	17-4-1795	27-8-1796	12-8-1819	22-7-1830	23-11-1841	—		1851
John Halliday (John Richard Delap Tollemache 1821)	1772	7-8-1795	—	19-9-1796	12-8-1819	22-7-1830	23-11-1841	—		16-7-1837
John Giffard		20-10-1790	1-2-1796	19-10-1796	12-8-1819	22-7-1830	23-11-1841	—	Retd. 1-7-1851	1855
John West (K.C.B. 1840, G.C.B. 1860)	28-7-1774	27-7-1793	7-9-1795	15-11-1796	12-8-1819	22-7-1830	23-11-1841	25-6-1858	{Retd. 28-8-1819: restd. 1840.}	18-4-1862
Joseph Bullen	14-4-1761	6-3-1778	20-11-1793	24-11-1796	12-8-1819	12-11-1840	23-11-1841	—		
Stephen Poyntz	1769	1-1-1791	3-10-1795	5-12-1796	12-8-1819	22-7-1830	23-11-1841	—		12-5-1847
Hon. John, Lord Colville	15-3-1768	29-7-1793	28-8-1795	6-12-1796	12-8-1819	22-7-1830	23-11-1841	—		22-12-1849
John Cochet	3-8-1760	26-8-1789	27-5-1795	9-12-1796	12-8-1819	22-7-1830	23-11 1841	—		1851
Archibald Collingwood Dickson (suc. as Bart. 1803)	30-6-1772	1791	1794	12-12-1796	12-8-1819					18-6-1827
Robert Winthrop	1762	1790	6-10-1795	16-12-1796	12-8-1819	22-7-1830	23-11-1841	—		10-5-1832
Henry Digby (C.B. 1815, K.C.B. 1831)	1769	1790	1795	19-12-1796	12-8-1819	22-7-1830	23-11-1841	—		18-9-1842
Charles Ekins (C.B. 1816, K.C.B. 1831)	1768	1790	18-6-1795	22-12-1796	12-8-1819	22-7-1830	23-11-1841	—		
John Sprat Rainier		1794	1794	22-12-1796	12-8-1819	—				
Benjamin William Page	7-2-1765	20-11-1784	12-4-1796	23-12-1796	12-8-1819	22-7-1830	23-11-1811	—		3-10-1845
Hon. Philip Wodehouse	16-7-1773	1794	1796	23-12-1796	12-8-1819	22-7-1830	23-11-1841	—		1838
Thomas Alexander (1)		19-11-1790		27-12-1796	12-8-1819	22-7-1830	23-11-1841	—		10-3-1843

Name	Born	Lieut.	Cdr.	Capt.	R.-Adm.	V.-Adm.	Adm.	Adm. of Fleet	Remarks	Died
Andrew Smith	20-3-1763	10-8-1790	1795	6-1-1797	19-7-1821					29-9-1831
Edward Berry (Kt. 1798, Bart. 1806, K.C.B. 1815)	1766	1794	1796	6-3-1797	19-7-1821					1831
William Prowse (1) (C.B. 1815)		1782	1796	6-3-1797	19-7-1821	10-1-1837				
Lord Mark Robert Kerr	12-11-1776	1794	8-7-1795	7-3-1797	19-7-1821	10-1-1837				9-9-1840
James Athol Wood (Kt. 1810, C.B. 1815)	1760	1794		27-3-1797	19-7-1821	10-1-1837				28-5-1841
Thomas Harvey (1) (C.B. 1815, K.C.B. 1833)	1775	1793	3-7-1796	27-3-1797	19-7-1821	10-1-1837				6-11-1842
Richard Hussey Moubray (later R. Hussey Hussey) (C.B. 1815, K.C.B. 1833, G.C.M.G. 1837)	16-3-1776		9-6-1794	10-4-1797	19-7-1821	10-1-1837			Retd. 1-7-1851.	
Henry Richard Glynn		28-10-1790	29-6-1795	10-4-1797	19-7-1821	10-1-1837	9-11-1846			
John Bligh (2) (C.B. 1815)		1791	8-3-1797	25-4-1797	19-7-1821	10-1-1837				
Peter Puget		1790	1795	29-4-1797	19-7-1821	10-1-1837				
Edward Hamilton (Kt. 1800, K.C.B. 1815, Bart. 1818)	12-3-1772	9-6-1793	11-2-1796	3-6-1797	19-7-1821	10-1-1837	9-11-1846		Dismd. 22-1-1802: restd. 6-1802.	20-3-1851
Thomas Baker (1) (C.B. 1815, K.C.B. 1831)		13-10-1792	24-11-1795	13-6-1797	19-7-1821	10-1-1837			Retd. 26-7-1821: restd. 1840.	26-11-1845
Henry Evans		1782	1794	20-6-1797	19-7-1821	12-11-1840				13-12-1842
Samuel Sutton	1760	1783	1795	27-6-1797	19-7-1821					1832
Hon. Courtenay Boyle (Kt., K.C.H. 1832)	3-9-1770	1790	4-1795	30-6-1797	19-7-1821	10-1-1837			Retd. 1821: restd. 1840	1836
Robert Laurie (suc. as Bart. 1804, K.C.B. 1831)	25-5-1764		25-6-1795	17-7-1797	19-7-1821	10-1-1837	9-11-1846			2-11-1826
William Hall Gage (Kt. 1834, G.C.B. 1860)	2-10-1777	11-3-1796	13-6-1797	26-7-1797	19-7-1821	10-1-1837	9-11-1846	20-5-1862	R.A. and V.A. of U.K.	
John Maitland (2)	1771	1794	1796	11-8-1797	19-7-1821					5-1-1864
Stair Douglas (2)	27-10-1764	1780	1795	13-9-1797	19-7-1821					13-7-1831
William Cuming (C.B. 1815)		7-12-1779	1795	13-10-1797	19-7-1821					1838
James Walker (2) (C.B. 1815)	1764	18-6-1781	1795	17-10-1797	19-7-1821	10-1-1837			Dismd. 1796: restd. 1797	1844
Hon. Charles Paget (Kt., K.C.H. 1819, G.C.H. 1832)	7-10-1778	17-10-1796	17-10-1797	17-10-1797	9-4-1823					27-1-1839
Robert Williams (1)		1797	1797	10-11-1797	9-4-1823	10-1-1837				
Richard Worsley	1768	1794	1794	29-11-1797	27-5-1825	10-1-1837				1838
Aiskew Pafford Hollis		1790	1-11-1796	1-11-1796	27-5-1825	10-1-1837				1844
Henry Heathcote (Kt. 1819)	20-1-1777	22-1-1781	11-8-1797	5-2-1798	27-5-1825	10-1-1837	9-11-1846		Retd. 1-7-1831	16-8-1851
Andrew Fitzherbert Evans		19-9-1796	1795	5-2-1798	27-5-1825	10-1-1837				2-8-1845
Edward William Campbell Rich Owen (K.C.B. 1815, G.C.H. 1832, G.C.B. 1845)		1-12-1787	19-9-1796	15-1-1798	27-5-1825	12-11-1840	11-12-1846			
George James Shirley	1768	6-11-1793	11-9-1797	23-4-1798	27-5-1825	10-1-1837			Retd. 1825: restd. 1840	20-5-1826
George Frederick Ryves (1)	8-9-1758	18-11-1780	10-1795	26-4-1798	27-5-1825	10-1-1837				21-12-1841
George Scott (1) (C.B. 1815, K.C.B. 1831)	1770	19-9-1796	19-9-1796	29-5-1798	27-5-1825	10-1-1837				1841
Thomas Dundas (K.C.B. 1831)	1768	2-9-1795	2-9-1795	15-6-1798	27-5-1825	12-11-1840				2-4-1832
George Fowke		1790	1795	9-7-1798	27-5-1825					1843
James Keith Shepard		28-5-1781	1796	9-7-1798	27-5-1825	12-11-1840				
Richard Harrison Pearson		19-9-1777	1793	12-7-1798	27-5-1825	10-1-1837			Retd. 1825: restd. 1840	
George Astle		1793	1794	7-8-1798	27-5-1825					9-1-1838
John Tremayne Rodd (C.B. 1815, K.C.B. 1832)		1794	1795	27-8-1798	27-5-1825	10-1-1837			Gov. of Green. Hosp. 1834.	4-10-1838
Thomas Masterman Hardy (Bart. 1806, K.C.B. 1815, G.C.B. 1831)	1769	1793	5-1797	2-10-1798	27-5-1825	10-1-1837				20-9-1839
William Cumberland		1790	1795	8-11-1798	27-5-1825					

List of Flag-Officers—*continued*.

Name.	Born.	Lieut.	Com.	Captain.	R.-Adm.	V.-Adm.	Admiral.	Adm. of Fleet.	Remarks.	Died.
Graham Eden Hamond (C.B. 1815, suc. as Bart. 1828, K.C.B. 1831, G.C.B. 1855)	30-12-1779	19-10-1795	20-10-1797	30-11-1798	27-5-1825	10-1-1837	22-1-1847	1862	R.A. and V.A. of U.K.	20-12-1862
Robert Honyman	1776	21-10-1790	13-8-1796	10-12-1798	27-5-1825	10-1-1837	19-2-1847		Retd. 1825: restd. 1840	7-1848
Robert Lewis Fitzgerald (Kt., K.C.H. 1835)	1774	1794	2-1797	24-12-1798		12-11-1840				17-11-1844
Volant Vashon Ballard (C.B. 1815)	29-10-1765	6-11-1795	26-7-1797	25-12-1798	27-5-1825	10-1-1837				12-10-1832
Hugh Downman		5-3-1790		25-12-1798	27-5-1825	10-1-1837	24-4-1847		R.td. 1-7-1851.	
Hon. Thomas Bladen Capel (C.B. 1815, K.C.B. 1832)	25-8-1776	5-4-1797	20-10-1798	27-12-1798	27-5-1825	10-1-1837	28-4-1847			4-3-1853
William Hanwell	1767	1793	1797	29-12-1798	27-5-1825					19-6-1834
Thomas Manby		1795		22-1-1799	27-5-1825	10-1-1837				3-7-1855
Lord James O'Bryen (G.C.H. 1831, suc. as Marq. of Thomond 1846)		11-1790	5-12-1796	14-2-1799	27-5-1825	10-1-1837	26-6-1847			19-3-1848
Richard Matson		15-10-1794	22-9-1797	22-3-1799	27-5-1825	10-1-1837			Retd. 1-7-1851	
Richard Raggett	1768	15-12-1778	1793	21-4-1799	27-5-1825	10-1-1837	26-7-1847		Retd. 1825: restd. 1840.	1854
John Mackellar		22-11-1790	5-7-1797	8-6-1799	27-5-1825	12-11-1840	27-12-1847			16-9-1853
George Barker		19-3-1782	19-12-1796	12-6-1799	27-5-1825	10-1-1837	8-1-1848			
Charles Adam (K.C.B. 1835)	6-10-1780	8-2-1798	16-5-1798	14-6-1799	22-7-1830	10-1-1837				2-1-1848
John Stiles	1769	12-9-1781	1797	22-7-1799	22-7-1830	10-1-1837				4-4-1845
William Granger		7-10-1793	10-5-1797	2-8-1799	22-7-1830	12-11-1840				11-4-1846
John Chambers White (K.C.B. 1841)	24-12-1770	22-11-1790	28-8-1795	16-9-1799	22-7-1830	10-1-1837	20-3-1848		Retd. 1830: restd. 1840	
Henry Garrett	1774	17-8-1795	27-12-1798	30-10-1799	22-7-1830	12-1-1840	1-6-1848			3-3-1849
Adam Drummond (K.C.H., Kt. 1837)		1782	29-5-1798	18-11-1799	22-7-1830	10-1-1837				11-4-1842
Robert Hall (1)	1765	22-11-1790	6-12-1796	6-12-1799	22-7-1830	17-8-1840				17-1-1846
Robert Lloyd (2)		24-7-1781	6-12-1799	26-12-1799	22-7-1830	28-6-1838			Retd. 1830: re-td. 1840.	
John Chesslyre	24-3-1765	22-11-1790	1794	13-1-1800	22-7-1830		1-6-1848			1834
Thomas Livingstone (suc. as Bart. 1795)		5-3-1795	26-12-1799	27-1-1800	22-7-1830					24-11-1835
Lucius Ferdinand Hardyman (C.B. 1815)		1793	8-8-1799	18-2-1800	22-7-1830	28-6-1838				24-1-1844
Joshua Sydney Horton	1772	1792	1795	22-4-1800	22-7-1830	1-7-1840				21-4-1844
Edward Brace (C.B. 1815, K.C.B. 1834)		1790	1797	25-4-1800	22-7-1830	28-6-1838				
Jahleel Brenton (2) (Bart. 1812, K.C.B. 1815)	22-8-1770	28-12-1792	3-7-1799	13-5-1800	22-7-1830	17-8-1840				
Francis William Austen (1) (C.B. 1815, K.C.B. 1837, G.C.B. 1860)	23-4-1774	21-9-1790	3-2-1799	15-5-1800	22-7-1830	28-6-1838	1-8-1848	27-4-1863	R.A. and V.A. of U.K.	10-9-1865
Bendall Robert Littlehales	1765	1782	27-9-1797	11-7-1800		17-8-1840				8-1847
Patrick Campbell (1) (C.B. 1815, K.C.B. 1836)	1773	1790	4-9-1797	11-8-1800	22-7-1830	28-6-1840			Retd. 1830: Restd. 1840	1841
Norborne Thompson	8-11-1768	29-10-1790	1795	11-8-1800	22-7-1830					
Michael Seymour (1) (Bart. 1809, K.C.B. 1815)			11-8-1795	11-8-1800	27-6-1832				(Retd. 14-1-1829: restd. 1832.)	9-7-1834
Edward Stirling Dickson	15-7-1778	9-7-1780	1796	6-9-1800	22-7-1830	23-11-1841				
Thomas James Maling		6-10-1797	24-12-1798		22-7-1830	23-11-1841				23-1-1849
John Acworth Ommanney (C.B. 1827, K.C.B. 1838)		20-5-1893	6-12-1796	16-10-1800	22-7-1830	23-11-1841	4-5-1849			

Name										
Henry Stuart	1768	1793	7-10-1799	16-11-1800	22-7-1830	23-11-1841	—	15-9-1849	Retd. 19-1-1852.	9-4-1840
Zachary Mudge	1775	24-5-1789	24-11-1797	15-11-1800	22-7-1830	23-11-1841	—			7-6-1849
Henry Hill	1767	17-12-1793	24-7-1795	1-1-1801	22-7-1830	23-11-1841	—		{ Retd. 22-7-1830: restd. 17-8-1840 }	19-2-1845
Charles Wollaston	1767	25-10-1790	6-12-1796	1-1-1801	17-8-1840	23-11-1841	—			
Alexander Wilmot Schomberg, K.C.H. 1833	1775	26-7-1793	2-4-1798	1-1-1801	22-7-1830	23-11-1841	—	9-10-1849	…	16-1-1862
Edward Durnford King (Kt., K.C.B. 1833)		5-9-1794	23-6-1796	8-1-1801	22-7-1830	23-11-1841	—	30-10-1849	…	3-1843
Henry Vansittart		1795	8-1798	3-2-1801	22-7-1830	23-11-1841	—		…	9-2-1861
George Mundy (C.B. 1815, K.C.B. 1837)	3-3-1777	11-3-1796	24-12-1798	10-2-1801	22-7-1830	23-11-1841	—	24-12-1849		27-11-1840
George Sayer (1) (C.B. 1815)		1793	1798	14-2-1801	22-7-1830		—		{ Retd. 22-7-1830: restd. 1840. }	
Charles Tinling		1793	1798	14-2-1801	17-8-1840		—			3-1-1841
Philip Bowes Vere Broke (Bart. 1813, K.C.B. 1815)	9-9-1776	1797	2-1-1799	14-2-1801	22-7-1830	23-11-1841	—			3-1-1841
Frederick Lewis Maitland (2) (C.B. 1815, K.C.B. 1830)	7-9-1776	5-4-1795	14-6-1799	21-3-1801	22-7-1830	23-11-1841	—			30-12-1839
Frederick Warren	3-1775	24-10-1794	10-8-1797	12-5-1801	22-7-1830	23-11-1841	—		{ Retd. 22-7-1830: restd. 1840. }	22-3-1848
Richard Peacocke		22-1-1796	28-1-1801	4-6-1801	17-8-1840	23-11-1841	—			24-4-1846
James Carthew		4-11-1790	4-6-1798	11-1-1801	22-7-1830	23-11-1841	—	14-1-1850	Retd. 21-3-1854.	
Thomas Briggs (G.C.M.G. 1833)	1780	28-9-1797	30-6-1800	24-7-801	27-6-1832	23-11-1841	—	2-9-1850	Retd. 1830: restd. 1832.	1837
John Broughton (1)		26-8-1795	7-1-1795	3-8-1801	22-7-1830		—			1834
Hon. George Heneage Lawrence Dundas (C.B. 1815)		1797	1800	3-8-1801	22-7-1830	23-11-1841	—			
Thomas, Lord Cochrane (K.B. 1809, *suc. as* Earl of Dundonald 1831)	14-12-1775	24-5-1796	28-3-1800	8-8-1801	2-5-1832	23-11-1841	—	21-3-1851	{ Dismd. 5-7-1814: restd. 1832. R.A. of U.K. First posted 12-12-1796: dismd. 11-1798: restd. 22-9-1801: retd. 22-7-1830: restd. 17-8-1840 }	31-10-1860
Nicholas Tomlinson		23-3-1782	30-11-1795	22-9-1801	17-8-1840	23-11-1841	27-4-1863			6-3-1847
William Parker (2) (C.B. 1815, K.C.B. 1834, G.C.B. 1842, Bart. 1844)	1781	5-9-1799	10-10-1799	9-10-1801	22-7-1830	23-11-1841	—	29-4-1851	R.A. of U.K.	13-11-1866
Tristram Robert Ricketts (Bart. 1828)	1772	1793	16-5-1798	9-10-1801	22-7-1830	23-11-1841	—	11-6-1851	Retd. 16-9-1851.	18-8-1842
George M'Kinley	5-7-1770	14-1-1782	16-5-1798	20-10-1801	22-7-1830	23-11-1841	—		{ Retd. 22-7-1830: restd. 1840. }	1852
James Katon	1-9-1765	18-2-1794	7-5-1801	2-11-1801	17-8-1840	23-11-1841	—		{ Retd. 22-7-1830: restd. 1840. }	14-12-1845
Charles Dashwood (Kt. 1825, K.C.B. 1840)	1772	20-6-1794	3-8-1799	7-11-1802	22-7-1830	23-11-1841	—		{ Retd. **v.a.** 1-7-1851: **a.** 8-7-1851. }	21-9-1847
Richard Curry (C.B. 1831)		7-4-1778	30-11-1794	7-1-1802	10-1-1837	9-11-1846	—			
William Skipsey	1756	1797	6-12-1796	18-3-1802	10-1-1837		—			18-3-1846
Hon. Frederick Paul Irby (C.B. 1831)	18-4-1779		1800	14-4-1802	10-1-1837		—			15-5-1844
John Wentworth Loring (C.B. 1815, K.C.B. 1840)	13-10-1775	24-5-1794	3-1-1799	28-4-1802	10-1-1837	9-11-1846	8-7-1851			1852
Robert Howe Bromley (*suc. as* Bart. 1808)	28-11-1778	22-1-1798	14-2-1801	28-4-1802	10-1-1837	9-11-1846	17-8-1851			8-7-1857
Hon. Duncombe Pleydell Bouverie	28-6-1780	17-2-1799	14-2-1801	28-4-1802	17-8-1840		—		{ Retd. 10-1-1837: restd. 1840. }	5-11-1850
Richard Poulden	12-2-1783		29-6-1795	29-4-1802	10-1-1837	9-11-1846	—		{ Retd. 10-1-1837: restd. 1840. }	16-3-1845
John Dick		4-8-1794	28-6-1796	29-4-1802	10-1-1837	9-11-1846	19-1-1852			
Peter Ribouleau	1769	31-8-1793	25-7-1796	29-4-1802	17-8-1840	9-11-1846	—		{ Retd. 10-1-1837: restd. 1840. }	16-12-1847

LIST OF FLAG-OFFICERS—*continued.*

Name.	Born.	Lieut.	Com.	Captain.	R.-Adm.	V.-Adm.	Admiral.	Adm. of Fleet.	Remarks.	Died.
Matthew Buckle (2)	3-5-1770	21-1-1791	6-12-1796	29-4-1802	17-8-1840	9 11-1846	—	—	Retd. 10-1-1837: restd. 1840: retd. a. 30-7-1852.	
John Allen (1)		10-12-1793	6-12-1796	29-4-1802	17-8-1840	9-11-1846	—	—	Retd. 10-1-1837: restd. 1840: retd. a. 30-7-1852.	
James Noble		9-3-1796	27-2-1797	29-4-1802	17-8-1840	9-11-1846	—	—	Retd. 10-1-1837: restd. 1840.	
Samuel Warren (2) (C.B. 1815, K.C.H., Kt. 1835)	9-1-1769	1790	3-1797	29-4-1802	17-8-1840	—	—	—	Retd. 10-1-1837: restd. 1840.	1839
Anselm John Griffiths		22-11-1790	8-3-1797	29-4-1802	10-1-1837	—	—	—		1842
Francis Holmes Coffin		1791	1797	29-4-1802	17-8-1840	—	—	—	Retd. 10-1-1837: restd. 1840.	
Jeffery (Baron von) Raigersfeld		1793	1797	29-4-1802	17-8-1840	—	—	—	Retd. 10-1-1837: restd. 1840.	
Christopher John Williams Nesham	1771	17-11-1790	2-1-1798	29-4-1802	17-8-1840	9-11-1846	—	—	Retd. 10-1-1837: restd. 1840: retd. a. 30-7-1852.	
Charles Bullen (C.B. 1815, K.C.H., Kt. 1835, K.C.B. 1839)	10-9-1769	9-8-1791	2-1-1798	29-4-1802	10-1-1837	9-11-1846	30-7-1852	—		1853
John Wight	1776	8-9-1796	3-1-1798	29-4-1802	17-8-1840	9-11-1846	—	—		
Henry Folkes Edgell	13-8-1767	16-11-1790	5-3-1798	29-4-1802	17-8-1840	—	—	—	Retd. 10-1-1837: restd. 1840.	14-6-1846
William Butterfield	1767	1794	4-1798	29-4-1802	17-8-1840	—	—	—	Retd. 10-1-1837: restd. 1840.	3-10-1842
Richard Byron (2) (C.B. 1815)	1769	1793	3-1798	29-4-1802	10-1-1837	—	—	—	Retd. 10-1-1837: restd. 1840.	2-9-1837
William Young (2)	27-8-1761	3-7-1783	3-7-1798	29-4-1802	17-8-1840	9-11-1846	—	—	Retd. 10-1-1837: restd. 1840.	11-2-1847
George Tobin	13-12-1768	22-11-1790	1798	29-4-1802	10-1-1837	—	—	—		10-3-1838
William Henry Webley (*later* W. H. W. Parry) (C.B. 1815)	1767	21-9-1790	1798	29-4-1802	10-1-1837	—	—	—		1837
Edward Galwey		1791	1798	29-4-1802	10-1-1837	—	—	—		
Jacob Walton		1793	1798	29-4-1802	17-8-1840	—	—	—	Retd. 10-1-1837: restd. 1840.	
John Hayes (1) (C.B. 1838)	1767	1793	1-3-1799	29-4-1802	10-1-1837	—	—	—		7-4-1838
Samuel Campbell Rowley	19-1-1774	30-1-1794	6-4-1799	29-4-1802	10-1-1837	—	—	—		28-1-1846
Bulkley Mackworth Prael		1-9-1793	21-4-1799	29-4-1802	17-8-1840	9-11-1846	—	—	Retd. 10-1-1837: restd. 1840.	
Samuel Motley (1)	1764	1782	29-4-1799	29-4-1802	17-8-1840	—	—	—	Retd. 10-1-1837: restd. 1840.	27-5-1841
Edward Walpole Browne	1767	9-11-1790	25-6-1799	29-4-1802	17-8-1840	—	—	—	Retd. 10-1-1837: restd. 1840.	15-10-1846

Name	Born	Lieut.	Com'r	Capt.	R.-Adm.	V.-Adm.	Adm.		Retired / remarks	Died
John Rouet Smollett		23-1-1794	28-8-1799	29-4-1802	17-8-1840			—	Retd. 10-1-1837: restd. 1840.	1842
Hon. William Le Poer Trench	7-1771	16-6-1793	19-11-1799	29-4-1802	17-8-1840			—	Retd. 10-1-1837: restd. 1840.	16-8-1846
Edward Sneyd Clay	1768	19-3-1794	3-12-1799	29-4-1802	17-8-1840			—	Retd. 10-1-1837: restd. 1840.	3-2-1846
Charles Carter (2)		22-11-1790	15-5-1800	29-4-1802	17-8-1840	9-11-1846		—	Retd. 10-1-1837: restd. 1840.	20-12-1847
Thomas Browne (1)		21-11-1790	11-8-1800	29-4-1802	10-1-1837	11-12-1846		—	Retd. 10-1-1837: restd. 1840.	1851
William Henry Brown Tremlett	15-11-1777	21-9-1795	1-1-1801	29-4-1802	17-8-1840	22-1-1847	17-12-1852	—	Retd. 10-1-1837: restd. 1840: retd. a. 17-12-1852.	
Samuel Pym (C.B. 1815, K.C.B. 1839)	1778	7-3-1795	10-2-1801	29-4-1802	17-8-1840	13-2-1847		—		8-5-1849
Samuel Butcher	30-10-1770	17-7-1794	19-2-1801	29-4-1802	10-1-1837	8-3-1847		—		9-6-1852
Robert Jackson (2)	4-1765	22-11-1790	6-10-1801	29-4-1802	10-1-1837			—		6-1841
Robert Barrie (C.B. 1815, K.C.H. 1834, K.C.B. 1840)	1774	1795	23-10-1801	29-4-1802	10-1-1837			—	Retd. 10-1-1837: restd. 1840.	2-3-1849
Charles Bayne Hodgson Ross (C.B. 1815)	5-9-1782	14-7-1796	11-6-1800	15-10-1802	10-1-1837	24-4-1847		—		1851
Charles Malcolm (Kt. 1827)	1778	12-1-1799	28-5-1802	29-12-1802	10-1-1837			—		28-3-1844
Francis William Fane		1801	28-4-1802	30-8-1803	10-1-1837	28-4-1847		—		
Hon. George Elliot (3) (C.B. 1831, K.C.B. 1862)	1-8-1784	12-8-1800	14-4-1802	2-1-1804	17-8-1840	13-5-1847	5-3-1853	—	Retl. 3-10-1855.	24-6-1863
James Hillyar (C.B. 1815, K.C.H. 1834, K.C.B. 1840)	1770	1794	16-4-1800	29-2-1804	10-1-1837			—		10-7-1843
Lord William Fitzroy (C.B. 1815, K.C.B. 1840)	1-6-1782	13-5-1800	7-1-1802	3-3-1804	10-1-1837	26-6-1847	2-4-1853	—	Dismd. 7-4-1811: restd. 22-8-1811.	13-5-1857
Lord George Stuart (C.B. 1815)	1-3-1780	1801	22-4-1802	3-3-1804	17-8-1840			—		19-2-1841
Matthew Godwin	25-12-1766	1-8-1794	15-1-1802	8-5-1804	10-1-1837	26-7-1847		—	Retd. 10-1-1837: restd. 1840.	
Hugh Pigot (3) (C.B. 1831, K.C.H., Kt. 1834, K.C.B. 1847)	1775	12-11-1794	29-4-1802	8-5-1804	10-1-1837	6-8-1847	4-7-1853	—		30-7-1857
Salusbury Pryce Humphreys (S. P. Davenport, 1838) (C.B. 1831, Kt., K.C.H. 1834)	26-11-1778	27-1-1797	29-4-1802	8-5-1804	17-8-1840			—	Retd. 10-1-1837: restd. 1840.	17-11-1845
John Tower (C.B. 1831)		1797	30-6-1803	8-5-1804	10-1-1837			—		11-1837
Edward Hawker		14-7-1796	9-10-1802	6-6-1804	10-1-1837	22-9-1847	17-9-1853	—		1860
Charles Richardson (C.B. 1815, K.C.B. 1841)		4-8-1794		27-9-1804	10-1-1837	17-12-1847	21-1-1854	—		19-1-1863
Francis Temple		8-10-1793	4-7-1803	12-3-1805	17-8-1840	21-12-1847		—		
Arthur Farquhar (1) (C.B. 1815, K.C.H. 1832, K.C.B. 1841)		1798	29-4-1802	8-4-1805	10-1-1837	27-12-1847		—	Retd. r.a. 10-1-1837: rest. 17-8-1840: retd. a. 21-1-1854.	
Henry Gordon		13-7-1798	29-4-1802	8-4-1805	17-8-1840	8-1-1848		—	Retd. 10-1-1837: restd. 1840: retd. a. 21-1-1854.	
James Alexander Gordon (1) (K.C.B. 1815, G.C.B. 1855)	1782	27-1-1800	3-3-1804	16-5-1805	10-1-1837	3-1-1848	21-1-1854	—	Retd. a. of f. 30-1-1868.	8-1-1869
Hon. Frederick William Aylmer (suc. as Lord Aylmer 1850) (C.B. 1816, K.C.B. 1855)	12-10-1777	17-12-1796	7-1-1802	18-5-1805	10-1-1837	8-1-1848		—	Retd. 1-7-1851: retd. a. 11-9-1854.	5-3-1858
Richard Thomas (2)		15-1-1797	18-1-1803	22-10-1805	10-1-1837		11-9-1854	—		1857

List of Flag-Officers—continued.

Name	Born	Lieut.	Com.	Captain	R.-Adm.	V.-Adm.	Admiral	Adm. of Fleet	Remarks	Died
James Richard Dacres (2).		15-11-1804	5-7-1805	14-1-1806	28-6-1838	20-3-1848			Retd. 28-6-1838: restd. 1840: retd. v.a. 23-3-1848; retd. a. 3-7-1855	1853
John Surman Carden	15-8-1771	24-7-1794	25-10-1798	22-1-1806	17-8-1840					22-4-1858
John Sykes (1)	25-5-1774	6-11-1795	18-6-1800	22-1-1806	28-6-1838	1-6-1848	3-7-1855			12-2-1858
John Hancock (1) (C.B. 1815)	1766	24-10-1794	2-4-1801	22-1-1806	28-6-1838				Retd. 28-6-1838: restd. 1810	12-10-1839
John Wentworth Holland	1766	1794	25-4-1801	22-1-1806	17-8-1840					1841
John Impey		7-11-1793	15-1-1802	22-1-1806	17-8-1840	1-8-1848			Retd. 28-6-1838: restd. 1840: retd. a. 4-7-1855.	
Henry Manaton Ommanney		10-4-1794	29-4-1802	22-1-1806	17-8-1840	24-1-1849			Retd. 28-6-1838: restd. 1840: retd. a. 4-7-1855	1857
Archibald Duff	1774	8-12-1798	29-4-1802	22-1-1806	17-8-1840				Re'd. 28-6-1838: restd. 1849: retd. v.a. 3-3-1849; retd. a. 4-7-1855	9-2-1858
Donald Hugh Mackay (suc. as Hon. 1841)	31-12-1780	27-3-1798	29-4-1802	22-1-1806	28-6-1838	4-5-1849				26-3-1850
Francis Mason (C.B. 1815, K.C.B. 1841)	19-2-1779	8-7-1799	29-4-1802	22-1-1806	28-6-1838	9-5-1849				27-5-1853
Major Jacob Henniker (suc. as Hon. 1832).	19-8-1780	23-7-1799	29-4-1802	22-1-1806	17-8-1840				Retd. 28-6-1838: restd. 1840	1843
Thomas Brown		24-10-1794	8-10-1802	22-1-1806	28-6-1838	8-6-1849	4-7-1855			
Alexander Shippard	1778	28-10-1793	3-3-1804	22-1-1806	28-6-1838					4-4-1841
Robert Henderson		29-5-1799	21-6-1804	22-1-1806	28-6-1838					
Lucius Curtis (C.B. 1815, suc. as Bart. 1816, K.C.B. 1862)	3-6-1786	11-8-1801	16-11-1804	22-1-1806	28-6-1838	15-9-1849	9-7-1855	11-1-1864		14-1-1869
John Louis (suc. as Bart. 1808)	1785	21-4-1801	28-2-1805	22-1-1806	28-6-1838	9-10-1849	27-9-1855		Retd. 2-5-1860	31-3-1863
Brian Hodgson		11-12-1799	8-4-1805	22-1-1806	28-6-1838	18-10-1849				1849
Hood Hanway Christian	23-7-1784	25-1-1800	21-3-1805	30-1-1805	28-6-1838	10-1849				20-6-1850
Josiah Cramer (Josiah Coghill Coghill 1817) (suc. as Bart. 1817)	1773	24-3-1800	7-5-1802	1-2-1806	23-11-1841					16-11-1844
Nathaniel Day Cochrane		26-12-1800	30-7-1805	26-3-1806	23-11-1841	24-12-1849	3-10-1855			1864
John Ayscough		6-11-1793	12-5-1797	18-4-1806	23-11-1841					
Thomas John Cochrane (Kt. 1812, C.B. 1839, K.C.B. 1847, G.C.B. 1860)	1789	14-6-1805	24-9-1805	23-4-1806	23-11-1841	14-1-1850	31-1-1856	12-9-1865	V.A. of U.K.	19-10-1872
William Furlong Wise (C.B. 1816)	21-8-1784	1-5-1804	1-11-1805	18-5-1806	23-11-1841					5-5-1844
Edmund Boger	1776	16-3-1795	27-1-1803	22-5-1806	23-11-1841					1845
William Jones Lye.	9-6-1783	15-1-1802	31-1-1806	22-5-1806	23-11-1841					7-3-1846
George Francis Seymour (C.B. 1815, K.C.H., Kt. 1831, G.C.H. 1834, K.C.B. 1852, G.C.B. 1860)	17-9-1787	12-10-1804	23-1-1806	29-7-1806	23-11-1841	27-3-1850	14-5-1857	20-11-1866	R.A. and V.A. of U.K.	20-1-1870

Name										Remarks	Died
Hon. George Poulett	10-5-1786	3-4-1804	12-10-1805	31-7-1806	23-11-1841	21-6-1850		—				10-2-1854
James Haldane Tait	1771	6-7-1796	29-4-1802	5-9-1806	23-11-1841			—				7-3-1845
William Beauchamp Proctor (*suc. as* Bart. 1827)	14-10-1781	25-2-1801	29-4-1802	5-9-1806	23-11-1841	6-11-1850		—			{Retd. v.a. 2-9-1850; retd. a. 18-6-1827}	14-3-1861
Charles James Johnston		26-2-1795	18-1-1803	5-9-1806	23-11-1841	6-11-1850		—			Retd. v.a. 15-4-1854	1856
Edward Ratsey		9-4-1795	4-2-1806	5-9-1806	23-11-1841			—			{Retd. v.a. 11-11-1850; retd. a. 18-6-1857}	1868
Richard Turner Hancock	23-6-1764	26-8-1789	4-9-1800	25-9-1806	23-11-1841			—				5-3-1846
Charles Philip Butler Bateman	1776	31-10-1795	29-4-1802	25-9-1806	23-11-1841			—				
Mauritius Adolphus Newton .e Starck		20-11-1790	1-5-1804	25-9-1806	23-11-1841			—				4-9-1848
Arthur Lysaght		3-8-1802	22-1-1806	25-9-1806	23-11-1841			—				
Hon. Josceline Percy (C.B. 1831)	29-1-1784	30-4-1804	22-1-1806	25-9-1806	23-11-1841	29-4-1851		—			{Retd. v.a. 21-3-1851; retd. a. 18-6-1857}	19-10-1856
Hon. Anthony Maitland (Earl Lauderdale 1860) (C.B. 1816, K.C.M.G. 1832, K.C.B. 1852)	10-6-1780	2-2-1805	6-5-1806	25-9-1806	23-11-1841	11-6-1851	18-6-1857	—			{Re'd. v.a. 8-4-1851; retd. a. 18-6-1857}	22-3-1863
Hon. Granville Leveson Proby (Earl of Carysfort 185..)	1781	24-10-1804	15-8-1806	28-11-1806	23-11-1841			—			{Retd. v.a. 16-6-1851; retd. a. 9-7-1857}	3-11-1868
Hon. Granville George Waldegrave (Lord Radstock 1825) (C.B. 1815)	24-9-1786	20-7-1804	22-1-1806	16-2-1807	23-11-1841	1-7-1851		—				11-5-1857
Hon. George Cadogan (Earl Cadogan 1832) (C.B. 1815)	5-5-1783	12-4-1802	4-5-1804	23-3-1807	23-11-1841	1-7-1851		—				15-9-1864
Edward Tucker (Kt. 1813, K.C.B. 1815)		21-5-1799	22-1-1806	23-3-1807	23-11-1841	8-7-1851	9-7-1857	—			Retd. 28-1-1858	1864
William Maude	1780	26-9-1800	11-12-1805	26-9-1807	23-11-1841		30-7-1857	—				18-6-1843
Samuel Hood Inglefield (C.B. 1839)	1783	26-7-1798	29-1-1802	6-10-1807	23-11-1841			—				23-11-1847
William Augustus Montagu (C.B. 1815, K.C.H., Kt. 1832)		14-11-1804	31-10-1805	12-10-1807	23-11-1841	17-8-1851		—				1852
Valentine Collard	1770	17-11-1793	8-3-1797	13-10-1807	23-11-1841			—				18-3-1846
Edward Chetham (E. C. Strode 1845) (C.B. 1815, K.C.H., Kt., 1837, K.C.B. 1845)	5-7-1775	18-8-1794	7-11-1800	13-10-1807	23-11-1841	19-1-1852	22-8-1857	—				11-4-1862
Reuben Cailland Mangin	1-11-1780	3-12-1800	8-5-1804	13-10-1807	23-11-1841			—				20-8-1846
William Croft	4-1782	22-12-1801	8-5-1804	13-10-1807	23-11-1841			—			{Retd. 1851: Retd. v.a. 8-3-1852; retd. a. 28-11-1857}	22-12-1846
Francis Beaumann	1778	26-10-1796	4-3-1805	13-10-1807	23-11-1841			—			Retd. 1851.	
James Robert Philips		10-12-1795	15-3-1805	13-10-1807	23-11-1841			—				29-1-1848
Pringle Stoddart	23-5-1768	16-4-1796	22-1-1806	13-10-1807	23-11-1841			—				1869
William Bowles (C.B. 1839, K.C.B. 1862)	1780	30-8-1803	22-1-1806	13-10-1807	23-11-1841	8-3-1852	28-11-1857	—			R.A. and V.A. of U.K.	26-5-1854
Hyde Parker (3) (C.B. 1839)		24-9-1804	22-1-1806	13-10-1807	23-11-1841	4-6-1852		15-1-1869				
Charles Sibthorp John Hawtayne		24-8-1799	31-1-1806	13-10-1807	23-11-1841	30-7-1852		—				3-10-1862
James Whitley Deans Dundas (J. W. Deans till 1808) (C.B. 1839, G.C.B. 1855)	4-12-1785	25-5-1805	8-10-1806	13-10-1807	23-11-1841	17-12-1852	8-12-1857	—				16-1-1845
Samuel Jackson (C.B. 1815)	1775	3-11-1796	18-8-1801	5-11-1807	23-11-1841			—				
Edward Thomas Troubridge (*suc. as* Bart. 1807, C.B. 1838)		22-2-1806	5-9-1806	28-11-1807	23-11-1841			—			{Retd. 1851: retd. v.a. 5-3-1853}	7-10-1852
Charles Gordon (1) (C.B. 1840)	11-3-1802		20-5-1806	21-12-1807	23-11-1841			—				
James Murray Gordon	6-3-1782	25-2-1803	1-2-1806	15-2-1808	9-11-1846			—				
William Henry Dillon (K.C.H., Kt. 1835)	8-8-1779	28-4-1797	8-4-1805	21-3-1808	9-11-1846	5-3-1853		—				17-3-1849
Thomas Searle (C.B. 1815)	29-5-1777	19-8-1796	26-11-1799	25-4-1808	9-11-1846			—				

LIST OF FLAG-OFFICERS—*continued.*

NAME.	BORN.	LIEUT.	COM.	CAPTAIN.	R.-ADM.	V.-ADM.	ADMIRAL.	ADM. OF FLEET.	REMARKS.	DIED.
Henry Hope (C.B. 1815, K.C.B. 1860)	1787	3-5-1804	22-1-1806	24-5-1808	9-11-1846	2-4-1853	20-1-1858			23-9-1863
Thomas Ussher (C.B. 1815, K.C.H., Kt. 1831)	1779	17-7-1797	18-10-1806	24-5-1808	9-11-1846					6-1-1848
William Ward (1)	21-11-1782	10-1-1800	23-7-1806	10-6-1808	9-11-1846				(Retd. 1851: retd. v.a. 22-4-1853.)	
Samuel John Brooke Pechell (C.B. 1815, *suc. as* Bart. 1826, K.C.H. 1833)	1-9-1785	1-4-1803	23-3-1807	16-6-1808	9-11-1846					3-11-1849
Robert Elliot	10-1769	13-7-1793	14-2-1801	27-6-1808	9-11-1846				Retd. 1-7-1851.	
Cuthbert Featherstone Daly (C.B. 1838)		30-9-1800	10-4-1806	18-8-1808	9-11-1846					
Hon. Fleetwood Broughton Reynolds Pellew (C.B. 1815, K.C.H., Kt. 1836)	13-12-1789	8-9-1805	12-10-1807	14-10-1808	9-11-1846	22-4-1853	13-2-1858			28-7-1861
Francis Augustus Collier (C.B. 1815, Kt. 1830, K.C.H. 1832)	1783	11-4-1803	25-1-1805	13-12-1808	9-11-1846					1849
Hon. James William King	6-3-1786	3-3-1804	15-8-1806	18-1-1809	9-11-1846					14-2-1848
Charles Napier (2) (C.B. 1815, K.C.B. 1840)	6-3-1786	29-7-1794	30-11-1807	22-5-1809	9-11-1846	28-5-1853	6-3-1858			5-11-1860
John Brett Purvis	12-8-1787	1-5-1805	9-8-1808	16-9-1809	9-11-1846	4-7-1853				1857
William Henry Shirreff	1785	3-3-1804	3-3-1806	15-11-1809	9-11-1846					1-12-1847
Richard Arthur (C.B. 1838)	1779	28-2-1800	1-11-1805	11-1-1810	9-11-1846	17-9-1853				1854
Phipps Hornby (C.B. 1815, K.C.B. 1852, G.C.B. 1861)	27-4-1785	1-8-1804	15-8-1806	16-2-1810	9-11-1846	21-1-1854	25-6-1858		R.A. of U.K.	19-3-1867
Hon. William Gordon (2)	1785	2-7-1804	24-4-1807	12-3-1810	9-11-1846	11-2-1854				3-2-1858
Charles John Austen (1) (C.B. 1840)	1779	18-12-1797	10-10-1804	10-5-1810	9-11-1846	11- -1854				1852
Philip Browne (2)	16-9-1772	22-12-1793	25-9-1806	19-6-1810	9-11-1846				(Dismd. 31-3-1814: restd. 1815: retd. 1851: retd. v.a. 16-4-1854.)	26-1-1860
Henry Prescott (C.B. 1815, K.C.B. 1856, G.C.B. 1869)	4-5-1783	28-4-1802	4-2-1808	25-7-1810	24-4-1847	15-4-1854	2-5-1860		Retd. 9-6-1860.	18-11-1874
Nisbet Josiah Willoughby (C.B. 1815, Kt., 1827 and 1832, K.C.H. 1832)	29-8-1777	13-1-1798	9-4-1808	5-9-1810	28-4-1847					19-5-1849
Edward Wallis Hoare	4-5-1779	4-8-1796	25-10-1804	16-10-1810	13-5-1847				(Retd. 1851: retd. v.a. 27-5-1854.)	
John Coode (C.B. 1816, K.C.B. 1855)	11-2-1779	6-5-1796	3-8-1802	21-10-1810	26-6-1847	27-5-1854			Retd. v.a. 10-12-1855.	19-1-1858
Thomas Fellowes (C.B. 1815, Kt. 1828)	1778	29-6-1807	16-9-1809	4-3-1811	26-7-1847				Retd. r.a. 1-7-1851.	
Edward Henry a'Court Repington (E. H. a'C. Repington, 1847)	10-12-1783	13-2-1804	10-6-1808	29-3-1811	6-8-1847				(Retd. 1851: retd. v.a. 11-9-1854.)	22-9-1855
John Pasco	20-12-1774	15-7-1795	24-12-1805	3-4-1811	22-9-1847					
William Fisher	18-11-1780	3-9-1801	25-9-1806	18-4-1811	2-12-1847					
Edward Harvey (K.C.B. 1861)	3-3-1783	24-7-1801	7-1-1808	18-4-1811	17-12-1847	11-9-1854	9-6-1860		Retd. v.a. 6-2-1855.	4-5-1865
William Fitzwilliam Owen		10-4-1802	20-5-1809	2-5-1811	21-12-1847	27-10-1854			Retd. v.a. 28-12-1855: retd. a. 1-11-1860.	1857
Manley Hall Dixon	8-6-1786	15-5-1800	10-2-1809	28-6-1811	27-12-1847	7-2-1855			(Retd. r.a. 1851: retd. v.a. 3-7-1855: retd. a. 1-11-1860.)	3-3-1864
Hon. Alexander Jones	9-3-1778	15-5-1800	22-1-1806	1-8-1811	3-1-1848	3-7-1855			Retd. v.a. 21-7-1856.	8-1-1862
Peter John Douglas	30-6-1787	11-6-1804	17-2-1807	26-11-1811	7-1-1848					

Name										
Barrington Reynolds (C.B. 1838, K.C.B. 1856)	1785	18-9-1801	3-10-1810	22-1-1812	8-1-1848	4-7-1855	1-11-1860	|		1861
Hon. George Alfred Crofton	20-8-1787	10-10-1804	9-2-1808	1-2-1812	30-1-1848	9-7-1855		|	Retd. v.a. 12-11-1856.	
Villiers Francis Hatton		31-1-1806	19-6-1808	7-2-1812	14-2-1848			|	{ Retd. 1851: retd. v.a. 27-9-1855. }	
Charles Sotheby	26-5-1788	25-1-1802	8-1-1810	23-2-1812	20-3-1848			|		
Augustus William James Clifford (C.B. 1815, Kt. 1830, Bart. 1838).	1785	25-6-1806	12-2-1811	23-7-1812	23-3-1848	27-9-1855		|	Retd. a. 1866.	8-2-1877
Joshua Ricketts Rowley (*suc. as* Bart. 1832)		9-4-1808	8-8-1810	30-9-1812	3-4-1848	3-10-1855	7-11-1860	|		18-3-1857
Alexander Renton Sharpe (C.B. 1815)		8-12-1806	25-3-1809	22-1-1813	1-6-1848	30-10-1855		|	Retd. a. 21-1-1858	1-5-1860
Gordon Thomas Falcon	1788	15-6-1800	8-3-1811	29-10-1813	1-8-1848			|	{ Retd. v.a. 28-12-1855: retd. a. 11-2-1861. }	
Watkin Owen Pell (Kt. 1837)		11-11-1806	29-3-1810	1-11-1813	5-9-1848			|	Retd. 1855	
William Fairbrother Carroll (C.B. 1815, K.C.B. 1852)	28-1-1784	15-5-1804	4-3-1811	6-12-1813	24-1-1849			|	{ Retd. 1851: retd. v.a. 31-1-1856. }	8-4-1862
Andrew Pellet Green (K.C.H., Kt. 1832)		8-8-1800	1-2-1812	12-4-1814	3-3-1849			|	{ Retd. 17-10-1856: retd. a. 11-2-1861. }	
William Bowen Mends	27-1-1781	9-4-1801	26-2-1811	26-5-1814	19-3-1849	31-1-1856		|	{ Retd. 1851: retd. v.a. 31-1-1856: retd. a. 11-2-1861. }	7-2-1864
George Ferguson		30-3-1805	27-12-1808	6-6-1814	4-5-1849			|		15-3-1867
George Rose Sartorius (Kt. 1844, K.C.B. 1865, G.C.B.)	1790	5-3-1808	1-2-1812	6-6-1814	9-5-1849	31-1-1856	11-2-1861	|	{ Retd. 1851: retd. v.a. 11-2-1861. }	13-4-1885
Robert Wauchope		21-12-1808	21-3-1812	6-6-1814	21-5-1849	21-7-1856	29-7-1861	|	{ Remd. 1832; restd. 1836: V.A. of U.K. }	14-6-1862
John Gordon Sinclair (*suc. as* Bart. 1795).	31-7-1790	7-7-1809	13-8-1812	6-6-1814	8-6-1849	17-10-1856	5-8-1861	3-7-1869		13-11-1863
George Edward Watts		1-5-1804	17-9-1807	7-6-1814	1-9-1849			|	{ Retd. 1851: retd. v.a. 21-10-1856. }	2-1-1860
James John Gordon Bremer (C.B. 1815, K.C.H., Kt. 1836, K.C.B. 1841)	26-9-1786	3-8-1805	13-10-1807	7-6-1814	15-9-1849			|		
Ralph Randolph Wormeley	29-10-1785	22-1-1806	16-2-1810	7-6-1814	9-10-1849			|		
Hayes O'Grady		21-3-1807	15-6-1810	7-6-1814	18-10-1849			|		1852
Maurice Frederick Fitzhardinge Berkeley (*suc. as* Earl Fitzhardinge, 1862) (C.B. 1840, K.C.B. 1855, G.C.B. 1861)	3-1-1788		19-12-1810	7-6-1814	30-10-1849	21-10-1856	15-1-1862	|	{ Retd. 1851: retd. v.a. 21-10-1856: retd. a. 15-1-1862. }	10-6-1864
David Dunn (Kt. 1835, K.C.H. 1837)		9-7-1808	13-3-1811	7-6-1814	5-11-1849			|		17-10-1867
Fairfax Moresby (C.B. 1815, K.C.B. 1865, G.C.B. 1865)	1786	12-7-1808	18-4-1811	7-6-1814	20-12-1849	12-11-1856	12-4-1862	21-1-1870	{ Retd. 29-10-1852: retd. v.a. 12-11-1856. }	
George Anson Byron (2) (*suc. as* Lord Byron, 1824)	8-3-1789	10-4-1806	1-2-1812	7-6-1814	24-12-1849			|	R.A. and V.A. of U.K.	21-1-1877
Edmund Lyons (K.C.H. 1835, Bart. 1840, G.C.B. 1844, Lord Lyons 1856)	21-11-1790	24-8-1807	21-3-1812	7-6-1814	14-1-1850	19-3-1857		|	{ Retd. 1851: retd. v.a. 19-3-1857: retd. a. 20-5-1862. }	1-3-1868
Charles Sullivan (*suc. as* Bart. 1814)	28-2-1789	22-11-1809	24-3-1812	7-6-1814	15-2-1850	12-5-1857		|		23-11-1858
John Marshall (2) (C.B. 1815, Kt., K.C.H. 1832)	1785	25-4-1808	24-10-1812	7-6-1814	27-3-1850		20-5-1862	|		21-11-1862
James Erskine Wemyss	1789	14-8-1808	1-2-1812	1-7-1814	21-6-1850	14-5-1857		|	Retd. 1851	3-4-1854
Francis Erskine Loch	4-1788	22-1-1806	6-1-1813	29-9-1814	2-9-1850		16-6-1862	|	Retd. 25-6-1863.	13-2-1868

LIST OF FLAG-OFFICERS—*continued.*

Name.	Born.	Lieut.	Com.	Captain.	R.-Adm.	V.-Adm.	Admiral.	Adm. of Fleet.	Remarks.	Died.
Edward Collier (1) (C.B. 1840, K.C.B. 1865)	1783	17-6-1803	25-7-1810	18-11-1814	1-10-1850	18-6-1857			{Retd. v.a. 27-11-1857: retd. a. 4-10-1862}	5-8-1872
David Price	1790	1809	6-12-1813	13-6-1815	6-11-1850					30-8-1854
Lord Algernon Percy (*suc. as* Lord Prudhoe 1817, *as* Duke of Northumberland 1847, K.G.)	15-9-1792	16-12-1811	8-3-1814	19-8-1815	11-11-1850				{Retd. 1851: retd. v.a. 9-7-1857: retd. a. 4-10-1852}	12-2-1865
John Toup Nicolas (C.B. 1815)	22-2-1788	1-5-1804	26-8-1809	26-8-1815	30-12-1850					1851
William Wilmot Henderson (C.B. 1840)		11-4-1806	13-3-1811	9-10-1815	21-3-1851					1854
John Hill (2) (Kt. 1831)		28-7-1814	28-10-1815	28-10-1815	11-6-1851	9-7-1857	4-10-1862			14-6-1864
Arthur Fanshawe (C.B. 1840, K.C.B. 1860)	5-2-1794	22-1-1813	2-10-1815	17-10-1816	16-6-1851	30-7-1857	10-11-1862			10-12-1875
Houston Stewart (C.B. 1840, K.C.B. 1855, G.C.B. 1865)	3-8-1791	1-8-1811	13-8-1814	10-6-1817	8-7-1851	22-8-1857	22-11-1862	20-10-1872		22-4-1865
James Stirling (1) (Kt. 1833)	1791	12-8-1809	19-6-1812	7-12-1818	27-8-1851	10-9-1857				13-2-1892
Lord John Hay (1) (C.B. 1837)		1-4-1812	17-6-1814	7-12-1818		10-9-1857				1875
Provo William Parry Wallis (K.C.B. 1860, G.C.B. 1873)	12-4-1791	30-11-1808	9-7-1813	12-8-1819	27-8-1851		23-3-1863	11-12-1875	R.A. and V.A. of U.K.	13-2-1892
William Walpole (2)	29-1-1789	8-8-1808	15-6-1814	7-12-1819	19-1-1852				{Retd. v.a. 26-2-1858: retd. a. 27-4-1863.}	8-7-1855
Armar Lowry Corry (1)		28-4-1812	13-6-1815	23-7-1821	8-3-1852					14-12-1863
William Edward Parry (Kt. 1829)	19-12-1790	6-1-1810	4-11-1820	8-11-1821	4-6-1852					1865
Henry William Bruce (K.C.B. 1861)	2-2-1792	5-1-1810	27-5-1814	16-11-1821	30-7-1852	2-10-1857	27-4-1863		Retd. v.a. 18-12-1858.	29-11-1863
William James Mingaye		6-7-1805	2-10-1817	29-1-1822	1-10-1852	4-11-1857				5-8-1861
James Hanway Plumridge (K.C.B. 1855)		28-8-1806	7-6-1814	9-10-1822	19-1-1852	8-12-1857	27-4-1863			19-6-1877
Thomas Herbert (K.C.B. 1841)	2-1793	10-10-1809	19-10-1814	25-11-1822	26-10-1852	5-1-1858	26-6-1863		Retd. 1866	1863
Hon. Henry John Rous	23-1-1795	18-5-1814	1-3-1815	25-4-1823	17-12-1852	20-1-1858	24-9-1863		Retd. v.a. 17-6-1859	11-7-1878
Edward Boxer	1784	8-1-1807	26-10-1813	23-6-1823	5-3-1853					1863
George Frederick Rich.		30-12-1805	9-9-1820	1-7-1823	2-4-1853	13-2-1858			R.A. of U.K.	11-7-1878
William James Hope Johnstone (K.C.B. 1862, G.C.B.)	28-7-1798	16-2-1810	8-2-1823	21-10-1823	22-4-1853	24-2-1858			{R.A. of U.K.: retd. a. 1-4-1870}	24-3-1895
William Fanshawe Martin (K.C.B. 1860, *suc. as* Bart. 1864, G.C.B. 1873)	5-12-1801	15-12-1820	23-6-1823	5-6-1824	28-5-1853	25-6-1858	14-11-1863			24-3-1895
Hon. Richard Saunders Dundas (C.B. 1841, K.C.B. 1856)	11-4-1802	18-6-1821	17-5-1823	17-7-1824	4-7-1853	21-11-1858			Retd. a. 9-2-1864	3-6-1861
Lord Adolphus Fitzclarence (G.C.H. 1832)	18-2-1802	23-4-1821	16-5-1823	24-12-1824	17-9-1853					17-5-1856
Henry Dumas	11-11-1798	7-12-1819	29-?-1822	9-2-1825	17-11-1853	18-12-1858				11-9-1863
Hon. Montagu Stopford (K.C.B. 1855)		17-7-1819	28-5-1813	8-4-1825	5-12-1853	17-6-1859	30-11-1863			10-11-1864
Henry Ducie Chads (C.B. 1826, K.C.B. 1855, G.C.B. 1865)	1788	5-11-1806	19-1-1822	25-7-1825	12-1-1854		3-12-1863			7-4-1868
George Robert Lambert (K.C.B 1853, G.C.B. 1865)	1796	5-5-1815	15-5-1823	8-8-1825	21-1-1854		15-12-1863		Retd. a. 5-3-1864	5-6-1869
Alexander Thomas Emeric Vidal		6-2-1815	13-6-1815	4-10-1825	27-1-1854					5-2-1863
John Leith		10-10-1809	13-6-1815	11-11-1825	11-2-1854					1854
Charles Hope (2)		20-10-1817	15-10-1822	26-1-1826	1-4-1854	17-6-1859				1870
Henry John Leeke (Kt. 1835, K.C.B. 1858)	1798	24-11-1810	15-6-1814	27-5-1826	15-4-1854	2-5-1860	11-1-1864			

Charles Howe Fremantle (K.C.B. 1857, G.C.B. 1867)	1-6-1800	11-12-1819	23-4-1822	4-8-1826	15-4-1854	9-6-1860	9-2-1864	—	V.A. of U.K.: retd. a. 1870.	25-5-1869
Michael Seymour (2) (K.C.B. 1855, G.C.B. 1859)	3-12-1802	12-9-1822	6-12-1824	5-8-1826	27-5-1854	1-11-1860	5-3-1864	—		23-2-1887
Henry Byam Martin (C.B. 1840, K.C.B. 1855)	6-1803	20-3-1823	8-4-1825	28-4-1827	13-7-1854	7-11-1860	15-6-1864	—		9-2-1865
Henry Eden (1)	1798	20-10-1817	23-10-1821	30-4-1827	7-8-1854	11-2-1861	16-9-1864	—	Retd. a. 1870.	30-1-1888
Frederick William Beechey	17-2-1796	10-3-1815	25-11-1822	8-5-1827	11-9-1854			—		29-11-1856
James Scott (2) (C.B. 1841, K.C.B. 1862)	18-6-1790	16-11-1809	19-10-1814	8-1-1828	26-10-1854	4-6-1861	10-2-1865	—	Retd. a. 2-4-1866	2-3-1872
Williams Sandom	1795	30-4-1808	15-6-1814	8-1-1828	27-10-1854			—	Retd. a.	
George William Conway Courtenay	23-8-1805	19-7-1813	26-12-1822	14-4-1828	24-11-1854	29-7-1861		—		31-3-1863
Hon. Frederick William Grey (C.B. 1843, K.C.B. 1857, G.C.B. 1865)	1796	7-4-1825	17-4-1827	19-4-1828	22-1-1855	5-8-1861	24-4-1865	—	Retd. v a. 2-11-1863: retd. a. 12-9-1865.	2-5-1878
Robert Lambert Baynes (C.B. 1827, K.C.B. 1860)	22-2-1785	8-4-1818	8-7-1828	16-9-1828	7-2-1855	15-1-1862	5-5-1865	—	Retd. v.a. 12-4-1862: retd. a. 12-9-1865.	7-9-1869
Thomas Bennett		9-12-1803	15-6-1814	28-10-1829	2-5-1855			—	Retd. a. 30-11-1865.	
Peter Richards (C.B. 1842, K.C.B. 1865)	1804	12-12-1807	16-9-1828	17-9-1828	6-6-1855	12-4-1862		—		18-1-1887
Henry Smith (2) (C.B. 1840, K.C.B. 1873)	12-12-1803	19-7-1821	8-9-1828	8-9-1828	3-7-1855	24-4-1862		—	Retd. r.a. 17-5-1862: retd. v.a. 1-10-1865. retd. a. 2-12-1865.	28-5-1877
Stephen Lushington (K.C.B. 1855, G.C.B. 1867)	1806	13-7-1824	13-5-1828	28-10-1829	4-7-1855	20-5-1862	12-9-1865	—	Retd. a. 1870	19-5-1882
John Alexander Duntze	8-4-1788	28-5-1825	19-4-1828	24-12-1829	9-7-1855	16-6-1862		—	Retd. a. 2-4-1866	
Frederick Thomas Michell (C.B. 1855, K.C.B. 1867)	3-7-1790	16-9-1816	9-5-1825	22-2-1830	9-7-1855	16-6-1862		—	Retd. a. 2-4-1866	
Thomas Hastings (Kt. 1839, K.C.B. Civ. 1859)	27-12-1802	17-1-1810	14-4-1828	22-7-1830	27-9-1855	4-10-1862	2-4-1866	—	Retd. a. 1870.	1870
Charles Ramsay Drinkwater Bethune (C.B. 1841)	1792	29-10-1823	17-4-1824	22-7-1830	3-10-1855			—	Retd. a.	
Charles Graham (C.B. 1846)	1-11-1801	9-7-1817	30-4-1827	4-11-1830	30-11-1855	22-1-1862		—		18-11-1857
Charles Talbot (K.C.B. 1862)	11-11-1789	7-1-1823	14-7-1815	25-4-1831	28-12-1855	6-2-1863		—	Retd. a. 20-11-1866.	8-8-1876
Thomas Wren Carter (C.B. 1855)	11-11-1789	18-4-1806	17-9-1828	24-5-1831	31-1-1856	22-1-1862	2-4-1866	—	Retd. a. 1870	13-2-1884
Sir Thomas Sabine Pasley, Bart.	26-12-1804	16-3-1824	29-7-1824	22-2-1832	31-1-1856	23-3-1863		—		29-1-1863
Christopher Wyvill	24-8-1794	5-7-1813	19-7-1822	27-8-1832	19-5-1856	23-3-1863		—		18-10-1864
Henry Francis Greville (C.B. 1855)	12-8-1803	4-2-1814	28-2-1828	19-7-1822	21-7-1856	1-4-1863		—	Retd. v.a. 7-4-1863	22-11-1879
Lord George Paulet (C.B. 1855)	1805	18-2-1828	15-11-1828	27-8-1832	17-10-1856	3-4-1863		—	Retd. a. 20-3-1867	21-5-1887
Lord Edward Russell (C.B. 1855)	1805	19-11-1833	8-11-1826	11-11-1833	21-10-1856	27-4-1863	20-3-1866	—	Retd. a. 18-10-1867.	
Henry Wolsey Bayfield	16-5-1809	20-3-1815	8-11-1826	4-6-1834	12-11-1856	26-6-1863	20-3-1867	—	Retd. a. 1-4-1866.	
Hon. George Grey (2)	17-2-1829	3-9-1831	14-6-1834	14-6-1834	12-11-1856			—		3-10-1891
James Clark Ross (Kt. 1843)	15-4-1800	26-12-1822	8-11-1827	28-10-1834	1-12-1856			—		3-4-1862

PUBLISHER'S NOTE
In the original edition the four photogravure plates and
four full-page illustrations faced the text pages as listed
on page xiii. In this edition these illustrations are
collected on the following pages in the order in which
they appeared in the first edition. The original position
indicators have been retained.

THE CAPTURE OF THE U.S.S. *CHESAPEAKE* BY H.M.S. *SHANNON*, JUNE 1st, 1813.

(From W. J. Bennett's engraving, after the picture which was painted by Whitcombe under the direction of Capt. Sir P. B. V. Broke, Bart., R.N.)

[*To face page* 80.]

CAPTURE OF THE U.S. BRIG *ARGUS* BY H.M. SLOOP *PELICAN*, AUG. 14TH, 1813.

(*From a painting by Whitcombe, formerly in the possession of Capt. Jno. Fordyce Maples, R.N.*)

[*To face page* 88.

Walter L Colls, Ph. Sc.

Admiral Sir David Milne, G.C.B,

Reproduced from an engraved family portrait, by permission of his
grandson, Capt. Sir Archibald Berkeley Milne, Bart R.N.

BOMBARDMENT OF ALGIER, AUG. 27TH, 1816.

(*From a painting by T. Whitcombe, after a plan by Capt. Sir James Brisbane, R.N.*)

[*To face page* 228.

Wm Little A.Se.

Napier's Defeat of the Squadron of Dom Miguel, Oct. 10th 1833.

From the engraving by E. Duncan, after the picture by W. J. Huggins.

Walter L. Colls, Ph. Sc.

Admiral the Hon. Sir Robert Stopford,
G.C.B. G.C.M.G.

By permission of the Lords of the Admiralty, from the portrait by
F.R. Say, in Greenwich Hospital

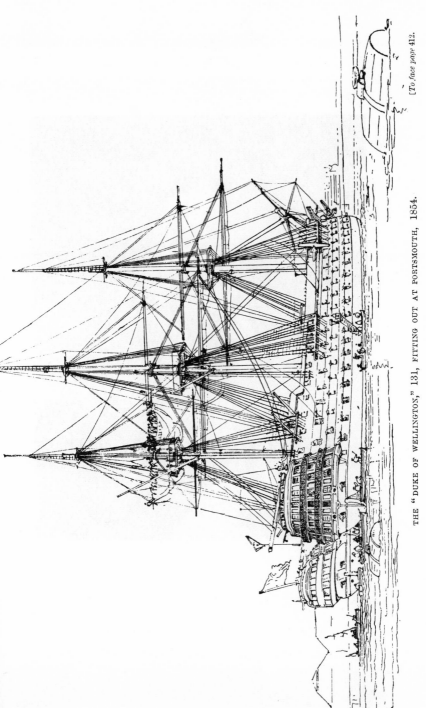

THE "DUKE OF WELLINGTON," 131, FITTING OUT AT PORTSMOUTH, 1854.

(*From a sketch by E. Duncan.*)

[*To face page* 412.

Walter L. Colls, Ph. Sc.

Admiral Sir Charles Napier, K.C.B.

By permission of his granddaughter, Mrs Safford, from a family portrait.

INDEX.

—

VOLUME VI.